PROPERTY IN THE MA

CW00540191

Having its origins in the process of transformation
take shape in South Africa at the end of the last c
analysis of property starts from deep inside the pr
distant or abstract perspective on property rules ana practices. rocusing on issues
of stability and change in a transformative setting and on the role of tradition and
legal culture in that context, the book argues that a property regime, including the
system of property holdings and the rules and practices that entrench and protect
them, tends to insulate itself against change through the security- and stability-
seeking tendency of tradition and legal culture, including the deep assumptions
about security and stability embedded in the rights paradigm, rhetoric and logic
that dominate current legal culture. The rights paradigm tends to stabilise the current distribution of property holdings by securing extant property holdings on the
assumption that they are lawfully acquired, socially important and politically and
morally legitimate. This function of the rights paradigm tends to resist or minimise change, including change brought about by morally, politically and legally
legitimate and authorised reform or transformation efforts. The author's goal is to
gauge the lasting power of the rights paradigm by investigating its effects in the
margins of property law and of society, by establishing the actual efficacy and
power of reformist or transformative anti-eviction policies and legislation aimed
at the protection of marginalised and weak land users and occupiers in areas such
as landlord–tenant law, eviction of unlawful occupiers of land and other restrictions on the landowner's power to enforce a stronger right to exclusive possession.
Ultimately the book's aim is to explore the possibility of opening up theoretical
space where justice-inspired changes to (or transformation of) the extant property
regime can be imagined and discussed more or less fruitfully from an unusual
perspective, a perspective from the margins which is valuable for any theoretical
consideration or discussion of property.

Property in the Margins

AJ van der Walt

·HART·
PUBLISHING

OXFORD AND PORTLAND, OREGON
2009

Published in North America (US and Canada) by
Hart Publishing
c/o International Specialized Book Services
920 NE 58th Avenue, Suite 300
Portland, OR 97213-3786
USA
Tel: +1 503 287 3093 or toll-free: (1) 800 944 6190
Fax: +1 503 280 8832
E-mail: orders@isbs.com
Website: http://www.isbs.com

Hart Publishing Ltd, 16C Worcester Place, Oxford, OX1 2JW
Telephone: +44 (0)1865 517530 Fax: +44 (0)1865 510710
E-mail: mail@hartpub.co.uk
Website: http://www.hartpub.co.uk

British Library Cataloguing in Publication Data
Data Available

ISBN: 978-1-84113-963-0

Typeset by Hope Services, Abingdon
Printed and bound in Great Britain by
CPI Antony Rowe, Chippenham, Wiltshire

For

Robert Feenstra, Klaus Stern, Frank Michelman and Kevin Gray

PREFACE

I

This book was extremely long in the making. I decided sometime in the 1990s to write something on property theory, but considered it necessary to first make an extensive study of existing theory. This resulted in a number of exploratory journal articles in which I attempted to review property theories and the debates that informed them in the literature from the 1980s and 1990s.[1] From these exploratory investigations it became clear that the direction I wanted to take was to consider the meaning of property theory for the process of transformation and land reform that was then just beginning to take shape in South Africa, rather than to add another more or less abstract theoretical analysis of property as an institution of social, political and economic ordering. A number of journal articles and essays followed in which I investigated the implications and effect of land reform for the established property system and for property law in a transformational setting. During this phase my interest in property theory was expanded by the foray into constitutional law that was more or less forced on all South African private law specialists during the late 1990s, and I therefore became particularly interested in issues surrounding the public/private divide and the relationship between private and constitutional law.[2] Important works on property theory from the time, such

---

[1] See eg AJ van der Walt, 'Property and Personal Freedom: Subjectivism in Bernhard Windscheid's Theory of Ownership' (1993) 56 *THRHR* 569–89; 'Unity and Pluralism in Property Theory: A Review of Property Theories and Debates in Recent Literature' 1995 *TSAR* 15–42; 'Subject and Society in Property Theory: A Review of Property Theories and Debates in Recent Literature' 1995 *TSAR* 322–45; 'Rights and Reforms in Property Theory: A Review of Property Theories and Debates in Recent Literature' 1995 *TSAR* 493–526; 'Marginal Notes on Powerful(l) Legends: Critical Perspectives on Property Theory' (1995) 58 *THRHR* 396–420. The three articles in 1995 *TSAR* were inspired by and constructed around SR Munzer, *A Theory of Property* (1990), but also drew heavily upon LS Underkuffler, 'On Property: An Essay' (1990) 100 *Yale LJ* 127–48; CM Rose, *Property and Persuasion: Essays on the History, Theory, and Rhetoric of Ownership* (1994); and some of the essays subsequently collected in MJ Radin, *Contested Commodities* (1996). The Underkuffler essay was later worked out further in LS Underkuffler, *The Idea of Property: Its Meaning and Power* (2003).
[2] See eg AJ van der Walt, 'Tradition on Trial: A Critical Analysis of the Civil-Law Tradition in South African Property Law' (1995) 11 *SAJHR* 169–206; 'Un-doing Things with Words: The Colonization of the Public Sphere by Private Property Discourse' 1998 *Acta Juridica* 235–81; 'Property Rights and Hierarchies of Power: A Critical Evaluation of Land Reform Policy in South Africa' (1999) 64 *Koers* 259–94; 'Modernity, Normality, and Meaning: The Struggle between Progress and Stability and the Politics of Interpretation (2000) 11 *Stell LR* 21–49; 226–43; 'Protecting Social Participation Rights within the Property Paradigm: A Critical Reappraisal' in E Cooke (ed), *Modern Studies in Property Law, Vol II* (2003) 27–41.

as Gregory Alexander's *Commodity and Propriety*[3] and Joseph William Singer's *Entitlement*,[4] convinced me that what I wanted to write was an analysis of property theory from deep inside the property regime, in other words a theoretical discussion that does not take a too distant or abstract perspective on property rules and practices as they function in a particular social and historical context, but starts out from that context. In this kind of theory, philosophical argument is secondary to contextual jurisprudential analysis, although philosophical reasoning remains important in the background. At the same time, I realised that I wanted to focus on issues of stability and change in a transformative setting and on the role of tradition and legal culture in that context. Following on from a few further exploratory journal articles and book contributions along those lines,[5] this book is the end result.

The purpose of the book and the theoretical approach are set out in chapter one and developed further in chapters two and three. In short, the argument is that what I describe as the property regime, including the current system of property holdings and the rules and practices that entrench and protect them, tends to insulate itself against change (including social and political transformation) through the security- and stability-seeking tendency of tradition and legal culture, including the deep assumptions about security and stability embedded in the rights paradigm, which I describe as the most important element of the doctrine, rhetoric and logic that dominate current legal culture. The rights paradigm tends to stabilise the current distribution of property holdings by securing extant property holdings on the assumption that they are lawfully acquired, socially important and politically and morally legitimate. This function of the rights paradigm tends to resist or minimise change, including change brought about by morally, politically and legally legitimate and authorised reform or transformation efforts.

My goal is to gauge the lasting power of the rights paradigm by investigating its effects in the margins of property law and of society, by establishing the actual efficacy and power of reformist or transformative anti-eviction policies and legislation aimed at the protection of marginalised and weak land users and occupiers. Eviction is the strong landowner's primary remedy for exclusive possession and therefore policies and legislation that restrict it for the sake of weak and marginal land users and occupiers will tend to undermine the paradigm. My central hypothesis is that the success of policy- and justice-driven protections against eviction

---

[3] GS Alexander, *Commodity and Propriety: Competing Visions of Property in American Legal Thought 1776–1970* (1997).

[4] JW Singer, *Entitlement: The Paradoxes of Property* (2000). See the discussion in ch 2.

[5] See eg AJ van der Walt, 'Rendition / Eviction: A Post-Apartheid Reflection' (2005) 15 *Law & Critique* 321–44; 'Transformative Constitutionalism and the Development of South African Property Law' 2005 *TSAR* 655–89, 2006 *TSAR* 1–31; 'Property Theory and the Transformation of Property Law' in E Cooke (ed), *Modern Studies in Property Law, Vol III* (2005) 361–80; 'Legal History, Legal Culture and Transformation in a Constitutional Democracy' (2006) 12 *Fundamina* 1–47; 'Property, Social Justice and Citizenship: The Transformation of Property Law in Post-Apartheid South Africa' (2008) 19 *Stell LR* 325–46; 'Property and Marginality' in G Alexander and E Penalver (eds), *Law and Community* (forthcoming, 2009).

would be an indication of the strength of the paradigm. The conclusions are set out and discussed in chapter seven: Although there are quite a few examples of strong reformist legislative efforts to protect weak and marginalised occupiers against eviction, these efforts are sometimes frustrated by restrictive judicial and doctrinal interpretation and application informed by the underlying assumptions of the rights paradigm. To the extent that the continued power of the paradigm frustrates reformist or transformative policies, it is difficult to imagine theoretical space where further and stronger justice-inspired reforms of the property regime can be developed. The purpose of the substantive chapters in the book is to iden-tify areas where protective policies and legislation challenge the integrity of the rights paradigm by preventing a landowner from enforcing her right to exclusive possession, on the understanding that these challenges to the paradigm open up theoretical space where meaningful reforms and transformative changes can be imagined and developed. At the same time, the analysis also identifies areas where such transformative space should have been opened up but was not, thereby per-haps suggesting an agenda for further change, particularly in the theoretical field.

The method followed in the book is to describe selected areas where eviction laws and practices feature prominently in South African law and to compare them with similar institutions in English and German law. The reasons and justification for this apparently counter-intuitive comparative choice are set out in chapter four, but on the whole the decision to focus on these jurisdictions was inspired by the complexity of similarities and differences between the respective legal cultures, consisting of their partially shared social and legal histories and contexts, the align-ment of their often similar economic and social policies and its effect on housing, the interplay between constitutional, public and private law and the influence of codification on the development and reform of the common law tradition in each of the three main systems I investigate. Obviously the purpose is not to describe any of the legal systems or the institutions I focus on comprehensively or even in great depth, but rather to set out just enough material on eviction in the selected areas to inform the discussion about stability and change. This means that there will inevitably be gaps where my treatment of foreign law remains superficial or unspecific; the references in the footnotes should ameliorate these shortcomings to a certain extent for the reader who wants to find out more about a specific legal system.

The ultimate goal of the book is not programmatic; I do not set out or claim to develop a new or even a coherent theory of property. Above all, I do not discuss or theorise either the justification for or the injustice of extant property holdings or the justice of particular no-property claims or interests. What I do is more mod-est, namely to explore the possibility of opening up theoretical space where justice-inspired changes to (or transformation of) the extant property regime can be imagined and discussed more or less fruitfully from an unusual perspective, namely the effect that enforcement of strong property rights has on marginalised property holders and users. My proposal is that imaginative and creative thinking about improving the justice content of property law is easier from a theoretical stance that does not focus exclusively or primarily on strong or central rights positions in property, but that also takes seriously the no-property interests of people and communities in the margins of society and in the margins of property law. In so far as the book does put forward any substantive theoretical claim, it is that the perspective from the margins is valuable for any theoretical consideration or discussion about property. Obviously this does not imply that I reject the perspective from the centre or deny the value of vested rights in property—strong property rights already enjoy strong protection in the legal system and I therefore do not concern myself with their justification; I merely accept that legal recognition and protection of property interests is an important facet of social ordering and then argue for a wider notion of what could be considered worthy of recognition as 'property interests'.

II

Many people and institutions have been instrumental in making this book see the light of day. First of all I want to thank the research assistants who have worked on the book with me over the last two years, when the major part of the writing was done. Elmien du Plessis provided much-needed research assistance when I seriously started writing two years ago and continued to give valuable and much appreciated support and encouragement after moving to another project in 2008. In the last year her work in checking references was taken over by Lee-Ann Kiewitz, who did a sterling job. At the same time Sue-Mari Maass took over as the research assistant who was primarily responsible for assisting me with the book, and she provided excellent and tireless assistance and support, always willing to go the extra mile to find the sources I required and to check the correctness of examples and arguments alluded to and the accuracy and consistency of references and citations. Her work was invaluable and is highly appreciated. Heiko Braun helped check the accuracy of my discussion of German legislation and cases. I owe them all a huge debt of gratitude for their support.

Apart from my assistants, I received selfless and invaluable assistance of another kind from some of my colleagues and friends. Frank Michelman and Gregory Alexander read early versions of the comparative chapters and provided valuable comments, especially on references to and discussions of US law. Kevin Gray and Susan Bright read the sections on English law (in some cases several times) and gave me the benefit of their expert knowledge, thereby helping me improve the accuracy and completeness of my analysis and saving me from unnecessary error and embarrassment. Susan was especially willing to keep suggesting improved and more accurate versions of my analysis of the extremely intricate legislation that makes up the bulk of English landlord–tenant law. She and Kevin also pointed me to further sources that were most helpful in developing the comparative chapters. I cannot thank them enough for their time and effort. Karin van Marle and Stewart

Motha read some of the draft chapters and discussed them with me during a couple of reading sessions, helping me to clarify and develop my thoughts and arguments. I am most grateful for their contribution and their time. My Stellenbosch colleagues Sandra Liebenberg and Juanita Pienaar discussed aspects of South African land reform and eviction law with me and provided valuable insights and comments from their expert knowledge of the field. Ms Melinda Heese of the Stellenbosch University Library throughout assisted us in finding elusive sources, both physical and electronic.

Amongst those colleagues and friends who helped me improve the draft chapters Brenna Bhandar deserves special mention. She not only kindly agreed to act as critical reader of the whole manuscript, but made time to read some chapters in several drafts and to give me detailed and thoughtful comments and criticism, which was invaluable in the final editing of the draft chapters and the writing of the final chapter. I was also fortunate enough to host her in Stellenbosch for a few weeks, during which we could discuss all the draft chapters in detail. Without the time she selflessly invested in reading and commenting on the draft chapters and in our discussions the book would have been much weaker and poorer, and for that I am greatly indebted to her. Obviously, whatever errors and shortcomings still plague the book remain despite the best efforts of the colleagues and friends mentioned above and I accept full responsibility for them.

My friendly and helpful publisher, Richard Hart, not only agreed to publish what might seem to be a somewhat esoteric book from a faraway country but was kind enough to provide encouragement and valuable editorial comments. I am grateful for his support. Other staff members of Hart Publishing Ltd, notably Managing Editor, Mel Hamill and copy editor, Jo Morton provided friendly and most valuable assistance in preparing the final manuscript, and I thank them for that.

The project benefited from financial support from several sources, especially over the last two years. I thankfully acknowledge the support of the Stellenbosch University Research Committee (Humanities and Social Sciences), the National Research Foundation (grant number GUN 2050532) and Trinity College, Cambridge, where I was fortunate enough to spend valuable research time in 2004 and 2008. The final stage of the writing process in 2008 was facilitated by the award of the South African Research Chair in Property Law, which is hosted by Stellenbosch University, funded by the Department of Science and Technology and administered by the National Research Foundation. I am also grateful for the support, especially by way of research leave and encouragement, from my faculty and the Dean, Professor Gerhard Lubbe. Obviously the views set out in the book are mine alone and should not be attributed to any of these persons or institutions.

References and sources in the bibliography and footnotes have been updated to the end of September 2008. In some chapters I have made use of sections and passages from a number of earlier journal articles and book contributions that were written in anticipation and during the development of this project; the relevant sources are acknowledged in the footnotes. All these materials have been reworked and updated for this publication.

III

I dedicate the book to four great lawyers, great masters of property and constitutional law, who have shaped my academic career and helped me to understand and treasure the intricacies of property law, constitutional law and property theory. Each of them entered into my academic life at a crucial stage and each directed me towards new sources and topics that provided impetus to my professional development. I take great pride and pleasure in acknowledging their support, encouragement and friendship.

I first encountered Professor (emeritus) mr Robert Feenstra in the early 1980s, when he agreed to be the co-promoter for my doctoral study. With the letter in which he agreed to co-supervise the thesis and invited me to spend research time with him in Leiden, he sent me offprints of two of his (then recent) publications on the historical development of ownership in Roman law.[6] Reading those articles opened up a wonderful new world, in which the history and development of ownership are traced through centuries of time and across national boundaries, helping us understand the nature and social function of ownership in its current historical and social context. Robert Feenstra taught me many things, but perhaps the most enduring of all is the importance of close attention to the social, political, economic and historical context within which law functions. Those first article offprints still stand on the shelf right next to my desk and I reread the from time to time, together with the other historical sources Robert introduced me to.

I made contact with Professor (emeritus) Dr Klaus Stern during the 1990s, just after the democratic changeover in South Africa, when I went to Germany to seek assistance in familiarising myself with German constitutional property law. I knew his monumental work on German constitutional law,[7] and I reckoned that as a

[6] R Feenstra, 'Historische Aspecten van de Private Eigendom als Rechtsinstituut' 1976 *RM Themis* 248–75; 'Hugo de Groot's Eerste Beschouwingen over *Dominium* en over de Oorsprong van de Private Eigendom: *Mare Liberum* en zijn Bronnen' 1976 *Acta Juridica* 269–82. To these he later added offprints of two further articles that were just as important for my development: R Feenstra, *Ius in Re: Het Begrip Zakelijk Recht in Historisch Perspectief* (Thorbecke-Colleges no 4) (1979); 'Der Eigentumsbegriff bei Hugo Grotius im Licht einiger mittelalterlicher und spätscholastischer Quellen' in O Behrends *et al* (eds), *Festschrift für Franz Wieacker zum 70. Geburtstag* (1978) 209–34. I dedicated an earlier publication on legal history and legal culture to Robert Feenstra; see AJ van der Walt, 'Legal History, Legal Culture and Transformation in a Constitutional Democracy' (2006) 12 *Fundamina* 1–47. Two Festschriften have, to my knowledge been dedicated to Robert Feenstra, of which the last was specifically of South African origin. They are JA Ankum *et al* (eds), *Satura Roberto Feenstra Sexagesum Quintum Annum Aetatis Complenti an Alumnus Collegis Amicis Oblata* (1985); and TJ Scott and D Visser (eds), *Developing Delict: Essays in Honour of Robert Feenstra* (2000) (also published as *Acta Juridica* 2000).

[7] K Stern, *Das Staatsrecht der Bundesrepublik Deutschland*, vols I–V (1994–2005). Apart from subsequently published volumes of the *Staatsrecht* (the important vol IV/I on fundamental rights appeared in 2005), he later added to my collection of Stern publications the important essay on the limits of fundamental rights: K Stern 'Die Grundrechte und ihre Schranken' in P Badura and H Dreier (eds), *Festschrift 50 Jahre Bundesverfassungsgericht, Vol 2 Klärung und Fortbildung des Verfassungsrechts* (2001) 1–34. As far as I am aware at least one Festschrift has been dedicated to Klaus Stern: J Burmeister *et al* (eds), *Verfassungsstaatlichkeit: Festschrift für Klaus Stern zum 65. Geburtstag* (1997).

private law specialist who needed to understand constitutional law in a hurry I could do worse than to learn from the German master himself. Klaus not only welcomed me to his institute several times over the next decade, but also went out of his way to explain the intricacies of German constitutional law to me and to direct me to sources and to other German colleagues who could provide more specialised assistance in the area of constitutional property law. This experience literally changed my life as it projected me into the then, for me, unknown territory of constitutional property law; a field that was foreign to South African property lawyers but that was obviously going to become immensely important in the new constitutional era. The most important thing I learned from Klaus was the value of comprehensive, detailed and painstaking analysis, an art to which the five volumes of Stern's *Staatsrecht* are a living monument. Thanks to him German law has become an important marker in all my work on property law. Stern's *Staatsrecht* stands on the bookshelf just behind me and I consult it often, together with the other German constitutional sources Klaus introduced me to.

Roughly at the same time when I made my first hesitant contacts with German constitutional law, I met Professor Frank Michelman for a drink in New York City, where he was visiting at the time. I knew his work from reading a few seminal articles on constitutional property,[8] and I realised that a South African property scholar who wanted to understand constitutional property law had to learn something about US property law. I also sensed that nobody would be a better teacher than Frank Michelman; hence the request to meet with him. Although he admits that my request came out of the blue, Frank responded warmly and over the next decade selflessly provided me with continued support, encouragement and endless discussions to help me understand US constitutional law, constitutional property law and property in general. Our sustained discussions and exchanges on property law in the shadow of the constitution, both in the US and in South Africa, remain an invaluable source of learning and insight, while Frank's immense knowledge and understanding of and commitment to the development of South African post-apartheid law is an inspiration. The most important thing I learned from him was to be aware of the deep connections between law, morality and politics. Apart from the sizeable collection of other articles and publications in my database, the core Michelman articles still occupy a special space on my shelf, within reach, and I reread them often.

Of the four masters of property law to whom I dedicate this book Professor Dr Kevin Gray is the closest to my own age. We first met at the Maastricht property

---

[8] FI Michelman, 'Property, Utility and Fairness: Comments on the Ethical Foundations of "Just Compensation" Law' (1967) 80 *Harvard LR* 1165–258; 'Property as a Constitutional Right' (1981) 38 *Wash & Lee LR* 1097–114; 'Possession vs Distribution in the Constitutional Idea of Property' (1987) 72 *Iowa LR* 1319–50; 'Takings, 1987' (1988) 88 *Columbia LR* 1600–29. Both he and I added Michelman articles to my collection subsequently; at present there are more than 50 in my personal database. I have dedicated an article to Frank Michelman before; see AJ van der Walt, 'A South African Reading of Frank Michelman's Theory of Social Justice' (2004) 19 *SAPL* 253–307; and I have been involved in a South African Festschrift dedicated to Frank Michelman: H Botha *et al* (eds) *Rights and Democracy in a Transformative Constitution* (2003).

conference I co-organised with Gerrit van Maanen in 1996, where Frank Michelman and other luminaries like Eltjo Schrage, Carol Rose, Peter Butt, Stephen Schnably, Gregory Alexander, Joe Singer and Jenny Nedelsky were also present. Of course, Kevin was invited to the conference on the strength of his standard text on English land law,[9] but personally I wanted to meet him because I admired his wonderfully imaginative and stimulating 1991 article on the elusive propertiness of property.[10] The meeting was highly satisfactory and since then Kevin has become a constant interlocutor and a much-valued source of information, understanding and inspiration, especially on the vagaries of English land law. The most valuable thing I have learned from Kevin is to combine really deep and thoroughgoing specialisation in private property law, in a deliberately comparative context, with a wide-ranging involvement in constitutional and theoretical issues; the apparent ease with which he practises this art remains an inspiration and an elusive ideal for others. The 'thin air' article remains on the shelf right next to my desk and I consult it regularly; the land law text stands right next to it and was a major source of information for this book.

Each of these masters of property and constitutional law influenced my work and my career in lasting ways and I am fortunate enough to now count them all as treasured friends. I dedicate the book to them because I owe each of them a huge debt of gratitude for their support and encouragement over decades and for the sheer volume of learning and understanding that they have opened up for me through their collegial and friendly assistance, advice, comments and criticism. They are obviously not responsible for my shortcomings or for the errors and misapprehensions that remain in this book. With their assistance and support I have now become grown up enough to take full responsibility for that.

André van der Walt
Stellenbosch
14 October 2008

---

[9] K Gray, *Elements of Land Law* (1987). The current edition is K Gray and SF Gray, *Elements of Land Law* (4th edn, 2005); a fifth edition is imminent at the time of writing.
[10] KJ Gray, 'Property in Thin Air' (1991) 50 *Cambridge LJ* 252–307.

CONTENTS

Preface   vii
Abbreviations   xvii
Table of Cases   xix
Table of Legislation   xxvii

1 **Property in a Transformative Setting**   1
   I. Facing up to Social and Political Transformation   1
   II. Property Theory in a Time of Transformation   12

2 **Property in the Centre: The Rights Paradigm**   27
   I. Property in the Rights Paradigm   27
   II. Three Illustrations   41

3 **Eviction in the Rights Paradigm**   53
   I. The Right to Evict as an Incident of Ownership   53
   II. Eviction, Socio-Economic and Political Power   60
   III. The Eviction Challenge   70

4 **Eviction in Landlord–Tenant Law**   77
   I. Introduction   77
   II. Tenant Protection: A Comparative Overview   82
   III. Tenant Protection in South African Law   114
   IV. Conclusion   130

5. **Eviction of Unlawful Occupiers**   133
   I. Introduction   133
   II. Eviction of Politically Inspired Urban Squatters   135
   III. Anti-eviction Protection in South African Land Reform Law   146
   IV. Eviction of Gypsies or Travellers   161
   V. Conclusion   166

6 **Limitations on Eviction in Other Contexts**   169
   I. Introduction   169
   II. Acquisitive Prescription and Adverse Possession   172
   III. Public Access to Private Property   188
   IV. Significant Building Encroachments   199
   V. Weak Owners   205
   VI. Conclusions   208

7 Conclusions   211
   I.   Property in the Context of Stability and Change   211
   II. Overview of Results   222
   III. Property in the Margins   230

Bibliography   249
Index   263

ABBREVIATIONS

ALR	American Law Reports
ASSAL	Annual Survey of South African Law
BuaNews	South African government news service
Buffalo LR	Buffalo Law Review
California LR	California Law Review
Cambridge LJ	Cambridge Law Journal
Canadian Journal of Law & Jur	Canadian Journal of Law and Jurisprudence
Cardozo LR	Cardozo Law Review
Columbia LR	Columbia Law Review
Cornell LQ	Cornell Law Quarterly
Cornell LR	Cornell Law Review
Edinburgh LR	Edinburgh Law Review
Environmental LR	Environmental Law Review
European Rev of Private Law	European Review of Private Law
Fundamina	Fundamina: A Journal of Legal History
Georgetown LJ	Georgetown Law Journal
Harvard Civil Rights–Civil Liberties LR	Harvard Civil Rights–Civil Liberties Law Review
Harvard LR	Harvard Law Review
Houston LR	Houston Law Review
Iowa LR	Iowa Law Review
J Planning & Env Law	Journal for Planning and Environmental Law
Lesotho LJ	Lesotho Law Journal
Loyola LR	Loyola Law Review
L&T Rev	Landlord and Tenant Review
LQR	Law Quarterly Review
Maryland LR	Maryland Law Review
McGill LJ	McGill Law Journal
NJB	Nederlands Juristenblad
NJW	Neue Juristische Wochenschrift
Northwestern Univ LR	Northwestern University Law Review
Political Science Qly	Political Science Quarterly
PL	Public Law
Rev Const Studies	Review of Constitutional Studies
RM Themis	Rechtsgeleerd Magazijn Themis
SAJHR	South African Journal on Human Rights
SALJ	South African Law Journal

SAPL	*South African Public Law*
S California LR	*Southern California Law Review*
Stanford LR	*Stanford Law Review*
Stell LR	*Stellenbosch Law Review*
Texas LR	*Texas Law Review*
The Economic History Rev	*The Economic History Review*
THRHR	*Tydskrif vir Hedendaagse Romeins-Hollandse Reg*
TSAR	*Tydskrif vir Suid-Afrikaanse Reg*
Univ Chicago LR	*University of Chicago Law Review*
Univ Miami LR	*University of Miami Law Review*
Univ Pennsylvania LR	*University of Pennsylvania Law Review*
Univ of Western Australia LR	*University of Western Australia Law Review*
Virginia LR	*Virginia Law Review*
Wash & Lee LR	*Washington and Lee Law Review*
Washington Univ LQ	*Washington University Law Quarterly*
William & Mary Bill of Rights J	*William and Mary Bill of Rights Journal*
Yale LJ	*Yale Law Journal*

TABLE OF CASES

AUSTRALIA

Griffiths and Another v Lands and Mining Tribunal [2003] NTSC 86
(http://www.austlii.edu.au) 207
Griffiths v Northern Territory of Australia [2003] FCA 1177
(http://www.austlii.edu.au) 207
Griffiths v Minister for Lands, Planning and Environment [2008]
HCA 20 (15 May 2008) 197, 205, 207
Mabo and Others v State of Queensland (No 2) (1992) 107 ALR 1 (HC) 38, 205
Minister for Lands, Planning and Environment v Griffiths and Others
[2002] NT LMT 26 (http://www.austlii.edu.au) 207
Minister for Lands, Planning and Environment v Griffiths [2004]
NTCA 5 (http://www.austlii.edu.au) 207

CANADA

Delgamuukw v British Columbia [1997] 3 SCR 1010 .... 38, 205

EUROPEAN COURT OF HUMAN RIGHTS

Blecic v Croatia (2004) 41 EHRR 185 165
Connors v United Kingdom (2004) 40 EHRR 189 .... 11, 51, 107–10,
112, 162, 164–5
Gillow v United Kingdom (1986) 11 EHRR 335 163
JA Pye (Oxford) Ltd v The United Kingdom [2005] ECHR 44302/02 (IV) 181
JA Pye (Oxford) Ltd and JA Pye (Oxford) Land Ltd v The United
Kingdom [2007] ECHR 44302/02 (GC) 181
James v United Kingdom [1986] 8 EHRR 123 244
McCann v United Kingdom [2008] ECHR 19009/04
(13 May 2008) 108–10, 112, 162

EUROPEAN COMMITTEE OF SOCIAL RIGHTS

European Roma Rights Centre v Greece (Complaint no 15/2003),
decision of 8 December 2004 165

European Roma Rights Centre v Italy (Complaint no 27/2004), decision of 7 December 2004 165

GERMANY

BGH NJW 1985, 789 203
BVerfGE 24, 367 (*Deichordnung*) [1968] 219
BVerfGE 37, 132 (*Wohnraumkündigungsschutzgesetz*) [1974].................... 46–7, 90
BVerfGE 38, 248 (*Zweckentfremdung von Wohnraum*) [1975] 47, 88, 89, 90
BVerfGE 42, 263 (*Contergan*) [1976] 219
BVerfGE 51, 193 [1979] 49
BVerfGE 58, 300 (*Naßauskiesung*) [1981]... 48
BVerfGE 65, 196 1983 49
BVerfGE 68, 361 (*Wohnungskündigungsgesetz*) [1985] 90
BVerfGE 74, 264 (*Boxberg*) [1986] 207
BVerfGE 79, 292 (*Eigenbedarfskündigung*) [1989] 47, 89, 90–91
BVerfGE 89, 1 (*Besitzrecht des Mieters*) [1993] 42, 47, 90–92
BVerfGE 89, 237 (*Eigenbedarfskündigung*) [1993].. 47, 89
BVerfGE 91, 294 (*Fortgeltung des Mietepreisbindung*) [1994]........................ 47, 90
BVerfG NJW 1994, 41 88
BVerfGE 100, 226 (*Rheinland-Pfälzische Denkmalschutzgesetz*) [1999] 49, 88

INDIA

Hemaji Waghaji Jat v Bhikhabhai Khengarbhai Harijan & Others 2008 AIOL 3789 (23/09/2008) (SC).. 179

NETHERLANDS

Arr Rb Middelburg 1 October 1980, 24 December 1980, 1981 *NJ*, 374 139
HR 16 December 1969, *NJ* 1971, 96... 139
HR 17 April 1970, *NJ* 1971, 89 202
HR 2 February 1971, *NJ* 1971, 385... 138
HR 16 November 1971, *NJ* 1972, 43 139
HR 16 November 1971, *NJ* 1972, 62 138
HR 4 January 1972, *NJ* 1972, 121 138
HR 24 June 1980, *NJ* 1980, 625 138
HR 26 June 1984, *NJ* 1985, 138 138

SOUTH AFRICA

ABSA Bank v Amod [1999] 2 All SA 423 (W) 43, 125, 152

Alexkor Ltd and Another v Richtersveld Community and Others 2004
  (5) SA 460 (CC) 38, 206

Baartman v Port Elizabeth Municipality 2004 (1) SA 560 (SCA) 153

Batchelor v Gabie 2002 (2) SA 51 (SCA) 125

*Bato Star Fishing (Pty) Ltd v Minister of Environmental Affairs and
  Others* 2004 (4) SA 490 (CC) 45, 151

Bekker and Another v Jika [2001] 4 All SA 573 (SEC) 125

Betta Eiendomme (Pty) Ltd v Ekple-Epoh 2000 (4)
  SA 468 (W) 44–5, 57, 121, 125

Bisschop v Stafford 1974 (3) SA 1 (A) 172–4

Blomson v Boshoff 1905 TS 429 58

Boshoff v Theron 1940 TPD 299 59

Brisley v Drotsky 2002 (4) SA 1 (SCA) 42, **43–6**, 56, 69, 72,
                          120–21, 123, 126, 131, 148, 153, 157, 240

*Cape Killarney Property Investments (Pty) Ltd v Mahamba and
  Others* [2001] 4 All SA 479 (A) 149

Chetty v Naidoo 1974 (3) SA 13 (A) 57–8

Chirwa v Transnet Ltd and Others 2008 (4) SA 367 (CC) 151

Christie v Haarhoff and Others (1886–1887) 4 HCG 349 200

Cillie v Geldenhuys (306/07) [2008] JOL 21782 (SCA) 173

City of Johannesburg v Rand Properties (Pty) Ltd 2007 (1)
  SA 78 (W) 68, 155, 159, 167

City of Johannesburg v Rand Properties (Pty) Ltd and Others 2007
  (6) SA 417 (SCA) 68, 69, 155

Conradie v Hanekom 1999 (4) SA 491 (LCC) 128

De Jager v Sisana 1930 AD 71 59

De Villiers v Kalson 1928 EDL 217 200

*Department of Land Affairs and Others v Goedgelegen Tropical Fruits
  (Pty) Ltd* 2007 (6) SA 199 (CC) 38, 206

Dique NO v Van der Merwe 2001 (2) SA 1006 (T) 128

Dreyer NO and Another v AXZS Industries (Pty) Ltd [2006] 3 All
  SA 219 (SCA) 57

Durban City Council v Kistan 1972 (4) SA 465 (N) 58

Ellis v Viljoen 2001 (4) SA 795 (C) 121, 125

Ex parte Menzies et Uxor 1993 (3) SA 799 (C) 57

FHP Management (Pty) Ltd v Theron and Another 2004 (3)
  SA 392 (C) 46

*First National Bank of SA Ltd t/a Wesbank v Commissioner, South African
  Revenue Service; First National Bank of SA Ltd t/a Wesbank v Minister of
  Finance* 2002 (4) SA 768 (CC) 198

Fredericks v Stellenbosch Divisional Council 1977 (3) SA 113 (C) 66

Fuel Retailers Association of Southern Africa v Director-General: Environmental Management, Department of Agriculture, Conservation and Environment, Mpumalanga Province, and Others 2007 (6) SA 4 (CC)............................ 151–2

Genna-Wae Properties (Pty) Ltd v Medio-Tronics (Natal) (Pty) Ltd 1995 (2) SA 926 (A).. 58–9, 116

Gien v Gien 1979 (2) SA 1113 (T) 32–3

Goudini Chrome (Pty) Ltd v MCC Contracts (Pty) Ltd 1993 (1) SA 77 (A) 57

Government of the Republic of South Africa and Others v Grootboom and Others 2001 (1) SA 46 (CC) 118, 150, 156, 158–9

Graham v Ridley 1931 TPD 476 57–9

Greeff v Krynauw (1899) 9 CTR 591 200

Haakdoornbult Boerdery CC v Mphela 2007 (5) SA 596 (SCA) 206

Hefer v Van Greuning 1979 (4) SA 952 (A) 58

Henning v Petra Meubels Bpk 1947 (2) SA 407 (T) 58

Ismail v Ismail and Others 2007 (4) SA 557 (EC) 59, 116

Jaftha v Schoeman and Others; Van Rooyen v Stoltz and Others 2005 (2) SA 140 (CC) 118, 159, 206

Jackpersad v Mitha 2008 (4) SA 522 (D) 155

Jeena v Minister of Lands 1955 (2) SA 380 (A) 57–8, 64

Joubert and Others v Van Rensburg and Others 2001 (1) SA 753 (W) 67, 121

Kendall Property Investments v Rutgers [2005] 4 All SA 61 (C) 57, 124, 129

Khuzwayo v Dludla 2001 (1) SA 714 (LCC) 125

Lombard v Fischer [2003] 1 All SA 698 (O) 199

Magodi and Others v Van Rensburg [2001] 4 All SA 485 (LCC)...................... 121

Malan v Nabygelegen Estates 1946 AD 562 172–3

Mangaung Local Municipality v Mashale and Another 2006 (1) SA 269 (O).. 118

Marcus v Stamper & Zoutendijk 1910 AD 58 .... 57, 59

MEC for Education: KwaZulu-Natal and others v Pillay 2008 (1) SA 474 (CC) 147

Meyer v Keiser 1980 (3) SA 504 (D) 200

Minister of Health and Another NO v New Clicks South Africa (Pty) Ltd and Others (Treatment Action Campaign and Another as Amici Curiae*)* 2006 (2) SA 311 (CC) 147, 151

Minister of the Interior v Lockhat 1961 (2) SA 587 (A) 67, 206

Minister of Public Works and Others v Kyalami Ridge Environmental Association and Another (Mukhwevo Intervening) 2001 (3) SA 1151 (CC).. 64, 150, 158

Minister van Landbou v Sonnendecker 1979 (2) SA 944 (A) 174

Mkangeli and Others v Joubert and Others 2002 (4) SA 36 (SCA) 121

Modderklip Boerdery (Pty) Ltd v Modder East Squatters and Another 2001 (4) SA 385 (W).. 150

Morkel's Transport (Pty) Ltd v Melrose Foods (Pty) Ltd and Another 1972 (2) SA 464 (W).. 172, 174

Mpedi and Others v Swanevelder and Another 2004 (4) 344 (SCA) 128

Mphela and 217 Others v Haakdoornbult Boerdery CC and Others
    2008 (7) BCLR 675 (CC) 38, 154, 206

Myaka v Havemann and Another 1948 (3) SA 457 (A) 58

Ndlovu v Ngcobo; Bekker v Jika 2003 (1) SA 113
    (SCA) 45, 46, 118, 125–6, 152–3, 158

Nhlabati and Others v Fick 2003 (7) BCLR 806 (LCC) 197–8

Nino Bonino v De Lange 1906 TS 120 58

Nkosi and Another v Bührmann 2002 (1) SA 372 (SCA) 197–8

Occupiers of 51 Olivia Road, Berea Township, and 197 Main Street,
    Johannesburg v City of Johannesburg and Others 2008 (3)
    SA 208 (CC) 61, 69, 151–2, 154–8

Oertel en Andere NNO v Direkteur van Plaaslike Bestuur en Andere
    1983 (1) SA 354 (A) 172

Pareto Ltd and Others v Mythos Leather Manufacturing (Pty) Ltd 2000
    (3) SA 999 (W) 57

Pedro and others v Transitional Council of the Greater George [2001]
    1 All SA 334 (C) 149

Pienaar v Rabie 1983 (3) SA 126 (A) 174–5

Port Elizabeth Municipality v Peoples Dialogue on Land and Shelter and
    Others 2000 (2) SA 1074 (SE) 150

Port Elizabeth Municipality v Peoples Dialogue on Land and Shelter and
    Others [2001] 1 All SA 381 (E) 149–51

Port Elizabeth Municipality v Various Occupiers 2005 (1) SA 217
    (CC) 45, 46, 62, 67, 69, 121, 149, 153–6, 158–60, 167, 242

Port Nolloth Municipality v Xhalisa and Others; Luwalala and Others v
    Municipality of Port Nolloth 1991 (3) SA 98 (C) 64

President of the Republic of South Africa and Another v Modderklip
    Boerdery (Pty) Ltd (Agri SA and Others, Amici Curiae*)* 2005 (5)
    SA 3 (CC) 155, 159

Pretoria City Council v Modimola 1966 (3) SA 250 (A) 201

Rand Waterraad v Bothma en 'n Ander 1997 (3) SA 120 (O) 199–200

Rikhotso v Northcliff Ceramics 1997 (1) SA 526 (W) 66

Ross v South Peninsula Municipality 2000 (1) SA 589 (C) 44, 45, 125

Ruskin NO v Thiergen 1962 (3) SA 737 (A) 57

Serole and Another v Pienaar 2000 (1) SA 328 (LCC) 197

Simonsig Landgoed (Edms) Bpk v Vers 2007 (5) SA 103 (C) 134, 148

Singh v Santam Insurance Ltd 1997 (1) SA 291 (A) 57–58

Skhosana and Others v Roos t/a Roos se Oord and Others 2000
    (4) SA 561 (LCC) 125

South African National Defence Union v Minister of Defence and
    Others 2007 (5) SA 400 (CC) 147

Swanepoel v Crown Mines Ltd 1954 (4) SA 596 (A) 172

Trustees, Brian Lackey Trust v Annandale 2004 (3) SA 281 (C) 199–200

Tswelopele Non-Profit Organisation v City of Tshwane Metropolitan Municipality 2007 (6) SA 511 (SCA) 65, 66, 151–2

Van Boom v Visser (1904) 21 SC 360 200

Vena v George Municipality 1987 (4) SA 29 (C) 65

Victoria & Alfred Waterfront (Pty) Ltd and Another v Police Commissioner, Western Cape, and Others (Legal Resources Centre as Amicus Curiae) 2004 (4) SA 444 (C) 195–6

Vulcan Rubber Works (Pty) Ltd v SAR&H 1958 (3) SA 285 (A) 57

Wade v Paruk (1904) 25 NLR 219 200

Welgemoed v Coetzer and Others 1946 TPD 701 172

Wormald NO and Others v Kambule 2006 (3) SA 562 (SCA) 148, 157

Yeko v Qana 1973 (4) SA 735 (A) 58

Zondi v Member of the Executive Council for Traditional and Local Government Affairs and Others 2005 (3) SA 589 (CC) 196

UNITED KINGDOM

Barrett v Morgan [2000] 2 AC 264 100

Beaulane Properties Ltd v Palmer [2005] 3 WLR 554 108

Belfast City Council v Miss Behavin' Ltd [2007] 1 WLR 1420 (HL) 111

Bradney v Birmingham City Council and Birmingham City Council v McCann [2003] EWCA Civ 1783 .... 108, 110

Bruton v London & Quadrant Housing Trust [2000] 1 AC 406 .... 98, 105

Butcher v Poole Corporation [1943] KB 48 99

Cowan v Department of Health [1992] Ch 286 54

Doherty v Birmingham City Council and another [2006] EWCA Civ 1739 .... 110, 113

Doherty (FC) and Others v Birmingham City Council [2008] UKHL 57 (HL) 108, 110, 111–13, 144, 161–4

Ezekiel v Orakpo [1977] QB 260 99

Haniff v Robinson [1993] QB 419 (CA) 105

Harrow London Borough Council v Qazi [2003] UKHL 43 58

Harrow London Borough Council v Qazi [2004] 1 AC 983 (HL). 11, 42, **50–51**, 55, 99, 107–10, 161–2, 164, 189

Holland v Worley (1884) 26 ChD 578 200

Hunter v Canary Wharf Ltd [1997] AC 655 (HL) 98

JA Pye (Oxford) Ltd and Another v Graham and Another [2000] 3 WLR 242 179

JA Pye (Oxford) Ltd v Graham [2001] 2 WLR 1293 (CA) 179, 181

JA Pye (Oxford) Ltd v Graham [2003] 1 AC 419 (HL) 173–4, 179–80

Jaggard v Sawyer and Another [1995] 2 All ER 189 (CA) 202

Kay and Others v Lambeth London Borough Council and Others [2004] 3 WLR 1396 (CA) 163

Kay and Another v London Borough of Lambeth and Others; Leeds City Council v Price and Others [2006] UKHL 10 (HL).............................. 51, 107–8, 110–13, 131, 144, 161–3

Lambeth London Borough Council v Howard [2001] 33 HLR 58; [2001] EWCA Civ 468 107

Lancashire City Council v Taylor [2005] 1 P & CR 2 107

Leeds City Council v Price [2005] 1 WLR 1825 (CA)..................................... 162–4

Manchester City Council v Romano [2004] 1 WLR 2775................................... 113

McPhail v Persons (Names Unknown) [1973] Ch 447 143

Newham London Borough Council v Kibata [2004] 15 EG 106............. 107–8, 110

North Devon Homes v Brazier [2003] L & TR 26................................... 113

Poplar HARCA v Donoghue [2001] 3 WLR 183 107

Price v Leeds City Council [2005] 1 WLR 1825 108

Shelfer v City of London Electric Lighting Co [1895] 1 Ch 287 (CA)........... 200–201

Smith v Secretary of State for Trade and Industry [2008] 1 WLR 394 .... 109, 207

Southwark London Borough Council v St Brice [2002] 1 WLR 1537 58

Southwark London Borough Council v Williams and Another; Southwark London Borough Council v Anderson and Another [1971] 2 All ER 175 (HL).. 143–4

Tuley v The Highland Council 2007 SLT (Sh Ct) 97 194

White v Knowsley Housing Trust [2007] EWCA Civ 404 102

UNITED STATES OF AMERICA

Armstrong v United States 364 US 40 (1960) 191

Berman v Parker 348 US 26 (1954) 206

Block v Hirsch 256 US 135 (1921).. 89

County of Wayne v Hathcock 684 NW2d 765 (Mich 2004)............................. 207

Hawaii Housing Authority v Midkiff 467 US 229 (1984)............................ 206, 244

Kaiser Aetna v United States 444 US 164 (1979)............................. 36, 53, 189, 192

Kelo v City of New London, Connecticut 545 US 469 (2005) 12, 206–7

Lindsey v Normet 405 US 56 (1972) 55

Loretto v Teleprompter Manhattan CATV Corp 458 US 419 (1982)..... 53, 189, 192

Pennell v City of San Jose 485 US 1 (1988)... 55–6

Poletown Neighborhood v Council v City of Detroit 304 NW2d 455 (Mich 1981).. 207

PruneYard Shopping Center v Robins 447 US 74 (1980).................... 53, 191–2, 195

Spector v Norwegian Cruise Line Ltd 545 US 119 (2005)................................ 192

Yee v City of Escondido 503 US 519 (1992) 36, 53

TABLE OF LEGISLATION

SOUTH AFRICA

Black Areas Regulations 1969.. 62
Black Communities Development Act 4 of 1984 62
Black Land Act 27 of 1913 62
Black Local Authorities Act 102 of 1982... 62
Blacks (Prohibition of Interdicts) Act 64 of 1956 .... 62, 66
Blacks (Urban Areas) Consolidation Act 25 of 1945 62
Communal Land Rights Act 11 of 2004 118
Communal Property Associations Act 28 of 1996 118
Community Development Act 3 of 1966.. 62
Constitution of the Republic of South Africa 1996 .... 19,39–40, 43–6, 56,
                        59, 62, 64, 66, 68–9, 72, 97, 113, 115–22, 126, 130,
                  146–50, 153–4, 156–60, 174, 197-8, 201, 206, 212, 227, 240
Deeds Registries Act 47 of 1937... 59, 201
Development Trust and Land Act 18 of 1936 62
Extension of Security of Tenure Act 62 of 1997 .... 45, 67, 115–16, 118,
                                                 122–3, 125–7, 134, 148, 197
Formalities in Respect of Leases of Land Act 18 of 1969 .... 59, 116
Group Areas Act 36 of 1966 62
Health Act 63 of 1977 .... 61, 62, 155
High Court Rules 58, 117
Housing Act 4 of 1966 62
Housing Act 107 of 1997 57
Interim Protection of Informal Land Rights Act 31 of 1996 .... 129, 147–8
Labour Relations Act 66 of 1995 147
Labour Tenants Act 3 of 1996 .... 118, 122, 129
Land Settlement Act 12 of 1912 64
National Building Regulations and Building Standards
    Act 103 of 1977 .... 155, 157–8
National Policy for General Housing Matters Act 102 of 1984........... 62
Physical Planning Act 88 of 1967 61–2
Population Registration Act 30 of 1950... 62
Pound Ordinance 32 of 1947 (Natal) 196–7
Prescription Act 18 of 1943 .... 172–3, 176
Prescription Act 68 of 1969 .... 172–3, 176

Prevention of Illegal Eviction from and Unlawful Occupation of
  Land Act 19 of 1998 .... 40, 43–6, 56, 61, 64, 69, 115, 118, 122–6,
                              134, 146–7, **147–51**, 152–4, 157, 166, 230–31
Prevention of Illegal Eviction From and Unlawful Occupation of Land
  Amendment Draft Bills published on 16 November 2007 (*GG* 30459)
  and 22 December 2006 (General Notice 1851, *GG* 29501). 152
Prevention of Illegal Squatting Act 52 of 1951 .... 62–4, 65, 66
Prevention of Illegal Squatting Amendment Act 104 of 1988 65
Promotion of Administrative Justice Act 3 of 2000 .... 147, 151
Promotion of Equality and Prevention of Unfair Discrimination
  Act 4 of 2000 140
Regulations for the Administration and Supervision of a Black Urban
  Residential Area and Related Issues 1968 62
Regulations for the Administration and Control of Townships in
  Black Areas 1962 62
Rental Housing Act 50 of 1999 .... 45, 57, 113, 114–16, 118, 123–9, 134
Rental Housing Amendment Bill 2007, http://www.info.gov.za/gazette/bills/
  1999/b29d-99.pdf (18 June 2008) 115
Rent Control Act 80 of 1976 .... 114–5, 128
Rents Act 33 of 1942 114
Rents Act 43 of 1950 114
Reservation of Separate Amenities Act 49 of 1953 62
Slums Act 76 of 1979 .... 61, 62
Trespass Act 6 of 1959 62

OTHER COUNTRIES

Americans with Disabilities Act of 1990 (USA) 192
Anti-Social Behaviour Act 1996 (UK) 103
Bankruptcy Act (*Konkursordnung*) (Germany) 87
Basic Law for the Federal Republic of Germany (*Grundgesetz
  fur die Bundesrepublik Deutschland* or *GG*) 1949 (Germany). 48–9, 90–3,
                                                            96, 113, 141
Caravan Sites Act 1968 (UK) 164
Chancery Amendment Act 1858 (UK) 201
Civil Rights Act of 1964 (USA) 192
Constitution of Ireland 1937 (Ireland) 40
Countryside and Rights of Way Act 2000 (UK) 194
Disability Discrimination Act 1995 (UK) 113
Dutch Civil Code 1938 (*Burgerlijk Wetboek* or *BW*)
  (Netherlands) 86, 203
Dutch Criminal Code (Netherlands) 138, 141
Dutch Civil Code (*Burgerlijk Wetboek*) (Netherlands) 89, 203–4

European Convention on Human Rights 1950
(Europe)/ 11, 50, 55, 84, 104, 106–14
135, 161–2, 164–6, 213, 220
European Social Charter (Europe) 165–6
General Equal Treatment Act 2006 (*Allgemeines Gleichbehandlungsgesetz*
or *AGG*, 14 Aug 2006, BGB1 I S 1897) (Germany) 113
German Civil Code (*Bürgerliches Gesetzbuch* or *BGB*)
(Germany) 48, 86–8, 92, 93, 141, 202–4
German Criminal Code (*Strafgesetzbuch* or *StGB*) (Germany) 141
Homestead Act of 1862 (USA) 183
Housing Act 1980 (UK) 103
Housing Act 1985 (UK) 98, 100, 102, 108–9
Housing Act 1988 (UK) 100, 102–3, 130
Housing Act 1995 (UK) 103
Housing Act 1996 (UK) 100
Housing Act 2004 (UK) 100
Human Rights Act 1998 (UK) 14, 16, 20, 55, 79, 84,
104, 106, 164–5, 213, 220
Insolvency Act (*Insolvenzordnung*) (Germany) 87
Irish Constitution 1937 (Ireland) 40
Landlord–Tenant Framework Act (*Mietrechtsrahmengesetz*) 2001
(Germany) 86
Land Reform Act 2003 (Scotland) 194
Land Registration Act 1925 (UK) 176, 181
Land Registration Act 2002 (UK) 176, 178–9, 182
Leegstandwet 1986 (Netherlands) 139, 141
Limitation Act 1980 (UK) 176, 179-81
Mobile Homes Act 1983 (UK) 164
Protection from Eviction Act 1977 (UK) 58, 101, 104, 106, 109
Sale in Execution Act (Gesetz über die Zwangsversteigerung und die
Zwangsverwaltung) (Germany) 87
Supreme Court Act 1981 (UK) 201
US Code (42 USC 3601; 3604) (USA) 113

1

Property in a Transformative Setting

I. Facing up to Social and Political Transformation   1
II. Property Theory in a Time of Transformation   12

I. Facing up to Social and Political Transformation[1]

AROUND 1989, WHEN real political change first appeared possible without a bloody revolution, South Africans[2] who acknowledged the injustices
of the apartheid state were caught between hope for much-needed political
reform and fear of an uncertain future. Despite rigorous state censorship, newspapers like *Vrye Weekblad*[3] and *Weekly Mail* carried news and opinion pieces
during the 1980s that challenged the state-sponsored certainties of the apartheid era
and an increasing number of people realised that the inequality, discrimination and
brutality that characterised the apartheid regime's institutionalised system of racial
segregation should not and could not survive. By the end of 1989, everybody who
held democratic values would have welcomed an end to the state of emergency;
many people were ready for true democracy and a black majority government;
and even for the most fearful amongst the white minority the end of apartheid
seemed less of a threat than it did just a decade earlier. Radical political change was
in the air.

However, for the privileged white minority the idea of radical political change
had not lost its threat completely. After centuries of racial discrimination and

---

[1] The first section of this chapter is loosely based on, and therefore resembles parts of, the introductory section of AJ van der Walt, 'Legal History, Legal Culture and Transformation in a
Constitutional Democracy' (2006) 12 *Fundamina* 1–47. The article, based on an early version of this
chapter, was written as background for a keynote address delivered at the annual conference of the
South African Society of Legal Historians, Pretoria, 24–26 January 2006.

[2] I am not claiming that apartheid privilege and power are exclusive to the white population as a
minority group or that all whites are privileged by apartheid; my arguments hold for all those who
benefited from the privileges of the apartheid system, directly or indirectly. However, that does not
change the fact that political power and economic privilege were distributed fundamentally unequally,
along racial lines, in the apartheid order and that whites were the primary beneficiaries. See nn 4–6.

[3] Max du Preez (political commentator and former editor of *Vrye Weekblad*) provides an overview
of the history and contents of this influential newspaper in *Oranje Blanje Blues: 'n Nostalgiese Trip—
Vrye Weekblad 88–94* (2005).

exploitation and four decades of institutionalised apartheid, white political power and social and economic privilege were largely secured by apartheid politics—the entrenchment of the huge divide, along racially defined lines, between material privilege and disadvantage was a central feature of the apartheid system.[4] Exclusive or privileged access to land and natural resources and the concomitant opportunity for white people to accumulate wealth, combined with the forced removals and the restrictions upon free movement and economic activity that accompanied state-enforced racial segregation,[5] helped to secure white privilege while at the same time politically and economically marginalising millions of black South Africans, inexorably reducing many of them to homelessness and poverty.[6] Consequently, even some of those who were in favour of political change by 1989 were concerned about the future, because it was clear that the abolition of apartheid and the establishment of a new democracy based on human dignity and equality inevitably had to be accompanied by a significant shift in the existing patterns of wealth distribution. In the absence of visible changes that would substantively improve the social and economic position of the majority, political change would be hollow and meaningless. At the same time, political change that included

[4] For general perspectives on the history during which white privilege was entrenched through the establishment of political and economic domination in South Africa see H Giliomee, *The Afrikaners: Biography of a People* (2003); SJ Terreblanche, *A History of Inequality in South Africa, 1652–2002* (2002); H Giliomee and R Elphick *The Shaping of South African Society, 1652–1840* (2nd edn, 1989).

[5] Approximately 3.5 million people were affected by forced removals between 1960 and 1983, but this figure does not reflect the impact that influx control had in the urban areas, or that of forced removals within the so-called 'homelands' or Bantustans. For more information see L Platzky and C Walker, *The Surplus People: Forced Removals in South Africa* (1985).

[6] The United Nations' *South Africa Human Development Report* (2003) shows that in 2003 48.5% of the South African population lived well below the national poverty line of R533 (around US$75) per adult per month. Furthermore, the Gini-coefficient that rates inequality has risen from 0.596 in 1995 to 0.635 in 2001 (a higher figure being more unequal): *South Africa Human Development Report* (2003) 5. According to UNICEF, 11% of the South African population was living on less than US$1 (ZAR 7.50) a day during 1994–2004. In the same period, the bottom 40% of the population shared in 10% of the total household income, while the top 20% of the population's share was 62%: http://www.unicef. org/infobycountry/southafrica_statistics.html (accessed 25 January 2008). This means that the income share of the richest 10% in South Africa was 65 times that of the poorest 10%: *South Africa Human Development Report* (2003) 284. In 1998 black people owned only 2% of economic wealth: *South Africa Human Development Report* (2003) 72. During 1994–98 white South Africans' Human Development Index (HDI) was on par with that of Canada or Israel, while the HDI for black South Africans compared to that of the citizens of Swaziland: *South Africa Human Development Report* (2003) 94. Some 2.4 million households lived in informal housing structures in 2005: Opening Address by LN Sisulu, Minister of Housing, Housing Indaba, Cape Town, 22 September 2005: http://www.housing.gov.za/ Content/Social%20Housing%20Contract/SPEECH%20AT%20THE%20HOUSING%20INDABA1. doc (accessed 25 January 2008), although the state announced early in 2007 that it planned to eradicate all informal housing by 2014 (which requires building 500,000 houses a year from 2007, in addition to the 2.5 million houses built since 1995): see *Business Report* of 29 January 2007 at http://www. busrep.co.za/ (accessed 29 January 2007). It is often said that apartheid resulted in a situation where more than 80% of the population was crammed into less than 13% of the land. Since 1994, over 1.2 million people have benefited from various state land reform programmes, representing delivery of more than 3 million hectares of land, but that still falls short of the goal of redistributing 30% of agricultural land by 2014: for more detail see the Address by Ms Thoko Didiza, Minister of Agriculture and Land Affairs, National Land Summit, Johannesburg, 27–30 July 2005: http://land.pwv.gov.za/ publications/news/speeches/Land%20Summit.2005.01.doc (accessed 25 January 2008).

substantive and meaningful social and economic reforms would inevitably threaten the social and economic security of the white minority.

Substantive corrective justice could therefore not be reached without a knock-on effect for those who enjoyed the benefits of the apartheid economy. Economic power and privilege are evident in every aspect of white South Africans' lives, from personal security to education, employment, housing, medical care and retirement. The beneficiaries of apartheid realised that substantial social and economic reforms might deprive them of these forms of material wealth and of the personal security and social stability embodied in it. In a very real sense, merely being a member of the privileged white minority had become a valuable property asset that was threatened by the prospect of transformation.[7] Ultimately, the fear that transformation would require material sacrifice was based on the realisation that property was at the heart of the economic and social divisions created and upheld by the apartheid state,[8] which implies that transformation—including the reversal of apartheid dispossessions and improvement of the general maldistribution of property and its social and economic consequences—inevitably had to bring about a significant shift in the distribution of property, wealth and privilege. The prospect of change therefore raised serious questions about the measurable or quantifiable effects of reforms for the privileged white minority: Exactly how much change would be required to abolish apartheid and to establish a non-racial democracy? Would restitution and reparation be required; would revenge and punishment be part of it? How much white privilege and personal security would have to be sacrificed for democracy and justice? Could legal and economic stability be preserved during the process of political and social transformation?

Some of the white anxiety and resistance inspired by the prospect of political reform was channelled into efforts to avoid or curb the most painful effects of change—in the face of inevitable social reform, damage control became an important part of supposedly progressive white legal theory and practice. The most disin-

[7] The structural interconnectedness of racial segregation and privilege was recognised in US Critical Race Theory in the literature on 'whiteness as property'; see CI Harris, 'Whiteness as Property' (1993) 106 *Harvard LR* 1707–91 (particularly 1731–6 on the property functions of whiteness); MR Mahoney, 'Segregation, Whiteness, and Transformation' (1995) 143 *Univ Pennsylvania LR* 1659–84 (particularly 1660–69 on the social construction of whiteness). See further L Alcoff and E Mendieta, *Identities: Race, Class, Gender, and Nationality* (2003) at 85–6: 'The relative economic, political and social advantages dispensed to whites under systematic white supremacy in the US were reinforced through patterns of oppression of blacks and Native Americans . . . These advantages became institutionalised privileges, became part of the settled expectations of whites . . . Through legal doctrine, expectation of continued privilege based on white domination was reified; whiteness as property was reaffirmed.' On a different level, the prospect of political change also threatened the marginal security of those who had never enjoyed any material privilege and who had never had access to wealth, in the sense that the political changes could close down avenues by which some black people managed, against all odds, to acquire a stake in the privileges of property. As is pointed out below, this argument is sometimes used to oppose change, but it does not counter the whiteness as property argument.

[8] The argument is formulated clearly by Gregory S Alexander, *The Global Debate over Constitutional Property: Lessons for American Takings Jurisprudence* (2006) 12: 'Perhaps more than in any other new democracy in the world today, in South Africa the status of property rights is at the very center of the nation's future. Whether and how South Africa will be able to fully transform itself and completely eradicate all vestiges of its apartheid past is substantially a matter of property.'

genuous damage-control argument acknowledges that apartheid was a political aberration that had to be abolished from society, but hastens to add that 'mistakes of the past had to be avoided in future' and that post-apartheid law should be free from all politics, including reformist political ideals to reverse the effects of apartheid or to transform society.[9] In other words, the necessity and even inevitability of transformation is accepted, provided it remains a political and not a legal process and it leaves existing rights largely unaffected—the injustices brought about by apartheid are blamed on the law being politicised in general, not on the politics of apartheid in particular. According to this strategy, transformation means depoliticisation of the law: Reforms in the property sphere should be restricted to the creation of new rights in property (especially land), without affecting existing rights. A related strategy is to recognise the need for limited reforms, but to balance the need for change against the need for (particularly economic) stability and security. Accordingly, proponents of this approach could be seen to support social and economic reform while still insisting that transformation should not threaten the stability of the status quo. One popular argument along these lines is that the security of investment and business confidence could increase the prospect of reducing poverty by ensuring economic growth and development, and that effective protection of existing property holdings is therefore especially necessary in a time of social and political transformation.[10] The assumption behind this argument is that transformation relies on economic stability and growth, which implies that existing property rights should be constitutionally protected and secured rather than threatened by transformation.[11] Inevitable reform had to be

---

[9] See to this effect JM Potgieter, 'The Role of the Law in a Period of Political Transition: The Need for Objectivity' (1991) 54 *THRHR* 800–97 at 802: 'It must be stressed that the basic assumption that the South African legal system as a whole has become illegitimate, is unfounded. The crisis in South Africa lies primarily in the socio-political rather than the legal sphere.'

[10] In June 1995 the Agricultural Employers Organization expressed similar concerns with regard to the imminent passing of the Land Reform (Labour Tenants) Bill, arguing that the proposed protection of labour tenants would be 'against the Constitution that guarantees ownership and property rights'. The Bill, it was averred, would change the idea of private ownership and frighten off foreign investors: P du Toit, 'Vrae oor Hanekom se Grondhervorming' *Finansies & Tegniek* (15 June 1995) 37. Ten years later, Agri SA stated that the state's land reform interventions in private landownership caused uncertainty and affected the economy unfavourably, especially in terms of labour and food security: L Bosman, 'Grondteikens Moet Ander Doelwitte in Ag Neem' *Landbouweekblad* (11 November 2005) 106. In early 2008 reactions in the media against the draft Expropriation Bill (tabled in the Portfolio Committee on Public Works on 26 March 2008; see the Parliamentary Monitoring Group's website at www.pmg.org.za) were also shaped by these arguments; in August the Bill was withdrawn because of the public reaction against it.

[11] It has been argued that the ANC government's economic policy has developed increasingly in the direction of neo-liberalism, which might seem to support this kind of counter-reform argument. See H Marais, *South Africa: Limits of Change. The Political Economy of Transformation* (1998) 146–7, referring to the discussion document on a new economic policy 'The State and Social Transformation' (1996), which set the scene for the government economic strategy known as the Growth, Employment, and Redistribution policy (GEAR). For more detail on GEAR see http://www.info.gov.za/otherdocs/1996/gear.pdf (accessed 12 February 2008). This argument relies on what Gregory S Alexander in *The Global Debate over Constitutional Property: Lessons for American Takings Jurisprudence* (2006) 24ff calls 'the formalist trap'; described as 'the assumption or claim that without constitutional protection, property rights are unlikely to enjoy the degree of security and stability that is necessary for a properly functioning liberal democracy as well as for an efficient free market economy'. Alexander argues, with

restricted to policy interventions in the form of creation of new rights and upgrading of existing rights, neither of which would threaten the continued security of existing rights or the stability of the legal and economic order.

Another related argument holds that global social and economic changes over the last decades have brought about shifts in the landscape of property, reducing the wealth-building and wealth-conserving role of land and fixed assets while increasing the significance of intangible sources and forms of property. Consequently, it is argued that social and economic transformation that focuses too strongly on land reform will inhibit growth and development prospects.[12] According to this view, the real purpose of transformation should be economic growth and not redistribution. Similar to the previous line of argument, the approach here is that redistribution should focus on the creation of new rights, particularly new-order rights that create and sustain wealth outside of the narrow sphere of land. Job creation, access to higher education and training, and black economic empowerment are singled out as special foci for attention. Again, the assumption is that transformation should not interfere with existing rights. Both these arguments restrict property reform to forward-looking—in other words, political—rather than backward-looking processes. The reform-inhibiting potential of this general line of argument has been pointed out, especially by critics of the comparable neo-liberal tendencies in the Mbeki government's economic policy. Apart from the criticism based on different economic perspectives and policies, it should also be clear that the approach embodied in these arguments would restrict property reform to political intervention rather than fundamental reform of the legal or the economic system: Law, as a protector of the security of vested and acquired rights and guarantor of the stability of the system, is primarily backward-looking.

The transformation fears of the privileged white population around 1989 were in stark contrast with the black majority's seemingly unshakeable determination that social and political change had to and would come about sooner or later and that it would bring about a meaningful redistribution of property. The overwhelming political message of the Mass Democratic Movement during the late 1980s and the early 1990s was that, despite concerns about an uncertain future, it was time to face up to inevitable political, social and economic reform and its implications. At least in part the rebellion of December 2007 against the Mbeki government should be seen in the light of a wish within the ANC (and its allies in the labour movement) to return to a more poverty-focused and a less growth-focused set of economic and social policies.

The peaceful transition that followed release of political prisoners and the unbanning of the ANC in 1991 was largely counter-intuitive, at least as far as many

reference to Canada and India, that constitutional entrenchment of property is not a requirement for a liberal democracy or for an efficient free market economy.

[12] M Robertson, 'Land and Human Rights in South Africa (A Reply to Marcus and Skweyiya)' (1990) 6 *SAJHR* 215–27 at 219 provides an interesting perspective on these arguments in his analysis of white resistance against land reform. Robertson discusses the need to balance 'black antagonism' and inevitable land reforms carefully against 'white security' and the protection of land rights as human rights.

leaders of the previously oppressed majority were concerned.[13] The possibility of a peaceful transition, during which at least some measure of stability and security could be guaranteed, was therefore initially no more than an unlikely ray of hope held out by a visionary minority of black leaders. This possibility formed the fragile but indispensable foundation for negotiations about a peaceful political transition: A political settlement could bring about a peaceful transition to a democracy based on human dignity and equality without necessarily destroying existing privilege. A peaceful transition therefore became possible on the basis of agreement that political change, while inevitable, need not be disastrous, but it was clear that such a transition would scarcely enjoy any legitimacy unless it could provide real benefits for poor and marginalised members and sectors of society. A peaceful political transformation thus inevitably had to include very substantial, even dramatic, corrective measures that would change the existing distribution of wealth visibly and substantively.[14] In the absence of real and significant social and economic transformation, a peaceful political settlement would be a hollow and meaningless gesture that could not bring lasting security or stability. A peaceful political transition was possible, but only at the cost of significant social and economic transformation, which would presumably have significant implications for the personal security and the systemic stability of the existing property regime. By the early 1990s this message was broadcast loud and clear in political circles. The remaining legal puzzle was how to structure a peaceful transformation that would simultaneously recognise and uphold vested property interests, at least up to a point where the risk of systemic instability was acceptably low, and also promote real and significant restitution and redistribution of property and wealth.

From the paragraphs above it appears that the prospect of political change elicited two apparently contradicting sets of reactions[15] that, between them, set the

[13] Recent struggle histories such as M Gevisser, *Thabo Mbeki: The Dream Deferred* (2007) and A Butler, *Cyril Ramaphosa* (2007) make it clear that this attitude was not generally or even widely accepted amongst either the ANC exile community or the broader democratic movement inside the country until well after the unbanning of the ANC and the release of political prisoners in 1991. Even after the first democratic elections in 1994 many high-placed and influential ANC leaders believed that some form of military conflict would be inevitable before true liberation would become possible.

[14] This realisation was reflected relatively early even in legal literature about property; see eg TW Bennett *et al* (eds), *Land Ownership—Changing Concepts* (1986) (also published as 1985 *Acta Juridica*), with a range of contributions on changing legal concepts of ownership and the effects of apartheid politics on landownership; A Sachs, *Protecting Human Rights in a New South Africa* (1990) (ch 9 at 104–38 deals with 'Rights to the Land'); CR Cross and RJ Haines (eds), *Towards Freehold: Options for Land and Development in South Africa's Black Rural Areas* (1988) (papers, mainly from economists and development specialists, many of whom spell out the effects of apartheid politics and economics on the development of the black rural areas); as well as articles by G Budlender and J Latsky, T Marcus, Z Skweyiya and M Robertson in a special section, entitled 'Debating the Land Issue', of (1990) 6 *SAJHR* 155–227. Other early publications of a similar nature are cited in these sources.

[15] AJ van der Walt, 'Dancing with Codes—Protecting, Developing, Limiting and Deconstructing Property Rights in the Constitutional State' (2001) 118 *SALJ* 258–311 describes the confrontation between these two postures regarding existing privilege and change (protective vs demanding, rights vs needs, rule of law vs justice, security vs transformation) as a static, fundamentally sterile dance according to different cultural (dancing) codes. See nn 12 and 14.

agenda for the early debate about transformation.[16] Amongst the privileged white
minority and their representatives, the transformation debate centred upon a core
of continued individual security and systemic stability: How do we restrict the
transaction cost of political change to levels that could render the prospect of
transformation personally and systemically acceptable or at least provisionally
reassuring? By contrast, amongst the formerly oppressed and marginalised black
majority and their representatives, the debate centred upon justice-driven reform
that would inevitably result in some discontinuity and change: How do we abolish
the apartheid system with maximum speed and efficiency, and how do we reverse
its legacy of oppression, inequality, injustice, poverty and marginalisation?

Although the contrast between those who feared change and those who insisted
on it appears stark and uncompromising, there was always room for efforts to
mediate between stability and change—some commentators who shared the
majority view that reform and change were paramount nevertheless argued that
transformation had to include a measure of social, economic and political stability, and they therefore favoured complex solutions that could dismantle
apartheid's legacy of poverty, marginalisation and structural inequality without
necessarily destroying all prospects for economic growth and without undermining the fragile political compromise that seemed to facilitate a peaceful transition.[17] The compromise made possible by these mediating or balancing arguments
nevertheless implied significant political change that unmistakably posed the
threat of real material sacrifice on the part of the previously advantaged and still
powerful white minority, who would not have supported a negotiated settlement
that eroded all or most of their security. Even in a transitional situation where the
moral and political justification for change is beyond dispute, this raises serious
questions about stability, which highlights the difficulties associated with the fundamental contradiction between stability and change.

The question was: Can transformation be promoted in a negotiated political settlement that avoids the worst outcome of the conflict between stability and change,
or is transformation only possible through revolution and uncompromising majority domination, with all the implications that revolutionary change would probably
have for the continued security of existing property holdings and for the prospects
of future economic growth and welfare? The solution that emerged from the South
African political negotiations appears misleadingly simple: The tension between stability and change that results from a negotiated peaceful transition cannot be
avoided or overcome altogether, but a contextually optimal, non-destructive and
possibly sustainable tension between the two forces can be approximated if real and
significant social and economic reform or transformation is a primary obligation

---

[16] See n 15. In Duncan Kennedy's terminology, this conflicting reaction and the tension it embodies can be described as an aspect of the fundamental contradiction between egoism and altruism, or
between our need for others and society, and our fear of the Other: see D Kennedy, 'Form and
Substance in Private Law Adjudication' (1976) 89 *Harvard LR* 1685--778 at 1713–24 (first describing
a 'sense of contradiction'); D Kennedy, 'The Structure of Blackstone's *Commentaries*' (1979) 28 *Buffalo
LR* 209–382 at 211–13 (relating this ambivalence to the notion of a fundamental contradiction).

[17] See n 14.

authorised and regulated by a democratic constitution based on human dignity, equality and freedom. Existing rights, including property rights, could continue to be recognised and protected legally and constitutionally, but would simultaneously be restricted, within the boundaries of the same constitutional framework that demands and enables significant reforms. This idea, associated by US academic Karl Klare with the notion of 'transformative constitutionalism',[18] represents a broad framework within which it was claimed that conflicting aspirations and concerns about transformation could be accommodated and reconciled and it embodies the preferred solution of many theorists who want to attain real and effective transformation via a peaceful, negotiated transition. Since 1994 a number of South African lawyers have attempted to analyse and expand upon this seemingly simple yet powerful formula for change that is at once effective and bearable.[19]

Although the notion of transformative constitutionalism is said to be capable of accommodating or negotiating the seemingly intractable tension between democratic majority rule and constitutional stability, even in a time of large-scale social and political reforms, participants in the transformation discourse have pointed out that it also evokes further questions: How does one explain the apparent contradiction of transformation in a constitutional democracy? After all, transformation implies change, while constitutionalism traditionally secures stability—can the two really be held in a creative tension, or is that just a theoretical delusion?[20]

---

[18] K Klare, 'Legal Culture and Transformative Constitutionalism' (1998) 14 *SAJHR* 146–88 at 166–7 coined and developed the phrase 'transformative constitutionalism' to describe a delicately balanced tension between democratic majority rule and constitutional checks and balances. I return to Klare's analysis in later chapters. At 150, Klare formulates the question discussed in the text above as follows: 'The major question . . . is whether it is possible to achieve this sort of dramatic social change [social and economic transformation] through law-grounded processes.'

[19] The notion of transformative constitutionalism has been taken up and developed further in publications such as H Botha, 'Metaphoric Reasoning and Transformative Constitutionalism' (2002) *TSAR* 612–27; (2003) *TSAR* 20–36; D Moseneke, 'The Fourth Bram Fischer Memorial Lecture: Transformative Adjudication' (2002) 18 *SAJHR* 309–19; H Botha, 'Freedom and Constraint in Constitutional Adjudication' (2004) 20 *SAJHR* 249–83; W le Roux, 'Bridges, Clearings and Labyrinths: The Architectural Framing of Post-Apartheid Constitutionalism' (2004) 19 *SAPL* 629–75; T Roux, 'Continuity and Change in a Transforming Legal Order: The Impact of Section 26(3) of the Constitution on South African Law' (2004) 121 *SALJ* 466–492; AJ van der Walt, 'Transformative Constitutionalism and the Development of South African Property Law' (2005) *TSAR* 655–89; (2006) *TSAR* 1–31; M Pieterse, 'What do we Mean when we Talk about Transformative Constitutionalism?' (2005) 20 *SAPL* 155–66; S Liebenberg, 'Needs, Rights and Transformation: Adjudicating Social Rights' (2006) 17 *Stell LR* 5–36; P Langa, 'Transformative Constitutionalism' (2006) 17 *Stell LR* 351–60. See further the contributions of H Botha, D Davis, J Froneman, J van der Walt and K van Marle in H Botha *et al* (eds) *Rights and Democracy in a Transformative Constitution* (2003), and compare the early analyses of C Albertyn and B Goldblatt, 'Facing the Challenges of Transformation: Difficulties in the Development of an Indigenous Jurisprudence of Equality' (1998) 14 *SAJHR* 248–76; P de Vos, 'A Bridge too Far? History as Context in the Interpretation of the South African Constitution' (2001) 17 *SAJHR* 1–33.

[20] Klare's solution is that this seemingly paradoxical combination of transformative constitutionalism is possible within a 'postliberal' reading of the South African Constitution; 'postliberal' referring to a departure from the liberal view that a constitution is primarily intended to secure individual self-determination, combined with a new reading that highlights the social redistributive, caring, positive, partly horizontal, participatory, multicultural and self-consciously transformative aspects of the Constitution: K Klare, 'Legal Culture and Transformative Constitutionalism' (1998) 14 *SAJHR* 146–88 at 153*ff*.

Is a democratic constitution that seems to entrench existing privilege and power workable in a political, social and economic situation that so palpably requires radical transformation? Can and should a constitution (and the judges who interpret and apply it) restrain democratic political and social transformation in a way that would reassure the previously privileged minority to a degree, without insulating existing privilege and inequality and frustrating the previously disadvantaged democratic majority? Is significant reform really possible within a process of peaceful, negotiated transformation?

The idea of transformative constitutionalism does not guarantee certainty or closure on questions about social, economic and political reform but, at most, can assist in opening the debates about them up for further critical analysis and discussion. From the early debates it emerged that the idea of transformative constitutionalism need not be seen as a grand post-apartheid narrative that provides undisputed responses and clear answers—at most, it is a useful and challenging hook upon which to hang a critical post-apartheid debate about reform, development, stability and change.[21] However, notions of democracy, constitutionalism and transformation remain contested and open to different interpretations.[22]

Fully recognising the open and contested aspects of these notions, I hang my discussion of property theory on the hook of transformative constitutionalism by investigating the meaning of property in the context of substantive social, economic and political transformation in a constitutional democracy. My point of departure is that South Africans, when forced by historical developments to face up to politically inevitable and morally justified large-scale social and political change, chose to do so in the context of transformation within a democratic constitutional system, which apparently offers opportunities for simultaneous accommodation of security and justice; stability and change. The notion of transformative constitutionalism is therefore a framework within which change, reform or development of legal rules, practices and institutions (such as private property) can be analysed and discussed with due recognition of their social and political context in a particular history. The South African example provides a discursive framework for a contextual argument that highlights the intrinsic links between politics, law, and property with reference to the tension between the security of existing property interests and the justice of reforming the property regime.[23] Property interests, the social and economic distribution of property and the social and political power associated with property occupy a significant

---

[21] On South African constitutional meta-narratives see P de Vos, 'A Bridge too Far? History as Context in the Interpretation of the South African Constitution' (2001) 17 *SAJHR* 1–33; compare M Pieterse, 'What do we mean when we Talk about Transformative Constitutionalism?' (2005) 20 *SAPL* 155–66.

[22] The questions raised here also involve issues about legal certainty, legitimacy and foundation that are discussed in subsequent chapters.

[23] I am using the term 'property regime' in roughly the same sense as Eduardo M Peñalver, 'Reconstructing Richard Epstein' (2006) 15 *William & Mary Bill of Rights J* 429–37 at 434: '[in contrast to a specific government practice or policy] a regime is an entire complex of interlocking practices that constitute the permissible operations of the state'.

position in the historical development and the social and political processes leading up to and inhabiting the South African transformation, and therefore the process of transformation in South Africa and the accompanying notion of transformative constitutionalism provide a useful backdrop for a theoretical analysis of property.

Against this backdrop, facing up to inevitable social and political transformation also means facing up to significant reform of the property regime, including reforms that will affect the security and protection of existing property interests. The changes and reforms that are clearly required, even in the restrictive context of the political settlement, can clearly not be limited to forward-looking political interventions in the form of upgrading existing rights and creating new rights—at some point, these reforms will inevitably have an impact upon existing rights and privileges created under and protected by the apartheid property regime. Moreover, the changes and reforms that are required include at least some reform of the system of property rules and practices as such, as opposed to interventions in the current distribution of property rights and privileges. Transformation requires change both in the distribution pattern of property holdings and in the law that governs the acquisition, transfer and protection of property rights. Change will affect both individual security and systemic stability.

From the introductory passages above it may appear as if my remarks about facing up to social and economic transformation—and, with it, the rest of my analysis of property—are particular to the South African post-apartheid context, but they have a wider application. In addition to the first signs that apartheid was nearing its end, 1989 also witnessed the fall of the Berlin Wall and signalled the demise of old-style communism in Eastern Europe. The transformative implications of these developments in Eastern and Central Europe and the similarities with developments in South Africa are clear even without any normative evaluation of their social or political justification. Like South Africa, all or most of the constitutional democracies that emerged in the aftermath of the velvet revolutions of 1990 also struggle with continuity and transformation; they also highlight the need to reconcile necessary social and economic reforms with access to and the security of private property interests, and the need for economic stability and growth in a globalised market; in many of them the apparently conflicting need for stability and the duty to transform are also embodied in a new democratic constitution.[24] Similar problems emerged in post-authoritarian South American and other post-colonial African democracies,[25] where relatively new legislatures and courts

---

[24] I refer to other sources below, but see eg GS Alexander and G Skàpska (eds), *A Fourth Way. Privatization, Property, and the Emergence of New Market Economies* (1994); IS Pogany, *Righting Wrongs in Eastern Europe* (1997); RG Teitel, *Transitional Justice* (2000).

[25] IS Pogany, *Righting Wrongs in Eastern Europe* (1997) concentrates on Eastern European democracies that recently made the switch from communist rule to constitutional democracy; he also focuses largely on restitution issues as opposed to the more general redistribution question and he includes non-property abuses and restitutions in his discussion. RG Teitel, *Transitional Justice* (2000) does not focus on property issues, although she does spend a chapter on reparatory justice; she also concentrates on Eastern European countries, but she does refer to African and South American examples.

are also struggling to come to terms with the legacy of unjust existing property regimes, the demands of a new constitutional democracy that requires corrective justice, and the requirements of economic growth and stability in a global market.[26] Even in older, stable democracies such as Canada, Australia and New Zealand, post-colonial restitution claims for land and other property lost by indigenous populations raise questions about the security and inviolability of vested property rights.[27] The so-called Aboriginal land claims and the case-law emerging from them provide ample illustrations of the way in which justice claims can threaten both the security of vested individual property rights and the stability of the current property system, especially when the restitution claims are based upon notions of justice and on rhetoric and logic that are foreign to the Western legal system. In Western European countries such as Germany and the Netherlands post-World War II legislative measures to alleviate the housing shortage have created conflicts between property owners and socially marginal-ised groups since the 1970s, amongst other effects resulting in demonstra-tive politically inspired unlawful occupation of unused buildings;[28] current conflicts over the residential use of land in the United Kingdom[29] and the United

---

[26] See eg TW Bennett *et al* (eds), *Land Ownership—Changing Concepts* (1986) (also published as 1985 *Acta Juridica*); JP Powelson, *The Story of Land. A World History of Land Tenure and Agrarian Reform* (1988); CR Cross and RJ Haines (eds), *Towards Freehold: Options for Land and Development in South Africa's Black Rural Areas* (1988); AJ van der Walt (ed), *Land Reform and the Future of Landownership in South Africa* (1991).

[27] See eg on cultural appropriation, which is a complicated post-colonial version of the land debate, B Ziff and PV Rao (eds), *Borrowed Power. Essays on Cultural Appropriation* (1997). Compare further RH Bartlett, *The Mabo Decision; With Commentary and the Full Text of the Decision in* Mabo and Others v State of Queensland (1993); S Swain and A Clarke, 'Negotiating Postmodernity: Narratives of Law and Imperialism' (1995) 6 *Law & Critique* 229–56; AJ van der Walt, 'Modernity, Normality, and Meaning: The Struggle between Progress and Stability and the Politics of Interpretation' (2000) 11 *Stell LR* 21–49; 226–243 at 28–49; H Mostert and P Fitzpatrick, '"Living in the Margins of History on the Edge of the Country"—Legal Foundation and the Richtersveld Community's Title to Land' (2004) *TSAR* 309–23, 498–510.

[28] See AJ van der Walt, 'De Onrechtmatige Bezetting van Leegstaande Woningen en het Eigendomsbegrip: Een Vergelijkende Analyse van het Conflict tussen de Privaat Eigendom van Onroerende Goed en Dakloosheid' (1991) 17 *Recht & Kritiek* 329–59. I return to the Dutch and German case-law and literature on this point in ch 5.

[29] Two interesting and conflicting cases that illustrate the point recently emerged from the UK. In *Harrow London Borough Council v Qazi* [2004] 1 AC 983 (HL) the House of Lords decided that Art 8 of the European Convention on Human Rights 1950 does not authorise judicial scrutiny of state hous-ing policy to determine the appropriateness of allowing a landlord to recover possession, based on the impact that eviction might have on the home life of the tenant. Proportionality issues, according to the majority, have already been decided at the legislative level and cannot be reopened for every individual case by the judiciary. K Gray and SF Gray, *Elements of Land Law* (4th edn, 2005) paras 2.70–2.75 at 137–40; paras 14.16–14.17 at 1495–7 point out that this decision appears to contradict the decision in *Connors v United Kingdom* (2004) 40 EHRR 189, where the European Court was willing to examine the proportionality of the eviction despite the fact that the local authority had already terminated the ten-ants' licence. Two recent publications on English law indicate that questions about security of the home are highly disputed and extremely relevant in English law, albeit in a slightly different context (com-pared with my discussion of the South African land issue): L Fox, *Conceptualising Home: Theories, Laws and Policies* (2007); S Bright, *Landlord and Tenant Law: Past, Present and Future* (2007). I return to the English cases and literature in ch 4.

States[30] emphasise the continued importance of struggles between long-standing property rights and the traditionally underrated interests of socially and economically marginalised groups. The broad assumptions of liberal economics and politics are subjected to searching criticism in the worldwide environmental and anti-globalisation movements and in postcolonial literature. Many of the issues and arguments brought into the public sphere by these movements relate directly or indirectly to the South African transformation debate. In this book I focus on the South African situation because I am more familiar with it and because it has obvious illustrative value, but many of the questions I discuss are neither restricted to post-apartheid South Africa nor interesting only in recently 'liberalised' or democratised nations, and therefore I relate them, wherever possible, to more general issues and to examples and literature from other jurisdictions.[31]

II. Property Theory in a Time of Transformation[32]

The point of the introductory section above is to show that the political option that South Africans chose as a way out of the confrontational stand-off created under apartheid, namely a negotiated political settlement that would establish a constitutional democracy based on human dignity, equality and justice, could only succeed if real and significant social and economic reforms were included under the fundamental and primary constitutional obligations to be placed upon

---

[30] There is a case to be made in support of the proposition that the decision of the US Supreme Court in *Kelo v City of New London, Connecticut* 545 US 469 (2005) illustrates a similar tension between economically marginalised and economically powerful legal interests. See K Gray, 'Human Property Rights: The Politics of Expropriation' (2005) 16 *Stell LR* 398–412 for an early discussion of *Kelo*. In *The Edges of the Field: Lessons on the Obligations of Ownership* (2000) JW Singer explores the tension between property rights and the interests of socially and economically marginalised groups in US law; GS Alexander, *Commodity and Propriety—Competing Visions of Property in American Legal Thought 1776–1970* (1997) does the same. A recent publication shows acute awareness of just the kind of social and economic shifts I have in mind and their implications for property theory and practice: HM Jacobs (ed), *Private Property in the 21st Century: The Future of an American Ideal* (2004). I return to these authors and their views in chs 4 and 5.

[31] In other jurisdictions, land issues may appear like simpler, more straightforward economic disputes between the commercial interests of investors and landlords and the personal interests of occupiers of residential property, whereas South African land disputes have a more obvious political aspect, embedded as they are in a history of apartheid and racial discrimination. This difference appears most strongly from the perspective of private or commercial law; compare eg L Fox, *Conceptualising Home: Theories, Laws and Policies* (2007); S Bright, *Landlord and Tenant Law: Past, Present and Future* (2007) (emphasis, as far as the most relevant case-law is concerned, on the conflict between occupiers of residential property and landlords and/or creditors). However, as both authors cited here point out and as appears more clearly from a stronger public-law or human-rights perspective, the differences are more apparent than real—the legal choice between protecting landowners and creditors as against occupiers and debtors is always a political decision with significant social and economic overtones and implications. I return to this point in later chapters.

[32] Parts of this section of the chapter rely on passages from ch 7 of AJ van der Walt, *Constitutional Property Law* (2005) at 410–27, where I first made the point that eviction is the paradigmatic context within which to discuss the transformation of property law, particularly in South Africa.

the legislature, the executive and the judiciary, as well as civil society, albeit in a different way. Because of the close historical and causal links between apartheid and remaining social and economic inequalities, it is an inevitable and non-negotiable prerequisite for success of the negotiated settlement that the new democratic government should bring about visible and significant social and economic reforms that would redress some of the direct effects of apartheid inequality and rectify the general maldistribution of social and economic privilege, wealth and power. It is also clear that reforms of this nature would inevitably have an impact upon the privileged protection and security of existing property interests, particularly in the area of land law, where apartheid had the most visible and lasting effects. Effectively, it had to be accepted that the success of a peaceful and negotiated transition depended in part upon reforms of the property regime that inevitably would have a negative effect on the continued security of existing property interests. It was furthermore necessary to acknowledge that the necessary reforms would inevitably go much further, at least in some instances, than the 'business-as-usual', so-called interstitial dogmatic shifts and adaptations that characterise 'normal' developments of the common law. At least in some instances, reform would imply significant changes to the current system of property rules and practices and have a negative impact upon existing property rights and interests.

Accepting the negative impact of social and political reform on existing property interests cannot be rationalised as a simple political or pragmatic trade-off that has little or no effect on legal principle or theory and that simply had to be accepted as a politically expedient anomaly that disturbs the aesthetic and logical coherence of pre-existing property law. In the historical context of the South African transition from apartheid to a constitutional democracy, making suitable adjustments in the existing property regime is a matter of moral and social obligation rather than purely political expediency—if anything, post-1994 reform of property law represents an effort to rectify politically expedient anomalies introduced by apartheid law. Apartheid was perhaps the most glaring example of purely ideological or political decision-making, but it nevertheless had deep and lasting effects on the very fabric of the law, including property law. Accordingly, the effects of transformation on existing property rights cannot be dismissed as being irrelevant for property law because they depend on arbitrary (or at least debatable) political whim—as far as their effects are concerned, the political processes that initiate and drive these reforms are comparable to and just as relevant as any other regulatory process that affects the distribution of privilege, wealth and power in society. The social and political reform of apartheid society (like the social and political reform processes that take place in other democracies) is a valid context for a theoretical analysis of property because it involves both the actual content and scope of property interests and the moral and political justification for amending the content and scope of those interests.

The central question in this book is whether it is possible to theorise property in the context of social and political transformation that highlights the fundamental tension between protection of established property interests and promotion of socio-economic justice through some form of redistributive politics. For the reasons set out in the introductory section above I contextualise this question within a society committed to large-scale political, social and economic reform away from injustice and inequality, and towards the establishment of a constitutional democracy based on human dignity, equality and justice. Obviously this focus fits well for property regimes that are affected by large-scale political and social reforms in emerging or new democracies, but similar considerations apply in other, established constitutional democracies to the extent that they also from time to time require or bring about (larger or smaller) social and economic reforms, for example by introducing or amending protective housing laws to satisfy membership requirements of the European Union or under the economic influence of globalisation.[33]

For the kind of analysis I have in mind it is necessary to follow a slightly different approach than has become customary in literature on property theory. To focus on property within the context of social, economic and political change is not an original idea, and a few theorists have recently discussed property questions with specific attention for political issues, but by and large it is still true that a substantial body of property theory tends to concentrate on different perceptions of the limits of property within a well-established and generally accepted (and therefore more or less stable) property regime. A significant part of recent property theory concerns itself with the tension between the (constitutional and private law) protection of existing property holdings and the (constitutional and private law) justification of regulatory limitations placed upon private property. Accordingly, recent writings on property theory tend to emphasise the paradoxical nature or aspects of property and the need to balance the protection of existing property interests with restrictions imposed upon property rights in the interests of the collective.[34]

What is absent from most recent writings on property is an effort to take the social and political challenges that resulted in the developments described above seriously enough to consider the possibility of fundamental challenges to the very foundations of the existing property regime. My point of departure is that some recent challenges to the security of vested property interests and to the stability of existing property regimes are serious enough, at least in South Africa but perhaps elsewhere as well, to warrant critical reconsideration of the way in which we think and argue about the property regime as such. Instead of investigating the possibility to establish a balance between vested property interests and the public interest, my purpose is to investigate the possibility of significant reforms in the

---

[33] Social, economic and political change, reform or transformation can assume many different forms and formats, but an obvious example that illustrates the relevance of these issues for established democracies is globalisation, including the social and legal processes involved in the formation and growth of the European Union, the effects of international human rights law on domestic legal systems, and the adaptations required in the UK since the adoption of the Human Rights Act 1998. As will appear from examples cited in this and other chapters below, each of these processes involves shifts towards greater equality and a notion of justice that, at some point, brings the apparently inviolate security of landowners' rights in conflict with the interests of weak or even unlawful occupiers.

[34] See examples of relevant literature in n 37.

very foundations of the existing property regime, possibly by way of establishing a balance between the forces involved in significant and meaningful structural reforms of society or of property law. Above all, my interest is focused on the implications that considering such a reform process might have for the way we conceptualise and argue about property in general. Justice often requires that property rules and practices be qualified or amended in a certain way, without thereby necessarily undermining or threatening the property regime consisting of rules and practices that constitute and uphold a particular distribution of property holdings. However, certain justice-driven qualifications of and amendments to the property regime are so fundamental that they cannot be accommodated within or explained in terms of the current doctrine—they require a rethink of the system, a reconsideration of the language, the concepts, the rhetoric and the logic in terms of which we explain and justify choices for or against individual security and systemic stability in the property regime. My aim is to distinguish between 'business-as-usual', 'normal' or systemically bearable limitations of property and qualifications of the property regime and the larger, system-threatening changes and qualifications that are sometimes required in a transformational setting, and to try and theorise the implications of this distinction.

According to libertarian and even classic liberal perceptions,[35] property is a basically unrestricted right that can accommodate restrictions—by way of exception—when the need for a restrictive measure is justified by a clear, immediate or overriding public interest (including the need to protect the rights of others).[36] Recent theory qualifies this so-called absolutist notion of property, usually by adding that property may be the most important and extensive right with regard to assets and wealth, but is nevertheless legitimately and routinely subjected, in the public interest, to sometimes extensive limitations and restrictions, provided they are legitimately imposed, properly authorised and proportional to the purpose for which they are imposed or allowed. In a number of cases this resulted in a property theory that underlines the tension between two conflicting visions or understandings of property, one emphasising the power of private property and the other qualifying that power with reference to morality or a broad notion of the

---

[35] The nuances of libertarian, liberal and utilitarian versions of this traditional approach are set out briefly and clearly by Eduardo M Peñalver 'Reconstructing Richard Epstein' (2006) 15 *William & Mary Bill of Rights J* 429–37. Perhaps the most illuminating nuance highlighted by Peñalver (at 430) is that Richard Epstein— widely regarded as a hard-core libertarian—distinguishes himself from traditional libertarians such as Robert Nozick in that Epstein embraces 'the notion that human beings are typically cooperative, social animals'; while he distinguishes himself from other liberals such as Ronald Dworkin in that Epstein sees property as a system that embodies and protects a libertarian conception of individual rights subject to utilitarian constraints, while Dworkin views individual rights as constraining an utilitarian conception of the common good.

[36] See P Birks, 'The Roman Law Concept of Dominium and the Idea of Absolute Ownership' (1985) *Acta Juridica* 1–37 for an introductory discussion of this notion, with further references. Compare AJ van der Walt, 'Marginal Notes on Powerful(l) Legends: Critical Perspectives on Property Theory' (1995) 58 *THRHR* 396–420. In Anglo-American law, similar perceptions relate back to libertarian readings of Blackstone; see CM Rose, 'Canons of Property Talk, or, Blackstone's Anxiety' (1998) 108 *Yale LJ* 601–32 and compare n 37.

public interest.[37] Generally speaking, the upshot of recent property theory has been to provide reasons for the argument that property is not absolute and that it can be and is regularly subjected to restrictive regulation based on valid considerations of morality and the public interest. Clearly this theoretical alignment against the notion of absolutism is highly relevant to the position of property in a transformational constitutional context,[38] but the property analysis I have in mind raises more fundamental issues by asserting that traditional notions of property do not suffice in transformational contexts, where the foundations of the property regime itself are or should be in question because regulatory restrictions, even when imposed in terms of a broadly conceived notion of the public good, simply cannot do all the transformative work that is required. In this perspective it is not sufficient to demonstrate that property is subject to (regular and often extensive but nonetheless exceptional) public-purpose restrictions; the point is to identify and explain instances where transformation justifies changes that question the very foundations upon which the current distribution of property rests.

Once the need for significant social and political transformation is either democratically accepted or constitutionally imposed,[39] social and economic reform will probably create (or foreground) so much or such a strong tension between the legal (and perhaps constitutional) obligation to protect existing property holdings and the political (and probably statutory and constitutional) duty to promote social and economic reform that it will inevitably affect existing property interests. The resulting collision between the political and constitutional commitment to bring about change and the 'normal' tendency of law to entrench the status quo and protect existing property holdings will often be accommodated in a doctrinal

---

[37] The most famous example is BA Ackerman, *Private Property and the Constitution* (1977), in which Ackerman describes the analytic conflict between the freedom of private property interests and the public interest in environmental regulation in terms of the difficult choice between two ideal types, described as 'Scientific Policymaking' and 'Ordinary Observing'. GS Alexander, *Commodity and Propriety—Competing Visions of Property in American Legal Thought 1776–1970* (1997) outlined what he described as the competing commodity and propriety visions of property, the former relating to the wealth-creating, economic aspect of private ownership and the latter to the status-oriented aspect of property as a mechanism for creating and maintaining social order and justice. Alexander borrowed the term 'propriety' from CM Rose, *Property and Persuasion: Essays on the History, Theory, and Rhetoric of Ownership* (1994) 58, who uses it to describe medieval and early modern practices according to which property ownership included certain responsibilities, some of which related to caring for the poor. See further CM Rose, 'Canons of Property Talk, or, Blackstone's Anxiety' (1998) 108 *Yale LJ* 601–32 at 603–4, where Rose indicates that Blackstone was well aware of and acknowledged this tradition. LS Underkuffler, *The Idea of Property: Its Meaning and Power* (2003) distinguishes between the common conception of property that describes the protected sphere of the individual as against the collective and the operative conception of property that incorporates change as part of the idea of property. Other theorists simply emphasise the paradoxical nature of property; compare eg RW Gordon, 'Paradoxical Property' in J Brewer and S Staves (eds), *Early Modern Conceptions of Property* (1996) 95–110; JW Singer, *Entitlement: The Paradoxes of Property* (2000).
[38] I return to these issues in ch 4, 5 and 6.
[39] This applies both to the obvious political transformations in South Africa or Eastern Europe and less obvious reforms, eg those that are brought about by alignment with the European Union (eg as a result of the Human Rights Act 1998 in the UK) or with global economic (and political) tendencies. Social, economic and political transformation does not have to involve large-scale changes to be significant.

shift or qualification that explains and recognises the resulting restrictions, without compromising the system of property rules and practices or the foundations of the property regime as such. However, sometimes the required shift will make it necessary to choose between stability and change on the basis of political or policy or moral considerations that are extraneous and foreign to the language, rhetoric and logic of 'technical' property doctrine;[40] in these cases, it will sometimes be impossible to explain the change within the framework of the current system. Experience in several jurisdictions suggests that, even when it is accepted that reforms are broadly justified by reformist legislation or constitutional obligation, established legal doctrine and tradition will require unambiguous and convincing reasons for allowing and accommodating the relevant changes, especially when they affect vested rights detrimentally. In borderline situations the courts and commentators will sometimes uphold the integrity of existing rights on the basis of legal doctrine, requiring the justification and authority for reforms to comply with and satisfy technical doctrinal requirements. However, in a transformative context it is arguable that the outcome of specific cases should not depend on purely 'scientific' or technical interpretation and application of more or less clear and uncontested rules or even on slightly more open balancing practices, but rather on open-ended, policy-oriented interpretation of contingent and contested standards that are formulated and applied very specifically with a view to the historical background and continued legitimacy of the property regime as a whole and the social and economic circumstances of the parties involved. Such a process clearly does not fit within the framework of the 'normal' adjudication of property disputes and therefore its acceptance as part of the transformation of property law or property holdings will sometimes entail questioning or reconsidering the very foundations of property law.

In many cases the underlying policy choice may be obscured by trite doctrinal positions that have been reified into seemingly immovable or uncontested rules and practices, with the result that judicial (or even legislative and executive) decision makers might find it difficult or impossible to see or imagine alternative outcomes. In those cases doctrinal reform might also be necessary to facilitate social and economic reform. When substantial doctrinal innovation or reform is required, the odds are stacked against significant and efficacious social and economic change because fundamental democratic institutions such as the division of powers and the rule of law by definition separate and insulate the main agents of doctrinal development, namely judges, practitioners and legal academics, from the sources, processes and dynamics of political change. Stated differently, legal doctrine that frustrates or inhibits the implementation of social and economic

---

[40] Compare in this regard the choice between Scientific Policymaking and Ordinary Observing in BA Ackerman, *Private Property and the Constitution* (1977) or the competition between commodity and propriety visions of property in GS Alexander, *Commodity and Propriety—Competing Visions of Property in American Legal Thought 1776–1970* (1997). LS Underkuffler, *The Idea of Property: Its Meaning and Power* (2003) specifically aligns stability with the common and change with the operative conceptions of property. I return to the tension between stability and change in chs 4, 5 and 6.

reforms is unlikely to change, simply because of political or policy considerations that have not been translated into the supposedly objective, neutral or scientific language that fits the doctrinal logic that most judges, practitioners and academics feel comfortable with. In a legal system where interpretation of the law depends upon professional judicial skills that are traditionally shaped and honed in the province of uncodified common law, this problem becomes critical, even (or especially) when the new democratic legislature introduces lavish amounts of new and innovative legislation in an attempt to force through the necessary reforms. In these instances legal tradition can play a major role in determining and circumscribing the possibilities for real and effective change. Politically necessary and constitutionally or statutorily authorised social and economic change could be frustrated by interpretive reluctance or doctrinal immobility shaped or informed by a legal culture that was developed in a supposedly apolitical environment but that was nevertheless almost certainly influenced by pre-reform (and very likely politically discredited) social and political thinking and attitudes. In a nutshell, lawyers who were trained in the supposedly apolitical doctrinal logic of the common law during the apartheid era and who are now confronted with open-ended policy choices that run directly against everything they have learnt will be caught between the strong normative thrust in favour of reform and their equally strong professional sensibilities in favour of what they might perceive as the neutrality, continuity and certainty of doctrinal logic; in some cases they might react by shying away from the foreign and unknown, thereby indirectly but effectively favouring the status quo and frustrating or inhibiting real change.[41] For the most part, these lawyers might well be unable to even understand, let alone acknowledge or question, the fact that they have acted upon and favoured one rather than another moral, political and theoretical approach to property.

All these modalities are present in post-apartheid South Africa. Large-scale social and economic reforms are morally justified and politically and legally authorised, and it is clear that they must have a significant impact on existing property holdings. Apartheid land law was a central feature of the apartheid system and therefore it is clear that the political and social transformation will have to include significant and substantive reforms of the property regime. At the same time private property is protected by a largely uncodified civil law system of private law rules that are doctrinally strongly inclined to protect individual interests against sweeping social policy interferences. The interpretation and adjudication of private law principles and rules are dominated by a professional set of skills and attitudes that traditionally avoid political and social policy standards, preferring to rely on supposedly clear-cut rules in what is regarded as a scientific system of rights and remedies. Recent experience shows that even lawyers and politicians who are in favour of significant reforms favour a forward-looking, political approach that avoids

---

[41] K Klare, 'Legal Culture and Transformative Constitutionalism' (1998) 14 *SAJHR* 146–88 at 166–72 first made this point about the transformation-inhibiting effect of legal culture in the South African context; see further in the same vein RJ Coombe, '"Same as it Ever Was"—Rethinking the Politics of Legal Interpretation' (1989) 34 *McGill LJ* 603–52.

backward-looking reassessment of and interference with existing rights and with the system of property law as such. Given the protective and confirming tendencies of doctrinal tradition, such a restrictive approach will very likely restrict or even prevent real change. Real and effective social and political reform is therefore bound to require a measure of doctrinal development and adaptation, which in fact is explicitly authorised and commanded by the Constitution.[42] At the same time, the constitutional provision that apparently reinforces the private law protection of existing property holdings also requires and mandates substantive reform of land law, which could pose a threat to existing land holdings.[43] The constitutional provision that explicitly deals with property thus deepens the tension between stability and reform because it embodies within itself an apparently contradictory set of provisions that represent the fundamental tension between protection of existing property holdings and reform of the property regime for the sake of social and economic justice. Instead of reading the provision as a whole that requires a completely different style of thinking and argument, lawyers both for and against change might find grounds for their particular approach in its paradoxical structure, thereby strengthening their respective choices for one or another of two conflicting views of and approaches to property in a time of transition.[44]

---

[42] Section 8 of the 1996 Constitution provides as follows:

8. (1) The Bill of Rights applies to all law, and binds the legislature, the executive, the judiciary and all organs of state.
    (2) A provision of the Bill of Rights binds a natural or a juristic person if, and to the extent that, it is applicable, taking into account the nature of the right and the nature of any duty imposed by the right.
    (3) When applying a provision of the Bill of Rights to a natural or juristic person in terms of subsection (2), a court

    —in order to give effect to a right in the Bill, must apply, or if necessary develop, the common law to the extent that legislation does not give effect to that right; and
    —may develop rules of the common law to limit the right, provided that the limitation is in accordance with section 36(1).

Section 39(2)–(3) adds:

'39. (2) When interpreting any legislation, and when developing the common law or customary law, every court, tribunal or forum must promote the spirit, purport and objects of the Bill of Rights.
    (3) The Bill of Rights does not deny the existence of any other rights or freedoms that are recognised or conferred by common law, customary law or legislation, to the extent that they are consistent with the Bill.'

[43] Section 25(1)–(3) of the 1996 Constitution protects property interests, while s 25(5)–(9) authorises and requires land reform. See in this regard AJ van der Walt, 'Striving for the Better Interpretation: A Critical Reflection on the Constitutional Court's *Harksen* and *FNB* Decisions on the Property Clause' (2004) 121 *SALJ* 854–78; AJ van der Walt, *Constitutional Property Law* (2005) 26–42.

[44] Interestingly, the government at least seems to be aware of the paradox and is attempting to deal with it. Compare, eg, the way in which land reform programmes are premised on the necessity to change land holding patterns and the obligation to respect existing rights. See eg S Benton, 'Section 25 of Constitution will Help Land Reform' *BuaNews*, 28 October 2005, http://www.eprop.co.za/news/article.aspx?idArticle=6472 (accessed 12 February 2008). *BuaNews* is a 'South African news service which provides quick and easy access to articles and stories aimed at keeping the public informed about the implementation of government's mandate' (www.buanews.gov.za) (accesssed 12 February 2008).

The restrictive effect that legal and property doctrine has on the possibility of real and effective reform could suggest that effective change is possible only through revolutionary action after all, but in my view the seemingly paradoxical structure of the South African constitutional property provision indicates that this need not be the case. As an essential part of the negotiated settlement that made the peaceful transition possible, this constitutional provision indicates that the conflict between stability and change, between security and justice and between property and reform cannot be avoided or denied—it is an inherent part of the politics of transformation. My central hypothesis for the purposes of this book is that the stand-off between the moral, political and constitutional obligation to change and the cultural, doctrinal and methodological tendency to resist, postpone or minimise change is not only a fruitful but an essential locus for critical reflection about property.

The rest of this book is predicated upon this hypothesis and its implications. In the first place I assume that transformational situations highlight the tension between stability and change in the sense (and to the extent) that they include a moral and political impulse to reform and a cultural and doctrinal tendency to resist or minimise change. Secondly, I assume that these situations and the tension they embody present an essential context for critical reflection upon property because property is so fundamentally socially, morally and politically shaped and determined and therefore paradoxical. In the introductory section I explained this hypothesis with reference to the ideas that social, economic and political factors help shape property regimes; that property regimes reflect the characteristics of their accompanying economic, social and political systems; and that property regimes are therefore fundamentally political in nature and prone to the effects of (larger or smaller) political processes of change and reform. Property regimes reflect the outcomes of political power but are simultaneously always open to political reform; hence they are constantly prone to transformative change.[45]

The peaceful transition to democracy and social justice in South Africa presents theorists with a fascinating real-life example of a large-scale politically driven and morally justified reform of the property regime within the framework of democratic transformative constitutionalism.[46] If it is at all possible to theorise property meaningfully in a transformative constitutional context, it should be possible— and it will also be valuable—to do so in the South African setting, although the same set of modalities are also at work in other societies and legal systems, both in

[45] This means that I discuss property within the context of political rather than doctrinal issues, although the discussion of property in a transitional context obviously has implications for doctrinal questions. I return to the relationship between law and politics in later chapters.

[46] As I emphasise in this chapter and demonstrate with reference to case-law and literature, the same aspects are also present in many other democracies, both in the context of obvious large-scale political, social and economic reforms (eg in Middle Europe, South America or elsewhere in Africa) and in instances where reforms and changes are smaller in scale or less obvious but nevertheless present (eg in the UK subsequent to adoption of the Human Rights Act 1998, in Western Europe following the formation of the European Union and in post-colonial democracies struggling to come to terms with restitution claims and with multiculturalism and globalisation in general).

countries that recently underwent or are currently going through an obvious political transition and in stable, established societies where change takes place on a smaller scale and at a slower rate.

Electing to discuss property in a transformative context has the additional methodological advantage that, in such a context, the principles, rules, practices and institutions of property law are stretched to the limit and challenged in the sense that they do not function 'normally'. Because of the transformational setting and the strong moral and political impulse to reform, interpretation and application of the law take place in circumstances that are by definition extraordinary; at the same time, moral pressure in favour of reform prevents interpreters from resorting to 'normal' doctrinal techniques of extension and development. At best, existing doctrine might be rendered inapplicable or irrelevant by overwhelming policy considerations; at worst, the very foundations of doctrinal positions or techniques might be in question because of its development during a now discredited political era. In either case the personal security and systemic stability normally guaranteed by well-established and known rules and logic and doctrinal tradition make room for personal uncertainty and systemic openness. In a time of political change, new policy directions require lawmakers and interpreters to take cognisance of uncertain and vague standards and considerations that otherwise might have been ignored or deemed unsuitable for legal reasoning. As a result of these and related results of the transformational setting, the principles, rules, practices and institutions of property law are placed under severe strain and it becomes possible to consider and analyse them from a different perspective, without the usual 'normalising' force of their established doctrinal logic and rhetoric.

In a very fundamental sense the transformational setting means that property loses its traditional central position and acquires a marginal character: As soon as property is considered in a transformational context, the monolithic presence of securely entrenched existing property interests and the insulated logic of current property rhetoric and doctrine loses its hegemonic grip on property discourse because of the intrusion of otherwise marginal considerations and issues that enter the debate as soon as past and present political and social evils and injustices are raised and condemned as part of the justification for reform. Acknowledging the social origins and nature of property also implies that social injustice affects and shapes the property regime; conversely, recognition of the need for social reform implies acceptance of the justification for reform of the property regime, whether it be on a smaller or larger scale. At the same time, marginal persons and groups (in the form of those who suffered under the injustices of the discredited regime or whose position must be taken seriously because of the political changes) become more important in a social and political debate that can no longer be dominated by purely technical legal issues. It is a central theme of my approach in this book to consider property from this marginal perspective and to develop the implications of such a perspective for property theory in general. For that purpose it is necessary to reflect on thinking about property, particularly thinking about the nature and function of change in property regimes.

In the terminology of Thomas Kuhn,[47] some challenges to existing theory can only be responded to adequately by scientific explanations that embody or rely on a fundamental shift in the theoretical framework of basic assumptions that underlie the relevant scientific endeavour. In the same spirit, I focus on property issues that challenge existing knowledge or thinking about property in a way that cannot be responded to adequately by the doctrinal developments that typify 'normal' science—these issues and the context in which they arise require a fundamental rethinking of traditionally accepted assumptions and truths about property rather than doctrinal refinement or adaptation. My point of departure is that property issues acquire a distinctive marginal aspect in the transformational situations described earlier and that they then pose fundamental challenges to the 'normal' theoretical assumptions and problem-solving tools of property law and the theoretical framework that underpins it. I am therefore interested in property issues that cannot be explained or solved adequately—in view of the political acceptance and constitutional authorisation of the need for reform—by 'normal' legal responses in the sense of small or incremental doctrinal adjustments or developments; issues that, instead, require solutions that depend upon or only become possible as a result of paradigmatic shifts in the very foundations of what was traditionally accepted as normal or true or valid about property.

Stated differently, I discuss property from the (disad)vantage point that Gerrit van Maanen once described as 'balancing on the edge of the legal system';[48] a place where one is precariously placed in such a way as to be constantly looking down into the abyss of problems that cannot be solved by 'normal' legal science. From this marginal position on the edge of the legal system it appears that certain problems cannot simply be treated as exceptions that require adaptations or developments of the existing doctrine; the problems themselves assume a central position that demands reconsideration of what was previously considered 'normal'. Or, framed within yet another theoretical discourse, I consider property not from the perspective of 'normal' property holders, 'normal' property relationships and 'normal' property issues, but rather from the perspective of persons, relationships and issues that are marginal in relation to—and marginalised by—the 'normal' regime of property holdings. In one sense, my approach resembles the one aspect of the 'bad man' example of Oliver Wendell Holmes,[49] where he famously argued that the

---

[47] TS Kuhn, *The Structure of Scientific Revolutions* (1962); I used and refer to the enlarged second edition (1970). Kuhn discusses the nature of 'normal science' in ch III and the nature of scientific revolutions in ch IX.

[48] See GE van Maanen, 'Balanceren op de Grens van de Rechtsorde' (1982) 8 *Recht & Kritiek* 467–71.

[49] In his ground-breaking speech of 1897, published as OW Holmes, 'The Path of the Law' (1897) 10 *Harvard LR* 457–78 and republished a century later in (1997) 110 *Harvard LR* 991–1009. Something similar could be read into the statement of PJ Proudhon, 'Avertissement aux Propriétaires' in C Bouglé and H Moysset (eds), *Oeuvres Completes de PJ Proudhon* (new edn, 1938) vol XIV at 200 that property is theft; a judgment that only makes sense when considered from the perspective of the landless labourer who adds value to the land but does not have title. (Proudhon's point is that the owner does not add any value beyond what has been added by the labourer, which belies Adam Smith's argument in support of private property.)

'bad man' or criminal who breaks the law and faces the consequences in a criminal trial and in prison understands the law more fundamentally than the academic lawyer who thinks about the law in abstract concepts. I do not subscribe to Holmes' pragmatist and consequentialist position on the 'bad man' perspective or to the instrumentalist connotations that have since been attached to the bad man example, and I would not argue that my approach overlaps with his to any significant extent, but his argument about the alternative perspective of the bad man does illustrate the point that the effect of legal rules on marginalised persons and groups in society discloses valuable insights that are unlikely or impossible in 'normal' circumstances. Mari Matsuda proposed something similar in what she called a 'new epistemological source', based on studying 'the actual experience, history, culture, and intellectual tradition of people'.[50] Matsuda is specifically interested in the actual experience of people of colour, but the same could hold for other forms of marginalisation such as poverty or gender, especially since these forms of marginality are connected. Her approach therefore points, for my purposes in this book, towards the possibility of theorising property not with reference to the central property status of property institutions or the property holdings of the advantaged, but rather with reference to the actual experiences of those who find themselves on the margins of society and of property distribution patterns. Again, Eric Hobsbawm's famous *Bandits*,[51] a socio-historical study that selects as its central focus the shady underworld of social bandits, illustrates something of my point that a study of property law could benefit from focusing not on the central figures of rich and powerful property owners, but rather on the marginal figures of those who do not share in wealth and power. Charles van Onselen did something similar in his celebrated socio-historical study of sharecropping in South Africa.[52] For sociologists and social historians it might appear reasonably obvious to select a marginal social group as their study; for lawyers even this first, tentative look towards the margins is a novel idea. To take the second, even more unfamiliar, step of assessing the validity and justifiability of mainstream legal dogma from the unfamiliar vantage point of the margins is obviously not only novel but threatening.

In the analysis to follow I focus on the marginal or powerless social and political position of persons and groups who were disadvantaged by apartheid and argue that the 'poor person's' experience of property law is particularly interesting for property theory, especially in so far as this experience involves conflict with the

---

[50] MJ Matsuda, 'Looking to the Bottom: Critical Legal Studies and Reparations' (1987) 22 *Harvard Civil Rights–Civil Liberties LR* 323–99 at 325. See particularly 323–6, where Matsuda explains her epistemological approach and contrasts it with the more abstract moral approach of J Rawls, *A Theory of Justice* (1971) and BA Ackerman, *Social Justice in the Liberal State* (1980). Rawls and Ackerman propose an abstract attempt to imagine oneself in the shoes of the poor or the black in some hypothetical world; Matsuda (citing A Gramsci, 'The Intellectuals' in *Selections from the Prison Notebooks* 5 (1972) and C West, *Prophesy Deliverance! An Afro-American Revolutionary Christianity* (1982) 121–2) proposes the more 'organic' epistemology of studying the actual experience of black (or poor) people.

[51] EJ Hobsbawm, *Bandits* (2nd edn, 2000).

[52] C van Onselen, *The Seed is Mine: The Life of Kas Maine, A South African Sharecropper 1894–1985* (1996).

powerful 'rich person', whose experience of the law is restricted to the law's function of protecting the existing hierarchy of vested property holdings.[53] My focus is
on property as it is experienced by those on the margins of society;[54] my argument
is that their experience of the law inherently involves conflict with privileged property positions and that marginality is therefore a vital element of property as a legal
institution. Accordingly, I argue that property can be analysed fruitfully from a
marginality perspective in a transformational setting. An important aspect of the
analysis in chapters to follow is that, although those on the margins usually hold
weak property rights or no property rights at all, marginality in itself does not
equal weakness—at least in some cases, marginality reveals a power of its own that
is highly relevant for property theory.

This perspective on property from the margins is exemplified in the most dramatic and illuminating manner by an issue that crops up repeatedly in both stable
and transitional societies: eviction of marginal, weak or unlawful occupiers from
immovable property. It is typical of eviction that it involves the enforcement of the
will of the powerful property rights holder against the will of persons whose property rights are weaker than those of the landowner, or who are unable to raise
property rights in their own defence. In the case of residential property, on which
I concentrate, eviction evokes powerful images of the indigent being evicted from
their home so that the owner can rent it out more profitably or redevelop the
property for capital gains.[55] In this sense, the eviction example embodies both the
power of property and the weakness or marginality of evictees, and hence it makes
it possible to contrast the traditional rights-dominated vision of property with the
marginal vision I have in mind. However, I also argue that marginality is not just
about weakness—marginal positions in property can sometimes be quite powerful because of the social and political context, and in those instances it is sometimes entrenched property rights or even established law and doctrine that could
be described as marginal.

---

[53] An interesting version of roughly the same perspective was developed, with reference to the relative positions and experiences of slave owners and slaves, by JB Baron, 'Property and "no Property"'
(2006) 42 *Houston LR* 1425–49.

[54] In this respect my approach could be compared to that of theorists who focus on marginality
from a philosophical perspective; see eg the literature on the needs-based constitutional argument
about social and economic justice. The classic US sources are M Tushnet, 'An Essay on Rights' (1984)
62 *Texas LR* 1363–1403; FI Michelman, 'The Supreme Court 1968 Term—Foreword: On Protecting
the Poor through the Fourteenth Amendment' (1969) 83 *Harvard LR* 7–59; and PJ Williams,
'Alchemical Notes: Reconstructing Ideals from Deconstructed Rights' (1987) 22 *Harvard Civil
Rights–Civil Liberties LR* 401–33; see the response from J Waldron, 'Rights and Needs: The Myth of
Disjunction' in A Sarat and TR Kearns (eds), *Legal Rights: Historical and Philosophical Perspectives*
(1997) 87–109. See further AJ van der Walt, 'A South African Reading of Frank Michelman's Theory
of Social Justice' in H Botha *et al* (eds), *Rights and Democracy in a Transformative Constitution* (2003)
163–211; D Brand, 'The "Politics of Need Interpretation" and the Adjudication of Socio-economic
Rights Claims in South Africa' in AJ van der Walt (ed), *Theories of Social and Economic Justice* (2005)
17–36. RG Teitel, *Transitional Justice* (2000) refers to the 'liminal' quality of justice in a transitional setting, highlighting a further aspect of what I describe as property in the margins.

[55] L Fox, *Conceptualising Home: Theories, Laws and Policies* (2007) demonstrates the same point
within the context of conflicts between occupiers and creditors in English law; see further on the same
issue S Bright, *Landlord and Tenant Law: Past, Present and Future* (2007).

In chapters two and three below I develop the working hypothesis that the conflict between stability and change (and with it the role of property in a transformational context) is illustrated most strikingly by the law regarding eviction and that a margin-sensitive analysis of property could therefore fruitfully be based upon critical reflection on eviction law. As a point of departure I sketch the contrast between the traditional property paradigm, which was dominated—at least in civil law—by the notion of ownership as the most valuable and important property right,[56] and eviction as a paradigmatic example of the marginal perspective on property. Thereafter I summarise a number of anti-eviction measures and their effect on 'normal' property discourse, before investigating (in the final chapter) the question whether the outlines of an alternative, marginality approach to land rights can be gleaned from the case-law and literature on eviction and whether it provides any useful perspectives on property law and practice. In addition to the analysis of eviction laws and cases (in chapters four and five), I also describe (in chapter six) four other areas in which the supposedly absolute or overriding right of ownership conflicts with the rights of persons whose position could, for purposes of property law, be described as weak or marginal.

[56] The difference between the traditional rights-dominated approach and my marginality approach is illustrated nicely by the case note of S Scott, 'Recent Developments in Case Law Regarding Neighbour Law and its Influence on the Concept of Ownership' (2005) 16 *Stell LR* 351–77. Scott (at 351–2) sets out to investigate the effect of recent developments in neighbour law on the concept of landownership and concludes (at 376) that case-law does not support the idea of a tendency to deviate from the traditional emphasis on the absoluteness of ownership. (She does not refer to literature in this respect but probably aims this observation at the absolutism debate mentioned in n 36 above.) As far as it goes, her examples do support her conclusion, but reflection suggests that the result of her study was predisposed by her focus. Neighbour law is by definition an area where development is restricted to 'normal science' (see n 47 above) that requires nothing more than small, incremental adaptations that improve, clarify or expand upon the well-settled doctrinal explanation of the reasonableness standard by which neighbouring landowners' rights are balanced or, occasionally, the slightly more complex reasonableness standard by which reciprocal regulatory limitations on the use of land are tested. By definition, these doctrinal developments take place within the sphere of equal privilege and power amongst neighbouring landowners. In both cases the purpose is balancing of the rights of subjects who are basically equally privileged and powerful—the issue is merely to establish the optimal balance between their rights in instances where those rights conflict because their exercise relates to contiguous land parcels so they are therefore likely to cause nuisance. The law in this regard is well developed and established in existing doctrine, but it does not have any relation to or effect on political conflicts about land reform or social and economic transformation, because neither of the parties involved in neighbour relationships was systemically marginalised by apartheid land law. In that sense Scott's project was, at least as far as she explains it as an investigation into changing concepts of landownership, theoretically misconstrued from the outset. In order to get a theoretically interesting perspective on politically inspired transitional changes in the notion of landownership it is necessary to take into account land relations that have been fundamentally structured and skewed by apartheid and post-apartheid politics. Ironically, Scott chooses to gloss over the one area where neighbour law does hold some interest for a marginal analysis of property, namely 'nuisance caused by squatters', where the rights of landowners conflict with the no-rights position of individuals and groups who have been marginalised by apartheid politics and who occupy land unlawfully. (I return to this issue in ch 5.) Scott's discussion of neighbour law cases highlights the theoretical futility of discussing transformation issues in terms of the traditional concepts and logic of property law and with reference to areas of property law that are relatively insensitive to transformational or marginal property politics because they concern only boundary conflicts between equally privileged and powerful beneficiaries of apartheid land law. Formulated differently, it is true but also meaningless to state that, judged strictly between neighbouring landowners, nothing much has changed in post-apartheid property law.

The three substantive chapters (four to six) suggest two sets of conclusions that are discussed further in the remaining chapters below and especially the final chapter. The first conclusion is that ownership and other supposedly strong property positions are in fact not nearly as strong as the rhetoric of the rights paradigm suggests. Ownership is regularly and routinely subjected to surprisingly many marginal, weak and other non-property interests for a number of policy reasons. The analysis shows that property rights are surprisingly often subjected to both 'normal', doctrinally explicable qualifications and more serious, system-challenging deviations for the sake of extra-legal social and political policy reasons. While the lesser qualifications can mostly be explained within the current property doctrine as exceptions or developments, the larger deviations can sometimes not be accommodated within or explained in terms of the doctrinal logic. However, since these qualifications and deviations are accepted for social and economic policy reasons, the resulting contradictions and inconsistencies are either explained away (sometimes unconvincingly) or simply ignored. However, interestingly, there is a worrying tendency to resist equally large, constitutionally sanctioned or required, doctrinal deviations resulting from political or transformational shifts by forcing them into the restrictive logic of 'normal' doctrinal development.

The second conclusion is that a corrective perspective on property, from the margins, needs to replace or at least complement the traditional strong-rights focus of property doctrine if real and meaningful transformation of the property is to be promoted effectively and systemically, because it is easier (and sometimes only possible) to imagine alternative property arrangements from outside the property paradigm. Within the strong-rights paradigm the larger changes that are sometimes required by significant political shifts and social transformations are more difficult to imagine because of the doctrinal tendency to restrict change or development to interstitial or incremental steps. In a transformative setting, development by incremental steps can often simply not do enough work to realise the reformist goals that drive the process of change; by preventing the necessary larger developments from taking place, the doctrinally restricted dynamics of incremental change could effectively scupper the entire transformative project.

2

Property in the Centre: The Rights Paradigm

I. Property in the Rights Paradigm   27
II. Three Illustrations   41

I. Property in the Rights Paradigm

IN THIS CHAPTER I set out the place and function of property interests in mainstream property doctrine. I describe the doctrinal framework within which property interests are traditionally considered and discussed as the rights paradigm, which is depicted as a set of doctrinal, rhetorical and logical assumptions and beliefs about the relative value and power of discrete property interests in the law and in society. For my purposes, the most interesting feature of this paradigm is that it justifies the more or less automatic rights-biased (and often ownership-biased) outcome of particular property disputes. In the rights paradigm, property interests are primarily valued according to their status as either property rights, personal rights or no-rights, and also as either strong rights, weak rights, or no-rights. The rhetoric and logic of this paradigm prescribes that property rights would usually be stronger than personal rights; that rights always trump no-rights; and that stronger rights always trump weaker rights or no-rights. Some strong rights (of which ownership is the main example) may have the status and force of trump rights, which means that they will practically always trump other rights because they are stronger than any other right. According to this paradigm, the most important issue in any dispute about property is whether any or all of the conflicting interests are recognised as rights; whether the rights that are recognised are property rights or personal rights and whether they are strong or weak rights; how the doctrinal hierarchy of property interests in a particular legal system is structured; whether a particular value (trump, strong right, weak right, no-right) is attached to a particular property interest; and which remedies are assigned to protect the stronger right in any particular conflict. These doctrinal questions usually determine the outcome of property disputes in terms of an abstract, syllogistic logic, in which contextual issues such as the general historical, social, economic or political context of the dispute and the personal circumstances of the parties have no relevance or effect. To the extent that the outcomes of concrete property disputes are determined by the power-rhetoric and the syllogistic logic of the paradigm, I describe the paradigm as abstract and hierarchical.

Although the hierarchical ordering and the legal protection of stronger or weaker property rights in civil law (Roman-Germanic) legal systems differ from those in common law (Anglo-American) systems,[1] significant features of the property rights paradigm are, at least for my purposes, shared by the two systems. The most significant features of the rights paradigm, for my purposes, are that property interests are ordered hierarchically, in the sense that some are more important than others, and abstractly, in the sense that doctrinal rhetoric and logic will determine how conflicts between different interests are decided in any specific instance, without reference to the concrete context or the personal circumstances of the parties. In both systems, the relative power of competing property claims (whether based on rights or on possession) is assessed in a stabilising, backward-looking way that is subject to the conceptual and syllogistic logic of legal doctrine; the legal rhetoric of stability and its doctrinal logic of subsumption are sharply distinguished from the forward-looking rhetoric of political intervention and the economic logic of calculation and measurement. In this and subsequent chapters I will argue that these features of the rights paradigm, in both the civil law and the common law traditions, are based on socio-political and socio-economic assumptions and rhetoric about the role of property in individual lives and in society, rather than purely on legal tradition or doctrine. In my analysis of property in the rights paradigm, the traditional and doctrinal differences between the two systems are therefore overshadowed by the similarities that are founded in their shared socio-political and socio-economic value systems. For the purposes of my argument, these shared characteristics are more important than the doctrinal differences.

I start this section off with a discussion of the paradigmatic role of ownership in civil law, which lends itself to a simpler and clearer explanation of the point I make about the power of property hierarchies. My analysis of the central role that ownership plays in civil law property regimes is followed by a few remarks about the ordering of property interests in Anglo-American law and, finally, by a discussion of the general features of property in the rights paradigm. In the second section of

[1] I am particularly indebted to Frank Michelman for his comments on an early draft of this chapter. His observations and the discussion that followed induced me to strive for a more nuanced and accurate analysis of the differences between the two systems. I am further indebted to Joseph William Singer and Kevin Gray for their helpful analyses of the relationship between property and ownership in Anglo-American law. The most obvious difference between Roman-Germanic or civil law systems and Anglo-American or common law systems is, of course, the fact that property interests are seen as relative claims to possession in the latter, which means that the stronger claim (which may sometimes not even be founded upon a property right, strictly speaking) should usually win any property dispute, whereas property interests are structured according to a more or less fixed hierarchy of property rights (ownership, limited real rights, personal rights in property, no-rights) in civil law. See in this regard also S Bright, *Landlord and Tenant Law in Context* (2007) at 48–9, citing W Swadling, 'Property: General Principles' in P Birks (ed), *English Private Law*, Vol I (2000) at 218: in a strict sense English land law has no concept of ownership since property in land is protected as possession. For purposes of English law, the strong claim to possession plays the same role that ownership does in civil law; both are characterised by the right to exclude.

the chapter I discuss three case studies from South Africa, Germany and the United Kingdom to illustrate the points made in the first section and to provide a backdrop for the detailed analysis of legislation and case-law in the following chapters.

In the civil law systems based on Roman law (including South African private law), ownership dominates the whole of property law—in a sense, all other property interests are defined with reference to the ways in which they derive from, yield to and fall short of ownership, thereby establishing a conceptual, institutional and rhetorical hierarchy of property interests. The property interests that are recognised by law and their respective places—and thus power or value—in the hierarchy are defined abstractly, that is without reference to the general context or the specific circumstances of any given property dispute. As the central property institution, ownership is the main focus of property law; the most valuable and important property relationship; and the model property arrangement that gives birth to all other property rights and against which their strengths and value—but also their shortcomings and weakness—are measured. In the civil law systems, ownership can be described as the pinnacle private law right; the paradigmatic example for rights in general. In a sense, property law is the law of ownership—although a (mostly strictly circumscribed) number of lesser property interests deriving from and based on temporary or partial use of ownership entitlements are recognised, they derive from and are dependent on ownership for their existence, content and limits. Perusal of any introduction to property law in a civil law system will show that the property interests or relations that are discussed, apart from ownership, are all somehow defined by their differences from ownership, their shortcomings as measured against ownership, or their origin in limited use rights being created out of ownership. Possession is defined as factual control of things and contrasted with ownership, which is defined as legal control that normally also includes factual control, unless the owner agreed to allow another person to exercise factual control. In a straight contest between ownership and possession not based on a right derived from ownership, possession will always lose out. The limited real rights (mainly real security and servitudes) are distinguished from ownership, which is the only unlimited real right and the origin or mother right from which the limited rights are derived. Personal rights are contrasted with real rights, of which ownership is the strongest and most comprehensive right. And so on.

This abstractly hierarchical line of thinking about property reflects the victory of modern civil law over feudal law, pivoting as it does on the idea that ownership entitlements should ideally be united in one hand (not split up, complete) and as free from burdens and restrictions as possible (unlimited). In a very real sense, the personal sovereignty (*dominium*) associated with the civil law notion of absolute ownership is rooted directly in the modern ideal of political and economic liberty, much of which was informed by the desire to be free from feudal burdens. Properly translated, this civil law notion should be described as *full* or *complete* rather than *absolute* ownership, although it is often defined with reference to the latter term. Its doctrinal roots are embodied in Hugo Grotius' effort to abandon the feudal notion of split ownership with an appeal to the medieval and scholastic Roman distinction between full and imperfect ownership.[2] Relying on the distinction as it was developed by the Spanish moral philosophers from whom he borrowed so much and relating it directly (and somewhat disingenuously) to the feudal distinction between direct and beneficial ownership, Grotius proposed that the concept 'ownership' be reserved for direct ownership unencumbered by real (or feudal) burdens (*dominium directum*) and that beneficial ownership (the real, or rather feudal, rights held and exercised by vassals, or *dominium utile*) should be known merely as 'rights' because the former was clearly the more valuable of the two kinds of *dominium*.[3] Consequently, the feudal notion of beneficial ownership was effectively robbed of all its power and relegated to the category of lesser, derivative or limited real rights of control and use, while all the doctrinal and rhetorical power of ownership was reserved for the direct owner (either the feudal overlord or, in some cases the beneficial owner), even when his right has been eroded by the granting of 'lesser' use rights. In establishing this hierarchy of property interests, Grotius not only signalled the demise of feudal property relationships in civil law but also disposed of the notion of relative title. As the dominant property institution, ownership was henceforth understood to trump all other competing rights and interests in the relevant object of property, subject only to restricting legislation and limitations agreed to or licences granted by the owner. Instead of having to compete with beneficial ownership rights for the status of relative title, direct ownership thus became the pinnacle of the property hierarchy in civil law. Henceforth, ownership was regarded as the most valuable of all property rights and it was understood to be burdened by only two categories of restrictions: those accepted by the owner herself through the granting of limited real or personal use rights, and those imposed by legislation, which can also be justified as being based on exercise of the owner's free will through democratic participation in the legislative process. Apart from the democratic argument, restrictions imposed on ownership by legislation are also justified with reference to the fact

---

[2] The distinction between *dominium plenum* and *dominium minus plenum* (later also *dominium perfectum* and *dominium imperfectum*) was created and established by the glossators (see the gloss *servitus sit* at D 50.16.25; compare D Willoweit, 'Dominium und Proprietas—zur Entwicklung des Eigentumsbegriffs in der mittelalterlichen und neuzeitlichen Rechtswissenschaft' (1974) *Historisches Jahrbuch des Görres-Gesellschaft* 131–56 at 142) and developed by the Spanish moral philosophers of the sixteenth century, who related it to ownership that was either unencumbered or encumbered by the granting of limited real rights such as servitude, respectively. See R Feenstra, 'Der Eigentumsbegriff bei Hugo Grotius im Licht einiger mittelalterlicher und spätscholastischer Quellen' in O Behrends *et al* (eds), *Festschrift für Franz Wieacker zum 70. Geburtstag* (1978) 209–34 at 222 on the classical and medieval roots and use of the terminology.

[3] H Grotius, *Inleidinge tot de Hollandsche Rechts-Geleerdheid* (1621) II.33; see further AJ van der Walt, 'Der Eigentumsbegriff' in R Feenstra and R Zimmermann (eds), *Das römisch-holländische Recht* (1992) 485–520. Through this conceptual sleight of hand Grotius indirectly discarded the medieval division of direct and beneficial ownership and confirmed the abolition of feudalism and the concomitant transition from medieval to modern property law. AFJ Thibaut, 'Über Dominium Directum und Utile' in *Versuche über einzelne Theile der Theorie des Rechts* (1817, reprint 1970) vol I, Part II at 67–9 did the same for German law, but only much later. See further n 2.

that they are often not only in the public interest but also reciprocal in the sense that they serve the mutual interests of all landowners by imposing identical restrictions on them all, for their common benefit. As is the case with lesser or so-called derivative limited real rights, ownership is regarded as the source of its own restrictions. This is entirely in line with the logic of the rights paradigm, in the sense that restrictions on the liberty associated with ownership can be explained with reference to exercises of the owner's free will and without having regard for external policy interventions from the side of the state. Within the paradigm, the rhetoric and logic of ownership remain firmly backward-looking, lawyerly, stabilising the status quo.

In some ways, this picture of ownership and of the rights paradigm is of course a caricature, in the sense that the paradigm and the actual practice of property disputes will not coincide perfectly. The abstract description of the paradigm is coloured by the political and social ideal underlying the paradigm—it draws upon and focuses very strongly upon mostly unarticulated assumptions about the nature of ownership and strong property rights and their role in society, without necessarily giving full account of the qualifications and nuances that in fact detract from the power of ownership or strong rights in the messy hustle and bustle of the legal system as it functions in society. However, as I argue below and in later chapters, these assumptions and their embodiment in the abstract depiction of the paradigm have real and lasting rhetorical power; they shape the way we think and argue about property, even if they are presented in a model that oversimplifies or exaggerates the status and power of ownership. In subsequent chapters I analyse some of the legal rules and practices that qualify ownership and conclude that, on the one hand, the existence of many qualifications and nuances show that the power of ownership is in fact restricted far more by social and political policy than is acknowledged by property rhetoric. On the other hand, however, the restricting or qualifying rules and practices do not necessarily reform the property regime sufficiently to challenge the paradigm, even when they were adopted specifically for that purpose, because they could not overcome the rhetorical power of the ideal notion of ownership presented by the rights paradigm in its abstract or absolute form. As a consequence, even restrictions that were adopted specifically to reform the current property regime often continue to function merely as limited exceptions and qualifications that do no more than circumscribe the traditional status and power of ownership, and then only in so far as these changes can be proven and justified with reference to explicit, properly authorised, legitimate and reasonable legislative measures or contractual agreements. As a rule, these qualifications are not seen as fundamental amendments of the property paradigm or challenges to the power of ownership.

In view of the introductory remarks it might be useful to rehearse the outlines of my main argument here, before returning to the discussion of the rights paradigm. The first part of the argument (in this chapter and chapter three) is that property relations are ordered and property conflicts are adjudicated within a paradigm that favours the protection of existing rights and the stability of the status quo through its abstract, acontextual, backward-looking, rights-privileging rhetoric and logic. The second part of the argument (in chapters four, five and six) is that there are, in fact, many examples of property rules and practices that apparently detract from or at least qualify the strong ownership or rights focus of the paradigm. The third part of the argument (in the same chapters) is that some of these examples do illustrate often quite significant qualifications of the rights paradigm, but that only a small number of them actually undermine or challenge the paradigm in a fundamental way. A fundamental challenge to the paradigm is defined (in this chapter and in chapter three, followed up in chapters four, five and six) as an instance where a party with a weaker right or without any property right is allowed to challenge and prevent eviction by the owner or a person with a stronger right (in property or to possession), purely because of contextual factors or personal considerations that are unrelated to the relative rights of the parties. The argument (in chapter one) that meaningful reform of the property regime will in some instances depend upon significant departures from the rights paradigm is followed up (in the final chapter) by discussing the possible value of a marginal focus or perspective on property, which could weaken or undermine the rights paradigm by emphasising the significant or fundamental challenges that already exist in property law and practice and perhaps support amendments that would have the same effect.

In the Roman-Dutch civil law tradition the doctrinal and hierarchical supremacy of ownership is often associated with the idea that ownership is absolute, which is understood either as an indication that ownership is the most complete real right or that it is unrestricted. Describing ownership as 'absolute' in the sense of the fullest, most complete and most valuable property right indicates that it grants the owner the most comprehensive collection of entitlements possible, including the right of exclusive possession.[4] In this perspective, ownership is described as hierarchically superior to limited real rights and personal rights in property in the sense that only ownership includes all the entitlements of ownership, including residuarity, whereas limited real rights or personal rights only grant a limited entitlement to use someone else's property temporarily and partially.[5] In this sense, ownership trumps other property interests in that limited real rights and personal rights in property can only derive from (and are therefore limited by) ownership as the mother right. In the property hierarchy that means that limited rights can never trump ownership—the holder of the limited right can only withstand an ownership claim if and to the extent that she can prove a valid and enforceable derivative right that was granted either by legislation or by the owner or her predecessors in title (and therefore imposed on the mother right

---

[4] It was arguably Grotius' intention to describe direct ownership as 'full' or complete in this sense, and not as absolute in the sense of free disposition; see n 3 above.

[5] For South African law see eg PJ Badenhorst *et al, Silberberg & Schoeman's The Law of Property* (5th edn, 2006) at 92; *Gien v Gien* 1979 (2) SA 1113 (T) 1120. On the notion of ownership as the fullest and most valuable property right in Roman-Dutch law see DV Cowen, *New Patterns of Landownership. The Transformation of the Concept of Landownership as Plena in Re Potestas* (1984).

by the owner herself). This understanding of absoluteness reflects the personal sovereignty aspect of ownership as *dominium*: non-owners cannot really challenge or withstand the right of ownership; only the owner herself can do that in the sense that she can grant derived rights to others that she must then honour as long and as far as they are valid.

Ownership is also described as absolute in the Roman-Dutch tradition to indicate that it permits the owner to do with the property what she likes or that ownership is presumed to be free of restrictions as a point of departure, with the result that restrictions can be imposed (by law or by consent) but will be treated as temporary and exceptional.[6] Once again this description of ownership as an absolute right indicates its position in the hierarchy of property interests: the owner's claim to use and dispose of the property can be challenged only by someone who can prove a valid and enforceable right or immunity, based on either legislation or consent of the owner, that restricts the owner's right. This perspective on the rights paradigm once again reflects the notion of *dominium* as personal sovereignty: Ownership can be limited by restrictions on use, but only if the restrictions are compatible with the owner's liberty, which could be exercised either by voluntarily accepting limitations through agreement or by acquiescing in legislative restrictions imposed through democratic processes. Furthermore, the rhetoric of the rights paradigm (as far as this particular version of the notion of absoluteness is concerned) insists that limitations are exceptional (they must be proven, they must rest on proper authority and they must be reasonable) and temporary (as soon as the limitation falls away ownership resumes its natural 'fullness').

The idea that all possible ownership entitlements are usually (or ideally) vested in one person—that there is just one owner for a particular item of property—and the view that the owner is entitled to exclusive (disposition over) possession and use of her property are traditionally associated with the civil law definition of

---

[6] For South African law see eg PJ Badenhorst *et al*, *Silberberg & Schoeman's The Law of Property* (5th edn, 2006) 91–2; *Gien v Gien* 1979 (2) SA 1113 (T) 1120; DV Cowen, *New Patterns of Landownership. The Transformation of the Concept of Landownership as Plena in Re Potestas* (1984). The Dutch Civil Code (*BW* 5:1) and the German Civil Code (*BGB* § 903) provide that the owner is free to use the property as she wishes and to the exclusion of everybody else, within the limits laid down by law—a definition that goes back to Bartolus de Saxoferrato in the fifteenth century (Bartolus on the *Digest* 41.2.17.1). This definition never meant and still does not mean that ownership is unrestricted or absolute; the real question is (as is demonstrated by the Depenheuer debate in the next section below) whether the legally imposed restrictions on use are regarded as fundamental limits or as subsequently imposed restrictions of a pre-existing right. The closer property theory remains to its liberal roots, the more likely it is that the rights paradigm will be understood as a reflection of absoluteness in the latter sense rather than the former. On modern Dutch and German law see WHM Reehuis and AHT Heisterkamp (with contributions from GE van Maanen and GT de Jong), *Pitlo Het Nederlands Burgerlijk Recht, Vol 3 Goederenrecht* (12th revised and expanded edn, 2006) 377–8; F Baur *et al*, *Sachenrecht* (17th edn, 1999) 269; for critical analysis of the Dutch debate see GCJJ van den Bergh, *Eigendom: Grepen uit de Geschiedenis van een Omstreden Begrip* (2nd edn, 1988); GE van Maanen, *Eigendomsschijnbewegingen: Juridische, Historische en Politiek-Filosofische Opmerkingen over Eigendom* (1987).

ownership as an absolute right, resulting in the broad assumption that the owner is generally entitled to exclude anyone else from access to and possession of her property, unless either the owner herself or the democratic legislature has granted access rights to someone else. In the civil law systems, non-ownership property rights are regarded as less complete, less valuable and less powerful than 'full' ownership, which is seen as the first prize, the trump card, the ultimate property right. Accordingly, ownership is not only held in higher esteem than non-ownership rights but is also protected more strongly. Above all, the fact that ownership is valued so highly and protected so jealously is directly linked to the exclusivity of ownership. Ownership is so valuable because it is exclusive, and it is exclusive because it allows the owner to exclude everybody else—both the state and other private parties—from access to and possession of the property. In other words, saying that ownership is absolute also implies that ownership is exclusive; given the status of ownership in the property hierarchy, that is tantamount to saying that the pinnacle of the property regime exists in the fact that a property owner can exclude anybody else from possession or use of that property, unless the other person can prove a valid and enforceable right to possess or to use, derived from either legislation or the consent of the owner and her predecessors in title. In short, the hierarchical supremacy of ownership as an absolute right vests in the owner of land the absolute right to exclude or to evict anybody who cannot prove a valid and enforceable right to occupy. Absent legislation or contractual licences to the contrary, the civil law notion of ownership in property relegates non-owners to the margins of property in land; they should in principle lose in any direct conflict with the owner.

At the risk of repetition one can say, in conclusion, that the civil law notion of absolute ownership accommodates qualifications and limitations in two different but related ways. Firstly, in so far as it is clear that ownership is often in fact restricted by legislation or by other rights granted by the owner, it is said that these restrictions do not detract from the notion of absoluteness because the restrictions were imposed upon ownership through the owner's consent, expressed either through the grant of a limited right or a licence or through democratic participation in the promulgation of statutory limitations imposed in the public interest. Secondly, the effect of limitations and restrictions is curtailed by depicting them as exceptional and temporary qualifications to the rule of absolutism.

In the civil law systems, limitations on ownership are also explained in a third way. When limitations and restrictions are imposed upon ownership (or other real rights) as a result of changing circumstances and policies, the rhetoric of the rights paradigm resorts to a dynamic version of the absolutism doctrine, in terms of which property rules and practices are said to be capable of incremental, interstitial development and qualification. Although limitations on ownership come from outside in this case, in the sense that they originate in contextual exigency and government policy and not in the owner's free will, they are nevertheless bound into the logic of the rights paradigm because they are applied (through interpretation of either uncodified common law or legislation) as interstitial or incremental developments that fit in with rather than disturb or upset the logic of the property regime. I revert to this aspect in later chapters.

The rights-focused line of thinking is generally stronger in Roman-Germanic civil law systems than in Anglo-American law because of the relatively late influence of feudalism in the latter. Two important features that distinguish Anglo-American common law from the features of civil law described so far are that the common law is based on the notion of relative title and, accordingly, as Gray and Gray describe it, the fact that 'the single most striking feature of English land law is precisely the absence, within its conceptual apparatus, of overarching notions of *ownership*'.[7] At least doctrinally, the notion of relative title, which still reflects something of the feudal origins of the common law, means that the common law does not acknowledge any single, absolute title that will always trump any conflicting interest or claim—any given property conflict will be won by the stronger of the conflicting claims on possession.[8] This obviously precludes or qualifies most of the absolutism talk characterising the ownership theory of civil law doctrine.

Moreover, the abstract 'completeness' characteristics ascribed to ownership in civil law are conspicuously absent from common law property analysis as well. Because of the feudal origin and heritage of English land law, the notion of relative title is so strong that absolutism talk seems out of place and inapplicable in the common law context, at least doctrinally speaking. In the United States, property doctrine was influenced by legal realism, which treats property as a bundle of rights that can be disaggregated into discrete entitlements that can be owned by different persons (instead of rights that inhabit a specific hierarchy because of the entitlements usually associated with them) and as power relationships between people (as opposed to relationships between people and things).[9] This doctrinal

[7] K Gray and SF Gray, 'The Idea of Property in Land' in S Bright and J Dewar (eds), *Land Law: Themes and Perspectives* (1998) 15–51 at 35 (italics in original). See further K Gray and SF Gray, *Elements of Land Law* (4th edn, 2005) at 109 (to the same effect).
[8] See S Bright, *Landlord and Tenant Law in Context* (2007) 48–9, citing W Swadling, 'Property: General Principles' in P Birks (ed), *English Private Law*, Vol I (2000) 218: in a strict sense English land law has no concept of ownership since property in land is protected as possession. Compare n 1. In a given instance the stronger claim to possession could, of course, even be made by an unlawful possessor, whose prior possession should trump the bare possession of any subsequent unlawful possessor. The statement that the common law does not acknowledge a single notion of absolute title must be qualified for the colonial context, where it has always been accepted that absolute title vests in the Crown. Apart from its association with sovereignty as *imperium*, the notion of Crown sovereignty can also refer to so-called radical title or sovereignty as *dominium*. See further in this regard n 16.
[9] Some of the most influential realist writings on property are WN Hohfeld, 'Some Fundamental Legal Conceptions as Applied in Judicial Reasoning' (1913) 23 *Yale LJ* 16–59; WN Hohfeld, 'Fundamental Legal Conceptions as Applied in Legal Reasoning' (1917) 26 *Yale LJ* 710–70 (property and other rights analysed and depicted as sets of legal relationships); RL Hale, 'Coercion and Distribution in a Supposedly Non-Coercive State' (1923) 38 *Political Science Qly* 470–94 (analysis of the reasons why the law does or does not protect specific vested rights in terms of underlying structures of power and coercion); MR Cohen, 'Property and Sovereignty' (1927) 13 *Cornell LQ* 8–30; FS Cohen, 'Transcendental Nonsense and the Functional Approach' (1935) 35 *Columbia LR* 809–49 (description of property 'in terms of what it does' instead of transcendental principles). See further JW Singer, 'Legal Realism Now' (1988) 76 *California LR* 467–544. For a definitive overview and analysis of the literature on property as relationship see SR Munzer, 'Property as Social Relations' in SR Munzer (ed), *New*

and theoretical difference reinforces the common law notion of relative title and steers common law property discourse further away from the civil law notion of absoluteness. In a doctrinal sense, it therefore makes no sense to discuss the hierarchical supremacy of ownership in a common law context—the terminology and the logic simply do not fit.

However, despite the differences between the Roman-law-based civil law system and the English common law system and despite the unique development of rights theory in the United States under the influence of legal realism, the notion of absolute ownership and the idea that property ownership occupies a superior position in the hierarchy of property interests are not unknown in common law property theory. On the contrary—Blackstone's reference to property as 'sole and despotic dominion' is often understood in a sense not unrelated to the civil law notion of absolute ownership,[10] and in fact it appears as if Blackstone described property as 'sole and despotic dominion' for much the same reason as Grotius discarded the medieval notion of split ownership, namely to 'put aside the earlier medieval traditions in which property ownership had been hemmed in'.[11] Despite the obvious and significant doctrinal differences between the two systems, the notion of absolutism is known (and critiqued) in English and US law[12] and, as Alexander explains, the idea of absolute ownership evokes the same associations with free disposition, exclusivity and being consolidated in one hand in US law as in continental civil law.[13] It should therefore come as no surprise that Justice O'Connor, writing for the US Supreme Court in *Yee v City of Escondido*,[14] could assert so boldly that 'the "right to exclude" is doubtless, as petitioners assert, "one

Essays in the Legal and Political Theory of Property (2001) 36–75. For post-realist critiques of the ownership paradigm see JW Singer, *Entitlement: The Paradoxes of Property* (2000) at 6*ff*; K Gray and SF Gray, *Elements of Land Law* (4th edn, 2005) at 100–11.

[10] See CM Rose, 'Canons of Property Talk, or, Blackstone's Anxiety' (1998) 108 *Yale LJ* 601–32; K Gray and SF Gray, *Elements of Land Law* (4th edn, 2005) at 105; GS Alexander, 'Critical Land Law' in S Bright and J Dewar (eds), *Land Law: Themes and Perspectives* (1998) 52–78 at 55–6; JW Singer, *Entitlement: The Paradoxes of Property* (2000) at 4–8, 12–13.

[11] CM Rose, 'Canons of Property Talk, or, Blackstone's Anxiety' (1998) 108 *Yale LJ* 601–32 at 603. Rose suggests that John Locke has probably done as much in the same cause. Within the context of the first taker (considered by Grotius, Locke, Blackstone), the liberalisation of ownership from feudal restrictions also prepared the way for appropriation of land in the colonies. See n 16.

[12] See eg K Gray and SF Gray, *Elements of Land Law* (4th edn. 2005) at 105; GS Alexander, 'Critical Land Law' in S Bright and J Dewar (eds), *Land Law: Themes and Perspectives* (1998) 52–78 at 55–6; CM Rose, 'Canons of Property Talk, or, Blackstone's Anxiety' (1998) 108 *Yale LJ* 601–32; JW Singer, *Entitlement: The Paradoxes of Property* (2000) at 4–8, 12–13.

[13] For various expositions and critiques of this view of ownership see JW Singer, *Entitlement: The Paradoxes of Property* (2000) 1–5; GS Alexander, 'Critical Land Law' in S Bright and J Dewar (eds), *Land Law: Themes and Perspectives* (1998) 52–78 at 55–6; P Schlag, 'Rights in the Postmodern Condition' in A Sarat and TR Kearns (eds), *Legal Rights: Historical and Philosophical Perspectives* (1997) 263–304 at 275–82; J Nedelsky, *Private Property and the Limits of American Constitutionalism: The Madisonian Framework* (1990) at 207–11; GS Alexander, *Commodity and Propriety: Competing Visions of Property in American Legal Thought, 1776–1970* (1997) at 10–12; CM Rose, 'Canons of Property Talk, or, Blackstone's Anxiety' (1998) 108 *Yale LJ* 601–32. See further FI Michelman, 'The Bill of Rights, the Common Law, and the Freedom-friendly State' (2003) 58 *Univ Miami LR* 401–48 at 419 (minimising privately engineered infringements of constitutionally super-valued interests).

[14] 503 US 519 (1992) at 528, citing *Kaiser Aetna v United States* 444 US 164 (1979) at 176.

of the most essential sticks in the bundle of rights that are commonly referred to as property"'. On one level, the doctrinal differences between the common law tradition and the civil law tradition should not blur the shared rhetorical and affective value that the notion of absolutism or stronger property rights represents in both systems. In the remaining chapters of this book it will be necessary continuously to emphasise the space between the doctrinal detail of property rules and practices on the one hand and the abstract, rhetorical and affective value of paradigmatic rights talk on the other, in order to illuminate the similarities between the common law and the civil law systems in the face of large doctrinal differences.

Johan van der Walt explains the apparent contradiction, namely that the civil law and common law systems are so different doctrinally but that the same or similar notions of absolute ownership or property rights nevertheless appear in both, with reference to the relative influence of political and economic liberalism.[15] He points out that European history left us with two discrete property paradigms; one that conceived of property as a private law right and one that treated it as a constitutional right. As a private law right, property was seen as an embodiment of economic liberty; as a political right, it was founded on political liberty. Although visions of property are embedded in liberty they might have developed in different directions, but the differences between the private and public notions of liberty were practically wiped out when economic liberty or privatist thinking triumphed over political thinking during the nineteenth century. The overbearing effect of economic liberalism on the rights paradigm goes some way in explaining the somewhat counter-intuitive similarities between civil and common law property systems: Both attach the qualities of power and centrality to individual or private property because of its importance for economic liberalism as a social system; the doctrinal differences are technical remainders that should not detract attention from the rhetorical and ideological similarities. When discussing narrow private law doctrine, talk of absolute ownership and hierarchical supremacy makes little sense in a common law setting, but these difficulties fade when considering the socio-economic and socio-political status and power of property interests—in the latter setting, notions of absolutism and power have a much

---

[15] See JWG van der Walt, 'The Critique of Subjectivism and its Implications for Property Law: Towards a Deconstructive Republican Theory of Property' in GE van Maanen and AJ van der Walt (eds), *Property Law on the Threshold of the 21st Century* (1996) 115–59 at 115–19. What Johan van der Walt describes as 'economic' and 'political' thinking corresponds almost perfectly with what GS Alexander, *Commodity and Propriety: Competing Visions of Property in American Legal Thought, 1776–1970* (1997) refers to as the 'commodified' and the 'proprietary' visions of property respectively. For purposes of US law, EM Peñalver, 'Reconstructing Richard Epstein' (2006) 15 *William & Mary Bill of Rights J* 429–37 at 429–30 explains the counter-intuitive nuances of liberal theory with reference to two major theorists: Richard Epstein is often portrayed as a hard-core libertarian, but he acknowledges 'that human beings are typically cooperative, social animals' and thus he is willing 'to limit the reach of individual property rights by utilitarian constraints'; in other words by considerations of the common good. Ronald Dworkin, on the other hand, 'views individual rights as constraining what otherwise appears to be a broadly utilitarian understanding of the common good'. Although both approaches resonate with the ownership model discussed here, Epstein's reflects the economic or privatist version more closely and Dworkin's the public or political version.

stronger appeal than narrower principles of relative title.[16] In view of this explanation, one might expect that the resilient absolutism rhetoric would, in both the common law and the civil law systems, feature prominently (and comparably) in property issues dominated by concerns about personal autonomy, market efficiency and related liberal economic values.

[16] The apparently comfortable fit between different private property interests in English common law has an interesting parallel in post-colonial land disputes. In private law, different property interests can exist simultaneously in the same piece of land because English land law, strictly speaking, does not have a concept of ownership—property in land is protected as possession. In this sense, one can, for example, say that the ownership interest is split up between the landlord and the tenant (S Bright, *Landlord and Tenant Law in Context* (2007) 48–50; see the other sources referred to in ch 4, n 47). In private law, the simultaneous existence of multiple interests is not a problem because the integrity of property is safeguarded in the 'sole and despotic dominion' of the right to exclude, which is protected as the stronger claim to possession. Similarly, original acquisition of ownership is justified by first possession (by theorists such as Locke and Blackstone), at least in what is presumed to be *terra nullius*. In cases where the landowner's claim to possession is thwarted by another, stronger, claim, that outcome would normally be justified by the fact that the owner had granted the competing claim in the first place; the owner also has the power to grant either rights that can compete with her own claim to possession or mere licences, which cannot, and the law will uphold this distinction. The appearance of multiple competing and overlapping rights should not blind us to the reality of their being locked into a single framework of power or sovereignty as *dominium*, expressed in the language of relative claims to possession but in fact founded on the basis of the right to exclude. In the public sphere, this picture finds its parallel in struggles about sovereignty as *imperium*. In famous cases like *Mabo and Others v State of Queensland (No 2)* (1992) 107 ALR 1 (HC) and *Delgamuukw v British Columbia* [1997] 3 SCR 1010, both the sovereign settlement of colonial land and subsequent recognition of Aboriginal or First Nation land claims based on colonial dispossession are framed and justified within the common law paradigm. Consequently, these land claims could be recognised inside the property framework of property as *dominium* without compromising state sovereignty or property as *imperium*, even in the post-colonial era, where post-colonial governments could distance themselves from racist colonial actions (establishing property as *dominium* on the basis that pre-existing native title is not recognised for racist reasons) while simultaneously absolving them from the obligation to pay compensation for actual post-colonial dispossessions of purportedly recognised Aboriginal rights (property as *imperium*). See AJ van der Walt, 'Modernity, Normality, and Meaning: The Struggle between Progress and Stability and the Politics of Interpretation (Part 1)' (2000) 1 *Stellenbosch LR* 21–49 at 41, where this strategy is described (with reference to the *Mabo* decision) as the politics of continuity. S Swain and A Clarke, 'Negotiating Postmodernity: Narratives of Law and Imperialism' (1995) 6 *Law & Critique* 229–56 at 237*ff* explain how *Mabo* finds a way to transcend the dichotomy of the racist past of colonial dispossession and the post-colonial pressure of non-discrimination and acknowledgement, by casting its recognition of the Aboriginal Other (with its pre-colonial land rights) within a metanarrative of emancipation, which ultimately reaffirms the Western colonial power as the subject, the speaker, the legislator. Recognition of Aboriginal or First Nations claims is granted from a position and a perspective of power that confirms the new post-colonial state's political unity and sovereignty, much in the same way that the right to exclude upholds the unity of the common law's seemingly fractured picture of overlapping property interests. MR Cohen, 'Property and Sovereignty' (1927) 13 *Cornell LQ* 8–30 at 12 already reminded us that private property rights confer on us power over others and that the essence of private property is the right to exclude. It is therefore unsurprising that Aboriginal title was recognised in *Mabo* as 'outside' rights that are not protected by the common law because they were not granted by the common law; a position that had to be rectified (because of the racially discriminatory implications) by legislation. It would be interesting to analyse more recent South African decisions like *Alexkor Ltd and Another v Richtersveld Community and Others* 2004 (5) SA 460 (CC); *Department of Land Affairs and Others v Goedgelegen Tropical Fruits (Pty) Ltd* 2007 (6) SA 199 (CC); *Mphela and 217 Others v Haakdoornbult Boerdery CC and Others* 2008 (7) BCLR 675 (CC) in the context of the post-colonial debate, but that would take the current discussion of eviction too far off course. Some of these cases are referred to again in ch 6.

For present purposes, I will focus on the broad assumptions of economic liberalism that influenced both civil and common law systems. It is telling that one of the principal critics of property theory and practice in the US, Joseph William Singer, has analysed property interests in terms that are immediately clear and understandable to civil law specialists. Singer described the view that ownership is the most important property right as 'the ownership model',[17] adding that it represents a pervasive way of thinking according to which strong protection of ownership is necessary and justified because it is assumed to enhance personal and civil liberty. According to Singer, the characteristic feature of this model is its presumptive power—it always places the burden to explain why ownership rights should not prevail or why they should be limited on the state (to justify the regulatory restrictions that it places upon ownership) and on those who do not own property themselves (to justify their competitive interferences with the property of those who do own property).[18] In other words, ideological assumptions about the personal and social importance of ownership translate into presumptive power for the individual property owner, whose right functions as a trump in that it is presumed free from regulatory restrictions and from competitive interferences or claims from non-owners (of that property). This line of thinking appears completely familiar and unexceptional to a lawyer schooled in the civil law tradition.

The presumptive 'absoluteness' of ownership, or the fact that it is presumed to be free from state restriction and competitive interference, finds expression in various procedural and substantive rules of law that almost always privilege the individual owner against competing claims.[19] Against those who do not hold any legally recognised property rights, the owner always wins; against those with a weaker property right, the owner wins unless the other party can show why her lesser right should prevail. The only reason that could successfully be raised for this purpose is that the non-owner was granted a valid right as against the owner, either by statute[20] or by consent of the owner. This result is easily comparable to the situation in most civil law systems.

---

[17] JW Singer, *Entitlement: The Paradoxes of Property* (2000) at 3. The same model has also been described, for purposes of Anglo-American common law, as the conventional or Blackstonian conception of property in land; see particularly CM Rose, 'Canons of Property Talk, or, Blackstone's Anxiety' (1998) 108 *Yale LJ* 601–32; compare further D Kennedy, 'The Structure of Blackstone's *Commentaries*' (1979) 28 *Buffalo LR* 209–382 at 262–64, 328, 334–5; G Alexander, 'Critical Land Law' in S Bright and J Dewar (eds), *Land Law: Themes and Perspectives* (1998) 52–78 at 53. Rose (at 603) argues that Blackstone's definition of ownership as exclusive dominion has the most lasting and effective influence on modern thinking about property as a metaphor and not as a literal description.

[18] JW Singer, *Entitlement: The Paradoxes of Property* (2000) at 3.

[19] The twin notions of exclusivity and absoluteness find their most authoritative expression, as far as English common law is concerned, in Blackstone's description of it as 'that sole and despotic dominion which one man claims and exercises over the external things of the world, in total exclusion of the right of any other individual in the universe': W Blackstone, *Commentaries on the Laws of England*, Book 2 (11th edn, 1791) at 2: 2; see further G Alexander, 'Critical Land Law' in S Bright and J Dewar (eds), *Land Law: Themes and Perspectives* (1998) 52–78 at 53–9; CM Rose, 'Canons of Property Talk, or, Blackstone's Anxiety' (1998) 108 *Yale LJ* 601–32; LS Underkuffler, *The Idea of Property: Its Meaning and Power* (2003) at 65–70.

[20] An example is the current South African land reform laws that either prevent or restrict eviction of even unlawful occupiers of homes in certain circumstances; see Constitution of the Republic of

The basis of the liberal ownership model described by Singer is the assumption that ownership occupies such a dominant position in the legal system because it is a central pre-political and pre-constitutional institution that guarantees individual independence and autonomy and safeguards cornerstones of the liberal society (such as individual self-determination, rational maximisation of personal preferences and the free market). As such, ownership is seen as a natural or rational phenomenon and not as a social or political construct,[21] and consequently it is deemed to pre-date any consensual (social, political, constitutional or statutory) amendment—inasmuch as property is considered subject to restriction at all, the relevant limitations have to be properly authorised (constitutionally and/or statutorily or by contract), justified (by legitimate state authority or consensual agreement) for serving an overriding public purpose, and reasonable (in terms of some kind of justiciable rationality or proportionality requirement). The ownership model therefore privileges ownership as against both regulatory state control and other property rights or claims and justifies this hierarchy with reference to a particular view of the relationship between individual and collective. Singer explains the political orientation and the moral deficiency of the ownership model as follows:

> Ownership, as we use the term, abhors obligation; for obligations, if they exist at all, are understood to limit ownership. In this conceptual framework, ownership and obligation are opposites, as are property and regulation. If property means ownership, and if ownership means power without obligation, then we have created a framework for thinking about property that privileges a certain form of life—the life of the owner. In the conceptual space framed by the life of the owner, we are invited to live as if we were the only ones that mattered. We are invited to live as if we were alone.[22]

Even in the doctrinal perspective on Anglo-American property law it can be said that the focus on relative title confirms the main features of the property rights paradigm, in the sense that the doctrine of relative title privileges the stronger right in any given property dispute in much the same way that ownership does in the civil law systems. Within the common law doctrine, the stronger possessory claim is associated with the same notions of strong privilege that characterise absolutism talk in the civil-law systems, because the ownership model, as Singer describes it, protects the same liberal economic values and interests in both systems.

South Africa 1996, s 26(3); Prevention of Illegal Eviction from and Unlawful Occupation of Land Act 19 of 1998, s 4. In the terminology of Hohfeld, this right not to be evicted would probably be described as an immunity; see WN Hohfeld, 'Some Fundamental Legal Conceptions as Applied in Judicial Reasoning' (1913) 23 *Yale LJ* 16–59; 'Fundamental Legal Conceptions as Applied in Legal Reasoning' (1917) 26 *Yale LJ* 710–70.

[21] A unique constitutional subscription to this notion appears in Art 43.1.1 of the Irish Constitution of 1937: 'The State acknowledges that man, in virtue of his rational being, has the natural right, antecedent to positive law, to the private ownership of external goods.' Remarkably, this strong liberal view of property is balanced out in Irish Constitutional law by what G Hogan and G Whyte, *JM Kelly: The Irish Constitution* (4th edn, 2003), para 7.7.01 at p 1969, fn 1; para 7.9.02 at p 2079 describe as 'Roman-Catholic social justice teaching' in the form of other constitutional provisions (Arts 43.2 and 45) that allow regulatory restrictions of property rights.

[22] JW Singer, *Entitlement: The Paradoxes of Property* (2000) at 6.

In this and subsequent chapters I describe this view of ownership as 'the rights paradigm', arguing that, where and in so far as it features in any legal system, it privileges absolute or strong property rights and interests and allows them to dominate the doctrinal structure, the rhetoric and the logic of the law (both property law and in general). Moreover, this paradigm also privileges the common law over legislation and even the constitution—it is a feature of the rights paradigm that the traditional property principles of private law in its historically received form are assumed to reflect and embody the presumptive power associated with property as a supposedly pre-political right, whereas restrictions emanating from the constitution or legislation are regarded as unnatural and therefore exceptional limitations that have to be authorised, justified and treated with a measure of scepticism and restraint. It is assumed that the traditional institutions of private property law, including the dominant role that private ownership plays in the property regime and the presumptive burdens it places on competing individual claims and social demands, safeguard central values and structures of liberal society such as individual autonomy and liberty and the free market. Historical 'novelties' such as democratic constitutions, bills of rights and regulatory legislation are assumed to safeguard, entrench and build upon rather than threaten or derogate from this tradition and therefore apparent threats or derogations that appear in these sources have to be scrutinised strictly and interpreted restrictively.

II. Three Illustrations

In this section of the chapter I discuss three cases that illustrate the power and influence of the rights paradigm on property thinking and that provide a backdrop for my analysis in subsequent chapters. The cases illustrate a point that is important for subsequent chapters: Doctrinally, ownership (or the stronger right to possession) is regarded as the strongest property right, and residential occupation interests (lawful tenancy or unlawful occupation) are seen as weaker rights or no-rights that usually defer to ownership (or possessory rights), although housing policies can and often do attach special socio-economic significance to residential occupation interests and therefore protect them in ways that place greater or smaller restrictions on the rights of landowners or holders of stronger possessory claims. The result is that doctrinal reasoning about property disputes sometimes seems to be in conflict with policy reasoning about the relative socio-political importance of those who occupy land for residential purposes and the effect that this policy emphasis inevitably has on landownership. My hypothesis is that this conflict is a fruitful locus for a theoretical debate about stability and change in property law, particularly in a transformative setting, where both policy and property issues often pivot on residential housing interests. More particularly, I am interested in instances where policy interventions undermine or overturn the paradigmatic hierarchy in that they restrict the possessory claims of landowners or holders of other strong possessory claims for reasons that have nothing to do with the relative legal strength of the conflicting interests.

The three examples I discuss derive from case-law that reflects the conflict mentioned earlier: *Brisley v Drotsky*[23] (a 2002 decision of the South African Supreme Court of Appeal); the 1993 *Landlord–Tenant* decision of the German Federal Constitutional Court[24] and *Harrow London Borough Council v Qazi* (a 2004 House of Lords decision).[25] I place the discussion of each case in context by referring to one or more other cases from the same jurisdiction and, in some instances, academic literature, but I do not discuss the cases themselves or the literature in detail, because all of them feature again and in more detail in later chapters. For the moment it is sufficient to see how these cases, together with related case-law and academic literature, demonstrate the doctrinal and rhetorical power of what Singer described as the ownership model. The selection and combination of these three cases further illustrate a point that is central to my approach in this book, namely that the theoretical argument I develop is illustrated by material from three different legal systems that display complex and interesting historical, contextual and doctrinal similarities and differences, namely South African, German and English law.

All three cases involve conflicts of interest between a landowner-landlord and a tenant or former tenant; a locus for property disputes that receive further, detailed analysis in chapter four. In landlord–tenant eviction cases, the widely assumed right to exclusive possession of the landowner (and the concomitant right to evict) suggests, within the rights paradigm, that a landlord who wishes to evict a tenant must prevail, unless the tenant can prove a legally recognised occupation right. Significantly, for present purposes, the owner's presumed right to exclude and evict is often restricted by a policy principle, sometimes derived from legislation, that it is (or should be) difficult to evict another person from property that is their home. This apparently dramatic qualification of ownership seems less problematic in the landlord–tenant context, where it is likely that the owner had created a conflicting right by consent, but recent policy suggests that it might even apply when the property is occupied unlawfully, for example when the former tenant is holding over or when the property was invaded unlawfully (a situation that is analyzed further in chapter five).[26] My central hypothesis in the book is that the conflict

---

[23] 2002 (4) SA 1 (SCA).

[24] *BVerfGE* 89, 1 (*Besitzrecht des Mieters*) [1993]. German cases do not usually have names; a name is sometimes attached to certain cases in the popular press and then that name is usually included when the case is cited. It is not usual to refer to the year in which German cases were decided either, but I include a reference to the year to give some sense of the socio-economic context.

[25] [2004] 1 AC 983 (HL).

[26] This argument finds support in constitutional provisions such as s 26(3) of the South African Constitution 1996 and Art 8 of the European Convention for the Protection of Human Rights and Fundamental Freedoms 1950 and in academic writing. For particularly interesting examples of recent academic writing on the point see L Fox, *Conceptualising Home: Theories, Laws and Policies* (2007); EM Peñalver, 'Property as Entrance' (2005) 91 *Virginia LR* 1889–972.

between landowner and tenant or between landowner and unlawful occupier presents an interesting context for purposes of theorising about property in a transformational situation, because the landlord would usually embody and represent the socio-economic power of the powerful and privileged propertied minority, while tenants and unlawful occupiers would possibly embody and represent the poor and socio-economically marginalised. The question posed by the cases discussed below (and in subsequent chapters) is whether the policy reasons for sometimes favouring the interests of tenants and unlawful occupiers are strong enough to undermine or challenge the hegemony of the rights paradigm, or whether they are simply accommodated within the rights paradigm as 'normal' regulatory restrictions on the exercise of rights. The point of the illustrations in the three cases discussed below is that legislation, introduced for policy reasons, that is designed specifically to amend the power hierarchy between landlords and tenants sometimes meet with doctrinal resistance in the courts, often with the result that the status quo is privileged and the reformist effect of the legislation curtailed. In the process the conflict between the interests of landlord and tenant becomes a useful and illuminating locus for debating the power and effect of the rights paradigm and its implications for social and economic transformation.

The South African case of *Brisley v Drotsky*

Brisley v Drotsky[27] dealt with a tenant who refused to vacate the premises subsequent to cancellation of the lease. In resisting the eviction, the tenant relied directly on the anti-eviction provision in section 26(3) of the Constitution.[28] At common law, the considerations that determined whether an eviction order should be granted were completely in the knowledge and under the control of the landowner, namely proof of ownership and the fact that someone else was in possession, presumably without the owner's consent. Once the landowner could prove these facts she would normally be entitled to an eviction order, unless the occupier could prove a valid and enforceable right to occupy. Section 26(3) seemingly changed the common law position by providing that a court may only grant an eviction order once it has considered all the circumstances, thereby potentially

---

[27] 2002 (4) SA 1 (SCA).

[28] Section 26(3) provides: 'No one may be evicted from their home, or have their home demolished, without an order of court made after considering all the relevant circumstances. No legislation may permit arbitrary evictions.' Relying directly on s 26(3) is a problematic strategy in view of the strong difference of opinion in earlier case-law about the effect of s 26(3) on existing private law (see n 31). An obvious explanation for the choice cannot be ascertained from the case report. It could be that the tenant was wary of the apparently strong authority of *ABSA Bank v Amod* [1999] 2 All SA 423 (W), where the Witwatersrand High Court decided that the Prevention of Illegal Eviction from and Unlawful Occupation of Land Act 19 of 1998 (PIE) was intended for cases where land was *settled* unlawfully, and not where originally lawful occupiers were holding over subsequent to the ground for lawful occupation falling away. This does not explain why the Court did not raise the applicability of PIE in *Brisley*, especially since it actually mentioned PIE as an example of a statute that could have changed the result—see the majority decision at para 43.

(but not explicitly) subjecting the granting of an eviction order to considerations that were irrelevant in eviction proceedings at common law, namely the general historical, social and economic context and the personal circumstances and hardship (poverty, old age, gender, homelessness) of the occupier. Taking these considerations into account before deciding whether to grant an eviction order would obviously bring about a serious restriction of the landowner's existing right, which was never subjected to a judicial discretion along those lines before. In its most radical form, a ruling to the effect that a landlord who could prove all the common law requirements would nevertheless fail to obtain an eviction order if it appeared that eviction would have an unjustifiably harsh effect on the tenant or occupier, given the general context or her personal circumstances, would amount to a significant challenge to the fundamentals of the rights paradigm as set out earlier in this chapter.

The practical issue was, therefore, whether an unlawful occupier could rely directly on section 26(3) to resist eviction, based purely on considerations that were out of the control of and possibly even unknown to the landowner, such as the general context or the occupier's personal circumstances. Allowing the evictee to rely directly on section 26(3) by raising an opposition based purely on the context or her personal circumstances, which is what section 26(3) seems to require on a superficial reading, would weaken the entitlement of a landowner to obtain an eviction order (and thus the power of the rights paradigm) significantly; denying the validity of such a defence based directly on section 26(3), in the face of a reasonably clear constitutional provision, would be an indication that this paradigm still has a strong grip on property thinking. In its simplest form, the question is whether section 26(3) would have a strong, direct and fundamental impact on the existing common law tradition (and the rights paradigm privileged by it) or merely a minor, indirect effect.

This issue was the subject of much confusion and strong difference of opinion in earlier case-law,[29] which indicates that South African courts find it difficult to determine whether, when and how far constitutional provisions such as section 26(3) should influence the application of common law (private law) eviction principles in various types of eviction cases. Some general principles are reasonably clear, depending on the context of eviction: When the evictee is an unlawful invader who never occupied the premises lawfully, the Prevention of Illegal Eviction from and Unlawful Occupation of Land Act 19 of 1998 applies; it explicitly overrides the common law and specifies personal considerations of the occupiers that have to be considered before the eviction order is granted. In these cases a direct defence based on section 26(3) is unnecessary, since the 1998 Act pre-

---

[29] Summarised by AJ van der Walt, 'Exclusivity of Ownership, Security of Tenure, and Eviction Orders: A Critical Evaluation of Recent Case Law' (2002) 18 *SAJHR* 372–420 at 394–404. Of the significant decisions, *Ross v South Peninsula Municipality* 2000 (1) SA 589 (C) decided that s 26(3) amended the common law with regard to eviction, while *Betta Eiendomme (Pty) Ltd v Ekple-Epoh* 2000 (4) SA 468 (W) held that it had no effect on common law.

scribes similar but more extensive and explicit grounds for the defence.[30] In these cases, the courts have been reasonably willing to accept a direct and fairly robust amendment of common law principles in line with the explicit provisions of the Act, although some restrictive interpretations indicate that the rights paradigm exerts strong influence to stabilise the common law tradition even in these cases. If the evictee is a lawful occupier of land, either the Extension of Security of Tenure Act 62 of 1997 (rural land) or the Rental Housing Act 50 of 1999 (urban land) could apply; both statutes require consideration of specified contextual matters before an eviction order is granted, but neither overrides the common law explicitly. In these instances it therefore makes little difference whether the landowner evicts in terms of the legislation or the common law, because it is not clear in either case that the restrictions of section 26(3) should apply. When none of these statutes applies, the clash between the common law and the constitutional provision in section 26(3) is even more evident, and it is with regard to these cases that the *Brisley* court decided (as is explained below) that section 26(3) does apply to eviction under the common law, although its practical effect is to leave the common law requirements unchanged. In effect, any eviction order granted in terms of the common law, without any reference to section 26(3), could undermine or frustrate the reformist aims of the legislation because the common law position is upheld regardless of the effect of the Constitution and the circumstances of the occupiers.

The Supreme Court of Appeal resorted to a surprising strategy in *Brisley*. First, the Court held that section 26(3) applies horizontally and that it therefore binds private persons; accordingly, this section does apply in landlord–tenant situations and the courts have to consider all relevant circumstances before granting an eviction order.[31] However, the Court then also argued that section 26(3) does not give the courts the discretion to refuse an application for an eviction order, since it does not specify the circumstances that could or should affect the 'normal' outcome. The 'normal' outcome, determined by common law tradition, is that an owner is entitled to an eviction order if she can prove ownership and possession, and this baseline situation cannot be amended by implication. In the absence of specified circumstances that would allow a court to deviate from the common law position, the only relevant circumstances to be considered as far as section 26(3) is concerned are therefore whether the applicant is owner and the respondent is in possession of the property—if so, the owner is entitled to possession and the court cannot refuse the application for an eviction order on extraneous considerations.[32]

---

[30] *Ndlovu v Ngcobo; Bekker v Jika* 2003 (1) SA 113 (SCA) and *Port Elizabeth Municipality v Various Occupiers* 2005 (1) SA 217 (CC) dealt with the Prevention of Illegal Eviction from and Unlawful Occupation of Land Act 19 of 1998 and are the most authoritative sources on this point. The Constitutional Court has established that specific legislation that gives effect to a right in the Bill of Rights should generally be applied before relying directly on the constitutional rights provision: *Bato Star Fishing (Pty) Ltd v Minister of Environmental Affairs* 2004 (4) SA 490 (CC), para 25.

[31] *Brisley v Drotsky* 2002 (4) SA 1 (SCA), paras 40, 41. This aspect of the decision explicitly rejected the approach adopted in *Betta Eiendomme (Pty) Ltd v Ekple-Epoh* 2000 (4) SA 468 (W); see n 24.

[32] 2002 (4) SA 1 (SCA), paras 41–6. This aspect of the decision explicitly rejected the approach followed in *Ross v South Peninsula Municipality* 2000 (1) SA 589 (C); see n 24.

In other words, section 26(3) does indeed affect landlord–tenant relationships, but it cannot in itself justify a direct constitutional defence against eviction and it does not in itself amend the common law requirements for eviction. Such a defence is only possible on the basis of clear and explicit legislation that grants the courts the discretion to deny an eviction application, specifying the considerations on which that discretion can be exercised.[33] As far as direct reliance on section 26(3) is concerned and in the absence of such more specific legislation, everything remains as it was under the common law.[34] The rhetorical and doctrinal power of the rights paradigm is evident in this decision.

The *Brisley* decision indicates that the rights paradigm still is a powerful factor in the property thinking of the South African Supreme Court of Appeal—rights, and particularly ownership rights, cannot be restricted purely on the basis of the personal circumstances of occupiers who are infringing upon those rights, even if the Constitution itself indicates (obliquely or indirectly, without stating explicitly) that such an amendment might be desirable. The duty of the courts is to protect property rights—particularly ownership—against infringements, regardless of the hardship that doing so might cause for those who are infringing upon the rights. This is a strong confirmation of the rights paradigm: rights always trump no-rights; where there is a right, there is a remedy; rights are not restricted purely because of the personal hardship eviction would cause or on the basis of the general context.

The German *Landlord–Tenant* case

The continued power of the ownership-focused rights paradigm also appears from German constitutional case-law concerning the law of landlord and tenant. In the aftermath of World War II and the concomitant housing shortage, the protection of residential tenants in German law was strengthened by legislation that regulates rent increases and evictions. In several cases the Federal Constitutional Court confirmed the validity of these restrictions on the constitutional principle that they successfully establish an equitable balance between the landowner's property rights and the public interest in housing.[35] Generally, termination of a lease and

---

[33] Such as the Prevention of Illegal Eviction from and Unlawful Occupation of Land Act 19 of 1998, which does contain such specific provisions to indicate circumstances to be considered, including old age, ill health, gender and the general social position of the occupiers.

[34] The *Brisley* decision was followed by two other significant decisions that apparently contradict it, but careful analysis indicates that these decisions actually did not bring about a reversal of *Brisley*. *Brisley* dealt with evictions under s 26(3) of the Constitution, and therefore neither *Ndlovu v Ngcobo; Bekker v Jika* 2003 (1) SA 113 (SCA) nor *Port Elizabeth Municipality v Various Occupiers* 2005 (1) SA 217 (CC), both of which dealt with evictions under the Prevention of Illegal Eviction from and Unlawful Occupation of Land Act 19 of 1998, which overrides the common law explicitly, could override it. In *FHP Management (Pty) Ltd v Theron and Another* 2004 (3) SA 392 (C) the Cape High Court professed to apply both *Brisley* and *Ngcobo/Jika* and ended up simply maintaining the common law, even though it in fact should have dealt with the 1998 Act.

[35] It is usually said that less room exists for interfering with private property through regulatory controls the closer it is to the intimate personal sphere, while more room for regulation exists when the property falls into the commercial sphere, as rental property does. See *BVerfGE* 37, 132

eviction are only allowed for limited reasons such as unacceptable behaviour by the lessee or when the landlord wants either to use the property herself or to change its purpose from residential to something else. In a series of cases the Federal Court of Justice in Civil Matters and the Federal Constitutional Court explored the standard of review that was admissible in the application of this legislation. Although these cases ostensibly concern the correct standard of review, they illustrate the power of the rights paradigm indirectly because stricter review indicates a greater willingness to accept restrictions on the right of the landlord.

In earlier cases the Federal Court of Justice in Civil Matters required the landlord's cancellation for own use to be reasonable, but in 1989 the Federal Constitutional Court decided[36] that it was unconstitutional for the civil courts to institute unrestricted investigations into the motives of the landlord for wanting to use the property herself since the landlord, as owner of the property, must be allowed to decide how she wants to use and dispose of her property. Tenant protection laws place considerable restrictions on ownership of rental property and therefore an interpretation that takes no account of the landlord's wish to use her property for her own purposes would be in conflict with the constitutional guarantee of ownership. Although the courts must verify that the landlord's need to use the property was real, overly strict review of the owner's wish to use the property herself would not be permissible—the courts' discretion to review the landlord's decision is limited and has to be exercised with restraint so as not to interfere with the owner's fundamental rights.[37] This line of argument and the outcome of the 1989 decision demonstrate the continued force of the ownership paradigm in German constitutional thinking.

In the 1993 *Landlord–Tenant* decision the Federal Constitutional Court reiterated that the landlord-owner's wishes had to be respected, but it softened its earlier stance slightly by indicating that the declared intention of the landlord to use the property for her own purposes was insufficient to justify cancellation. Even though the courts could not institute unlimited review of the owner's motives, the landlord's decision has to be reasonable and feasible and the courts have some scope to inquire into these aspects of the landlord's prospective own use of the property.[38] This decision evoked a storm of protest in academic literature, partly because the Court's argument was said (with some justification) to be doctrinally flawed and partly because it was perceived to undermine the ownership model. The underlying ideological or political cause of the outcry (resistance against a move that subjects ownership to stricter review and therefore to more fundamental statutory restrictions for policy reasons) and the basis on which the strongest

---

(*Wohnraumkündigungsschutzgesetz*) [1974]; BVerfGE 38, 248 (*Zweckentfremdung von Wohnraum*) [1975]; BVerfGE 68, 361 (*Wohnungskündigungsgesetz*) [1985]; BVerfGE 79, 292 (*Eigenbedarfskündigung*) [1989]; BVerfGE 89, 1 (*Besitzrecht des Mieters*) [1993]; BVerfGE 89, 237 (*Eigenbedarfskündigung*) [1993]; BVerfGE 91, 294 (*Fortgeltung des Mietpreisbindung*) [1994].

[36] BVerfGE 79, 292 [1989].
[37] BVerfGE 79, 292 [1989] at 304–5.
[38] BVerfGE 89, 1 [1993] at 9–10.

arguments against the decision were founded, namely doctrinal inconsistency, are illuminating.

Perhaps the clearest example of doctrinal criticism that supports ideological objections against the decision came from property theorist Otto Depenheuer, who chastised the German Federal Constitutional Court for decisions that tend, in his view, to erode the position of private ownership as a cornerstone and guarantor of the free market.[39] His criticism is primarily aimed at two property cases decided by the Federal Constitutional Court, the *Groundwater* and *Landlord–Tenant* cases respectively.[40] Depenheuer is particularly critical of the *Landlord–Tenant* decision because the Court described a tenant as a kind of property owner; something that might sound trite to common law ears but that is doctrinally questionable for civil law traditionalists. According to Depenheuer, this decision splits ownership up between the holders of different entitlements (the owner and the tenant) and thereby erodes the unitary, abstract ownership right that forms the backbone of the free market system according to civil law orthodoxy.[41] However, in his view, the problem started even earlier, in the Court's famous *Groundwater* case.

In the *Groundwater* case the Federal Constitutional Court said that Article 14 of the German Basic Law, which grants the legislature the power to determine the content and boundaries of ownership,[42] means that the statutes that are in force at a particular moment determine what is recognised as property (ownership)[43] for purposes of the Basic Law. According to the standing jurisprudence of the Court, the property that is guaranteed by the Basic Law is therefore defined (and restricted) by legislation; with the result that regulatory restrictions placed on private ownership through legislation only require constitutional justification if they are arbitrary or disproportionate.

Depenheuer rejects this argument—in his view, the Basic Law itself is founded upon the pre-political and pre-constitutional primacy of the individual property owner, and therefore every legislative determination of the content or limits of ownership requires justification.[44] Contradicting the Court's view, Depenheuer

[39] O Depenheuer, 'Entwicklungslinien des verfassungsrechtlichen Eigentumsschutzes in Deutschland 1949–2001' in T von Danwitz *et al*, *Bericht zur Lage des Eigentums* (2002) 109–213 at 118. The next few paragraphs are loosely based on sections of AJ van der Walt, 'Property Theory and the Transformation of Property Law' in E Cooke (ed), *Modern Studies in Property Law*, Vol III (2005) 361–80.

[40] *BVerfGE* 58, 300 (*Naßauskiesung*) [1981]; *BVerfGE* 89, 1 (*Besitzrecht des Mieters*) [1993].

[41] Thereby reversing the move away from feudalism, initiated by Grotius and completed, as far as German law is concerned, by Thibaut; see n 3 above.

[42] Article 14 II of the Basic Law provides that the content and limits of ownership are determined by the legislature.

[43] Both § 903 of the German Civil Code (*BGB)* and Art 14 of the German Basic Law (*GG*) refer to *Eigentum*, the technical translation of which is 'ownership' rather than 'property'. However, for purposes of the constitutional text, this term is interpreted as 'property': *BVerfGE* 58, 300 (*Naßauskiesung*) [1981] 335. See AJ van der Walt, *Constitutional Property Clauses: A Comparative Analysis* (1999) 151–3. (For purposes of private law it is interpreted more narrowly as 'ownership', inter alia because German private law—embodied in § 903 of the Civil Code—restricts property to tangible things.)

[44] O Depenheuer, 'Entwicklungslinien des verfassungsrechtlichen Eigentumsschutzes in Deutschland 1949–2001' in T von Danwitz *et al*, *Bericht zur Lage des Eigentums* (2002) 109–213 at 166–70. At 167 Depenheuer describes § 903 of the Civil Code, which defines ownership as the right that allows the owner to dispose of the property as he wishes and to exclude everybody else from its use, as the '*magna charta*'

argues that the pre-political content and limits of ownership are derived from the civil law tradition and embodied in the Civil Code's definition of ownership as the right of free disposal and exclusivity (absoluteness). In Depenheuer's view, the legislature's power to restrict owners' entitlements in terms of the Basic Law is therefore subsidiary to a pre-politically private-law determined ownership framework.[45] Accordingly, Depenheuer argues that decisions of the Federal Constitutional Court that over-emphasise the powers of the legislature (such as *Groundwater*) or exceed the boundaries of legitimate judicial activity (such as *Landlord–Tenant*) by allowing and justifying the imposition of extraneous restrictions and limitations upon ownership erode the constitutional property guarantee and undermine the security of property as the backbone of individual autonomy and the free market system. In his view, the security of private property can be guaranteed only if the liberal private law concept of property forms the basis of the constitutional property provision, so that every state determination that affects the content and scope of ownership has to be justified with reference to legitimate public interests and the proportionality principle.[46] In the context of eviction, this would entail that the landowner's entitlement to evict unlawful occupiers may be

---

of the constitutional right in Art 14 of the Basic Law (on this definition of ownership compare n 4). The point of departure is that constitutional property is established on the basis of private law property in the Civil Code, in other words in the tradition of the 'unitary, abstract notion of ownership as shaped by Roman law'. The idea that the constitutional concept of ownership is developed with the private law institution as its starting point derives from the Federal Constitutional Court's decision in *BVerfGE* 65, 196 [1983] at 209. However, it is unlikely that the Court intended to establish a hierarchical relationship or institutional foundation as is assumed by Depenheuer—although the Court reasoned that development of the constitutional property concept had to take the private law concept as its starting point, it added that the constitutional institution had to develop according to its own requirements and context: *BVerfGE* 51, 193 [1979] at 218. Underplaying this qualification and then criticising the Court for developing a separate constitutional institution that differs from private law is disingenuous and begs the question. Depenheuer's view is contested; see M Ruffert, *Vorrang der Verfassung und Eigenständigkeit des Privatrechts* (2001) at 371ff for the counter-argument, and J Dietlein, *Die Lehre von den grundrechtlichen Schutzpflichten* (1992) at 49 (a fixed, pre-constitutional notion of ownership is foreign to the German Basic Law).

[45] This is the heart of Depenheuer's argument; see O Depenheuer, 'Entwicklungslinien des verfassungsrechtlichen Eigentumsschutzes in Deutschland 1949–2001' in T von Danwitz *et al*, *Bericht zur Lage des Eigentums* (2002) 109–213 at 168–70. Limitation of constitutional rights can be justified only if it serves a legitimate public interest and satisfies the proportionality requirement in the constitutional *Übermaßverbot* (prohibition against disproportionate regulation), which requires an equitable balance between the interests of the property owner and the public interest.

[46] Despite his criticism of individual cases, O Depenheuer, 'Entwicklungslinien des verfassungsrechtlichen Eigentumsschutzes in Deutschland 1949–2001' in T von Danwitz *et al*, *Bericht zur Lage des Eigentums* (2002) 109–213 at 213 concludes that the Federal Constitutional Court can overall be said to protect private property adequately. He specifically approves of the decision in *BVerfGE* 100, 226 (*Rheinland-Pfälzische Denkmalschutzgesetz*) [1999] because it subjected legislative and administrative regulatory actions that could have qualified, in terms of the *Groundwater* decision, as legitimate determinations of the content and scope of property to constitutional scrutiny, indicating that statutory determinations are measured against some extra-statutory baseline. The issue was whether the owner could be forced to bear the cost of maintenance of a property that has no private or commercial use or value because of preservation restrictions. The owner's application for demolition was turned down because of the restrictions, leaving her with no use option and high expenses. In such a case, the Court held, the state either had to allow development to make the property usable, or expropriate it in the public interest.

restricted only on the authority of a law that not only spells out the considerations upon which the courts could deny an application to evict, but also satisfies a strict legitimacy (serving a legitimate public purpose) and proportionality (establishes a fair balance between public and individual interests) test.

The English *Qazi* case

English common law developed along different lines and consequently property in English law differs from ownership in the civil law systems, not least because feudal land law was abolished later and less comprehensively in English law than in the civil law countries. However, because of the pervasive influence of economic liberalism the rights paradigm—and the centrality of ownership in that paradigm—nevertheless features large in the Anglo-American legal tradition. Gray and Gray confirm the influence of the ownership paradigm in English law when they describe the landlord's common law right of re-entry as 'the ultimate affirmation of the landlord's proprietary power' and characterise the outcome of the *Qazi* eviction case in the House of Lords as 'a resolute defence of proprietary sovereignty in the face of a much more open-textured form of proprietary morality stemming from a European source'.[47]

In the *Qazi* case, the House of Lords refused to concede that the right to housing that is protected by the European Convention on Human Rights could derogate from proprietary and contractual rights acquired under domestic law, thereby confirming the presumptive power of ownership[48] as it is enshrined in the rights paradigm. *Qazi* dealt with the question whether English courts, in deciding the validity of a claim for possession under Article 8(2) of the European Convention on Human Rights 1950, should balance the rights of the tenant against the rights of the owner, in line with the proportionality test employed by the European Court of Human Rights in adjudicating Article 8.[49] The House of Lords decided that English courts do not have to balance the landowner's rights against the housing interests of the tenant, since that balancing has already been done in the suitable political forum, namely the legislature.[50] Accordingly, once it has been established that the

---

[47] K Gray and SF Gray, *Elements of Land Law* (4th edn, 2005) at 1489, referring to *Harrow London Borough Council v Qazi* [2004] 1 AC 983 (HL). I return to the *Qazi* decision in subsequent chapters. The notion that property is a pre-political or pre-constitutional phenomenon shaped by natural law and embodied in private law also finds support in JW Harris, *Property and Justice* (1996); compare A Brudner, *The Unity of the Common Law: Studies in Hegelian Jurisprudence* (1995), Part II 'The Unity of Property Law'; HM Jacobs (ed), *Private Property in the 21st Century: The Future of an American Ideal* (2004).

[48] The phrase 'presumptive power' is used by LS Underkuffler, *The Idea of Property: Its Meaning and Power* (2003) at 70*ff* to refer to the traditional assumption that ownership rights trump 'lesser' competing rights and public interests in the imposition of restrictions. See further JW Singer, *Entitlement: The Paradoxes of Property* (2000) at 3, who also emphasises the evidentiary burdens that the ownership paradigm imposes on the regulatory state and on non-owners as a matter of course.

[49] See T Allen, *Property and the Human Rights Act 1998* (2005) at 241–5 on *Qazi*; at 210–11, 241–3 on the proportionality test applied to Art 8.

[50] *Harrow London Borough Council v Qazi* [2004] 1 AC 983 (HL), para 72.

landowner is entitled to an order for possession in terms of domestic law, there is nothing further to investigate. Effectively this decision confirms the same principle as in the South African *Brisley* case, namely that the presumptive power of the landowner's right is not automatically upset by constitutional provisions that promote or protect the housing rights of tenants or unlawful occupiers—in the absence of explicit legislative authority to the contrary, the courts will not and need not depart from the tradition according to which a landowner is entitled to eviction as soon as she proves a right to possession under private law.

Interestingly, the European Court of Human Rights refused to revisit the *Qazi* decision, even though the European Court was willing, in the later decision of *Connors v The United Kingdom*,[51] to review the proportionality of a similar eviction despite the fact that the local authority in that case had also already terminated the tenants' licence and was therefore, in terms of the *Qazi* logic, entitled to evict. As Gray and Gray point out, the later decision in *Connors* suggests that the earlier decision in *Qazi* might have been wrong, but the European Court has declared further proceedings in *Qazi* inadmissible, which rules out the possibility of it being overturned in Strasbourg.[52] The whole matter, including the apparent conflict between *Qazi* and *Connors*, was revisited by the House of Lords in *Kay and Another v London Borough of Lambeth and Others; Leeds City Council v Price and Others*[53] (discussed in chapter four), in which the House of Lords confirmed the *Qazi* position by holding that the courts may assume that landlord–tenant legislation establishes a fair balance between the interests of the landlord and those of the tenant. Unless the validity of a specific statute is challenged in terms of human rights standards, the existing balance between the conflicting property interests is therefore to be assumed just and equitable and it is not up to the courts to interrogate the effects of an eviction to which a landlord is entitled under existing law.

English eviction law is more complex than is suggested by this single example (I return to English law in chapter four), but as Gray and Gray correctly point out, the House of Lords' 'resolute defence of proprietary sovereignty' in *Qazi* at least shows quite strikingly that the rights paradigm, and particularly a rights paradigm that places emphasis on ownership, is alive and well in modern English law.

Evaluation

The three cases discussed above indicate that the rights paradigm, at least in some instances clearly dominated by the central figure of ownership, is still influential in property law, even though it is regularly critiqued and albeit that even its supporters often hold on to varying and even conflicting versions of the paradigm. I rely on the general persuasiveness and wide acceptance of this paradigm, particularly

[51] (2005) 40 EHRR 189; see K Gray and SF Gray, *Elements of Land Law* (4th edn, 2005) at 137–9; 1497.
[52] K Gray and SF Gray, *Elements of Land Law* (4th edn, 2005) at 1497.
[53] [2006] UKHL 10 (HL).

in the context of landownership disputes, to support my thesis that real and significant reform of the property regime requires a doctrinal, methodological and rhetorical paradigm shift that would dilute and undermine the influence of the rights paradigm in 'normal' property thinking. An important aspect of this reform would have to involve reconsideration of the relative significance of ownership in the rights paradigm, particularly with reference to land rights, since it is clear from the examples above that ownership-focused thinking plays an important part in upholding the paradigm and the socio-economic structures entrenched by it.

However, it is also necessary to point out from the outset that the rights paradigm itself is deeply ambiguous and even paradoxical.[54] In subsequent chapters I discuss various aspects and permutations of the landlord–tenant conflicts in the three cases discussed earlier and conclude that the law with regard to eviction has changed to such an extent over the last century that it is often difficult to maintain the central tenets of the paradigm. First of all, in chapter three I discuss the nature of eviction as the landowner's strongest and most valuable weapon and arguably the most eloquent symbol of the rights paradigm. In chapters four and five (dealing with tenants, and unlawful occupiers or squatters, respectively) I consider reform legislation intended to regulate eviction and to protect occupiers of residential premises against unlawful or unwanted eviction. In chapter six I discuss four other aspects of property law involving eviction in a more indirect way (adverse possession or acquisitive prescription; public access to private property; subversion of ownership rights through encroachment; and the position of weak owners, respectively) to illustrate the fact that the rights paradigm is qualified and even sometimes undermined by rules and practices that restrict the landowner's right of eviction in ways that cannot always be explained satisfactorily within the doctrinal framework of the paradigm. Once again I structure my discussion around the situation in South African law, with references to similarities and differences in other systems.

---

[54] This point has been made by a number of theorists; see ch 1, nn 24, 30 for references. CM Rose, *Property and Persuasion: Essays on the History, Theory, and Rhetoric of Property* (1994) at 58 uses the term 'propriety' to describe medieval and early modern practices according to which property ownership included responsibilities, some of which related to caring for the poor. See further CM Rose, 'Canons of Property Talk, or, Blackstone's Anxiety' (1998) 108 *Yale LJ* 601–32 at 603–4, where Rose indicates that Blackstone was well aware of and acknowledged this tradition. Compare further JW Singer, *The Edges of the Field: Lessons on the Obligations of Ownership* (2000); GS Alexander, *Commodity and Propriety: Competing Visions of Property in American Legal Thought 1776–1970* (1997).

3

Eviction in the Rights Paradigm

I.   The Right to Evict as an Incident of Ownership   53
II. Eviction, Socio-economic and Political Power   60
III. The Eviction Challenge   70

I. The Right to Evict as an Incident of Ownership

IN PRIVATE LAW,[1] ownership of land is generally protected strongly and the owner can evict unwanted occupiers fairly easily, at least in principle. This strong and straightforward right to evict is said to be based on a central incident of ownership, namely the owner's right to undisturbed and exclusive possession of her property,[2] and it kicks in whenever someone else occupies the property

---

[1] This section is drafted mainly with reference to civil law; the differences and similarities in English law are pointed out mainly in the footnotes. This section of the chapter is loosely based on rewritten passages from AJ van der Walt, 'Exclusivity of Ownership, Security of Tenure, and Eviction Orders: A Model to Evaluate South African Land-Reform Legislation' (2002) *TSAR* 254–89, and AJ van der Walt, *Constitutional Property Law* (2005) at 410–16. The main features of my overview of South African law are confirmed by the most important source on the law of landlord and tenant: WE Cooper, *Landlord and Tenant* (2nd edn, 1994) at 372–4.

[2] On South African law see nn 12*ff* below; for German private law see ch 4 below and compare further HJ Wieling, *Sachenrecht* (1992) at 156*ff*; F Baur *et al*, *Sachenrecht* (17th edn, 1999) at 97*ff*; F Quack (ed), *Münchener Kommentar zum BGB* Band IV *Sachenrecht* (1986) 877*ff*. For Dutch law see ch 4 below and compare further P Abas, *Asser's Handleiding tot de Beoefening van het Nederlands Burgerlijk Recht: Bijzondere Overeenkomsten* (2007) 'Huur', Art 199. Despite the obvious conceptual and institutional differences (see n 3 below), a comparable principle holds in Anglo-American common law, albeit that the focus is on the stronger right to possession rather than the stronger property right. AM Honoré, 'Ownership' in AG Guest (ed), *Oxford Essays in Jurisprudence* (1961) 107–47 at 113 describes the right to have exclusive physical control of the property as 'the foundation on which the whole superstructure of ownership rests'; see further C Lewis, 'The Modern Concept of Ownership of Land' in TW Bennett *et al* (eds), *Land Ownership: Changing Concepts* (1986) 241–66 at 254. Although possessory disputes are adjudicated in the context of relative title in English and US law (see ch 4 below and compare further n 3 below), the right to exclude—and hence to possession—is considered an essential element of ownership in these systems as well; compare ch 2, n 9, and see K Gray, 'Property in Thin Air' (1991) 50 *Cambridge LJ* 252–307; K Gray and SF Gray, *Elements of Land Law* (4th edn, 2005) at 117 (with further references to US and Australian law). On US law see especially *Kaiser Aetna v United States* 444 US 164 (1979); *PruneYard Shopping Center v Robins* 447 US 74 (1980); *Loretto v Teleprompter Manhattan CATV Corp* 458 US 419 (1982). In *Yee v City of Escondido* 503 US 519 (1992) at 528 Justice O'Connor stated that 'the "right to exclude" is doubtless, as petitioners assert, "one of the most essential sticks in the bundle of rights that are commonly referred to as property"' (citing *Kaiser Aetna v United States* 444 US 164 (1979) at 176).

against the owner's will or without her permission. Because the right to evict is based on the owner's stronger right to the property,[3] the courts normally do not have a wide or general discretion to refuse an application for an eviction order once the basic requirements have been met, nor do they have a discretion to take the social or economic circumstances of the occupier or other general policy considerations into consideration in refusing to grant an eviction order—the landowner who can prove the basic requirements is entitled to relief regardless of the personal circumstances of the occupier and the political, social or economic context within which the dispossession or occupation took place. The landowner's right can only be resisted by a person with a valid and recognised right of occupation, which could either be a personal or a real right and could only derive from legislation or from a right, permission or licence granted by the owner.

Despite the obvious differences, I will argue in this and the following chapters that the general principle that the owner's right to evict is based on her strong (and even dominant) position in the property hierarchy, regardless of the context or circumstances, is borne out by examples from English common law,[4] the largely

---

[3] In this regard, K Gray and SF Gray, *Elements of Land Law* (4th edn. 2005) at 109 point out the fundamental difference between English common law and the civil law systems: In the absence of a singular concept of *dominium* or direct ownership of land, the common law traditionally parcels up various degrees of socially recognised control over land (*ibid* at 106), with the result that both the fee simple owner and the lessee can claim property in the same land, albeit that each of them holds a different parcel of property (at 109). Eviction depends on the relatively stronger right to possession rather than ownership; see further ch 4 below and compare ch 2, nn 6, 7. The same applies in US law; see JW Singer, *Property Law: Rules, Policies, and Practices* (1993) at 696; C Rose, 'The Comedy of the Commons: Custom, Commerce, and Inherently Public Property' (1986) 53 *Univ Chicago LR* 711–81 at 711–17. This split between the property rights of owner and lessee is not possible in civil law systems—the extent to which the German Federal Constitutional Court seemed to apply the same construction was at the heart of the controversy in the *Landlord-Tenant* case (see ch 2, nn 30–35 and accompanying text). On the one hand this distinction could suggest that the eviction example discussed here applies only in civil law systems because the fundamental doctrinal hierarchy of landowner vs occupier does not feature in English law; however, the eviction example is relevant for English law as well, although the landlord–tenant relationship is described in different terms because of the different conceptual approach. Although property disputes in English law are determined by the relatively stronger title in every case, the central issues dominating eviction in landlord–tenant situations, *viz* the owner's presumptive power to exclude and the landlord's right of re-entry, compare quite usefully with the landowner's supposedly absolute right to exclude and to evict in civil law; see further ch 4 below; compare n 2 above and see K Gray and SF Gray, *Elements of Land Law* (4th edn, 2005) at 116, and the discussion below. Although I do not wish to ignore or minimise the differences between the two systems, I assume for present purposes that the similarities are sufficiently strong to support the general points that I make.

[4] The landlord's right to evict is strong in English law—if the tenant has committed a breach of covenant the common law allows the landlord 'to re-enter the premises and forfeit the lease or tenancy' as if it had not been made. K Gray and SF Gray, *Elements of Land Law* (4th edn, 2005) at 1485 describe this harshest remedy that a landlord can use against a tenant who breached the covenant of the landlord as 'draconian', even though it is heavily qualified by the court's discretion to grant relief against forfeiture (see ch 4). Written leases more often than not include forfeiture clauses that aid the landlord in enforcing the covenants of the lease. Although the English focus on possession implies that the power of eviction, in the landlord–tenant context, is exercised by landlords rather than landowners, it is clear (from a socio-economic perspective) that landlords are landowners to a degree that renders the comparison with civil law eviction by landowners useful. From the statement in *Cowan v Department of Health* [1992] Ch 286 at 295G (Gray and Gray at 1486; see further at 1488–9 with regard to the legal nature of the right) that the landlord's right of re-entry 'is what gives value and substance to the . . . freehold reversion' it is clear that the right of re-entry is premised upon the same kind of property

codified continental civil law systems[5] and largely uncodified (and mixed) South African law.[6] This comparability argument is strengthened by the fact that many of the statutory changes that have been introduced to amend the legal relationship between landowners and other interested parties in civil and in common law systems are often quite similar. Landlord–tenant relationships are heavily regulated in most contemporary legal systems, partly by post-World War II landlord–tenant legislation explicitly intended to protect tenants against exploitation in socially and economically trying conditions. In the process of promoting social welfare and housing policy, for example to stimulate the development and provision of new residential housing stock or to protect existing access to limited private rental housing—a legislative purpose which is generally regarded as a legitimate regulatory public interest[7]—regulatory legislation restricts landowners' interests and entitlements, including the right to evict. In some instances landlords' rights are

hierarchy that informs the civil law right to evict or, as Gray and Gray (at 1489) describe it, 'the ultimate affirmation of the landlord's proprietary power'. The force of the ownership paradigm in English law is also illustrated by the decision of the House of Lords in *Harrow London Borough Council v Qazi* [2004] 1 AC 983 (HL) to the effect that the Human Rights Act 1998 (and through it Art 8 of the European Convention on Human Rights) did not create or authorise 'some new form of judicial scrutiny as to the appropriateness of the landlord's recovery of possession', based on the impact of the eviction on the tenant—the proportionality issue has already been decided by the legislature that promulgated the relevant housing legislation and cannot be reopened in every case by a judicial examination of the social merits of the individual tenant's eviction (Gray and Gray at 1495–6). Gray and Gray at 1497 describe the decision as 'a resolute defence of proprietary sovereignty in the face of a much more open-textured form of proprietary morality stemming from a European source', by which they confirm the judicial force, in English law, of what I describe as the rights paradigm in eviction cases. I return to the *Qazi* decision in ch 4. In the US, the landlord is entitled to evict the tenant if she breaches material terms of the lease; most states have statutes that provide summary eviction proceedings and although some state courts allow tenants to raise an increasing number of defences in summary proceedings, the US Supreme Court has upheld the practice of not allowing such defences, describing it as not fundamentally unfair: JW Singer, *Property Law: Rules, Policies, and Practices* (3rd edn, 2002) at 760, referring to *Lindsey v Normet* 405 US 56 at 68 (1972). This decision and the availability of summary eviction proceedings arguably find support in the rights paradigm, as does Scalia J's dissenting opinion in *Pennell v City of San Jose* 485 US 1 (1988) at 16–25 to the effect that the rent control provision in issue effected a taking of property without just compensation. The position is broadly similar in Australian law (see P Butt, *Land Law* (3rd edn, 1996) at paras 15127–31) and Canadian law (see B Ziff, *Principles of Property Law* (4th edn, 2006) at 282–7).

[5] In German law the basic principle is that the owner's superior right to possession trumps any occupier's right unless the occupier can raise a defence based on a right that is valid specifically against the owner: See ch 4 below and compare further HJ Wieling, *Sachenrecht* (1992) at 159; F Baur *et al, Sachenrecht* (17th edn, 1999) at 98; F Quack (ed), *Münchener Kommentar zum BGB* Band IV *Sachenrecht* (1986) at 879. In Dutch law eviction is based on a similar principle, although the Civil Code specifies that the judge has to consider whether eviction would be fair and just in the circumstances: See ch 4 below and compare further P Abas, *Asser's Handleiding tot de Beoefening van het Nederlands Burgerlijk Recht: Bijzondere Overeenkomsten* (2007), 'Huur', Arts 199–236. For further comparative references to landlord–tenant legislation see further ch 4.

[6] South African legislation has not amended the common law situation intrinsically; see n 14 below and compare in more detail ch 4. Despite the fact that tenancy of residential property is heavily regulated in continental civil law systems, regulation did not seriously challenge the ownership paradigm in those systems either; see ch 4. I discuss anti-eviction legislation in chs 4 and 5.

[7] This holds even in relatively cautious or openly ownership-oriented decisions, although the tendency then is to analyse the relationship (and justify the unrestricted power of eviction) in utilitarian (eg law and economics) terminology. See eg the minority opinion of Scalia J in *Pennell v City of San Jose* 485 US 1 (1988) at 16–25, where he explains why regulatory wealth transfers should preferably be achieved through invisible, 'off-budget' transfers such as tax increases combined with rent subsidies.

restricted quite severely, particularly as far as termination of the tenancy and the actual enforcement of an eviction order are concerned. However—and this is a central theme in the chapters to follow—even quite dramatic restrictions imposed by legislative regulation of the landlord–tenant relationship mostly fail to undermine[8] the hierarchical power of the landowner's common law property rights in two crucial respects. Firstly, legislative protection is mostly limited to tenants and other lawful occupiers of residential property; instances where legislation restricts landowners' rights for the protection of *ab initio* unlawful occupiers (land invaders or 'squatters', as opposed to tenants or former tenants holding over) are far less common.[9] Secondly, even the anti-eviction protection that is afforded to tenants and other lawful occupiers in legislation usually turns on factors that are within the landowner's control, such as non-payment or other breaches of the tenancy agreement, changes in the current use of the rental property or the landowner's changing needs and plans with regard to the property, but the landowner's right to evict is seldom curtailed purely with reference to the general socio-economic context or the personal or economic circumstances of the tenant.[10] It can therefore be said that eviction is still largely based on the hierarchical power of the landowner's superior right to possession, even when that right has been restricted quite severely for public policy considerations related to the regulation of the rental housing market.[11]

According to South African common law[12] a landowner evicts unwanted occupiers using the most important Roman-Dutch remedy for the protection of

---

[8] In the sense that the restrictions do not affect the hierarchy that privileges ownership over non-ownership rights, even when the relationship is regulated very heavily. The rights of landowner/landlords are undoubtedly restricted, often quite severely, by legislation that regulates the circumstances and conditions under which property may be rented out for residential purposes, the kind and quality of residential properties that may be rented out, conditions under which rent levels may be altered, contractual provisions and guarantees that have to be complied with and conditions for cancellation or termination of tenancies and for evictions to be carried out. In some instances legislation places additional burdens upon owners who allow their property to stand empty and unused in times and areas where there is a scarcity of residential property. For a general overview of legislation see ch 4.

[9] See ch 5 for a discussion of relevant legislation.

[10] The US case of *Pennell v City of San Jose* 485 US 1 (1988) is an interesting example where such an amendment was (unsuccessfully) attacked for being unconstitutional; see ch 4. The South African case of *Brisley v Drotsky* 2002 (4) SA 1 (SCA) is an example of an unsuccessful attempt to interpret s 26(3) of the South African Constitution in such a way that it would make the personal and social circumstances of the evictee relevant; see ch 2, nn 28–35 and accompanying text, and ch 4. On the other hand, the South African Prevention of Illegal Eviction from and Unlawful Occupation of Land Act 19 of 1998 (PIE) is an example of legislation that explicitly grants the courts a discretion to refuse an application for an eviction order purely on the basis of the evictee's personal or social circumstances; see ch 5.

[11] See n 8.

[12] I use the term to refer to the largely uncodified system of rules received from Roman-Dutch civil law, together with case-law in which those rules have been explained, analysed and developed. In the process of development, elements of English law were imported, resulting in a mixed system that should be distinguished from English common law and from European civil law. However, the law relating to the *rei vindicatio* was received from uncodified Roman-Dutch law (in South African law regularly described as 'common law') and developed more or less unaffected by English law. For an introduction and references to further literature see R Zimmermann and DP Visser, 'Introduction: South African Law as a Mixed Legal System' in R Zimmermann and DP Visser (eds), *Southern Cross: Civil Law and Common Law in South Africa* (1996) 1–30.

ownership, namely the *rei vindicatio*.[13] The requirements were set out in *Chetty v Naidoo*:[14]

> It is inherent in the nature of ownership that possession of the *res* should normally be with the owner, and it follows that no other person may withhold it from the owner unless he is vested with some right enforceable against the owner (eg a right of retention or a contractual right). The owner, in instituting a *rei vindicatio*, need, therefore, do no more than allege and prove that he is the owner and that the defendant is holding the *res*—the *onus* being on the defendant to allege and establish any right to continue to hold against the owner.[15]

A plaintiff relying upon the *rei vindicatio* must simply prove that she is the owner of property held by the defendant.[16] In an eviction case the owner would typically prove that the property occupied by the defendant is registered in the plaintiff's name;[17] the onus is then on the occupier to prove that he has a valid right of

---

[13] The Roman law notion of vindication (the process by which the owner reclaims possession, based on the superiority of her entitlement to possession, from whomsoever is in possession) still underlies eviction in the continental civil law systems, although the relevant civil codes now provide the legal framework of the eviction process: see HJ Wieling, *Sachenrecht* (1992) at 159; F Baur *et al*, *Sachenrecht* (17th edn, 1999) at 98; F Quack (ed), *Münchener Kommentar zum BGB* Band IV *Sachenrecht* (1986) 879 (Germany); P Abas, *Asser's Handleiding tot de Beoefening van het Nederlands Burgerlijk Recht: Bijzondere Overeenkomsten* (2007), 'Huur', Arts 199–236 (Netherlands) (see n 5 above). In English common law the underlying notion is the landlord's right 'to re-enter the premises and forfeit the lease or tenancy', which is also based on the (albeit relative) superiority of the owner's right to possession, although the remedy is now regulated by legislation in many common law countries; see nn 4, 20.

[14] 1974 (3) SA 13 (A); most recently confirmed by the SCA in *Dreyer NO and Another v AXZS Industries (Pty) Ltd* [2006] 3 All SA 219 (SCA) at 221f–g, para 4. See PJ Badenhorst al, *Silberberg & Schoeman's Law of Property* (5th edn, 2006) at 242–53; WE Cooper, *Landlord and Tenant* (2nd edn, 1994) at 372–4. The South African common law situation was not fundamentally amended by legislation, except for specific interventions in land reform laws, which are discussed in chs 4 and 5. The Housing Act 107 of 1997 (intended to promote the facilitation of a sustainable housing development process: see the preamble) does not contain an explicit eviction provision, but the Act does require (s 2(1)(h)(i)) the national, provincial and local spheres of government to respect, protect, promote and fulfil the rights in ch 2 of the Constitution, including the prohibition against judicially unauthorised and arbitrary evictions in s 26 of the Constitution. The Rental Housing Act 50 of 1999 (which is restricted to rental property for residential purposes) protects tenants of rental housing against eviction by requiring that termination of a lease should not constitute an unfair practice: *Kendall Property Investments v Rutgers* [2005] 4 All SA 61 (C); compare ch 4.

[15] 1974 (3) SA 13 (A) at 20A. This passage was cited and followed most recently in *Pareto Ltd and Others v Mythos Leather Manufacturing (Pty) Ltd* 2000 (3) SA 999 (W) at para 5; *Betta Eiendomme (Pty) Ltd v Ekple-Epoh* 2000 (4) SA 468 (W) at para 9. See further PJ Badenhorst et al, *Silberberg & Schoeman's Law of Property* (5th edn, 2006) at 242–6; R Keightley, 'The Impact of the Extension of Security of Tenure Act on an Owner's Right to Vindicate Immovable Property' (1999) 15 *SAJHR* 277–307 at 283–4; AJ van der Walt, 'Exclusivity of Ownership, Security of Tenure, and Eviction Orders: A Model to Evaluate South African Land-Reform Legislation' 2002 *TSAR* 254–89 at 256–8. The considerations upon which eviction is based are similar in other legal systems; see nn 4 and 5 above, and ch 4.

[16] See *Graham v Ridley* 1931 TPD 476; *Marcus v Stamper & Zoutendijk* 1910 AD 58 at 72; *Jeena v Minister of Lands* 1955 (2) SA 380 (A); *Vulcan Rubber Works (Pty) Ltd v SAR&H* 1958 (3) SA 285 (A) at 289; *Ruskin NO v Thiergen* 1962 (3) SA 737 (A) at 744; *Chetty v Naidoo* 1974 (3) SA 13 (A) at 20; *Singh v Santam Insurance Ltd* 1997 (1) SA 291 (A).

[17] Eg by producing the title deeds in court. See *Goudini Chrome (Pty) Ltd v MCC Contracts (Pty) Ltd* 1993 (1) SA 77 (A) at 82A; *Ex parte Menzies et Uxor* 1993 (3) SA 799 (C) at 804F.

occupation that is enforceable against the owner.[18] The owner does not have to prove unlawfulness or animus on the part of the defendant[19]—once ownership has been established, the plaintiff is entitled to possession unless the defendant can prove a valid right of occupation. More specifically, the baseline rule was that the general historical, social and economic context and the individual and personal circumstances of the owner and the occupier could have no direct influence on the outcome of an eviction action—both civil law and common law courts have repeatedly confirmed that (in the absence of legislation) they have no discretion to deprive a landowner of an eviction order that she would otherwise have been entitled to, purely because of the context, the personal circumstances of the occupier or the unfair effect that eviction would have on the occupier or her family.

Even though landowners cannot evict without legal process in South African law,[20] the protection afforded by the eviction action under the 'normal' common law rule is strong, as it is based on the fundamental assumption that the owner is entitled to exclusive possession of his or her property—this is the normal state of affairs that would most likely be upheld in the absence of a valid defence.[21] This

---

[18] See *Jeena v Minister of Lands* 1955 (2) SA 380 (A) at 383A; *Durban City Council v Kistan* 1972 (4) SA 465 (N) at 487E–F; *Chetty v Naidoo* 1974 (3) SA 13 (A) at 20; *Hefer v Van Greuning* 1979 (4) SA 952 (A) at 959H; *Singh v Santam Insurance Ltd* 1997 (1) SA 291 (A). There is no legal obligation upon the landowner to allege that the occupier had a right of occupation (for example in terms of a lease) that lapsed or was cancelled, but should she raise such a ground for occupation the owner has to prove that the right no longer exists or is no longer enforceable: *Graham v Ridley* 1931 TPD 476; *Henning v Petra Meubels Bpk* 1947 (2) SA 407 (T) at 412; *Myaka v Havemann and Another* 1948 (3) SA 457 (A); *Chetty v Naidoo* 1974 (3) SA 13 (A) at 21. The mere assertion that the occupier is in occupation unlawfully or against the will of the owner does not trigger the additional burden of proof—the additional onus will be placed on the owner only in cases where she relies on the termination of the right of occupation from the outset or acknowledges the existence of that right, and if the defendant relies on the right as a defence: *Chetty v Naidoo* 1974 (3) SA 13 (A) at 20C, 21. The owner would normally satisfy the additional onus by proving that the lease or other right has expired or has been terminated.

[19] *Chetty v Naidoo* 1974 (3) SA 13 (A) at 20; *Singh v Santam Insurance Ltd* 1997 (1) SA 291 (A).

[20] Rule 6 of the High Court Rules does not allow *ex parte* applications for eviction; see JM Pienaar, 'Recent Developments Relating to Automatic Review Proceedings in the Land Claims Court' (2001) 34 *De Jure* 162–71 at 169. Contractual terms permitting forcible eviction are unlawful and unenforceable: *Blomson v Boshoff* 1905 TS 429; *Nino Bonino v De Lange* 1906 TS 120. The common law does not permit self-help to restore possession, even against allegedly unlawful and illegal occupiers: *Yeko v Qana* 1973 (4) SA 735 (A). The English law with regard to harassment or unlawful eviction that constitutes a breach of the implied covenant for quiet enjoyment has a similar restraining effect; although the landlord's right of re-entry establishes a strong right to evict, evictions are heavily regulated in English law (see K Gray and SF Gray, *Elements of Land Law* (4th edn, 2005) at 1440–41, 1490–97 on the restrictions). Protection from Eviction Act 1977 (UK), s 3(1) makes it unlawful for an owner to enforce his right to possession by other means than by court proceedings; see *Harrow London Borough Council v Qazi* [2003] UKHL 43 at 36; *Southwark London Borough Council v St Brice* [2002] 1 WLR 1537 at para 32. Most US state courts also hold that self-help evictions are unlawful and that the landlord must evict through court proceedings: JW Singer, *Property Law: Rules, Policies, and Practices* (3rd edn, 2002) 759. In German and Dutch law eviction is possible only in accordance with the relevant statutory provisions; see ch 4 and compare n 5 above.

[21] The lessee's security of tenure is generally ensured against sale of the property and change of ownership. In the civil law tradition, the *huur gaat voor koop* rule (lease trumps sale) states that an existing short-term lease of immovable property is not automatically terminated by sale of the property: The purchaser of the property is substituted for the lessor by operation of law, and the lessee cannot be evicted by the new owner during the term of the lease as long as the lessee continues to fulfil his or her obligations under the lease; see *Genna-Wae Properties (Pty) Ltd v Medio-Tronics (Natal) (Pty) Ltd* 1995

rule and its underlying assumptions formed part of Roman-Dutch law and early South African law,[22] and it still formed the baseline point of departure when anti-eviction measures were introduced in the land reform legislation of the 1990s and the 1996 Constitution. It also forms the point of departure for eviction law in most other legal systems (for the common law, Singer and Underkuffler describe it as the 'presumptive power' of ownership).[23] In the sense that this rule upholds the superiority and exclusivity of ownership, it entrenches the individual security of vested and acquired rights and the stability of the established regime of property rights. By the same token, any deviation from the rule that qualifies or undermines this rule by qualifying the formal right to evict regardless of context or circumstances threatens the individual security and the systemic stability of established property rights. In chapter four I argue that legislative amendments have apparently qualified the power of the right to evict, but that they only seldom amount to really serious challenges to the rule.

By way of preliminary conclusion one can say that eviction, as a tool with which to protect and enforce the exclusivity of ownership via the owner's (absolutely or relatively) superior right to possession, is a powerful instrument that underlines the social force of the rights paradigm. The most striking characteristic of the owner's right to eviction is the presumptive power of ownership which forces anybody who wants to resist eviction to prove a right that can withstand the owner's strong claim to exclusive possession. The existence and power of such a right can derive from the landlord's grant or from legislation, but usually not from the context or the parties' personal circumstances.

The political force of the presumptive power assigned to ownership through the right to eviction was demonstrated most vividly in the South African apartheid era, when eviction (also described as forced removals to indicate the scale of eviction programmes that affected whole communities)[24] was used to promote the exclusionary racial politics of the apartheid government. Once the relative power positions of owner and evictee were associated with social and political roles in the racially determined apartheid order, the presumptive power embodied in eviction law became irresistible and it was easier to both authorise and justify politically

---

(2) SA 926 (A). Short-term lessees are also protected by the doctrine of knowledge if the requirements are met. Registered long-term leases of immovable property (10 years or longer and registered in accordance with the Deeds Registries Act 47 of 1937) establish real rights and are protected as such. Unregistered long-term leases are protected (according to the Formalities in Respect of Leases of Land Act 18 of 1969) under the *huur gaat voor koop* rule for the first 10 years and under the doctrine of knowledge for the whole term if the requirements are fulfilled (confirmed in *Ismail v Ismail and Others* 2007 (4) SA 557 (EC)). For more detail on the requirements see B Wunsh, 'May Lessee Quit Premises on Sale of Them?' (1990) 107 *SALJ* 384–7; *De Jager v Sisana* 1930 AD 71; *Boshoff v Theron* 1940 TPD 299.

[22] JW Wessels, *History of the Roman-Dutch Law* (1908) at 484–5 regards Grotius (and specifically his views on the owner's superior right to vindication; see ch 2, n 4) as the link between received Roman law and South African law. See further M Josson, *Schets van het Recht van de Zuid-Afrikaanse Republiek* (1897) 407; AFS Maasdorp, *The Institutes of Cape Law*, Part 3 *The Law of Things* (1903) 31. The same approach was followed in early case-law; see eg *Marcus v Stamper & Zoutendijk* 1910 AD 58 at 72; *Graham v Ridley* 1931 TPD 476 at 479.

[23] See ch 2, n 16 and accompanying text; see further nn 4 and 5 above.

[24] See ch 1, n 5 on forced removals.

inspired forced removals without much resistance from private law. However, even in communities and at times when property holdings are not directly related to some evidently discriminatory political programme such as apartheid, it is still true that ownership of residential land that is rented out in a more or less free market represents significant social and economic power. As a general rule, people who rent residential property will have less power and be more open to arbitrary (or at least non-negotiable) exercises of social and economic power by others, unless the rental market is pointedly and specifically regulated in some way to prevent or restrict those exercises of power. Eviction inevitably has to be considered within the framework of political power. The increasing amount of attention given to eviction from one's home in case-law under domestic and international human rights instruments suggests that there is political understanding for the potential social and economic harm that can result from residential evictions but, once again, these policy-inspired qualifications of the right to evict establish qualifications of the established power hierarchies within the property regime and consequently they often meet with staunch resistance. Nowhere is this link between eviction and political power as clear as in the history of South African land law.

II. Eviction, Socio-Economic and Political Power

Under apartheid land law, the scope of the power to evict was extended far beyond its already considerable common law applications. In the process it became clear that eviction was not a neutral legal process through which abstract principles were applied objectively, but an exercise of social and political power. At common law the right to evict was supposedly based purely on the landowner's stronger right to possession, which reinforces the impression that the common law remedy merely protected the stronger of competing, private individual rights in an objective, neutral and legitimate fashion. As an expression of the protection of private ownership, eviction appears not only relatively harmless and normal but even positively laudable, even essential for the security of private autonomy and the stability of social and economic order. However, when applied in the context of apartheid land policy it soon became obvious that eviction is a political instrument that not only serves a general socio-political purpose in that it entrenches the existing hierarchy of owners and non-owners, but that could also be used to further less wholesome and far more contentious ideological goals, such as racial segregation and oppression. Moreover, highlighting the nature and scope of forced removals under apartheid not only confirms the evil of apartheid—it also underlines the role of eviction law in entrenching and upholding social and economic inequalities and injustices in the existing property system, whether it is tainted by apartheid ideology or not. Apartheid and racial oppression emphasised the ugliest side of social and economic power but it does not monopolise it.

In its apartheid guise, eviction mostly assumed the form of forced removals; the process by which (sometimes large) groups of people were forcibly removed from land for the sake of creating and maintaining the apartheid regime of 'reserving' land use within state-appointed segregated land parcels for different race groups.[25] Despite their general political and (under apartheid) specifically state-sponsored ideological nature, forced removals were carried out not only by the state, since private evictions were also reinforced by legislation that furthered the aims of apartheid ideology. Furthermore, the state often carried out evictions in its capacity as private landlord, a felicitous position created by the systematic abolition and feudalisation of customary and even private Black land rights. This characterised eviction during the apartheid era as a special blend of regulatory and private power, combined for the efficacious promotion of the apartheid ideology.

Obviously, the regulatory state power of forced removals was not unique to apartheid law—in general, eviction always illustrates the political nature of decisions to either uphold or dismiss property claims.[26] Furthermore, as part of the state's power to regulate land use (especially in the urban planning and the residential housing context), most governments can remove people from land when state security, public health or the public interest demands it; powers of this nature were vested in the state before the apartheid era[27] and, like most other democratic governments, the new democratic South African government has similar powers.[28] I return to this point in the discussion of recent South African case-law towards the end of this section. However, during the apartheid era the state's regulatory power of control over the use of land was amended in extraordinary ways that helped shape the Draconian character of the apartheid property regime. The changes in South African eviction law that took place under the influence of apartheid ideology pushed eviction law way beyond anything that one would expect to find in a democratic constitutional state and therefore they were unique to the apartheid state, but at the same time they helped to highlight the general problems with and the power of eviction in the rights paradigm more clearly than 'normal' eviction cases would. Eviction law was clearly abused by the apartheid government, but in the absence of constitutional and statutory controls and qualifications the right to

---

[25] See ch 1, fn 5 on forced removals, and compare further C Murray and C O'Regan (eds), *No Place to Rest: Forced Removals and the Law in South Africa* (1990).

[26] My hypothesis that eviction could be discussed fruitfully and sensibly, in the context of this book, with reference to other legal systems than South Africa hinges on this point.

[27] Seemingly 'normal' eviction provisions in statutes such as the Physical Planning Act 88 of 1967, the Health Act 63 of 1977 and the Slums Act 76 of 1979 relate to the health, public safety and public interest functions for which a state organ may sometimes require the right to evict (eg to remove people from a dangerous building or flood plain), but in the apartheid era these laws were applied on a racial basis and so served the agenda of apartheid rather than public health and safety. See AJ van der Walt, 'Towards the Development of Post-Apartheid Land Law: An Exploratory Survey' (1990) 23 *De Jure* 1–45 at 32. Eviction in the health and safety context and the way in which it should be approached in the South African democratic and constitutional context was again highlighted in *Occupiers of 51 Olivia Road, Berea Township, and 197 Main Street, Johannesburg v City of Johannesburg and Others* 2008 (3) SA 208 (CC); see the discussion below and compare ch 5, section III.

[28] Apart from health and safety laws, the obvious example is the Prevention of Illegal Eviction from and Unlawful Occupation of Land Act 19 of 1998; see the discussion in ch 5.

evict is open to such abuse exactly because of the strong hierarchical assumptions and power implications of the traditional, paradigmatic institution of eviction as a context-neutral right to enforce the stronger right to possession.

Eviction law underwent three major changes under the influence of apartheid, in each case relying on and deepening the hierarchical and power facets of the right to evict. Firstly, the state's regulatory powers to evict in the process of regulating and protecting public health and safety were used—or abused—for a very specific and extraordinarily problematic and contested political purpose under apartheid, namely to establish and maintain racially-based segregation of land use. Even when acknowledging the inherent political nature of eviction powers, one should recognise that the political purpose for which it was exercised under apartheid is unique in that the purpose of racial segregation is not justified by widely-shared democratic views about legitimate exercises of the police power. Apartheid land law was entrenched in more than a hundred laws, the most important of which, the Prevention of Illegal Squatting Act 52 of 1951 and the Group Areas Act 36 of 1966,[29] criminalised the use and occupation of land on the basis of race: Anybody who occupied land designated for a different race group committed a crime. The power to control the use of land and to remove people from land to protect public health, safety and well-being was therefore abused for the sake of the state ideology of racial segregation, which established a strong and lasting negative link between racial discrimination and eviction. My first substantive point is thus that apartheid evictions were not remarkable for their political motivation but for the particular politics relied upon in and served by the evictions.[30] In other words, apartheid evictions were not evil because they were politically inspired but because they were inspired by a particular politics, namely racial segregation founded in discrimination and inequality, or apartheid. This created a lasting negative connotation between eviction and apartheid—part of my argument about transformation is that this negative link was not and could not be extinguished simply by abolishing the apartheid laws and practices, because it left a legacy that still has to be dealt with and, more importantly, that can only be dealt with in an overtly political manner. The argument that transformation should avoid the mistakes of the

---

[29] See further the Black Land Act 27 of 1913; Development Trust and Land Act 18 of 1936; Blacks (Urban Areas) Consolidation Act 25 of 1945; Population Registration Act 30 of 1950; Prevention of Illegal Squatting Act 52 of 1951; Reservation of Separate Amenities Act 49 of 1953; Blacks (Prohibition of Interdicts) Act 64 of 1956; Trespass Act 6 of 1959; Regulations for the Administration and Control of Townships in Black Areas 1962; Group Areas Act 36 of 1966; Community Development Act 3 of 1966; Housing Act 4 of 1966; Physical Planning Act 88 of 1967; Regulations for the Administration and Supervision of a Black Urban Residential Area and Related Issues 1968; Black Areas Regulations 1969; Health Act 63 of 1977; Slums Act 76 of 1979; Black Local Authorities Act 102 of 1982; Black Communities Development Act 4 of 1984; National Policy for General Housing Matters Act 102 of 1984; and compare AJ van der Walt, 'Towards the Development of Post-Apartheid Land Law: An Exploratory Survey' (1990) 23 *De Jure* 1–45.

[30] This point finds support in *Port Elizabeth Municipality v Various Occupiers* 2005 (1) SA 217 (CC) at paras 8–10, where Sachs J explains the 'intensely racialised' political foundation and purposes of the Prevention of Illegal Squatting Act 52 of 1951 and the explicit purpose of s 26(3) of the Constitution (and other land reform laws) to reverse the legacy of that particular history.

past and shy away from politics altogether[31] is therefore doubly mistaken: Not only can politics not be avoided in land law in general, but on top of that the very legacy of apartheid land law requires a specific type of restorative politics if it is to be transformed or reformed at all.

The second amendment of eviction law was to establish a negative link between abuses of the apartheid state's regulatory power and the private law foundations of eviction. Associating apartheid land law with Roman-Dutch common law may appear counter-intuitive, but in fact the seemingly easy accommodation of discriminatory apartheid practices in the Roman-Dutch-dominated private law of the apartheid era continues to shape negative perceptions of and attitudes towards the South African common law tradition.[32] In a general sense, Roman-Dutch common law was and still is blamed for not offering stronger resistance to the injustices perpetrated through its supposedly neutral and scientific application during the apartheid era. It could well be argued that private law specialists accepted too easily that the dogmatic structure of eviction law, with its hierarchical assumptions about the vindication of the stronger private right, was hijacked and adapted for contested ideological purposes by casting the state and white landowners in the paradigmatic role of evictor whose legitimate property and autonomy rights had to be vindicated, while Black land users were cast as temporary, no-rights users who could be evicted whenever the social, economic or political interests of the rights holder demanded. In the slippage from private law institution to instrument of political power, eviction and its private law foundations were tainted by apartheid ideology. However, an even more direct link between common law eviction and apartheid land law was forged in a roundabout way: The Prevention of Illegal Squatting Act 52 of 1951 promoted apartheid by granting extensive and arbitrary powers of eviction to state organs and the

---

[31] See ch 1, n 9 and accompanying text.

[32] I am indebted to Frank Michelman for first challenging my views on this point and alerting me to the need to argue it more explicitly to overcome scepticism. In the much earlier AJ van der Walt, 'Ownership and Personal Freedom: Subjectivism in Bernhard Windscheid's *Theory of Ownership*' (1993) 56 *THRHR* 569–89 I worked out some of the historical background for the link between private ownership and personal autonomy and power over others in the Romanist tradition. The examples in this section illustrate the way in which the inherent inequality and social power that results from this particular perspective on property were used under apartheid to exploit the doctrinal weakness of Black landowners and users by translating it into political weakness. It might have been expected that negative attitudes towards the Roman-Dutch tradition would have shaped political sentiments against the retention of Roman-Dutch law, but influential commentators such as (now Constitutional Court judge) Albie Sachs supported the retention of the common law at a crucial time and thereby probably diluted stronger reactions against it; see A Sachs *Protecting Human Rights in a New South Africa* (1990) ch 8 ('The Future of South African Law') at 90–103. Compare further former Chief Justice MM Corbett, 'Trust Law in the 90s: Challenges and Change' (1993) 56 *THRHR* 262–70 at 264; former Chief Justice I Mahomed, 'The Future of Roman-Dutch Law in Southern Africa, Particularly in Lesotho' 1985 *Lesotho LJ* 357–65 at 360. For a very interesting complementary view see further current Chief Justice P Langa, 'Transformative Constitutionalism' (2006) 17 *Stell LR* 351–60 (focused on the development rather than just the preservation of the common law). In other civil law systems the same question was never raised in the same way, partly because they were not exposed to apartheid ideology and partly because the private law power inherent in the Romanist tradition was tempered by codification and (at least in German law after 1950) a constitutional Bill of Rights.

police,[33] but it also obliged white landowners to evict 'unlawful squatters' from their land and provided them with wide-ranging powers for that purpose.[34] Although the consolidation of the race-specific 'white' and 'Black' land pockets was largely accomplished through police-enforced removals from state land, this statutory innovation allowed the state to rely on private evictions to accomplish a substantial percentage of its forced removal goals, especially with regard to private land, thereby presumably lending an air of legitimacy to the eviction process. During the 1970s and 1980s, private evictions were mostly carried out in terms of the Prevention of Illegal Squatting Act 51 of 1952 (or related legislation)[35] and not the common law, because the Act made eviction so much easier and practically prevented unlawful occupiers from successfully resisting eviction. However, the rather tenuous link with private eviction created the impression that the 'squatter' legislation reinforced the common-law right of private landowners to protect their rights against illegal land invasions, thereby establishing an insidious association between common-law protection of private landownership and state control over racial segregation. In some instances the state, when evicting 'unlawful squatters' from state-owned land, acted as private landowner rather than as a state organ,[36] thereby reinforcing the impression that apartheid evictions were a 'normal' part of the protection of private ownership against unlawful land invasions and dispossessions. The resulting co-opting of the common law by apartheid politics coloured the private law rules and practices of eviction in a lasting way. Once again this connection was not and could not be extinguished by the abolition of apartheid; it left the common law tainted and the process of transformation has to concern itself with this fact. The attitude that transformation or reform or development of the law should leave the common law 'untouched' as far as

[33] *Port Nolloth Municipality v Xhalisa and Others; Luwalala and Others v Municipality of Port Nolloth* 1991 (3) SA 98 (C): A municipal authority attempted to evict and remove people who were living in tents in an emergency camp established by the municipal authority on land owned by the municipal authority. The Act allowed the local authority to identify these people as 'unlawful squatters' and forcibly remove them; the local authority consequently dumped them on open ground outside the boundaries of the local authority's jurisdiction (where they would of course be vulnerable to similar treatment by whoever owned that land), but the Cape Supreme Court (as it then still was) refused to allow the eviction (termed a 'civil deportation').

[34] C Lewis, 'The Prevention of Illegal Squatting Act: The Promotion of Homelessness?' (1989) 5 *SAJHR* 233–9 at 235 indicates that eviction of illegal squatters was not always mandatory; it was rendered so by the amended s 3 and the new s 3A, inserted by the Prevention of Illegal Squatting Amendment Act 104 of 1988. Section 3A made it an offence for the owner or lessee to permit the building or occupation of unapproved structures on the land; s 3B allowed the owner or lessee, together with the local authority, to demolish such structures. See further n 37 below.

[35] See eg *Jeena v Minister of Lands* 1955 (2) SA 380 (A): In this case eviction took place in terms of the Land Settlement Act 12 of 1912.

[36] This phenomenon still occurs and I return to it in ch 4. See particularly the Constitutional Court decision in *Minister of Public Works and Others v Kyalami Ridge Environmental Association and Another (Mukhwevo Intervening)* 2001 (3) SA 1151 (CC) (the state has the same rights in respect of state land as a private landowner in respect of private land). Land reform laws such as the Prevention of Illegal Evictions from and Unlawful Occupation of Land Act 19 of 1998 (PIE) now explicitly distinguish between private and state evictions.

possible[37] is consequently clearly misguided: Effective and significant transformation that can change the lingering effects of apartheid land law inevitably requires
incisive and critical reassessment and, where necessary, amendment of the common law, including amendments that might have less to do with a perceived
return to the purity of Roman-Dutch tradition than with a decisive move away
from the weaknesses that allowed the tradition to be co-opted and abused under
apartheid.

The third amendment of the common law tradition brought about by apartheid
evictions was that eviction law acquired an air of arbitrariness that related back to
but extended far beyond the traditional context-insensitivity of common law evictions. In the South African common law framework eviction was supposedly
always allowed regardless of the occupier's personal circumstances because the
paradigm within which eviction was adjudicated was ostensibly dominated by the
superiority of the landowner's right to possession, but under apartheid the per-
ception of 'neutrality' was abandoned wholesale. This followed because apartheid
legislation created a situation in which Black occupiers and users of land were
legally classified as unlawful occupiers (or 'squatters')—who could therefore be
evicted without any conceivable defence—by the very legislation that allowed and
regulated eviction of unlawful occupiers in the first place or, even worse, by the
same authorities who had established and housed them in a particular location.
The Prevention of Illegal Squatting Act 51 of 1952 introduced a wide-ranging definition of 'unlawful squatting' that included people who were originally permitted
(or even forced) to settle on the land by the public authority or the landowner,
thereby placing the identification of individuals and groups to be affected by eviction and forced removal in the complete and arbitrary discretion of the landowner
or the state.[38] The Act was also amended repeatedly in an effort to oust the courts'

---

[37] See ch 1, n 12 and accompanying text. This argument also underscores the reasons why the
Supreme Court of Appeal missed a golden opportunity to develop, invigorate and legitimise the common law in *Tswelopele Non-Profit Organisation v City of Tshwane Metropolitan Municipality* 2007 (6)
SA 511 (SCA). The court decided that an unlawful and unconstitutional eviction by state officials had
to be overturned and that the evicted squatters had to be reinstated, but refused to amend the common
law spoliation remedy (*mandament van spolie*) to reach this goal, preferring to leave the common law
'untouched' and develop a new constitutional remedy for the purpose. The doctrinal argument on
which this decision hinges was that the common law remedy could not be used when the original building materials had been destroyed. For a full discussion see AJ van der Walt, 'Developing the Law on
Unlawful Squatting and Spoliation' (2008) 125 *SALJ* 24 36 and compare n 40 below.
[38] *Vena v George Municipality* 1987 (4) SA 29 (C): The Act rendered occupiers 'unlawful squatters'
if the structures they occupied—mostly self-built shacks—did not comply with building regulations.
Of course, the informal housing of people most at risk never complied with these regulations, allowing
the local authorities to evict and remove them at will, even when they have been settled on that land
and in those structures by the same local authority in the first place. In the *Vena* case, the Cape Supreme
Court (as it then still was) refused to treat as unlawful squatters people who had been settled on the
land by the local authority and who were paying rent to the local authority. The Act was amended soon
after (by the Amendment Act 104 of 1988; see n 33) to render the lawfulness or title in terms of which
the occupier occupied the land irrelevant and to oust the courts' jurisdiction to consider any aspect of
eviction unless bad faith was proved on the side of the applicant. See AJ van der Walt, 'Towards the
Development of Post-Apartheid Land Law: An Exploratory Survey' (1990) 23 *De Jure* 1–45 at 30.

jurisdiction to review evictions in terms of the Act.[39] During the 1980s, some judges resisted the implementation of increasingly harsh eviction proceedings and forced removals and the ousting of the courts' jurisdiction to review state evictions,[40] but inevitably their efforts merely resulted in further amendments to the legislation and further limitations of the courts' powers.[41] This third characteristic of eviction under apartheid law, namely its arbitrariness, is perhaps the one that could most easily be rectified through reforming legislation—section 26(3) of the Constitution and land reform laws to the same effect clearly have to be read as efforts to attain exactly that goal.[42]

Through the combined effect of these changes in the common law tradition, eviction law was meant to acquire an air of tough but normatively unavoidable and formally irresistible, 'objective' application of apparently 'normal' legal rules and procedures, while in fact it hid from view completely arbitrary state action that was informed purely by the ideological whim of the apartheid government. Formally, the pretence was upheld that eviction served the perfectly normal and legitimate purpose of vindicating recognised property and security rights against perceived threats of invasion, chaos and lawlessness, but in fact the institution was abused cynically to create and uphold a socially engineered, state-sponsored and state-enforced system of racially segregated land use. In the constitutional post-1994 era, this characteristic of land law and the role that eviction played in it obviously became untenable, adding to the other considerations that required reconsideration and amendment of eviction law in general.

---

[39] The most infamous ouster clauses were the regularly amended and extended s 3B(4)(a) of the Prevention of Illegal Squatting Act 52 of 1951 (requiring proof of bad faith before a court could consider or grant any order, judgment or relief founded upon the exercise of the powers under the section) and the Blacks (Prohibition of Interdicts) Act 64 of 1956 (prohibiting black persons from obtaining an interdict to prevent or terminate allegedly unlawful or invalid state action under certain laws as identified by proclamation in the government gazette). See AJ van der Walt, 'Towards the Development of Post-Apartheid Land Law: An Exploratory Survey' (1990) 23 *De Jure* 1–45 at 29–32 for more detail; compare C Lewis, 'The Prevention of Illegal Squatting Act: The Promotion of Homelessness?' (1989) 5 *SAJHR* 233–9.

[40] In *Tswelopele Non-Profit Organisation v City of Tshwane Metropolitan Municipality* 2007 (6) SA 511 (SCA) the Supreme Court of Appeal decided that a state eviction, which was carried out unlawfully and in contravention of s 26(3) of the Constitution, had to be reversed and that the former unlawful occupiers had to be reinstated in temporary shelters, if necessary by using replacement materials since the original materials had been destroyed. In giving this decision, which clearly promotes 'the spirit, purport and objects of the Constitution', the Court crafted a new constitutional remedy since it held (confirming *Rikhotso v Northcliff Ceramics* 1997 (1) SA 526 (W)) that the Roman-Dutch *mandament van spolie* could not be employed when restoration required use of replacement materials. However, it could be argued that this attitude denies the bravery of courts who 'developed' and used remedies available to them under the common law, including the *mandament van spolie*, to defy state evictions and forced removals, as appears from the well-known decision in *Fredericks v Stellenbosch Divisional Council* 1977 (3) SA 113 (C). See n 37.

[41] See nn 36–7. AJ van der Walt, 'Towards the Development of Post-Apartheid Land Law: An Exploratory Survey' (1990) 23 *De Jure* 1–45 at 26–32 'Criminalized Tenure', refers to some of the dozens of other cases. See 27–29 (cases relating to the Group Areas Act 36 of 1966), 29–31 (cases relating to the Prevention of Illegal Squatting Act 52 of 1951); compare further AJ van der Walt, 'Squatting and the Right to Shelter' 1992 *TSAR* 40–55 for a discussion of later case-law.

[42] See chs 4 and 5 below for an overview of the anti-eviction provisions.

Through the amendments described above, the already powerful common law right to evict was transformed into an even stronger remedy that not only protected individual landowners, but also sanctioned the arbitrary exercise of state power (often undertaken by private landowners) to establish and entrench a basically feudal relationship between the state and black occupiers of land, in terms of what was clearly a racially inspired and discriminatory land-use politics. To a large degree, the current land and housing crisis was created because apartheid land law allowed the state to evict and forcibly remove people from land and to marginalise and undermine the security of their occupancy, for the sake of promoting the ideology of racial separation.[43] Racially based land laws, backed up by often uncontrolled state force, denied most black occupiers of land any meaningful security of tenure and allowed the state to determine, as a matter of political expedience, whether individuals and groups should be removed from land and 'settled' elsewhere as part of the 'huge social experiment' known as 'separate development' or apartheid.[44] Increasingly, racially based land legislation ousted the courts' power to review, prevent or control evictions and removals.

The power to enforce politically motivated, legislatively sanctioned and state-sponsored eviction and (on a larger scale) forced removals thus became a cornerstone of apartheid land law. This represented a significant shift away from common law eviction principles, both quantitatively (creating more, stronger powers to evict and allowing less judicial control) and qualitatively (evictions became more openly politically and ideologically inspired and authorised by public rather than private law), thereby transforming the traditional common law notion of eviction as a remedy that protects the private landowner's right to undisturbed possession into a more overtly political notion of eviction as an exercise of state power to manipulate social relationships through control over land holdings and use.[45] In the process, eviction law in general inevitably became a major focus of the post-apartheid land reform process. One result of this shift was that eviction in general, including private-law eviction aimed at protecting private landownership against unlawful dispossession and occupation, became strongly associated with arbitrary and state-sponsored forced removals aimed at furthering the ideology of apartheid. Inevitably, the brute force whereby the will and autonomy of the rights holder could be enforced on the weaker occupier or user of land washed back into private law, thereby also raising questions about the legitimacy and the

---

[43] This view is not shared universally; see *Joubert and Others v Van Rensburg and Others* 2001 (1) SA 753 (W) at paras 35–42, where Flemming DJP describes the effect of the Extension of Security of Tenure Act 62 of 1997 as 'arbitrary deprivation' of existing ownership, 'allowing people to choose to stay on another's property wherever they choose and simply because they so choose, at the expense of lawful rights, [which] is clearly not land reform' (at para 43.6).

[44] In *Minister of the Interior v Lockhat* 1961 (2) SA 587 (A) at 602D apartheid was described as 'a colossal social experiment and a long term policy' that must 'inevitably cause disruption and, within the foreseeable future, substantial inequalities', the political wisdom of which had to be left for the supreme legislature as policy-making body to decide upon, and was not for the courts to judge.

[45] The Constitutional Court recently subscribed to this evaluation; see *Port Elizabeth Municipality v Various Occupiers* 2005 (1) SA 217 (CC) at para 10.

justifiability of eviction as a purely private (and racially indifferent) instrument of settling land disputes, especially in situations where one party is socially and economically stronger than the other. Through its association with apartheid, eviction law has become a generally contested and problematic legal institution.

The analysis above demonstrates the fact that eviction, under apartheid, was used to serve a particularly abhorrent political programme. However, eviction always embodies an exercise of power and this power always has a political aspect—apartheid forced removals were not objectionable because they were politically inspired but because of the politics that inspired them. Even in the absence of apartheid politics, eviction still represents power and therefore it is always political and hence open to scrutiny and questioning. Although directly politically inspired evictions are not nearly as prevalent or as problematic in other democracies—particularly in established and relatively wealthy democracies—as they were in apartheid South Africa, there is still enough evidence in the newspapers and in the reported case-law to indicate that state-supported or state–enforced evictions occur in other countries and that they are sometimes highly contested and politically charged. Some examples of case-law from other jurisdictions are discussed in subsequent chapters, particularly chapters four and five. It is also clear that, even now, in the aftermath of the first democratic elections and under the auspices of the new Constitution, state-enforced eviction still features prominently in South African society. Some of the new legislation that is supposed to change this situation and some of the case-law that emerged under the new Constitution and legislation are discussed in subsequent chapters. For the moment it is sufficient to note that eviction still occurs, that it is still politically charged and contested, and that it almost always involve the exercise of force and superior power against people who can only be described as vulnerable and marginalised.

In a recent demonstration of the continued relevance of the observations above, the City of Johannesburg attempted to evict occupiers from state and private land on the authority of building, health and safety regulations. On the surface, these evictions seemed a world away from the racially based forced removals of the apartheid era, but beneath the surface they were equally problematic because of the lingering effects of apartheid economics and the political power stigma of eviction. The Witwatersrand High Court refused to grant an eviction order[46] but this decision was overturned by the Supreme Court of Appeal.[47] The Supreme Court of Appeal argued that the City's powers to order the vacation of unsafe buildings are not dependent upon its being able to offer alternative housing to the occupants. One of the assumptions the court relied upon in arriving at this conclusion was that the Constitutional Court has not yet given a binding decision on the meaning of 'relevant circumstances' in section 26(3) of the Constitution, nor has it indicated 'whether a court has a general discretion after having considered the "relevant circumstances"' to deny an applicant the eviction order it would

---

[46] *City of Johannesburg v Rand Properties (Pty) Ltd and Others* 2007 (1) SA 78 (W).
[47] *City of Johannesburg v Rand Properties (Pty) Ltd* 2007 (6) SA 417 (SCA).

normally be entitled to.[48] Relying on its own tradition-upholding decision in *Brisley v Drotsky*,[49] the Court insisted that in eviction applications not covered by the Prevention of Illegal Eviction from and Unlawful Occupation of Land Act 19 of 1998 (PIE), courts do not have a general discretion to refuse an eviction application purely based on what is just and equitable: According to the *Brisley* decision, section 26(3) of the Constitution does not grant or necessarily imply such a discretion.[50] In other words, the Supreme Court of Appeal held that eviction law still applied in its seemingly neutral and abstract traditional form, unless it has been explicitly and clearly amended by reform legislation such as PIE. The common law tradition was seemingly left unaffected by apartheid and its aftermath in the democratic reforms of the 1996 Constitution, even when the power of eviction is exercised by the state.

In a surprising and fascinating development, the Constitutional Court overturned the Supreme Court of Appeal's decision on the eviction, although it declined to consider the Supreme Court of Appeal's holding with regard to the applicability of PIE.[51] Following its own decision in *Port Elizabeth Municipality v Various Occupiers*,[52] the Constitutional Court decided that evictions like the one in *City of Johannesburg* cannot proceed unless the local authority has engaged with the occupiers meaningfully and in good faith to see whether all or some of the issues surrounding the eviction can be solved.[53] Such engagement should involve the reasons for the eviction, the short- and long-term availability of alternative housing, as well as the possibility of rendering the presently occupied properties safer and healthier for the occupants in the interim. In the *City of Johannesburg* case, the Court initially gave an interim order that forced the parties to engage in negotiations and subsequently approved the agreement that was reached between the parties during negotiations. It was clear that much of the hardship usually caused by eviction was prevented or at least alleviated through the process of negotiation, which forced the local authority to take its constitutional obligations regarding provision of housing more seriously. The implications of the decision and the attitude adopted by the Court are vast—I return to the decision and some of its implications in later chapters. For present purposes, the most significant implication is that the *Johannesburg City Council* decision of the Constitutional Court, like its predecessor in *Port Elizabeth Municipality*, overtly recognises and acknowledges the political nature of eviction and the social and political power exercised in an eviction and attempts to ameliorate that power by forcing the state, at least, to take its housing obligations seriously and to treat the individuals who are subjected to eviction with dignity. This represents a significant shift in

---

[48] *City of Johannesburg v Rand Properties (Pty) Ltd* 2007 (6) SA 417 (SCA) at para 40.

[49] 2002 (4) SA 1 (SCA). See the discussion of this decision in ch2, section II and in ch 5.

[50] *Brisley v Drotsky* 2002 (4) SA 1 (SCA) at para 40.

[51] *Occupiers of 51 Olivia Road, Berea Township, and 197 Main Street, Johannesburg v City of Johannesburg and Others* 2008 (3) SA 208 (CC).

[52] 2005 (1) SA 217 (CC).

[53] *Occupiers of 51 Olivia Road, Berea Township, and 197 Main Street, Johannesburg v City of Johannesburg and Others* 2008 (3) SA 208 (CC) at paras 14–23.

traditional thinking about eviction in the rights paradigm, moving away from the traditional exclusive focus on the rights of the landowner (or the state as regulator) and instead taking cognisance of the social and personal circumstances of those affected by eviction and the detrimental effect that eviction might have for them and their families.

The analysis above indicates that eviction is a major tool in the process of upholding and securing the exclusivity of established property rights, particularly ownership, and in stabilising the supposedly legitimate current distribution of property holdings. In view of the discussion in chapter two it appears that constitutional and legislative or administrative efforts to curb the granting and implementation of eviction orders can give a useful indicator of the strength of the rights paradigm. The conflict between efforts to uphold and enforce the right to evict and constitutional or legislative efforts to restrict that right for the sake of considerations and circumstances out of the control of the landowner, such as the general social and economic situation in the country or the specific social and economic circumstances of the occupiers, is therefore an instructive and useful locus for critical thinking about property in the margins.

III. The Eviction Challenge

The rights paradigm obviously does not exist in a 'pure' or unadulterated form in the sense that ownership or stronger property rights in fact always and inevitably trump state regulation or competing property interests. Depending on the view one takes, the rights paradigm in its abstract form either never reflected the reality of property law accurately or, if it did, property law has been modified by changing conditions and newly created restrictions to such an extent that the rights paradigm now overstates the power that ownership or strong property rights exercise in fact. In any event it is clear that ownership and other property rights in land are in fact subject to numerous and often quite extensive and onerous restrictions, including restrictions on a landowner's right to evict. Governments routinely use legislation to amend or regulate the hierarchical domination of property ownership according to social, economic and political circumstances and requirements;[54] in the modern regulatory state, many of these restrictions replaced or expanded the common-good restrictions that common law has always imposed on the use of property.[55]

---

[54] The power of the legislature to impose statutory restrictions of this nature is often referred to as the police power, which indicates that these restrictions can bring about burdensome limitations on the owner's use of the property, without compensation, because the restrictions are imposed to promote public safety and health purposes normally associated with the police power. See further AJ van der Walt, *Constitutional Property Law* (2005) at 132–7 and comparative sources referred to there.

[55] The obvious example is neighbour law, particularly in its pre-legislation common law version. As in the case of statutory police power limitations, neighbour law limitations are characteristically reciprocal in the sense that they impose restrictions that simultaneously and mutually burden and benefit all affected owners.

Irrespective of the position that one takes on the 'erosion of ownership' thesis,[56] it is clear that police power-type restrictions on the use of private property exist as a matter of fact, both at common law and in legislation; that these common-good or police power restrictions are often quite extensive; that in some cases they may impose a very significant burden on the property owner; and that, with few exceptions, compensation is not payable for them.[57] It is also clear that control over the availability and commercial exploitation of residential property and housing in general is nowadays regarded as a legitimate public purpose for which the state may use its regulatory police power, much in the same way that the state would regulate the use of property to protect public health and safety more directly.[58]

However, recognising the existence of common law and statutory restrictions on ownership does not necessarily diminish the power of the rights paradigm or of

---

[56] According to this thesis ownership is being eroded by a growing number of increasingly burdensome restrictions, particularly in areas that arguably did not and should not fall within the sphere of the police power, such as land-use planning and environmental conservation regulation. The issue is not necessarily whether there was an actual starting point where ownership was more or less unencumbered, but rather whether restrictions are increasing in number and impact, and whether they are nearing the point where the essence of ownership as an absolute right is being eroded. This thesis is often forwarded from a libertarian perspective to argue against the imposition or enforcement (without compensation) of what are regarded as increasingly burdensome land-use planning and environmental conservation regulations. In response it is sometimes argued either that ownership was never absolute or unrestricted and that common-good restrictions are both historically and conceptually inherent to ownership of particularly land (eg AJ van der Walt and DG Kleyn, 'Duplex Dominium: The History and Significance of the Concept of Divided Ownership' in DP Visser (ed), *Essays on the History of Law* (1989) 213–60), or that the institution of property ownership is indeed undergoing a radical transformation in society (including its being restricted more than before) and that it is the absolutist doctrinal view of ownership that requires updating, because the existence and scope of the restrictions are socially and morally above criticism (eg LK Caldwell, 'Rights of Ownership or Rights of Use? The Need for a New Conceptual Basis for Land Use Policy' (1975) 6 *Environmental LR* 409–25; DP Visser, 'The "Absoluteness" of Ownership: The South African Common Law in Perspective' 1985 *Acta Juridica* (also published separately as TW Bennett *et al* (eds), *Land Ownership: Changing Concepts* (1986)) 39–52; DV Cowen, *New Patterns of Landownership. The Transformation of the Concept of Landownership as Plena in re Potestas* (1984) at 76–7; CH Lewis, 'The Modern Concept of Ownership of Land' 1985 *Acta Juridica* (also published separately as TW Bennett *et al* (eds), *Land Ownership: Changing Concepts* (1986)) 241–66 at 257; AJ van der Walt, 'The Effect of Environmental Conservation Measures on the Concept of Landownership' (1987) 104 *SALJ* 469–79). In German constitutional law it is accepted as a matter of principle that ownership, like all property rights, is restricted. References to the absoluteness of ownership in German law therefore relate either to its general enforcement ('against the whole world', as opposed to personal enforcement of rights based on contractual or other obligations) and not to the notion that it is unrestricted; or to the exclusivity or indivisibility of ownership in civil law systems: F Baur *et al*, *Sachenrecht* (17th edn, 1999) at 29–31.

[57] The Swiss Constitution explicitly provides for compensation in case of what is called 'material expropriations'; see AJ van der Walt, 'The Property Clause in the New Federal Constitution of the Swiss Confederation 1999' (2004) 15 *Stell LR* 326–32. Some other jurisdictions allow compensation for what are known as 'regulatory takings' in US constitutional jurisprudence, while others explicitly do not; see AJ van der Walt, *Constitutional Property Law* (2005) at 213–21 and comparative literature referred to there; AJ van der Walt, 'Compensation for Excessive or Unfair Regulation: A Comparative Overview of Constitutional Practice Relating to Regulatory Takings' (1999) 14 *SAPL* 273–331. In a few instances non-expropriatory compensation is possible; in German law this is known as equalisation benefits because it is meant to spread the financial burden caused by exceptionally harsh or unfair non-expropriatory (and hence uncompensated) regulatory restrictions; see AJ van der Walt, *Constitutional Property Law* (2005) at 221–4; GS Alexander, *The Global Debate over Constitutional Property: Lessons for American Takings Jurisprudence* (2006) at 236–9.

[58] For a comprehensive theoretical analysis of the property aspects of the home see L Fox, *Conceptualising Home: Theories, Laws and Policies* (2007).

ownership as a particularly powerful (dominant) property right. Particularly in the continental civilian tradition, mainstream lawyers tend to preserve the doctrinal integrity of the paradigm by insisting that ownership is an absolute or unlimited right in principle, although it can accommodate temporary restrictions, just like a rubber ball can accommodate temporary indentation without thereby permanently losing its characteristic spherical shape.[59] When elasticity or residuarity is seen as a (or the main) characteristic of essentially unrestricted ownership,[60] restrictions and limitations upon ownership are recognised, but by definition they are regarded as temporary and exceptional.[61] The doctrinal implications of this approach are that there is a presumption against the existence of limitations and an interpretive rule according to which limitations, once proven, have to be interpreted in such a way as to impose the smallest possible burden on the owner. To the extent that the presumption against restrictions and the interpretive rule against expansive interpretation of restrictions are recognised and enforced, the mere existence of actual statutory or regulatory limitations on the right to evict does not detract from the fact that the rights paradigm continues to exist and that ownership and other strong property rights enjoy a privileged hierarchical position in that paradigm that enables them to dominate the adjudication of property disputes.[62]

---

[59] The doctrinal argument that ownership is an absolute right that is capable of absorbing temporary and partial limitations is based on the same assumptions about the pre-political origin and nature of ownership as the privileging of common law over legislation; see the discussion in ch 2. In South African private law doctrine this is known as the 'elasticity of ownership'; see eg PJ Badenhorst *et al*, *Silberberg & Schoeman's The Law of Property* (5th edn, 2006) at 91–5. The rubber ball metaphor was popularised in South African literature by DV Cowen, *New Patterns of Landownership. The Transformation of the Concept of Landownership as Plena in re Potestas* (1984) at 76–7. It stands in direct contrast with the description (popularised by the realists) of ownership or property as a bundle of sticks that can be split up, so that rights can be rearranged according to requirements and circumstances. The bundle of sticks metaphor so often relied on in common law jurisdictions does not allow for a notion of abstractness or elasticity in the way the rubber ball metaphor of civil law doctrine does.

[60] Logically, the notion of absoluteness and the notion of elasticity or residuarity are not identical and they need not even necessarily go together, but the libertarian combination of the two aspects as constituting an inviolate pre-political right is interesting for discussing the status of ownership in the rights paradigm. AM Honoré, 'Ownership' in AG Guest (ed), *Oxford Essays in Jurisprudence* (1961) 107–47 at 128 argues against the idea that residuarity is the essential characteristic of ownership; see DV Cowen, *New Patterns of Landownership. The Transformation of the Concept of Landownership as Plena in re Potestas* (1984) at 77, and CH Lewis, 'The Modern Concept of Ownership of Land' 1985 *Acta Juridica* (also published separately as TW Bennett *et al* (eds), *Land Ownership: Changing Concepts* (1986)) 241–66 at 257–8 for criticism of Honoré's view.

[61] Restrictions are said to be temporary because of the residual character of ownership that always returns to its unrestricted state as soon as restrictions fall away, since ownership itself is not subject to time limits (see the literature referred to in n 49). Restrictions are said to be exceptional because it is assumed that the natural state of ownership is to be free of restrictions.

[62] The most striking illustration of the continued power of the ownership paradigm in South African law is the decision of the Supreme Court of Appeal in *Brisley v Drotsky* 2002 (4) SA 1 (SCA) at paras 42–6; see the three illustrations discussed in ch 1. In that decision, the SCA held that the landowner is normally entitled to an eviction order against unlawful occupiers of her land, except in so far as that right is limited by the Constitution, another law or contract; although s 26(3) of the Constitution clearly affected the availability of evictions, the courts do not have the discretion to refuse an eviction order to which the owner would have been entitled at common law, purely because of external considerations not clearly identified in the provision.

I focus on eviction as a core entitlement associated with ownership and argue that the law of eviction is fundamentally shaped by the rights paradigm. Eviction is a legal process by which a landowner relies on her (absolute or relative) entitlement of exclusive or undisturbed possession and employs the power of the courts and the law enforcement agencies to eject unwanted occupiers from her land. To the extent that the eviction is successful, it serves to secure existing property rights and to stabilise the current regime of property holdings as a matrix of social, economic and political power. The landowner seeks to enforce a legally recognised right from a position of relative legal, social and economic power within which that right is recognised as legitimate and worthy of protection; the occupier is often on the land either unlawfully or on the basis of a precarious and temporary permission or licence (that may have lapsed or could be terminated) and therefore resists eviction from a position of relative legal, social and economic weakness or vulnerability. The effect of the rights paradigm in eviction law is that the owner's right to eviction is usually privileged purely on the basis of the owner's stronger right, regardless of the social and economic circumstances (and specifically the weakness or vulnerability) of the occupier. Enforcing the law 'normally', 'neutrally' or 'objectively' will therefore more often than not privilege the protection of existing rights and result in more or less mechanical eviction of unlawful occupiers.

Eviction law has been codified or supplemented by legislation in many jurisdictions, mostly in legislation intended to protect lessees against unfair and arbitrary eviction. At least in some cases, these statutory interventions have left the rights paradigm intact in the sense that, although termination of the right to occupy and the actual enforcement of an eviction order may be regulated, the success of an application for an eviction order still depends purely or largely on the owner's stronger right and is allowed regardless of the surrounding circumstances. In other cases, the legislation brings about more substantive challenges to or qualifications of the paradigm in the sense that either termination of the right to occupy or eviction might be precluded purely because of the surrounding circumstances or because of the effect it would have on the occupier.

In chapter four I discuss legislative interventions that have qualified or amended the rights paradigm in landlord–tenant situations by allowing or requiring courts to take judicial notice of the social and economic context or of the specific personal circumstances of the tenants before granting an eviction order. Obviously, when and in so far as these statutory amendments force or allow the courts to deprive the landowner of an eviction order she might otherwise have been entitled to, purely because of the personal circumstances of the tenant, the legislation represents a significant qualification of the rights paradigm. However, in cases where the landowner can insist upon eviction purely because of her relatively stronger right, and regardless of the circumstances or the effects of the eviction, the paradigm can be said to remain intact, despite regulatory control. In chapter four I argue that the rights paradigm has generally been qualified by landlord–tenant legislation, in some cases quite radically, but without necessarily bringing about any really significant paradigmatic shift.

In chapter five I discuss eviction of persons who occupy land without any legally recognised right, permission or licence, concluding that the rights paradigm has hardly been affected at all by legislative reforms in this area. Apartheid has shown that the definition of an unlawful occupier is very much a matter of political choice; in so far as the identification of unlawful occupiers remains in the power of the regulatory state or powerful landowners, eviction law has not been transformed significantly, despite regulatory controls over the enforcement of eviction orders. However, in chapter five I also discuss a small number of examples where legislation has brought about really deep or significant changes in that eviction is sometimes precluded or delayed purely because of the personal circumstances of the occupiers, the general historical, social or economic context or the detrimental effects of eviction on the individual, her family or the community. In line with my central argument I discuss these examples as instances that signify a (smaller or larger) paradigm shift in eviction law.

South African eviction law is unique because of its apartheid history. At the very time when European countries were implementing special legislation to impose rent control and protect residential lessees from exploitation and unfair treatment, South African eviction law was sharpened by racially motivated legislation that facilitated the eviction of both lawful and unlawful occupiers of land for the sake of forced removals aimed at the establishment of spatial segregation. Despite its uniqueness, this development is relevant for present purposes because it represents a special, overtly political and ideologically supercharged version of the rights paradigm, upon which it also relies. In a transformative situation, social justice may require the state to have more empathy with the position of occupiers, particularly if they belong to a weak, marginalised and previously disadvantaged group in society. In such a situation the state might be enjoined (constitutionally or otherwise) to enforce the law in favour of property owners while simultaneously attempting to promote social justice and social and economic transformation for the sake of weak and marginalised individuals and groups. In some cases, it might even be necessary or possible to suspend the protection normally afforded to landowners, purely in order to protect the interests of vulnerable occupiers of land. In such a transformative setting, eviction could therefore present a situation within which 'normal' property law reaches its margins, where lawyers are forced to fall back on equity decisions, policy calls and compromises shaped by extra-legal (political, social and economic) considerations that are traditionally excluded from 'rational' or 'scientific' legal analysis and decision-making as it is seen in the rights paradigm.

South African pre-reform-era land law reflects the liberal, common law based view of the rights paradigm, namely that existing land rights (and particularly ownership) should be protected against unlawful intrusions without the landowner first having to assert or prove the socio-political legitimacy of his or her right and without reference to 'extra-legal' social, economic or political circumstances that might have a bearing on the justice or morality of the eviction. In this context, it is left to the occupier to raise and prove a valid right that could resist the owner's eviction claim. Interestingly, in common and civil law jurisdictions where special rent control and other protective legislation has been introduced during or after the post-World War II housing shortages, eviction law is sometimes (albeit rarely and often weakly) influenced by the personal and social circumstances of the occupier, although this leniency generally does not apply equally when the owner wants to evict unlawful occupiers.[63] A discussion of eviction law that accepts the paradigm as its starting point remains locked into a debate about the legitimacy of state regulation that restricts or infringes upon existing land rights by placing qualifications upon the landowner's right to evict unlawful occupiers, pretty much along the lines of Depenheuer's argument about the justification of restrictions on ownership.[64]

By contrast, the South African post-apartheid land reform programme and the case-law dealing with it breaks away from the rights paradigm at least partially in the (admittedly limited number of) cases where legislation highlights the egalitarian, reformist view that the common law rules and practices of land law entrench—through its protection of existing property holdings—unfair patterns of social domination and marginalisation that need to be amended on a fundamental level. Certain anti-eviction measures that were introduced in other jurisdictions, especially in Western Europe after the end of World War II, are based on similar approaches and can raise similar questions. The most interesting facet of these anti-eviction measures for present purposes is that they sometimes require reconsideration of the paradigm within which we discuss and adjudicate property rights in general. The articulation between a landowner's common law right to sue for eviction and reform-driven legislative protection of vulnerable occupiers against eviction illustrates a central difficulty of transformation, namely the paradoxical need to accept the uncertainties caused by inevitable social and economic reform, while preserving some certainty about the continued validity and protection of existing rights.[65] In this sense, eviction law forces the confrontation between the stabilising, protective impulse of the law and the reformist obligations of a transitional situation out into the open and enables theorists to consider the implications of the tension between stability and change in a way that is simultaneously concrete, practical and theoretically sophisticated.

The South African examples that I rely on as the backbone of my descriptive analysis demonstrate a point that may be valid for other social and political contexts as well, albeit at varying levels of intensity, but that is easier to explain in the South African context. This point is that the tendency to uphold the rights paradigm and its abstract, a-contextual enforcement of the stronger right to exclusive possession inevitably entrenches the individual security of established property

---

[63] In the terminology of CM Rose, 'Canons of Property Talk, or, Blackstone's Anxiety' (1998) 108 *Yale LJ* 601–32, the traditional strategy of dealing with eviction issues within the rights paradigm can be explained as soothing the doubts raised with reference to the position of socially and economically weak and marginalised occupiers with an appeal to doctrinal tradition or social and economic utility. See chs 4 and 5 on anti-eviction measures.

[64] See ch 2, nn 29–35 and accompanying text.

[65] See AJ van der Walt, 'Exclusivity of Ownership, Security of Tenure, and Eviction Orders: A Model to Evaluate South African Land-Reform Legislation' (2002) *TSAR* 254–89 at 254.

rights and the systemic stability of the current property regime, while at the same time resisting changes that threaten either the security of individual property rights or the stability of the extant property regime (or both). In line with the argument in chapter one, this means that significant reforms of the property regime would necessarily have to involve a paradigmatic shift that would reduce the right to enforce eviction in an abstract, a-contextual manner. Stated differently, it means that instances where the right to enforce a stronger claim on exclusive possession without attention to the context or circumstances indicate that reform of the current distribution of property rights will be difficult, whereas areas where this right has already been eroded or undermined by legislation might offer better reform possibilities.

The following three chapters will focus on instances where the law may or may not allow smaller or more significant restrictions on the landowner's right to enforce the exclusivity of possession through eviction. In chapters four and five I discuss the continued power of the rights paradigm with reference to the granting and enforcement of eviction orders in residential situations, arguing that more or less unrestricted enforcement of the right to evict would indicate that the rights paradigm still enjoys a high profile, whereas common law or statutory restrictions that prevent a landowner from evicting unlawful occupiers at will indicate challenges to and qualifications of the paradigm. These qualifications can be smaller or larger in scope and effect. Chapter four deals with restrictions on eviction within the context of landlord–tenant relationships, while chapter five concentrates on the position of unlawful occupiers or squatters. In chapter six I discuss four developments that are not directly related to eviction but that also indicate qualifications of the rights paradigm in the sense that they uphold or protect non-rights interests against the exclusivity interests of the property owner, often in ways and for reasons that cannot be explained comfortably within the rights paradigm. These restrictions are significant, not because they impose a large or heavy burden on ownership, but rather because they strike at the very essence of ownership as it is defined according to the paradigm. The first and third restrictions concern possibilities according to which unlawful occupiers or trespassers may acquire ownership through prescription or adverse possession and encroachment and therefore undermine the security of ownership; the second involves public access to private property and therefore undermines its exclusivity. The fourth example concerns the position of owners whose rights are undermined or restricted with apparent impunity because of their weak social and political status.

4

Eviction in Landlord–Tenant Law

I.   Introduction   77
II. Tenant Protection: A Comparative Overview   82
III. Tenant Protection in South African Law   114
IV. Conclusion   130

I. Introduction

IN CHAPTER TWO it was said that the rights paradigm, in the civil law tradition, presents ownership as the strongest property right. In the English common law tradition the stronger claim to possession plays a similar role, despite the differences between the two legal systems. The paradigmatic focus on fundamentally stronger and more important property interests tends to create a hierarchy within which ownership (and other strong property rights) dominate the doctrinal structure, the rhetoric and the logic of property law, thereby potentially entrenching unequal socio-economic power relations in favour of current holders of paradigmatically dominant property interests.

Chapter three illustrated the practical effect of this hypothesis with reference to eviction law, explaining that both the civil and the common law traditions generally allow a landowner to evict unwanted occupiers[1] from her land quite easily and, more particularly, without consideration for the socio-economic context or the personal circumstances of the occupiers. The fact that ownership is allowed to trump lesser occupation rights and occupation interests not backed up by rights in this way, regardless of the context, is described as a property hierarchy, according to which great value and power attach to ownership or strong property rights, compared with property interests that are not backed up by a strong, legally recognised right. In the sense that this paradigmatic focus privileges existing rights over

---

[1] For purposes of eviction, unwanted occupiers can be subdivided into the two groups discussed in this chapter and the next respectively: formerly lawful occupiers (such as tenants) whose occupation becomes unlawful when their tenancy or permission to occupy is terminated (this chapter); and squatters or other unlawful occupiers who never had any legal ground for occupation (ch 5). As is indicated in the text below, the issues in the former case (termination of the lease, due process and fairness) differ from those in the latter (just due process and fairness), albeit that the distinction between the two categories is often unclear and disputed.

weaker interests and non-rights, and to the extent that it stabilises the status quo and hence assumes that the existing distribution of property is fair and equitable, the hierarchy between ownership as the overriding right and vulnerable occupation interests symbolises the paradigmatic privileging of existing social and economic power over non-ownership positions. In chapter three I explained that this hierarchical privileging of rights tends to secure extant individual property holdings and to stabilise the regime of property rules and practices and the current distribution pattern of property holdings. In a society characterised by social, economic and political inequality and marginalisation, paradigmatic support for the power hegemony of the privileged could restrict or frustrate social and economic reform.

The rights paradigm obviously does not exist in a 'pure' or unadulterated form in the sense that ownership (or other strong property rights) inevitably and always trumps supposedly inherently weak property interests. Despite the apparent hegemony of the private law tradition and its sceptical attitude towards constitutional and statutory intervention, governments routinely use legislation to amend or regulate the hierarchical domination of property ownership in response to social, economic and political circumstances and requirements. One significant example of such intervention is the embodiment of anti-eviction policies in legislation, usually in an effort to stabilise housing rights. In some cases, anti-eviction legislation is required or bolstered by constitutional housing provisions; in others, it is not necessarily required or supported by the constitution and the courts might find it necessary to determine whether the protective legislative intervention is constitutionally legitimate and properly authorised. In some instances (German law) the whole of private law, including landlord–tenant legislation, is codified, which could simplify the relationship between constitutional and private law; in uncodified systems (English and South African law) the relationship could be more complicated. In either case the proper fit between common (or private) law, normally inspired by the rights paradigm, and statutory pro-tenant or pro-poor amendments, often in conflict with the rights paradigm, poses difficult doctrinal and interpretive questions for the judiciary. Being the outcome of efforts to restrict the institutional or systemic domination of landownership over other interests in (particularly residential) property, anti-eviction legislation can reduce or undermine the power of ownership and stronger rights in the rights paradigm, so that the number, extent and efficacy of anti-eviction measures that exist in fact and that are effectively enforced allow us to evaluate the power of the rights paradigm in current law. The power of the rights paradigm will also be affected by the tug of war between reformist legislatures and courts, as appears from the analysis in this chapter. In chapter three I argued that reformist legislation that regulates the landlord–tenant relationship could either qualify the power and the paradigmatic privileging of the landlord to a lesser extent (for instance by merely regulating the processes whereby rights to occupy are terminated and eviction is carried out), or it could have a more fundamental impact on the relationship by disallowing eviction in cases where the landowner could prove all the normal requirements for an eviction order. The former instances were described as qualifications of the rights paradigm, while the latter were characterised as potential indications of a paradigm shift. In chapter three I also indicated, referring back to chapter one, that really significant reforms of the current property regime would be almost impossible in the absence of either existing indications of or space for such a paradigm shift because the effect of the hierarchical privileging of stronger property rights is not only to secure individual property interests but also to stabilise the current property regime as a system of property rules and practices that uphold an established distribution pattern.

In this chapter, constitutional and statutory anti-eviction measures and judicial interpretations that amend the ownership paradigm are evaluated in the context of landlord–tenant law. Anti-eviction legislation that protects the interests of tenants against unfair, arbitrary or unlawful eviction has become a common feature of many Western legal systems, at least since World War II,[2] and one of the aims of this chapter is to show how far the rights paradigm is qualified, or is being challenged, in those systems by anti-eviction legislation that undermines the central characteristics of the paradigm. As appears from the discussion of English and South African law, the extent to which tenants are protected by legislation varies with time and changes in government policy—in English law, tenant protection that was introduced by earlier governments has been cut back since the 1980s by the process of privatisation (combined with weaker protection of short-term tenancies in private housing) and a concomitant decline in public housing, whereas the introduction of the Human Rights Act 1998 seems to indicate a move in exactly the opposite direction. On the other side of the globe, the newly elected democratic South African legislature has attempted to increase protection of tenants and other residential occupiers of land since 1994. The chapter will show that judges often find it difficult to respond to these legislative and policy changes, given the doctrinal hegemony of the rights paradigm and its pervasive influence on lawyerly sensibilities, which are not always sensitised or responsive to socio-economic changes that inspire policy changes and legislative interventions, especially in systems (like English and South African law) where the larger part of private law remains uncodified. Court cases dealing with landlord–tenant legislation are therefore discussed together with the overview of legislation. Since the focus in this book is on shifts in the rights paradigm inspired by social policy with regard to housing, this chapter concentrates on residential rather than commercial, industrial or agricultural tenancies.

In the discussion of English and South African law the goal is to contrast socio-economically inspired anti-eviction legislation with the 'background' law as it

---

[2] K Gray and SF Gray, *Elements of Land Law* (4th edn, 2005) at 1446 point out that the English common law was first amended by socio-economically inspired state interventions during the Industrial Revolution, when 'the bleaker aspects of the common law rule [regarding habitability] came to be qualified by a number of [statutory] exceptions'. Obviously, many tenant-protective laws were initiated after World War I, but for current purposes I concentrate upon post-World War II legislation and case-law.

existed prior to these changes and to show how statutory interventions are accommodated through (largely interpretive, in other words judicial) reinterpretations or changes of the 'background' law. The biggest problem in these systems is to explain the fit between pre-existing common law and statutory amendment in a doctrinally satisfactory way, particularly in view of strong constitutional or policy pressure to protect occupiers of residential property against eviction. Shifts in the governments' housing policies (such as privatisation under the Thatcher governments in the UK in the 1980s and the focus on social support in post-1994 South Africa) therefore obviously play a large role in the promulgation and the interpretation of housing legislation. In the case of German law the contrast between settled property doctrine and policy shifts is less obvious because changes in landlord–tenant law are accommodated within the structure of the civil code; doctrinal fit is also less problematic because the overall relationship between constitution and civil code has been worked out more or less satisfactorily in German case-law. However, the link between systemic or doctrinal changes inspired by policy developments and the constitution does arise in all three systems under discussion. Accordingly, a number of constitutional (or constitutional-type) court decisions from all three jurisdictions are discussed to illustrate the shape in which this question emerged in each system and to explain the solutions developed by each. In all three cases it will be argued that the problem of constitutional fit and the solutions that have been developed indicate doctrinal resistance against significant shifts in the rights paradigm.

Logically, tenants are lawful occupiers during the term of a tenancy, and they therefore usually have a valid defence against eviction. Eviction of tenants usually becomes possible only once the tenancy relationship is terminated[3]—in this respect, eviction in the landlord–tenant situation is significantly different from eviction of unlawful occupiers who never had a right to occupy (discussed in chapter five) in the sense that the landlord–tenant situation always involves an additional step (and hence an additional stage of protection), namely lawful termination of the lease, before eviction becomes possible.[4] South African post-1994 anti-eviction laws by and large concentrate on subjecting the eviction process to due process and fairness restrictions without bringing about sweeping or significant restrictions of the landowner's right to terminate the lease. In English and German law the eviction process is also subjected to due process requirements, but in some areas substantive restrictions have also been imposed on the right to terminate the tenancy. For present purposes, I focus on paradigm-challenging anti-eviction legislation that restricts or delays termination of a tenancy as well as legislation that subjects eviction, once it is allowed, to due process and fairness controls. Obviously, in line with the analysis in chapter three, the most significant restrictions are those that pivot on considerations that are outside the control, or

---

[3] If these former tenants remain in occupation when their tenancy is terminated they are sometimes described as former tenants holding over.

[4] In many ways the procedural restrictions that apply during the eviction phase are similar to the restrictions that apply in the case of unlawful occupiers (ch 5).

even the knowledge, of the landowner, such as the personal or social circum-stances of the tenant or the availability of alternative accommodation. Generally speaking, significant legislative interventions that pose a real challenge to the logic of the rights paradigm occur more frequently in the form of restrictions on the right to terminate a lease. However, as the analysis of English law shows, due process controls can also have significant doctrinal effects that pose real challenges to the paradigm.

My approach in this chapter is to describe the ways in which various statutory amendments of eviction law in the landlord–tenant context qualify the rights par-adigm. Obviously, as has been pointed out earlier, the rights paradigm does not exist in an abstract, absolute form; it usually presents itself as a locus of tension between the rights of the landowner and the interests of tenants and other occu-piers or users of the land. However, I have argued in chapter three that there is a general tendency to privilege existing and established property rights (and the property status quo) in the sense that the current regime of property rules and practices, bolstered by property rhetoric, logic and doctrine, attaches presumptive power to those rights as against other property interests. This tendency establishes a property hierarchy that makes it much easier for owners and holders of strong property rights to prevail against weaker or marginal property interests. To the extent that this property hierarchy is upheld by the rhetoric, logic and doctrinal structure of current property rules and practices I have described it as a rights paradigm, while the statutory protections that strengthen the claims of weak or marginal property interests are described as larger or smaller qualifications of or challenges to the paradigm.

Logically, the most minimal qualification of the rights paradigm would be rep-resented by statutory interventions that merely impose due process controls over the eviction of former tenants, without placing any special emphasis on the per-sonal or social circumstances of the occupiers. Due process controls have been introduced in all three systems to regulate lawful termination of the tenancy and to control eventual eviction; their effect varies from a slight qualification of to a serious challenge to the paradigm. More extensive due process qualifications are present when the eviction process is delayed for due process considerations that emphasise the social or historical context within which eviction takes place or the personal circumstances of the occupiers and the effects that eviction would have on them.

An even more extensive qualification of the rights paradigm is present when regulatory controls are also imposed on the landowner's 'normal' private law right to terminate the tenancy, especially when the general socio-economic context and the personal circumstances of the tenant are allowed, in a context-sensitive adju-dicative situation where the judicial officer exercises a discretion, to prevent own-ership from trumping non-ownership interests in residential property.

If the right to evict is qualified by fairly widespread and strong controls of this nature the legislative intervention could go further than merely qualifying the rights paradigm; in some cases the qualification could be so significant that one has to acknowledge that it challenges or undermines the integrity of the paradigm and that it perhaps indicates a paradigm shift. As I argued in chapter three, the incidence of serious challenges to the rights paradigm could be seen as an indication of space for significant reforms of the property regime, while the relative absence or weakness of such indications could suggest that significant reforms would be impossible or very difficult to achieve.

In this chapter, as in the others, my approach is to build the argument around evidence and examples from South African law, complemented by comparative references to the situation in English and German law. In this case I start off with German and English law, followed by a discussion of South African law. The section on German law refers to comparable aspects of Dutch law, and the section on English law includes some references to US law. In the section on South African law I refer to pre-reform (Roman-Dutch) common law, but by and large the focus is on post-1994 legislative reforms. The chapter concludes with an effort to construct an explanation of the effect and implications of the legislation and case-law discussed in this chapter on the rights paradigm. In the final section of the chapter I evaluate the anti-eviction legislation and conclude, provisionally, that the vast majority of legislative interventions in landlord–tenant law amount to nothing more than (more or less drastic) qualifications of and exceptions to the rule of ownership dominance (or the dominance of relatively stronger rights) over weak or marginal interests in residential property. However, in a few significant instances there are unmistakable signs that legislative interventions in the landlord–tenant relationship go much further and either seriously challenge or undermine the rights paradigm, particularly if not only the content but also the social and economic scope and impact of the legislation is taken into consideration.

II. Tenant Protection: A Comparative Overview

A. Introduction

There are many examples outside of South African law of statutory restrictions on the eviction of tenants (or former tenants). Most anti-eviction laws focus on procedural controls over the actual eviction process, but some eviction controls in German and English law also regulate the landlord's right to terminate the lease and reclaim possession, the approach being that eviction is impossible as long as termination is prohibited or delayed. Once the lease is terminated lawfully, eviction may follow and procedural controls generally take over to ensure due process and fairness, but in many cases the substantive blocks in the way of termination of the lease are more significant. In some of these cases termination of the landlord–tenant relationship is subjected to legislative control, in others the courts exercise a judicial discretion, derived from the legislation, whether to allow termination in view of the potential impact that termination and eviction will have, considering all the relevant circumstances, on the tenant and her family or on the community. In a small number of cases, the relevant circumstances to be considered in exercising this discretion include factors that are outside the landowner's knowledge and control, such as the general historical or economic context and its impact on the availability of housing, the personal or social circumstances of the tenant or the availability of alternative accommodation. The landowner is therefore not allowed simply to terminate the lease and evict the tenants on the basis of her stronger right to possession—even in situations where the lease would normally have expired or the owner would have been entitled to terminate the lease in accordance with the lease agreement or the general principles of contract or property, termination is sometimes prohibited or restricted and the lease relationship is allowed to continue, or else termination is allowed but eviction is suspended, purely because it is judged that summary termination and eviction would under the circumstances have an unjustifiably harsh impact on the tenant. In line with the general approach set out in chapter three, I regard these controls as significant interventions that not only qualify the hierarchical assumptions and the stabilising effects of the rights paradigm but pose a serious challenge to its doctrinal, rhetorical and logical integrity. Explaining these statutory qualifications satisfactorily might warrant or require paradigmatic shifts that could open up valuable space for further reforms of the property regime. It is therefore important not only to identify significant qualifications that challenge the core assumptions of the rights paradigm and to distinguish them from qualifications that leave those assumptions unchallenged, but also to assess the actual scope and impact of these changes within the larger social and economic context—apparently significant statutory interventions that apply to a vanishingly small number of public housing tenants might have far less paradigmatic and reformist impact than their textual form might suggest.

The anti-eviction measures discussed below were mostly inspired by general housing shortages. Obviously housing shortages in Europe had their origins in circumstances that cannot be compared to apartheid land policy and practice, but the similarities between the European post-World War II and the South African post-apartheid motivations for protecting tenants in occupation hold far enough to make the comparison interesting. In post-World War II Europe the existence and scope of housing shortages created a strong impulse to protect tenants in occupation; this impulse was strengthened under the tenant-friendly or social welfare-oriented housing policies of labour or social democratic governments during the economic upswing of the 1970s. Landlord–tenant legislation promulgated in German and English law since the 1970s embodies protective interventions of this kind. The social welfare politics of the post-1994 South African democratic government point in the same direction, although tenant-friendly policies in this case were strengthened significantly by reformist land policies inspired or justified by the particular history of apartheid South Africa.

In both the German and the South African cases, this impulse to protect housing rights and to favour social welfare interests was fortified by more or less explicit constitutional provisions. Although similar constitutional provisions do not exist in English law, there are indications that a similar effect could be created under the influence of the European Convention on Human Rights 1950, at least since the introduction of the Human Rights Act 1998.

Regardless of the constitutional context, tenant-friendly and reformist policies were more or less difficult to implement in all three systems because of the strong influence of the rights paradigm in established legal tradition, including private law doctrine, legal rhetoric and legal methodology. In the end, the somewhat counter-intuitive comparison between German, English and South African law is justifiable because of the ways in which the tension between constitutional or policy obligation to protect housing interests, the legislative regulation of eviction and the doctrinal force of traditional private law (including the rights paradigm) works out in each system. For purposes of this book I am primarily interested in the general characteristics of this tension between the reform-driven (and constitutionally entrenched or supported) anti-eviction measures and the ownership-friendly private law tradition and its implications for reform and not in the detail of the measures; my discussion is therefore not intended as an exhaustive analysis of the legislation or the case-law but rather as an illustration of legislative and judicial tendencies in reacting to the housing shortage and the constitutional context in each case.

B. German law

German law provides a particularly interesting comparative source because of its doctrinal similarities with the South African situation.[5] On the one hand both the South African and German systems derive from the Roman-Germanic civil law tradition, which is characterised by a strong ownership-dominated version of the rights paradigm, developed in nineteenth-century Pandectism.[6] Consequently, both systems are doctrinally more tolerant of easy and even arbitrary eviction and less tolerant of regulatory restrictions on the right to evict. The doctrinally significant German distinction between private law and constitutional law also resembles the South African position,[7] as does the doctrinal emphasis on the differences

---

[5] Obviously, the social, economic and political situations are very different. The doctrinal and structural similarities pertain mostly to the law, as is set out in the rest of the paragraph below. Regarding most of the aspects mentioned in this paragraph, the same could in principle be said for Dutch law, but since the Dutch Constitution does not include an entrenched, justiciable property clause in a bill of rights the comparison is less interesting. For that reason I refer to applicable Dutch landlord–tenant laws in the footnotes in this section below, but I do not discuss the details in the text. In the next chapter, on eviction of unlawful occupiers, Dutch law acquires greater significance because of historical considerations, and it is discussed more extensively.

[6] See generally AJ van der Walt, 'Ownership and Personal Freedom: Subjectivism in Bernhard Windscheid's Theory of Ownership' (1993) 56 *THRHR* 569–89.

[7] The same is not necessarily true of English or US law, but in English law the tension between municipal law and European Convention law (under the Human Rights Act 1998) is equally instructive. The distinction between public and private law is much less evident in US law, but there are indications in case-law that a certain tension exists between constitutional and state (private) law. English law is discussed separately in the next section of this chapter, with references to US law in the footnotes.

between ownership and non-ownership interests (like those of tenants and other lawful occupiers of land) in private law.[8] In both the South African and the German systems, the statutory regulation of housing (and hence eviction) is dominated by the influence of a constitution that includes a property clause (guaranteeing the protection of property interests) but that also imposes strong social obligations (including the obligation to promote and protect access to housing).[9] As appears from the analysis the balance between these apparently conflicting constitutional duties has been worked out quite thoughtfully by the German federal Constitutional Court, while there are signs that the South African Constitutional Court is in the process of developing a comparable balancing approach.

On the other hand, German private law has been codified since 1900 (*Bürgerliches Gesetzbuch* or *BGB*), while South African private law remains largely uncodified. The analysis below demonstrates that the legacy of the rights doctrine is weaker in modern German law because of the codification of private law, which allowed quite pertinent, comprehensive and strongly promoted social welfare policies to be introduced by the social democratic governments that dominated early post-World War II German politics until the 1980s. Significant legislative amendments introduced to regulate the landlord–tenant relationship in German law are largely accommodated in the Civil Code, which includes or controls all property legislation and therefore tends to reduce the tension between the doctrinal force of the rights paradigm and 'external' regulatory legislation because it renders the contrast between the status quo and policy shifts less visible. In this respect, the German constitutional principle that property rights are shaped by the laws (including legislation) contributed significantly to the erosion of the rights paradigm's doctrinal force. An important aspect of the combination of socially responsible constitution, codified private law and closely regulated housing law in German law is that the amendments of landlord–tenant law that were introduced by post-World War II legislation received the imprimatur of the Federal Constitutional Court and are now accepted as a normal part of German property law. Furthermore, although social welfare and housing policies again shifted during the 1980s under the Christian Democratic government and the subsequent Social Democratic and broad coalition governments, these shifts were not strong or large enough to have a significant impact on the direction indicated by earlier constitutional and legislative choices. The overall effect was significantly to reduce the force of the rights paradigm and, simultaneously, to reduce the tension between constitution and private law. Although there are strong

[8] Again, this aspect does not have much meaning in English or US law. The German and South African doctrinal positions highlight a point that is much less obvious in English or US law but that does play an under-the-surface role via the significance that is attached to property ownership as a power relationship (economic liberty) in those systems—compare ch 2.

[9] This aspect features in all the systems discussed below: South Africa, Germany and the US have entrenched bills of rights with property clauses, while English law has something similar via the Human Rights Act 1998 (which incorporates the European Convention on Human Rights 1950 into English law). However, the constitutional dispensations are not necessarily all reformist in nature, as appears from the discussion of English law. For an enlightening comparison that emphasises the social responsibility aspect see GS Alexander, *The Global Debate over Constitutional Property: Lessons for American Takings Jurisprudence* (2006), especially chs 3 and 4.

similarities between the German and the South African systems, these distinctive features set them apart sufficiently to make comparison interesting.

The most important issues in German landlord–tenant law, for present purposes, are that termination (through expiration or cancellation) of a residential lease is sometimes prevented or delayed by German legislation purely to avoid unjustifiable hardship for the tenant or her family; and that the effect of these amendments of the rights paradigm have been accepted—subject to certain qualifications—by the German Federal Constitutional Court as legitimate and justifiable restrictions on ownership. In what follows I discuss the provisions that prevent or delay termination of a lease briefly, pointing out that a few of them are highly significant for my analysis because they apply purely on the basis of preventing unjustifiable hardship for the tenant or her family. Finally, I discuss the case-law of the Federal Constitutional Court concerning judicial review of the landlord's decision to cancel the lease because the landlord wants to use the property herself. Although this body of case-law concerns just one aspect of the landlord–tenant legislation, it shows that the Federal Constitutional Court has accepted that, while leases cannot be cancelled in certain circumstances (a restriction that qualifies the rights paradigm), a landlord can legitimately cancel the lease for some purposes, such as her own need to use the property (confirming the power of the rights paradigm); that this decision is subject to judicial review (imposing a restriction that qualifies the paradigm); but that judicial review is not unlimited and must leave some scope for the autonomy of the landlord (again confirming the essentials of the rights paradigm, but within a constitutional framework characterised by social binding and responsibility). The overall picture demonstrates that tenant-protection legislative changes are authorised and justified in terms of the constitution; that quite strong legislative changes have been introduced in the Civil Code and ancillary legislation; and that they are interpreted by the courts in a way that construes an inclusive, co-operative (rather than antagonistic) relationship between constitution and private law in the creation, shaping, limitation and protection of rights (including the rights of both landlord and tenant). In the process, the rights paradigm is qualified significantly in view of social housing obligations, but without necessarily amounting to a full-scale paradigm shift.

The Civil Code and ancillary legislation[10] protect lessees and their families against termination of the lease (and ultimately against eviction) in different sets of circumstances, the most important of which are sale of the property to a third party; sale of the property in execution or in case of liquidation or insolvency of the owner; death of the lessee; expiration of a lease concluded for a fixed term; and cancellation of the lease by the lessor.

---

[10] The core of civil law protection appears in the provisions on landlord and tenant (§§ 535–80) in the German Civil Code (*Bürgerliches Gesetzbuch*, or *BGB*). In addition to the Civil Code, the landlord–tenant relationship is controlled by special legislation, the most important being the Landlord–Tenant Framework Act (*Mietrechtsrahmengesetz*) 2001. Similar provisions apply in the Dutch Civil Code (*Burgerlijk Wetboek*, or *BW*), where the landlord–tenant relationship is regulated in Book 7 (*BW* 7), Title 4, Arts 7:201–7:282; see the references below.

Like most civil-law systems, German law protects lessees' interests by providing that a lease is not automatically terminated when the property changes hands; as long as the lessee continues to comply with her obligations under the lease, the lease continues and the purchaser simply steps into the legal position of the previous lessor.[11] German legislation contains similar provisions to protect lessees in cases where the property is sold in execution or in cases of liquidation or insolvency of the lessor,[12] although the purchaser of property sold in execution may in certain instances have a limited right to cancel the lease.[13] Furthermore, the Civil Code provides that a residential lease is not automatically terminated by the death of the lessee either; if they so wish, the spouse, other family members or other persons with whom the deceased lived in a communal household can continue in the lease relationship, either on their own (when they and the deceased had concluded the lease together as co-lessees) or in the lessee's place (when the deceased was the actual lessee).[14] However, although a lease survives the death of the lessee, either the landlord or the heirs can terminate the lease under certain (prescribed and regulated) conditions.[15]

Apart from the instances mentioned above, a residential lease can come to an end either when the lease is cancelled or when the term expires. In German law, an indefinite (periodic) lease comes to an end when either of the parties cancels in accordance with the agreed (contractual) and prescribed (statutory) requirements,[16] whereas a lease for a fixed term comes to an end when the term (agreed upon in the lease contract) expires. The Civil Code protects residential lessees in both instances: cancellation of a lease is possible only when the Civil Code or subordinate legislation allows it and provided that the cancellation complies with the requirements and prescriptions set out in the legislation;[17] while a lease for a fixed

---

[11] *BGB* § 566. The Dutch position is similar: *BW* 7:226. This rule originated in Roman-Germanic law prior to the Civil Code; see in this regard EJH Schrage, *Koop Breekt Geen Huur: Enige Grepen uit de Geschiedenis van het Geleerde Recht inzake de Gevolgen van de Vervreemding van een Verhuurde Zaak* (1984). The South African common law rule is also that *huur gaat voor koop* (lease trumps sale): see ch 3, n 21 and section III. below.

[12] See further the discussion in section III. below. The relevant German measures appear in § 57 of the Sale in Execution Act (*Gesetz über die Zwangsversteigerung und die Zwangsverwaltung*), § 21 of the Bankruptcy Act (*Konkursordnung*) and §§ 108 and 111 of the Insolvency Act (*Insolvenzordnung*). F Baur *et al*, *Sachenrecht* (17th edn, 1999) at 350 point out that these provisions are essentially similar to *BGB* § 566, which applies to sale of the property; see text accompanying n 11 above.

[13] Such a right is granted by § 57a of the Sale in Execution Act (*Gesetz über die Zwangsversteigerung und die Zwangsverwaltung*), but this right is limited by *BGB* §§ 573 and 574. See further § 111 of the Insolvency Act (*Insolvenzordnung*), which also grants a limited right to cancel the lease in cases of insolvency. In cases where the tenant fails to prevent cancellation of the lease she may have a claim for compensation against the former landlord according to the general provisions regarding breach of contract: *BGB* §§ 535, 281 and 283.

[14] *BGB* §§ 563, 563a, 563b. The Dutch position is similar: *BW* 7:229, 7:268. The Dutch *BW* 7:266 further determines that the lessee's spouse or partner who uses the property as his/her main residence is legally a co-tenant and takes the lessee's place when the tenancy comes to an end as far as the original lessee is concerned (see further *BW* 7:267 regarding cohabiting partners).

[15] *BGB* §§ 563, 563a, 564, 573c.

[16] *BGB* § 542(1); *BW* 7:271.

[17] *BGB* § 568 requires cancellation to be in writing. Cancellation is normally only possible for a legitimate ground as set out in *BGB* § 573; in extraordinary instances, simplified (§ 573a) or summary

---

term will not necessarily terminate when the term expires—it can be extended (or terminated earlier) according to the applicable statutory prescriptions and requirements.[18]

Cancellation of a residential lease follows different routes in abnormal and in normal situations. In abnormal cases the lessor is allowed to cancel for a reason that is so important that the notice terms laid down in the agreement or by law are not enforced (summary cancellation); in normal cases the lease must be cancelled in accordance with the agreed and prescribed notice terms.[19] Summary cancellation is generally only possible when the lessee is guilty of specified serious actions (or omissions) that render continuation of the lease impossible;[20] in these situations the lessee cannot prevent cancellation or eviction but she is still protected by law in the sense that summary cancellation is restricted to the grounds in the Civil Code and the actual eviction is subject to prescribed procedural controls.

In normal situations, protection against cancellation is stricter in that the landlord can only cancel for certain specified reasons.[21] Even more interestingly, the lessee can object to cancellation and demand continuation of the lease on the

(§ 569) cancellation might be possible. Cancellation is never allowed purely in order to raise the rent: *BGB* § 573. The Dutch position is similar: *BW* 7:271.

[18] *BGB* § 542(2); *BW* 7:271. The Dutch *BW* 7:228 provides that a lease for a fixed term ends without cancellation when the term expires, but *BW* 7:271 overrides this general provision for purposes of residential leases.

[19] *BGB* § 573 sets out the requirements for normal cancellation; §§ 543, 569 cover extraordinary, summary cancellations. See F Baur *et al*, *Sachenrecht* (17th edn, 1999) at 347. The Dutch situation is regulated in *BW* 7:274.

[20] *BGB* §§ 543, 569. The grounds are unlawful or dangerous use of the lease property (see *BVerfG NJW* 1994, 41 on overcrowding as a ground for summary cancellation); continuous disturbance of the peace; neglect of the property that causes damage for the owner; non-payment of substantial amounts of rent; and other actions that render continuation of the lease impossible. Similar grounds are recognised for cancellation in Dutch law: *BW* 7:274.

[21] The most important grounds are: that the lessee had committed serious and culpable breaches of her obligations under the lease; that the landlord requires the property for use by herself, her family members or other members of her household; and that continuation of the lease would cause serious damage to the landlord by preventing her from making suitable economic use of the property. The latter consideration allows the lessor to prove that she could make more profitable use of the property in another way, but not if that simply involves charging a higher rent: *BGB* § 573. The comparable Dutch provision is *BW* 7:274. In the discussion that follows I focus on instances where the landlord wanted to cancel the lease because she wanted to use the property herself; my focus on this one aspect was inspired by the fact that this ground enjoyed more attention in case-law than the others. Because of the principle that regulation of property use is reviewed more strictly when the property is used for personal purposes (such as an own dwelling) and less strictly when it is used commercially (such as for renting out; see AJ van der Walt, *Constitutional Property Law* (2005) at 134), reliance on the economic use ground for cancellation has enjoyed less prominence in the case-law. However, in *BVerfGE* 100, 226 (*Rheinland-Pfälzische Denkmalschutzgesetz*) [1999] the fact that the regulatory scheme (historical preservation of buildings) destroyed all economic use of the property was considered relevant in deciding whether the regulatory scheme was invalid for regulatory excess (*Übermaßverbot*). Because of the principle that regulation of commercial property can be stricter than in the case of personal property it is unlikely that economic use potential would be allowed to trump the residential rights of tenants, unless the owner can satisfy the statutory requirements for changing the use of the property; see in that regard *BVerfGE* 38, 248 (*Zweckentfremdung on Wohnraum*) [1975]. Interestingly, this approach corresponds with ECHR decisions regarding the regulation of residential rights; see n 93 below and accompanying text.

ground that termination would bring about hardship for the lessee or her family and that such hardship cannot be justified, even when the lawful interests of the lessor are taken into account.[22] Unless the landlord can show that continuation would be unreasonable or that the lessee had not complied with the requirements, the lease then continues on the terms agreed to or subsequently determined by the court. In these cases the interests of the tenant are therefore balanced against (and potentially upheld against) those of the landlord. This is a significant qualification of the rights paradigm in the sense that the rights of the landlord are not only prevented from trumping tenant rights, but are actually subjected to socially important considerations that are out of the landlord's control and irrelevant to the logic of the rights paradigm, namely personal and social circumstances that would cause termination of the lease and eviction to translate into unjustifiable hardship for the tenant and her family.

The most important legal grounds for cancellation of a residential lease in normal situations are that the landlord needs the property for her own use[23] or intends lawfully to change the use of the property.[24] In either case the lessor's reasons for wanting to cancel the lease are subject to review. The civil courts have initially been rather strict in their scrutiny of the owner's reasons for cancellation,[25] but more recently the Federal Constitutional Court has decided that these controls and the limitation that they place upon the property interests of the landowner are constitutionally justified, provided that they give sufficient

---

[22] *BGB* § 574. Procedural aspects of the objection and its effects are regulated by *BGB* §§ 574a–c. The opportunity to object does not apply when the landlord has a ground for extraordinary summary cancellation. In Dutch law the lessee has to agree to the cancellation; if not, the landlord must ask the court to ratify cancellation: *BW* 7:272. If the court ratifies cancellation on one of the admissible grounds, it must also determine when the property should be vacated. If it does not ratify cancellation the lease is extended by law and the court must indicate whether it is extended indefinitely or for a fixed term: *BW* 7:273.

[23] The central provision is *BGB* § 573. The principle is that the hardship caused for the lessee by cancellation is justified if the owner has a lawful interest in own use of the property. The Federal Constitutional Court has set out its interpretation of this protective provision in several cases: *BVerfGE* 79, 292 (*Eigenbedarfskündigung*) [1989]; *BVerfGE* 89, 237 (*Eigenbedarfskündigung*) [1993]; *BVerfGE* 89, 1 (*Besitzrecht des Mieters*) [1993]; see the discussion of these cases below. The Dutch Civil Code also allows the courts the discretion to allow termination of a residential lease if cancellation, considered against all the circumstances, would be fair because the lessor requires the property for her own use: *BW* 7:274. The US Supreme Court has also upheld a constitutional challenge against a rent control ordinance that protects tenants against eviction at the end of their lease terms at the rent determined by a local authority, unless the owner wants the property for occupation by herself or her family: *Block v Hirsch* 256 US 135 (1921); see JW Singer and JM Beerman, 'The Social Origins of Property' (1993) 6 *Can Journal of Law & Jur* 217–48 at 225.

[24] This principle is that justifiability of the hardship caused by cancellation has to be evaluated with due recognition of the lawful interests of the owner. This test would not be satisfied if enforced continuation of the lease would cause serious loss for the lessor by preventing her from making reasonable economic use of it, for instance by changing the economic use of the property from residential to commercial or by renovating and upgrading the property. However, the fact that the owner can charge higher rent for renovated property may not be taken into consideration: *BGB* § 573. The Federal Constitutional Court has set out its interpretation of this protective provision in *BVerfGE* 38, 248 (*Zweckentfremdung von Wohnraum*) [1975].

[25] See the discussion in the text below.

recognition to the lawful interests of the landlord.[26] In the process, the Federal Constitutional Court has developed case-law that indicates how the conflicting interests of the landowner and residential occupiers should be held in balance to give effect to the constitutional protection of property within a social obligations framework. This series of decisions and the balance that they establish qualify the rights paradigm significantly in so far as they balance social housing obligations (and the social and economic context within which they are realised) against the abstract individual property interest of the landowner.

The central question in these cases was how closely the courts may scrutinise the landlord's reasons for cancellation when she wants the property for her own use.[27] In earlier cases the Federal Court of Justice in Civil Matters required the landlord's cancellation for own use to be reasonable, but in 1989 the Federal Constitutional Court decided[28] that it was unconstitutional for the civil courts to review the motives of the landlord for wanting to use the property herself too strictly or in an overly aggressive fashion. The Court explained its approach by reiterating its long-standing principle that a landlord, as a property owner, must be allowed to take her own decisions about how she wants to control and develop her life through the use and disposal of her property; the courts cannot take those decisions for her because that would interfere with her personal autonomy.[29] The Court pointed out that tenant protection laws place considerable restrictions on ownership of rental property and decided that, while these laws were constitutionally justifiable because they served the social obligation purposes of the Basic Law, an interpretation of these laws that takes no account of the landlord's wish to use her property for her own purposes would be in conflict with the constitutional guarantee of ownership. Accordingly, overly strict review of the owner's wishes to use the property herself is not permissible. The courts have to verify that the landlord's need to

---

[26] The German Federal Constitutional Court's interpretation and application of the landlord–tenant provisions are set out in a series of important decisions between 1974 and 1994: *BVerfGE* 37, 132 (*Wohnraumkündigungsschutzgesetz*) [1974]; *BVerfGE* 38, 248 (*Zweckentfremdung von Wohnraum*) [1975]; *BVerfGE* 68, 361 (*Wohnungskündigungsgesetz*) [1985]; *BVerfGE* 79, 292 (*Eigenbedarfskündigung*) [1989]; *BVerfGE* 89, 237 (*Eigenbedarfskündigung*) [1993]; *BVerfGE* 89, 1 (*Besitzrecht des Mieters*) [1993]; *BVerfGE* 91, 294 (*Fortgeltung der Mietepreisbindung*) [1994]. In these cases the Court developed the general principle that legislative control over rent increases and eviction is constitutionally valid because housing laws are regulatory limitations of the content and limits of property in terms of Arts 14 I 2 and 14 II of the Basic Law and as such they are justified by the public interest in dealing with the housing shortage. In *BVerfGE* 91, 294 (*Fortgeltung der Mietepreisbindung*) [1994] the continuation of rent control in the former East Germany was upheld. The rent control system in the former East Germany was eventually phased out and assimilated into the West German system in 1997: see C Flockton, 'Employment, Welfare Support and Income Distribution in East Germany' in C Flockton and E Kolinsky (eds), *Recasting East Germany: Social Transformation after the GDR* (1999) 33–51 at 46. Almost 20% of rental housing in the former East Germany is social housing: HD Vilhjálmsdóttir, 'Housing Support and Public Housing Funds in Iceland and Abroad' (2004) 4 *Monetary Bulletin* at http://www.sedlabanki.is/lisalib/getfile.aspx?itemid=2866 (accessed 9 June 2008).

[27] The following paragraphs are loosely based on revised passages from AJ van der Walt, 'Ownership and Eviction: Constitutional Rights in Private Law' (2005) 9 *Edinburgh LR* 32–64.

[28] *BVerfGE* 79, 292 [1989].

[29] As will appear from the discussion below this autonomy-cum-dignity in the social setting argument is the guideline according to which the German courts decide all constitutional property cases; see n 35.

use the property is real and not merely a ruse to get rid of the tenant, but the courts' discretion to decide whether the landlord's needs are reasonable is limited and it has to be exercised with restraint so as not to interfere with the owner's fundamental right to take responsibility for her own life.[30]

In 1993 the Federal Constitutional Court reiterated that the landlord's wishes with regard to own use of her property had to be respected, but it again qualified the 1989 decision by pointing out that the bare declared intention of the landlord to use the property for her own purposes was insufficient on its own to justify cancellation of the lease. Even though the courts could not institute unlimited review of the owner's motives, the intention to use the property for oneself has to be reasonable and feasible, and the courts have some scope to inquire into the landlord's prospective own use of the property.[31]

In the cases referred to, the Federal Constitutional Court established what it regarded as a fair balance, in accordance with the relevant statutory provisions, between the interests of landlords (individual landowners) and the public interest in protecting the interests of vulnerable tenants in a context where provision of adequate housing is a national priority. The owner's interest in her property can trump the interests of tenants, but unless the owner can prove a reasonable intention to use the property personally, the interests of lessees who will suffer a hardship if evicted will prevail.

In the sense (and to the extent) that the outcome of a landlord–tenant dispute does not depend purely on the stronger ownership rights of the landlord but, at least in some cases, will be determined with reference to the hardship that the tenant will suffer if evicted, the German Federal Constitutional Court's interpretation of the landlord–tenant provisions in the Civil Code has, for the sake of secure housing rights, brought about a significant qualification of the rights paradigm. In a sense the Court stuck its neck out in the 1993 decision by not only balancing the rights of the landlord against those of the tenant but overtly attempting to lift the housing interests of the tenant onto the same plane as those of the landlord. As appears from the discussion of this case below (and in chapter two), this effort by the Court to push property doctrine and rhetoric forward encountered little resistance in the sphere of constitutional property law, but it met with vehement opposition and criticism in private law dogma, which is the home turf of the rights paradigm.

This evaluation of the statutory provisions and case-law found an interesting echo in academic discussions about the 1993 *Landlord–Tenant* decision of the Federal Constitutional Court. The result in the 1993 decision was more or less

---

[30] *BVerfGE* 79, 292 [1989] at 304–5. See nn 29, 35.

[31] *BVerfGE* 89, 1 [1993] at 9–10. The case is known as the *Besitzrecht des Mieters* decision. DP Kommers, *The Constitutional Jurisprudence of the Federal Republic of Germany* (2nd edn, 1997) at 255 calls it the '*Landlord–Tenant Case*'. The tenant brought this case under Art 14, which was unusual; in previous cases (see n 26) it was always the owner-landlord who instituted the constitutional complaint, arguing that legislation protecting tenants infringed upon the landowner's ownership rights and was therefore in conflict with Art 14 of the Basic Law. See also on this case GS Alexander, *The Global Debate over Constitutional Property: Lessons for American Takings Jurisprudence* (2006) at 125–7.

uncontroversial in constitutional circles, but in private law circles strong criticism was levelled at the property status that the Court ascribed to the tenant in coming to its result.[32] The Court concluded that the tenant's interest in using the property qualified as an independent constitutionally protected property interest and not merely as a restriction on the owner's property interest,[33] based on two arguments.[34] The uncontroversial constitutional part of the decision was that a tenant's right to continued possession and use qualifies as property (in the wide sense, that is, not as ownership) because it fulfils the constitutional purpose of

---

[32] For the criticism see: O Depenheuer, 'Entwicklungslinien des verfassungsrechtlichen Eigentumsschutzes in Deutschland 1949–2001' in T von Danwitz *et al*, *Bericht zur Lage des Eigentums* (2002) 109–213 at 124–6, 129–31, 186–7; O Depenheuer, 'Der Mieter als Eigentümer' (1993) 46 *NJW* 2561–4; M Ruffert, *Vorrang der Verfassung und Eigenständigkeit des Privatrechts* (2001) at 366–92. The case and Depenheuer's criticism are also referred to in ch 2, section II.

[33] The issue has more poignancy in German law than is suggested by the Anglo-American term 'property'. Both § 903 of the German Civil Code (*BGB*) and Art 14 of the Basic Law (*GG*) refer to '*Eigentum*', which, strictly speaking, translates as 'ownership' rather than 'property'. In the Roman-Germanic tradition, 'ownership' in this narrow sense is a much more restricted notion than 'property', because the distinction between ownership and (non-proprietary) possession is fundamental to all of civilian property law. More particularly, in the civil law systems there can only be one owner of any given property at one point in time (indivisibility principle). In this tradition, a lessee's occupation of the lease premises is seen as lawful use or possession (at best) and not as ownership; hence the criticism that the 1993 decision of the Federal Constitutional Court destroyed the basic logic of private law by negating this fundamental distinction: O Depenheuer, 'Entwicklungslinien des verfassungsrechtlichen Eigentumsschutzes in Deutschland 1949–2001' in T von Danwitz *et al*, *Bericht zur Lage des Eigentums* (2002) at 128–31, 186–7; further O Depenheuer, 'Der Mieter als Eigentümer' (1993) 46 *NJW* 2561–4. Compare M Ruffert, *Vorrang der Verfassung und Eigenständigkeit des Privatrechts* (2001) 366–92. Commentators from an Anglo-US common law background find this controversy hard to follow, even when they are well versed in German constitutional property law. GS Alexander, *The Global Debate over Constitutional Property: Lessons for American Takings Jurisprudence* (2006) at 126 describes the doctrinal objection against this aspect of the decision as 'ultimately without merit', apparently because he failed to value the doctrinal strength of the objection in German private law. It is one thing for the German courts to accept, for constitutional property purposes, that the interest of a lessee qualifies as *property* under Art 14 of the Basic Law; for German private lawyers that proposition has constitutional meaning only and it does not mean (or require) that the same interest should also be regarded or described as *ownership* in private law. Similarly, the courts and academic commentators are willing to accept that constitutional and social policy reasons justify the protection of tenants' rights and the concomitant limitation of landlords' rights, but that does not mean that they should also (or will) accept a doctrinal explanation of this development that goes against the grain of the still important distinctions between public and private law or between ownership and possession. The importance of this debate is that it illustrates, for all of civil law, the necessity of explaining shifts in the rights paradigm in a way that does not unnecessarily conflict with general doctrinal fundamentals; the development of tenant protection should be construed as far as possible in a way that fits in with general doctrinal distinctions. See further on the conceptual difficulties AJ van der Walt, *Constitutional Property Law* (2005) at 89, fn 112.

[34] *BVerfGE* 89, 1 [1993] at 5. The Court rejected the tenant's argument that the eviction order infringed his property right under Art 14 II of the Basic Law and reiterated the standard view that this provision does not grant any rights—it merely places an obligation on the legislature to promulgate laws that embody the social obligations and protect the public interest as foreseen in Art 14 II, read with Art 14 I 2. It could therefore not be said that the tenant has any right deriving from Art 14 II that could be infringed by the eviction order. Art 14 I 1 provides that ownership (property) is guaranteed; Art 14 I 2 that the content and limits of ownership (property) are determined by legislation. (Art 14 I: 'Das Eigentum und das Erbrecht werden gewährleistet. Inhalt und Schranken werden durch die Gesetze bestimmt'; Art 14 II: 'Eigentum verpflichtet. Sein Gebrauch soll zugleich dem Wohle der Allgemeinheit dienen'.)

protecting property in terms of Article 14 of the Basic Law, namely to enable the property holder (tenant) to take responsibility for her own life within the social framework.[35] Constitutional protection of the tenant's right means that it serves the tenant in the same way that ownership of tangible property serves others; security which the tenant derives from rent control laws can be enforced against everybody, including the landlord, and accordingly the tenant is enabled to take control over her own life through exercise of her property interests. Accordingly, the statutory provisions that protect the tenant are interpreted in view of the general constitutional requirement that an equitable balance has to be struck between the landlord's and the tenant's separate *constitutional* property interests. In constitutional property law this argument explains the Court's decision in an uncontroversial way that allows for significant tenant-friendly statutory interventions without conflicting with private law doctrine. It is widely accepted that *Eigentum*—the term used in both the Civil Code and the Basic Law—has a wider meaning in constitutional than in civil law: It refers to *ownership* of tangibles only in civil law and to *property* (which includes certain non-ownership interests and applies to intangibles as well) in constitutional law, and it includes both ownership and lesser rights in constitutional law, while it has a specific and very limited meaning that excludes all limited real rights and personal rights in the private law setting.[36] Describing a tenant's interest as property is therefore uncontroversial in constitutional law, but it is meaningless in private law. It is clear, however, that describing such a lesser right as property for purposes of constitutional law does not translate into calling it ownership for purposes of private law.

Accordingly, the second, private law part of the Court's argument was widely regarded as both unnecessary and controversial. The second part of the argument was that the tenant's interest in continued possession and use qualified as *private law* property (in the narrow sense, that is as ownership) because the tenant, like the landowner, was said to also enjoy an (albeit more limited) right of disposal with regard to the property. Critics argued that this aspect of the decision was bad in law because in German law it is simply not true that the lessee acquires an (even partial) right of disposal—in fact she acquires nothing more than a limited right of use and occupation as described in the lease agreement, while the right of disposal remains with the landlord, who holds and exercises it exclusively.[37]

---

[35] According to a long line of constitutional cases, the fundamental characteristic of property in terms of the property guarantee is that it provides the holder with a secured area of freedom in the patrimonial sphere, where she can take responsibility for the development and control of her own life within society. In this perspective, the family home is so important that it can be described as the core of human existence: See AJ van der Walt, *Constitutional Property Clauses: A Comparative Analysis* (1999) at 151–7, 139. GS Alexander, *The Global Debate over Constitutional Property: Lessons for American Takings Jurisprudence* (2006) 111–13 describes this aspect of German constitutional property law as a commendable approach that might be instructive for US scholars.

[36] See n 29 above; compare AJ van der Walt, *Constitutional Property Clauses: A Comparative Analysis* (1999) at 151. M Ruffert, *Vorrang der Verfassung und Eigenständigkeit des Privatrechts* (2001) at 366–92 provides the most consistent explanation of the dogmatic position.

[37] O Depenheuer, 'Der Mieter als Eigentümer' (1993) 46 *NJW* 2561–4. For the arguments used to establish that the tenant has a right of disposal see *BVerfGE* 89, 1 [1993] at 7.

Furthermore, critics considered this argument superfluous because it was sufficient to state that the tenant enjoyed property for purposes of Article 14; he did not have to enjoy ownership (in the narrow private law sense) to be protected by Article 14. It is unclear whether the Federal Constitutional Court added the second argument purely by mistake or whether it wanted to strengthen the private law position of tenants and so push private law property doctrine and rhetoric forward. The Court's intention to emphasise the competing force of tenants' rights (and thereby undermine the presumptive power of ownership) is reasonably clear, however, and in that sense the decision is significant.

The second part of the decision and the criticism against it demonstrate how the rights paradigm resists amendments of private law doctrine, even when a significant departure from the paradigm has been sanctioned through legislative intervention and accepted in case-law. It further illustrates the close connection between liberal economic ideology, the rights paradigm and doctrinal orthodoxy. Critics argued that this part of the German Federal Constitutional Court's argument brought about a functional splitting of ownership between the landlord and the tenant,[38] which is said to threaten the modern civil law institution of private ownership (and with it the free market economy) and to push society back towards feudalism.[39] These critics are not necessarily questioning the legitimacy of the legislative policy decision to promote protection of tenants—their point is that the interpretation of the legislation in this case was unnecessarily unconventional for purposes of private law and that it rested upon questionable doctrinal logic. The problem was therefore not that the tenant was protected against the owner, but rather that his protection was explained on the basis that he had a private law ownership interest on the same level as the owner's. The more conventional private law argument—that statutory protection of tenant's rights had to be accepted and explained as restrictions that are placed upon the landowner's ownership in

---

[38] A functional splitting of ownership is far more contentious in Roman-Germanic legal systems than in Anglo-American law, where remnants of feudal land law are still common. In English land law functional splitting is more or less acceptable because of the late (and incomplete) abolition of feudal remainders in property law; in US law it is less contentious because of the influence of legal realist and law and economics reasoning. However, neither realism nor law and economics had much influence in continental private law theory, and consequently efficiency arguments in favour of functional splitting are relatively unknown and doctrinally frowned upon. One exception is C Engel, 'Die Soziale Funktion des Eigentums' in T von Danwitz *et al, Bericht zur Lage des Eigentums* (2002) 9–107. Engel justifies the functional splitting of ownership in this decision on the basis of law and economics efficiency analysis, but ultimately his argument is unconvincing. See AJ van der Walt, 'Property Theory and the Transformation of Property Law' in E Cooke (ed), *Modern Studies in Property Law*, Vol 3 (2005) 361–80 at 367–8. See n 39 below.

[39] O Depenheuer, 'Entwicklungslinien des verfassungsrechtlichen Eigentumsschutzes in Deutschland 1949–2001' in T von Danwitz *et al, Bericht zur Lage des Eigentums* (2002) 128–31, 186–7; O Depenheuer, 'Der Mieter als Eigentümer' (1993) 46 *NJW* 2561–4; M Ruffert, *Vorrang der Verfassung und Eigenständigkeit des Privatrechts* (2001) 366–92. The decisive turn of German private law against functional splitting of ownership came when Thibaut rejected the medieval categories of direct and beneficial ownership (and the remnants of feudalism) in 1817: AFJ Thibaut, 'Über Dominium Directum und Utile' in *Versuche über einzelne Theile der Theorie des Rechts* (1817, reprint 1970), vol I, part II, 67–9. The same move was made much earlier in Roman-Dutch law when Grotius argued away the medieval distinction between direct and beneficial ownership; see ch 2, n 3.

the public interest, even when these restrictions are quite extensive—is clearly more acceptable in civil law than an explanation that evaluates the tenant's interest as private law ownership. In this sense, constitutional amendments of the rights paradigm have been assimilated and even welcomed in legal practice, but they are preferably explained in a way that fits in with existing private law doctrine. This attitude could perhaps be described as low-intensity doctrinal resistance against constitutional or statutory reforms of established private law doctrine. The most important aspect of the reaction against doctrinal change in the *Landlord–Tenant* case is that the rhetorical, logical and doctrinal effects of even constitutionally sanctioned and widely accepted legislative changes are restricted to the area of policy and public (constitutional) law, while their effect on private law strictly speaking is either denied or resisted.

In conclusion it may be said that German private law, in the form of the Civil Code and ancillary landlord–tenant legislation, has brought about certain significant statutory amendments of the traditional relationship between landlord and tenant. While some of these amendments amount to little more than formal procedural control over the cancellation of a lease and eviction procedures, others involve significant qualifications of the rights paradigm in that they not only restrict the landlord's right to cancel a lease and evict the former tenant, but in certain instances even prevent the owner from exercising those rights purely because of the hardship that doing so would cause for socially weak and marginalised tenants or their families. These amendments of the private law relationship between landowners and tenants involve a significant qualification of the rights paradigm in the sense that they no longer allow eviction purely on the logic of the landlord's stronger right to possession, but instead sometimes allow tenants' interests and personal circumstances to trump the landlord's rights. More specifically, a landlord is prevented from terminating a tenancy through cancellation if it can be shown that doing so would bring about unjustifiable hardship for the tenant and her family while upholding and continuing the tenancy would not place an unconscionable burden upon the landowner. In accordance with German constitutional doctrine this result is explained and accepted in landlord–tenant situations to the extent that the landlord's interest in the property is commercial, as opposed to the personal stake that an owner-resident has in the property. The constitutional privileging of personal over commercial property interests also explains why the landlord is allowed to cancel the lease when she requires the property for her own use (as opposed to the commercial use of renting it out).

It is an interesting feature of German constitutional law that the landowner's right is balanced against the interests of the tenant, with the result that one can describe the German constitutional and legislative qualifications of the rights paradigm, in the landlord–tenant context, as follows: If cancellation of a residential lease and eviction of the tenant would cause significant hardship for the tenant or her family, the German courts will not automatically allow the landowner to cancel the lease and evict the tenant, unless the owner can prove that the resulting limitation of her ownership rights would be unjustifiable in view of her legitimate, personal needs. There is an interesting paradox at work in German constitutional property theory in the sense that the constitutional justification for protecting the property interests of both the landlord and the tenant is still founded upon the same liberal vision of individual autonomy that underlies the rights paradigm—in adjudicating these property cases the Federal Constitutional Court relies on a long-established practice of insisting that property is protected by the Basic Law in order to allow the holder to make autonomous decisions in arranging her affairs. However, it is equally clear from the line of cases in which this practice has been worked out that individuals are allowed and expected to take autonomous decisions about property and about their own affairs in a social setting, and not, as Singer commented on the ownership model, 'as if we were alone' (see chapter two). The situatedness of autonomous property decisions explains the German privileging of personal above commercial property uses and also provides a framework for the liberty assumptions within which property is protected. The result is that the focus shifts away from entrenching individual security of current property owners and stability of the existing property system towards the constitutional and statutory obligation to ensure individual security of all property holders, including landlords and tenants, and long-term, sustainable stability of the property system in the sense of making changes, in some cases even radical changes, that are necessary to bring about a more just and equitable system, on the assumption that a fairly distributed property system has better prospects for long-term stability than a system that might be entrenched by strong rights, but that is plagued by deep injustices and inequalities.

The validity and legitimacy of statutory amendments that protect tenants against exploitation and arbitrary eviction have been accepted in German private and public law and they are applied by both civil and constitutional courts. At the same time traditional private law resists the conclusion that doctrine has to adapt to these changes—the preferred explanation is that they are politically legitimate and constitutionally valid exceptions to the private law rule and they are accommodated as such, without any fundamental implications for the dogmatic structure of property rights.

C. English Law[40]

At first it might seem strange to compare English landlord–tenant law with German and South African law, but there are reasons for such a comparison. English law shares with South African law the feature that the private law of property consists largely of uncodified common law, part of which has been amended explicitly by landlord–tenant legislation (although the volume of legislation is vastly larger in English law). The two systems also share the common feature that this mix of

---

[40] I am particularly indebted to Susan Bright for explaining the intricacies of English landlord–tenant law to me and painstakingly reading and commenting on early drafts of this section. Remaining errors are nevertheless mine.

uncodified background law and reformist legislation is now interpreted with reference to the social responsibility provisions in the South African Constitution 1996 and the English Human Rights Act 1998 respectively, thereby triggering a process of push-and-pull between constitutional (or constitution-type) reform principles and the inherent stability-preserving tendencies of uncodified private law. In South African law, some of the reformist legislation predates the 1993 and 1996 Constitutions, but the more significant legislation is explicitly constitution-driven in that it was promulgated and is justified in terms of the new constitutional dispensation. In English law, the overwhelming majority of legislative interventions pre-date the Human Rights Act 1998. In both cases, the relevant constitutional instruments were adopted at a relatively late stage, subsequent to promulgation of the protective social legislation during the 1970s and at a time when the global tendency was to privatise housing and to cut back on state-sponsored social support systems. As a result of these policy shifts, both English and South African case-law suggest that courts find it difficult to navigate the apparent conflict between new liberal housing policies and social responsibility obligations introduced at a relatively late stage by constitutional or similar instruments. On a different level, the interpretation problems that arise in court cases in English and South African law because of the influence of doctrine in a largely uncodified private law system offer interesting perspectives compared to the slightly less fraught relationship between constitutional, legislative and judicial reform processes in German law, where private law is codified. Simultaneously, English and German landlord–tenant law originated at roughly the same time and under comparable circumstances and the substantive content of their tenant protection provisions is roughly similar, while South African legislation is much younger and less developed. The comparison between the three systems is therefore justified by strong similarities in certain key contextual, doctrinal and historical features, while stark differences in other areas render the comparison interesting.

As is the case in modern German law, English law also protects tenants in two ways, on the one hand by ensuring due process and fairness when the landlord wants to cancel a lease and again when eviction occurs, and on the other hand— more fundamentally—by sometimes either delaying or actually preventing termination of the tenancy and eviction.[41] Normally, a lease or tenancy can come to an end in a number of ways in English law, the most important of which, for present purposes, are effluxion of time, notice to quit and forfeiture.[42] The death of the tenant does not in itself terminate a tenancy in English law; in the absence of legislative intervention, the residue of the tenancy devolves either in accordance with the former tenant's will or according to intestate succession.[43] Susan Bright

---

[41] It is impossible to give even the vaguest overview of the complex legislative framework; see in general S Bright, *Landlord and Tenant Law in Context* (2007) at 141–235; K Gray and SF Gray, *Elements of Land Law* (4th edn, 2005) at 1590–610.

[42] K Gray and SF Gray, *Elements of Land Law* (4th edn, 2005) at 563*ff.*

[43] S Bright, *Landlord and Tenant Law in Context* (2007) at 546–51; K Gray and SF Gray, *Elements of Land Law* (4th edn, 2005) at 565.

indicates that the inheritance of a long leasehold can be valuable, whereas transmission on death of a short-term contractual lease is of little significance; succession to protected periodic tenancies is more important. Succession rights are treated differently in the private and the public housing sectors. In the private sector, the Housing Act 1988 grants succession rights to the spouse or civil partner of an assured periodic tenant if the spouse or partner was occupying the premises as his or her only or principal home.[44] In the public sector, succession rights are granted to a broader range of persons: The Housing Act 1985 provides that a person who occupies a dwelling together with the tenant as her only or principal home at the time of the tenant's death qualifies to succeed the tenant under a secure tenancy if she is the tenant's spouse or civil partner or another member of the tenant's family who has resided with the tenant throughout the 12 months preceding the tenant's death.[45] As in German law, spouses, partners and other family members of a tenant therefore enjoy limited statutory security upon the tenant's death.

One security issue that arises in civil-law systems, namely whether a tenancy is terminated by sale of the land, does not pose the same problems in English law because of the doctrine of estates in land. Because of what Gray and Gray describe as 'the proprietary principle: *nemo dat quod non habet*',[46] sale of the freeholder's interest (or the property interest of any other person in the same land) to a third party will (subject to priority rules and registration principles) not affect a tenant who owns an independent leasehold.[47] In civil law systems, special principles had to be developed to protect a tenant under these circumstances, but because of the doctrine of estates, a tenant does not need special protection to be developed in English law.

---

[44] S Bright, *Landlord and Tenant Law in Context* (2007) at 547. Only one succession is allowed and if the survivor of a joint tenancy becomes the sole tenant, that counts as succession. If there is nobody with succession rights the assured tenancy will pass to the tenant's estate, but then the landlord has the right to end the tenancy within 12 months of the tenant's death, thereby preventing the periodic tenancy from continuing indefinitely.

[45] Section 87. If there is more than one successor, preference is given to the spouse or civil partner over other family members. As in the private sector, only one succession is allowed. See S Bright, *Landlord and Tenant Law in Context* (2007) at 547–9; K Gray and SF Gray, *Elements of Land Law* (4th edn, 2005) at 565. Susan Bright discusses the Law Commission's proposals for amendments to this situation: *ibid* at 549–51.

[46] K Gray and SF Gray, *Elements of Land Law* (4th edn, 2005) at 461, citing *Bruton v London & Quadrant Housing Trust* [2000] 1 AC 406.

[47] S Bright, *Landlord and Tenant Law in Context* (2007) at 48–50 usefully explains this characteristic of English land law in a section with the heading 'Leases as split-ownership'. Citing W Swadling, 'Property: General Principles' in P Birks (ed), *English Private Law*, Vol I (2000) at 218; *Hunter v Canary Wharf Ltd* [1997] AC 655 (HL) at 703; D Clarke, 'Long Residential Leases: Future Directions' in S Bright (ed), *Landlord and Tenant Law: Past, Present and Future* (2006) 171–90 at 171, Bright explains that land law, strictly speaking, does not have a concept of ownership, since property in land is protected as possession. In this sense, one can say that the ownership interest is split up between the landlord and the tenant—exactly the effect against which German commentators reacted so sharply subsequent to the *Landlord–Tenant* case (see nn 36–40 and accompanying text above). Crucially, in English law the tenant is the one holding the right to exclude during the life of the lease. For the effect of sales in execution on housing rights compare L Fox, *Conceptualising Home: Theories, Laws and Policies* (2007) at chs 2–3.

What remains to consider are legislative amendments of the common law position with regard to termination of a lease and eviction. For present purposes, legislation that affects termination of a lease through effluxion of time, notice to quit and forfeiture are of most interest, as those were the most important ways in which a lease or tenancy could be ended in English common law. Forfeiture was traditionally the most dramatic way in which a landlord could bring a lease or tenancy to an end, demonstrating the power of the rights paradigm by allowing the landlord to exercise his right to possession in a high-handed and demonstrative fashion. The right to forfeit, which is traditionally entrenched in most written leases, allows the landlord to re-enter premises occupied by a tenant in breach of the covenant and thereby forfeit the lease by acting as if it had never existed. Demonstrating the significance of forfeiture for the rights paradigm, Kevin Gray and Susan Gray describe this right as 'the most draconian weapon in the armoury of the landlord whose tenant has committed a breach of the covenant' and 'the ultimate affirmation of the landlord's proprietary power'.[48] According to the common law, a landowner could reclaim possession of her property, through re-entry and forfeiture of the lease, as part of the exercise of her proprietary rights—this forceful demonstration of the stronger right to possession reflects what is referred to as the owner's absolute power of exclusion in civil law systems. Originally a landowner could evict a tenant in breach in this way without a court order by simply exercising his right of physical re-entry, even using reasonable force when necessary.[49] However, the common law situation was amended by two lines of statutory development.[50] On the one hand, increasingly strict statutory due process regulation was imposed on the landlord's common law right to forfeit the lease for breach by the tenant; on the other hand, legislation increasingly provided certain tenants with greater security of tenure, which enabled them to resist the landlord's efforts to end the lease. The landlord's common law right to forfeit was traditionally exercised by simply re-entering the premises, whereby the tenancy was forfeited and the tenant's right of occupation terminated. Through the

---

[48] K Gray and SF Gray, *Elements of Land Law* (4th edn, 2005) at 1485, 1489, referring to *Harrow London Borough Council v Qazi* [2004] 1 AC 983 (HL). See ch 2, nn 19–20 and accompanying text.

[49] *Butcher v Poole Corporation* [1943] KB 48 at 53; *Ezekiel v Orakpo* [1977] QB 260. See C Harpum, *Megarry & Wade The Law of Real Property* (6th edn, 2000) at § 14-042; K Gray and SF Gray, *Elements of Land Law* (4th edn, 2005) at 1485–6. The Law Commission, *Report on Forfeiture of Tenancies*, (1985) Law Com No 142; *Termination of Tenancies Bill*, (1994) Law Com No 221 recommended that the whole be replaced with a single statutory scheme that will govern the termination of tenancies for breach of covenant; see C Harpum, *Megarry & Wade The Law of Real Property* (6th edn, 2000) at § 14-167. A new proposal *Termination of Tenancies for Tenant Default*, (2006) Law Com No 303, more recently proposed the abolition and reform of a large part of the law in this field, focusing on the termination of tenancies because of default on the side of the tenant. For the time being the system remains complex; K Gray and SF Gray, *Elements of Land Law* (4th edn, 2005) at 1434–5 note that 'This corpus of legislation has grown both unwieldy and convoluted and there now exists an overwhelming case for the replacement of all landlord and tenant rules by the enactment of a more simple consolidated code of landlord–tenant relations.' The 2006 Law Commission Report (Law Com No 303 at 11) confirms the urgent need for reform and indicates that almost all academics and practitioners subscribe to this view.

[50] I am indebted to Susan Bright for bringing this distinction to my notice and helping me understand the intricacies of the relevant legislation.

increased imposition of due process regulation, the original function of the forfeiture process was watered down to the point where it no longer makes sense, and
therefore the Law Commission recommended in 2006 that forfeiture be abolished
altogether and replaced with a statutory scheme for termination of tenancies on
the basis of tenant default.[51] The strong and immediate claim on possession
embodied in the right to forfeit by re-entry was therefore eroded by due process
requirements of notice and judicial oversight, while legislation increasingly provided certain tenants with greater security of tenure.[52] In the process, the termination of leases and tenancies was not only subjected to due process controls but
also brought under a comprehensive scheme of statutory control. In particular,
the limited statutory protection afforded to tenants in case of death of the tenant
was expanded to other tenants, both public and private, against arbitrary and
unfair termination of the lease and, ultimately, eviction. These developments
provide a striking example of how due process limitations on termination and
eviction could, over time, bring about a significant qualification of the rights
paradigm.

In English common law, expiration of the term of a tenancy for a fixed term
automatically terminated the tenancy, without notice, although a fixed-term tenancy could be ended by forfeiture prior to the expiration date.[53] This position was
amended by legislation that now requires a court order for ending a tenancy; the
legislation also provides that a periodic tenancy comes into existence at the end of
a fixed-term residential tenancy (with the same parties, on the same terms and for
the same period as the previous fixed-term tenancy). In the private sector this is
known as a statutory periodic assured tenancy.[54] In either case, the terms of the
new periodic tenancy can be varied and the new periodic tenancy can be ended in
the same way as other protected periodic tenancies (described below). More
specifically, both private and public leases can be ended by forfeiture only if there
is a statutory ground for possession.[55] Tenancies for a fixed term are therefore no
longer automatically terminated through effluxion of time or ended by forfeiture—at the end of the fixed term a periodic tenancy is created that can only be
ended, like all other periodic tenancies, if there is a statutory ground for possession
and if the prescribed procedure is followed.[56]

---

[51] Law Commission, *Termination of Tenancies for Tenant Default* (2006), Law Com No 303, Part 2:
Overview of the Scheme; see 12. I discuss the Law Commission's proposals below.

[52] Special categories such as secure tenancies in terms of the Housing Act 1985 and assured tenancies
under the Housing Act 1988 were created for this purpose. The 1996 Housing Act did not alter the situation regarding assured tenancies; the default position since 1996 is that a new tenancy will be an
assured shorthold tenancy. The 2004 Housing Act does not change the situation with regard to eviction.

[53] K Gray and SF Gray, *Elements of Land Law* (4th edn, 2005) at 656, citing *Barrett v Morgan* [2000]
2 AC 264. See further S Bright, *Landlord and Tenant Law in Context* (2007) at 596.

[54] See S Bright, *Landlord and Tenant Law in Context* (2007) at 596; K Gray and SF Gray, *Elements of
Land Law* (4th edn, 2005) at 565–6.

[55] S Bright, *Landlord and Tenant Law in Context* (2007) at 596–7.

[56] The grounds for possession in the private and public sectors overlap to a degree: S Bright,
Landlord and Tenant Law in Context (2007) at 599–602. Bright classifies the grounds for possession into
three broad categories that are not reflected directly in the legislation: occupier default, social policy
grounds (anti-social behaviour, domestic violence), and estate management. In the public sector,

At common law a periodic tenancy is ended by serving a notice to quit, the length of notice depending on the period of the tenancy in so far as it has not been prescribed by legislation.[57] This position has also been amended by legislation. Apart from common law due process rules, the power to quit by notice has been amended by the Protection from Eviction Act 1977, which prescribes due process and fairness rules for the termination of residential tenancies by notice to quit. Other landlord–tenant statutes provide further amendments that affect the land-lord's common law power to end the tenancy by notice.[58] Secure and assured peri-odic tenancies can now only be ended by court order, which can only be granted if a statutory ground for possession exists. In the public sector, where tenancies are protected more strongly than in the private housing sector, an order for possession can, in certain cases, only be given if the court considers it reasonable or if suitable alternative accommodation is available.[59] Moreover, in the case of (public) secure tenancies there are no mandatory grounds for possession, and considerations of reasonableness or the availability of suitable alternative accommodation (or both) will be taken into account in granting the possession order.[60] For (private) assured tenancies the protection is somewhat weaker and the courts are sometimes bound to grant possession on mandatory grounds; in other cases the order can be given on discretionary grounds that turn on reasonableness. For an assured shorthold tenancy, which enjoys the weakest protection, the fact that the tenancy has come to an end (subject to a six-month minimum) and notice will be sufficient to secure an order for possession.[61]

The salient features of the statutory protection set out above are that possession can only be regained by way of a court order, that there must be a statutory ground for possession to obtain a court order, and that the courts must—with the excep-tion of certain short-term private (assured) tenancies—often consider either rea-sonableness or the availability of suitable alternative accommodation in granting such an order. Mandatory grounds for possession feature only in the private sec-tor, where the availability of suitable alternative accommodation is never a factor; mandatory grounds usually apply to the landowner's use of the property for own

---

possession can be granted for some reasons only if the court considers it reasonable; for some reasons only if suitable alternative accommodation will be available for the tenant; and for some reasons only if the court considers the order reasonable and suitable alternative accommodation is available. In the private sector, some reasons for possession are mandatory and some are available only if the court considers it reasonable. Many of the mandatory reasons in the private sector are designed to ensure that the landlord will be able to recover possession when requiring the property for his or her own pur-poses; a purpose that resembles the most important German reason for allowing private landlords to terminate the lease. In English law private landlords can now attain this purpose by using the assured shorthold tenancy, which grants only minimal security.

[57] S Bright, *Landlord and Tenant Law in Context* (2007) at 669.
[58] S Bright, *Landlord and Tenant Law in Context* (2007) at 597–8.
[59] S Bright, *Landlord and Tenant Law in Context* (2007) at 596, 599–600. Bright shows that rea-sonableness of granting a possession order is a requirement that confers a wide discretion on a trial judge.
[60] S Bright, *Landlord and Tenant Law in Context* (2007) at 596, 599–602.
[61] S Bright, *Landlord and Tenant Law in Context* (2007) at 596.

purposes.[62] Reasonableness or the availability of suitable alternative accommodation (or both) always features in public tenancies; in some private tenancies reasonableness is also a factor. When reasonableness has to be considered, the courts have to look at the case as a whole, including factors that pertain to the personal circumstances of the tenant, although there is evidence that this does not really work in practice, in the sense that the participation of tenants and the courts' actual consideration of the reasonableness factors are very limited in fact.[63] Apart from considering extraneous factors such as reasonableness and the availability of suitable alternative accommodation, the courts have some leeway to suspend or postpone possession orders subject to conditions that give tenants time and opportunity to remedy the landlord's complaint, combined with conditions the court may consider reasonable.[64]

An interesting and puzzling feature of the statutory scheme is the notion of a tolerated trespasser. In the public sector, a secure tenant often remains in the property after the tenancy has ended, in accordance with the Housing Act 1985, on the date for possession given in the possession order, but before a warrant for possession has been executed.[65] As long as the former tenant keeps paying the rent the landlord might well be perfectly happy for this situation to continue; in certain areas there are apparently large numbers of former tenants finding themselves in continuing occupation of the premises under these conditions. A tolerated trespasser has no statutory rights and no security, yet may remain in occupation and continue paying rent for a considerable time. Gray and Gray describe the tolerated trespasser's position as precarious but not wrongful.[66] The continued occupation of tolerated trespassers, combined with the courts' wide discretion under section 85(2) of the Housing Act 1985, apparently gives rise to the prospect that a secure tenancy may be revived through a court order to suspend or postpone possession in terms of the Housing Act 1985. In the private sector, the notion of tolerated trespasser is apparently also possible in the case of assured tenants in terms of the Housing Act 1988.[67] A tolerated trespasser obviously occupies a strange and contradictory status in landlord–tenant law and, although its application is limited, it demonstrates a quite remarkable deviation from the norm under the rights paradigm.

In evaluating the protective legislation it is important to take note of shifts in government housing policy. On the one hand, public sector tenancies, which

[62] S Bright, *Landlord and Tenant Law in Context* (2007) at 599; see the lists of grounds at 600. The mandatory grounds in the private sector cases relate to owner-occupiers, mortgagee repossession, out-of-season holiday home lettings, educational institutions' vacation lettings, minister of religion, demolition or reconstruction, periodic tenancy recently inherited, and rent arrears. See n 23 above concerning German and US law on the role of the landowner's wish to use the property herself.

[63] S Bright, *Landlord and Tenant Law in Context* (2007) at 599, 601–602.

[64] S Bright, *Landlord and Tenant Law in Context* (2007) at 601. This relates particularly to non-payment of rent.

[65] S Bright, *Landlord and Tenant Law in Context* (2007) at 605–8; K Gray and SF Gray, *Elements of Land Law* (4th edn, 2005) at 504.

[66] K Gray and SF Gray, *Elements of Land Law* (4th edn, 2005) at 504.

[67] S Bright, *Landlord and Tenant Law in Context* (2007) 607–8, citing *White v Knowsley Housing Trust* [2007] EWCA Civ 404.

enjoy stronger protection, have been eroded since the 1980s by a shift in housing policies that resulted in large-scale privatisation of public housing; on the other hand, the protective measures have been reduced even with regard to public tenancies. Susan Bright explains that, although private sector tenants had enjoyed security for most of the twentieth century, and public sector tenants have been protected by statute since 1980, the statutory security provided to tenants has generally been reduced over the last 20 years.[68] An important policy shift took place when the protection of secure tenancies (granted to public sector tenants under the Housing Act 1980) was reduced through provision for termination of a lease and eviction because of anti-social behaviour of the tenant in terms of the Housing Act 1995 (introductory tenancy) and the Anti-Social Behaviour Act 1996 (demoted tenancy). In the private sector, the various schemes of legislation[69] that provided tenants with security throughout most of the twentieth century were cut back significantly when the Housing Act 1988 introduced assured shorthold tenancies, which are protected for six months only (except if the contractual term is longer). Almost 90% of new private rented lettings available to the public are now subject to shorthold tenancies,[70] which means that a very significant percentage of tenants in the private sector are excluded from the substantive statutory protections described earlier. In addition, new housing policies since the 1980s have resulted in a large part of previously public housing being privatised, thereby reducing the protection that tenants of public housing enjoyed under the protective schemes set out above.

In view of these considerations it could be said that English legislation had brought about both procedural and substantive amendments to the common law of landlord and tenant, thereby moving away—at least in some instances—quite decisively from the rights paradigm (which, in English land law, is the paradigm of possessory rights), but that some of these amendments have recently been undone by new legislation that reduced the scope of tenant protection, especially in the private sector. At the same time, the reduction of public sector housing under the influence of new liberal economic policy has eroded the tenant protections put in place during the 1970s and 1980s quite considerably.

The English Law Commission recently proposed its own tenancy termination scheme for tenants in default.[71] The proposal sets out a court-based statutory termination scheme which is always preceded by written notice to the tenant, informing her of the nature of the default on which the complaint is based and the action (if any) the landlord requires the tenant to take. Written notice would be required even in the rare cases where the landlord is allowed to follow the

---

[68] S Bright, *Landlord and Tenant Law in Context* (2007) at 593. Bright usefully distinguishes between security (instances where the landlord is prevented from terminating the lease and the tenant is entitled to stay on) and eviction (following once a lease has been terminated) at 591–666 and 667–742 respectively.

[69] S Bright, *Landlord and Tenant Law in Context* (2007) at 183–222.

[70] S Bright, *Landlord and Tenant Law in Context* (2007) at 595.

[71] Law Commission. *Termination of Tenancies for Tenant Default* (2006), Law Com No 303; see 21–9 for an overview.

summary termination procedure.[72] The default notice system proposed in the scheme is intended to encourage the parties to negotiate a suitable outcome rather than merely push for and against a termination order; consequently, a range of orders, apart from mere termination, would be available once the court was satisfied that the tenant default had in fact occurred. Once it was satisfied that a tenant default had indeed occurred, the court would have the discretion to make such an order as it thought appropriate and proportionate in the circumstances.[73] In exercising this discretion the court must take into account certain prescribed considerations, including the conduct of the parties (including a person with a qualifying interest in the tenancy), the nature and terms of any qualifying interest in the tenancy and the circumstances in which it was granted, the extent to which action to remedy the default has been or can be taken, the extent to which any deadline in the tenant default notice for remedial action is reasonable, any other remedy available to the landlord, and any other matter which the court considers relevant. The Law Commission explicitly states in its report that it considered the proposed scheme compatible with the Human Rights Act 1998 and the European Convention on Human Rights.[74]

Apart from substantive protections tenants also enjoy due process protection. Only tenancies that fall outside of the statutory schemes or residential tenancies excluded from the Protection from Eviction Act 1977 are governed purely by the common law and the contract, and it is only in those exceptional cases that a court order is not required for eviction.[75] For the rest, legislation prescribes due process requirements and requires all evictions to take place by way of a court order. As was indicated earlier, these due process controls had a very significant substantive effect in practically rendering the common law right of forfeiture redundant. Generally speaking, the due process controls relate to notice requirements and the requirement that eviction be based on a court order. Section 5 of the Protection from Eviction Act 1977 requires that residential tenants, including occupiers holding a so-called periodic licence to occupy premises as a dwelling, must be given at

---

[72] The summary procedure is available when a tenant has no realistic prospect of persuading the court not to make a termination order and there are no other reasons why the trial should take place. The summary order must still be preceded by written notice, so that the tenant can object by way of application for a discharge order, in which case the summary termination order is suspended and the landlord would have to rebut a statutory presumption in favour of discharge. The summary procedure is intended to assist landlords in case of abandoned buildings and is therefore not available in certain prescribed situations, eg when someone lawfully resides in the premises or when the unexpired term of the tenancy exceeds 25 years.

[73] Without limiting the range of orders the court can make, six orders are mentioned specifically: a termination order that brings the tenancy and all rights from it to an end; a remedial order to require the tenant to remedy any default; an order for sale of the tenancy and distribution of the proceeds; an order for the tenancy to be transferred to any person; a new tenancy order (only for a holder of a qualifying interest in the tenancy); and a joint tenancy adjustment order. In addition to the order selected, the court can impose conditions.

[74] Law Commission, *Termination of Tenancies for Tenant Default* (2006), Law Com No 303 at 19.

[75] S Bright, *Landlord and Tenant Law in Context* (2007) at 680.

least four weeks' notice and prescribes formalities for such notice.[76] Section 3 of the Act provides that it is unlawful to enforce a right of re-entry or forfeiture or otherwise to evict a tenant other than by court order when the property is lawfully occupied.[77] Once a tenancy has been ended lawfully and the former tenant fails to vacate the premises, the landowner cannot re-enter the premises physically but has to obtain a warrant of possession, whereafter she has to enforce the warrant of possession according to statutory procedures.[78] Although it may sometimes be necessary to prove reasonableness to obtain a possession order, the landlord usually does not have to prove that it is reasonable to execute the order and in many cases the warrant of possession is obtained without even giving the occupier further notice.[79] The Law Commission's 2006 proposed statutory scheme for termination of tenancies for tenant default continues the trend to prefer regulated, court-based evictions procedures.[80]

This brief overview indicates that legislation enacted to protect residential tenants in English law has resulted in qualifications of the rights paradigm in much the same way as in German law: Tenancies for a fixed term are transformed into periodic tenancies and thus continue under certain circumstances; in some circumstances, landlords are prevented from terminating a tenancy and claiming possession purely because the court considers it unreasonable to allow termination and eviction; and when termination of a tenancy is allowed, landlords are mostly expected to proceed with eviction according to procedural requirements that could involve lengthy stays of execution and suspensions, purely because of

---

[76] S Bright, *Landlord and Tenant Law in Context* (2007) at 674. Certain categories of excluded tenancies and licences are enumerated in the section. The fact that tenant protection has been cut back recently does not mean that tenants are left without protection, even when they fall within the now more vulnerable categories. In *Bruton v London & Quadrant Housing Trust* [2001] 1 AC 406 (HL) the House of Lords held that a tenancy existed where the claimant, an impoverished resident of social housing not belonging to the landlord, did not occupy the land merely on the basis of a licence as was alleged. It was emphasised that title, which is founded on possession in English law, is relative and that the landlord–tenant relationship also depends on possession. Even when the landlord had no title to the land, the grant of exclusive possession usually creates a tenancy, unless surrounding circumstances indicate otherwise (at 413).

[77] S Bright, *Landlord and Tenant Law in Context* (2007) at 675–8; *Haniff v Robinson* [1993] QB 419 (CA). Interestingly, Frank Michelman has described a similar process in US law, arguing that the courts have developed a substantive public housing entitlement on the basis of fairly slim due process requirements, while failing to do so—on the basis of similar due process requirements—in the sphere of public employment, possibly because of what Michelman describes as our intuition that there is something special about the need for adequate housing: F Michelman, 'Formal and Associational Aims in Procedural Due Process' in JR Pennock and JW Chapman (eds), *Due Process (NOMOS XVIII)* (1977) at 126–71; see further AJ van der Walt, 'A South African Reading of Frank Michelman's Theory of Social Justice' in H Botha *et al* (eds), *Rights and Democracy in a Transformative Constitution* (2003) 163–211 at 188–9.

[78] 1977 Act, s 3.

[79] S Bright, *Landlord and Tenant Law in Context* (2007) at 608.

[80] Law Commission, *Termination of Tenancies for Tenant Default* (2006), Law Com No 303 makes it clear that, apart from greater simplicity and transparency, continued movement towards judicial enforcement rather than self-enforcement was one of the driving forces behind the case for reform: see the report at 11–12.

the circumstances of the tenant and her family members.[81] Despite the fact that especially private sector tenancies have been excluded from many of the statutory protections through the introduction of assured shortholds, English statutory law provides a protective scheme within which at least public-sector tenants enjoy both substantive and due process protection against eviction. At least in some instances, these protections amount to a significant qualification of the rights paradigm in the sense that the landlord is not permitted to end the tenancy or evict the occupier, purely because of extraneous considerations such as reasonableness or the availability of suitable alternative accommodation. The Law Commission's proposal to abolish the doctrine of forfeiture completely and to replace it with a statutory termination scheme points in the same general direction and develops the protective scheme even further away from the traditional paradigm. However, as has been noted before, the impact of some of these protective measures has been reduced by changes brought about by new housing policies since the 1980s.

Potentially, the position was complicated further and the rights of tenants protected even more strongly when the Human Rights Act 1998 became operative, making Article 8 of the European Convention for the Protection of Human Rights and Fundamental Freedoms 1950 (ECHR) applicable to English law. Article 8(1) ECHR provides that 'Everyone has the right to respect for his private and family life, his home and his correspondence'. In the jurisprudence of the European Court of Human Rights it has become practice to protect tenants (and even unlawful occupiers) of residential premises against eviction in terms of this provision.[82] Since introduction of the Human Rights Act 1998 the English courts have struggled with the applicability of the Act and its impact on the common law, particularly in cases where it seems as if application of Article 8 could create an additional judicial discretion that would require (or legitimise) a judicial weighing-up of landlords' rights against the rights of tenants or unlawful occupiers. It has been argued that Article 8 does not apply to 'normal' landlord–tenant disputes about possession because the rights of the tenant are already sufficiently protected by the Protection from Eviction Act 1977 or other applicable legislation, but in a number of cases this argument was rejected and it was decided that a claim

---

[81]   In US law the principle is also that a landowner is permitted to evict a tenant only once the lease has been terminated lawfully and that the lease may only be terminated if the landowner has the right to do so. The right to cancel the lease is granted either by statute or by the lease agreement and usually it is based upon a breach of the lease agreement by the tenant; statutes in different states vary on the grounds that are required to establish a breach that would entitle the landowner to cancel. Normally, the landowner would terminate the lease by giving the tenant notice, according to the applicable statute, to either cure the breach within a specified time or vacate the premises. Should the tenant fail to cure the breach and to vacate the premises, she becomes an unlawful detainer of the property ('holding over'). In most states the owner would then have a summary court action for possession; in some states the owner also has the right to enter the premises without the court order, provided she does so peaceably, although an increasing number of jurisdictions require the landlord to resort to legal procedures rather than self-help if the lessee holds over. See generally R Cunningham *et al*, *The Law of Property* (1984) at 393–9. On the question of dispossession without legal process see PA Agambin, 'Right of Landlord Legally Entitled to Possession to Dispossess Tenant without Legal Process' 6 *ALR* 3d 177 (2006) 1–7.

[82]   See T Allen, *Property and the Human Rights Act 1998* (2005) at 227–31 for examples.

for possession triggers Article 8 and that the courts may grant a possession order only if Article 8(2) ECHR is complied with.[83] In subsequent decisions it was decided that, where a landlord has a legal right to possession, respect for a person's home in terms of Article 8(1) does not require the court to balance the tenant's rights or interests against the landlord's right in terms of Article 8(2)—even when Article 8 has been triggered by an eviction, the landlord's right to possession prevails if she is able to prove a legal right to possession.[84] The argument was that balancing of landlords' rights against the housing interests of tenants is a legislative function that has already been exercised in drafting the applicable legislation: Courts are neither positioned nor trained to do this kind of policy-based balancing and should therefore not indulge in second-guessing the legislature on the suitability or wisdom of its policy choices.

A number of decisions demonstrate the difficulties raised by this debate about Article 8 and its importance for the current evaluation of eviction law. As will appear from the discussion, it is difficult to keep eviction cases against tenants and unlawful occupiers (squatters) apart in discussing the English case-law, because the cases often do not make this distinction as clearly as it is presented in this book (this chapter dealing with tenants and chapter five with unlawful occupiers). Some of the relevant European Court cases deal with gypsies or travellers, a group that sometimes features in the case-law as lawful tenants and sometimes as unlawful squatters.[85]

In *Harrow London Borough Council v Qazi*[86] the House of Lords decided that the English courts, in deciding the validity of a claim for possession under Article 8(2) ECHR, do not have to apply a full-scale proportionality test involving balancing of the landowner's rights against the housing interests of the tenant, since that balancing has already been done in the suitable political forum, namely the legislature.[87] Accordingly, once it has been established that the landowner (including a public landowner) is entitled to an order for possession in terms of domestic law, Article 8 cannot be relied upon to defeat the landowner's right to possession and there is nothing further to investigate.[88] The majority argued that it does not matter whether the landlord's right to possession trumps the former tenant's

---

[83] *Poplar HARCA v Donoghue* [2001] 3 WLR 183; *Lambeth London Borough Council v Howard* [2001] 33 HLR 58; [2001] EWCA Civ 468; see J Luba, 'Residential Possession Proceedings and Article 8 (Part 2): The Impact on the Private Sector' (2002) 6(2) *L&T Rev* 9–12.

[84] *Harrow London Borough Council v Qazi* [2004] 1 AC 983 (HL); see further *Newham London Borough Council v Kibata* [2004] 15 EG 106; *Lancashire City Council v Taylor* [2005] 1 P & CR 2; *Leeds City Council v Price* [2005] 1 WLR 1825 (CA). It has been said that the decision of the House of Lords in *Qazi* is incompatible with the subsequent decision of the European Court of Human Rights in *Connors v United Kingdom* (2004) 40 EHRR 189; see the discussion below.

[85] *Kay and Another v London Borough of Lambeth and Others; Leeds City Council v Price and Others* [2006] UKHL 10 (HL) at para 51.

[86] [2004] 1 AC 983 (HL). The former husband and wife in *Qazi* occupied a council house under a joint tenancy, which was terminated when the marriage broke down and Ms Qazi served notice to quit. Mr Qazi was refused a sole tenancy because the house was originally allocated to a family. He continued to occupy the house unlawfully with his new family.

[87] [2004] 1 AC 983 (HL), at para 23.

[88] [2004] 1 AC 983 (HL), at para 108.

interests because there was no infringement of the Article 8(1) right to respect for the tenant's home, or whether Article 8(1) was engaged but Article 8(2) was automatically satisfied by the strength of the owner's right to possession—in the view of the House of Lords it comes to the same thing.[89] The House of Lords did refer to the possibility that an occupier could apply for judicial review if she believed that the local authority was acting from improper or ulterior motives in applying for possession, but since nothing of the sort was proved in *Qazi* the matter ended there. The decision in *Qazi* was followed in later cases where it was again decided that Article 8 ECHR did not bring about a departure from the traditional principles that apply once a landowner has proven her proprietary rights.[90] Significantly, the European Court refused to admit an appeal from the House of Lords decision in *Qazi*.

The majority approach in *Qazi* was criticised in the minority opinion of Lord Steyn and in subsequent decisions and in academic literature.[91] One of the most important points raised in criticism is the question whether the *Qazi* decision conflicts with the European Court of Human Rights decision in *Connors v United Kingdom*.[92] In *Connors*, the European Court held that the granting of a possession order against a gypsy family had violated Article 8 under circumstances where it was clear that the measures taken were in accordance with the law and pursued a legitimate government aim; the only issue for decision was therefore proportional-

---

[89] *Harrow London Borough Council v Qazi* [2004] 1 AC 983 (HL) per Lord Millett at para 103; Lord Scott at paras 137, 149. See S Bright, 'Ending Tenancies by Notice to Quit: The Human Rights Challenge' (2004) 120 *LQR* 398–403 at 399.

[90] *Newham London Borough Council v Kibata* [2004] 15 EG 106; *Bradney v Birmingham City Council and Birmingham City Council v McCann* [2003] EWCA Civ 1783. *McCann* was later overturned by the European Court of Human Rights; see *McCann v United Kingdom* [2008] ECHR 19009/04 (13 May 2008) (n 104). The *Qazi* line of argument was confirmed in later House of Lords decisions; see *Kay and Another v London Borough of Lambeth and Others; Leeds City Council v Price and Others* [2006] UKHL 10 (HL); *Belfast City Council v Miss Behavin' Ltd* [2007] 1 WLR 1420 (HL) at para 36; *Doherty (FC) and Others v Birmingham City Council* [2008] UKHL 57 (HL) at paras 22, 42.

[91] See the minority opinion of Lord Steyn in *Harrow London Borough Council v Qazi* [2004] 1 AC 983 (HL) at paras 26–33. See further S Bright, *Landlord and Tenant Law in Context* (2007) at 271–96, 610–13, 670–73; K Gray and SF Gray, *Elements of Land Law* (4th edn, 2005) at 130–32; D Hughes and M Davis, 'Human Rights and the Triumph of Property: The Marginalisation of the European Convention on Human Rights in Housing Law' (2006) Nov/Dec *Conveyancer & Property Lawyer* 526–52. In 'Human Rights and Property Law' (Nov 2005, www.landmarkchambers.co.uk/upload/docs/Blundell_elvin_june-2006.pdf) (accessed 18 June 2008), David Elvin QC (Landmark Chambers) indicates that the decision of the ECHR in *Connors v United Kingdom* (2004) 40 EHRR 189, like the decisions of the High Court in *Beaulane Properties Ltd v Palmer* [2005] 3 WLR 554 and of the Court of Appeal in *Price v Leeds City Council* [2005] 1 WLR 1825 (CA), suggests strong opinions to the contrary.

[92] (2004) 40 EHRR 189. In *McCann v United Kingdom* [2008] ECHR 19009/04 (13 May 2008) at para 50 the European Court of Human Rights refused to restrict the effect of the *Connors* decision to cases involving the eviction of gypsies or cases where the applicant sought to challenge the law itself (as opposed to the application of the law in her case). *McCann* involved a case for possession where the secure joint tenancy was terminated when the local authority convinced the departing partner in a domestic violence situation to serve notice to quit, thereby ending the tenancy and depriving the remaining partner of the statutory protection he would have enjoyed in a possession case under the Housing Act 1985. The Court concluded that any person at risk of losing her home is entitled to have the proportionality of the measure determined by an independent tribunal in view of Art 8 principles and that the bypassing of the statutory scheme by the local authority was disproportionate.

ity under Article 8(2). The Court was willing to indulge in proportionality analysis under Article 8(2), arguing that it was for the national authorities to decide what was necessary initially, but that the final evaluation of whether the reasons for the interference were relevant and sufficient remains subject to review. A margin of appreciation is left to national authorities to formulate policy in terms of their own, better placed evaluation of local conditions and needs. This margin will tend to be narrower when the right at stake is crucial to the individual's effective enjoyment of intimate or key rights, whereas the margin is wider in spheres involving the application of social and economic policies.[93] Accordingly, judicial proportionality evaluation and review of those policy choices remains possible and necessary.

Gray and Gray describe the outcome of the *Qazi* case in the House of Lords as 'a resolute defence of proprietary sovereignty in the face of a much more open-textured form of proprietary morality stemming from a European source'.[94] Susan Bright points out that the ownership-friendly decisions like *Qazi* arose in a situation where the tenancy was terminated when the tenant gave notice to quit to the landlord, which was a local council, and that the procedure followed and the argument underlying the majority decision in *Qazi* have serious consequences for such notice to quit situations.[95] In all these cases, the problem with the *Qazi* approach is not so much the fact that the landlord's right to possession cannot be challenged on proportionality grounds but the fact that a remaining occupier, who has no independent right of occupation,[96] need not be informed of the intention to serve notice to quit, nor does she necessarily get an opportunity to apply for a new tenancy or to state her case for continued occupation. This is particularly the case when a couple occupied the property as their common home and one of them

---

[93] *Connors v United Kingdom* (2004) 40 EHRR 189 at paras 81, 82. The *Connors* decision and other cases dealing with the position of gypsies or travellers are discussed in ch 5, section IV. The tendency to adapt the margin of appreciation to the sphere of activity regulated (personal vs commercial) corresponds with German constitutional theory; see n 21. It is remarkable that palpably unfair evictions often affect weak and marginal individuals or groups; compare ch 6, section V and see *Smith v Secretary of State for Trade and Industry* [2008] 1 WLR 394, involving compulsory acquisition of land occupied by Romani Gypsy and Irish Travellers for 'economic development and regeneration' of the land in preparation for the 2012 Olympic Games.

[94] K Gray and SF Gray, *Elements of Land Law* (4th edn, 2005) at 1489, referring to *Harrow London Borough Council v Qazi* [2004] 1 AC 983 (HL). The notion that property is a pre-political or pre-constitutional phenomenon shaped by natural law and embodied in private law also finds support in JW Harris, *Property and Justice* (1996); compare A Brudner, *The Unity of the Common Law: Studies in Hegelian Jurisprudence* (1995), Part II 'The Unity of Property Law'; HM Jacobs (ed), *Private Property in the 21st Century: The Future of an American Ideal* (2004).

[95] See S Bright, 'Ending Tenancies by Notice to Quit: The Human Rights Challenge' (2004) 120 *LQR* 398–403 at 400–3; S Bright, *Landlord and Tenant Law in Context* (2007) at 610–13, 670–73. See further D Elvin QC (Landmark Chambers), 'Human Rights and Property Law' (Nov 2005) (available at www.landmarkchambers.co.uk/upload/docs/Blundell_ elvin_June-2006.pdf) (accessed 18 June 2008) at 19*ff*. See further *McCann v United Kingdom* [2008] ECHR 19009/04 (13 May 2008) (n 92).

[96] The joined tenancy came to an end when the one spouse filed a notice to quit in accordance with s 5 of the Prevention of Eviction Act 1977: *Harrow London Borough Council v Qazi* [2004] 1 AC 983 (HL) at para 41. Compare the situation in *McCann v United Kingdom* [2008] ECHR 19009/04 (13 May 2008), where one party was convinced by the local authority to serve notice to quit, thereby ending the tenancy and freeing the local authority from a more arduous possession action under the Housing Act 1985; compare n 92.

leaves when the relationship breaks down—regardless of whether the ex-partner who cancels was a sole tenant or whether they were joint tenants, the notice to quit ends the tenancy and with it the remaining partner's right to remain in occupation.[97] By encouraging a partner to serve notice to quit the local council can effectively avoid the statutory protection that the remaining partner enjoys under normal possession proceedings, as long as the argument in *Qazi* is followed.[98]

In a subsequent decision on evictions in terms of Article 8, *Kay and Another v London Borough of Lambeth and Others; Leeds City Council v Price and Others*,[99] the House of Lords explained the apparent conflict between *Qazi* and *Connors* in a way that would uphold the central sentiment of the *Qazi* decision while creating the impression that this decision was in line with European Court jurisprudence on Article 8.[100] The House of Lords was invited by the appellants in this case to reconsider and depart from its decision in *Qazi* but declined to do so, holding that neither of the two sets of appellants had any prospect of succeeding with a defence based on Article 8. The House of Lords confirmed that Article 8(2) was activated in the *Kay* case and that the eviction should have been seen as an interference with the appellants' right to respect for their homes, but found that there was no reasonable prospect of the case being decided differently if remitted to the county court for reconsideration under Article 8, since the appellants had no right under domestic law to occupy the premises, nor did they fall into one of the categories of tenants protected by legislation—the local authority would therefore inevitably succeed with a claim for possession against them. The appellants in the *Price* appeal never had a home interest in the premises they briefly and unlawfully occupied with their caravans, and therefore eviction in their case never activated Article 8 at all.[101]

---

[97] S Bright, 'Ending Tenancies by Notice to Quit: The Human Rights Challenge' (2004) 120 *LQR* 398–403 at 400 points out that the ex-partner was a sole tenant in *Newham London Borough Council v Kibata* [2004] 15 EG 106, whereas s/he was a joint tenant in *Harrow London Borough Council v Qazi* [2004] 1 AC 983 (HL) and *Bradney v Birmingham City Council and Birmingham City Council v McCann* [2003] EWCA Civ 1783. See further *McCann v United Kingdom* [2008] ECHR 19009/04 (13 May 2008) (n 92).

[98] S Bright, 'Ending Tenancies by Notice to Quit: The Human Rights Challenge' (2004) 120 *LQR* 398–403 at 401–3. Bright was proved right by the decision in *McCann v United Kingdom* [2008] ECHR 19009/04 (13 May 2008); see n 95.

[99] [2006] UKHL 10 (HL). *Kay/Price* is interesting in that it, like other English cases on this issue, resists the distinction between eviction of tenants and unlawful occupiers respectively that underlies the division of chs 4 and 5 of this book; the two cases were consolidated in the House of Lords appeal and decided together despite the fact that Kay was a former tenant and Price was one of a group of unlawful squatters or trespassers. See S Bright, *Landlord and Tenant Law in Context* (2007) at 610–13. For a useful summary of the *Kay/Price* decision and the two so-called 'gateways' to an Art 8 challenge, see *Doherty v Birmingham City Council and Another* [2006] EWCA Civ 1739 at para 22. I am indebted to Kevin Gray for bringing this decision to my notice. *Doherty* was confirmed in part and overruled in part in the House of Lords; see *Doherty (FC) and Others v Birmingham City Council* [2008] UKHL 57 (HL).

[100] *Kay and Another v London Borough of Lambeth and Others; Leeds City Council v Price and Others* [2006] UKHL 10 (HL) at paras 107, 112, 166–7.

[101] *Kay and Another v London Borough of Lambeth and Others; Leeds City Council v Price and Others* [2006] UKHL 10 (HL) at paras 47, 48, 148. See S Bright, *Landlord and Tenant Law in Context* (2007) at 610–13.

In deciding these cases the House of Lords pointed out that the English legislature has already made extensive provision for the protection of certain categories of tenants against eviction, although eviction of those tenants is still possible if the statutory requirements are met. If the statutes protect a tenant but provide for eviction, and if the requirements for obtaining possession are met, the occupier will only gain additional protection from Article 8 in highly exceptional circumstances.[102] In other words, if the necessary weighing up of the interests of landlords and tenants has already been undertaken by the legislature, it is unlikely that the European Convention should give the courts the power to revisit that balancing exercise on their own. Under the jurisprudence of the European Court this sentiment is justified to the extent that the Court grants local legislatures quite a wide 'margin of appreciation' in devising regulatory schemes in terms of their own knowledge and understanding of local conditions and requirements, asking only that sufficient safeguards and due process protections should be built into the system to ensure that citizens who feel that they have been treated badly could have their case heard by an independent judiciary.

A particularly interesting aspect of the *Kay/Price* decision, for present purposes, is the House of Lords' firm rejection of the proposition that the personal and social or economic hardship of the evictees should have any bearing on the matter, especially if there are public services available to deal with and alleviate the problems (such as ill health) in question.[103] This line of argument indicates that the House of Lords is firmly supporting the rights paradigm—it is a central hypothesis in this book that a significant qualification of the rights paradigm is indicated when the courts have (and exercise) the discretion to prevent or delay eviction purely on consideration of the personal, social or economic hardship of the evictees. It could be said that the House of Lords did not reject the idea that a landowner's right to possession could be restricted purely on the basis of the personal hardship of the evictees, but rather the idea that such a discretion has to be exercised a second time, by the courts, when it has already been exercised once, by the legislature, in drafting the legislation pertaining to social housing. The courts' discretion, in such a case, would then be restricted to testing whether the legislation was sufficient in protecting the rights in question and whether the legislation was complied with. In *Kay/Price* the evictees fell outside of the protective legislative framework; a fact that in view of the decisions in *Qazi* and *Kay/Price* should be seen as a conclusive indication that the legislature has taken a decision on the status of those groups

---

[102] *Kay and Another v London Borough of Lambeth and Others; Leeds City Council v Price and Others* [2006] UKHL 10 (HL) at paras 33–6, 53. See S Bright, *Landlord and Tenant Law in Context* (2007) at 610–13. The House of Lords has subsequently confirmed this reading of its central decision in *Qazi* and in *Kay/Price*: *Belfast City Council v Miss Behavin' Ltd* [2007] 1 WLR 1420 (HL) at para 36; *Doherty (FC) and Others v Birmingham City Council* [2008] UKHL 57 (HL) at para 22.

[103] *Kay and Another v London Borough of Lambeth and Others; Leeds City Council v Price and Others* [2006] UKHL 10 (HL) at paras 38, 172. It is true that the vulnerable position of gypsies has been taken into account specifically in some cases, but gypsies are often treated as unlawful occupiers (squatters) rather than tenants; their position is therefore discussed in ch 5, section IV. See further S Bright, *Landlord and Tenant Law in Context* (2007) at 282.

and that its decision should be respected.[104] The House of Lords made this clear when it confirmed that courts should in future proceed on the assumption that domestic law strikes a fair balance as intended in and is compatible with Article 8. If the court is satisfied that the domestic law requirements have been met it should grant a possession order unless the occupier shows that it is seriously arguable, in exceptional and highly unlikely circumstances, either that the law that authorises the possession order is incompatible with the European Convention or that, considering the occupier's personal circumstances, the local authority's exercise of its power to seek a possession order was an unlawful act as meant in Article 6.[105] With this decision, domestic law on eviction was practically immunised against all but the most exceptional and extreme attacks on the basis of Article 8, thereby restricting the protection of tenants against eviction to domestic law as amended by legislation. In this way, the potential effect that Article 8 of the European Convention might have had on English law (namely to accentuate the protection of tenants under landlord–tenant legislation and thereby perhaps help to shift the relative common law power positions of the landlord and the tenant) was restrained quite decisively.[106] The *Kay/Price* decision confirms that a public landowner's unquali-

[104] *Kay and Another v London Borough of Lambeth and Others; Leeds City Council v Price and Others* [2006] UKHL 10 (HL) at para 75; *Doherty (FC) and Others v Birmingham City Council* [2008] UKHL 57 (HL) at paras 56–7. In *Doherty* at para 9 (following *Kay/Price* at para 110) the House of Lords confirmed that the personal circumstances of the tenant could be considered only when the domestic law that governs the tenancy provides accordingly; but when the public landlord's right to recover possession is unqualified there are only two instances (so-called 'gateways') where a challenge could be brought namely if the challenge is that the law under which the possession order is sought is incompatible with Art 8 (eg for excluding the relevant category of occupiers from its protection) or where the public authority's action in bringing the claim for possession is so unreasonable as to be unlawful. The House of Lords was informed of the decision in *McCann v United Kingdom* [2008] ECHR 19009/04 (13 May 2008), where the European Court of Human Rights held (at para 50) that '[t]he loss of one's home is a most extreme form of interference with the right to respect for the home. Any person at risk of an interference of this magnitude should in principle be able to have the proportionality of the measure determined by an independent tribunal in light of the relevant principles under Article 8 of the Convention, notwithstanding that, under domestic law, his right of occupation has come to an end', and invited to abandon the approach it had followed in *Kay/Price*. The House of Lords resisted this invitation and accepted a solution that would apply and to some extent develop the reasoning of the majority in *Kay/Price* so as to bring it in line with both *Connors* and *McCann* (*Doherty* at para 19). The House of Lords therefore confirmed in *Doherty* at para 22 that, unless the legislation itself can be attacked, it is not open to a court, once it has decided that the effect of legislation is that a public housing authority's right to possession is unqualified, to hold that the exercise of that right could be denied purely because of the occupier's circumstances. The rights paradigm is therefore upheld as 'the basic rule' 'which can be applied to all cases of this type generally'. The case in *Doherty*, which resembled *Connors* in almost all respects, was found to prompt a slight development of the *Kay/Price* principle in that a challenge against the actions of the local authority (gateway (b)) was not restricted to common law judicial review grounds but could extend to the question whether the decision to recover possession was one that no reasonable person would consider justifiable: para 55.

[105] *Kay and Another v London Borough of Lambeth and Others; Leeds City Council v Price and Others* [2006] UKHL 10 (HL) at paras 39, 109. Compare the summary of this decision in *Doherty (FC) and Others v Birmingham City Council* [2008] UKHL 57 (HL) at para 8.

[106] See D Hughes and M Davis, 'Human Rights and the Triumph of Property: The Marginalisation of the European Convention on Human Rights in Housing Law' (2006) Nov/Dec *Conveyancer & Property Lawyer* 526–52 at 550; compare K Gray and SF Gray, *Elements of Land Law* (4th edn, 2005) at 1489.

fied property right provides the justification required by Article 8(2): in a normal case, where the legislation that governs the tenancy does not allow for consideration of the tenant's personal circumstances by requiring reasonableness, there is no need for a public authority to plead or provide individual justification.[107]

In sum, the English common law had been amended significantly through legislation that protects tenants from eviction.[108] Some amendments involve no more than procedural controls over the eviction process, but others amount to significant qualifications of the rights (in this case possession) paradigm in that they prevent a landlord from exercising her right to terminate a tenancy, which in turn affects her right to claim possession.[109] The most significant amendments resemble the German examples in that the courts exercise a discretion whether or not to allow termination of a lease and a claim for possession, based on an assessment of all the circumstances, including (in some instances) the availability of alternative suitable accommodation for the evicted former tenants.[110] However, some of the changes brought about by tenant-friendly legislation have subsequently been undone, especially in the private sector, while both the size and the protection of the public housing sector have been reduced in view of new liberal economic policy.

In English case-law there are signs of resistance against a rhetorical and doctrinal shift away from the rights paradigm, mostly based on judicial scepticism about

[107] *Doherty v Birmingham City Council and Another* [2006] EWCA Civ 1739 at para 22, referring to *Kay and Another v London Borough of Lambeth and Others; Leeds City Council v Price and Others* [2006] UKHL 10 (HL) at para 24. *Doherty* was confirmed in part and overruled in part in *Doherty (FC) and Others v Birmingham City Council* [2008] UKHL 57 (HL), compare n 104.

[108] C Harpum, *Megarry & Wade The Law of Real Property* (6th edn, 2000) at 843, fn 85 points out that the Law Commission initially advised that the right of peaceable re-entry should be abolished altogether, but later amended its advice to say that this right should merely be regulated statutorily.

[109] Civil law theorists might be tempted to conclude that English law has already left the ownership paradigm behind, considering the fact that the tenant is regarded as having a property interest in the land (see n 95). In German law, this would be regarded as a very significant departure from the traditional paradigm; see nn 70–72 and accompanying text. However, this impression is misleading—describing the tenant's interest as a property interest or not is a question of doctrinal and structural semantics as far as the differences between common law and civil law systems are concerned. In common law systems it is historically unproblematic to hold that different property interests can co-exist with regard to the same property; the same statement would raise civil law eyebrows if 'property' were to be translated or understood as 'ownership' in private law, but not if it were translated as 'real rights' (for private law purposes) or 'property' for constitutional purposes.

[110] A point that bears mentioning is the fact that the landlord–tenant relationship—and the freedom to dominate this relationship usually ascribed to the owner—is also severely curtailed by equality legislation and case-law. The US Code (42 USC 3601*ff* is popularly known as the Fair Housing Act) proscribes discrimination on the grounds of race, colour, religion, sex, family status, national origin and any handicap: 42 USC 3604. This restriction has more effect on the conclusion of a lease agreement than its termination and is not pursued here. A similar prohibition against discrimination was brought about in the UK by s 24 of the Disability Discrimination Act 1995; see *North Devon Homes v Brazier* [2003] L & TR 26; *Manchester City Council v Romano* [2004] 1 WLR 2775. For further detail see K Gray and SF Gray, *Elements of Land Law* (4th edn, 2005) at 1484. In South African law, s 4(1) of the Rental Housing Act 50 of 1999 gives effect to s 9(4) of the 1996 Constitution by prohibiting unfair discrimination against prospective tenants, tenants, their households and certain categories of visitors. In line with the general prohibition against discrimination in Art 3 III of the German Basic Law, § 2(1)8 of the General Equal Treatment Act 2006 (*Allgemeines Gleichbehandlungsgesetz AGG* 14 Aug 2006, BGBI I S 1897) provides that discrimination shall be unlawful in the provision of public goods and services, including housing.

the suitability of the proportionality analysis introduced by Article 8(2) of the European Convention on Human Rights and conservatism regarding the scope of judicial review rather than unwillingness to accept legislative changes of the relationship between ownership and residential occupation rights. For the largest part, this resistance can be related to the courts' view that the necessary weighing has already been undertaken by the legislature and that a second balancing process in the courts is unwarranted, at least unless it is authorised by the legislation. If it appears that the legislature has already decided to treat a certain category of tenants in a specified way as far as actions for possession by the landlord are concerned, the English courts are unwilling to undertake a further weighing of the interests of landlords against those of tenants, particularly if the challenge is based purely on the personal and social or economic hardship of the tenant. This attitude is in line with long-established English doctrine about separation of powers and the scope of judicial review. In view of the recent shifts in housing policy and the conservative approach adopted by the courts in eviction disputes it must therefore be concluded that the qualification of the rights paradigm in English law is less decisive and smaller in its ultimate effect than might be expected on first view of the rather impressive array of landlord–tenant legislation.

III. Tenant Protection in South African Law[111]

The rights paradigm was strong in South African law during the apartheid era, but its hegemony was never complete. Even Roman-Dutch law[112] protected tenants against unfair eviction by despotic landowners,[113] and since 1942 this protection was continued and extended by statutory control over eviction of tenants.[114] The

---

[111] This section of the chapter is based loosely on revised passages from AJ van der Walt, 'Exclusivity of Ownership, Security of Tenure, and Eviction Orders: A Model to Evaluate South African Land-Reform Legislation' 2002 *TSAR* 254–89; AJ van der Walt, 'Ownership and Eviction: Constitutional Rights in Private Law' (2005) 9 *Edinburgh LR* 32–64; AJ van der Walt, *Constitutional Property Law* (2005) at 308–53, 416–19, 424–7.

[112] I use the term to refer to the Roman-Dutch law as it was received in South Africa during the seventeenth century and subsequently developed, partly through case-law and partly through legislation.

[113] Several examples are mentioned in ch 3: Landowners are generally not allowed to evict without legal procedure, which usually includes judicial oversight (compare ch 3, n 47) and lessees generally enjoy some measure of security of tenure as against new purchasers of the land (compare ch 3, n 48). I return to these protections below.

[114] The 1950 Rents Act repealed the 1942 Act and consolidated rent control legislation. The 1950 Act controlled residential as well as business premises, but provided only limited protection for lessees facing eviction. Government notices increasingly limited the jurisdiction of the Act and eventually business premises were excluded from the Act. On the other hand premises occupied before 1 June 1966 as well as certain garages and parking lots were included under the jurisdiction of the Act. Changes were consolidated in the 1976 Rent Control Act, which increased protection for lessees of dwellings and business premises in affected areas. Rent boards were established in many urban areas, but only affected white tenants. Statistical evidence is hard to find, but commentators agree that the rent control scheme only ever affected a very small percentage of poor white tenants in urban areas. The 1976 Act was repealed by the Rental Housing Act 50 of 1999. See n 115.

most important pre-1994 piece of rent-control legislation, the Rent Control Act 80 of 1976, restricted landowners' right to cancel a lease and imposed some due process controls over eviction, but the Act only applied in areas where rent control boards had been established.[115] The 1976 Act was repealed by the Rental Housing Act 50 of 1999, which again provides tenants with a measure of protection. This protection is based upon and authorised by the 1996 Constitution and complemented by anti-eviction provisions in other post-1994 land reform legislation that applies to residential tenants. The discussion below is restricted to the position at common law and its amendment by the 1996 Constitution and post-1994 legislation, particularly the Extension of Security of Tenure Act 62 of 1997 and the Rental Housing Act 1999.

A few preliminary remarks are necessary before embarking on a discussion of anti-eviction provisions in post-apartheid landlord–tenant law. Firstly, it is necessary to repeat that eviction and forced removals played a central role in the apartheid era and that this background had a decisive influence on the direction and tenor of post-apartheid land reform law.[116] The 'normal' legislative purpose of adjusting the potentially unequal power relationship between landlords and tenants acquired a special poignancy in South African law because of the apartheid context and the close links between apartheid land policy and eviction.[117] Secondly, the post-1994 land reform legislation distinguishes between different categories of occupiers; two distinctions that have a bearing on this discussion are lawful versus unlawful occupiers, and occupiers of urban versus occupiers of rural land.[118] This chapter and the next reflect the broad distinction between eviction of tenants (lawful occupiers) and unlawful occupiers respectively. The distinction between land reform measures that apply to urban or to rural land implies that both the Extension of Security of Tenure Act 62 of 1997 (rural land) and the Rental Housing Act 1999 (urban land) have to be considered for purposes of this chapter. Thirdly, it is necessary to keep in mind that doctrinal resistance against statutory amendments of the common law sometimes coincides with or resembles—but does not necessarily equal—political resistance against land reform.[119] In the South African land reform context, differences of opinion about the question whether a particular land reform law applies may be inspired by anti-reform sentiments, but it may also simply be the result of confusion or uncertainty about the 'correct' interpretation of legislation that ostensibly brings about amendments to the common law

---

[115] The 1999 Act repealed the 1976 Act in its entirety. The three-year period for which certain provisions (especially s 28) of the 1976 Act still applied expired on 1 August 2000; see PJ Badenhorst *et al*, *Silberberg & Schoeman's The Law of Property* (5th edn, 2006) at 429, fn 21. The Rental Housing Amendment Bill 2007 confirms revocation of the 1976 Act; see http://www.info.gov.za/gazette/bills/1999/b29d-99.pdf (20 April 2008).

[116] See ch 2, section III for a fuller discussion.

[117] See ch 2, section III for detail.

[118] Some land reform laws, such as the Rental Housing Act 50 of 1999 and the Extension of Security of Tenure Act 62 of 1997 (ESTA) apply only to lawful occupiers of (mainly urban) residential and agricultural land respectively. The Prevention of Illegal Eviction from and Unlawful Occupation of Land Act 19 of 1998 (PIE) applies only to unlawful occupiers of either urban or residential land; see ch 5.

[119] The majority of land reform laws do not overrule the common law; see n 102.

and existing practices. This consideration is particularly relevant in cases where anti-eviction laws amend the common law—doctrinal conservatism inspires judges to opt for interpretations that bring about the smallest possible change in existing legal positions. In this respect the South African debate resembles the English debate post-*Qazi* and the German academic debate about the *Landlord–Tenant* case referred to in chapter two, section II.

For purposes of landlord–tenant law, the protection of tenants against termination of the tenancy and eviction must therefore be considered against the background of what remains of the common law, together with the 1996 Constitution (particularly section 26) and the most important pieces of legislation, namely the Extension of Security of Tenure Act 62 of 1997 and the Rental Housing Act 1999.

As far as the common law is concerned, the only significant protection afforded to tenants is that their occupation rights under the lease are not extinguished when the rental property is sold to a third party—in South African common law, the position of the tenant is protected by upholding the lease in certain circumstances. In the case of a long-term lease (for more than 10 years), tenants are protected by a combination of the Formalities in Respect of Leases of Land Act 18 of 1969, the doctrine of knowledge and the rule that lease is not broken by sale of the rented property (*huur gaat voor koop*).[120] Long leases are valid against third parties (and thus against purchasers of the land) if they have been registered against the title deed of the land; once registered, the long lease creates real rights that are enforced against third parties regardless of their knowledge of the lease and independent of the tenant's possession. Unregistered long leases are also enforced against third parties for the first 10 years of the lease on the basis of the rule that sale does not break lease (*huur gaat voor koop*), but this protection depends on the tenant already having taken possession of the rental property. An unregistered long lease also binds purchasers of the land who had knowledge of the existence of the lease (doctrine of knowledge); in this case the protection extends beyond the first 10 years of the lease.[121] Short leases (for less than 10 years) are normally not registered and the tenants cannot therefore be protected by registration. However, they enjoy the protection of the *huur gaat voor koop* principle. Tenants also enjoy the protection of the rule if the property is sold in execution, unless the highest bid is

---

[120] The rule (also translated as 'lease trumps sale') is explained in *Genna-Wae Properties (Pty) Ltd v Medio-Tronics (Natal) (Pty) Ltd* 1995 (2) SA 926 (A) at 931G–932G: Sale of the leased property does not terminate the lease; the purchaser steps into the shoes of the former landlord by operation of law; as long as the lessee pays the rent and observes all other obligations under the lease, the purchaser acquires all the rights and obligations of the landlord under the lease; the lessee is bound by the lease and cannot resile from it as long as the new owner acknowledges it. The rule applies only once the tenant has taken possession by occupying the premises, and it applies only to a lease of land and buildings. There has been much debate in South African law about the question whether this rule provides the tenant with a limited real right (which would be against normal Roman-Dutch doctrine, which requires registration for the creation of a real right in land) and whether it simply binds third parties to a personal right for policy purposes. This debate has some doctrinal interest but does not really affect the current discussion.

[121] PJ Badenhorst *et al*, *Silberberg & Schoeman's The Law of Property* (5th edn, 2006) at 430–31; *Ismail v Ismail and Others* 2007 (4) SA 557 (EC); see ch 3, n 21.

insufficient to cover the mortgaged debt, in which case the property will be sold free from the lease and the tenant will be left to pursue her contractual remedies against the former landlord.[122] In all these instances, the tenant is protected against termination of the lease and eviction by a new purchaser of the rental property. However, outside of the limited protection afforded by the Rent Control Acts discussed earlier, the South African common law did not allow the tenant any protection against the landlord in the form of a right to uphold or extend the term of the lease without the landlord's consent. The only protection the tenant enjoyed against the landlord is that even before 1994 landowners were not allowed to evict tenants without legal process.[123]

The common law position has been amended, as far as the protection of tenants is concerned, by or under the influence of three sets of provisions in the 1996 Constitution, pertaining to tenure reform, the negative housing obligation and the prohibition against arbitrary eviction, respectively. The legal basis for tenure reform[124] is section 25(6) (read with section 25(9)) of the Constitution, which places a duty on the state to improve the security of tenure of certain occupiers of land by promulgating appropriate legislation.[125] The thinking behind tenure reform policy is that black land interests were rendered vulnerable by apartheid land laws that denied them appropriate legal recognition and that the land reform process therefore requires legal redefinition and strengthening of these rights for the sake of increased security. Tenure reform laws strengthen and secure weak and vulnerable interests in land, in some cases regardless of their lawfulness, by restructuring them or by establishing new, suitably protected rights for specific

---

[122] PJ Badenhorst *et al*, *Silberberg & Schoeman's The Law of Property* (5th edn, 2006) at 433.

[123] Rule 6 of the High Court Rules does not allow ex parte applications for eviction; see JM Pienaar, 'Recent Developments Relating to Automatic Review Proceedings in the Land Claims Court' (2001) 34 *De Jure* 162–71 at 169. See ch 3, n 20. Similar due process rules applied under the Rent Control Act 80 of 1976, but as was pointed out above, this Act had limited application.

[124] Eviction control forms part of tenure reform, one of the three pillars of post-1994 land reform in South Africa. It is intended to ensure that individuals and groups from disadvantaged communities who do have access to land do not lose it unnecessarily, unfairly or in an arbitrary manner. The other pillars (restitution—giving back land rights taken away under apartheid—and redistribution—improving access to land) return or redistribute state or private land to claimants; tenure reform adjusts and strengthens previously weak or vulnerable use and occupation rights. See Department of Land Affairs, *White Paper on South African Land Policy* (1997) at heading 2.3 'The three elements of the land reform programme' at http://land.pwv.gov.za/legislation_policies/white_papers/_docs/White%20Paper%20land%20policy.doc (11 March 2008). For an overview of land reform laws compare G Budlender *et al*, *Juta's New Land Law* (1998) *passim*; D Carey Miller (with A Pope), *Land Title in South Africa* (2000) 282–555; AJ van der Walt, 'Property Rights and Hierarchies of Power: A Critical Evaluation of Land-Reform Policy in South Africa' (1999) 64 *Koers* 259–94 at 281; AJ van der Walt, *Constitutional Property Law* (2005) 308–53.

[125] Section 25(6) (read with s 25(9)) of the Constitution places an obligation on the state to improve security of tenure by way of appropriate legislation: 'A person or community whose tenure of land is legally insecure as a result of past racially discriminatory laws or practices is entitled, to the extent provided by an Act of Parliament, either to tenure which is legally secure or to comparable redress.' See D Carey Miller (with A Pope), *Land Title in South Africa* (2000) at 456–61; compare the Department of Land Affairs, *White Paper on South African Land Policy* (1997) at ch 10 for a summary of the principles that drive government policy on tenure reform.

needs and by imposing restrictions on eviction of vulnerable occupiers.[126] Part of this process involves providing (permanent or temporary) security of tenure for weak and marginalised persons and families who lawfully occupy urban and rural land for residential purposes, inter alia by imposing both substantive restrictions and procedural controls over eviction of these occupiers. A number of laws have been promulgated in compliance with this constitutional obligation.[127] Some of these reform laws subject evictions, in so far as they are allowed within the new constitutional framework, to procedural controls; others impose substantive restrictions by either making eviction impossible or rendering it more difficult to obtain an eviction order against certain kinds of occupiers and under certain circumstances or by imposing restrictions on the termination of the lease in the first place.

The general principle of tenure reform is complemented by two provisions in section 26 of the Constitution. Firstly, section 26(1), which (read together with section 26(2)) places an obligation on the state progressively to increase access to housing within its budget, has been interpreted to establish a so-called negative obligation, placed upon the state, to desist from action that would unnecessarily deprive persons who already have housing from their occupation rights.[128] This negative obligation weighs against eviction of people who already have access to housing and who would, if evicted, become homeless and increase the already heavy burden of providing housing to the homeless. However, until now the negative obligation has been employed mostly to counter eviction of unlawful occupiers; it is not entirely clear how it could strengthen tenants' rights against eviction, except in the general sense of supporting the promulgation of tenant protection legislation. The third relevant constitutional provision is the general anti-eviction provision in section 26(3), which determines that no one may be evicted from their home[129] without a court order; that a court order shall only be granted 'after considering all the relevant circumstances'; and that no law shall

---

[126] See DL Carey Miller (with A Pope), *Land Title in South Africa* (2000) at 155; AJ van der Walt, *Constitutional Property Law* (2005) at 308.

[127] The most important are the Land Reform (Labour Tenants) Act 3 of 1996, the Communal Property Associations Act 28 of 1996, the Extension of Security of Tenure Act 62 of 1997 (ESTA), the Prevention of Illegal Eviction from and Unlawful Occupation of Land Act 19 of 1998 (PIE), the Rental Housing Act 50 of 1999 and the Communal Land Rights Act 11 of 2004. See AJ van der Walt, *Constitutional Property Law* (2005) at 308–38 for an overview of the legislation.

[128] See particularly *Government of the Republic of South Africa and Others v Grootboom and Others* 2001 (1) SA 46 (CC) at para 46; confirmed and followed in *Jaftha v Schoeman and Others; Van Rooyen v Stoltz and Others* 2005 (2) SA 140 (CC) at paras 25–6; see further S Liebenberg, 'The Right to Social Assistance: The Implications of *Grootboom* for Policy Reform in South Africa' (2001) 17 *SAJHR* 232–57.

[129] The provision applies to homes only and not to non-residential property or structures: *Ndlovu v Ngcobo; Bekker and Another v Jika* 2003 (1) SA 113 (SCA) at para 20; *Mangaung Local Municipality v Mashale and Another* 2006 (1) SA 269 (O), at para 11. The question whether a particular structure is a 'home' is controversial, but it has to be determined as a matter as fact and not of law, which means that the lawfulness of the occupation and compliance with legal requirements for residential property cannot be decisive.

permit arbitrary evictions.[130] Section 26(3) must now be seen as the constitutional source of the due process rule in South African law as far as eviction is concerned: nobody may be evicted without a court order; a court order allowing eviction may not be given unless the court has considered all the circumstances; and no law may permit arbitrary eviction. This provision is also the main inspiration behind and authority for the anti-eviction provisions in a wide range of post-1994 land-reform laws.

Given the seemingly explicit nature of the provision, one might expect it to have a direct and forcible bearing on all eviction cases, but to date the constitutional anti-eviction provision has not by itself brought about a substantial departure from the pre-constitutional position in case-law, where the rights paradigm proved more resilient than might have been expected. The most troubling issue has been to determine the impact and effect of section 26(3)—like section 25(5), it has had a marked influence on the promulgation of new legislation but, unlike the so-called negative obligation that has been distilled from section 26(1), section 26(3) has had little or no direct impact on eviction disputes outside of eviction of unlawful occupiers of land. On the face of it, one might expect that the anti-eviction principle in section 26(3) of the Constitution should be the point of departure in all eviction disputes[131] and that all evictions, whether based on the common law or on the land-reform laws and whether dealing with lawful or unlawful occupiers, should be subject to its apparently general and direct pro-hibitory and regulatory language. Direct application of section 26(3) would bring about a significant qualification of the rights paradigm because it would transform the apparently strong right of a landowner to evict any occupier, without having to give reasons, unless the occupier can prove an enforceable occupation right, into a discretionary right that could be refused by a court on the basis of consid-erations wholly outside of the owner's control or even knowledge. The High Courts have signalled uncertainty about their power, in the absence of much clearer legislation, to exercise such a dramatic impact on common law rights, and the Supreme Court of Appeal has opted for a safer, more familiar interpretation that upheld the common law as far as possible, insulating it from a significant par-adigm shift inspired by the Constitution.

The most difficult question has been whether section 26(3) applies directly to landlord–tenant situations. As could be expected in a constitutional text, section 26(3) is couched in general terms and it does not indicate whether it applies to eviction of lawful or unlawful occupiers; what the circumstances are that have to

---

[130] Section 26(3) provides: 'No one may be evicted from their home, or have their home demol-ished, without an order of court made after considering all the relevant circumstances. No legislation may permit arbitrary evictions.' On s 26(3) see T Roux, 'Continuity and Change in a Transforming Legal Order: The Impact of Section 26(3) of the Constitution on South African Law' (2004) 121 *SALJ* 466–92; AJ van der Walt, *Constitutional Property Law* (2005) at 308–11, 416–18.

[131] See s 8(1) of the Constitution: 'The Bill of Rights [chapter 2 of the Constitution] applies to all law and binds the legislature, the executive, the judiciary, and al organs of state;' compare AJ van der Walt, 'Exclusivity of Ownership, Security of Tenure, and Eviction Orders: A Critical Evaluation of Recent Case Law' (2002) 18 *SAJHR* 372–420.

be considered by a court before granting an eviction order; or whether it applies directly or is supposed to be mediated by legislation. Most importantly, the provision does not make it clear that it grants courts the discretion to refuse an eviction order on any of the circumstances that have to be considered. Theunis Roux has pointed out that it is plausible to read section 26(3) restrictively, to the effect that a court hearing an application for an eviction order can consider nothing more than the common law requirements, but that it is equally plausible to read the provision in any of the other more expansive interpretations suggested by Geoff Budlender.[132] As Roux has shown, the most interesting interpretation implies that the common law was amended by section 26(3), the only question being whether the amendment merely changes the pleading requirements and/or onus of proof with regard to additional circumstances or whether it grants the courts the discretion to refuse or stay execution of an eviction order.[133] In either case the amendment of the common law and the concomitant qualification of the rights paradigm would be significant. However, in reality the courts were hesitant to adopt the alternative interpretations identified by Budlender,[134] at least as far as the landlord–tenant situation is concerned, instead opting for a more conventional approach that pushed section 26(3) into the background and allowed the common law to continue dominating eviction proceedings in so far as the situation had not been amended explicitly or clearly by legislation. At least as far as the landlord–tenant relationship is concerned, section 26(3) was not considered clear enough to amend the common law significantly and, accordingly, in the landlord–tenant context the presumptive power of the rights paradigm survived the direct impact of the constitutional provision.

The decision that prevented section 26(3) from having immediate or direct effect was *Brisley v Drotsky*.[135] Initially, the Supreme Court of Appeal Court held that section 26(3) of the Constitution was horizontally enforceable[136] and that an eviction order may indeed only be granted once all relevant circumstances have been considered. This part of the decision creates the impression that a significant departure from the ownership paradigm was about to take place, but the Court further decided that section 26(3) did not clearly grant the courts the discretion to deprive a landowner of an eviction order that she would have been entitled to at common law, simply because the personal circumstances of the occupier and her

---

[132] T Roux, 'Continuity and Change in a Transforming Legal Order: The Impact of Section 26(3) of the Constitution on South African Law' (2004) 121 *SALJ* 466–92 at 473, referring to G Budlender, 'Justiciability of the Right to Housing: The South African Experience' in S Leckie (ed) *National Perspectives on Housing Rights* (2003) 207–19 at 210–12.

[133] T Roux, 'Continuity and Change in a Transforming Legal Order: The Impact of Section 26(3) of the Constitution on South African Law' (2004) 121 *SALJ* 466–92 at 474.

[134] See the discussion and references below; T Roux, 'Continuity and Change in a Transforming Legal Order: The Impact of Section 26(3) of the Constitution on South African Law' (2004) 121 *SALJ* 466–92 at 475–92 analyses and discuses the cases at greater length and in detail, but comes to similar conclusions.

[135] 2002 (4) SA 1 (SCA) at paras 35–46. The case deals only with the effect of s 26(3) and not with any of the land reform laws.

[136] *Brisley v Drotsky* 2002 (4) SA 1 (SCA) at paras 39–40.

family or the availability of alternative accommodation might weigh against eviction. In the absence of explicit statutory provisions, the personal circumstances of the occupier and the availability of alternative accommodation are therefore not 'relevant circumstances' that section 26(3) forces or allows the courts to take into consideration when deciding whether to grant an eviction order.[137] Effectively, the decision therefore confirms that section 26(3) did not bring about a paradigm shift—any real changes would have to be engineered by more specific legislation.

The point of departure in *Brisley* was the rights paradigm's preference for the status quo as it is stabilised by the established rules and practices of the common law: A landowner is entitled to possession and hence to eviction, and in the absence of a clear legal or statutory right of occupation this entitlement (and the right to evict based on it) cannot be denied purely because of the occupier's personal situation or the unavailability of alternative accommodation. The decision set the tone for a common law-based approach that inhibits the transformative effect of section 26(3) of the Constitution, requiring unambiguous statutory authority for any amendment of the common law right of a landowner to obtain an eviction order purely on the strength of her stronger right. The Supreme Court of Appeal has overturned decisions that displayed judicial resistance against land reform and can therefore not be accused of judicial obstructionism,[138] but the *Brisley* decision did nothing to dispel the impression that the common law continues to be the subsidiary law that applies unless it is excluded or amended explicitly.[139] The position at common law is taken as given, as clear and fair, which implies that the property holdings protected by it are normal, to be upheld unless the opposite is proven.[140] The effect is failure to acknowledge the reformist view of law as a social construct and an instrument of social and political power; and it denies the role that property law and eviction law played in the construction and entrenchment of apartheid hierarchies of privilege and poverty, power and marginality that still characterise South African society. At least as far as the landlord–tenant situation is concerned, the *Brisley* decision refused to acknowledge the demand in section 26(3) for a direct, significant and decisive transformative qualification of the rights paradigm.[141]

---

[137] *Brisley v Drotsky* 2002 (4) SA 1 (SCA) at paras 42–6; Olivier JA dissenting at para 87.

[138] In *Joubert and Others v Van Rensburg and Others* 2001 (1) SA 753 (W) the trial court reasoned that existing land rights had to be upheld against a perceived threat of land invasion and lawlessness, which was associated with land reform. In *Mkangeli and Others v Joubert and Others* 2002 (4) SA 36 (SCA) at para 24 the Supreme Court of Appeal repudiated the remarks of the trial court concerning the suitability of the Act, stating that these remarks were unwarranted and 'should have been avoided': para 25. See further *Magodi and Others v Van Rensburg* [2001] 4 All SA 485 (LCC).

[139] Eg *Joubert and Others v Van Rensburg and Others* 2001 (1) SA 753 (W) at para 25.4.2.

[140] In *Betta Eiendomme (Pty) Ltd v Ekple-Epoh* 2000 (4) SA 468 (W) this attitude is clear: para 6.2. See further *Ellis v Viljoen* 2001 (4) SA 795 (C) at 805E–H.

[141] In the subsequent decision of the Constitutional Court in *Port Elizabeth Municipality v Various Occupiers* 2005 (1) SA 217 (CC), Sachs J noted that the considerations that required a court to grant an eviction order at common law now 'merely trigger the court's discretion' and that the courts can no longer 'establish a hierarchical arrangement between the different interests involved, privileging in an abstract and mechanical way the rights of ownership over the right not to be dispossessed of a home' (para 23). This remark may well have been directed at the Supreme Court of Appeal's decision in

Apart from the constitutional provisions, the common law position with regard to eviction was amended by a number of land reform laws. Generally, the courts have been less hesitant to recognise and apply the changes brought about by legislation. This is hardly surprising, since the relevant legislation is more detailed and specific, thereby overcoming the objections that have been levelled against direct application of section 26(3). Since 1996 a range of anti-eviction provisions has been promulgated, in different land reform laws, to control eviction and promote security of tenure according to the constitutional anti-eviction principle.[142] Despite a general lack of coordination, the anti-eviction provisions in the land reform laws display a shared policy with regard to the question when eviction should be allowed and how it should be controlled and carried out. The main features of these control measures can be summarised as follows:[143] Existing occupation rights must be terminated lawfully and fairly before eviction can even be considered; and when eviction is allowed (either when the occupation was always unlawful or after existing occupation rights have been terminated lawfully and fairly), it must be authorised by a court order and, once such an order has been obtained, its execution is subject to strict procedural requirements.

Like the German and English measures discussed earlier, these laws impose both due process and substantive controls over eviction. The due process controls impose notice and time requirements on landowners to ensure that eviction is carried out only when it has been authorised by a court that has considered all the circumstances and that the occupiers are given a fair opportunity to defend themselves. These procedural controls qualify the presumptive power of the rights paradigm but do not necessarily challenge or subvert its logic—the availability of eviction remains largely in the hands of the landowner who, despite being subjected to stricter procedural requirements, is still entitled to an eviction order provided she satisfies the common law substantive requirements and the new statutory due process standards.

However, some land reform laws shift the adjudication of occupation conflicts away from a mechanical process dominated by landownership trumps towards a substantive process aimed at fairness in the larger socio-economic and political context. In terms of the anti-eviction provision in section 26(3) of the Constitution (and

Brisley, but *Port Elizabeth Municipality* dealt with eviction in terms of the Prevention of Illegal Eviction from and Unlawful Occupation of Land Act 19 of 1998 and therefore it can be distinguished from eviction cases involving lawful occupiers such as tenants.

[142] The land reform statutes generally define 'eviction' widely to include actions that have the effect of terminating, frustrating or effectively preventing some aspect of the normal occupation and use of the premises: s 1 of the Land Reform (Labour Tenants) Act 3 of 1996 defines 'eviction' to include 'the deprivation of a right of occupation or use of land'; s 1 of the Extension of Security of Tenure Act 62 of 1997 defines 'evict' as 'to deprive a person against his or her will of residence on land or the use of land or access to water which is linked to a right of residence in terms of this Act'; s 1 of the Prevention of Illegal Eviction from and Unlawful Occupation of Land Act 19 of 1998 defines 'evict' as 'to deprive a person of occupation of a building or structure, or the land on which such building or structure is erected, against his or her will'.

[143] AJ van der Walt, 'Exclusivity of Ownership, Security of Tenure, and Eviction Orders: A Model to Evaluate South African Land-Reform Legislation' (2002) *TSAR* 254–89.

in the land reform laws promulgated in accordance with it), the granting of eviction orders is only possible after due consideration has been given to relevant circumstances, which are sometimes set out in some detail, including the social and economic context and the personal circumstances of the occupiers, even when they are occupying the plaintiff's land unlawfully.[144] In at least two pieces of legislation, the Extension of Security of Tenure Act 62 of 1997 and the Prevention of Illegal Eviction from and Unlawful Occupation of Land Act 19 of 1998, the circumstances that have to be considered are spelled out in some detail, thereby overcoming the objections raised in *Brisley*. The courts have been more willing to exercise their discretion to refuse an eviction order in applying these laws and have refused or suspended an eviction order if the circumstances indicated that granting it might be unjustifiable. At least in principle these provisions create the possibility that a court can refuse to grant an eviction order simply because of the weak, vulnerable or marginal position of the occupiers, thereby removing the success of the eviction application from the exclusive control of the landowner and out of the logic of the rights paradigm. By requiring the courts to consider the social context and the personal circumstances of occupiers before granting an eviction order, the anti-eviction provisions qualify the rights paradigm, sometimes even radically:[145] The landowner can lose an eviction struggle because of considerations that are out of her control, and therefore the value and strength of ownership is no longer the only or the central consideration in allowing an eviction. Instead, considerations that are deemed marginal or irrelevant in the rights paradigm, such as the social or economic status and circumstances of the occupier and the availability of alternative accommodation, can influence the decision whether to allow eviction in a specific case. This represents a significant qualification of and perhaps even a challenge to the rights paradigm.

However, when the legislation fails to make it clear that it intends to amend the common law situation in a specified way, the courts have rarely been willing to depart from the ownership-friendly common law position. The judicial attitude seems to be that when the common law is not excluded explicitly it is not clear how the anti-eviction principle should apply or, more particularly, how it should

---

[144] Of the land-reform laws that include anti-eviction measures, the Extension of Security of Tenure Act 62 of 1997 and the Rental Housing Act 50 of 1999 are intended specifically to protect lawful occupiers. By contrast, the Prevention of Illegal Eviction from and Unlawful Occupation of Land Act 19 of 1998 is specifically designed to assist and protect unlawful occupiers. The latter situation is discussed in ch 5.

[145] The landlord–tenant legislation that most clearly illustrates this move away from the ownership paradigm is the Extension of Security of Tenure Act 62 of 1997, which (in addition to procedural safeguards) provides that eviction may be allowed only when existing permission to occupy agricultural land has been cancelled lawfully in terms of the Act and requires that certain substantive requirements be met before permission to occupy may be cancelled lawfully. The substantive reasons for an eviction are considered with reference to a distinction between occupiers who already had consent to occupy on 4 February 1997 (s 10) and occupiers who acquired consent only afterwards (s 11). Occupiers who had consent to occupy before 4 February 1997 may in certain instances be evicted only if alternative accommodation is available; in other circumstances eviction may be slightly easier for the landowner. See in general AJ van der Walt, 'Exclusivity of Ownership, Security of Tenure, and Eviction Orders: A Model to Evaluate South African Land-Reform Legislation' 2002 *TSAR* 254–89 at 275–81 for an overview; compare T Roux, 'Chapter 7: The Extension of Security of Tenure Act' in G Budlender *et al*, *Juta's New Land Law* (1998) at 7A-17-26. See the discussion below.

influence the common law in a given situation and then the common law is applied. The statute that made its intention to change the common law the clearest, the Prevention of Illegal Eviction from and Unlawful Occupation of Land Act 19 of 1998, applies to unlawful occupation of land and is therefore not obviously applicable to landlord–tenant cases; obvious landlord–tenant legislation is less clear about its effect on the common law and therefore had less direct impact. Consequently, case-law initially displayed a striking lack of consensus on the impact that the anti-eviction laws should have on the common law in 'normal' landlord–tenant cases. The result was that landlord–tenant evictions were not consistently subjected to the new anti-eviction framework as set out in either the Constitution or the legislation. As should perhaps be expected, landowners are often unaware of (or simply ignore) the land reform laws and continue to apply for eviction in terms of the common law—traditional attitudes favour proceeding in terms of the common law, where the landowner-plaintiff knows exactly what is required when suing for eviction, whereas the land reform laws could complicate the landowner-plaintiff's case. The high courts' initial reaction to the questions that ensued was uncertain and evasive. When questions about the priority of common law or statutory law were raised the courts often restricted their decisions to practical matters such as jurisdiction[146] and burden of proof rather than entering into the difficult substantive issues.[147]

The major question in landlord–tenant eviction cases was whether a landowner can elect to institute eviction proceedings in terms of common law or whether she is bound to do so in terms of one of the land reform laws. In cases where the occupiers were unlawful land invaders who settled on the land without any right to do so, the courts have no difficulty in applying the Prevention of Illegal Eviction from and Unlawful Occupation of Land Act 19 of 1998 (PIE) rather than the common law,[148]

---

[146] Different courts have jurisdiction with regard to different land reform laws, and the landowner might find it difficult in some instances to decide in which forum to institute the application. See AJ van der Walt, 'Exclusivity of Ownership, Security of Tenure, and Eviction Orders: A Model to Evaluate South African Land-Reform Legislation' 2002 *TSAR* 254–89 at 263–89; A Gildenhuys, 'Evictions: A Quagmire for the Unwary' *Butterworths Property Law Digest* (Sep 1999) 5–11 at 11.

[147] Land reform laws invariably set higher standards of proof than the common law and require additional information that is often not readily available to the landowner. Furthermore, the landowner might not want to admit indirectly, by proceeding in a certain forum and in terms of a certain statute, that the occupier enjoys or enjoyed a certain protected status (eg as residential tenant or labour tenant). See AJ van der Walt, 'Exclusivity of Ownership, Security of Tenure, and Eviction Orders: A Critical Evaluation of Recent Case Law' (2002) 18 *SAJHR* 372–420.

[148] See s 4(1) of the Prevention of Illegal Eviction from and Unlawful Occupation of Land Act 19 of 1998: 'Notwithstanding anything to the contrary contained in any law or the common law, the provisions of this section apply to proceedings by an owner or person in charge of land for the eviction of an unlawful occupier.' Compare s 13(10) of the Rental Housing Act 50 of 1999: 'Nothing herein contained precludes any person from approaching a competent court for urgent relief under circumstances where he or she would have been able to do so were it not for this Act, or to institute proceedings for the normal recovery of arrear rental, or for eviction in the absence of a dispute regarding an unfair practice.' In *Kendall Property Investments v Rutgers* [2005] 4 All SA 61 (C) the court held that the landlord must prove that the lease has been terminated, that such termination was not an unfair practice and that the grounds of termination are specific to the lease, thereby creating the impression that the common law can prevail only in limited and circumscribed situations; see ch 2, n 41. See further AJ van der Walt,

but since the land reform laws dealing with tenants—who are lawful occupiers—do not override the common law explicitly, complications arise when a landowner wants to evict occupiers who occupy or have at some stage previously occupied the property lawfully but whose occupation has become unlawful. This question primarily arose in situations of holding over, where former tenants failed to vacate the premises after the lease had expired or been cancelled. In a series of decisions the High Courts granted common law eviction orders against former tenants who were holding over, arguing that the Prevention of Illegal Eviction from and Unlawful Occupation of Land Act 19 of 1998 (PIE) was not intended to apply to them[149] and that none of the other land reform laws that could apply explicitly overrules the common law.

In the absence of clear provisions to override the common law, the applicability of other land-reform laws—apart from PIE—and their impact on the common law was a moot point. The argument that won the day stated that PIE overrides the common law explicitly but does not apply to holding over, while the other land reform laws could apply to specific lawful occupiers but do not explicitly override the common law. In principle, lawful occupiers of rural land (many of whom would qualify as residential tenants) could enjoy the protection of the Extension of Security of Tenure Act 62 of 1997 (ESTA), but it was decided in several cases that ESTA does not deprive a landowner of the possibility of evicting occupiers in terms of the common law, because the Act prescribes its own eviction requirements and procedures but does not override the common law explicitly.[150] Similarly, occupiers of urban and rural rental property could be protected by the Rental Housing Act 50 of 1999, which requires a rental lease to be terminated in accordance with the Act before eviction may take place. However, it may be possible to evict urban residential tenants from rental housing in terms of the common law as well, because the Rental Housing Act does not override the common law explicitly either.[151] In

'Exclusivity of Ownership, Security of Tenure, and Eviction Orders: A Critical Evaluation of Recent Case Law' (2002) 18 *SAJHR* 372–420.

[149] The most important cases are *ABSA Bank Ltd v Amod* [1999] 2 All SA 423 (W); *Ellis v Viljoen* 2001 (4) SA 795 (C); *Betta Eiendomme (Pty) Ltd v Ekple-Epoh* 2000 (4) SA 468 (W). In *Bekker and Another v Jika* [2001] 4 All SA 573 (SEC) the High Court held that PIE did apply to holding over; this decision was eventually upheld on appeal in the decision that settled the matter as far as unlawful occupiers are concerned: *Ndlovu v Ngcobo; Bekker v Jika* 2003 (1) SA 113 (SCA) (see the discussion below, compare ch 5). In *Ross v South Peninsula Municipality* 2000 (1) SA 589 (C) the court decided *obiter* that PIE applied to 'normal' rent situations. Compare AJ van der Walt, 'Exclusivity of Ownership, Security of Tenure, and Eviction Orders: A Critical Evaluation of Recent Case Law' (2002) 18 *SAJHR* 372–420 at 375–90; T Roux, 'Continuity and Change in a Transforming Legal Order: The Impact of Section 26(3) of the Constitution on South African Law' (2004) 121 *SALJ* 466–92; JM Pienaar and H Mostert, 'Uitsettings onder die Suid-Afrikaanse Grondwet: Die Verhouding tussen Artikel 25(1), Artikel 26(3) en die Uitsettingswet (Deel 1)' 2006 *TSAR* 277–99 at 281–95.

[150] The relevant cases are *Skhosana and Others v Roos t/a Roos se Oord and Others* 2000 (4) SA 561 (LCC); *Khuzwayo v Dludla* 2001 (1) SA 714 (LCC).

[151] The Act does not explicitly exclude the common law. The landlord's rights against the tenant are set out in s 4(5), the phrasing of which could indicate that the landlord's common law rights, where they have not been amended or excluded, remain in force. See *Batchelor v Gabie* 2002 (2) SA 51 (SCA); compare A Mukheiber, 'The Effect of the Rental Housing Act 50 of 1999 on the Common Law of Landlord and Tenant' (2000) 21 *Obiter* 325–50 at 329.

effect, therefore, it is not entirely clear that anti-eviction provisions in land reform laws that apply to lawful occupiers protect former tenants who are holding over; instead, the common law seems to be available to landowners in all or most of these situations. Given the choice, landowners prefer to proceed according to the common law, if only because they and their lawyers are more familiar with it and the land reform laws impose stricter, time-consuming and costly controls. The result was that lawful occupiers whose occupation became contested found themselves in a worse position than unlawful land invaders in that they could be denied the substantive and procedural protection that the land reform laws offer against eviction. In the process the effect of the anti-eviction principle in section 26(3) of the Constitution on landlord–tenant evictions was restricted because it had been decided in *Brisley* that this principle could only amend the common law and impose regulatory controls upon landowners indirectly, through legislation that applies to landlord–tenant relationships and that overrides the common law explicitly or by necessary implication. In so far as the applicable legislation does not exclude common law evictions either, the effect of section 26(3) is very limited indeed.

On the face of it, the decision in *Brisley v Drotsky* to the effect that section 26(3) applies horizontally could have solved the problem.[152] However, in *Brisley* the court was concerned only with the direct effect of section 26(3) and not with any of the land reform laws. Eventually, the Supreme Court of Appeal settled the matter in *Ndlovu v Ngcobo/Bekker v Jika*,[153] deciding that the anti-eviction provisions in the Prevention of Illegal Eviction from and Unlawful Occupation of Land Act 19 of 1998 (PIE) indeed applied to a tenant who is holding over subsequent to the lawful termination of his lease. The majority of the court decided that it could not be discounted that the legislature intended to extend the applicability of PIE to holding over by tenants and similar occupiers whose right of occupation had been terminated or expired.[154] This decision attracted a great deal of criticism, especially in the popular press, because of the threat it was said to pose for the residential housing market. At the time of writing, amending legislation was being prepared to regularise the situation by determining when PIE and other related legislation apply to 'normal' landlord–tenant and similar situations of holding over, where the occupier's occupation of the premises was initially lawful.[155]

In the end, the two reform laws that affect residential tenants directly (apart from eviction of tenants holding over) are the Extension of Security of Tenure Act 62 of 1997 (ESTA), which applies to lawful occupiers of rural land,[156] and the

---

[152] 2002 (4) SA 1 (SCA) at paras 35–46.

[153] 2003 (1) SA 113 (SCA).

[154] 2003 (1) SA 113 (SCA) at paras 21–3.

[155] The legislature has been working on amending legislation since 2006, but nothing final has been produced yet. See ch 5, n 67.

[156] The Extension of Security of Tenure Act 62 of 1997 applies only to land outside the urban areas, ie rural and peri-urban land which is used for non-commercial purposes (s 2) and provides security of tenure to lawful occupiers of agricultural land. T Roux, 'Chapter 7: The Extension of Security of Tenure Act' in G Budlender *et al, Juta's New Land Law* (1998) at 7A-3 has said that the Act treats the relationship between owners and lawful occupiers of agricultural land as one between traditional landlords and tenants. The Act allows eviction only once existing rights to occupy have been terminated lawfully and

Rental Housing Act 50 of 1999, which applies to residential leases.[157] The Extension of Security of Tenure Act 62 of 1997 (ESTA) protects lawful occupiers of rural land against eviction by firstly regulating the termination of their permission to occupy and secondly imposing due process controls over eviction, once termination is allowed.[158] The major premise of the Act is that eviction is allowed only once existing rights to occupy have been terminated lawfully, in accordance with the Act (as described below); lawful and fair termination of occupation rights must precede eviction. Section 6 ensures that occupiers who resided on and used land on 4 February 1997 can continue exercising their rights unless the tenancy is terminated, on lawful grounds, provided that contractual requirements and the fairness requirements in the Act are complied with.[159] Factors that should be taken into account in deciding whether termination of an occupation right is fair are specified in the Act, and special requirements apply to certain categories such as occupiers whose rights of residence arise solely from employment contracts, long-term protected occupiers,[160] and family members and dependants of long-term

---

in accordance with the strict procedural requirements in the Act; if termination of existing occupation rights complies with contractual and fairness requirements in the Act; and if a court order has been obtained to authorise the eviction: ss 6(1), 8(1), 9(1). The Act is intended to benefit occupiers who have permission (or on 4 February 1997 or thereafter have had permission) to occupy land belonging to someone else. The scope of the Act is restricted in that it applies mainly to rural and peri-urban areas; it excludes labour tenants, persons who use or intend to use the land in question mainly for industrial, mining, commercial or commercial farming purposes and persons with an income exceeding a specified amount per month. See s 1(1) of the Act. See in general AJ van der Walt, 'Exclusivity of Ownership, Security of Tenure, and Eviction Orders: A Model to Evaluate South African Land-Reform Legislation' 2002 *TSAR* 254–89 at 275–81 for an overview; compare T Roux, 'Chapter 7: The Extension of Security of Tenure Act' in G Budlender *et al, Juta's New Land Law* (1998) at 7A-17-26.

[157] The Rental Housing Act 50 of 1999 provides that tenants of rental housing may be evicted only once the lease has been terminated lawfully. The Act does not specify that it applies to urban land only, but it is restricted to rental property for residential purposes and will therefore largely affect residential property on urban land. A landlord has the right to terminate a lease in respect of rental housing property on grounds that are specified in the lease, provided they do not constitute an unfair practice as defined in the Act: s 4(5)(c). Eviction is possible provided that a court order has been obtained first, and a court order can only be obtained once the lease has been terminated in accordance with the contract and the requirements in the Act. See in general AJ van der Walt, 'Exclusivity of Ownership, Security of Tenure, and Eviction Orders: A Model to Evaluate South African Land-Reform Legislation' 2002 *TSAR* 254–89 at 275–81 for an overview; compare T Roux, 'Chapter 7: The Extension of Security of Tenure Act' in G Budlender, J Latsky and T Roux *Juta's New Land Law* (1998) at 7A-17-26.

[158] Chapter IV. See in general AJ van der Walt, 'Exclusivity of Ownership, Security of Tenure, and Eviction Orders: A Model to Evaluate South African Land-Reform Legislation' 2002 *TSAR* 254–89 at 275–82; AJ van der Walt, *Constitutional Property Law* (2005) at 318–19.

[159] Section 8. See AJ van der Walt, 'Exclusivity of Ownership, Security of Tenure, and Eviction Orders: A Model to Evaluate South African Land-Reform Legislation' 2002 *TSAR* 254–89 at 276; AJ van der Walt, *Constitutional Property Law* (2005) at 319–20.

[160] This category consists of persons who have resided on the land in question or other land belonging to the same owner for at least 10 years and who have either reached the age of 60 or are employees or former employees who have become unable to supply labour because of ill health or disability. See AJ van der Walt, 'Exclusivity of Ownership, Security of Tenure, and Eviction Orders: A Model to Evaluate South African Land-Reform Legislation' 2002 *TSAR* 254–89 at 276–7, fn 113; AJ van der Walt, *Constitutional Property Law* (2005) at 319–20.

protected occupiers.[161] Once occupation rights have been terminated lawfully and in accordance with the Act it becomes possible for the landowner or person in charge of the land to evict the occupiers, but only on the authority of a court order, and even then the eviction process is subjected to fairness requirements set out in the Act.[162] Four requirements are laid down for an eviction under the Act: The occupier's occupation right must have been terminated in accordance with the Act; the occupier must not have vacated the premises voluntarily; the substantive grounds for an eviction in the Act (set out earlier) must be satisfied; and the mandatory notice and other due process requirements must have been met. The protection offered by the Act is strong, although it does allow farm owners to cancel labour contracts and then terminate the housing rights of their former labourers as long as they proceed in accordance with the Act.

Section 28 of the Rent Control Act 80 of 1976 provided that, as long as a tenant continued to pay the agreed rent within seven days after the termination of the lease and continued to comply with other terms of the lease, a court could not order ejectment of the tenant or repossession of the premises by the landlord unless certain circumstances prevailed.[163] The effect was that the tenant became a statutory tenant when the lease expired, similar to the position in English and German legislation with regard to certain categories of tenants. However, the effect of the Rent Control Act was always limited because of its restricted application, and the Act was eventually repealed by the Rental Housing Act 50 of 1999.[164] The new Rental Housing Act also restricts landlords' right to terminate a lease. According to section 4(5)(c) of the Rental Housing Act 50 of 1999, the landlord has the right to terminate the lease on grounds that do not constitute an unfair practice and that are specified in the lease.[165] Termination of the lease is therefore placed under statutory control, much as in the case of English and German law, and termination for certain reasons (labelled unfair practice) is prohibited. The Act allows fixed-term tenancies to continue as periodic tenancies under certain

---

[161] On the special requirements see T Roux, 'Chapter 7: The Extension of Security of Tenure Act' in G Budlender *et al, Juta's New Land Law* (1998) at 7A-20–7A-27. On the position of family members see *Conradie v Hanekom* 1999 (4) SA 491 (LCC); *Dique NO v Van der Merwe* 2001 (2) SA 1006 (T); T Roux, 'Pro-Poor Court, Anti-Poor Outcomes: Explaining the Performance of the South African Land Claims Court' (2004) 20 *SAJHR* 511–43 at 525–7.

[162] Section 9. The Supreme Court of Appeal held in *Mpedi and Others v Swanevelder and Another* 2004 (4) 344 (SCA) at para 1 that even lawful termination of the right of residence does not entail eviction as of right; the court must still determine whether the requirements for granting an eviction order have been satisfied. See further AJ van der Walt, 'Exclusivity of Ownership, Security of Tenure, and Eviction Orders: A Model to Evaluate South African Land-Reform Legislation' 2002 *TSAR* 254–89 at 277; AJ van der Walt, *Constitutional Property Law* (2005) at 320.

[163] Section 28(a)–(d); compare E Kahn *et al, Principles of the Law of Sale and Lease* (1998) at 96, 97.

[164] Section 18. See n 115 above.

[165] See s 15(1)(f) for a list of unfair practices; the most salient ones are causing damage to the property; causing a nuisance; unlawful activities on the premises; overcrowding and health threats; and the landlord's intention to demolish and convert the property. According to s 13(9), any dispute in respect of an unfair practice must be determined by the tribunal (instituted in terms of s 7) unless proceedings have already been instituted in any other court. See PHJ Thomas, 'The Rental Housing Act' (2000) 33 *De Jure* 235–47 at 244–7; A Mukheiber, 'The Effect of the Rental Housing Act 50 of 1999 on the Common Law of Landlord and Tenant' (2000) 21 *Obiter* 325–50 at 343.

(very limited) circumstances, thereby protecting the occupation interests of persons who already have access to housing against unnecessary termination. Normally, the landlord is entitled to terminate a fixed-term lease without good reason; renewal is subject to consent from both parties.[166] However, if the tenant remains in the dwelling on expiration of a fixed-term lease with the consent (express or tacit) of the landlord, the parties are deemed to have entered into a periodic lease on the same terms and conditions as the expired lease; at least one month's written notice must then be given by either party of their intention to terminate the lease.[167] This continuation provision is more restricted than the examples from English and German law referred to earlier, because (express or implied) consent from the landlord is required. In line with the tendency elsewhere, eviction of tenants is possible only once the lease has been terminated lawfully in terms of the Act, and then only in accordance with prescribed due process requirements. It has been confirmed in case-law that the Rental Housing Act 50 of 1999 restricts a landowner's common law right, as against tenants, in pursuance of the state's constitutional housing mandate in section 26[168] and also that the Act establishes a fair balance between the interests of the landowner and the tenant in exercising its constitutional obligation towards housing.

Apart from the two statutes discussed above, the Interim Protection of Informal Land Rights Act 31 of 1996 also protects the rights of a range of holders of so-called informal land rights by providing that these occupiers of land may not be deprived of their rights without their consent.[169] In effect the Act merely prevents cancellation or termination of really weak and vulnerable occupation rights created under apartheid land law. These rights are nothing more than precarious licences to occupy; they can be terminated, without reason, unilaterally by the landowner; accordingly, regulatory control can establish only the flimsiest due process controls. The Land Reform (Labour Tenants) Act 3 of 1996 protects a specific category of persons, defined as labour tenants, who occupy agricultural land on the basis of vulnerable labour tenancy contracts, against unfair or arbitrary eviction.[170]

In summary it can be said that the post-1994 South African legislation rather surprisingly provides residential tenants with less protection against eviction than might have been expected in view of the apartheid history. Despite indications of strong anti-eviction sentiments in the Constitution and the concerted effort to redress the ills of apartheid land law through legislation, tenants enjoy less protection than unlawful occupiers of land, except in so far as tenants holding over are still regarded as unlawful occupiers. Neither the Constitution nor land reform laws could succeed in bringing about significant changes to the rights paradigm as

---

[166] Ph J Thomas, 'The Rental Housing Act' (2000) 33 *De Jure* 235–47 at 241

[167] Section 5(5).

[168] *Kendall Property Investments v Rutgers* [2005] 4 All SA 61 (C) at 64. See further further PJ Badenhorst *et al*, *Silberberg & Schoeman's The Law of Property* (5th edn, 2006) at 429.

[169] The Act was supposed to have lapsed on 31 December 1997, but its validity has been extended repeatedly and it remains in operation, apparently until the commencement of the Communal Land Rights Act 11 of 2004; see AJ van der Walt, *Constitutional Property Law* (2005) at 311.

[170] AJ van der Walt, *Constitutional Property Law* (2005) at 312.

far as tenants are concerned, although there are statutory controls over eviction that protect especially weak and vulnerable tenants against arbitrary action. Although it would be overstating the case to claim that there was judicial resistance against landlord–tenant reforms, judicial hesitation and doctrinal conservatism did play a role in preventing the reformist legislation from having a greater impact upon existing rights than might have been expected.

IV. Conclusion

From the analysis and discussion above it may be concluded that the rights paradigm is qualified more extensively in landlord–tenant law than might have been expected, but that it has by no means been subjected to substantive challenges through the imposition of protective legislation. Legislative regulation, imposed or interpreted in terms of constitutional housing obligations, has generally qualified the doctrinal domination of ownership (or the stronger right to possession, as far as English law is concerned) by imposing often extensive due process controls over the termination of the lease and over the eviction procedure. As a general rule these procedural controls imply that eviction cannot take place without judicial process and that it can be contemplated only once the lease has been terminated lawfully. In some cases, legislative amendments have also imposed substantive restrictions on termination of the lease, thereby either postponing or even preventing eviction. The most extensive protections imply that termination is suspended or prevented purely because of the prejudicial effect that eviction would have for the tenant and her family, in other words on subjective grounds that are out of the landowner's control and traditionally irrelevant in terms of the rights paradigm. However, there are also indications that these protective measures are either restricted in scope or are being eroded by changing economic policies and that their effect is sometimes minimised by hesitant and sceptical judiciaries. The rhetorical and doctrinal power of the rights paradigm obviously plays an important role in inspiring or supporting judicial reticence to treat eviction as a discretionary right that can be disallowed purely because of the subjective circumstances of the occupier.

In English law, the protection afforded to tenants by the legislative system introduced since the 1970s was reduced by legislation that provided for termination of a lease and eviction because of anti-social behaviour of the tenant and especially when the Housing Act 1988 introduced assured shorthold tenancies, which now represent the majority of private sector tenancies but enjoy very limited protection. In South African law the abolition of earlier rent control statutes also brought about a reduction in the statutory protection of tenants, albeit that the earlier laws applied to a very small number of rental properties in selected areas. Post-apartheid legislative efforts to increase statutory protection of tenants in South African law were rather less extensive than might have been expected, particularly because the laws that apply specifically to tenants fail to exclude common law eviction completely and because the courts have been unwilling to allow section 26(3) of the Constitution to affect landlord–tenant relationships directly.

English and South African case-law on the statutory protection of tenants also demonstrates the difficulties of accommodating the changes brought about by the legislation in question in the context of a largely uncodified private law system and a constitutional (or comparable) obligation to promote and protect housing or home interests. In German law the doctrinal pressure is significantly reduced by the simplified relationship between constitution, civil code and ancillary legislation, but both English and South African case-law show that the courts find it difficult to explain the effect of legislative changes on uncodified common law doctrine and precedent, especially if the changes are inspired and authorised by constitutional principles that may be in direct or indirect conflict with private law doctrine. In these cases the tendency seems to be to restrict the effects on uncodified private law doctrine to the minimum that is required by explicit or otherwise very clear legislative language. The academic reaction to the German *Landlord–Tenant* decision shows that doctrinal reaction to statutory intervention in landlord–tenant law is often stronger than actual political conservatism, an impression that is echoed by the English House of Lords decisions in *Qazi* and *Kay/Price* and the South African decision in *Brisley*.

However, the doctrinal conservatism of courts should not be accepted uncritically as an inevitable side-effect of lawyerly training and practice. Even when the outcome of cases is determined purely by doctrinal conservatism and not by political resistance, the result is effectively also a political choice in the sense that it upholds the existing distribution of property against democratic or executive intervention, which suggests that the status quo is seen as or assumed to be fundamentally justified and normal. In a transformative setting, this could have a negative effect on the promotion and implementation of reformist policies and legislation.

Despite these reservations and qualifications, there are some significant qualifications of the rights paradigm in German, English and South African landlord–tenant law. The rights paradigm is particularly qualified, sometimes quite dramatically, by legislation implemented in terms of national housing policies. Even in jurisdictions where large-scale constitutionally driven transformation is not a high priority, but where housing shortages and social and economic circumstances have contributed to a tenant-friendly housing policy, legislation has been introduced to protect tenants against unnecessary, unfair and arbitrary termination of the lease and eviction. At least two significant qualifications of the rights paradigm are highlighted by tenant-friendly housing policies in all three jurisdictions discussed here, namely that a landowner is generally not allowed to use self-help to regain possession of the rental property after cancellation of the tenancy and that the landowner is not allowed to cancel a tenancy arbitrarily or without any reason. Instead, due process regulation has generally been imposed on the process of termination of the lease and the process of eviction, while some substantive regulation has been imposed on the cancellation of a lease. These amendments have qualified the rights paradigm; in cases where legislation restrict the grounds upon and circumstances under which a lease may be terminated with reference to the history of land rights or the social and economic context, the qualification can sometimes be described as significant.

In a small number of cases where these restrictions pivot purely upon the personal circumstances of the tenant or the effect that it would have for her the protective legislation obviously poses a serious challenge to the logical integrity of the rights paradigm to the extent that the success of an eviction application no longer depends purely on the stronger right of the landlord or landowner. It is not possible to explain the more radical protections that prevent a landowner from regaining possession for reasons that are outside of her control, and unrelated to the strength of her right, within the rights paradigm. It is possible to explain some restrictions on ownership as public interest or policy limitations that establish an exception to the rule that strong rights trump weaker rights and that rights trump no-rights, but when the relative merit of the respective competing claims plays no role and the dispute is decided purely with reference to socio-economic or policy considerations a substantive challenge to the paradigm is indicated. The analysis in this chapter shows that doctrinal resistance against amendments that embody such a significant deviation is strong, but also that such a development is indeed at least under discussion in all three legal systems considered here. All three systems provide for instances where a landowner's right to regain possession is qualified so strongly that the force of the rights paradigm is challenged. It is only the limited scope and exceptional nature of these examples that prevent them from shaking the paradigm in its foundations. In some cases the legislature and policy changes hold the exceptions in check; in others their effect is restricted by conservative adjudication and by the force of rhetoric and doctrinal logic.

5

Eviction of Unlawful Occupiers

I.   Introduction   133
II. Eviction of Politically Inspired Urban Squatters   135
III. Anti-eviction Protection in South African Land Reform Law   146
IV. Eviction of Gypsies or Travellers   161
V.   Conclusion   166

I. Introduction

I N CHAPTER TWO it was said that the paradigmatic privileging of existing
social and economic hierarchies by the rights paradigm could, in a society
characterised by social, economic and political inequality and marginalisation,
frustrate social and economic reform. The rights paradigm's preference for stability and tradition would, if applied uncompromisingly, ensure that the common
law effectively insulates ownership and other strongly vested property rights
against statutory and even constitutional transformation and reform initiatives. It
was pointed out earlier that the question is whether effective social and economic
reform is possible; significant challenges to the rights paradigm could create or
indicate space for reform, but in the absence of space reform will inevitably be
more difficult. In the previous chapter, constitutional and statutory amendments
of landlord–tenant law and judicial reactions to those amendments were evaluated
and it was pointed out that some of these changes have qualified the rights paradigm to a certain extent, while a smaller number of amendments have brought
about more serious challenges to the paradigm in so far as they restrict or even suspend the right to obtain an eviction order purely because of the general social and
economic context or because of the personal circumstances of the occupier,
instead of on the basis of the relative rights of the parties to obtain or to retain possession. It was also pointed out that, even when landlords' right to obtain possession has been restricted by protective legislation, courts sometimes find it difficult
to square the statutory shifts with established rhetoric and doctrine that entrench
existing rights.

Anti-eviction legislation and case-law reveals even more interesting qualifications of and challenges to the rights paradigm in an area that cannot strictly be

considered part of landlord–tenant law, namely the eviction of unlawful occupiers. Most landlord–tenant evictions take place in the context of 'holding over', when the tenancy has either expired or been cancelled and the former tenant's continued occupation therefore amounts to (or at least is treated as) unlawful occupation (in the passive sense of failure to vacate the property),[1] but apart from such 'normal' residential evictions landowners and holders of other rights in land sometimes attempt to evict persons who have occupied (in the active sense of invaded or settled) the premises unlawfully in the first place, without any legal cause.[2] These unlawful occupiers are described as 'land invaders' or 'squatters' in South African and English law; in Dutch and German law unlawful occupiers of uninhabited or unused buildings are known as '*krakers*' or '*Hausbesetzer*'. The position of the so-called gypsies or travellers is in some cases comparable to that of land invaders (in the sense of unlawful occupiers who settled on land without any current or prior right to do so) or of the politically inspired squatters; some cases dealing with their position are also referred to in this chapter.

Eviction of the unlawful occupiers identified above is legally and socially different from eviction in the landlord–tenant situation and in some instances it acquired a political aspect that renders these evictions controversial for reasons that do not necessarily apply to 'normal' tenant evictions. In a few instances, including post-apartheid South African land reform law, eviction of unlawful occupiers has been subjected to regulatory controls that were at least in part introduced to protect unlawful occupiers from abuse and arbitrary eviction. The restriction on eviction brought about by these controls obviously constitutes a more intrusive and controversial restriction of ownership and land rights than is the case with anti-eviction controls in 'normal' landlord–tenant legislation, because one would expect that a landowner (or holder of another land right) should find it easier to evict unlawful occupiers and land invaders than to evict tenants or former tenants. Consequently, the statutory measures that restrict eviction of unlawful occupiers and the case-law dealing with them establish a particu-

---

[1] In *Simonsig Landgoed (Edms) Bpk v Vers* 2007 (5) SA 103 (C) the Cape High Court decided that the eviction of former lawful occupiers (tenants and their families) whose occupation had become unlawful because the tenancy was terminated by the death of the tenant had to be carried out in terms of the legislation that regulated their tenancy while still lawful (Extension of Security of Tenure Act 62 of 1997, ESTA) and not the legislation that regulates eviction of unlawful occupation (Prevention of Illegal Eviction from and Unlawful Occupation of Land Act 19 of 1998, PIE). Compare ch 4, n 154. Many of the significant recent English landlord–tenant cases on eviction were also decided in the context of holding over; compare ch 4, section II.

[2] South African legislation is organised according to the distinction between lawful and unlawful occupation of land, so that eviction of lawful (or formerly lawful, see n 1) occupiers is regulated by the Extension of Security of Tenure Act 62 of 1997 (ESTA, applicable to rural land) or the Rental Housing Act 50 of 1999, whereas eviction of unlawful occupiers (mostly in the sense of unlawful land invaders and squatters) is regulated by the Prevention of Illegal Eviction from and Unlawful Occupation of Land Act 19 of 1998 (PIE). As appears from the discussion, unlawful invasion or settlement of the land could have taken place long ago or more recently; a factor that plays an important role in deciding whether eviction would be justifiable and whether availability of alternative accommodation is an issue.

larly instructive backdrop for the discussion of challenges to the rights paradigm: If a landowner is prevented from evicting unlawful occupiers and squatters purely because of their personal circumstances or the effect that eviction would have on them, that would be a much stronger indication of a challenge to the paradigm than is the case when a landlord is prevented from evicting a tenant for the same reasons. Some examples of controls of this nature, from different jurisdictions, are set out in this chapter, once again together with examples from case-law.

The next section of this chapter starts off with a discussion of politically inspired unlawful occupation of unused and empty-standing urban buildings during the 1970s and 1980s and unlawful sit-ins on property in the United States during the 1960s. These intentionally unlawful occupations formed part of political and social protest against racism and mismanagement of scarce urban land and housing; at least in some instances they had a marked effect on the direction of land use management and regulatory control over the use of valuable urban housing stock, even in the private market, during the 1980s. The case-law and literature on this phenomenon therefore provides a useful barometer of social and political reaction to state regulation of the availability and use of urban housing. The third section of the chapter provides an overview of South African constitutional and legislative control over eviction of unlawful occupiers of land in the post-1994 era. This system of regulatory controls covers both urban and rural land, but in a sense it also reflects current reactions to the same problems that were highlighted by the Western European political protests of the 1970s and 1980s. The fourth section of the chapter provides a brief overview of recent European and English case-law on eviction of a specific category of unlawful occupiers, namely the so-called gypsies or travellers, in terms of the limited protection they enjoy under the European Convention on Human Rights. Given the recent recognition of gypsies as a particularly marginalised and vulnerable social group, the case-law is instructive for purposes of this chapter. The chapter concludes with an effort to construct an alternative way in which the legislation and case-law discussed in this chapter could be explained more satisfactorily than in the rights paradigm, according to which the anti-eviction legislation and case-law discussed in this chapter are nothing more than exceptions and aberrations.

II. Eviction of Politically Inspired Urban Squatters

A. Introduction

A series of events that took place in Western Europe during the 1970s and 1980s, during which English, German and Dutch courts grappled with issues surrounding the eviction of persons who unlawfully occupied unused buildings as part of political protest against housing policies, provides a useful background for this chapter.[3] This phenomenon of political or 'expressive' squatting,[4] known as *kraken* in Dutch and *Hausbesetzungen* or *Instandbesetzungen*[5] in German literature, involved unlawful invasion and occupation of uninhabited buildings in urban areas by or under the inspiration of political activists who wanted to highlight unresolved social and political problems related to urban homelessness and poverty. The buildings targeted by these invasions were often deliberately left unused by investors waiting for the right time or for permission to demolish the buildings and redevelop the land for the sake of greater profit, while at the same time people in the area were homeless or unable to afford housing because of the housing shortage and the government's inadequate housing and development policies.

The significant characteristic of these invasions was that they were overtly political, as far as both their goals and their methods were concerned. In this regard the political squatting examples discussed in this section must be distinguished from unlawful squatting that is undertaken purely from necessity, because the squatters have nowhere to go and desperately need shelter. Obviously squatting from necessity also has political implications, but the political is not their primary function or focus. By contrast, although a side-effect of the political squatting movement was that homeless persons could find temporary shelter in the unused buildings, the purpose was always to highlight the social problems caused by homelessness and the political reasons for these social and economic problems. In the Netherlands and in Germany the invaders were organised in movements with clear political aims; these movements often provided infrastructure and organised the occupations and efforts to avoid civil litigation and criminal prosecution.[6]

The Western European urban squatting movement is discussed together with politically inspired unlawful occupation of property in the US during the 1960s. The US civil rights movement was a reaction against racial segregation rather than housing policy as such, although the two movements were of course linked socially,

---

[3] The following paragraphs are loosely based on passages from AJ van der Walt, 'De Onrechtmatige Bezetting van Leegstaande Woningen en het Eigendomsbegrip: Een Vergelijkende Analyse van het Conflict tussen de Privaat Eigendom van Onroerend Goed en Dakloosheid' (1991) 17 *Recht & Kritiek* 329–59 (translated from English by R Bakker).

[4] The very useful term 'expressive outlaws' is used by EM Peñalver and SK Katyal, 'Property Outlaws' (2007) 155 *Univ Pennsylvania LR* 1095–186 at 1114 to refer to people who intentionally occupied property unlawfully to make a political point, such as the lunch counter sit-ins to protest against segregation in the 1960s. The term is obviously also applicable to residential squatters. I return to the Peñalver and Katyal article below.

[5] In the German literature the term *Hausbesetzung* is used to refer to unlawful invasion and occupation of a property, while *Instandbesetzung* is used to indicate that the occupiers not only occupied the property but also made repairs and improvements to make it habitable.

[6] In Dutch and German civil law it was difficult at the time to institute private law action unless an unlawful occupier could be identified; the occupiers therefore often went to great lengths to remain anonymous, eg by only moving about at night, wearing masks or balaclavas and frequently moving around from one occupied property to another. Organised squatting groups also operated in the UK and in surprisingly many other countries, even where one would not expect a housing crisis, like Switzerland and the Scandinavian countries. Compare the discussion below and see the overview at http://en.wikipedia.org/wiki/Squatter (15 May 2008).

historically and ideologically. The political orientation of these unlawful occupations renders them particularly interesting for comparison with the South African situation, where the phenomenon of unlawful occupation also has a strong political aspect, albeit in a different political set-up and often without the organised political strategy that characterised the European examples. The comparison is even more interesting because the unlawful occupiers could and did make use of (albeit limited) legal protection against unlawful eviction, a situation that (just like in post-apartheid South Africa) resulted in direct conflict between the right of the landowner and the (occasionally) legally protected but doctrinally unclear interest of the unlawful occupier, thereby putting the power of the rights paradigm to the test in an unusually direct way. Almost inevitably this conflict inspired speculation about the question whether the occupiers could be said to have some kind of legal right that entitled them to occupation in defiance of the landowner, which again challenged the rights paradigm. As will appear from the evaluation at the end of this section, the legal effort to construe a kind of right to squat from the partial successes of the political housing movement was largely unsuccessful; in the end, the rights paradigm prevailed against all efforts to construe a legal right to squat. However, this movement was not entirely unsuccessful: Housing laws in Western European countries affected by the movement were amended in a more or less direct response to the political squatting movement. The failure of the theoretical and the relative success of the political aspects of the political squatting movement highlight an important aspect of this chapter, namely that challenges to the rights paradigm (and its impact in housing policies and laws) can and will not always be legal—in some cases, the law cannot do enough and political action is required. Of course these examples of political squatting and the theorising about them are not cited to justify unlawful behaviour, but to emphasise the importance of political action, in addition to legislative intervention and judicial interpretation, in the creation of space for significant legal reforms.

Although the movement still exists and many buildings around the world are still occupied by housing activists,[7] the political squatting movement reached its zenith during the 1970s and 1980s. In the following overview of the cases and literature the focus is therefore on the 1980s; subsequent developments are discussed either in the later sections of this chapter or in chapter four.

B. Dutch Law

In the Netherlands the *kraken* movement of the 1970s and 1980s was inspired by a serious housing shortage, especially in certain urban areas. According to Dutch law a landowner is entitled to evict unlawful occupiers from her property, but in

---

[7] Politically inspired squatting is a surprisingly widespread phenomenon, even in the relatively wealthy social democracies of Western Europe and Scandinavia; even though the movement had its heyday in the 1970s and 1980s, invasions of this nature still occur and many buildings are still occupied. For more general information see http://en.wikipedia.org/wiki/Squatter (15 May 2008).

practice it proved difficult and often impossible to evict unlawful *krakers,* espe-cially if they took care to remain anonymous and moved around frequently.[8] Accordingly, landowners preferred to evict *krakers* by way of the prohibition against breach of peace[9] in § 138 of the Dutch Criminal Code.[10] On the face of it, this criminal law provision afforded the perfect remedy against unlawful invaders and occupiers, but the *krakers* had some success in strategically opposing the evic-tions. Their legal response to the criminal evictions relied on a decision in which the Dutch Hoge Raad had interpreted the phrase 'used by another person' in § 138 restrictively, so that an invasion of property would not be unlawful unless it was actually being used by another person at the time it was occupied.[11] This obviously excluded dilapidated, unused or investment property left standing unoccupied and unused by its owners and, accordingly, although it was possible to close the loopholes created by the *Hoge Raad* decision of 1971 through other legislation and local ordinances, *krakers* of unused buildings in certain cities were effectively regarded as being more or less immune against criminal prosecution and eviction under the Criminal Code.

The *kraken* movement regarded this and similar decisions as important victo-ries, but in legal terms they were based on purely technical and procedural points and therefore they merely imposed procedural restrictions on landowners' enti-tlements to use their properties as they saw fit and to evict unwanted occupiers without any reference to the circumstances or the context. Important as they were for the *kraken* movement, these victories did not bring about a significant depar-ture from the rights paradigm, particularly since the battle was fought on the turf of criminal rather than private law. These conflicts did, however, inspire the national government to enact legislation to discourage owners from leaving their property standing unoccupied and unused in areas where there was a housing

[8] Dutch civil procedure required that a respondent in civil matters be cited by name. Some courts allowed alternative methods of citation, eg using fictitious names and/or photographs to identify *krakers,* but this was not accepted universally and was criticised by academics; see RM Schutte and JBM Vranken, 'Gebruik van Woonruimte en Woonrecht' in JJM de Vries *et al, Eigendom en Woonrecht* (1981) 65–127 at 100–2; J ten Berg-Koolen, 'Invoering van de Naamloze Dagvaarding; de Kraker Gekraakt?' (1987) 10 *NJB* 306–14. See details in AJ van der Walt, 'De Onrechtmatige Bezetting van Leegstaande Woningen en het Eigendomsbegrip: Een Vergelijkende Analyse van het Conflict tussen de Privaat Eigendom van Onroerend Goed en Dakloosheid' (1991) 17 *Recht & Kritiek* 329–59 at 334.

[9] *Huisvredebreuk* in Dutch.

[10] § 138 of the Criminal Code makes it a crime to unlawfully invade or occupy a home, an enclosed premises or land that is used by another person. See details in AJ van der Walt, 'De Onrechtmatige Bezetting van Leegstaande Woningen en het Eigendomsbegrip: Een Vergelijkende Analyse van het Conflict tussen de Privaat Eigendom van Onroerend Goed en Dakloosheid' (1991) 17 *Recht & Kritiek* 329–59 at 334–5.

[11] HR 2 February 1971, *NJ* 1971, 385. This interpretation of the Hoge Raad met with furious criti-cism, but in a series of other decisions the Hoge Raad expanded upon the initial finding, explaining that a house could not be assumed to be in use by another person merely because that person had left mov-able property in it (HR 16 November 1971, *NJ* 1972, 62); that a house would be assumed to be in use by another person if the owner had left the house in the hands of labourers working on it (HR 24 June 1980, *NJ* 1980, 625; HR 26 June 1984, *NJ* 1985, 138), or if the owner or tenant was in hospital (HR 4 January 1972, *NJ* 1972, 121). Details in AJ van der Walt, 'De Onrechtmatige Bezetting van Leegstaande Woningen en het Eigendomsbegrip: Een Vergelijkende Analyse van het Conflict tussen de Privaat Eigendom van Onroerend Goed en Dakloosheid' (1991) 17 *Recht & Kritiek* 329–59 at 335, fnn 34, 35.

shortage.[12] The legislation enacted for this purpose was not intended to facilitate squatting: It declared *kraken* a misdemeanour and provided for anonymous summons procedure in civil evictions, but it did change the legal framework within which property could be left unused or exploited at the cost of the homeless. In that respect the *kraken* movement won an important political victory.

The *kraken* movement also relied on another, even more controversial decision in which the Hoge Raad decided that the initial invasion or occupation of property would not be unlawful, even if it occurred without permission and against the will of the owner, if the occupation was justified by extraneous considerations.[13] This decision opened the door for attempting to justify the actions of the *krakers* by weighing their circumstances and interests against those of the property owner who allowed her property to remain uninhabited and unused, which would amount to a significant challenge to the rights paradigm because it would mean that eviction cases would no longer be decided purely on the strength of the owner's right to possession and the weakness of the occupier's right of occupation. Accordingly, this decision was cited in many efforts during the 1970s to convince the courts that a particular unlawful occupation should be justified because the property was uninhabited and unused and the occupiers were homeless. However, until 1980 these efforts were in vain and unlawful occupiers were often evicted by extra-legal means, while cases that did reach the courts were mostly decided on technical points and not on the basis of weighing the interests of the landowner against those of the unlawful occupiers.[14]

The situation changed in 1980 when a district court decided that *kraken* could be lawful even though it involved an infringement of the owner's right.[15] The

---

[12] The legislation that was enacted was the *Leegstandwet* 1986. The Act provided that local authorities could, under certain circumstances, use residential property that was left unused by its owners to provide accommodation for the homeless, without the owner's agreement, but against payment of a kind of rent to the owner. The provisions that criminalised *kraken* met with strong political criticism and never came into force. The rest of the Act came into operation between 1 January 1986 and 1 January 1987. For details and references to literature see AJ van der Walt, 'De Onrechtmatige Bezetting van Leegstaande Woningen en het Eigendomsbegrip: Een Vergelijkende Analyse van het Conflict tussen de Privaat Eigendom van Onroerend Goed en Dakloosheid' (1991) 17 *Recht & Kritiek* 329–59 at 336, fnn 42–6.

[13] HR 16 December 1969, *NJ* 1971, 96; HR 16 November 1971, *NJ* 1972, 43.

[14] The possibility that *kraken* might be lawful if the occupiers acted in an acute emergency situation and the owner could not show an interest in immediate eviction was raised in a number of summary actions, but these actions were decided on the basis of temporary civil order measures and not by way of a legal process that involves weighing up the interests of the owner against those of the occupiers. If the owner could prove an interest in immediate eviction in such a summary action, her right would trump the emergency interest of the occupiers anyway. Despite the arguments of certain academics, these decisions could therefore not provide sufficient authority for the general legal proposition that an unlawful occupier's interest in a housing emergency could be weighed up against the interests of a landowner. Details may be found in AJ van der Walt, 'De Onrechtmatige Bezetting van Leegstaande Woningen en het Eigendomsbegrip: Een Vergelijkende Analyse van het Conflict tussen de Privaat Eigendom van Onroerend Goed en Dakloosheid' (1991) 17 *Recht & Kritiek* 329–59 at 335–6.

[15] *Arr Rb Middelburg* 1 October 1980, 24 December 1980, 1981 *NJ*, 374. The case elicited critical response; see A Schotmans, 'De Middelburgse Fopspeen Herwogen' (1982) 8 *Recht & Kritiek* 463–6; GE van Maanen, 'Balanceren op de Grens van de Rechtsorde' (1982) 8 *Recht & Kritiek* 467–71. Further references to literature may be found in AJ van der Walt, 'De Onrechtmatige Bezetting van Leegstaande Woningen en het Eigendomsbegrip: Een Vergelijkende Analyse van het Conflict tussen de Privaat Eigendom van Onroerend Goed en Dakloosheid' (1991) 17 *Recht & Kritiek* 329–59 at 335–7, fn 49.

Middelburg Court pointed out that ownership was not an unrestricted right and that an infringement of the landowner's right might therefore be lawful if the owner herself acted irresponsibly, for instance by leaving scarce residential property uninhabited and unused without good cause and for a prolonged period during a housing shortage. If such a property was then occupied unlawfully by someone who did not have access to housing, and provided the *kraker* acted responsibly, for example by maintaining the property in good order, paying rent and declaring herself willing to evacuate the premises within a reasonable time if it were sold, the law could treat the *kraken* of the property as lawful. Most academic commentators were surprised by the decision and some criticised it, but one or two academics recognised the critical space opened up by the decision and proceeded to investigate its theoretical potential for mounting a challenge against the rights paradigm. The most interesting of these critical reactions argued that it was acceptable to deny a landowner the normal protection of the law when she used her property in a socially irresponsible manner, for example by leaving residential property unoccupied for speculative reasons while others were homeless, if the property was then occupied unlawfully by a person or persons who acted for socially understandable and justifiable reasons, such as acute homelessness.[16]

Gerrit Van Maanen[17] acknowledged that there was very little doctrinal room for arguing in favour of something like lawful *kraken* because of the strong and undifferentiated notion of ownership in the Roman-Dutch tradition. He argued, without actually using the words, that a satisfactory doctrinal explanation of a sympathetic solution to the *kraken* cases was prevented or inhibited by the ownership paradigm, even though criticism against this paradigm was gaining momentum in academic literature. Van Maanen's proposed solution was to plead for a differentiated notion of ownership that would allow legal recognition of different, legally protected, property interests in the same property.[18] Van Maanen's solution would not necessarily have posed a serious challenge to the rights paradigm, but in so far as it amounted to a plea for a differentiated notion of property it would have undermined the hierarchical supremacy of ownership in the rights paradigm. If the interests to be recognised and protected under the new property concept included unlawful interests in terms of domestic law, Van Maanen's pro-

---

[16] The most interesting comments came from RM Schutte and JBM Vranken, 'Gebruik van Woonruimte en Woonrecht' in JJM de Vries *et al, Eigendom en Woonrecht* (1981) 65–127; JF Bruinsma, 'Ongehoorzaam in en buiten de Rechtsorde' (1983) *NJB* 125–8; PH Bakker Schut *et al*, 'Politiek Protest in de Rechtszaal' (1984) 10 *Recht & Kritiek* 33–62; GE van Maanen, 'Kraken als Onrechtmatig Daad, of: De Grensoverschrijdende Speculant' (1981) 7 *Recht & Kritiek* 5–17 at 6–8; GE van Maanen, 'Balanceren op de Grens van de Rechtsorde' (1982) 8 *Recht & Kritiek* 467–71. Further references to literature may be found in AJ van der Walt, 'De Onrechtmatige Bezetting van Leegstaande Woningen en het Eigendomsbegrip: Een Vergelijkende Analyse van het Conflict tussen de Privaat Eigendom van Onroerend Goed en Dakloosheid' (1991) 17 *Recht & Kritiek* 329–59 at 335–7, fn 49.

[17] GE van Maanen, 'Kraken als Onrechtmatig Daad, of: De Grensoverschrijdende Speculant' (1981) 7 *Recht & Kritiek* 5–17 at 14–15.

[18] GE van Maanen, 'Kraken als Onrechtmatig Daad, of: De Grensoverschrijdende Speculant' (1981) 7 *Recht & Kritiek* 5–17 at 14; GE van Maanen, *Eigendomsschijnbewegingen. Juridische, Historische en Politiek-Filosofische Opmerkingen over Eigendom in Huidig en Komend Recht* (1987) at 150–7.

posal would have been even more radical. In view of subsequent developments this argument was never worked out further. Schutte and Vranken,[19] while agreeing with Van Maanen's socio-political view of the Middelburg decision, concluded that Dutch law did not create a subjective right to housing—at most it could be said that the *Leegstandwet* had an indirect, 'reflexive effect' that might benefit homeless persons in particular cases in that their personal circumstances might be taken into account in postponing eventual eviction in summary proceedings. Their proposal amounted to a strong qualification to the rights paradigm, but in the end the rights paradigm proved too strong to be displaced by the sympathetic but doctrinally inconclusive court decisions that favoured unlawful *krakers* and the debate died down when some of the problems highlighted by the squatters were solved through new legislation.

C. German Law

Like their Dutch counterparts, German *Hausbesetzer* also operated anonymously to frustrate civil eviction,[20] and landowners also preferred to employ criminal eviction proceedings in terms of § 123 of the German Criminal Code against the unlawful occupiers.[21] Although § 123 of the German Criminal Code resembles § 138 of the Dutch Criminal Code in essential respects, it was applied differently: Whereas the Dutch provision regarding breach of the peace was interpreted as a measure to ensure public order and eviction was therefore restricted to cases where the property was already occupied and used by someone, the German provision was seen as a guarantee of *Hausfrieden* as a private interest, which essentially entitles the person in control of premises to allow or restrict entry to the premises, whether they actually occupied or used the premises or not.[22] The object of this

---

[19] RM Schutte and JBM Vranken, 'Gebruik van Woonruimte en Woonrecht' in JJM de Vries *et al*, *Eigendom en Woonrecht* (1981) 65–127 at 107–14.

[20] § 985 of the German Civil Code (*Bürgerliches Gesetzbuch; BGB*) provides a property owner with a strong civil action with which to vindicate her property; § 854 *BGB* provides an additional claim for unlawful possession. In both cases eviction was rendered difficult by the evasive tactics of the squatters. The German guarantee of property in Art 14 of the Basic Law (*Grundgesetz; GG*) functions vertically and cannot be enforced against another private person to protect landownership against unlawful occupation; owners were therefore most likely to succeed with eviction proceedings under the Criminal Code (*Strafgesetzbuch; StGB*). For further references to literature see AJ van der Walt, 'De Onrechtmatige Bezetting van Leegstaande Woningen en het Eigendomsbegrip. Een Vergelijkende Analyse van het Conflict tussen de Privaat Eigendom van Onroerend Goed en Dakloosheid' (1991) 17 *Recht & Kritiek* 329–59 at 339–40.

[21] The prohibition against *Hausfriedensbruch* in § 123 is similar in all essential textual respects to § 138 of the Dutch Criminal Code; see n 7 and compare for more detail AJ van der Walt, 'De Onrechtmatige Bezetting van Leegstaande Woningen en het Eigendomsbegrip: Een Vergelijkende Analyse van het Conflict tussen de Privaat Eigendom van Onroerend Goed en Dakloosheid' (1991) 17 *Recht & Kritiek* 329–59 at 341–2.

[22] For detail and references to literature see AJ van der Walt, 'De Onrechtmatige Bezetting van Leegstaande Woningen en het Eigendomsbegrip: Een Vergelijkende Analyse van het Conflict tussen de Privaat Eigendom van Onroerend Goed en Dakloosheid' (1991) 17 *Recht & Kritiek* 329–59 at 341–2. On post-unification developments in the housing situation in the former East Germany see C Flockton,

right is the individual's freedom to exercise her free will in allowing or preventing others from entering into or remaining on the premises, and therefore even unin-habited and unused property is subject to it—the Dutch Hoge Raad interpretation that allowed a loophole for unlawful occupation in these cases could not be recog-nised in German law as long as the owner or lawful occupier retained secure and visible control over the premises by means of security walls, gates, locks and the like.[23] Some critics disagreed with this formalistic and dogmatic, narrow interpre-tation of § 123,[24] but after limited success in some lower courts their view was rejected and the narrow interpretation was confirmed by the higher courts.[25] Subsequently promulgated German legislation prohibits the abuse of (including failure to use) scarce residential property, but by and large the German *Hausbesetzung* movement was less successful in the courts than their Dutch coun-terparts and therefore they were reduced to political action, often assuming the form of civil disobedience and opportunism. In German law, even more than in Dutch law, adherence to the rights paradigm and doctrinal rigour was too strong to allow the development of an interpretation that would accommodate the inter-ests of unlawful *Hausbesetzer*.[26]

Since the German squatting conflicts were decided purely on the basis of crim-inal law and without the slightly more open-ended approach to the notion of breach of peace that was followed by the Dutch courts, it had no discernible effect on or interest for property law, although the civil disobedience displayed by the

'Employment, Welfare Support and Income Distribution in East Germany' in C Flockton and E Kolinsky (eds), *Recasting East Germany: Social Transformation after the GDR* (1999) 33–51. The gen-eral trend after unification was to assimilate housing in the two parts of Germany, but a decade after unification there were still huge differences in the respective housing situations. Two interesting fea-tures are that a large percentage (almost 30%) of housing in the former East Germany was social hous-ing and that empty and unoccupied residential property was much more prevalent in East Germany: C Flockton, 'Policy Agendas and the Economy in Germany and Europe' in C Flockton *et al* (eds), *The New Germany in the East: Policy, Agendas and Social Developments since Unification* (2000) 761–86 at 78; H Tomann, 'Germany' in P Balchin (ed), *Housing Policy in Europe* (1996) 51–68 at 51; HD Vilhjálmsdóttir, 'Housing Support and Public Housing Funds in Iceland and Abroad' (2004) 4 *Monetary Bulletin* at http://www.sedlabanki.is/lisalib/getfile .aspx?itemid=2866 (accessed 9 June 2008).

[23] So-called *befriedetes Besitztum*; see especially H Schall, 'Hausbesetzungen im Lichte der Auslegung des § 123 StGB' (1983) 3(6) *Neue Zeitschrift für Strafrecht* 241–47; further references to lit-erature may be found in AJ van der Walt, 'De Onrechtmatige Bezetting van Leegstaande Woningen en het Eigendomsbegrip: Een Vergelijkende Analyse van het Conflict tussen de Privaat Eigendom van Onroerend Goed en Dakloosheid' (1991) 17 *Recht & Kritiek* 329–59 at 342, fn 87.

[24] Particularly E Küchenhoff, 'Zur Strafbarkeit von Hausbesetzungen' 1981 *Demokratie und Recht* 300–1; E Küchenhoff, 'Demonstrative Hausbesetzungen' (1981) *Berliner Mieter-Zeitung* 9–10; H Schall, 'Hausbesetzungen im Lichte der Auslegung des § 123 StGB' (1983) 3(6) *Neue Zeitschrift für Strafrecht* 241–7; for further references to literature see AJ van der Walt, 'De Onrechtmatige Bezetting van Leegstaande Woningen en het Eigendomsbegrip: Een Vergelijkende Analyse van het Conflict tussen de Privaat Eigendom van Onroerend Goed en Dakloosheid' (1991) 17 *Recht & Kritiek* 329–59 at 343, fn 93.

[25] For references see AJ van der Walt, 'De Onrechtmatige Bezetting van Leegstaande Woningen en het Eigendomsbegrip: Een Vergelijkende Analyse van het Conflict tussen de Privaat Eigendom van Onroerend Goed en Dakloosheid' (1991) 17 *Recht & Kritiek* 329–59 at 343, fnn 95, 96.

[26] Unlawful occupiers confronted by eviction proceedings often made use of defences based on necessity. For references see AJ van der Walt, 'De Onrechtmatige Bezetting van Leegstaande Woningen en het Eigendomsbegrip: Een Vergelijkende Analyse van het Conflict tussen de Privaat Eigendom van Onroerend Goed en Dakloosheid' (1991) 17 *Recht & Kritiek* 329–59 at 343–4.

squatters had an indirect effect (as it also had in the Netherlands) on the direction of housing policy and legislation. To a large extent the public debate about housing issues shifted from the arena of political action and demonstration to policy changes, the promulgation of social housing legislation and the legitimisation of new laws by the constitutional courts (discussed in chapter 4, section II).

D. English Law

Political squatting also occurred in the United Kingdom, and in the *Southwark* cases of 1971 the English courts had an opportunity to consider the dilemma of a homeless person being evicted from an uninhabited and unused residential building belonging to a local council that has a responsibility to provide public housing.[27] In an action for possession instituted by the London Borough of Southwark on the basis of trespass to land, the unlawful occupiers in the *Southwark* cases relied on the defence of necessity, arguing that they had been unable to find accommodation from the local authority, which allowed residential property belonging to it to stand unused. A squatters' association helped them to occupy two empty-standing houses belonging to and considered unsuitable for residential purposes by the Borough, which had boarded up the windows of the houses and blocked the toilets with cement. The families unlawfully occupying the houses had made them more or less habitable. The Borough wanted the families evicted and the houses boarded up again as it did not plan to repair the houses for social housing within two or three years.

According to the English common law tradition a landowner may evict trespassers herself, even using force if necessary, provided she does so in the period before the trespass matures into possession and that she uses no more force than is reasonably necessary.[28] However, self-help is not recommended because it can lead to violence and, accordingly, the landowner must normally turn to the courts to evict trespassers.

The squatters in the *Southwark* cases relied on the doctrine of necessity to justify their unlawful action in occupying the houses without permission.[29] The Court of Appeals decided that the doctrine of necessity was recognised within very narrow limits in English law and that homelessness does not constitute the sort of emergency for which the doctrine could be invoked. In case of great and imminent

---

[27] *Southwark London Borough Council v Williams and Another; Southwark London Borough Council v Anderson and Another* [1971] 2 All ER 175 (HL); see AJ van der Walt, 'De Onrechtmatige Bezetting van Leegstaande Woningen en het Eigendomsbegrip: Een Vergelijkende Analyse van het Conflict tussen de Privaat Eigendom van Onroerend Goed en Dakloosheid' (1991) 17 *Recht & Kritiek* 329–59 at 330–2.

[28] K Gray and SF Gray, *Elements of Land Law* (4th edn, 2005) 240; *McPhail v Persons (Names Unknown)* [1973] Ch 447 at 456. The law of adverse possession is also relevant to the issue of squatting; see ch 6, section II.

[29] *Southwark London Borough Council v Williams and Another; Southwark London Borough Council v Anderson and Another* [1971] 2 All ER 175 (HL) at 177.

danger the doctrine of necessity could permit encroachment on private property, but to prevent it from being abused it had to be carefully circumscribed. According to the Court, homelessness, like hunger, could not be allowed as an excuse, because then no one's house would be safe. The Court therefore considered itself bound to take a firm stand, to reject the plea of necessity and to uphold the title to property for the sake of law and order.[30] The decision was clearly motivated by the ownership paradigm's assumption that the strict protection of ownership in itself was a guarantee of law and order.

E. American 'Property Outlaws'

Eduardo Peñalver and Sonia Katyal[31] use the expressive term 'property outlaws' to refer to persons who break or flout the laws of property openly and intentionally, arguing that the overwhelmingly negative view of property lawbreakers in the typically individualist, capitalist political culture of Western societies tends to overlook the important role that property lawbreakers have played, often as catalysts for needed legal change, in the evolution and transfer of property entitlements. Their argument supports the point made earlier in this chapter concerning the Dutch *krakers*, namely that necessary change in the property regime is sometimes achieved not through legal processes but through political action, which may in some instances involve unlawful occupation of property. They associate one category of property outlaws directly with the civil rights movement, pointing out that the lunch counter sit-ins to protest against segregation during the 1960s were essentially transgressions of property laws.[32] Interestingly, these sit-ins had the same purpose as the politically inspired squatting actions, namely to protest against the social effect (racial segregation) of property laws; in other words, to bring about larger social changes through changes in the (status or interpretation and application of) property laws. Just like the political squatters in Western Europe, the lunch counter sit-ins were 'intentionally disregarding the very property rights they sought to change'.[33] Flouting and challenging property rights and the laws that protect them openly was intended to bring about social and legal transformation. Like the Western European political squatters, the politically inspired or 'expressive' actions of the sit-in outlaws initially met with stern rejec-

---

[30] *Southwark London Borough Council v Williams and Another; Southwark London Borough Council v Anderson and Another* [1971] 2 All ER 175 (HL) per Lord Denning MR at 179–80; per Edmund Davies LJ at 181. The broad outline of this decision has been upheld in subsequent House of Lords decisions where it was decided that, as soon as it is clear that a public landlord's right to possession is unqualified, an occupier cannot rely on personal circumstances to challenge the eviction: see ch 4, n 104, compare *Kay and Another v London Borough of Lambeth and Others; Leeds City Council v Price and Others* [2006] UKHL 10 (HL) at para 110; *Doherty (FC) and Others v Birmingham City Council* [2008] UKHL 57 (HL) at para 9. On the defence of necessity in trespass cases see further K Gray and SF Gray, *Elements of Land Law* (4th edn, 2005) at 235.

[31] EM Peñalver and SK Katyal, 'Property Outlaws' (2007) 155 *Univ Pennsylvania LR* 1095–186.

[32] EM Peñalver and SK Katyal, 'Property Outlaws' (2007) 155 *Univ Pennsylvania LR* 1095–186 at 1114.

[33] EM Peñalver and SK Katyal, 'Property Outlaws' (2007) 155 *Univ Pennsylvania LR* 1095–186 at 1115.

tion and disapproval and with largely unsympathetic legal action,[34] although they obviously were more successful in the long run as far as changes in the legal system are concerned.

Apart from the lunch counter sit-ins, Peñalver and Katyal also describe another category of property outlaws that resembles the Western European political squatters more closely, namely the urban squatters who occupied unused buildings in the urban centres since the 1970s.[35] Much like their Western European counterparts, many of these squatters were activists protesting against inefficient and inadequate federal and local state housing programmes, claiming that state reactions to poverty and homelessness were exacerbating rather than combating the housing shortage and resulting urban decay. Peñalver and Katyal describe these urban squatters as 'intersectional squatters' to indicate that their actions were neither purely politically expressive nor purely acquisitive—their actions were partially politically inspired and partially really aimed at obtaining or providing desperately needed housing.[36]

F. Evaluation

The brief overview of politically inspired unlawful invasion and occupation of urban residential property above shows that squatting was widely used in the 1960s, 1970s and 1980s to protest against inadequate state housing programmes and policies and to force the state to amend and develop the laws, including property laws, so as to prevent anti-social abuse (non-use) of valuable and scarce residential housing and to increase access to housing. The overview also shows that the doctrinal efforts to construe a right to squat (or a defence against eviction, based on necessity) from the partial successes of the movement was unsuccessful. The most striking successes that the movement had in a couple of Hoge Raad decisions and the Middelburg court were restricted to Dutch law; moreover, they featured in summary judicial processes that do not allow any substantive conclusions about the relative value or strength of the occupiers' interest in the occupied property. Despite some interesting theoretical analyses by the likes of Gerrit van Maanen, and RM Schutte and JBM Vranken, the inevitable end result was that it was not possible to argue that homeless persons could acquire some kind of right to occupy uninhabited and unused premises belonging to someone else purely on the strength of social and economic circumstances.

However, the housing activists who initiated the political squats of the 1970s and 1980s were not entirely unsuccessful: They succeeded in inspiring amendments to housing law in at least two ways. Firstly, regulatory laws in both the

[34] EM Peñalver and SK Katyal, 'Property Outlaws' (2007) 155 *Univ Pennsylvania LR* 1095–186 at 1116–122.

[35] EM Peñalver and SK Katyal, 'Property Outlaws' (2007) 155 *Univ Pennsylvania LR* 1095–186 at 1122–6.

[36] EM Peñalver and SK Katyal, 'Property Outlaws' (2007) 155 *Univ Pennsylvania LR* 1095–186 at 1122–6.

Netherlands and Germany were amended in the 1980s to regulate non-use of valuable urban property, especially in the residential market. In the process one of the activists' main objectives, namely to protest against calculated neglect of urban property in order to ensure planning permission for demolition or renewal, was achieved. Secondly, most of the jurisdictions affected by strong political activism in the housing sphere introduced wide-ranging new housing legislation during the 1980s, at least partially in response to the protests—many of the central housing laws of the Netherlands, Germany and the United Kingdom date from that period. Similarly, the lunch counter sit-ins helped to inspire the eventual abolition of racial segregation laws and custom in the US.

III. Anti-eviction Protection in South African Land Reform Law[37]

A. Introduction

In chapter three it was pointed out that post-apartheid tenure reform laws protect both lawful and unlawful occupiers against unfair and arbitrary eviction. This seemingly extraordinary land reform strategy is best understood in the South African context of apartheid land law, where black people's occupation of land, both in urban and in rural areas, was often rendered unlawful by the technicalities of apartheid legislation or by the legacy of apartheid policy. Technically, apartheid laws classified (especially but not exclusively informal) occupation of land or structures on land as unlawful either because they did not comply with planning and building regulations that were designed for formal white urban developments, or because arbitrary changes in the government's classification of areas for separate development had rendered previously lawful occupation unlawful. Politically, apartheid policy directly and indirectly caused widespread landlessness and poverty, two of the social and economic factors that contribute to continuing unlawful land invasions and unlawful occupation of property. (The term 'land invasion' is not as common elsewhere as in South Africa; I use it here to refer to situations where people, sometimes from necessity and sometimes as a political act of protest, settle on and occupy land without any prior or current right to do so.) By protecting even unlawful occupiers of land against arbitrary and unfair eviction, the Constitutional Assembly (in adopting section 26(3) of the Constitution) and the legislature (in adopting the Prevention of Illegal Eviction from and

---

[37] This section of the chapter is loosely based on revised passages from AJ van der Walt, 'Exclusivity of Ownership, Security of Tenure, and Eviction Orders: A Model to Evaluate South African Land-Reform Legislation' 2002 *TSAR* 254–89; AJ van der Walt, 'Ownership and Eviction: Constitutional Rights in Private Law' (2005) 9 *Edinburgh LR* 32–64; AJ van der Walt, *Constitutional Property Law* (2005) at 308–53, 416–19, 424–7.

Unlawful Occupation of Land Act 19 of 1998, or PIE) acknowledged the role that apartheid and apartheid-inspired or -sanctioned eviction played in causing and exacerbating poverty and landlessness. The social construction of property relations and the political nature of homelessness are thus recognised in an overtly political effort at reform and reconstruction through imposing fairness and due process restrictions upon eviction of unlawful occupiers. This historical context shows the importance of recognising the political aspect of squatting. Once it is acknowledged that occupation and use of land is sometimes rendered unlawful by political intervention in the first place, it becomes easier to see that homelessness is generally a function of political decisions to recognise, uphold and protect certain interests above others. Once the law entrenches these political decisions, legal action might be ineffective in promoting the cause of those who are affected by them, and then it is clear that political action (not necessarily lawful) might be justified, at least in the political sense, as a means to bring about changes in the legal regime that created or exacerbated homelessness in the first place. For present purposes my goal is not primarily to engage the moral or political arguments for and against unlawful political action (including squatting), but rather to point out that this line of thinking highlights the fallacy of abstract, a-contextual enforcement of eviction orders in terms of the rights paradigm and the political significance and legitimacy of legislative and judicial interventions that take cognisance of the general historical, social and economic context within which eviction takes place and the personal circumstances of the occupiers.

B. Prevention of Illegal Eviction from and Unlawful Occupation of Land Act 19 of 1998 (PIE)

The principal statute that protects unlawful occupiers against eviction is the Prevention of Illegal Eviction from and Unlawful Occupation of Land Act 19 of 1998 (PIE).[38] The Act was promulgated to give effect to the constitutional right not to be evicted from one's home or have one's home demolished without a court order, which can be made only after considering all the relevant circumstances.[39]

---

[38] The Act applies to urban and rural land, and to factual occupation of land that is not based on permission of the landowner or some other right to occupy the land, but excludes (from the definition of 'unlawful occupier') a person who is an occupier in terms of the Extension of Security of Tenure Act 62 of 1997, and a person whose informal land rights are protected by the Interim Protection of Informal Land Rights Act 31 of 1996: s 2 read with s 1(xi). See JM Pienaar and A Muller, 'The Impact of the Prevention of Illegal Eviction from and Unlawful Occupation of Land Act 19 of 1998 on Homelessness and Unlawful Occupation within the Present Statutory Framework' (1999) 10 *Stell LR* 370–96; JM Pienaar and H Mostert, 'Uitsettings onder die Suid-Afrikaanse Grondwet: Die Verhouding tussen Artikel 25(1), Artikel 26(3) en die Uitsettingswet (Deel 1)' 2006 *TSAR* 277–99.

[39] Section 26(3) of the 1996 Constitution. In *Minister of Health and Another NO v New Clicks South Africa (Pty) Ltd and Others (Treatment Action Campaign and Another as* Amici Curiae*)* 2006 (2) SA 311 (CC) at paras 95–6, 434–7 with regard to s 33 and the Promotion of Administrative Justice Act 3 of 2000; confirmed in *South African National Defence Union v Minister of Defence and Others* 2007 (5) SA 400 (CC) at para 51 with regard to s 23(5) (right to collective bargaining) of the Labour Relations Act 66 of 1995; *MEC for Education: KwaZulu-Natal and Others v Pillay* 2008 (1) SA 474 (CC) at para 39

Like the other land reform laws, the Act establishes a threshold of due process requirements for eviction in accordance with the principle laid down in section 26(3) of the Constitution. Firstly, eviction is possible only once it has been proven that an occupier is an unlawful occupier as defined in the Act[40] and that she has no valid defence.[41] Once it had been established that the occupier is liable to be evicted in terms of the Act, eviction has to be authorised by a court order.[42] Thirdly, the court order authorising eviction has to be based on the court's judgment that, having consideration of all the relevant circumstances, granting such an order is just and equitable under the circumstances.[43] Finally, the granting and execution of eviction orders is subjected to strict procedural prescriptions.[44] Against the background of apartheid land law and taking into account the general tendency towards due process of law in the new constitutional order, it is not surprising that even unlawful occupiers of land are protected against arbitrary eviction in this fashion. As appears from the previous section of this chapter and from chapter four, it is customary in most jurisdictions to subject eviction of all occupiers to due process and judicial control.

with regard to s 9 (equality) and the Promotion of Equality and Prevention of Unfair Discrimination Act 4 of 2000, the Constitutional Court developed the view that once legislation has been promulgated to give effect to a particular constitutional right, a litigant cannot circumvent the legislation and rely directly on the constitutional right. The same logic must apply to PIE, which was enacted specifically to give effect to the rights in s 26(3). This aspect is discussed further below.

[40] Section 1 defines 'unlawful occupier' as 'a person who occupies land without the express or tacit consent of the owner or person in charge, or without any other right in law to occupy such land', excluding those already protected by the Extension of Security of Tenure Act 62 of 1997 and the Interim Protection of Informal Land Rights Act 31 of 1996.

[41] Section 4(8). Since the Act applies only to unlawful occupiers and unlawful occupiers have no right to occupy, the Act makes no provision for the termination of existing occupation rights, as is the norm with other land reform laws that control eviction of lawful occupiers. In *Simonsig Landgoed (Edms) Bpk v Vers* 2007 (5) SA 103 (C) the Cape High Court decided that the eviction of formerly lawful occupiers (tenants and their families) whose occupation had become unlawful because the tenancy was terminated by the death of the tenant had to be considered in terms of the legislation that regulated their tenancy while still lawful (Extension of Security of Tenure Act 62 of 1997; ESTA) and not PIE.

[42] Section 8(1) renders unauthorised evictions an offence under the Act.

[43] This summary of the requirements was confirmed by the Supreme Court of Appeal in *Wormald NO and Others v Kambule* 2006 (3) SA 562 (SCA) at para 10: 'PIE therefore requires a party seeking to evict another from land to prove not only that he or she owns such land and that the other party occupies it unlawfully, but also that he or she has complied with the procedural provisions and that on a consideration of all the relevant circumstances (and, according to the *Brisley* case, to qualify as relevant the circumstances must be legally relevant), an eviction order is "just and equitable"'. As is indicated in the text below (n 152 and accompanying text), the reference to the *Brisley* qualification in the quote above is inapposite, because *Brisley* was decided with reference to s 26(3) of the Constitution, which does not spell out the circumstances that should be considered, whereas the *Wormald* case dealt with PIE, where the circumstances are spelled out quite clearly, thereby overriding the SCA's objections in *Brisley*.

[44] Section 4(1) specifies that the Act applies to eviction proceedings by the owner or person in charge against an unlawful occupier. Section 4(2) contains notice requirements (the occupier plus the responsible municipality), ss 4(3) and (4) prescribe serving requirements. Section 4(5) prescribes information to be included in the notice (nature of proceedings is for eviction, date and time of hearing, grounds for proposed eviction, state the unlawful occupier's right to appear and defend the case and to legal aid).

However, like some other land reform laws[45] this Act goes further and subjects eviction of unlawful occupiers to substantive fairness requirements that extend beyond procedural controls. These substantive fairness requirements are peremptory and because they require consideration of the occupier's position, an eviction order will not be given ex parte.[46] The substantive requirements identify the social and political background of the housing shortage and the social and personal circumstances of the occupiers as factors that have to be considered before an eviction order is granted, thereby indicating that the Act brings about a significant qualification of the rights paradigm. In some instances this qualification might pose a serious threat to the integrity of the paradigm if the courts exercise a general discretion to prevent eviction, even though the landowner could prove all the common law and the statutory requirements, purely because of the circumstances of the occupier and the effect that eviction would have on her and her family.

First of all, a court considering an application for eviction of an unlawful occupier must distinguish between unlawful occupiers who have occupied the land in question, at the time when the proceedings are initiated, for less than six months, and unlawful occupiers who have occupied the land for more than six months.[47] In the sense that the duration of occupation affects the level of protection this distinction resembles other procedural fairness requirements, but the Act also imposes substantive fairness requirements in specifying the circumstances to be considered for each of the two groups of occupiers. When the occupation has lasted for less than six months, a court may grant the eviction order if it is of the opinion that it is just and equitable to do so, after considering all the relevant circumstances, including the rights and needs of the elderly, children, disabled persons and households headed by women.[48] If the occupation has been for longer than six months, a court must, in addition to deciding whether an eviction order would be just and equitable considering all the relevant circumstances (again including the rights and needs of the elderly, children, disabled persons and households headed by women), also consider the question whether land has been made available or can reasonably be made available by a municipality or other organ of state or another landowner for the relocation of the unlawful occupiers.[49] This requirement is waived only in instances where the land is sold in execution

---

[45] Compare the eviction of tenants in ch 4.

[46] *Pedro and Others v Transitional Council of the Greater George* [2001] 1 All SA 334 (C); confirmed in *Cape Killarney Property Investments (Pty) Ltd v Mahamba and Others* [2001] 4 All SA 479 (A).

[47] In *Port Elizabeth Municipality v Peoples Dialogue on Land and Shelter and Others* [2001] 1 All SA 381 (E), the Eastern Cape High Court full bench held that this provision is intended to protect the community of people who are to be evicted, and that it is their duty to provide the court with information. This question was the cause of differences of opinion in case-law and literature; see n 92 and compare the discussion of case-law below, particularly with regard to the Constitutional Court decision in *Port Elizabeth Municipality v Various Occupiers* 2005 (1) SA 217 (CC).

[48] Section 4(6).

[49] Section 4(7). As in the case of similar provisions in other land reform laws, the question is who should supply this information and what the court should do if no information is available. See n 92 and compare the discussion of case-law below, particularly the Constitutional Court decision in *Port Elizabeth Municipality v Various Occupiers* 2005 (1) SA 217 (CC).

pursuant to a mortgage.[50] When granting an eviction order, the court must determine a just and equitable date on which the unlawful occupier must vacate the land, as well as a date on which the eviction order may be carried out if the unlawful occupier fails to vacate the land,[51] taking into account all relevant factors, including the period the unlawful occupier and his or her family have resided on the land.[52] The court may also make an order regarding the demolition and removal of buildings and structures occupied by the unlawful occupier,[53] including any conditions the court may consider reasonable.[54]

The provisions set out thus far apply to eviction proceedings instituted by landowners, but the Act also makes provision for evictions at the instance of an organ of state with regard to land that falls within its area of jurisdiction.[55] The court may grant an eviction order in these cases,[56] where the organ of state applies for an eviction order not as landowner but as regulating authority,[57] if it is just and equitable to do so considering all the relevant circumstances,[58] and if the consent of the organ of state is required for the erection of a building or structure on the

[50] Section 4(7).

[51] Section 4(8).

[52] Section 4(9). See n 92.

[53] Section 4(10).

[54] Section 4(12). The court may also authorise any person to assist the sheriff in carrying out the eviction and demolition: s 4 (11).

[55] Section 6(1). Once again this does not apply when the unlawful occupier is a mortgagor and the land is sold in a sale of execution pursuant to a mortgage. A landowner who has been given notice by a state organ in terms of s 6(4) to institute eviction proceedings against unlawful occupiers of the private land is not burdened by the duties placed on the state by s 6—the private landowner only has to satisfy the requirements of s 4(6) or s 4(7): *Modderklip Boerdery (Pty) Ltd v Modder East Squatters and Another* 2001 (4) SA 385 (W) at para 1.

[56] Section 6(4)–(6) prescribes notice and procedural requirements for these cases. The decision in *Port Elizabeth Municipality v Peoples Dialogue on Land and Shelter and Others* 2000 (2) SA 1074 (SE) dealt with a situation under this provision.

[57] In *Port Elizabeth Municipality v Peoples Dialogue on Land and Shelter and Others* [2001] 1 All SA 381 (E), the Eastern Cape High Court full bench held that this provision was primarily intended for situations where the local authority acted as regulatory organ of state and not as landowner, but in cases where the local authority was also the landowner it could bring an application for an eviction order in the alternative, first as landowner under s 4 and then as state organ under s 6, with the result that a state organ which is also landowner is not disbarred from relying on s 6. Compare *Minister of Public Works and Others v Kyalami Ridge Environmental Association and Another (Mukhwevo Intervening)* 2001 (3) SA 1151 (CC) (the state has the same rights in respect of state land as a private landowner in respect of private land); see ch 3, n 36.

[58] For this purpose, the court must have regard to the circumstances under which the unlawful occupier occupied the land and erected the structure or building, the period for which the unlawful occupier and his or her family have occupied the land, and the availability of suitable alternative accommodation or land: s 6(3). In *Port Elizabeth Municipality v Peoples Dialogue on Land and Shelter and Others* 2000 (2) SA 1074 (SE) (confirmed on this point on appeal by the full bench in *Port Elizabeth Municipality v Peoples Dialogue on Land and Shelter and Others* [2001] 1 All SA 381 (E)) the Eastern Cape High Court held that the unlawful invasion of land which was earmarked for housing development must weigh heavily against the unlawful occupiers when an eviction order against them is considered, because they cannot be allowed to frustrate the overall development effort or to 'jump the housing queue' or to hold the process to ransom by their unilateral action. It is a question whether and how far this view accords with or can be reconciled with the Constitutional Court decision regarding emergency housing in *Government of the Republic of South Africa and Others v Grootboom and Others* 2001 (1) SA 46 (CC).

land or for the occupation of the land, and the unlawful occupier is occupying a building or structure without such permission, or if it is in the public interest[59] to grant such an order.[60]

C. Effect on the Common Law and Early Case-law

From the brief summary above it is clear that the Act goes far beyond mere proce-dural protection of unlawful occupiers. Even unlawful occupiers who have been in occupation for a relatively short period (less than six months) can, in terms of the Act, only be evicted when a court considers it just and equitable to do so, consid-ering the personal and social circumstances of the occupiers and all other relevant factors. The explicitly enumerated factors to be considered in exercising this dis-cretion, namely the rights and needs of the elderly, children, disabled persons and households headed by women, indicate that the Act departs from the common law in a way that poses a serious challenge for the rights paradigm—the economic and legal value of the landowner's right no longer automatically or presumptively trumps the interests of the occupiers. Instead, the personal and social circum-stances of the occupiers, specifically their weaknesses and vulnerability, have to be considered by a court in exercising its discretion whether or not to allow eviction (and, if it does, in determining the conditions under which the eviction should take place). The Act therefore foresees the possibility that a landowner might not succeed with an eviction application, even when she has satisfied all the common law and statutory requirements, purely because of the hardship that the occupiers would suffer if evicted. This is a significant departure from the common law posi-tion and it undermines the central logic of the rights paradigm. The question is how to construe the intended effect of the Act on the common law, where the owner's right to possession was considered a trump unless the occupier could prove a stronger right to occupy.[61]

The Act explicitly overrides the common law right to evict and therefore one might expect that it would simply replace the common law,[62] but in a number of cases the application of the Act and its reforming effect on the common law was restricted by judicial cautiousness.[63] Applicability of the Act caused the most

---

[59] 'Public interest' includes, for this purpose, the interest of the health and safety of those occupy-ing the land and of the public in general: s 6(2). In *Port Elizabeth Municipality v Peoples Dialogue on Land and Shelter and Others* [2001] 1 All SA 381 (E), the Eastern Cape High Court full bench held that in a situation where an unlawful land invasion is preventing the local authority from proceeding with the development of the land for housing, it is clearly in the public interest to grant an eviction order, to enable the local authority to go ahead with development plans.

[60] Section 6(1)(a)–(b).

[61] Compare ch 4.

[62] Section 4(1).

[63] In principle, one would expect the subsidiarity principle worked out in *Bato Star Fishing (Pty) Ltd v Minister of Environmental Affairs and Others* 2004 (4) SA 490 (CC) at para 25; *Minister of Health and Another NO v New Clicks South Africa (Pty) Ltd and Others (Treatment Action Campaign and Another as* Amici Curiae*)* 2006 (2) SA 311 (CC) at para 96 with reference to the Promotion of Administrative Justice Act 3 of 2000 (PAJA), and confirmed in *Chirwa v Transnet Ltd and Others* 2008 (4) SA 367 (CC)

serious problems with regard to eviction of occupiers who once occupied the land lawfully, but whose right of occupation had been cancelled or terminated. In *ABSA Bank Ltd v Amod*[64] it was held that the Act applies only to unlawful invasions of vacant land and unlawful occupation of structures erected in conflict with planning and buildings laws and regulations, and not to formalised housing or to 'normal' common-law rent or lease agreements. The result was that the Act was considered not to be applicable in cases of former tenants holding over. This decision was followed in several subsequent cases.[65] In *Ndlovu v Ngcobo; Bekker v Jika*[66] the Supreme Court of Appeal held that PIE does apply to a tenant who is holding over subsequent to the lawful termination of her lease and that an eviction order cannot be given without considering the personal and socio-economic circumstances of the occupiers as prescribed in the Act. The SCA accepted the reformist intention of the Act and its implications for the common law by arguing that the legislature intended that the Act should protect weak and vulnerable members of society against unfair eviction and that ex-tenants or formerly lawful occupiers should be included in the protected category.[67]

---

at para 23; *Fuel Retailers Association of Southern Africa v Director-General: Environmental Management, Department of Agriculture, Conservation and Environment, Mpumalanga Province, and Others* 2007 (6) SA 4 (CC) at para 37, to the effect that, once legislation has been enacted to give effect to a right in the Bill of Rights and to 'cover the field', that legislation should be regarded as a kind of codification and the common law can no longer be seen as an alternative, parallel system of law in the field, to apply to eviction of unlawful occupiers as well, especially since it is clear that PIE is legislation so enacted to give effect to s 26(3) and since this subsidiarity principle is a kind of flipside of the principle already mentioned in n 39. However, nothing has been decided on this point yet and several Supreme Court of Appeal (*Tswelopele Non-Profit Organisation v City of Tshwane Metropolitan Municipality* 2007 (6) SA 511 (SCA)) and Constitutional Court decisions (*Occupiers of 51 Olivia Road, Berea Township, and 197 Main Street, Johannesburg v City of Johannesburg and Others* 2008 (3) SA 208 (CC)) are difficult to square with it. On subsidiarity see generally L du Plessis, '"Subsidiarity": What's in the Name for Constitutional Interpretation and Adjudication?' (2006) 17 *Stell LR* 207–31.

[64] [1999] 2 All SA 423 (W).

[65] The relevant cases are discussed in ch 4, section III. and below. For an extensive discussion of the case-law see further AJ van der Walt, 'Exclusivity of Ownership, Security of Tenure, and Eviction Orders: A Critical Evaluation of Recent Case Law' (2002) 18 *SAJHR* 371–419; T Roux, 'Continuity and Change in a Transforming Legal Order: The Impact of Section 26(3) of the Constitution on South African Law' (2004) 121 *SALJ* 466–92; JM Pienaar and H Mostert, 'Uitsettings onder die Suid-Afrikaanse Grondwet: Die Verhouding tussen Artikel 25(1), Artikel 26(3) en die Uitsettingswet (Deel 1)' 2006 *TSAR* 277–99.

[66] 2003 (1) SA 113 (SCA). The following paragraphs are based loosely on rewritten and amended sections from AJ van der Walt, 'Ownership and Eviction: Constitutional Rights in Private Law' (2005) 9 *Edinburgh LR* 32–64.

[67] The SCA argued that there was not a sufficiently clear indication of legislative intention to the contrary, and that it could not be discounted that the legislature intended to extend the applicability of PIE to cases of holding over: *Ndlovu v Ngcobo; Bekker v Jika* 2003 (1) SA 113 (SCA) at paras 21–3. Since that decision there have been several attempts to amend PIE. The most recent Prevention of Illegal Eviction From and Unlawful Occupation of Land Amendment Bill of 2007 was published on 7 March 2008, being a direct consequence of earlier Draft Bills published on 16 November 2007 (*GG* 30459) and 22 December 2006 (General Notice 1851, *GG* 29501) respectively. The most important aim of the 2007 Bill is to restrict the scope of PIE by excluding from the scope of the Act persons who occupied land as tenants; in terms of any other agreement; and owners who continue to occupy after the basis for their occupation has lapsed. Notwithstanding these provisions, depending on the particular circumstances, the court may direct that the proceedings ought to be under PIE although the application was brought under the common law.

The contrast between the Supreme Court of Appeal's obviously reform-friendly decision in *Ndlovu/Bekker* and its earlier decision in *Brisley v Drotsky*[68] is striking and may appear puzzling. In *Brisley* the SCA refused to acknowledge that section 26(3) of the Constitution has a direct reforming effect on the common law with regard to eviction; in *Ndlovu/Bekker* it readily accepted that PIE has exactly that effect. The key to the apparent contradiction between the two decisions is the fact that PIE explicitly overrides the common law and obliges the courts to depart from the common law by exercising a judicial discretion in considering whether to allow eviction or not; PIE also specifies the considerations to be taken into account when exercising that discretion and therefore overcomes the scepticism of *Brisley*. The objection in *Brisley* was that section 26(3) does not explicitly grant the courts a discretion or specify the circumstances to be taken into account and that the courts are therefore not authorised to 'deprive' the landowner of a right to evict that she would normally have had in terms of common law; under PIE this objection falls away and the courts can refuse to allow eviction simply because of what they consider just and equitable with reference to the circumstances of the occupier.[69]

Despite the apparent clear intention of the legislature to change the law with regard to eviction, early case-law about the purpose and effect of PIE creates the impression of uncertainty and lack of a coherent vision. Such a vision has been developed in more recent case-law of the Constitutional Court, albeit that the latest and most interesting of these decisions was handed down without considering the question whether PIE was applicable to the case and what the relationship between section 26(3) of the Constitution and PIE was.

D. Recent Case-law

In *Port Elizabeth Municipality v Various Occupiers*,[70] a groundbreaking decision that includes a historically and context-sensitive analysis of the relationship between the constitutional anti-eviction provision (section 26(3)) and the constitutional protection of property (section 25) in post-apartheid law, the Constitutional Court confirmed that courts exercise a judicial discretion in deciding whether it is just and equitable to grant an eviction order in terms of PIE[71] and that they should take special steps to obtain relevant information regarding the interests of vulnerable persons and groups and the availability of alternative accommodation.[72] Secondly,

---

[68] 2002 (4) SA 1 (SCA) at paras 35–46. See the discussion of *Brisley* in ch 2, section II. and ch 4, section III.

[69] In *Baartman and Others v Port Elizabeth Municipality* 2004 (1) SA 560 (SCA) the Court also displayed a strong awareness of the historical, social and economic context within which the legislation was promulgated and had to be interpreted, and assumed that its discretion in considering the eviction application was quite wide. PIE also clearly applied to this case and thus the same logic as in *Ndlovu/Bekker* was at work.

[70] 2005 (1) SA 217 (CC).

[71] *Port Elizabeth Municipality v Various Occupiers* 2005 (1) SA 217 (CC) at paras 31–2.

[72] *Port Elizabeth Municipality v Various Occupiers* 2005 (1) SA 217 (CC) at paras 32, 36.

the Court pointed out that land reform laws can be interpreted and applied for the sake of transformation only when they are explicitly and purposively understood in their historical framework (the role of evictions and forced removals under apartheid) and their constitutional framework (the transformative purpose of the Constitution and the land reform laws).[73]

In *Port Elizabeth Municipality*, the Constitutional Court laid down the foundation for all decisions about eviction under PIE, placing special emphasis on the importance of contextual and purposive interpretation and application of the Act. Section 26(3) of the Constitution and the anti-eviction legislation promulgated in terms of it are intended to rectify eviction abuses of the apartheid past and to prevent their recurrence.[74] In the historical and constitutional context of these provisions it is necessary to establish an appropriate constitutional relationship between the protection of property rights (section 25) and the protection of access to housing (section 26).[75] The Constitution challenges the courts to avoid the traditional hierarchical view of property and housing rights and to reconcile them in as just a manner as possible, taking into account all the interests involved and paying proper attention to the circumstances of each case.[76] In some instances, such a contextual analysis could imply that a landowner might not be able to obtain or enforce an eviction order, even though she is able to satisfy the common law and statutory requirements, simply because the court deems eviction unjustified in view of the general social and the particular personal circumstances of the unlawful occupiers. However, the Court also made it clear that the anti-eviction measures do not imply that it becomes impossible for a landowner to obtain an eviction order—in cases where it is justified, eviction orders will still be granted, even if it means that people will lose their home. The Court emphasised that the decision whether to allow eviction is a highly case-specific one that has to be taken anew in every individual case, taking into account all the circumstances.[77] This statement can be seen as a more or less straightforward rejection of the central tenets of the rights paradigm as far as eviction is concerned.

The constitutional approach set out in *Port Elizabeth Municipality* was subsequently followed in a number of cases, the most interesting of which, *Occupiers of 51 Olivia Road, Berea Township, and 197 Main Street, Johannesburg v City of Johannesburg and Others*,[78] involved an effort by a local authority to evict unlawful

---

[73] *Port Elizabeth Municipality v Various Occupiers* 2005 (1) SA 217 (CC) at paras 8–23.

[74] *Port Elizabeth Municipality v Various Occupiers* 2005 (1) SA 217 (CC) at paras 11, 14.

[75] *Port Elizabeth Municipality v Various Occupiers* 2005 (1) SA 217 (CC) at para 19. This contextual approach to eviction was reiterated by the Court in a subsequent decision: *Mphela and 217 Others v Haakdoornbult Boerdery CC and Others* 2008 (7) BCLR 675 (CC).

[76] *Port Elizabeth Municipality v Various Occupiers* 2005 (1) SA 217 (CC) at para 23.

[77] *Port Elizabeth Municipality v Various Occupiers* 2005 (1) SA 217 (CC) at para 31. The Court indicated that it would ordinarily not be just and equitable to grant an eviction order unless proper discussions and, where suitable, mediation had been attempted to settle the matter: para 43.

[78] 2008 (3) SA 208 (CC). The case had its origin in plans of the City of Johannesburg, in line with its Inner City Regeneration Strategy, to evict the occupiers from three premises in the Johannesburg municipal area. The evictions were justified by allegations that the premises in question presented dangerous living conditions, including health and fire hazards, and that it would promote public health

occupiers from inner city premises in terms of its powers to promote public health and safety, used in this case to reverse inner city decay and eradicate dangerous and unhealthy living conditions.[79] In first deciding the case the Witwatersrand High Court followed the example of the *Port Elizabeth Municipality*[80] and *Modderklip*[81] decisions of the Constitutional Court, emphasising that eviction is fundamentally a political matter and that eviction cases therefore have to be decided in terms of the historical and contextual approach set out by the Constitutional Court. Even when the post-apartheid democratic state exercises its legitimate police power to maintain or protect public health and safety it must reconcile that duty with its constitutional duty towards the housing needs of the poor and the destitute.[82] In terms of the constitutional approach, the personal circumstances of occupiers have to be considered before an eviction can be granted, both when the landowner applies for eviction to enforce her property rights and when the local authority applies for eviction to exercise its police powers in ensuring public health and safety. The mere fact that premises appear to be unsafe or unhealthy does not automatically or mechanically justify eviction by the local authority—the degree of desperation of the people living under those circumstances and the length of time of their occupancy have to be considered as well.[83] The Constitution requires that the state should ensure that everyone has access to affordable and acceptable housing; among other things this means not destroying existing access to housing unless it can be justified with reference to constitutional requirements and values.[84]

This High Court decision was overturned by the Supreme Court of Appeal[85] but later confirmed by the Constitutional Court.[86] The interesting aspect of the Constitutional Court decision is that it was made in an unusual way. Two days after the application for leave to appeal was heard, the Constitutional Court surprisingly issued an interim order to ensure that the city and occupiers 'would engage with each other meaningfully' on certain issues involved in the eviction. As

and safety to 'evacuate' the premises as part of the process of reversing inner city decay. In certain instances the eviction notices were accompanied by notices directing the owners to demolish, alter or 'evacuate' the buildings in question. Another interesting High Court decision in which the balancing approach was followed is *Jackpersad v Mitha* 2008 (4) SA 522 (D).

[79] Relying on its powers in the National Building Regulations and Building Standards Act 103 of 1977, the Health Act 63 of 1977 and local fire by-laws.

[80] *Port Elizabeth Municipality v Various Occupiers* 2005 (1) SA 217 (CC).

[81] *President of the Republic of South Africa and Another v Modderklip Boerdery (Pty) Ltd (Agri SA and Others,* Amici Curiae*)* 2005 (5) SA 3 (CC).

[82] *City of Johannesburg v Rand Properties (Pty) Ltd and Others* 2007 (1) SA 78 (W) at paras 26, 28.

[83] *City of Johannesburg v Rand Properties (Pty) Ltd and Others* 2007 (1) SA 78 (W) at para 29.

[84] *City of Johannesburg v Rand Properties (Pty) Ltd and Others* 2007 (1) SA 78 (W) at paras 50, 52. The city was ordered to devise and implement, within its available resources, a coordinated programme that would progressively realise the right of residents of the inner city to have access to adequate housing. Pending the implementation of this programme or provision of alternative adequate accommodation the city was interdicted from evicting the residents: See the Court's order (following para 67).

[85] *City of Johannesburg v Rand Properties (Pty) Ltd and Others* 2007 (6) SA 417 (SCA). The SCA granted the eviction orders and combined them with an order that the local authority should provide temporary accommodation for certain occupiers.

[86] *Occupiers of 51 Olivia Road, Berea Township, and 197 Main Street, Johannesburg v City of Johannesburg and Others* 2008 (3) SA 208 (CC).

the court subsequently explained in the reported decision,[87] this order was ultimately founded on and justified by section 26 of the Constitution and based on the line of approach adopted in its earlier decisions.[88] A city (local authority) has constitutional obligations towards the occupants of residential property in its jurisdiction, including the obligation to respect, protect, promote and fulfil the rights in the Bill of Rights, the most important of which are the rights to dignity and life.[89] In view of these obligations, a municipality that evicts people from their homes without first meaningfully engaging with them to search for a solution 'acts in a manner that is broadly at odds with the spirit and purpose of the constitutional obligations'.[90] The duty to engage with people who may be rendered homeless by eviction is also 'squarely grounded' in the state's constitutional obligation (section 26(2)) to take reasonable measures, within its available resources, to achieve the progressive realisation of the right of access to housing.[91] Meaningful engagement between a municipality and people who may be rendered homeless by eviction is a two-way process with an open-ended list of objectives, including determining what the consequences of eviction might be; whether the city could help to alleviate dire consequences of eviction; whether it is possible to render unsafe or unhealthy buildings relatively safe and conducive to health for an interim period; whether the city had any obligations towards the occupiers in the prevailing circumstances and when and how the city could or would fulfil those obligations. Engaging in meaningful discussion about these issues might be a burdensome task but is by no means impossible for the local authority; at the same time, the occupiers must cooperate and not engage in intransigent and unreasonable attitudes.[92]

The Constitutional Court had issued the interim order 'because it was not appropriate to grant any eviction order against the occupiers, in the circumstances of this case, unless there had at least been some effort at meaningful engagement. ... The ejectment of a resident by a municipality in circumstances where the resident would possibly become homeless should ordinarily take place only after meaningful engagement.'[93] Accordingly, the court emphasised, meaningful engagement should in future cases like this take place prior to litigation unless it is

---

[87] *Occupiers of 51 Olivia Road, Berea Township, and 197 Main Street, Johannesburg v City of Johannesburg and Others* 2008 (3) SA 208 (CC) at paras 9–23.

[88] *Government of the Republic of South Africa and Others v Grootboom and Others* 2001 (1) SA 46 (CC) and *Port Elizabeth Municipality v Various Occupiers* 2005 (1) SA 217 (CC).

[89] *Occupiers of 51 Olivia Road, Berea Township, and 197 Main Street, Johannesburg v City of Johannesburg and Others* 2008 (3) SA 208 (CC) at para 16.

[90] *Occupiers of 51 Olivia Road, Berea Township, and 197 Main Street, Johannesburg v City of Johannesburg and Others* 2008 (3) SA 208 (CC) at para 16.

[91] *Occupiers of 51 Olivia Road, Berea Township, and 197 Main Street, Johannesburg v City of Johannesburg and Others* 2008 (3) SA 208 (CC) at paras 17, 18.

[92] *Occupiers of 51 Olivia Road, Berea Township, and 197 Main Street, Johannesburg v City of Johannesburg and Others* 2008 (3) SA 208 (CC) at paras 14, 19, 20.

[93] *Occupiers of 51 Olivia Road, Berea Township, and 197 Main Street, Johannesburg v City of Johannesburg and Others* 2008 (3) SA 208 (CC) at para 22.

impossible for some compelling reason.[94] In view of this decision the Court confirmed the so-called post-engagement agreement reached by the parties, but it declined the invitation to decide on a number of outstanding issues, including the general reach and applicability of section 26 of the Constitution, whether the Prevention of Illegal Eviction from and Unlawful Occupation of Land Act 19 of 1998 (PIE) applied to the case and the relationship between PIE and section 26.[95]

The Constitutional Court confirmed that the power to evict under section 12(4)(b) of the National Building Regulations and Building Standards Act 103 of 1977 and the right to adequate housing in section 26 were not reciprocal and that the former is neither dependent nor conditional on the latter. However, it would be wrong to assume that there is no relationship at all between section 26 and section 12(4)(b), even if an occupier would be rendered homeless by eviction. The Constitutional Court therefore explicitly rejected the false impression that the municipality could simply ignore the effect of eviction on the occupier:[96] The city must simultaneously take responsibility for safe and healthy buildings and for the welfare of its residents; it cannot just carry out the one obligation and ignore the other.[97] In what appears to be a rejection of the Supreme Court of Appeal's view in *Brisley v Drotsky*,[98] that non-rights based considerations (such as the effect of

---

[94] *Occupiers of 51 Olivia Road, Berea Township, and 197 Main Street, Johannesburg v City of Johannesburg and Others* 2008 (3) SA 208 (CC) at para 30.

[95] *Occupiers of 51 Olivia Road, Berea Township, and 197 Main Street, Johannesburg v City of Johannesburg and Others* 2008 (3) SA 208 (CC) at paras 24–6, 28, 29, 31–8. The question whether PIE applied to the case and the relationship between s 26(3) and PIE would have been important issues if they were considered, considering the subsidiarity approach that was adopted in earlier cases: see fnn 30, 39 above.

[96] *Occupiers of 51 Olivia Road, Berea Township, and 197 Main Street, Johannesburg v City of Johannesburg and Others* 2008 (3) SA 208 (CC) at para 43.

[97] *Occupiers of 51 Olivia Road, Berea Township, and 197 Main Street, Johannesburg v City of Johannesburg and Others* 2008 (3) SA 208 (CC) at para 44.

[98] 2002 (4) SA 1 (SCA). See particularly the discussion in ch 2, section II. and again in ch 4, section III. In *Wormald NO and Others v Kambule* 2006 (3) SA 562 (SCA) the Supreme Court of Appeal seemed to follow the Constitutional Court's guidelines as set out in *Port Elizabeth Municipality*, but in fact it followed the narrower approach of *Brisley*, as appears from the statement in para 11 that the considerations must be 'legally relevant'. *Brisley* dealt with an application under s 26(3) and not PIE and was therefore not authority for the eviction under PIE in *Wormald*. The outcome of the case is also less clear-cut than it may appear. The woman who occupied the property used to live there with a man with whom she was allegedly married according to customary law before his death. The man was married to another woman in a civil union, who apparently disapproved of the second 'wife', causing the husband to move her to the present location: item 6 4, para 6. The property belonged to a close corporation, of which the deceased man was the only member, and was heavily mortgaged. The administrators of the deceased estate wanted to sell the property and offered the 'widow' alternative accommodation, either for life (if a customary union was proved) or for six months (if not); she declined the offer: paras 19, 21. The SCA concluded that it was just and equitable to grant an eviction order, considering that the woman was not obviously indigent or 'in dire need of accommodation and does not belong to the poor and vulnerable class of persons whose protection was obviously foremost in the Legislature's mind when it enacted PIE': paras 19–21. The SCA considered the estate's offer of alternative accommodation reasonable and the woman's rejection unreasonable, but the question was never asked whether she would have been rendered homeless if unable to prove a valid customary union. (Proof of such a union would entitle her to a maintenance claim against the estate; the deceased did not make any provision for her in his will.) Although the financial state of the deceased's estate is never made

eviction on the occupier) are irrelevant in eviction cases, the Constitutional Court concluded that the Supreme Court of Appeal failed to 'wholly embrace the inter-relationship between section 12(4)(b) of the Act and section 26(2) of the Constitution' by regarding this case as being '"only peripherally about the constitutional duty of organs of state towards those who are evicted from their homes and are in a desperate condition" '.[99]

The 'significant engagement' process introduced in this decision is of great importance for all evictions involving local authorities or other state bodies. In view of the clear purpose of section 26 this approach is a logical development of the case-law since *Grootboom*[100] and *Port Elizabeth Municipality*.[101] There is enough flexibility in the engagement requirements to prevent them from becoming an impossible burden on local authorities and other state bodies doing their best to manage land use and provision of housing.[102] The significance of the *Port Elizabeth Municipality* decision and the judgments that followed it is that the Constitutional Court explicitly acknowledged the political nature of property rela-

---

clear, there are hints that the situation was not as sound as the woman might perhaps have been led to believe by the way in which the husband kept her during his lifetime; if the estate should turn out to be in financial trouble and if the woman should be unable to prove the existence of a valid customary union, she might well turn out to be not only indigent but indeed in dire need of accommodation and, in the absence of dependants, without a social safety-net. Considering that she was a 59-year-old single woman who depended upon a man living at least partly according to customary law, but without the benefit of a valid customary marriage, it could be asked whether sufficient weight had indeed been given to all the relevant circumstances. On the face of it she appears to be one of the many marginalised women who are rendered effectively powerless by the unorthodox social and economic dealings of their men. At the very least it must be doubtful whether she was really 'essentially no different from that of the "affluent tenant" occupying luxurious premises, who is holding over', used in the *Bekker* case to exemplify those who clearly do not deserve the protection of the anti-eviction legislation and who just want to exploit it while already enjoying the benefits of economic and social security: para 20, referring to *Ndlovu v Ngcobo; Bekker and Another v Jika* 2003 (1) SA 113 (SCA) at para 17.

[99] *Occupiers of 51 Olivia Road, Berea Township, and 197 Main Street, Johannesburg v City of Johannesburg and Others* 2008 (3) SA 208 (CC) at para 45. The Constitutional Court also overturned the SCA's decision concerning the constitutional validity of s 12(6) of the Act. This provision permits the issuing of an administrative order to vacate unsafe or unhealthy buildings; in the event of non-compliance it provides for a criminal sanction. The SCA found this constitutionally unobjectionable, but the Constitutional Court disagreed (paras 48–9). The effect of s 26(3) of the Constitution, which prohibits eviction from someone's home without a court order, would be rendered 'virtually nugatory and would amount to little protection' if people could be compelled to leave their homes by an administrative order, supported by criminal sanction, without a court order. The Court decided that s 12(6) of the Act could not be set aside because it serves legitimate purposes; the problems caused by its conflict with s 26(3) could be rectified by reading into the section a proviso that reads 'This subsection applies only to people who, after service upon them of an order of court for their eviction, continue to occupy the property concerned' (paras 49, 50).

[100] *Government of the Republic of South Africa and Others v Grootboom and Others* 2001 (1) SA 46 (CC).

[101] *Port Elizabeth Municipality v Various Occupiers* 2005 (1) SA 217 (CC).

[102] Courts should, however, be alert to the possibility that local authorities and state organs might try and evade the responsibilities imposed by this approach by evicting unlawful occupiers in their private capacity as landowners, instead of their public capacity as state organs with constitutional responsibilities under section 26. In this regard a qualification of (or gloss on) the Constitutional Court's decision in *Minister of Public Works v Kyalami Ridge Environmental Association* 2001 (3) SA 1151 (CC) might yet be necessary.

tions and the political background of evictions during apartheid, and that it explicitly linked adjudication of eviction cases under section 26(3) and PIE to due consideration of this background. Land reform and the anti-eviction measures cannot be understood or applied properly unless this background is acknowledged and taken into account clearly and explicitly. As the Court pointed out, that does not mean that eviction becomes impossible, but it does require a completely different approach to eviction conflicts and, by implication, a different approach to property relations and their regulation in a transitional setting. The point is highlighted in the *City of Johannesburg* decision, where the High Court pointed out that eviction cannot be approached or regarded as a 'normal' property case—the constitutional approach means that evictions have to be adjudicated from the marginal perspective of the occupiers to be evicted. Seen from their perspective, eviction is not simply a matter of property but also one of dignity and poverty,[103] and this fact has to be discounted in order to promote the transformative purposes of the Constitution as set out in the *Grootboom* case.[104]

An aspect that deserves to be highlighted is that the recent important decisions of the Constitutional Court, like a number of the significant House of Lords decisions discussed in chapter four, were concerned specifically with eviction actions instituted by a local authority and not (like the significant German decisions discussed in chapter four) with private evictions. In principle it should be easier to accept imposition of heavier restrictions on public landowners who want to evict, purely because of their greater responsibility with regard to provision of housing. The fact that these cases impose or accept heavier restrictions does not necessarily mean that the same burden would have been acceptable in private eviction cases although, as the German cases in chapter four indicate, restrictions on eviction imposed in terms of social obligations could also affect private landowners, albeit perhaps in a different way.

E. Overview

The decisions referred to in the previous section could create the impression that the post-1994 turn in property law means that unlawful occupiers are now favoured above landowners and that landownership is undervalued or denied protection because of the history of apartheid. However, this is not true. In its *Modderklip* decision the Constitutional Court[105] indicated that the protection of

---

[103] With reference to *Jaftha v Schoeman and Others; Van Rooyen v Stoltz and Others* 2005 (2) SA 140 (CC) at para 30; see *City of Johannesburg v Rand Properties (Pty) Ltd and Others* 2007 (1) SA 78 (W) at para 30. The *Jaftha* case is discussed in ch 3, section IV. Compare further *Port Elizabeth Municipality v Various Occupiers* 2005 (1) SA 217 (CC) at para 18, and see *City of Johannesburg v Rand Properties (Pty) Ltd and Others* 2007 (1) SA 78 (W) at para 57.

[104] *Government of the Republic of South Africa and Others v Grootboom and Others* 2001 (1) SA 46 (CC); see *City of Johannesburg v Rand Properties (Pty) Ltd and Others* 2007 (1) SA 78 (W) at paras 51, 62.

[105] *President of the Republic of South Africa and Another v Modderklip Boerdery (Pty) Ltd (Agri SA and Others,* Amici Curiae*)* 2005 (5) SA 3 (CC).

occupiers against eviction will not necessarily take place at the cost of the landowner—when a landowner is entitled to an eviction against unlawful occupiers but prevented from obtaining and executing the eviction order because of the sheer number and the personal circumstances of the occupiers, it is unacceptable for the state to just stand by and leave it to the owner to solve the problem. If the landowner is expected to bear the continued unlawful occupation of her land for an extended period until the state can provide an effective remedy (inter alia by providing alternative accommodation for the occupiers), the owner might have a claim for compensation against the state. In *Port Elizabeth Municipality* the Court again confirmed that the constitutional and contextual approach does not mean that eviction becomes impossible—it merely means that eviction is not to be taken lightly and that a court order cannot be granted until all the relevant considerations have indeed been considered. Eviction of unlawful occupiers is possible, but in view of the political and social history of evictions and forced removals it cannot function as it traditionally did—the Constitution and the land reform laws now constitute a new set of parameters within which eviction takes place. Within these parameters landownership is still a powerful and well-protected right; it is now even protected in the Constitution; but it was also placed within a very specific social, political and constitutional context that affects its adjudication in cases where traditional common law perceptions and enforcement of the landowner's right conflict with the constitutional obligation to protect the land rights and interests of socially, economically and legally marginalised and vulnerable members of society. The new paradigm for adjudication of land rights does not mean that the landowner always loses in such a conflict, but it does mean that he does not automatically win, as he did in common law. What changes is that, at least in some circumscribed cases, the context plays a role in determining whether eviction would be just and equitable.

The considerations that now dominate the decision to grant an eviction order according to the Constitutional Court's interpretation of the anti-eviction laws represent a significant departure from apartheid eviction law and even from pre-apartheid common law, primarily in that the granting of an eviction order now depends not only on the landowner's stronger right to possession, but also on the social and economic personal circumstances of the unlawful occupiers and on the social and economic history and the reform policies of the government. Whereas the unlawfulness of the occupation traditionally indicated that the landowner must inevitably be entitled to an eviction order, it now indicates that the occupier's social context and her personal circumstances need to be considered before evicting her. This shift of focus means that eviction law is no longer dominated by the rights-based perspective of the landowner at the centre of the property picture, but rather by the needs-based or marginality perspective of the often weak and vulnerable unlawful occupier who is to be evicted. Ownership and the stronger right to undisturbed possession no longer suffice to justify eviction; social and economic justice requires a wider inquiry into circumstances that are out of the landowner's control and probably outside of her knowledge as well. Through land reform, eviction law has become sensitive to social, economic and political marginality, weakness and vulnerability. This represents a major shift, not only in approach but also in terminology, language, metaphor and logic. The shift brought about by land reform legislation poses a serious challenge to the rights paradigm in so far as this shift implies that eviction is decided with reference to the context and the circumstances of the occupier and no longer purely on the basis of the owner's stronger right.

However, introduction of the statutory changes did not change the law in one fell swoop. Eviction law demonstrates that change is often resisted by the force of rhetoric and that transformation of the law requires squaring up to not only social and political reform but also a rethinking of the traditional language and methodology of private law. The rights paradigm is still powerful to the extent that it dominates the rhetoric, logic and doctrine of the law, and experience shows that courts often fall back on established paradigmatic solutions rather than implement apparently radical changes that will affect established property rights negatively. In that sense the rights paradigm still exercises a stabilising effect that can inhibit reforms of the property regime.

IV. Eviction of Gypsies or Travellers

A. English Case-law

Apart from the *Southwark* cases English law is also interesting for the cases in which attempted eviction of so-called gypsies, travellers or Roma[106] was countered with an appeal to Article 8 of the European Convention on Human Rights 1950.[107] The gypsies cases arose when local authorities wanted to evict persons unlawfully occupying land to which the plaintiffs had absolute rights of possession or, in some instances where the local authority terminated permits or licences in terms of which the gypsies occupied the land lawfully. In each case the defendants relied upon their only available defence, namely that eviction would infringe their rights under Article 8 of the European Convention. The issue in each case was whether a defendant under these circumstances could raise, by way of defence against an action for possession, the plea that the obtaining of possession would infringe her

---

[106] The English cases and literature mostly refer to this group as gypsies or sometimes as travellers; in the European Union cases and literature the term of preference is Roma, which of course has a cultural connotation that does not necessarily apply to the groups named gypsies or travellers in English law. I retain the terminology used by the most important cases.

[107] The most interesting cases are discussed below: *Harrow London Borough Council v Qazi* [2004] 1 AC 983 (HL); *Connors v United Kingdom* (2004) 40 EHRR 189; *Kay and Another v London Borough of Lambeth and Others; Leeds City Council v Price and Others* [2006] UKHL 10 (HL); *Doherty (FC) and Others v Birmingham City Council* [2008] UKHL 57 (HL). These cases are also discussed in ch 4, section II. See further ch 6, section II. on adverse possession.

rights under Article 8 of the Convention.[108] This question became acute because of the apparent conflict between the House of Lords decision in *Harrow London Borough Council v Qazi*,[109] where the answer was negative, and the decision of the European Court of Human Rights in *Connors v United Kingdom*,[110] where the answer was positive. Importantly, *Qazi* involved an action for possession in a notice to quit situation and not a traveller situation like *Connors*.[111] In *Kay and Another v London Borough of Lambeth and Others; Leeds City Council v Price and Others*[112] the House of Lords heard and decided two eviction cases together, one dealing with a lawful tenant and the other with an unlawful squatter, and attempted to square the *Qazi* and *Connors* decisions into the bargain.

In *Qazi* the House of Lords decided that the English courts, in deciding the validity of a claim for possession under Article 8(2) ECHR, do not have to apply a full-scale proportionality test involving balancing of the landowner's rights against the housing interests of the tenant, since that balancing has already been done by the legislature. Accordingly, once it has been established that the landowner is entitled to an order for possession in terms of domestic law, there is nothing further to investigate.[113] In *Connors*, the European Court of Human Rights followed the exact opposite approach, deciding that the national authorities had to decide what was necessary initially, but that the final decision whether the reasons for interference were relevant and sufficient remains subject to review.[114] On the face of it, the two decisions appeared to adopt contradictory approaches but, interestingly, the European Court declined the opportunity to hear a further appeal in *Qazi*.

In *Leeds City Council v Price*[115] the Court of Appeal held that the decision in *Connors* was indeed incompatible with the decision in *Qazi* to the extent that the latter established that 'the exercise by a public authority of an unqualified propri-

---

[108] For a discussion see M Edwards, 'Application for Order for Possession of Land: Whether Defendant could Raise as Defence a Claim of Infringement of Art. 8 of the European Convention on Human Rights' (2005) *J Planning & Env Law* 1241–52.

[109] [2004] 1 AC 983 (HL). See the discussion of this case in ch 2, section II. and ch 4, section II.

[110] (2004) 40 EHRR 189.

[111] Mrs Qazi, a joint tenant with Mr Qazi under a secure tenancy, gave the council notice to quit in accordance with the tenancy agreement, which brought the tenancy to an end. Mr Qazi was informed that the tenancy had come to an end and his application for a sole tenancy failed. The council instituted possession proceedings when he failed to vacate the premises as requested. See the discussion in ch 2, section II. and ch 4, section II, and compare S Bright, 'Ending Tenancies by Notice to Quit: The Human Rights Challenge' (2004) *LQR* 120(Jul) 398–403 on the implications of the *Qazi* decision under notice to quit circumstances. In *Leeds City Council v Price* [2005] 1 WLR 1825 (CA), as in *Connors v United Kingdom* (2004) 40 EHRR 189, the defendants were travellers who occupied the land without permission or licence. See n 107.

[112] [2006] UKHL 10 (HL). In *Doherty (FC) and Others v Birmingham City Council* [2008] UKHL 57 (HL) the House of Lords again decided an application for eviction of gypsies in terms of its earlier decisions in *Qazi* and *Kay/Price*; see ch 4, n 104. In this case it was also necessary to square the earlier decisions with the European Court decision in *McCann v United Kingdom* [2008] ECHR 19009/04 (13 May 2008), which did not concern gypsies but an eviction of secure tenants following a notice to quit, similar to the situation in *Qazi*.

[113] [2004] 1 AC 983 (HL) at 1020–21.

[114] *Connors v United Kingdom* (2004) 40 EHRR 189 at paras 81, 82. The *Connors* decision is discussed in more detail in section IV.B below.

[115] *Leeds City Council v Price* [2005] 1 WLR 1825 (CA).

etary right under domestic law to repossess its land will *never* constitute an interference with the occupier's right to respect for his home, or will *always* be justified under Article 8(2)'.[116] The Court of Appeals argued that the decision in *Connors* did not merely identify a discrete exception to the general rule propounded in *Qazi*; the two decisions are indeed incompatible.[117] The appropriate solution in such a situation, where the Court of Appeals is faced with a later European Court decision that is in conflict with an earlier House of Lords decision, is to follow the latter (that is, *Qazi*) and, should the matter arise, eventually allow an appeal to the House of Lords, where the conflict could be dealt with further if required. The Court therefore followed the restrictive decision in *Qazi* as a matter of being bound to an earlier decision of a higher court.[118]

Inevitably, the *Price* case did come up for appeal in the House of Lords, where it was heard and decided together with an appeal in the case of *Kay and Others v London Borough of Lambeth and Others*.[119] The appellants in *Kay* were former lawful occupiers whose lease had been terminated, but the appellants in *Price* were gypsies, trespassers who never had permission or a right to occupy and who occupied the site in question for a very brief period in any event. Purely on the facts, *Price* was probably never a good case to argue on the basis of Article 8 of the European Convention, because the appellants had only parked their caravans on the recreation grounds for a few days before they were evicted, making it very difficult to argue that the site was ever their home in the sense intended by Article 8. Even considering their vulnerable position as gypsies, it was difficult to argue that they had been on the site long enough to establish the kind of possession that could justify a defence under Article 8.[120] The House of Lords upheld the *Qazi* decision that, once it was clear that the public authority landlord had an unqualified right to possession, the claim for possession could not be challenged purely on the basis of the personal circumstances of the occupier, adding that in such a case there were only two gateways to a challenge against eviction in such a case, namely to challenge the law that governs eviction directly or to apply for judicial review of the local authority's decision to apply for possession.[121] In the latest decision dealing with eviction of gypsies the House of Lords again upheld its earlier decisions in *Qazi* and *Kay/Price*, although it developed them to the extent that judicial review of the local authority's decision to apply for possession is not restricted to common law review, but extends to a more general test whether the decision was one that any reasonable person would regard as reasonable and justifiable.[122]

---

[116] *Leeds City Council v Price* [2005] 1 WLR 1825 (CA) at para 26; italics in the original.

[117] *Leeds City Council v Price* [2005] 1 WLR 1825 (CA) at para 30. With reference to *Kay v Lambeth London Borough Council* [2004] 3 WLR 1396 (CA) at para 106, the Court refused to accept the argument that *Connors* applied only to cases involving eviction from gypsy sites.

[118] *Leeds City Council v Price* [2005] 1 WLR 1825 (CA) at para 33.

[119] [2004] 3 WLR 1396 (CA). See the discussion in ch 4, section II.

[120] The sufficient and continuing links test relied on by the English courts for this conclusion was formulated in *Gillow v United Kingdom* (1986) 11 EHRR 335 at para 46.

[121] *Kay and Another v London Borough of Lambeth and Others; Leeds City Council v Price and Others* [2006] UKHL 10 (HL). See ch 4, section II.

[122] *Doherty (FC) and Others v Birmingham City Council* [2008] UKHL 57 (HL). See ch 4, section II.

In its recent case-law the House of Lords insists that gypsies present an exceptional case and that eviction of gypsies therefore has to be treated with special care because they are a marginal and discriminated group,[123] but this statement has to be approached with some care. Although it is certainly true that gypsies are members of a unique and socially vulnerable group that therefore deserves special protection against eviction, the House of Lords was arguably emphasising this point in *Doherty* to underline the similarities between *Doherty* and the earlier European Court decision in *Connors*, thereby strengthening its efforts to justify the apparent contradictions between the *Connors* decision (which also involved gypsies) and *Qazi* (which did not). In the process the House of Lords was also allowing itself to take distance from the subsequent European Court decision in *McCann* (which did not involve gypsies and resembled *Qazi*) and its own decision in *Doherty* (which involved gypsies and resembled *Connors*). It was important for the House of Lords in *Doherty* to establish this distance from *McCann* because it attempted to restrict the potentially radical implications of the clear finding in *McCann* that all occupiers (and not just gypsies) have the right to have the effect of eviction on them tested in terms of an independent judicial proportionality analysis.[124] In this way the House of Lords could try and restrict the scope of the challenge that the European Court decisions potentially pose for the rights paradigm and, through it, the stability of the current property framework.

B. European Case-law

Since the Human Rights Act 1998 made the European Convention on Human Rights applicable in English law, European Court case-law featured large in English case-law on the eviction of gypsies. In *Connors* the Court held that the eviction of a family of gypsies from a camping site they were licensed to occupy so long as they did not cause a nuisance violated Article 8 of the Convention because the requisite procedural safeguards were not in place. Having terminated the Connors family's licence to occupy the gypsy site in question,[125] the local council regarded them as trespassers and obtained an order for possession. The local council argued that it had good reason, within the existing statutory regime, to evict the Connors family, while the family argued that the state had to show, in terms of Article 8 of the European Convention, that the eviction was necessary and

---

[123] *Doherty (FC) and Others v Birmingham City Council* [2008] UKHL 57 (HL) at paras 25–33.

[124] See the discussion of *Harrow London Borough Council v Qazi* [2004] 1 AC 983 (HL); *Connors v United Kingdom* (2004) 40 EHRR 189; *McCann v United Kingdom* [2008] ECHR 19009/04 (13 May 2008) and *Doherty (FC) and Others v Birmingham City Council* [2008] UKHL 57 (HL) in ch 4, section II and (as far as the ECHR cases are concerned) below.

[125] The Mobile Homes Act 1983 provides that a person who lives on a privately owned caravan site in a caravan or mobile home that is his only or main residence may only be evicted by court order and on a number of specified grounds. The Caravan Sites Act 1968a gives local authorities an unconditional right to terminate a licence on 28 days' notice, although a court order is necessary for obtaining possession. The local authority in *Connors* terminated the Connors family's licence to occupy because of action that constituted a nuisance; see *Leeds City Council v Price* [2005] 1 WLR 1825 (CA) at para 19.

proportionate. The European Court emphasised that the national states had a margin of appreciation in fixing the regulatory schemes within which they permitted interference with Article 8 rights, but that a reviewing court still had to judge whether the states remained within their margin of appreciation in acting upon the relevant statutory regime. Furthermore, the vulnerable position of gypsies as a minority group in society means that special consideration has to be given to their needs in the regulatory framework and in reaching judicial decisions under that framework.[126]

In applying these considerations to the case, the European Court took cognisance of the special social and physical challenges facing a gypsy family and the effect that eviction would have on them. In the Court's opinion, the seriousness of the effect that eviction would have for the Connors family required 'particularly weighty reasons of public interest by way of justification and the margin of appreciation to be afforded to the national authorities must be regarded as correspondingly narrowed'.[127] In the Court's view, the existing legal framework did not afford the gypsies sufficient procedural protection of their rights and, judging from domestic decisions since the Human Rights Act 1998 came into operation, English courts seemed reluctant to trespass on the legislative function and therefore did not provide additional support for the justification of the existing legal regime.[128] Accordingly, eviction of the Connors family 'was not attended by the requisite procedural safeguards, namely to establish proper justification for the serious interference with his [Mr Connors'] rights and consequently cannot be regarded as justified by a "pressing social need" or proportionate to the legitimate legal aim pursued'.[129] The conclusion was that the Connors eviction constituted a violation of Article 8.[130]

Apart from the European Court, the European Committee of Social Rights, established under Article 25 of the European Social Charter, has held in at least two cases[131] that the insufficiency and inadequacy of camping sites that are available to them; the forced evictions and other sanctions they are vulnerable to; and the lack of permanent dwellings available to Roma in the countries involved (Italy and Greece) constituted violations of Article 31.1, 31.2 and 31.1 with Article 31E of the European Social Charter, respectively. Similar complaints have been lodged with the Commission in relation to France and Bulgaria, and other complaints relating to the housing rights of children of illegal immigrants and of the extremely poor have also been lodged against France and the Netherlands. In all these cases, complainants relied on the right to housing guaranteed in Article 31 of the

---

[126] *Connors v United Kingdom* (2004) 40 EHRR 189 at para 84.

[127] *Connors v United Kingdom* (2004) 40 EHRR 189 at para 86.

[128] *Connors v United Kingdom* (2004) 40 EHRR 189 at para 91.

[129] *Connors v United Kingdom* (2004) 40 EHRR 189 at para 95.

[130] The other recent ECHR case considered serious authority by the English courts, *Blecic v Croatia* (2004) 41 EHRR 185, was not a gypsy case but concerned a tenancy that had been terminated because of absence of the tenant, who claimed to have a justifiable reason for her absence.

[131] *European Roma Rights Centre v Greece* (Complaint no 15/2003), decision of 8 December 2004; *European Roma Rights Centre v Italy* (Complaint no 27/2004), decision of 7 December 2004.

Charter. In terms of Article 31, parties to the Charter undertake to take measures designed to promote access to housing of an adequate standard; to prevent and reduce homelessness with a view to its gradual elimination; and to make the price of housing accessible to those with adequate resources. Obviously, in so far as member states adopt responsibilities under the Charter additional restrictions are placed upon their power to regulate housing. However, at this stage it seems unlikely that these international law instruments will bring about a significant shift in traditional private law dogma, and hence their effect on the rights paradigm is limited.

V. Conclusion

Four general preliminary conclusions or observations are possible on the evidence of the legislation and case-law discussed in this chapter. The first is that unlawful occupiers, in the sense of persons or groups who occupy land without ever having had permission or any other legal ground to do so, are obviously more vulnerable to eviction than tenants who have—or at one point had—lawful occupation rights.

Secondly, having said that, it is surprising how much protection unlawful occupiers enjoy against eviction. In many cases the protection amounts to little more than due process protection to ensure that they are not evicted arbitrarily and unfairly, but at least in some cases legislative interventions offer more substantive protection that can delay or even prevent eviction of unlawful occupiers purely on the basis of its effect on the occupiers. The most striking examples of these substantive protections are contained in legislation, like the South African Prevention from Illegal Eviction from and Unlawful Occupation of Land Act 19 of 1998, Article 8 of the European Convention on Human Rights and Article 31 of the European Social Charter, which protect the home interests of unlawful occupiers regardless of their status and in excess of due process. The most interesting protections are ones that focus on factors or considerations that are outside of the landowner's power and knowledge and that do not relate in any way to the traditional elements of an eviction action, namely the fact of possession and the stronger right to possession, but rather on social and economic considerations related to the vulnerable and marginalised status of the occupiers and the impact that eviction would have on them. In terms of the theoretical framework set out in chapter three these protective measures do not fit in with and in fact flatly contradict the essential tenets of the rights paradigm, and to that extent they pose a serious challenge to the paradigm, opening up space for significant reforms of the current property regime.

Thirdly, the most significant observation from the overview above is the fact that meaningful protections of unlawful occupiers against eviction always relate to the history and context of the person or group involved. In the South African context, the history of forced removals and racial prejudice in the entrenchment of vested land interests plays a central role in sharpening the focus of the remedial legislation on the position of weak and vulnerable individuals and groups such as black people in general and on the elderly, children, women and families headed by children in particular. In the Western European context, the special focus of the European Court of Human Rights and the European Committee of Social Rights on the vulnerable and marginalised status of the Roma or gypsies points in the same direction. In this respect it is interesting to note that some courts (including some South African courts and some English courts) find it difficult to accommodate this new focus within their established dogmatic structures and procedures, requiring special and clear statutory authority before they are willing to deviate from established norms on onus of proof. The *Port Elizabeth Municipality* and *City of Johannesburg* decisions of the South African Constitutional Court are all the more important for their clarity on the effect that the remedial shift in focus from rights to vulnerability must have in 'normal' law. In the end, courts will have an enormous influence on the success (or lack of it) of these novel and unfamiliar anti-eviction laws and principles.

A final point that deserves mention in this chapter is the fact that this analysis of anti-eviction measures and their benefit for unlawful occupiers demonstrates the explicit and pronounced political nature of property in general and of eviction in particular. The political squatters of the 1970s and 1980s, the South African homeless land invaders and the Roma all embody, in different ways, the essentially political conflict between those who own and control land and those who, because of their lack of access to money and power, are deprived of one of the most basic needs of humanity, namely secure shelter and a home. In the sense that social marginality and homelessness are always somehow related to political decisions regarding the privileging of certain property interests above others, both the rights paradigm that allows eviction, and statutory interventions or judicial interpretation that restrict or prevent it are political, which underlines the importance of taking the social and historical context within which eviction takes place into account before deciding whether it is justifiable. In the same vein it is important to note that challenges to the rights paradigm and the legal property regime that entrenches it can take place in two different ways: either by way of legal challenges that seek to open up and exploit the gaps and spaces left by qualifications of the paradigm or, when that fails, political action, which may include intentionally unlawful occupation of property as a form of protest against the immutability of the current regime.

6

Limitations on Eviction in Other Contexts

I.   Introduction   169
II.   Acquisitive Prescription and Adverse Possession   172
III. Public Access to Private Property   188
IV.   Significant Building Encroachments   199
V.   Weak Owners   205
VI.   Conclusions   208

I. Introduction

IN CHAPTER TWO it was said that the rights paradigm presents ownership (or the strongest right to possession) as the strongest and most important property interest, which means that strong property rights, particularly ownership, dominate the doctrinal structure, the rhetoric and the logic of property law in such a way and to such an extent that it entrenches existing unequal socio-economic power relations in favour of current property owners. In the civil law tradition, the common law[1] allows a property owner to exclude others from possession and use of her property and to evict unwanted occupiers from her land purely because of the superior value and power that normally attach to ownership and without consideration for the socio-economic context or the personal circumstances of the occupiers. Even in the Anglo common law tradition,[2] where the focus falls on the stronger right to possession rather than ownership, the rights paradigm supports the hierarchical privileging of strong property rights characterised by the power to exclude and evict. In the rights paradigm it is assumed that the dominant role that private ownership plays in the property regime and in society is both inevitable and legitimate because it ensconces important social and economic values.

---

[1] Here I use the term 'common law' to refer to the uncodified version of Roman-Germanic civil law, which still forms the bulk of what is described as the South African common law; see R Zimmermann and DP Visser, 'Introduction: South African Law as a Mixed Legal System' in R Zimmermann and DP Visser (eds), *Southern Cross: Civil Law and Common Law in South Africa* 1996) 1–30 and compare ch 2, fnn 3, 15, 16 on South African, Dutch and German law; fnn 2, 5, 21–5 on US and English law.

[2] Here I use the term to refer to the Anglo-American common law tradition. I discuss the features of the rights paradigm in this tradition in ch 2.

In this chapter I discuss four sets of situations that have an indirect rather than a direct bearing on eviction in the rights paradigm in that they demonstrate significant limitations on the exclusivity of landownership, in the sense that either the state or (lawful or unlawful) occupiers of land can override or have defences against enforcement of the right to exclude. These examples represent serious restrictions on the right to exclude and evict and they raise fundamental questions about the scope and force of the rights paradigm because they are based not on legislation but on established and long-standing civil and common law tradition.

The first example discussed below is the loss of ownership that follows from the rules regarding acquisitive prescription or adverse possession, particularly in favour of a possessor in bad faith such as a knowing trespasser or a squatter. According to the ancient principles of acquisition of ownership through prescription or adverse user, a possessor acquires ownership of property by operation of law, without the consent or cooperation of the previous owner, when a certain set of requirements are met, the most important being open and unchallenged (and possibly adverse) possession of the property over a relatively long period of time. The rights paradigm does offer explanations of acquisitive prescription to describe how this phenomenon fits in with its own assumptions about the doctrinal status and power of property ownership, but explaining prescription and adverse user practices within the rights paradigm becomes particularly challenging when the person who acquires ownership is a possessor in bad faith. The beneficial effect that adverse possession may have for bad faith possessors is controversial and often regarded as contradictory and counterintuitive; both courts and academic commentators in various jurisdictions have described it as anomalous and difficult to justify. My argument is that acquisitive prescription by bad faith possessors undermines the doctrinal force and consistency of the rights paradigm.

The second example concerns public access to private property, particularly the circumstances under which an owner of private land may be prohibited or prevented from excluding the public from her property or from ejecting them once they have access. For the purposes of this chapter I am not interested in trespass or squatting that has some kind of residential purpose (I discuss this in chapter five); the focus is rather on brief and intermittent access such as one would usually associate with the commercial, recreational or related uses of property that is at least partly open to the public. In the rights paradigm exclusivity is emphasised as a central aspect of ownership and therefore contested instances where the law restricts a landowner's right to exclude (certain members of) the public pose doctrinal difficulties for the paradigm. The instances that I refer to below illustrate the problems that arise when landowners grant the public access to their property for commercial or recreational purposes and members of the public who gain access to the property then use it or conduct themselves on it in ways that do not correspond with the landowner's intention or wishes, or that cause a threat, nuisance or loss for the landowner or for other members of the public. When the actions that give rise to the conflict are neither illegal nor unlawful as such and have some legitimate personal or public purpose, the question is whether the landowner should be able to exclude the users or uses in question. Rules or practices that allow the landowner to exclude these users at will indicate the force of the rights paradigm; rules and practices that prevent the landowner from exercising her right to exclude against them could indicate a qualification of the paradigm.

The third example concerns instances where a landowner's right to exclude others is limited by the rules regarding significant building encroachments. In at least some cases the landowner is prevented, for various reasons, from ordering removal of encroachments, with the result that the affected owner either loses use of the land permanently or is forced to sell the affected land to the encroacher. The reason for upholding the encroachment, even when it was made unlawfully, against the will of the landowner is usually linked to the balance of convenience or to the investment that the encroacher has made in the property. Obviously these examples represent a significant qualification of the rights paradigm in the sense that they illustrate how the owner's right to exclude and evict is limited for commercial or other policy reasons.

The fourth example concentrates on the phenomenon of weak owners. If the rights paradigm reflects the force and inviolability of ownership positions in law correctly, all owners of land should in principle enjoy at least comparatively strong respect for and protection of their rights, but in fact the state itself will sometimes be able to ride roughshod over the ownership rights of certain categories of landowners, in circumstances that cannot be explained satisfactorily as normal exercises of either the state's power of eminent domain or its police power. The examples discussed in the final section of the chapter suggest that the common thread that links these examples is the social, economic and political weakness of the owners in question. If these examples prove, as I suggest, that the lack of respect and protection offered to these owners is due to their socio-economically and politically weak position, it would imply that some persons are protected more strongly than others, even when both groups formally have ownership, purely because of the personal position or status of the respective rights holders, which is directly in conflict with the basic premises of the rights paradigm.

These examples differ from the material in earlier chapters in that they do not concern eviction directly. Of course, in so far as the adverse possessors, trespassers and encroachers who populate the examples in this chapter are unlawful occupiers or trespassers they are in principle liable to be evicted, and in that sense this chapter does link up with the preceding ones. Similarly, landowners are always liable to be evicted when their land is acquired by another through prescription or when it is expropriated for a public purpose. The main thrust of the book is that property law provides surprisingly many examples of serious restrictions on the owner's presumed strong right to exclude that are difficult to explain within the rights paradigm; the discussion about prescription, public access, encroachment and weak owners supports the argument by indicating that the paradigm is weaker and less pervasive in some areas of property law than might be expected and that landowners may sometimes not only fail to obtain an eviction order but actually lose their rights to persons who would otherwise be described as squatters, trespassers and supposedly more efficient users of the land. In this sense, the law regarding adverse possession, public accommodations and encroachment indicates that existing institutions of law and their application in practice demonstrate a significant qualification of the rights paradigm. Similarly, the examples of weak owners in the last section of the chapter indicate that ownership is sometimes unable to withstand the greater power of political and economic force, even in instances where state expropriation of land is difficult to justify with reference to the public interest.

II. Acquisitive Prescription and Adverse Possession

A. South African Law

The South African law regarding acquisitive prescription is based on Roman law,[3] but the process is now largely governed by legislation,[4] which provides that ownership of land is acquired originally[5] by someone who can prove openly exercised civil possession[6] of another person's property[7] for an uninterrupted period of

---

[3] On the Roman law see M Kaser, *Das römische Privatrecht* (2nd edn, 1971) vol I at 125; JAC Thomas, *Textbook of Roman Law* (1976) at 157–65; *Bisschop v Stafford* 1974 (3) SA 1 (A) 77D–H. In Roman law both *usucapio* and *praescriptio* required *bona fides*, although not necessarily *iusta causa*. The position in other Roman-law based civil jurisdictions is discussed at the end of section II.B below in the context of the European aftermath of the English *Pye* case.

[4] The relevant legislation is the Prescription Act 18 of 1943 and the Prescription Act 68 of 1969. The later Act came into operation on 1 December 1970; the former still applies to prescriptive periods that started before that date. See PJ Badenhorst *et al*, *Silberberg & Schoeman's The Law of Property* (5th edn, 2006) 160–73.

[5] In other words, independent of the consent or cooperation of the previous owner.

[6] Both statutes describe the possession requirement in a way that echoes the traditional Roman description of possession (civil possession or *possessio civilis*), which includes a physical and a mental element. The mental element has to assume the form of owner's intention (*animus domini*) to qualify, which automatically excludes possession on the strength of a precarious or revocable permission. The 1943 Act requires that possession should be exercised with the intention of becoming owner, *nec vi, nec clam, nec precario* (s 2(1)). The 1969 Act requires that possession should be exercised openly and as if the possessor were the owner of the property (s 1). See PJ Badenhorst *et al*, *Silberberg & Schoeman's The Law of Property* (5th edn, 2006) at 162–9.

[7] The question whether adverse user is also a requirement in South African law has caused some controversy. In *Morkel's Transport (Pty) Ltd v Melrose Foods (Pty) Ltd and Another* 1972 (2) SA 464 (W) at 467F Colman J, referring to *Swanepoel v Crown Mines Ltd* 1954 (4) SA 596 (A) at 603–4, said that the 1943 Act was not intended to codify the common law and that common law provisions not in conflict with the statutes were still in force. This was confirmed in *Oertel en Andere NNO v Direkteur van Plaaslike Bestuur en Andere* 1983 (1) SA 354 (A) at 367D. The Court added (at 467G) that the requirements for acquisitive prescription included those in the 1943 Act (see n 6 above) and two additional common law requirements, namely that possession must be adverse to the rights of the true owner (citing *Malan v Nabygelegen Estates* 1946 AD 562 at 574) and that it must be full civil possession or *possessio civilis* (citing *Welgemoed v Coetzer and Others* 1946 TPD 701 at 711–12). The Court explained this requirement by holding that possession is not adverse, for purposes of acquisitive prescription, unless the owner has a legal right to prevent it (at 479A). In *Malan v Nabygelegen Estates* 1946 AD 562 at 573–4 it was said that the adverse user requirement does not mean that possession must have been without consent in general; it meant that possession under a precarious or revocable permission would be excluded: 'In order to create a prescriptive title, such occupation must be a user adverse to the true

30 years. My purpose in this section is not to set out the doctrinal details and technicalities of prescription, but to highlight just two aspects that are interesting for present purposes: firstly, the fact that bad faith possessors are also allowed to benefit from prescription; and, secondly, the reasons for recognising this form of acquisition of ownership, particularly in case of bad faith possessors.

In South African law acquisitive prescription is described as an original method of acquisition of ownership, which indicates that the previous owner is neither merely prevented from reclaiming possession, nor is her title simply extinguished—a fresh title vests in a new owner (the possessor) automatically, by operation of law, without the consent or cooperation of the previous owner. In the process the focus has shifted from merely preventing the owner from asserting her rights to the acquisition of rights by the possessor. The previous owner loses ownership against her will and without her consent or cooperation, simply because a possessor, who may be in good or in bad faith, occupied and used the property as if she were owner, continuously for a relatively long period of time.[8]

It stands to reason that the security and exclusivity of ownership is undermined by this process, especially in cases where the possessor occupied and used the property in bad faith, knowing well that someone else owned it and that she had no right to occupy or use it. In the context of US law these possessors have been described as 'acquisitive [property] outlaws' to indicate that they may well be consciously and deliberately using the law regarding adverse possession to 'steal' property from the 'paper owner' without paying for it.[9] Considering the social importance attached to the sanctity and security of property ownership in the rights paradigm, allowing bad faith unlawful possessors to acquire ownership through acquisitive possession represents a significant qualification of the paradigm. It is therefore not surprising that judges and commentators have expressed their dismay at being forced to acknowledge the fact that a bad faith possessor had acquired ownership through prescription or adverse possession.[10] However,

---

owner and not occupation by virtue of some contract or legal relationship . . . which recognises the ownership of another.' This interpretation of the requirements was confirmed in *Bisschop v Stafford* 1974 (3) SA 1 (A) at 8B–9B, where the *nec precario*, adverse user and civil possession requirements were treated as synonymous. With reference to the decision in *Malan v Nabygelegen Estates*, some courts decided that adverse user was a separate requirement in addition to the *nec precario* requirement of the 1943 Act and the civil possession requirement of the 1969 Act, while others regarded it as synonymous with civil possession. See PJ Badenhorst *et al, Silberberg & Schoeman's The Law of Property* (5th edn, 2006) at 166–9 for an overview of case-law. In *Cillie v Geldenhuys* (306/07) [2008] JOL 21782 (SCA) the Supreme Court of Appeal linked the adverse possession requirement to the doctrine of notice and pointed out that it has no role to play in original acquisition of servitudes through prescription.

[8] The Prescription Act 18 of 1943 and the Prescription Act 68 of 1969 prescribe 30 years.

[9] EM Peñalver and SK Katyal, 'Property Outlaws' (2007) 155 *Univ Pennsylvania LR* 1095–186 at 1105–13. See section II.C below.

[10] The clearest recent example is the sentiments expressed by the trial judge in the *Pye* case (UK, see section 2.B below), referred to and echoed by Lord Bingham in *JA Pye (Oxford) Ltd v Graham* [2003] 1 AC 419 (HL) at para 2; see further the remarks of Lord Browne-Wilkinson (at para 49) and Lord Hope (at para 67).

strong arguments in support of this tradition have also been voiced in the wake of the English *Pye* case.[11]

In Roman law good faith was required for the acquisition of ownership through prescription, but in modern South African law both *bona fide* and *mala fide* possession satisfy the requirements, as long as the bad faith possessor's recognition of her own status as non-owner (a *mala fide* possessor knows that she is not owner but still holds as if she were) is consistent with the required intention of civil possession or *possessio animo domini*. In other words, it makes no difference that the possessor is aware that someone else is in fact owner, as long as she does not hold under some precarious permission or licence and provided she holds openly and as if she were the owner or with the intention to become owner through prescription. In either case, the required *animus domini* can co-exist with *mala fides*.[12] Apart from the fact that this interpretation is supported by the fairly clear wording of the Prescription Acts, it reflects the reasons most often cited for departing from Roman law tradition and recognising acquisitive prescription in favour of *mala fide* possessors, namely to punish neglectful owners and to bring legal title in line with actual use over a long time—if the purpose is not purely to reward a diligent and enterprising possessor, the state of mind of the possessor who benefits from prescription is considered irrelevant.[13]

In *Pienaar v Rabie*[14] the Appellate Division of the Supreme Court[15] recognised that punishment of neglectful owners was often cited as a justification for the existence of acquisitive prescription in general; the Court also indicated that there are indications in some Roman-Dutch authorities that such an explanation might have enjoyed some currency during the development of Roman law. However, the Court pointed out that other justifications for acquisitive prescription are also mentioned by the authorities, including the fact that it promotes legal certainty by bringing the legal position into line with a long-standing factual situation. Although punishment of a neglectful owner is therefore acknowledged as a reason for allowing acquisitive prescription, especially in favour of *mala fide* possessors, it is not the only or the most important reason and, more pertinently, this consideration has not played such a large role in prescription that it resulted in a separate requirement that the owner must have been neglectful for prescription to run, nor

---

[11] See LA Fennell, 'Efficient Trespass: The Case for "Bad Faith" Adverse Possession' (2006) 100 *Northwestern Univ LR* 1037–96 at 1047–9; R Caterina, 'Some Comparative Remarks on *JA Pye (Oxford) Ltd v. The United Kingdom*' (2007) 15 *European Rev of Private Law* 273–9. Fennell's argument against negative assessment of the practice to let bad faith possessors benefit from prescription is discussed in section II.C below.

[12] *Morkel's Transport (Pty) Ltd v Melrose Foods (Pty) Ltd and Another* 1972 (2) SA 464 (W) at 474E–F. In *Minister van Landbou v Sonnendecker* 1979 (2) SA 944 (A) at 947C–E (*obiter dictum*) the Appellate Division considered this interpretation of the possession requirement in the 1969 Act possible without deciding the issue, but in *Bisschop v Stafford* 1974 (3) SA 1 (A) at 8B–9B the matter was apparently put beyond doubt.

[13] *Morkel's Transport (Pty) Ltd v Melrose Foods (Pty) Ltd and Another* 1972 (2) SA 464 (W) at 468B–F, 477H–478A.

[14] 1983 (3) SA 126 (A). The relevant part of the decision appears at 135A–139A.

[15] Now the Supreme Court of Appeal; see s 166 of the 1996 Constitution.

did it create a separate defence to the effect that an owner who can show that she was not neglectful could thereby escape prescription.[16]

If punishment of neglectful owners is a reason, but not the only or the most important reason, for allowing acquisitive prescription in favour of bad faith possessors, the question remains whether this form of original acquisition of ownership is compatible with the hierarchically superior position of ownership in the rights paradigm. Promoting legal certainty by bringing the legal situation into line with a long-standing factual situation could arguably support rather than undermine the rights paradigm, especially since the requirement of open civil possession does seem to confirm that the possession has been stable and uncontested and that it has given the owner a reasonable chance to assert her rights against the possessor. This purpose is clearly served when prescription settles inaccurate border descriptions or when it confirms the ownership of someone who acquired a defective title in good faith. However, even then, and given the South African courts' partial reliance upon the punishment motivation, a lingering sense remains that the sanctity and supremacy of ownership as absolute and indefeasible legal title is perhaps not quite as secure as it seems when bad faith possessors can acquire ownership through effluxion of time. It has been pointed out that adverse possession arguably creates as much or more uncertainty and insecurity as it is supposed to overcome, at least in the sense that it undermines the security of ownership.[17]

Extinguishing existing legal title and vesting a new title in an adverse possessor creates an opening for the possibility that recognition of legal title could also follow—and succumb to—open and long-standing factual control in other situations where social stability and economic efficiency require or justify such a shift,[18] particularly if such a development would promote legal certainty and if it allows sufficient protection for existing interests and therefore does not offend one's sense of justice and fairness.[19] Stated differently, if pragmatic or utilitarian

[16] *Pienaar v Rabie* 1983 (3) SA 126 (A) at 138H–139A. These reasons are also raised in English and in US law; see sections II.B and II.C below. For a critical discussion of the reasons see section II.D below.

[17] LA Fennell, 'Efficient Trespass: The Case for "Bad Faith" Adverse Possession' (2006) 100 *Northwestern Univ LR* 1037–96 at 1063 mentions that the 'quieting of titles' or legal certainty argument is undermined by the fact that adverse possession creates and maintains at least as many uncertainties, in the form of murky titles, as it is supposed to settle through bringing title into line with actual possession and use. See section II.C.

[18] For instance in the context of land reform. Interestingly, there is a historical precedent in Roman-Germanic law of just such a development in the form of the so-called shifting of landownership; a process by which recognition of legal title 'shifted' from the feudal landlords to their former vassals who actually occupied and used the land for their own benefit and whose payment of rent to the landlords had over time become an economically meaningless ritual, especially in cases where the landlords were prevented from raising or neglected to raise the rent. On the shifting of ownership in Roman-Germanic law see W van Iterson, 'Beschouwingen over Rolverwisseling of Eigendomsverschuiving' in *Verslagen en Mededelingen van de Vereniging tot Uitgave der Bronnen van het Oud-Vaderlandsch Recht* XIII, no 3 (1971) at 407–66. Van Iterson's explanation of the historical process was not uncontested, although most of the critics also accepted that rights had been acquired by the formerly landless; see PWA Immink, '"Eigendom" en "Heerlijkheid": Exponenten van Tweërlei Maatschappelijke Structuur' (1959) 27 *Tijdschrift voor Rechtsgeschiedenis* 36–74.

[19] I extrapolate these considerations from what has been said in the case-law on acquisitive prescription as described above.

considerations such as legal certainty, economic efficiency and censuring of neglectful owners could justify a shift in landownership whenever one's sense of justice and fairness was satisfied that general criminal and civil rules against trespass protect the interests of the owner of record sufficiently, there do not seem to be obvious reasons why prescription or adverse user should be restricted to innocuous instances such as conveyancing errors and boundary squabbles. In a context where a significant maldistribution of wealth and lack of housing characterise the social and legal order, this configuration holds interesting possibilities that could be developed in favour of land redistribution, but development of these possibilities would clearly both rely on and contribute to a significant challenge to the rights paradigm. Such a wider application of the legal certainty argument, especially in combination with the punishment of neglectful owners argument, could indeed bring about a significant qualification of or departure from the rights paradigm; by opening the door (even just partially) for such a wider argument the rules and practices regarding prescription offer an interesting critical and undermining perspective on the rights paradigm.

B. English Law

The English law of adverse possession is grounded in the common law notion of the relativity and fundamental defeasibility of title. The common law principle that prior possession is stronger than later possession means that a current possessor could always be challenged by a prior possessor, which would render land titles subject to indefinite conflict. To solve this problem the principle of limitation was introduced during the seventeenth century, imposing arbitrary time limits to curtail the prior possessor's right to reclaim possession. As a consequence of this principle, now embodied in the Limitation Act 1980, a landowner is prevented, following expiration of a legally stipulated limitation period,[20] from enforcing her stronger claim to possession against the current possessor.[21] If the right to recover the land is barred in terms of the Limitation Act 1980, the title of the paper owner of unregistered land is extinguished;[22] in the case of registered land the title is not extinguished but the registered owner is thereafter deemed to hold the land in trust for the squatter.[23] In either case the landowner effectively loses her title.

Adverse possession extinguishes prior title, whereas prescription also includes a fiction of or an actual grant of new title.[24] In the context of relative title, the lim-

---

[20] K Gray and SF Gray, *Elements of Land Law* (4th edn, 2005) at 366. The Limitation Act 1980, s 15 requires 12 years.

[21] Although the Land Registration Act 2002 has brought about significant changes to the law of statutory limitation and reduced the importance and practical impact of adverse possession, the limitation principle still applies to titles that have not been registered: K Gray and SF Gray, *Elements of Land Law* (4th edn, 2005) at 366–7. See below for a brief explanation of the changes brought about by the 2002 Act.

[22] Section 17.

[23] Section 75(1) of the Land Registration Act 1925.

[24] K Gray and SF Gray, *Elements of Land Law* (4th edn, 2005) discuss the differences at 377. The South African Prescription Acts do not merely extinguish the prior title but grant new title to the possessor.

itation principle primarily means that the former possessor is prevented from enforcing a stronger claim to possession against the current possessor, but that does not vest an indefeasible title in the current possessor because other persons can still raise a stronger claim against her. However, the limitation principle does in effect mean that the current possessor's title 'ripens into an unimpeachable fee simple title' once the assertion of all older titles becomes barred through the effluxion of time, so that the current possessor does in fact acquire a right through adverse possession, even if her possession was initially unlawful.[25] Gray and Gray describe this process, through which 'adverse possession generates a "property" in land', even when the current possessor's title was wrongful in its inception, as 'one of the greatest paradoxes in the law of realty—an uncompensated shift of economic value to the squatter or interloper'.[26] It is in this paradoxical shift of economic value that the threat for the rights paradigm is hidden: Adverse possession over a long period can result in a bar to enforcement of the former owner's right of exclusive possession and eventually in the loss of that right, without the cooperation and against the will of the former owner and without receiving value or compensation.

Gray and Gray discuss a number of reasons for allowing unlawful possession to develop into a lawfully recognised right if it has existed unchallenged for a relatively long time. Prominent amongst these are legal recognition of the psychological bond between the long-term possessor and the land (and the concomitant loss of such connection as far as the neglectful owner is concerned);[27] restriction of endless and costly litigation about titles ('quieting' of land disputes); creating legal certainty and security of land title, both for the adverse possessor and for those who dealt with her in reliance upon the expectations created by her long-standing possession; bringing legal title into line with actual possession and so avoiding or restricting information and transaction cost; and punishing the sluggish and neglectful landowner while rewarding the person who beneficially uses the land.[28] Moreover, as Gray and Gray point out,[29] the practice of barring prior possessors at some point from challenging long-standing, sustained and unchallenged possessory control is entirely consistent with the common law's pragmatic approach to title as being a relative and defeasible claim to possession. In view of the negative

---

[25] K Gray and SF Gray, *Elements of Land Law* (4th edn, 2005) at 366.

[26] K Gray and SF Gray, *Elements of Land Law* (4th edn, 2005) at 367. LA Fennell, 'Efficient Trespass: The Case for 'Bad Faith' Adverse Possession' (2006) 100 *Northwestern Univ LR* 1037–96 at 1037 also refers to this result as 'an anomalous figure in the law'.

[27] This argument derives from US judge and academic Oliver Wendell Holmes; see 'The Path of the Law' (1897) 10 *Harvard LR* 457–8 at 476–7. This argument has been critiqued by R Posner, *Economic Analysis of the Law* (6th edn, 2003) at 78, 83; see further LA Fennell, 'Efficient Trespass: The Case for "Bad Faith" Adverse Possession' (2006) 100 *Northwestern Univ LR* 1037–96 at 1048. For a critical discussion of the reasons for adverse possession see section II.D below.

[28] K Gray and SF Gray, *Elements of Land Law* (4th edn, 2005) at 368–71, with references to literature and case-law. These reasons are also relied on in South African and in US law; see section II.A above and section II.C below. For a critical discussion of the reasons for adverse possession see section II.D below.

[29] K Gray and SF Gray, *Elements of Land Law* (4th edn, 2005) at 371–2.

effect that the Limitation Act 1980 has on the landowner's claim to recover the land it is relevant that some of these justifications, notably the ones relating to legal certainty and security, apply more clearly in case of unregistered land but less so with regard to registered land.

It is significant, for the purposes of this chapter, that adverse possession and the limitation principle allow 'interlopers' such as trespassers and squatters, in other words unlawful occupiers in bad faith, to trump the title of a neglectful landowner and to acquire a relatively or even absolutely indefeasible title through their unchallenged and long-time possession of the land. However, adverse possession was always more important in disputes about defective conveyancing information or inadvertent encroachments than in cases of squatting. Gray and Gray point out that 'it is likely that consciously wrongful seizure of land nowadays constitutes [the] least likely form' of adverse user and that it is much 'more frequently invoked to resolve ownership disputes which originate either in relatively innocent circumstances of entry under colour of title or in defective conveyancing practice'.[30] Moreover, the significance of adverse possession in squatting cases is also reduced by the fact that the institution of adverse possession has lost much of its relevance in English law because of recent developments. The Land Registration Act 2002 now provides that the mere lapse of time no longer bars the right of the registered proprietor of land, which makes it much harder for a squatter in possession of registered land to obtain title against the wishes of the proprietor, and consequently adverse possession is now practically limited to unregistered land.[31] A squatter who has been in adverse possession of registered land for 10 years may apply to be registered as proprietor, but such application can normally be defeated by a simple objection from the landowner.[32]

The shift brought about by the 2002 Act can be seen as an effort to bolster the rights protected by the rights paradigm against infringements that are allowed by what has been described here as qualifications of the paradigm. According to Gray and Gray, the Land Registration Act 2002 'has shifted the fundamental paradigm of English land law from the reality of *possession* towards the ideology of *ownership*',[33] a shift away from the factual link between possession and title, and from the fundamental relativity and defeasibility of title based on the stronger claim to possession, towards greater identifiability and security of proprietorship based on registration of 'abstractly defined proprietary entitlements'.[34] Although common law title could always survive a temporary loss of possession, it was inherently relative and defeasible because it depended on which of two claimants could prove the superior claim to possession. By contrast, the Land Registration Act 2002 aims to confer, through registration of title, a generally indefeasible title to a specified

---

[30] K Gray and SF Gray, *Elements of Land Law* (4th edn, 2005) at 372.

[31] K Gray and SF Gray, *Elements of Land Law* (4th edn, 2005) at 380.

[32] K Gray and SF Gray, *Elements of Land Law* (4th edn, 2005) at 381–3. Adverse possession by a tenant is possible, but the controls favour the landlord: *ibid* at 388.

[33] K Gray and SF Gray, *Elements of Land Law* (4th edn, 2005) at 354, 364; italics in the original.

[34] K Gray and SF Gray, *Elements of Land Law* (4th edn, 2005) at 354, 355, 356.

parcel of land on the registered proprietor.[35] This shift brings English land law closer to systems where original acquisition of land through acquisitive prescription is less relevant because title is not a relative and defeasible claim to possession but an indefeasible right based on registration.[36] In the words of Gray and Gray, 'estate ownership as constituted by the register record, becomes a heavily protected phenomenon, leaving little room for the operation "off the record" of some ancient and pragmatic principle of long possession'.[37] In a sense this could be regarded as a reconfirmation of the rights paradigm by removal or sidelining of an institution that initially (and perhaps traditionally) undermined the security of ownership but was no longer as important as it used to be.

Issues surrounding acquisition of title in land through adverse possession nevertheless recently resurfaced—and caused strong reaction—in the wake of the *Pye* case,[38] which was decided on the law as it stood before the Land Registration Act 2002. Graham, a farmer, had been using registered land belonging to Pye, a property development company, for grazing over a number of years on the basis of a written grazing licence. The licence was renewed a number of times but at a certain point Pye no longer responded to requests for renewal and Graham just went on using the land as before. After 12 years he registered cautions at the Land Registry against Pye's title to the land on the basis that he had obtained title through adverse possession. Pye then commenced action for possession against the widow and representative of Graham, who had died. The trial court dismissed the action, arguing that possession with the requisite intention to possess the land was not inconsistent with the squatter being willing to accept a new licence, but the court noted its lack of enthusiasm for the finding.[39] The Court of Appeal overturned the decision on the basis that Graham did not have the necessary intention to dispossess Pye within the meaning of the 1980 Act.[40] The House of Lords again

---

[35] K Gray and SF Gray, *Elements of Land Law* (4th edn, 2005) at 356, 358, 364.

[36] K Gray and SF Gray, *Elements of Land Law* (4th edn, 2005) at 365 note that '[t]he major registered estates are elevated into something approaching [civilian] absolute ownership of land' and that the effect of the 2002 Act is 'to weld together concepts of "title", "estate" and "proprietor" into a form of statutory ownership of land which begins to resemble the civilian model of proprietorship . . . thereby demonstrating, in effect, an inexorable drift towards the hitherto alien continental concept of *dominium*'.

[37] K Gray and SF Gray, *Elements of Land Law* (4th edn, 2005) at 364.

[38] I discuss the sequence of decisions in *Pye* in more detail at the end of this section below. The three English decisions are *JA Pye (Oxford) Ltd and Another v Graham and Another* [2000] 3 WLR 242 (trial court); *JA Pye (Oxford) Ltd v Graham* [2001] 2 WLR 1293 (Court of Appeal); *JA Pye (Oxford) Ltd v Graham* [2003] 1 AC 419 (House of Lords) For a discussion of the decision and its implications see K Gray and SF Gray, *Elements of Land Law* (4th edn, 2005) at ch 6. I rely on Gray and Gray extensively for my overview of the English law of adverse possession. On the position in Australia and New Zealand see P O'Connor, 'The Private Taking of Land: Adverse Possession, Encroachment by Buildings and Improvement under a Mistake' (2006) 33 *Univ Western Australia LR* 31–62. On the position in other civil law jurisdictions see the more detailed discussion of the *Pye* decisions at the end of this section. In a recent case the Supreme Court of India also expressed its disapproval of bad faith acquisition of land through adverse possession and requested the Indian legislature to consider amending the law: *Hemaji Waghaji Jat v Bhikhabhai Khengarbhai Harijan & Others* 2008 AIOL 3789 (23/09/2008) (SC). I am indebted to Roddy Paisley (Aberdeen) for bringing this decision to my attention.

[39] *JA Pye (Oxford) Ltd and Another v Graham and Another* [2000] 3 WLR 242 at 271.

[40] *JA Pye (Oxford) Ltd v Graham* [2001] 2 WLR 1293.

reversed the decision, confirming that there would be 'dispossession' of 'the paper owner' of land, for purposes of paragraph 1 of Schedule 1 to the Limitation Act 1980, if a squatter assumed possession of the land in the ordinary sense of the word and the paper owner failed to discontinue possession.[41] The decision confirmed that adverse possession requires a combination of factual possession and the intention to possess, the latter being expressed by the outward conduct of the possessor.[42] To qualify, the adverse possession must be continuous for the required period.[43] Good faith is not required and consequently a squatter or possessor in bad faith also qualifies.[44] Factual possession must be open, peaceful and not by consent of or licence from the owner. It must also be exclusive in the sense that the possessor must 'reserve the right to exclude all others from the land', at least for the moment being.[45] However, the possessor apparently does not have to intend to exclude the owner completely and permanently; intention to possess the land to the exclusion of all others for the moment being and to resist the owner as strongly as possible will suffice. The intention that is required is the intention to possess and not to be owner.

In a sense the House of Lords decision watered the possession requirement down to nothing more than the intention to possess the land on one's own behalf and for one's own benefit; a position that is even compatible with recognising the 'paper owner's' title and being willing to pay her if required. As a result of this friendly interpretation of the possession requirement, the House of Lords overturned the Court of Appeal's decision and reinstated the trial court's decision that Pye had indeed lost and Graham acquired ownership through adverse possession, even though it was clear that Graham had not resisted or challenged Pye's ownership in the period after termination of the lease agreement and that he would have been perfectly happy to continue paying for use of the land under the licensing agreement.[46]

The House of Lords decision was later overturned by the Fourth Chamber of the European Court of Human Rights, only to be reconfirmed by the Grand

[41] *JA Pye (Oxford) Ltd v Graham* [2003] 1 AC 419 (HL) at paras 42, 46.

[42] The possession requirement was analysed extensively in the opinion of Lord Browne-Wilkinson in *JA Pye (Oxford) Ltd v Graham* [2003] 1 AC 419 (HL) at paras 40–46. See K Gray and SF Gray, *Elements of Land Law* (4th edn, 2005) at 411–24.

[43] Limitation Act 1980, s 15 requires 12 years, although longer terms apply to certain claims, and some land is immune from adverse possession; see K Gray and SF Gray, *Elements of Land Law* (4th edn, 2005) at 373.

[44] *JA Pye (Oxford) Ltd v Graham* [2003] 1 AC 419 (HL) at para 42; see K Gray and SF Gray, *Elements of Land Law* (4th edn, 2005) at 419.

[45] K Gray and SF Gray, *Elements of Land Law* (4th edn, 2005) at 403; *JA Pye (Oxford) Ltd v Graham* [2003] 1 AC 419 (HL) at paras 38, 41.

[46] *JA Pye (Oxford) Ltd v Graham* [2003] 1 AC 419 (HL) at paras 46, 71; see K Gray and SF Gray, *Elements of Land Law* (4th edn, 2005) at 418–21. This weaker interpretation of the possession requirement is not only different from South African law, but also from other civil law jurisdictions such as Dutch and Italian law, where the occupier Graham would have been regarded as a *detentor* rather than a *possessor*; compare R Caterina, 'Some Comparative Remarks on *JA Pye (Oxford) Ltd v The United Kingdom*' (2007) 15 *European Rev of Private Law* 2739 at 273; JM Milo, 'On the Constitutional Proportionality of Property Law in The Netherlands' (2007) 15 *European Rev of Private Law* 255–63 at 261.

Chamber.[47] The Fourth Chamber decided that Article 1 of the First Protocol to the European Convention on Human Rights 1950 was activated by Pye's loss of ownership; that the relevant statutes[48] deprived Pye of its substantive property rights in the sense of the second sentence of Article 1 (expropriation); and that the deprivation was disproportionate in view of the absence of compensation and the effect it had on the former landowner.[49] The Grand Chamber decided that the interference with property brought about by the statutes had to be considered in terms of the second paragraph of Article 1 (regulation of the use of property) and not under the second sentence of the first paragraph (expropriation) and that the fair balance between the public interest and the individual interest had not been disturbed by the relevant statutes.[50] The extinction and acquisition of title through adverse user under the 1925 and 1980 statutes were thus not in conflict with the European Convention.

The *Pye* case evoked heated debate and controversy. When the House of Lords decision was overturned by the Fourth Chamber of the European Court a number of academic commentators noted that this turn of events could have significant effects in other member states of the European Union, unless the decision was regarded as one narrowly tailored to the English situation. In particular it was pointed out that the law of adverse possession or acquisitive prescription plays an important role in other jurisdictions and that the nature of the registration system was significant in evaluating both its purpose and its effect.[51] In the civil-law systems acquisitive prescription is often important because it brings the legal position (acquisition of ownership) in line with the registration system in situations where registration is either faulty because of a mistake or where the acquisition was ineffective because of a shortcoming in the predecessor's title. In both cases the protection offered by prescription is mainly aimed at good faith possessors, but there are instances where civil law systems allow acquisition of ownership through prescription by bad faith possessors, albeit usually over longer prescriptive periods

---

[47] The two European decisions are *JA Pye (Oxford) Ltd v The United Kingdom* [2005] ECHR 44302/02 (IV); *JA Pye (Oxford) Ltd and JA Pye (Oxford) Land Ltd v The United Kingdom* [2007] ECHR 44302/02 (GC).

[48] The Limitation Act 1980 and the Land Registration Act 1925.

[49] *JA Pye (Oxford) Ltd v The United Kingdom* [2005] ECHR 44302/02 (IV) at para 75. See further on this decision K Gray and SF Gray, *Elements of Land Law* (4th edn, 2005) at 411–24; C Norman, 'Compulsory Purchase Compensation: Limitation after *Pye v United Kingdom*' 2006 (Apr) *J Planning & Env Law* 454–62; GL Gretton, '*Pye*: A Scottish View' (2007) 15 *European Rev of Private Law* 281–8; O Radley-Gardner, '*Pye (Oxford) Ltd v. United Kingdom*: The View from England' (2007) 15 *European Rev of Private Law* 289–308.

[50] *JA Pye (Oxford) Ltd and JA Pye (Oxford) Land Ltd v The United Kingdom* [2007] ECHR 44302/02 (GC) paras 66, 74, 83.

[51] In South African, Belgian, Dutch and Italian law, Graham's holding and use of the land would not have qualified as possession because he lacked the necessary intention—the decision of the Court of Appeal in *JA Pye (Oxford) Ltd v Graham* [2001] 2 WLR 1293 was closest to the majority consensus in these countries. See V Sagaert, 'Prescription in French and Belgian Property Law after the *Pye* Judgment' (2007) 15 *European Rev of Private Law* 265–72; R Caterina, 'Some Comparative Remarks on *JA Pye (Oxford) Ltd v. The United Kingdom*' (2007) 15 *European Rev of Private Law* 273–9; JM Milo, 'On the Constitutional Proportionality of Property Law in The Netherlands' (2007) 15 *European Rev of Private Law* 255–63; compare section II.A above.

(for example 30 instead of 20 years). In the *Pye* decisions the focus was entirely on the characteristics and effects of the English registration system, and since acquisitive prescription serves different purposes and has different effects depending on whether the registration system is positive (as in Germany) or negative (as in Belgium), several commentators pointed out that the effect of the decision should be restricted to English law prior to the 2002 Act.[52]

C. Adverse Possession in the American Midwest

Original acquisition of land through adverse possession is also possible in US law, which poses the same questions as in South African and English law.[53] The statute of limitations, which functions on the same broad limitation principle that underlies adverse possession in English law, effectively prevents the owner from reclaiming possession from a possessor who can prove adverse possession for the prescribed period. Some US states require good faith for acquisition through adverse use; in those states squatters or trespassers (according to the subjective intention test) cannot benefit from their adverse use,[54] but in other states it is possible to acquire ownership through adverse possession in bad faith.[55] According to commentators, the objective standard that allows both mistaken (good faith) and knowing (bad faith) encroachers to obtain title through adverse possession is the majority rule that applies most widely,[56] even though bad faith possessors in fact seem to be treated more strictly by (and to fare much worse in) the courts than one might expect purely with reference to the abstract doctrine.[57] Academic commentators are mostly against the inclusion of bad faith trespassers under the adverse possession rules[58] and it could be argued that judicial reliance on the objective

---

[52] V Sagaert, 'Prescription in French and Belgian Property Law after the *Pye* Judgment' (2007) 15 *European Rev of Private Law* 265–72 at 270; R Caterina, 'Some Comparative Remarks on *JA Pye (Oxford) Ltd v. The United Kingdom*' (2007) 15 *European Rev of Private Law* 273–9 at 278.

[53] JW Singer, *Property Law: Rules, Policies, and Practices* (1993) at 143–72 explains that 'unprivileged entry on property possessed by another is a *trespass*' (emphasis in original). However, when one person possesses another's property exclusively, openly, without the owner's permission (adversely) and continuously for a period prescribed by state law, she acquires title.

[54] JW Singer, *Property Law: Rules, Policies, and Practices* (1993) at 158.

[55] In the sense that the possessor is fully aware that she is not in fact owner but intends to act as if she were owner or to become owner.

[56] LA Fennell, 'Efficient Trespass: The Case for "Bad Faith" Adverse Possession' (2006) 100 *Northwestern Univ LR* 1037–96 at 1047, citing the authoritative J Dukeminier and JE Krier, *Property* (5th edn, 2002) at 139.

[57] LA Fennell, 'Efficient Trespass: The Case for "Bad Faith" Adverse Possession' (2006) 100 *Northwestern Univ LR* 1037–96 at 1047, citing RH Helmholz, 'Adverse Possession and Subjective Intent' (1983) 61 *Washington Univ LQ* 331–58 at 331–2.

[58] LA Fennell, 'Efficient Trespass: The Case for "Bad Faith" Adverse Possession' (2006) 100 *Northwestern Univ LR* 1037–96 at 1048, referring to RA Epstein, 'Past and Future: The Temporal Dimension in the Law of Property' (1986) 64 *Washington Univ LQ* 667–722 at 686; TW Merrill, 'Property Rules, Liability Rules and Adverse Possession' (1985) 79 *Northwestern Univ LR* 1122–54 at 1126; RH Helmholz, 'More on Subjective Intent: A Response to Professor Cunningham' (1986) 64 *Washington Univ LQ* 65–106 at 75; MJ Radin, 'Time, Possession, and Alienation' (1986) 64 *Washington Univ LQ* 739–58 at 749; R Posner, *Economic Analysis of the Law* (6th edn, 2003) at 78.

standard is probably traditionally motivated by extraneous considerations that do not in fact benefit bad faith possessors as much as it seems.[59]

Eduardo Moisés Peñalver and Sonia K Katyal[60] refer to those who unlawfully hold land in adverse possession as 'acquisitive outlaws' to indicate that at least part of their purpose in defying property rules and vested rights is to derive a benefit from their unlawful possession in the form of acquiring ownership of the land. Their analysis presents an instructive perspective on acquisition of ownership through adverse possession by pointing out the ironies of one particular instance during the nineteenth century when this institution was employed to promote the equitable distribution of large tracts of state-held land in the American Midwest.[61] Local governments and state courts favoured the interests of settlers above those of land speculators and did what they could within the framework of the law to promote the interests of occupiers above those of absentee landlords; one of the results was that the law regarding adverse possession was 'liberalised'[62] in favour of the unlawful settlers or squatters by not requiring good faith. This example illustrates the point made earlier, namely that enforcement (or not) of the presumption against restrictions and of rules of interpretation that favour less burdensome restrictions indicate how strong the rights paradigm is—by not requiring good faith the courts departed from the conservative construction rules that uphold the paradigm. Eventually the US government adapted its own policies and started distributing land directly to settlers and amending the law to reflect its acceptance of the rights of the settlers, finally resulting in the 1862 Homestead Act that allowed free acquisition of federal land by occupiers who could satisfy the five-year residency and improvement requirements.[63] Ironically, these settlers, who were originally regarded as outlaws and lawless criminals, eventually acquired

---

[59] LA Fennell, 'Efficient Trespass: The Case for "Bad Faith" Adverse Possession' (2006) 100 *Northwestern Univ LR* 1037–96 at 1048, referring to RH Helmholz, 'Adverse Possession and Subjective Intent' (1983) 61 *Washington Univ LQ* 331–58 at 339–41. Helmholz argues that courts prefer the objective standard because it does not disadvantage the good faith claimant and that they applied it in a way that in fact burdened the bad faith claimant more heavily than one would expect.

[60] In 'Property Outlaws' (2007) 155 *Univ Pennsylvania LR* 1095–186.

[61] EM Peñalver and SK Katyal, 'Property Outlaws' (2007) 155 *Univ Pennsylvania LR* 1095–186 at 1105–13 indicate that the occupations took place within the framework of a policy debate between conflicting visions about disposition of vast tracts of land acquired by the state in the western territories. One group, mostly consisting of or representing existing property holders and speculators, favoured using the land to raise revenue by selling it off to the highest bidder; another group, including the settlers themselves, favoured giving it away for free or at very low cost to a large group of small landowners who could swell the ranks of the republican electorate. While public policy was still largely dictated by existing property interests in the east, the government initially favoured the first option and criminalised squatting to make the land as attractive to potential purchasers as possible. The significance of this example for my analysis is restricted by the fact that the history described by Peñalver and Katyal relates specifically to federal state land acquired and initially used for unpopular speculative purposes; it is unlikely that large-scale intentional, bad faith acquisitive squatting on private land would have met with the same indulgence and that it would have had the same effect on the development of the law of adverse user.

[62] EM Peñalver and SK Katyal, 'Property Outlaws' (2007) 155 *Univ Pennsylvania LR* 1095–186 at 1109–13.

[63] EM Peñalver and SK Katyal, 'Property Outlaws' (2007) 155 *Univ Pennsylvania LR* 1095–186 at 1113 show that pre-emption statutes of 1841 and 1862 preceded the 1862 Homestead Act.

the status of pioneers, the heroes of American mythology about settlement of the West.[64]

The reasons for adverse use acquisition of ownership that are traditionally relied on in US doctrine include the promotion of legal certainty through 'quieting' of titles, punishment of neglectful landowners and the economic notion of encouraging maximum utilisation of land.[65] Interestingly, two recent publications by academic commentators suggest that critical reconsideration of these reasons points towards greater liberalisation (rather than limitation) of the law regarding adverse possession, particularly in favour of bad faith possessors, knowing trespassers and squatters. Both normative and economic reasons are given for this counter-intuitive conclusion.

Peñalver and Katyal[66] discuss two perspectives on accommodating responses to unlawful squatting resulting in acquisition of land, utilitarian and retributive, and argue that both offer arguments in support of a measure of indulgence. Utilitarians are generally unwilling to sanction lawbreaking, but involuntary transfers of property can sometimes be justified if the lawbreaker places a much higher value on the property and if there is an obstacle to consensual transfer—this would typically be the case when the existing distribution of property is extremely skewed and the context favours legal reform: 'In cases of extreme want, it is possible that permitting forced transfers will enhance utility, even over the long run.'[67] Moreover, in social and economic conditions of that nature it is possible that forced transfers might actually increase and stabilise rather than undermine public and legal order and lawfulness, particularly when the squatters not only occupy but improve and develop the land beneficially. Utilitarian theory could therefore support the possibility that bad faith squatters could acquire prescriptive title through adverse possession, provided that the forced transfer is justified by an extremely skewed social and economic context and that the acquirer beneficially improves the property. Counter-intuitively, wider application of the principles of adverse possession

---

[64] EM Peñalver and SK Katyal, 'Property Outlaws' (2007) 155 *Univ Pennsylvania LR* 1095–186 at 1113. Of course, prior land rights belonging to indigenous groups or individuals were extinguished or overrun by Western settlement in places such as the US, Canada, Australia, New Zealand and South Africa, and in those instances Western law (mostly the common law) is traditionally relied on to justify the acquisition of Western title and the extinguishment of indigenous title, either through conquest or by treaty. As a result, the survival of indigenous rights has to be justified specifically, giving rise to the vast body of literature and case-law on indigenous or Aboriginal rights. Since the link between these two processes is tangential and I am specifically interested in the notion of adverse possession in common or civil law tradition I will not discuss indigenous rights here. However, see section V below.

[65] For a discussion of the reasons see JW Singer, *Property Law: Rules, Policies, and Practices* (1993) at 166–71; LA Fennell, 'Efficient Trespass: The Case for "Bad Faith" Adverse Possession' (2006) 100 *Northwestern Univ LR* 1037–96 at 1059–65.

[66] EM Peñalver and SK Katyal, 'Property Outlaws' (2007) 155 *Univ Pennsylvania LR* 1095–86 at 1145–1158. R Home, 'Land Titling and Urban Development in Developing Countries: The Challenge of Hernando de Soto's *The Mystery of Capital*' (2003) 2 *Journal of Commonwealth Law & Legal Education* 73–88 at 77 shows that there is a paradox in allowing formalisation of land title grounded in initial unlawful occupation: Registered title should be indefeasible, and therefore land titles that have been recognised should be defended against further squatting attempts.

[67] EM Peñalver and SK Katyal, 'Property Outlaws' (2007) 155 *Univ Pennsylvania LR* 1095–186 at 1150–51.

would in those cases support rather than undermine legal certainty and the stability of individual title.

In discussing the retributive perspective on intentional unlawful squatting Peñalver and Katyal[68] rely on broad contextual analysis that does not focus exclusively on the subjective intention of the lawbreaker, but also takes cognisance of the objective content of the law and the social facts against which it operates. With an appeal to Aquinas,[69] they argue that a retributive perspective on this kind of acquisitive property outlaw has to affect our evaluation of her action; at the very least, we have to acknowledge the informational value of squatters persisting with their unlawful conduct in the face of possible criminal and civil prosecution. Peñalver and Katyal favour extending this analysis beyond extreme and immediate personal need, referring to Amartya Sen's definition of poverty that takes into account the need not only to survive but also to participate, even minimally, in the life of the community.[70] Again, the argument is that wider and more radical application of adverse possession as a tool of social redistribution would, in the long run, stabilise rather than undermine the property regime as a whole because a just and equitable property regime is more sustainable than a seriously unfair one. In this case, security of individual title does not coincide exactly with the stability of the system. Regardless of whether one agrees with the Peñalver and Katyal argument regarding the use of adverse possession as redistributive tool, it has to be said that their normative evaluation, namely that increased systemic fairness would stabilise the property regime as a whole, even at the cost of individual security of title, goes a long way to explain why institutions such as adverse possession are accommodated (albeit apparently uncomfortably) in the rights paradigm.

Lee Anne Fennell similarly argues in favour of developing the law of adverse possession in the direction of 'efficient trespass', which she describes as a legal process of 'moving land into the hands of parties who value it much more highly than do the record owners, where markets cannot do so'.[71] Describing the mental state of a knowing trespasser as 'bad faith', she argues, is irrelevant because it is not the trespasser who actually 'steals' the land from the record owner; the transfer is brought about and sanctioned by government policy and the background state power that recognise and uphold the institution of adverse possession for policy reasons that have nothing to do with stealing.[72] The mental state of the knowing trespasser is reprehensible, but that is already dealt with in the very serious remedies, both

---

[68] EM Peñalver and and SK Katyal, 'Property Outlaws' (2007) 155 *Univ Pennsylvania LR* 1095–186 at 1152–8.

[69] *Summa Theologiae* IIa IIae Q 66; see EM Peñalver and SK Katyal, 'Property Outlaws' (2007) 155 *Univ Pennsylvania LR* 1095–186 at 1153. They also refer to similar arguments by Jeremy Waldron in *Liberal Rights: Collected Papers, 1981–1991* (1993) at 240–41; see to much the same effect JW Singer, *The Edges of the Field: Lessons on the Obligations of Ownership* (2000).

[70] EM Peñalver and SK Katyal, 'Property Outlaws' (2007) 155 *Univ Pennsylvania LR* 1095–186 at 1156, referring to A Sen, *Resources, Values, and Development* (1984) at 336–7.

[71] LA Fennell, 'Efficient Trespass: The Case for "Bad Faith" Adverse Possession' (2006) 100 *Northwestern Univ LR* 1037–96 at 1040.

[72] LA Fennell, 'Efficient Trespass: The Case for "Bad Faith" Adverse Possession' (2006) 100 *Northwestern Univ LR* 1037–96 at 1053, 1055–6.

criminal and civil, for trespass that are available to the landowner before the statute of limitations runs out. The question is therefore why the legal system countenances the acquisitive effect of adverse possession, even when it benefits knowing or bad faith unlawful occupiers or trespassers. In Fennell's opinion, some of the reasons forwarded for this result simply make no sense in that they are misconceived[73] or could be (and are) served much better by other means;[74] the only reason for upholding adverse possession that stands up to scrutiny is a properly conceived and formulated version of the argument that adverse possession punishes a neglectful landowner. Stated properly, this amounts to saying that the law moves land into the hands of the person who values the land more highly than the owner of record, under circumstances where markets cannot effect such a transfer.[75] In other words, the institution of adverse possession provides for rectification of a market failure by ensuring efficiency through a non-market transfer. Considered in this perspective, adverse possession should actually not be available to so-called *bona fide* (mistaken) occupiers or trespassers at all[76] and it should be restricted to instances of knowing trespass, where the unlawful occupier knows full well that she has no right and that she is trespassing. Given the strong criminal and civil remedies against trespass and the requirement that adverse possession must be open and non-fraudulent, the owner of record has every opportunity to enforce her right; failure to do so demonstrates that she attaches less value to the property than the trespasser does. At the same time the risks that the occupier knowingly runs by openly occupying the property demonstrates the higher value that she attaches to it.

Fennell's analysis has interesting implications for the position of squatters (in the sense of persons who knowingly and unlawfully occupy private land owned by someone else because they have no other option, being destitute and homeless). In line with her general point that adverse possession could serve the goal of moving property to higher-valuing users when markets cannot effect that transfer, Fennell argues that adverse possession could also 'respond to a more fundamental short-

---

[73] LA Fennell, 'Efficient Trespass: The Case for "Bad Faith" Adverse Possession' (2006) 100 *Northwestern Univ LR* 1037–96 at 1063 mentions that the 'quieting of titles' or legal certainty argument is undermined by the fact that adverse possession creates and maintains at least as many uncertainties, in the form of murky titles, as it is supposed to settle through bringing title into line with actual possession and use.

[74] LA Fennell, 'Efficient Trespass: The Case for "Bad Faith" Adverse Possession' (2006) 100 *Northwestern Univ LR* 1037–96 at 1059.

[75] This is the heart of Fennell's argument. See LA Fennell, 'Efficient Trespass: The Case for "Bad Faith" Adverse Possession' (2006) 100 *Northwestern Univ LR* 1037–96 at 1038, 1059–60, 1064. B Bouckaert and BWF Depoorter, 'Adverse Possession: Title Systems' in B Bouckaert and G de Geest (eds), *Encyclopedia of Law and Economics*, http://encyclo.findlaw.com/ (accessed 15 June 2008) 1200: 18–31 at 22 agree with Fennell that there are efficiency reasons to retain a rule of adverse possession, although they would make it available to both good faith and bad faith possessors and extend the prescription period for the latter (at 25). JG Sprankling, 'An Environmental Critique of Adverse Possession' (1994) 79 *Cornell LR* 816–84 critiques the institution from an environmental perspective, arguing that it is 'dominated by a prodevelopment nineteenth century ideology that encourages and legitimises economic exploitation' and environmental degradation of wild and fallow lands.

[76] Because it would encourage inefficient trespass in the sense of neglectful and ignorant behaviour where the relevant information is readily available. See LA Fennell, 'Efficient Trespass: The Case for "Bad Faith" Adverse Possession' (2006) 100 *Northwestern Univ LR* 1037–96 at 1066, 1071.

coming of markets' by providing a 'proxy for transactions that advance social welfare'.[77] In the case of great wealth disparities, Fennell argues, people without any conventional wealth resources could arguably use the opportunities offered by adverse possession by deliberately 'scouting out' parcels of land that have fallen in disuse and 'documenting' their adverse possession by making 'some nontrivial permanent improvement' to the land as an indication of their knowing, open and notorious possession of the land.[78] Fennell thus relies on the economic efficiency argument to substantiate development of the institution of adverse possession that would in effect undermine the security and exclusivity of existing individual landownership holdings while promoting the redistribution of land towards the landless and destitute, which would improve the overall fairness of the property regime and therefore stabilise it in the long run. In other words, adverse possession could function as a system-preservative tool to advance land reform (and social reform policies associated with it) without in any way affecting our disapproval of or legal response to trespass or to general lawlessness.

D. Conclusions

The brief overview of prescription and adverse possession law and practice above highlights a number of considerations that point towards a significant qualification of the rights paradigm in the sense that the security of ownership is reduced or undermined for reasons that are essentially out of the control of and even unrelated to the owner and her rights. Firstly, the fact that bad faith (or knowing) occupiers can benefit from prescription or adverse possession is arguably in itself already an indication that the security and exclusivity of ownership is sometimes sacrificed for the sake of another policy goal such as legal certainty or economic efficiency. Secondly, at least some of the reasons that are most often advanced for allowing this process to move property interests from the owner of record to a non-owner remain relevant, even in legal systems where land is registered, outside of the policy grounds that protect good faith possessors who obtained an imperfect title (or whose rights have been registered subject to a registration error). Quite a few commentators argue that it is beneficial and even necessary to leave room for acquisition of title by bad faith possessors through adverse possession, albeit in a small number of cases and in extraordinary circumstances. Thirdly, the policy argument that economic efficiency is the most coherent and convincing reason for adverse possession transfers, namely as a policy incentive to move property towards the person who values it the highest, when the market fails to effect such movement through market transactions, without thereby sanctioning lawless behaviour in general, represents a significant qualification of the rights paradigm.

---

[77] LA Fennell, 'Efficient Trespass: The Case for "Bad Faith" Adverse Possession' (2006) 100 *Northwestern Univ LR* 1037–96 at 1080.
[78] LA Fennell, 'Efficient Trespass: The Case for "Bad Faith" Adverse Possession' (2006) 100 *Northwestern Univ LR* 1037–96 at 1082–3.

Other considerations that are often cited as reasons for prescriptive transfers, such as legal certainty or 'quieting of titles', can arguably be justified and accommodated within the rights paradigm, but an efficiency argument fundamentally undermines the security and exclusivity of the rights paradigm and opens the door for further policy or efficiency arguments that could further erode the paradigm.

On the basis of these considerations it has been argued quite convincingly that it is not only permissible and consistent to include bad faith occupation or knowing trespass in the institution of prescriptive transfers, but that it might even be more efficient to concentrate the focus of prescription on knowing trespass and to exclude good faith occupation or inadvertent encroachment. In the same spirit it could be efficient and normatively legitimate to allow destitute, landless and homeless squatters to benefit from prescription practice, particularly if certain doctrinal refinements are introduced to ensure that they concentrate on disused land and document their intent by possessing the land openly and by making non-trivial and permanent improvements to the land. Even though courts and academic commentators tend to associate bad faith adverse possessors with outlaws, thieves and thugs, historical evidence suggests that similar prescriptive transfers to knowing and deliberate trespassers and squatters have been allowed in the past and that the settlers who benefited from them are now seen as heroes rather than villains. This line of argument represents a very strong qualification of the rights paradigm and a potentially fruitful approach for the development of property theory outside of the narrow constraints of that paradigm.

III. Public Access to Private Property

A. Exclusivity as a Core Characteristic of Property Ownership

Exclusivity is often described—even in English law—as one of the core entitlements that characterise ownership and that distinguish it from other, lesser rights with regard to property. In South African law this characteristic is captured in the principle that the owner is entitled to exclusive possession and use of her property and that nobody else may interfere with her exercise of that entitlement. This description is the foundation of eviction as it was described in chapter two: since the owner is entitled to exclusive possession, she can evict anyone who is in possession without her permission and without any other valid legal cause.[79] English

---

[79] PJ Badenhorst *et al*, *Silberberg and Schoeman's The Law of Property* (5th edn, 2006) at 92 refer to this characteristic as the 'individuality' of ownership and explain that it 'denotes the idea that the owner, in principle, has exclusive control over the thing which he or she can enforce against the whole world'. Both the principles of individuality and exclusivity (entitlement of possession) are also recognised as core characteristics of ownership in German private law, although holders of lesser real rights such as pledgees can also use the vindicatory action (compare § 985 *BGB* with §§ 1065, 1227); see F Baur *et al*, *Sachenrecht* (17th edn, 1999) at 30–31, 97.

law, while much more complicated because of the relativity of title and the import-ance of the 'network of relationships between "possession", "property", "title" and "estate" ',[80] nevertheless also recognises the importance of exclusivity by accepting that factual possession over land 'points towards ownership of one or other of the possessory estates'; exclusive possession is jealously protected because it generates a common law freehold.[81] Accordingly, the exclusivity of factual possession is pro-tected in English law by granting the possessor a right against anyone who is not in possession and who cannot prove a stronger right.[82] The US Supreme Court described exclusivity as one of the most important sticks in the bundle of rights that make up property ownership, crafting a *per se* or 'bright line' rule to the effect that compensation is required for any permanent physical invasion of property, regardless of the actual physical extent of the invasion or the actual loss or suffer-ing it imposes on the owner.[83]

Academic commentators also describe exclusivity as a central characteristic of ownership or at least refer to its significance in mainstream doctrine. This view is captured in two rightly acclaimed and influential articles. Honoré lists the right to possess as the first of what he describes as the 'standard incidents of ownership' and describes the right 'to have exclusive physical control of a thing' as 'the foun-dation on which the whole superstructure of ownership rests', adding that, in the absence of some rules and procedures to ensure firstly that the owner is placed in exclusive control and secondly that she remains in exclusive control, a legal system cannot be said to protect ownership.[84] Kevin Gray has demonstrated the related but more sophisticated point that, when deciding whether or not and how to 'propertise' a certain bundle of rights (and thereby remove it from the commons and insulate its exclusivity with nuisance and trespass rules), the 'propertiness' of property is usually determined with reference to its 'excludability'.[85] It is therefore

---

[80] K Gray and SF Gray, *Elements of Land Law* (4th edn, 2005) at 203.

[81] K Gray and SF Gray, *Elements of Land Law* (4th edn, 2005) at 206, 209–210.

[82] K Gray and SF Gray, *Elements of Land Law* (4th edn, 2005) at 211–12, referring to the decision in *Harrow London Borough Council v Qazi* [2004] 1 AC 983 (HL) (discussed in ch 2, section II., ch 4, sec-tion II.C and ch 5, section II.D).

[83] *Loretto v Teleprompter Manhattan CATV Corp* 458 US 419 (1982); *Kaiser Aetna v United States* 444 US 164 (1979). *Loretto* is particularly significant because the physical invasion (installation of tele-vision cables on private apartment buildings) was slight. In *Loretto*, the Supreme Court described the exclusivity of ownership as 'one of the most essential sticks in the bundle of rights that are commonly characterised as property' and as 'one of the most treasured strands in an owner's bundle of property rights'; see *Loretto v Teleprompter Manhattan CATV Corp* 458 US 419 (1982) at 433, 435. See further on these cases AJ van der Walt, *Constitutional Property Clauses: A Comparative Analysis* (1999) at 430–32; GS Alexander, *The Global Debate over Constitutional Property* (2006) at 76; LS Underkuffler, *The Idea of Property: Its Meaning and Power* (2003) at 26.

[84] AM Honoré, 'Ownership' in AG Guest (ed), *Oxford Essays in Jurisprudence* (First Series) (1961) 107–47 at 113. See further C Rose, 'The Comedy of the Commons: Custom, Commerce, and Inherently Public Property' (1986) 53 *Univ Chicago LR* 711–81 at 711–17.

[85] Gray's point is more sophisticated in that he demonstrated significant restrictions on thus recog-nising and protecting one person's right to exclude others from access to certain resources: K Gray, 'Property in Thin Air' (1991) 50 *Cambridge LJ* 252–307. The discussion of 'excludability' appears at 266–92, where Gray discusses physical, legal and moral considerations that render certain resources non-excludable, and 292–5, where he considers the characterisation of property as control over access. It is obvious from this note that Gray emphasises the limits of excludability and hence of exclusivity; this

justified to conclude that the supposed strength and value of ownership, as the strongest and most valuable property interest, are directly linked to the owner's power to exclude others from entering onto and using her property.

From the preceding introductory remarks it can be inferred that, on the one hand, exclusivity and control over access is an important aspect of legal recognition and protection of ownership interests over property while, on the other hand, there are well-known and widely recognised limits to legal enforcement and protection of the right to exclude. Gray has shown that the grounds for these limits may be physical, legal or moral in nature;[86] others have explained the same phenomenon in different ways.[87] In the following sections I discuss examples of instances where a landowner might be expected to have the right to exclude outsiders,[88] but where that right is either not recognised or enforced by law or, at the very least, successfully contested by certain users of the land. My contention is that these examples illustrate a point that Gray also makes, albeit in a slightly different context,[89] namely that the right to exclude, said to be a central and essential pillar of the rights paradigm, is often not as strong or as extensive as one might expect judging purely from the rhetoric of the rights paradigm.

B. Public Accommodations in US Law

Joseph William Singer explains an important limit on the landowner's right to control exclusive access to her property as a matter of the relationship between property and equality.[90] In making this connection Singer refers to an aspect of what is known as public accommodations law in the United States, namely the anti-discrimination rules (constitutional or otherwise) that restrict a landowner's control over access to her property in order to prevent discrimination based on

aspect is discussed again below. The links between the Gray argument about excludability and Margaret Jane Radin's argument about commodification are complex but significant: MJ Radin, 'Market-Inalienability' (1987) 100 *Harvard LR* 1849–937.

[86] See n 85 above.

[87] LS Underkuffler, *The Idea of Property: Its Meaning and Power* (2003) at 16–33 refers to the 'four dimensions' of property (theory, space, stringency of protection, and time) in construing a different explanation for the reasons why certain aspects of property are sometimes protected more strongly than others; see further MJ Radin, 'Market-Inalienability' (1987) 100 *Harvard LR* 1849–937.

[88] That is, persons who have no contractual relationship with the landowner that could found some right or claim to enter onto or occupy or use the land in any way.

[89] The difference is that Gray's article is mainly focused on the 'propertisation' of resources, in other words the decision to recognise a bundle of rights as property and so remove it from the commons and allow an individual holder to control access to it. Gray argues that there are physical, legal and moral limits that constrain that decision. My argument is based on much the same underlying assumptions and attitudes, but focuses on the fact that a property right, once recognised, will often not allow the owner to control access freely or at all, despite the fact that it has been removed from the commons.

[90] JW Singer, 'No Right to Exclude: Public Accommodations and Private Property' (1996) 90 *Northwestern Univ LR* 1283–497; JW Singer, 'Property and Equality: Public Accommodations and the Constitution in South Africa and the United States' (1997) 12 *SAPL* 53–86. In the following paragraphs I rely extensively on Singer, who refers to and analyses the literature and case-law. See further on this topic PJ Williams, 'Spirit-Murdering the Messenger: The Discourse of Fingerpointing as the Law's Response to Racism' (1987) 42 *Univ Miami LR* 127–57.

one of the prohibited grounds such as race, disability and gender. When privately owned property is used as a business that offers certain goods or services to the public, public accommodations laws require the owners to grant these services to the public without unjust discrimination. By proscribing discriminatory use of private property used as a business that serves the public, the public accommodations laws prevent a landowner from exercising her right to control access to the property in a manner that constitutes unjust discrimination.

Singer explains that the general view in the United States is that property owners have the right to exclude others from their property, even if that property is used as a business that serves the public, unless it falls within the limited class of businesses that historically had the duty to serve the public (public inns, common carriers and public utilities) or the right to control access is limited by a civil rights (anti-discrimination) statute. The common law in most states in the United States allows most businesses to exclude certain persons from the premises for any reason, including arbitrary and discriminatory reasons. Although the common law rule has been modified by legislation, the situation varies from state to state and often it is not absolutely clear whether the statutory amendments apply to all businesses. At the same time, Singer argues, case-law shows unequivocally that no judge in the United States will allow a retail store that is open to the public to exclude customers on the basis of race alone.[91]

The notion of public accommodations extends beyond unjust discrimination; in certain cases it might also indicate that the exclusivity of ownership is limited by other rights such as free speech. In such a case the owner might also find that her right to control access to the property is curtailed purely because the owner invited the public onto the property or because the property is generally used for a purpose that is open to the public. In *PruneYard Shopping Center v Robins*[92] the question was whether a state could make legislation which requires owners of private shopping centres to give access to people who want to exercise their right of free speech and petition in the shopping centre. The majority of the US Supreme Court confirmed that the right to exclude others from property is regarded as one of the essential sticks in the bundle making up property and concluded that this right would be destroyed by allowing freedom of expression rights to the public on the premises of a privately owned shopping centre. However, in previous decisions the US Supreme Court had established that not every destruction of or injury to property by governmental action amounts to a taking in the constitutional sense; the question is whether the restriction on private property 'forces some people to bear alone public burdens which, in all fairness and justice, should be borne by the public as a whole'.[93] This entails consideration of factors such as the nature

---

[91] JW Singer, 'Property and Equality: Public Accommodations and the Constitution in South Africa and the United States' (1997) 12 *SAPL* 53–86 at 58–60.

[92] 447 US 74 (1980). See AJ van der Walt, *Constitutional Property Clauses: A Comparative Analysis* (1999) at 432–43. The following paragraphs are based on AJ van der Walt, *Constitutional Property Law* (2005) at 176–7.

[93] *PruneYard Shopping Center v Robins* 447 US 74 (1980) at 83, quoting from *Armstrong v United States* 364 US 40 (1960) at 49, 80.

and economic impact of the regulation and its interference with reasonable investment-backed expectations. In the circumstances of *PruneYard* the requirement that petitioners be allowed to exercise their state-protected rights of free speech and petition in the shopping centre did not amount to an unconstitutional infringement of the owner's property rights under the takings clause, because the property owner was free to adopt and enforce regulations with regard to the time, place and manner in which these activities would be permissible, so as to minimise interference with the regular activities of a shopping centre. In this perspective, the Court decided, the actions of the petitioners could not be described as a physical invasion of the property. The property owner failed to demonstrate that the right to exclude others from the premises was so essential to the use or economic value of the property that the state-allowed limitation amounted to a taking of the property.[94] In view of the fact that physical invasions of private property need to be permanent to establish a *per se* taking according to the *Loretto* approach, this is not a surprising result and it demonstrates that there are limits to the exclusivity of private ownership, even in a jurisdiction where exclusivity is regarded as an essential and core aspect of ownership.[95]

Eduardo Moisés Peñalver and Sonia K Katyal[96] relate another story that also demonstrates the limits of the exclusivity of ownership in a context where property and equality interests were in conflict, namely the lunch counter sit-in demonstrations with which students and other activists, as part of the Civil Rights Movement, protested against race discrimination at shops in the United States during the 1960s. Peñalver and Katyal refer to these activists as 'expressive outlaws' to indicate that their conscious and deliberate transgression of private property exclusions had no acquisitive purpose but served to protest against an infringement of their civil rights. The students technically committed a trespass on private land by sitting at segregated lunch counters in a well-organised, non-violent but persistent manner, intentionally disregarding the property rights that they perceived as discriminatory in a conscious effort at changing those rights or the laws that supported them.[97] Despite initial opposition and disapproval, the sit-ins succeeded eventually; the owners of private shops desegregated their premises and the Civil Rights Act of 1964 reduced the opportunities for discriminatory exercise of property rights dramatically. As Peñalver and Katyal[98] point out, more recent

---

[94] *PruneYard Shopping Center v Robins* 447 US 74 (1980) at 84: Rehnquist J contrasted this aspect of the case with the position in *Kaiser Aetna v United States* 444 US 164 (1979). See JW Singer, 'Property and Equality: Public Accommodations and the Constitution in South Africa and the United States' (1997) 12 *SAPL* 53–86 at 66*ff*. See *Spector v Norwegian Cruise Line Ltd* 545 US 119 (2005) on the application of Title III of the Americans with Disabilities Act of 1990 (ADA), 42 USC § 12181*ff*, which prohibits discrimination based on disability in places of 'public accommodation', to foreign flag cruise ships.

[95] See in this regard GS Alexander, *The Global Debate over Constitutional Property: Lessons for American Takings Jurisprudence* (2006) at 76, referring to the categorical rule laid down in *Loretto v Teleprompter Manhattan CATV Corp* 458 US 419 (1982). See n 78 above.

[96] In 'Property Outlaws' (2007) 155 *Univ Pennsylvania LR* 1095–186.

[97] EM Peñalver and SK Katyal, 'Property Outlaws' (2007) 155 *Univ Pennsylvania LR* 1095–186 at 1125.

[98] In 'Property Outlaws' (2007) 155 *Univ Pennsylvania LR* 1095–186 at 1114–18.

urban squatters who occupy unused buildings deliberately and intentionally to make a political point have taken a leaf from the book of the lunch counter demonstrators, albeit that Peñalver and Katyal refer to the urban squatters as 'intersectional outlaws' to indicate that their intentional transgression of property laws and rights have both acquisitive and demonstrative purposes.[99]

C. The Right to Roam in English Law

In English law, an interesting commons-type limitation on the exclusivity of private land is the right to roam. Gray and Gray[100] indicate that this right, which comprises the right of access to private land for recreational purposes such as hiking, is related to several other categories of relatively weak, 'quasi-proprietary' public rights of access to private land such as the public right to use the highway, walkway agreements, the public right of passage in navigable waterways, the public right of fishing, local customary access rights and others. The point I am making in this section can be made with reference to any or all of these rights, but the right of recreational access is particularly enlightening, firstly because it was not recognised at common law but has now been extended dramatically by legislation, and secondly because it is the source of much controversy and conflict.

The common law does not confer a general right of recreational access to and use of private land for recreational purposes although, as Gray and Gray indicate, 'substantial de facto access has tended to be enjoyed in a rather ill-defined way'.[101] In particular the common law did not grant or recognise a general right to wander at large—the wide freedom of access and use suggested by such a right is too closely connected with ownership itself for such a right to exist comfortably within the rights paradigm.[102] The de facto access that does exist was enjoyed on the basis of 'fragile and arbitrarily revocable licence from the landowner' and not by right.[103] Although political appeals for increased access rights are often substantiated with references to the detrimental effects of emparkment and enclosure, Willmore pointed out that the modern drive for greater recreational access to

[99] EM Peñalver and SK Katyal, 'Property Outlaws' (2007) 155 *Univ Pennsylvania LR* 1095–186 at 1122–6. These and other politically inspired urban squatters are discussed in ch 5, section II.

[100] K Gray and SF Gray, *Elements of Land Law* (4th edn, 2005) at 315–35.

[101] K Gray and SF Gray, *Elements of Land Law* (4th edn, 2005) at 336; see further C Willmore, 'The "Right to Roam": An Empty Dream?' in P Jackson and DC Wilde (eds), *Property Law: Current Issues and Debates* (1999) at 14–47. On access through expansion of the national footpaths network, long user, rights over commons and waste lands, municipal parks and the Commons Registration Act 1965 see further K Gray and SF Gray, *Elements of Land Law* (4th edn, 2005) at 340–48.

[102] K Gray and SF Gray, *Elements of Land Law* (4th edn, 2005) at 337.

[103] K Gray and SF Gray, *Elements of Land Law* (4th edn, 2005) at 337; see further C Willmore, 'The "Right to Roam": An Empty Dream?' in P Jackson and DC Wilde (eds), *Property Law: Current Issues and Debates* (1999) 14–47 at 16.

natural areas should not be conflated with the agricultural access for use rights that were lost during enclosure.[104]

As Gray and Gray explain,[105] recreational access has been gradually expanded over the last few decades, mostly through a combination of activism, voluntary grants and licences and legislation. The most dramatic expansion of access rights—and simultaneous restriction of landowners' right to control access—was brought about by the Countryside and Rights of Way Act 2000.[106] According to Gray and Gray, this Act 'effectuates a quite remarkable social and environmental initiative' in that it 'gives legislative force to an entitlement which the common law could never recognise, ie a generalised right of self-determining pedestrian access to open land'.[107] An even more far-reaching right of access was established for Scotland in the Land Reform (Scotland) Act 2003.[108] The 2000 English Act defines public access to access land fairly widely but imposes strict limits on it. Because the Act explicitly establishes a fair balance between public access rights and the private

---

[104] See C Willmore, 'The "Right to Roam": An Empty Dream?' in P Jackson and DC Wilde (eds), *Property Law: Current Issues and Debates* (1999) 14–47 at 16–17. During the enclosure movement, land formerly held in common was either acquired by or transferred to individual holders and literally enclosed, with the result that thousands of former users were stripped of their rights. Enclosure of agricultural land started in the early sixteenth century in the form of establishing individual title (either freehold title or lifelong leases) to land previously held in common by agreement; see JR Wordie, 'The Chronology of English Enclosure 1500–1914' (1983) 36 *The Economic History Rev* 483–505 at 484, 487. The enclosure movement proper started in 1750 and was regulated by Acts of Parliament; from 1750 onwards 21% or roughly 7 million acres of land was enclosed with the assistance of 5,000 statutes: see http://www.surreycc.gov.uk/sccwebsite/sccwspages.nsf/LookupWebPagesByTITLE_RTF/ Parliamentary+enclosure?opendocument (accessed 18 June 2008) and http://www.achr.net/ Evictions%20Asia/Eviction%20Law.html (accessed 16 July 2008). In terms of these Acts a landlord could apply for enclosure awards that, if successful, would result in her being registered as individual owner of the identified pocket of enclosed land. These Acts annulled the leases previously held in terms of enclosure agreements and tenants could only get their smallholdings back at the mercy of the new owner, often against rent that would be out of their reach: JR Wordie, 'The Chronology of English Enclosure 1500–1914' (1983) 36 *The Economic History Rev* 483–505 at 504. Tenants were forced to move to the villages and cities, where they went to work as labourers. Some historians regard these evictions as a crucial part in the creation of the labour force during the Industrial Revolution, when the landless became the working class: http://www.achr.net/Evictions %20Asia/Eviction%20Law.html (accessed 16 July 2008).
[105] K Gray and SF Gray, *Elements of Land Law* (4th edn, 2005) at 340–53. See further on consensual access (voluntarist schemes, licences, etc) C Willmore, 'The "Right to Roam": An Empty Dream?' in P Jackson and DC Wilde (eds), *Property Law: Current Issues and Debates* (1999) 14–47 at 18–20.
[106] See K Gray and SF Gray, *Elements of Land Law* (4th edn, 2005) at 348–53. In 1999 C Willmore, 'The "Right to Roam": An Empty Dream?' in P Jackson and DC Wilde (eds), *Property Law: Current Issues and Debates* (1999) 14–47, discussing the lobbying for and early drafts of legislation that would create a 'right to roam', still despaired that such a statutory right was no more than an 'empty dream'.
[107] See K Gray and SF Gray, *Elements of Land Law* (4th edn, 2005) at 348.
[108] See K Gray and SF Gray, *Elements of Land Law* (4th edn, 2005) at 348, 353. Again, in 1999 J Rowan-Robinson, 'Working Together for Access' in P Jackson and DC Wilde (eds), *Property Law: Current Issues and Debates* (1999) 1–13 was still sceptical about the possibility of drafting legislation that could provide such a right of access for recreational purposes. In *Tuley v The Highland Council* 2007 SLT (Sh Ct) 97 the Sheriff's Court (Grampian) held that it could not be said with certainty that any use of a path by horse riders would be irresponsible or an unreasonable interference with the owners' rights and that speculative and premature erection of barriers by a landowner wanting to prevent damage caused by horses therefore prevented the legitimate exercise of access rights in terms of s 14(2) of the Land Reform (Scotland) Act 2003 (at 110J–K).

rights of the landowners it could effectively and successfully deprive landowners, without providing for compensation, of their right to sue in trespass anyone who enters the land without their permission. The rights of landowners are accommodated in that the right of public access is subjected to strict conduct prescriptions and requirements; members of the public who exceed or violate the requirements and conditions are liable to be ejected and sued for compensation for any damage they may have caused. Furthermore, owners are entitled to develop and use their land within the normal planning and other legislation. From the information available it seems as if the legislation, suffering from shortcomings though it may be, succeeded in establishing a public right of recreational access over private land in such a way that a fair balance between private and public interests can be maintained, thereby avoiding the rather bleak picture that Willmore painted in 1999.[109]

D. Excludability in Post-apartheid South African Law

Three examples from post-1994 South African case-law illustrate judicial efforts, outside of eviction law, to restrict landowners' general right to exclude others, thereby acknowledging and reinforcing the property interests of socially and economically weak individuals and groups who have been marginalised by apartheid. Some of these examples are related to what would be regarded as public accommodations or public access issues in the United States or in England; others are uniquely part of the South African land reform context.

In the *Victoria & Alfred Waterfront* case[110] the Cape High Court followed the US Supreme Court decision in *PruneYard Shopping Center v Robins*[111] by deciding that the private owner of premises open to the general public does not have an absolute right to exclude certain persons, even when they make a nuisance of themselves on the premises and do not enter the premises as clients. The owners of the Victoria & Alfred Waterfront in Cape Town, a popular tourist destination, applied for a permanent interdict to prohibit certain panhandlers from ever again entering the premises, based on evidence and unsubstantiated hearsay that these persons had been threatening, harassing and attacking staff and customers of establishments on the premises over a period of time. The owners relied on their right of ownership, but the Cape High Court argued that owners of premises do

---

[109] See generally K Gray and SF Gray, *Elements of Land Law* (4th edn, 2005) at 350–53. In 1999 C Willmore, 'The "Right to Roam": An Empty Dream?' in P Jackson and DC Wilde (eds), *Property Law: Current Issues and Debates* (1999) 14–47 anticipated that such a statutory deprivation of one of the owner's entitlements, without compensation, might intrinsically fall foul of the expropriation jurisprudence of the European Court of Human Rights (in view of the applicability of the European Convention in England once the Human Rights Act was introduced in 1998).

[110] *Victoria & Alfred Waterfront (Pty) Ltd and Another v Police Commissioner, Western Cape, and Others (Legal Resources Centre as* Amicus Curiae*)* 2004 (4) SA 444 (C). Of course the South African case is different in that it establishes a right of informal economic activity in a public place rather than a non-discrimination right to be served or a free speech right. The following paragraphs are based on passages from AJ van der Walt, *Constitutional Property Law* (2005) at 428–30.

[111] 447 US 74 (1980). See n 82 and accompanying text.

not have an absolute right of exclusion[112] and refused to grant a permanent interdict. Instead, the court granted an order that prohibited the affected persons from behaving in certain specified ways or doing certain specified things on the premises.[113] In the court's view, a blanket prohibition against entry and free movement should not be granted unless there is no other way of achieving the lawful and justifiable goal of protecting the custom and business interests of the owners and the physical integrity and security of their customers and employees.[114] In reaching this result the Court stated that conflicts between property owners and socially marginalised non-owners cannot be decided purely with reference to the rights of the owners, even when the non-owners have been acting unlawfully and causing a nuisance. Instead, the marginalised social position of the non-owners and the effect of a blanket exclusionary order against them have to be considered against the social and political history of the country in striving for a decision that is justifiable in view of the relevant constitutional provisions and principles.

Zondi[115] demonstrates the importance of post-apartheid restrictions on the landowner's right of exclusivity in a somewhat more roundabout way, especially since it was decided without reference to either the constitutional property or housing clauses. The case concerned the Pound Ordinance 32 of 1947 (Natal), which gave (mostly white) landowners the power to seize and impound (mostly black-owned) livestock found trespassing on their land. Under the Ordinance, both the impounding and sale of livestock took place without a court order. The Constitutional Court considered the social, economic and political role that the Ordinance played in establishing and reinforcing the unequal positions of white landowners and black people under apartheid land law.[116] While the exclusivity and integrity of landowners' property had to be respected and protected, this protection simultaneously had to be interpreted and applied with sensitivity for historical hierarchies of power and marginalisation and therefore certain provisions of the Ordinance were declared unconstitutional, but at the same time the legislature was given time to rectify the situation while still sensitively respecting and protecting the rights of landowners against stray animals.[117]

The Pound Ordinance could not be evaluated in isolation from the ownership-favouring common law; nor could the ostensibly apolitical regime of white land rights and the hierarchical structure of which it forms the pinnacle be separated

---

[112] *Victoria & Alfred Waterfront (Pty) Ltd and Another v Police Commissioner, Western Cape, and Others (Legal Resources Centre as* Amicus Curiae*)* 2004 (4) SA 444 (C) at 449A, 451E.

[113] *Victoria & Alfred Waterfront (Pty) Ltd and Another v Police Commissioner, Western Cape, and Others (Legal Resources Centre as* Amicus Curiae*)* 2004 (4) SA 444 (C) at 452G*ff.*

[114] *Victoria & Alfred Waterfront (Pty) Ltd and Another v Police Commissioner, Western Cape, and Others (Legal Resources Centre as* Amicus Curiae*)* 2004 (4) SA 444 (C) at 452E–G.

[115] *Zondi v Member of the Executive Council for Traditional and Local Government Affairs and Others* 2005 (3) SA 589 (CC).

[116] *Zondi v Member of the Executive Council for Traditional and Local Government Affairs and Others* 2005 (3) SA 589 (CC) at paras 38–42.

[117] The declaration of invalidity was suspended for 12 months to give the provincial legislature an opportunity to amend the Ordinance in a suitable way, and various rulings were made to provide for interim justice: *Zondi v Member of the Executive Council for Traditional and Local Government Affairs and Others* 2005 (3) SA 589 (CC) at paras 126–31.

from the political ideals of the apartheid land rights system. Instead, proper consideration of the historical, social, economic and political background and context shows that these laws were used to establish and reinforce the superiority of white landownership vis-à-vis black owners of livestock, thereby creating an intricate web of strong common law land rights, weak feudal-like customary law positions with regard to land and movable property, and strong state powers to uphold and enforce this hierarchy of strong and weak, powerful and marginalised, rich and poor.[118] Apartheid law has established strong property positions of privilege and weak property positions of marginality; consequently, developing the common law in line with the Constitution requires sensitivity not only for rights but also for weakness and marginality. Far from being politically neutral law that merely protected the exclusivity of a landowner's property against stray cattle, the Pound Ordinance was a political instrument that had a specific role in the creation and entrenchment of social and economic inequality during the apartheid era. The social and political context within which the Pound Ordinance was promulgated can therefore not be ignored in the new constitutional dispensation. Statutory protection of agricultural land against stray cattle is a legitimate purpose and therefore the Ordinance was not simply declared invalid, but the discriminatory potential of the Ordinance had to be minimised by amendment, even if that restricted landowners' right to exclude.

Nhlabati[119] dealt with a constitutional challenge against the Extension of Security of Tenure Act 62 of 1997. The Act grants farm labourers and lawful occupiers of agricultural land the right to bury their family members on the farm without consent and against the will of the landowner.[120] The occupier enjoys this burial right subject to reasonable conditions that may be imposed by the owner or person in charge. In the *Nhlabati* case the owner argued that the section of the Act that allows burial was unconstitutional because it violated the protection given to property by section 25 of the Constitution.[121] The Land Claims Court decided that

---

[118] In the recent Australian case of *Griffiths v Minister for Lands, Planning and Environment* [2008] HCA 20 (15 May 2008) at paras 87–149 Kirby J, in his minority judgment, argued for a similarly contextualised approach to the question whether expropriation of land subject to aboriginal land rights is legitimate (see section V. below).

[119] *Nhlabati and Others v Fick* 2003 (7) BCLR 806 (LCC). The following paragraphs are based on AJ van der Walt, *Constitutional Property Law* (2005) at 344–7.

[120] In two earlier decisions (*Serole and Another v Pienaar* 2000 (1) SA 328 (LCC); *Nkosi and Another v Bührmann* 2002 (1) SA 372 (SCA)) it had been decided that the legislature did not intend to include the right to establish a grave in the specific use rights originally listed in s 6(2) of the Act. Subsequently, the Act was amended to insert the new s 6(2)(dA), which now includes the right to bury a deceased occupier or member of the occupier's family (who, at the time of that person's death, was residing on the land) in accordance with their religion or cultural belief, if an established practice in respect of the land exists. 'Established practice' is defined in s 1 of the Act as a practice in terms of which the owner or person in charge of the land or his or her predecessor in title routinely gave permission to people living on the land to bury deceased members of their family on that land in accordance with their religion or cultural belief. The amendment and its history are discussed by the court in *Nhlabati and Others v Fick* 2003 (7) BCLR 806 (LCC) at paras 16–19.

[121] A similar argument was raised and considered but not clearly decided in one of the earlier decisions on burial rights, where it was said that it would amount to an appropriation if an occupier were allowed to take a gravesite without permission and against the will of the landowner: *Nkosi and Another*

section 6(2)(dA) does not authorise arbitrary appropriation (deprivation) of a grave,[122] because the right to appropriate a grave is balanced with the right of the owner, which could in certain circumstances outweigh the right to a grave.[123] In the Court's view the Act established a fair balance because an occupier has the right to establish a grave only if there is an established practice of giving permission for burials in the past, which presupposes some kind of pre-existing consensus between the landowner and the occupiers about burials;[124] and considering that the establishment of a grave would constitute a relatively minor intrusion into the landowner's property rights[125] and that the right to bury an occupier or a family member according to section 6(2)(dA) was enacted to fulfil the state's constitutional mandate to provide occupiers with legally secure tenure. Considering the importance of the religious or cultural beliefs of occupiers regarding burial of family members close to their residence, the constitutional mandate would in most cases be sufficient to justify the deprivation of some incidents of ownership.[126]

The court also considered the argument that section 6(2)(dA) might constitute or authorise an unconstitutional expropriation of property. Without deciding that the section indeed amounted to expropriation,[127] the court concluded that the statutory obligation of a landowner to allow an occupier to appropriate a gravesite on his or her land without compensation would be reasonable and justifiable as meant in section 36 even if it did amount to expropriation without compensation.[128] The constitutional challenge against section 6(2)(dA) was dismissed with reference to the social context and the reform-oriented nature of the Act, instead

v Bührmann 2002 (1) SA 372 (SCA) at para 38. In *Serole and Another v Pienaar* 2000 (1) SA 328 (LCC) at para 16 it was said that the granting of such a right would amount to granting of a servitude. See *Nhlabati and Others v Fick* 2003 (7) BCLR 806 (LCC) at paras 27, 32.

[122] This part of the decision was based on the analysis of the phrase 'arbitrary deprivation' in the Constitutional Court decision in *First National Bank of SA Ltd t/a Wesbank v Commissioner, South African Revenue Service; First National Bank of SA Ltd t/a Wesbank v Minister of Finance* 2002 (4) SA 768 (CC) at para 100. *FNB* requires the court to consider the possibility of unconstitutional deprivation first, while raising the issue of unconstitutional expropriation only if there is no such deprivation or if it could be justified under s 36.

[123] *Nhlabati and Others v Fick* 2003 (7) BCLR 806 (LCC) at para 31.

[124] *Nhlabati and Others v Fick* 2003 (7) BCLR 806 (LCC) at para 31. It is not required that the owner must have allowed the occupier or family involved in a specific dispute to bury their family members in the past—the question is merely whether burials of occupiers took place in the past or not. Moreover, it is the owner of the land in the abstract sense that is involved and not the specific owner at the time of a particular dispute, with the result that a practice would also be established if previous owners allowed burials.

[125] *Nhlabati and Others v Fick* 2003 (7) BCLR 806 (LCC) at para 31.

[126] *Nhlabati and Others v Fick* 2003 (7) BCLR 806 (LCC) at para 31.

[127] *Nhlabati and Others v Fick* 2003 (7) BCLR 806 (LCC) at paras 32–5.

[128] The same circumstances that determined the first part of the decision were again considered decisive: the right does not constitute a major intrusion on the landowner's property rights; the right is subject to balancing with the landowner's property rights and would not necessarily outweigh them; the right exists only where there is an established past practice with regard to gravesites; and the right will enable occupiers to comply with religious or cultural beliefs that form an important part of their security of tenure, and giving statutory recognition to their security of tenure is in accordance with the constitutional mandate. See *Nhlabati and Others v Fick* 2003 (7) BCLR 806 (LCC) at para 35.

of simply on the basis of the presumed inviolability of the common law right of ownership. *Nhlabati* therefore accepts an important physical intrusion on privately owned agricultural land, authorised by land reform laws, without compensation, on the basis of social and historical context.

E. Conclusions

The examples above illustrate the fact that landowners' right to control access to and exclude others from their property is not as extensive as one might think purely on the rhetoric of the rights paradigm. In fact landowners often find either that they cannot exclude certain people from their property or that they cannot evict persons who have gained access. The reasons for the common law and statutory restrictions that prevent owners from exercising the right to evict vary from public accommodations considerations that are largely inspired by equality (and sometimes free speech) principles to public access and use considerations that are based on principles of public health, civic and religious freedoms and social and economic justice. It is particularly significant that landowners are sometimes prevented from evicting persons even when the latter have gained access to the property unlawfully or are conducting themselves on the property in a way that poses a threat or a nuisance for the landowner, her livelihood, her employees or her customers.

IV. Significant Building Encroachments[129]

A. South African Law

In the Roman-Dutch tradition, the remedy for permanent building works that encroach significantly on neighbouring land was to have the encroachment demolished.[130] In recent cases,[131] South African courts refused to grant a demolition order

---

[129] This section is based on selected passages from AJ van der Walt, 'Replacing Property Rules with Liability Rules: Encroachment by Building' (2008) 125 *SALJ* 604–40. I do not expand on comparative sources, but see P O'Connor, 'An Adjudication Rule for Encroachment Disputes: Adverse Possession or a Building Encroachment Statute?' in E Cooke (ed), *Modern Studies in Property Law IV* (2007) 197–217; P O'Connor, 'The Private Taking of Land: Adverse Possession, Encroachment by Buildings and Improvement by Mistake' (2006) 33 *Univ of Western Australia LR* 31–62 for further information on other common law jurisdictions.

[130] JB Cilliers and CG van der Merwe, 'The "Year and a Day Rule" in South African Law: Do our Courts Have a Discretion to Order Damages instead of Removal in the Case of Structural Encroachments on Neighbouring Land?' (1994) 57 *THRHR* 587–93. See further on the law regarding encroachment A Pope, 'Encroachment or Accession? The Importance of the Extent of Encroachment in Light of South African Constitutional Principles' (2007) 124 *SALJ* 537–56; S Scott, 'Recent Developments in Case Law Regarding Neighbour Law and its Influence on the Concept of Ownership' (2005) 16 *Stell LR* 351–77 at 359–67.

[131] *Rand Waterraad v Bothma en 'n Ander* 1997 (3) SA 120 (O); *Trustees, Brian Lackey Trust v Annandale* 2004 (3) SA 281 (C); compare *Lombard v Fischer* [2003] 1 All SA 698 (O).

and awarded compensation instead, despite the fact that the affected landowners were permanently deprived of the use of their land. This raises the question whether these owners have been forced into a compulsory transfer of their land (or of rights in their land).

In *Rand Waterraad*,[132] the High Court decided that courts have the discretion to grant either demolition or compensation. This conclusion was justified with reference to the general reasonableness standard of neighbour law[133] and the assumption that this standard in South African neighbour law is similar to the equity principle in English law. In *Brian Lackey Trust*[134] the High Court also relied on English law, where the courts employ a 'working rule' to the effect that a damages award can be granted instead of injunctive relief in exceptional circumstances, where the injury to the affected landowner is small and can be compensated by a small money payment. It is said in English law that the alternative form of relief in damages is exceptional and cannot be used to oblige the affected landowner to sell his land against compensation.[135]

Neither the *Bothma* nor the *Brian Lackey Trust* decision ruled on the status of the land affected by the encroachment, and yet the encroachments in both cases were significant enough to imply, once the demolition order was denied, that the affected landowners would be prevented from using their land. In neither case was it established that (or considered whether) the encroacher acquired any rights in the land affected by the encroachment, nor was the question asked whether the land could or should be transferred to the encroacher by way of a forced sale. Before these cases were decided, Van der Merwe had stated that the courts can, if they judge it fair, order the encroacher to take transfer of the land upon which she encroached, the only question being the amount of compensation for the compulsory sale.[136] Van der Merwe found support for this view in older decisions, one of which stated that compensation was the primary remedy and that transfer of the affected land was incidental thereto.[137] On the face of it, these older decisions create the impression that the courts have the authority to order transfer of the affected land to the encroacher, in addition to compensation, when it is practicable to do so,[138] but in

---

[132] *Rand Waterraad v Bothma en 'n Ander* 1997 (3) SA 120 (O) at 133D–F.

[133] *Rand Waterraad v Bothma en 'n Ander* 1997 (3) SA 120 (O) at 133F–134E.

[134] *Trustees, Brian Lackey Trust v Annandale* 2004 (3) SA 281 (C).

[135] *Trustees, Brian Lackey Trust v Annandale* 2004 (3) SA 281 (C) at para 22, referring to Chancery Amendment Act 1858, s 2 and to *Shelfer v City of London Electric Lighting Co* [1895] 1 Ch 287 (CA); *Jaggard v Sawyer and Another* [1995] 2 All ER 189 (CA); *Holland v Worley* (1884) 26 ChD 578 at 587. English law is discussed in more detail in section IV.B below.

[136] CG van der Merwe, *Sakereg* (2nd edn, 1989) at 202–3.

[137] *Meyer v Keiser* 1980 (3) SA 504 (D) 507. See further *Christie v Haarhoff and Others* (1886–1887) 4 HCG 349; *Greeff v Krynauw* (1899) 9 CTR 591; *Van Boom v Visser* (1904) 21 SC 360; *Wade v Paruk* (1904) 25 NLR 219; *De Villiers v Kalson* 1928 EDL 217.

[138] In *Meyer v Keiser* 1980 (3) SA 504 (D) the plaintiff challenged the assumption that the court had the authority to grant such an order, but the challenge was overruled on the authority of CG van der Merwe, *Sakereg* (1979) at 129; JE Scholtens, 'Infringement and Protection of Ownership' 1956 *ASSAL* 129–36; *Christie v Haarhoff and Others* (1886–1887) 4 HCG 349. In *Christie v Haarhoff and Others* (1886–1887) 4 HCG 349 at 356 the court remarked that *solatium* had to be paid because the transfer 'practically amounts to a compulsory expropriation'.

reality there is little support in these cases for the conclusion. Ordering compulsory sale of land requires an exceptional judicial authority, especially in South African law, where the power of expropriation is reserved for the state and available only when granted by authorising legislation[139] and exercised for a public purpose.[140] There is no conclusive indication that such a power existed at common law, and section 33 of the Deeds Registries Act 47 of 1937 merely creates the registration procedure for bringing the deeds register in line with original changes in ownership;[141] it does not grant such a power to the courts.

The current situation is therefore that the courts apparently tend, even in some instances where the encroachment is significant and where it effectively deprives the affected landowner of use and enjoyment of her land, to grant compensation rather than demolition of building encroachments, without making an order with regard to the status of any rights in the land. At the same time it appears, despite some remarks to the contrary, that the courts do not have the power to actually order transfer of the land to the encroacher.

B. English Law

In English law the erection of an unlicensed building or structure upon neighbouring land constitutes a continuing trespass, for which the courts could award either injunctive relief or damages.[142] Injunctive relief is said to be a prima facie right because a landowner is normally entitled to an injunction to restrain trespass on her land, but Gray and Gray argue that the remedy of injunction is no longer necessarily the best remedy, pointing out that the courts increasingly order payment of compensation. This tendency is explained with reference to the modern equivalent of Lord Cairns' Act (Chancery Amendment Act 1858),[143] which allows the courts to withhold injunctive relief in favour of an award of equitable damages in respect of future or continuing acts of trespass.[144] These changing circumstances support the shift of emphasis in English law from injunctive to compensatory relief in trespass cases, despite the fact that damages is an inadequate form of relief for future and continuing acts of trespass, which encroachment inevitably causes.

In *Shelfer*[145] the court reiterated that landowners, especially landowners who are certain of their title, have a prima facie right to injunctive relief. However, the

---

[139] A Gildenhuys, *Onteieningsreg* (2nd edn, 2001) at 9 10; *Pretoria City Council v Modimola* 1966 (3) SA 250 (A) at 258G.

[140] Section 25(2) of the 1996 Constitution.

[141] Brought about by legitimate expropriation or acquisitive prescription.

[142] K Gray and SF Gray, *Elements of Land Law* (4th edn, 2005) at 247–52. See further, on Australian and New Zealand law, P O'Connor, 'An Adjudication Rule for Encroachment Disputes: Adverse Possession or a Building Encroachment Statute?' in E Cooke (ed), *Modern Studies in Property Law Vol IV* (2007) 197–217; P O'Connor, 'The Private Taking of Land: Adverse Possession, Encroachment by Buildings and Improvement by Mistake' (2006) 33 *Univ of Western Australia LR* 31–62.

[143] Section 50 of the Supreme Court Act 1981 (UK).

[144] K Gray and SF Gray, *Elements of Land Law* (4th edn, 2005) at 248.

[145] *Shelfer v City of London Electric Lighting Co* [1895] 1 Ch 287.

court also formulated the 'good working rule' later relied upon by South African courts, according to which the courts should exercise their discretion in choosing between injunctive relief and compensation on the basis of equity, taking into account factors such as the scope of the injury caused to the landowner's rights, whether the injury can be estimated in money and compensated adequately by payment of a sum of money, and whether it would be oppressive to the defendant if an injunction were granted. In *Jaggard*[146] the Court of Appeal emphasised that encroachers cannot expect to have an unlawful continuing trespass committed by them legitimised and continued simply because they are willing to pay for it; on the other hand, a landowner subjected to a continuing trespass cannot expect automatically to be able to have the building work demolished simply because they wanted undisturbed possession. In some cases the encroachment might just have to be accepted by the affected landowner as a fait accompli, particularly when the encroaching buildings are houses now occupied by people and families, and then compensation might be a better solution.

On the basis of case-law Gray and Gray argue that monetary relief is preferred to injunctive relief when the encroachment has had no more than a slight impact on the affected landowner; when compensation is easy to calculate; when the claimant has delayed in seeking injunctive relief; or when the affected landowner unreasonably demands excessive compensation or refuses to consider reasonable compensation offers.[147] Preference for monetary compensation instead of injunctive relief could imply that the courts are authorising the continuation of an unlawful state of affairs or that they allow the trespasser to purchase immunity for his unlawful actions, but the English courts have accepted that they are sometimes forced to follow this route to avoid granting injunctive relief that would deliver the trespasser 'bound hand and foot' to the claimant, exposing him to extortionate compensation demands.[148]

C. Dutch and German Law

In modern Dutch and German private law a landowner is entitled, in principle, to exclusive possession and use of her land and therefore she can claim removal of encroaching building works.[149] However, neither Dutch nor German law would allow the affected landowner to exploit the situation or to enforce evidently unfair results by insisting upon demolition.[150] Accordingly, both Civil Codes provide

[146] *Jaggard v Sawyer* [1995] 2 All ER 189 (CA) at 280, 282.
[147] K Gray and SF Gray, *Elements of Land Law* (4th edn, 2005) at 250.
[148] K Gray and SF Gray, *Elements of Land Law* (4th edn, 2005) at 252.
[149] The German Civil Code (*Bürgerliches Gesetzbuch; BGB*) therefore provides for demolition as the default remedy: §§ 93, 94, 946, 1004.
[150] See F Baur *et al, Sachenrecht* (17th edn, 1999) 278; WHM Reehuis and AHT Heisterkamp, *Pitlo Het Nederlands Burgerlijk Recht, Vol 3 Goederenrecht* (12th edn, 2006) at 446; see further HR 17 April 1970, *NJ* 1971, 89.

that compensation can be paid for certain building encroachments in lieu of demolition.[151]

Article 5:54 of the Dutch Civil Code is written from the perspective of the encroacher: The landowner can claim removal, but if removal would bring about greater loss for the encroacher than would be suffered by the landowner if the encroachment were left intact, the encroacher can demand that the encroachment be left intact against payment of compensation. Thereafter, the perspective switches to the landowner and the choice of legal construction for the respective rights affected by the surviving encroachment is left to her: Normally, a real servitude would be created over the affected landowner's land in favour of the encroacher, but the affected landowner has the option to choose that the relevant piece of land should be transferred to the encroacher against compensation.

In § 915 of the German Civil Code the choice is left to the affected landowner, who can at any time demand that the encroacher should buy the affected piece of land from her against a price that reflects its value when the encroachment first occurred, whereafter the rights and liabilities of the parties are determined by the provisions of the sale. German law therefore upholds the encroachment in all cases, regardless of the balance of loss or inconvenience. Judging from the provisions regarding the payment of compensation, a limited real right is not initially created in favour of the encroacher, but in favour of the affected landowner, with reference to her right to receive compensation. From the literature it appears as if the accepted construction is that attachment of the encroachment is suspended, so that the encroacher remains owner of the encroaching building, even where it encroaches upon the land that belongs to the neighbour.[152]

D. Conclusions

The results brought about by significant building encroachment are extraordinary, particularly if they are considered in the context of the rights paradigm.

---

[151] Article 5:54 of the Dutch Civil Code (*Burgerlijk Wetboek: BW*) determines that, if a building or construction is erected partly or completely upon or under the land of another person, and if the owner of the building or works would suffer greater loss from demolition or removal than the landowner would suffer if it were left intact, the owner of the building or works can claim, against suitable compensation, that a real servitude should be created in her favour to maintain the status quo or, if the owner of the land prefers, that the relevant part of her land be transferred to the owner of the building or works. This provision does not apply if the builder had a right to build or if she was malicious or grossly negligent. In the German Civil Code, §§ 912–13 provide that, if the encroacher has built across the boundary line onto the land of a neighbour without malice or gross negligence and, unless the affected landowner immediately objected to the encroachment, the affected landowner must accept the existence of the encroachment, against annual payment of a compensation amount in the nature of a rent or annuity. The amount of compensation is calculated according to the provisions of the Civil Code and the right to receive compensation overrides all other rights in the land. Although it is preferable that the right to receive compensation be entered in the land register, this does not happen automatically: § 914 *BGB*. Like Dutch law, §§ 912–15 *BGB* do not apply if the encroacher acted with malice or gross negligence or if the affected landowner immediately objected to the encroachment.

[152] F Baur *et al*, *Sachenrecht* (17th edn, 1999) at 279, citing § 95 *BGB* and the decision of the German Civil Court in BGH NJW 1985, 789.

Through no fault of their own and against their will, owners of land are forced to sacrifice all or part of their land to a careless neighbour whose building works encroach upon their land. The policy reasons for sometimes allowing the encroachment to stand and merely compensating the affected landowner are obviously so strong that the modern Dutch and German Civil Codes make explicit provision for the monetary solution, even as a default option and in German law regardless of the balance of inconvenience. In English and South African law the motivation for and the results of a choice for compensation are less clear-cut, but even in the absence of a formal transfer of land or rights, owners affected by significant encroachments are still forced to suffer serious infringements on their rights.

The legitimacy of the judicial tendency to leave even significant building encroachments intact and compensate the affected landowner with a monetary award is obviously relative to the force of the policy reasons for resorting to it. Indications are that the (mainly economic) policy reasons for this tendency are strong, at least in some cases, and therefore the pressure is on the legislature to promulgate suitable regulatory laws. The Dutch and German Civil Codes offer useful examples.

For present purposes, the point is that supposedly strong ownership rights are subjected, apparently quite easily and sometimes even without convincing judicial authority, to significant restrictions prompted by policy reasons that have been explored only superficially, at least in English and South African law. One may assume that the Dutch and German legislatures have considered the policy reasons for their amendments of the civil law and decided to amend the law so as to reflect the interests of the party benefiting from the balance of convenience, but these reasons have not featured very prominently in the English or South African cases where landowners have been forced to sacrifice their rights to encroachment or in the literature. Given the lack of clarity in the case-law one is left to speculate that the main reasons for allowing value to transfer to the builder in significant encroachment cases is economic efficiency or, in slightly different terms, the balance of convenience. Given the fact that the circumstances are relatively comparable one could also speculate that the reasons for allowing encroachment against compensation are similar to those for allowing acquisition of ownership through prescription or adverse possession; in both cases the losing owner was able to prevent the loss by simply taking better care of her property and not allowing adverse possession or encroachment to take place. At least in this instance, the hierarchical power of ownership is apparently less overpowering than the rights paradigm suggests. Landowners are sometimes forced to sacrifice the entitlement to exclusive use and enjoyment for other interests over which they have no control, even in circumstances where the infringement was caused by another person acting unlawfully, in breach of the owner's rights.

V. Weak Owners

One of the implications of the rights paradigm is that strong rights are protected more strongly than weak rights; another is that strong rights (and particularly ownership) are protected uniformly strongly. Of course all rights are subject to legitimate state interference in the form of either expropriation or regulation, but outside of that area of exception it is to be expected that owners of land should, in principle, enjoy more or less equal levels of respect and protection.

Property lawyers know that this is not true: Even strong rights in land have not always been respected or protected by Western legal systems, particularly if the rights were held by persons or exercised in a form unknown to Western law. Colonial powers blithely ignored and wiped out existing rights of indigenous occupiers and users of land, often on the excuse that the underlying cultures and legal systems were too barbaric or undeveloped to deserve recognition and that the land could therefore, in terms of superior colonial law, legitimately be regarded and treated as *terra nullius*.[153] More recently, in the wake of a number of ferociously litigated native land claims cases, courts in some jurisdictions have acknowledged, sometimes grudgingly, that colonial settlement and imposition of colonial law did not necessarily extinguish native land titles.[154]

Apart from colonial settlement, apartheid land law obviously provides another example of instances where strong land rights, including both customary land rights and full Western ownership, were treated with disdain and disrespect. Although a large part of apartheid policies and practices involved denying black people the property rights enjoyed by other landowners and forced removal of black people with weak property rights, there were also many instances where strong land rights, including Western ownership, enjoyed by black people were destroyed by forced removals. In some instances these removals were facilitated by what appeared, on the surface, to be voluntary sale and transfer of the land. Some forced removals were accompanied by formally valid expropriation and compensation; in others there was insufficient or no compensation. Common to them all was a single feature, recently described by the Constitutional Court as a 'grid of

---

[153] I will not discuss the massive literature on so-called indigenous, native or aboriginal land claims here. In AJ van der Walt, 'Modernity, Normality, and Meaning: The Struggle between Progress and Stability and the Politics of Interpretation' (2000) 11 *Stell LR* 21–49; 226–43 I discuss the central Australian decision in *Mabo and Others v State of Queensland (No 2)* (1992) 107 ALR 1 (HC) and some of the literature on it. Compare ch 2, n 16 and see further S Swain and A Clarke, 'Negotiating Postmodernity: Narratives of Law and Imperialism' (1995) 6 *Law & Critique* 229–56; *Delgamuukw v British Columbia* [1997] 3 SCR 1010.

[154] The ratio of the decision in *Mabo and Others v State of Queensland* (1992) 107 ALR 1 (HC) was that native title is recognised and protected by the common law in the sense that state annexation or colonisation does not automatically extinguish native title. However, this concession is qualified by the decision that native title is not derived from the Crown and therefore not protected by it either and that further, explicit state dispossessions could take place without any duty to compensate. The impact of the qualification was proven by the recent decision in *Griffiths v Minister for Lands, Planning and Environment* [2008] HCA 20 (15 May 2008) (n 162 below).

integrated repressive laws that were aimed at furthering the government's policy of racial discrimination' which 'materially affected and favoured the ability of the [state or private landowners] to dispossess the applicants' of their rights.[155] Regardless of the exact form that forced removals and 'black spot' clearances appeared to assume under apartheid land law, the vulnerability of black land users and owners and their inability to resist removal was a direct result of this grid of repressive laws and of the weak social and political status that it afforded them.[156] In other words, ownership is a strong right, arguably perhaps even the strongest property right, unless you happen to be a member of a oppressed social or political group, in which case the force and value of your rights are as strong as your political and social status. Like the colonial dispossessions, this conclusion about apartheid land law obviously undermines the central premise of the rights paradigm.[157]

We cannot dismiss this flaw in the rights paradigm by blaming it on the political fallacies of colonial settlement and apartheid racial policies. Even now, in the post-colonial and post-apartheid era, there are still weak owners whose rights are not afforded the same measure of respect and protection enjoyed by other, more powerful owners. The most obvious example is perhaps the recent *Kelo* decision of the US Supreme Court, in which an individual landowner who obviously lacked social, economic or political clout was forced to sacrifice her home for the sake of economic development.[158] It is trite that the American courts do not question the legislative or executive decision that a certain expropriation is for a public purpose too closely, as long as the exercise of the state's power of eminent domain is rationally related to a conceivable public purpose,[159] but the close split of the Supreme Court in *Kelo* shows that there is a measure of discomfort with the idea that private property—and particularly private homes—should be subjected to expropriation purely for the sake of economic development that would benefit another

---

[155] *Department of Land Affairs and Others v Goedgelegen Tropical Fruits (Pty) Ltd* 2007 (6) SA 199 (CC) at para 70. Compare further *Alexkor Ltd and Another v Richtersveld Community and Others* 2004 (5) SA 460 (CC); *Haakdoornbult Boerdery CC v Mphela* 2007 (5) SA 596 (SCA); *Mphela and 217 Others v Haakdoornbult Boerdery CC and Others* 2008 (7) BCLR 675 (CC).

[156] In *Minister of the Interior v Lockhat* 1961 (2) SA 587 (A) at 602D apartheid was described as 'a colossal social experiment and a long term policy' that must 'inevitably cause disruption and, within the foreseeable future, substantial inequalities'. Compare JT Schoombee, 'Group Areas Legislation: The Political Control of Ownership and Occupation of Land' 1985 *Acta Juridica* 77–118.

[157] The South African Constitutional Court decision in *Jaftha v Schoeman and Others; Van Rooyen v Stoltz and Others* 2005 (2) SA 140 (CC) offers an interesting counterpoint. The case involved the forced sale of houses, resulting from enforcement of attachment and execution legislation in order to satisfy small personal debts of indigent persons. In this case the debts were unconnected to the houses, which were bought with state subsidies, and not secured by bonds. The Court insisted that the relevant legislation should be read restrictively so as to require judicial oversight that could ensure protection of the homeowners' housing rights in terms of s 26 of the Constitution. Owners who were socially and economically weak were therefore protected against abusive legal process, but on the strength of the housing provision in the Constitution, not because of the inherent power of ownership.

[158] *Kelo v City of New London, Connecticut* 545 US 469 (2005).

[159] *Berman v Parker* 348 US 26 (1954) at 32–3; *Hawaii Housing Authority v Midkiff* 467 US 229 (1984) at 241; see further AJ van der Walt, *Constitutional Property Law* (2005) at 261–7.

private person (or company).[160] At least some judges simply do not feel comfortable with the proposition that weak owners can be forced, through the power of eminent domain, to sacrifice their homes so that other private persons can make money or so that the state can gather higher taxes from more efficient use of the land.

As Kevin Gray has shown, similar dispossessions of socially or politically weak landowners are allowed for the sake of economic development outside of the United States as well.[161] In Australia, a recent decision by the High Court now apparently allows expropriation of land that is subject to aboriginal land rights to go ahead, despite the fact that the expropriation would infringe upon or even destroy the aboriginal rights, in order to benefit other private parties involved in a commercial enterprise.[162] Similarly, in the United Kingdom an expropriation of land and concomitant eviction of gypsies and travellers from a lawful site where some of them had been living for as long as 20 years was allowed for the purpose of regenerating the area and developing the land for the 2012 London Olympics.[163]

These cases demonstrate that ownership is only as strong as the social, economic and political status and power of its holders allows. Far from being the strongest and most invulnerable right in the hierarchy of property interests, ownership is possibly just as vulnerable to overriding political and economic power as any other property interest. This conclusion suggests that the force and power of ownership, considered the strongest property right, is a function not so much of its elevated position in the hierarchical framework of the rights paradigm as of the social, economic and political status of its holder. Ownership (and strong property rights) are not necessarily strong in themselves; it is strong owners that are strong. Of course this conclusion flies right in the face of the central tenets of the rights paradigm.

[160] An expropriation similar to that in *Kelo* was allowed by the Supreme Court of Michigan in *Poletown Neighborhood v Council v City of Detroit* 304 NW2d 455 (Mich 1981); but subsequently the same court overruled this decision and reverted to a stricter public use test: *County of Wayne v Hathcock* 684 NW2d 765 (Mich 2004) at 786–7. See further K Gray, 'There's no Place like Home!' (2007) 11 *Journal of South Pacific Law* 73–88 at 78–80. The minority judgment of Kirby J in *Griffiths v Minister for Lands, Planning and Environment* [2008] HCA 20 (15 May 2008) shows that he was also uncomfortable with the effect of the majority decision. In German law a similar expropriation also failed because the German Federal Constitutional Court applies a slightly stricter public purpose test: *BVerfGE* 74, 264 (1986) (*Boxberg*); compare AJ van der Walt, *Constitutional Property Law* (2005) at 254–61.
[161] K Gray, 'There's no Place like Home!' (2007) 11 *Journal of South Pacific Law* 73–88 at 85–8.
[162] See K Gray, 'There's no Place like Home!' (2007) 11 *Journal of South Pacific Law* 73–88 at 85–8, referring to *Minister for Lands, Planning and Environment v Griffiths and Others* [2002] NT LMT 26 (http://www.austlii.edu.au); *Griffiths and Another v Lands and Mining Tribunal* [2003] NTSC 86 (http://www.austlii.edu.au) (Angel J); *Griffiths v Northern Territory of Australia* [2003] FCA 1177 (http://www.austlii.edu.au); *Minister for Lands, Planning and Environment v Griffiths* [2004] NTCA 5 (http://www.austlii.edu.au) (all accessed 16 October 2008). These cases have now come to a head in *Griffiths v Minister for Lands, Planning and Environment* [2008] HCA 20 (15 May 2008), where the High Court of Australia dismissed an appeal against a decision by the Federal Court that allowed an expropriation of land that is subject to aboriginal land rights to go ahead. The expropriation forms part of a scheme that would eventually benefit private persons.
[163] *Smith v Secretary of State for Trade and Industry* [2008] 1 WLR 394. I am indebted to Kevin Gray for bringing these cases to my attention.

VI. Conclusions

At first, the qualifications of the rights paradigm touched upon in this chapter appear difficult to explain on their own and difficult to compare to the qualifications discussed earlier. Generally, the rights paradigm (as explained in chapter three) stands for the fairly straightforward propositions that rights are stronger than no-rights, that strong rights are stronger than weak rights, and that ownership is the strongest right of all. In view of the link between strong rights and exclusivity (set out in chapter two) it is therefore to be expected that landowners and holders of other strong rights should be able to exclude or evict holders of weak rights or no-rights from their land, regardless of the context or the personal circumstances of the occupiers. Even the qualifications set out in chapters four and five can, to an extent, be explained within this paradigm as exceptions that are necessitated by legitimate housing and other state policies. At least to the extent that the qualifications in landlord–tenant law do not amount to ignoring the right of the landowner completely, they can be accommodated within the rights paradigm as justifiable limitations. However, the examples discussed in this chapter are more difficult to explain in the same terms. The examples show that some owners' supposedly strong rights are in fact weaker than others and that ownership interests are sometimes subjected to the no-right interests of bad faith squatters, trespassers and encroachers, often without great clarity about the policy reasons for these qualifications. When policy reasons are provided for these qualifications, the reasons are often completely different from (and sometimes contrary to) the justice considerations (involving care for weak, marginal or vulnerable persons or groups, especially in the residential housing market) encountered in chapters four and five.

It is striking that all the exceptional cases in this chapter, except for the weak owners, are characterised by the fact that the owners whose rights are curtailed are or were at some stage in a position to avoid the negative effects of the qualification of their rights, provided they pay attention and look after their property diligently. Owners who look after their property with reasonable care should, so the argument goes, be able to act in good time and efficaciously to prevent adverse possession or encroachment interests from vesting in their land, and owners of property that is open to the public should also be able, through the timely formulation and imposition of legitimate and suitable access rules and regulations, to prevent trespassers from coming onto or acting on their land in a way that could unreasonably damage their property interests. With the exception of the weak owners all these qualifications could therefore be explained with reference to lack of care and attention on the owner's side, an explanation that fits neatly into the autonomy language that underlies the rights paradigm. As long as the landowner has the power, in principle, to prevent loss or harm the threat that these qualifications pose to the rights paradigm is relatively minor.

The clearest reasons that are most often given for the existence of these qualifications of the rights paradigm are efficiency and utility. Encroachment and adverse possession transfers are specifically widely explained in terms of efficiency or utility in the sense that these involuntary transfers cause less harm than would be the case if they were not allowed; while the cost for the individual owner in terms of loss of security or value is justified with reference to the fact that the owner was in a position to protect her individual interests but failed to do so. The apparent ease with which the rights of weak owners are overridden for the sake of others is less simple to explain in terms of utility or efficiency.

Seen in this light, the qualifications described in this chapter differ from those described in chapters four and five in important ways. Both sets of qualifications are deviations from the paradigmatic rule that strong rights are protected against no-rights and weak rights, but in this chapter some deviations are tolerated because they are efficient in or useful for the property regime as a system of rules and practices that uphold the current distribution of property, while the examples in chapters four and five are deviations that are tolerated even though they might challenge or threaten that regime for the sake of equity, justice or fairness towards the holders of no-rights or weak rights. Some examples in this chapter (such as the *Nhlabati* gravesite case) could belong in either category.

It remains to explain the existence of the qualifications that suggest that all owners are not protected equally strongly. Clearly these qualifications do not fit the picture of anti-eviction qualifications in chapter four or chapter five, because they do not protect weaker or lesser property interests; in fact, they do exactly the opposite in the sense that they undermine the value of the supposedly strong property interests held by weak owners. They do not fit the efficiency or utility picture painted by the other qualifications in this chapter comfortably either, because the justification for the utility examples, namely that the affected owner had or has the choice to protect her interests and failed to do so, is absent in the case of weak owners.

It is possible to argue (as Fennell and Peñalver and Katyal have done with regard to adverse possession) that systemic sustainability (rather than just short-term stability) of the existing property regime is the justification for all exceptions to and qualifications of the rights paradigm, in the sense that a property regime that is more or less just and equitable is more stable in the long run than one that is fundamentally unjust. In that case, one could argue, smaller and even larger exceptions, deviations and qualifications that protect weaker property interests or marginal social groups for reasons of justice and fairness and that apparently undermine or erode the hierarchical supremacy of strong property rights are not only capable of being accommodated in but positively necessary for the long-term stability of the system. This explanation would make it possible to explain both the anti-eviction examples in chapters four and five and the utility qualifications in this chapter, but the weak owners example would still not fit this explanation easily because the examples undermine rather than protect the interests of weak and vulnerable groups and individuals.

Against that background the weak owners qualification discussed in this chapter could be explained either as an uncomfortable remainder an of earlier, more overtly racist, colonial version of the rights paradigm, or as a rather cynical version of the rights paradigm according to which the long-term stability of the property regime (and the property interests of the powerful owners who are its primary beneficiaries) is superior to the individual security of socially, economically or politically weak property owners. In either case this version of the rights paradigm stands in rather stark contrast with the qualifications and the more serious challenges to the paradigm brought about by reformist legislation discussed in chapters four and five.

7

Conclusions

I.   Property in the Context of Stability and Change   211
II. Overview of Results   222
III. Property in the Margins   230

I. Property in the Context of Stability and Change

A. Theoretical Background

IN CHAPTER ONE I described a property regime as an existing system of acquired or vested property holdings and the legal rules and practices that uphold and regulate them. I also stated that the stand-off between moral, political or constitutional obligation or pressure to bring about change in a particular property regime and the cultural, doctrinal and methodological tendency to resist, postpone or minimise such change is not only a fruitful but an essential locus for critical reflection about property. This hypothesis does not mean that property equals injustice, as Proudhon would have it, or that all existing property holdings need to be changed *tout court*, or even at all. The point is rather that property, being a fundamentally social and political institution, plays a central role in both establishing or maintaining and in changing or transforming the social, political and legal structures that represent and uphold inequality and injustice in society. Therefore, once a moral or political case has been made for justice-inspired change in a particular property regime, one could expect the social and political forces for and against change to play out in a confrontation between legal institutions that entrench and protect extant property holdings and political and legal efforts to reform or transform the property regime. My point is that we should not uphold the status quo without even considering the implications for justice.

In stating this hypothesis I am not primarily debating the moral or political case for changing or transforming this or that particular property regime, except in so far as such a case has already been made adequately and convincingly. In the case of post-apartheid South Africa, a strong moral and political case for large-scale transformation of society—including the inequitable property regime established as part of apartheid politics—has been made and enshrined in the new constitutions of

1993 and 1996. In other places, similar or different pressures might exist for smaller or larger changes in the property regime. However, such a case in favour of reform or transformation of a property regime cannot be argued abstractly. The historical, socio-economic and political context and the actual effect of established property regimes on the lives of individuals and communities are important in making normative judgments about the justification of either upholding or changing them. The fact that property regimes are shaped in part by social, economic and political factors and that they therefore reflect their context means, on the one hand, that their moral and political legitimacy can only be determined with reference to their context; on the other hand it means that they are fundamentally social and political in nature and therefore prone to the effects of (larger or smaller) political processes that require or imply change and reform. Important for my purposes in this book, extant property holdings within a property regime cannot be regarded as inviolable rights predicated upon and justified by pre-social or pre-political acquisitions, nor can the rules and practices that uphold and protect them be seen as immutable or immune against political change.

An important implication of this hypothesis is that any significant indication of injustice or inequality in the social structure or the property regime could, at least in principle, justify government action (within the boundaries of the particular constitutional and legal system) to adjust the property regime accordingly. Change brought about by such reformist state intervention could affect only the rules and practices of property law or, in more extreme cases, bring about adjustments in the current distribution of property holdings. In really radical cases the whole property regime might be overturned and replaced with something else, although this kind of revolutionary change tends to be frowned upon in the era of globalised human rights. Generally speaking, international human rights values and standards play a significant role in supporting and controlling changes of this kind. In the South African context, where the injustices to be rectified are vast and systemic in nature and where remedial state action takes place within an explicitly transformative constitutional framework, the process of reform has been described, from a particular theoretical perspective, as 'transformative constitutionalism'.[1] In other jurisdictions and conditions, adaptations of the property regime could take place on other grounds and on a different scale, and obviously the confrontation between forces of change and stability can be explained from different theoretical perspectives. However, I assume that the hypothesis above and the analysis that follows from it are relevant in any legal system where the property regime is adapted for justice reasons.

On the basis of my first hypothesis as stated above, this project is primarily about stability and change and the way in which these two opposing forces affect property's capacity to either entrench or uproot existing social and economic inequality and injustice. I said in chapter one that the tension between stability

---

[1] K Klare, 'Legal Culture and Transformative Constitutionalism' (1998) 14 *SAJHR* 146–88 at 166–7; see ch 1, n 18.

(protection of existing property holdings) and change (state intervention that affects existing property holdings) is inherent to and ubiquitous in property law, particularly in so far as the state intervenes in the property regime for 'normal' regulatory reasons (for example planning, building and development controls; licensing and regulation of firearms, businesses selling controlled medicines or the rental housing market). However, this tension becomes more visible and contentious in situations where large-scale adaptations to the property regime are required for justice reasons that exceed the 'normal', day-to-day business of state regulatory action. In any property regime, the restrictions that need to be placed upon existing property holdings for day-to-day regulatory reasons can be accommodated and explained within the established rules and logic of 'normal' property doctrine without making fundamental changes to or threatening the doctrinal system or tradition. In this respect (small, day-to-day) change is easily assimilated as a 'normal' part of the property regime, thanks to the stabilising effect of more or less flexible doctrinal tradition. The security provided by the doctrinal framework, which is related to the rule of law principle and the value of legal certainty, renders it feasible to allow a measure of flexibility that can accommodate some regulatory change, without challenging or reconsidering existing values or assumptions about the place and role of property in society.

However, in a time of radical social and political change many or all of the established doctrinal traditions and the foundations of the property regime as such might well be discredited as part of the process of change, as indeed was the case in post-apartheid South Africa and in the post-communist states of Central Europe. Radical political change might then require new lawmakers to introduce new policies that are in conflict with the established doctrinal tradition; at the very least they might amend the property regime by introducing uncertain new standards (often emanating from international human rights instruments) that are foreign to or deemed unsuitable for traditional legal reasoning.[2] In either event, the rules, practices and institutions of established property law will be placed under strain by these 'abnormal', large-scale changes to the extent that the existing doctrine cannot assimilate the changes without abandoning, distorting or departing from central characteristics or tenets of the current regime. In such a case one could say that the stability of the property regime is threatened by the nature or the extent of change. This kind of conflict between stability and change can occur either when the reform undermines the central certainties or values of the regime (for example by placing the security of a central right such as landownership in question without a cause that would have been recognised by existing doctrine as legitimate), or when the reform places issues or values (for example such as poverty or social vulnerability) that are considered irrelevant or marginal in the current property regime at the centre of its new policy focus. In some cases these two could coincide, for example when a landowner is prevented from enforcing

---

[2] It was argued in chs 4 and 5 that the introduction of the Human Rights Act 1998 in the UK had a comparable effect in so far as it made property and housing provisions in the European Convention on Human Rights 1950 applicable in the UK.

her property rights against someone else who has no legally valid property interest, purely because the latter is poor or otherwise socially vulnerable. A major premise of my argument is that examples of this kind are inevitable when social or political change demands or inspires relatively large-scale reforms of the existing property regime, and that they tend to challenge the integrity of existing doctrine and even of the entire theoretical paradigm within which the rhetoric and logic of the property regime function.

A second major premise in the argument is that examples like this, where political or constitutional obligations bring about reforms that have the effect that strong or central property rights are restricted or prevented from being enforced for reasons that are irrelevant or marginal according to the established doctrine, are extremely informative for property theory because they enable us to consider and analyse property conflicts from a different perspective, without the usual 'normalising' force of established doctrinal logic and rhetoric. In chapter one I argued that a transformative setting provides a useful starting point for theorising about property because established property doctrine loses its traditional central position and acquires a marginal status when the debate is informed by considerations of political and social injustice and the need for significant reform. At the same time, marginal persons and groups (who suffered the injustices of the discredited regime or whose position must be taken seriously because of the social and political changes) become more important in a debate no longer dominated by purely technical or doctrinal legal rhetoric and logic or by the interests of previously dominant or privileged groups. In these circumstances, I argued, the extraordinary tension that is placed on the flexibility and adaptability of the existing property regime may open up valuable space for imagining and theorising further or other reforms, or it might facilitate reform that has been legitimised but that has proven difficult to implement.

In chapter one I therefore proposed to focus on marginal or powerless persons and groups who were disadvantaged by social, political or economic policies and practices, arguing that the 'poor person's' experience of property law is particularly interesting for property theory in so far as it involves conflict with the powerful 'rich person', who expects property law merely to secure and protect the existing hierarchy of vested property holdings. My argument is that those on the margins of society experience the law differently from those who hold privileged property positions and that their marginal perspective could be instructive in thinking about the tension between stability and change in transformational contexts and about the need for and the possibilities of meaningful change.

In chapter one and chapter three I further argued that this perspective on property from the margins is exemplified most usefully by an issue that features in both stable and transitional societies: eviction of weak and unlawful occupiers from immovable property. Eviction normally enforces the rights of powerful property holders against persons whose property claims are weak or who are unable to raise property rights in their defence. In the case of residential property, on which I concentrate, eviction of weak and indigent persons from their homes also highlights the conflict between the powerful and the weak, the rich and the poor, in a context (housing, shelter, personal security and dignity) where justice considerations are obviously relevant. When moral, political or constitutional pressure is brought to bear to amend existing legal rules and practices with regard to eviction, the resulting tension between stability (protection of existing property rights) and change (promoting non-property interests in residential property) is instructive for property theory.

B. Stability and Change in Property Law

It appeared from chapter one that change—or reform—is sometimes inevitable in a property system, but also that change is sometimes difficult to bring about, even when it is morally legitimate, politically required or constitutionally authorised. Change is often resisted by requiring clear and unambiguous authority for it and, once the authority to change has been demonstrated, by reading it restrictively so as to limit the change to the minimum that is clearly required and authorised and that would cause the smallest possible harm or loss to existing rights. The reasons for resistance against change vary, but in chapter one the most important reason, for my purposes, has been identified as the tendency, in law generally and in property law in particular, to seek and promote security and stability.

In chapter one the tendency to resist change was associated, on the level of individual property holdings, with security: property rights that are secure against unwanted change signify personal security in so far as they protect individually acquired property holdings and the attributes that Margaret Jane Radin refers to as 'personhood'.[3] On the larger scale, within the property regime, the tendency to resist change was associated with stability: A stable property regime not only secures and protects the individual property rights recognised by it on a systemic level, but also stabilises the status quo in the sense that it creates certainty and trust in the social, economic and political system characterised as the 'liberal market economy', which is regarded as a pivotal institution that guarantees individual freedom and autonomy. In this sense, stability is associated with terms such as 'rule of law' and 'legal certainty'; it creates trust and encourages investment of resources and effort in the acquisition, development and useful exploitation of property.[4] It was pointed out in chapter one that the ideal of systemic stability is grounded on the assumption that the property regime, including the current distribution of property, privilege and power, the liberal market economy within which property is accumulated and traded and the system of legal rules and practices that regulates it, is largely legitimate and thus worthy of protection.

Within this picture, change—any change, large or small—represents a potential threat to personal security and to the systemic stability of the property regime,

---

[3] MJ Radin, 'Property and Personhood' (1982) 34 *Stanford LR* 957–1015.
[4] CM Rose, 'The Comedy of the Commons: Custom, Commerce, and Inherently Public Property' (1986) 53 *Univ Chicago LR* 711–81.

whenever and in so far as the change is not brought about by the autonomous will of property owners, exercised in accordance with the 'normal' processes of the market and the 'normal' legal rules that regulate acquisition and transfer of property interests. The point of departure is that changes in the existing property regime are legitimate if they are brought about by consensus in the form of either agreement or democratic participation in the legislative process. A landowner who agrees with her neighbour to accept the imposition, by way of servitude or easement, of certain limitations on her entitlements of use and enjoyment is freely participating in the market; a landowner whose entitlements of use and enjoyment are restricted by the statutory imposition of reciprocal limitations to preserve the character of a residential neighbourhood can arguably be assumed to be in a similar position, the legislation having been imposed by state intervention to correct a market failure caused by high transaction costs in bringing about consensus between a large number of residents, assuming that they all agreed or would have agreed to the change or that they would have availed themselves of democratic means of protest if not. In both these cases, neither individual rights nor the stability of the property regime are threatened by the change.

However, in order to discuss the effects of change on stability it is necessary to distinguish between different kinds of change in a property regime. Some of the distinctions below coincide; some overlap but do not coincide. The first important distinction is between small and large-scale changes. Obviously large-scale transformations of the property regime inspired by political, social and legal change are different from smaller changes inspired by small shifts in government policy or by relatively small interventions to stabilise the market or to correct market failures (development planning; regulating subdivision of agricultural land or possession of dangerous materials).[5] The distinction between large-scale and small processes of change can also be related to the distinction between reformist or transformative and regulatory state interventions in the property regime, respectively. The latter kind of change, brought about by 'normal' or day-to-day regulatory interventions in the property system, could hardly be described as transformation or even reform, since it usually does not affect the integrity or the general features of the property regime, nor is it usually inspired by social or political changes of direction. As a rule, this kind of change is simply accommodated within the property system, although the legitimacy of certain kinds or levels of regulatory intervention might be questioned in libertarian circles. Transformative change, on the other hand, is necessitated by large policy shifts; normally, they would require large and fundamental amendments of the property regime. For that reason they are often said to fall within the province of legislatures rather than judiciaries.

A second, related, distinction is that between incremental and systemic change. Legal and property regimes are used to and comfortable with change that assumes the form of incremental developments, without challenging the framework within

---

[5] I am using the language of economic analysis here to demonstrate the fit between the stability argument and the assumptions of the mainstream paradigm, not because I buy into it as being the best or even a valid analytic tool.

which it happens. However, change will sometimes be of such a nature and magnitude that it undermines or threatens fundamental assumptions, the structure, the rhetoric or the systemic logic of the entire property regime. Radical social and political transformation might bring about change that requires a complete overhaul or scrapping and replacement of the doctrinal system of laws and practices that regulate property holdings. Even small regulatory interventions that regulate property holdings can reach a cumulative level where the foundations of the property system are threatened.

However, not every threat to the security of individual property holdings is a threat to the stability of the property regime; hence it is also necessary to distinguish between state interventions that affect the security of individual property holdings and state interventions that affect the stability of the whole property regime. The assumptions upon which any private property regime is founded allow for state interventions that interfere with the security of private property in order to protect and stabilise the property regime as a whole—the notion of regulatory or 'police power' control over the use and exploitation of property is based on this assumption. More contentious, but nevertheless accepted within most private property systems, is complete sacrifice of the security of individual property holdings for the sake of the regime—the notion of expropriation or compulsory state acquisition of private property is based on this assumption, as are other examples of restrictions on the right to exclude in chapter six. The potential cumulative threat that the power of eminent domain poses for the entire regime is counterbalanced by subjecting the state's expropriation power to public purpose, due process and compensation requirements. In any event systemic stability is considered important enough to justify, in exceptional cases and subject to requirements, the sacrifice of personal security in individual property.[6] The point is that the sacrifice of individual property holdings and the security locked up in them does not in itself present a threat to the property regime; instead, these sacrifices are justified when and because they help to stabilise the regime. However, when the individual sacrifices required of individual property owners for the sake of stability of the property regime reach a certain level of cumulative magnitude the stability of the system might be endangered as well.

A further important distinction is that between change that threatens the security of property holdings or the stability of the property regime and change that challenges the rhetorical or logical integrity of property doctrine. Generally speaking, change will pose a really serious threat to the integrity of property doctrine only if it also threatens the stability of the property regime; change that threatens the security of individual property holdings is normally easily accommodated in the rhetoric and logic of the doctrine. To that extent, this distinction coincides with that between incremental and systemic change. In the terminology of Thomas

---

[6] As was pointed out in ch 6, the ease with which weak owners' rights are sometimes ignored or destroyed for the sake of systemic stability is not explained adequately by the same argument, because the purpose of these sacrifices is not as clear as in the case of expropriation, nor are there any counterbalancing controls.

Kuhn, incremental changes of the property regime, in the sense that they require finer qualifications of property doctrine, can be described as developments that constantly take place within the system, whereby 'normal science' adapts to reflect new knowledge and insights. By contrast, large systemic upheavals that cannot be explained by way of nuances and qualifications of the doctrine could indicate that a 'scientific revolution' is necessitated by new knowledge or insights that cannot be accounted for in the old paradigm.[7] In a different perspective, accommodation of small changes in property doctrine and practice can be explained as so-called 'interstitial developments' that are a 'normal' part of the (judicial or doctrinal) development of the common law, while large, reformist or transformative changes to the property system might be impossible to accommodate within the existing doctrinal framework or paradigm. Theoretically, these large changes can cause paradigmatic revolutions rather than mere interstitial developments. Politically, they might have huge systemic implications, which is why these changes are traditionally not brought about by judges but left to democratic legislatures.[8] In the context of the current discussion, small, interstitial or incremental changes in property rules or practices are easily accommodated in the rhetoric and logic of the mainstream doctrine without challenging the underlying assumptions or integrity of mainstream doctrine, while large, systemic reforms of property rules and practices are difficult or impossible to accommodate in or reconcile with mainstream doctrine and therefore threaten the integrity of the rights paradigm.

There is some slippage in the passages above between the notions of change that threatens the existing theoretical framework of property law because it is difficult to explain within the current doctrinal framework and change that threatens the stability of the property regime as a whole. The link between the two is the assumption that property doctrine is a coherent explanation of property rules and practices that legitimately entrench and protect individual property holdings and the market economy within which they function. Change that can be assimilated within the doctrine by way of interstitial developments or small adaptations does not threaten either the doctrine or the stability of the property regime. However, change that is so significant that it cannot be explained or assimilated in the doctrinal framework by definition also threatens the stability of the property regime, because it undermines or negates the central assumptions upon which the entire regime of property rules and holdings is founded. In this sense, property doctrine can be seen as a barometer of the property regime's capability to assimilate change.

However, current or traditional property doctrine only fulfils this barometer function in so far as one accepts its underlying assumptions. On one level it is certainly arguable that small but arbitrary and capricious state interventions in private property can reach a level where doctrine no longer adequately explains the way in which the property regime functions and where the stability of the entire system is also endangered—a ruinous system of redistributive taxation would be

---

[7] TS Kuhn, *The Structure of Scientific Revolutions* (2nd edn, 1970) at 52.
[8] The notion of 'interstitial', incremental developments that fill up small gaps in the received doctrine, on a case-by-case basis, is based on HLA Hart, *The Concept of Law* (1961) at 37–8.

an example of a regulatory scheme that cumulatively endangers the foundations of a property regime grounded in the notions of individual property and a free market. On the other hand, property doctrine might be flexible enough to accommodate even significant changes that superficially seem to threaten the property regime as such. The point is that not every change in the property regime that challenges property doctrine also indicates a threat to the property regime. Furthermore, property doctrine is flexible and develops, so that new directions in property theory might well be accommodated within doctrine if they do not undermine the fundamentals. In current property theory it is quite acceptable to argue that some of the central tenets of mainstream property doctrine are no longer either theoretically tenable or necessary for a system of property based on individual rights and a free market.[9] In this perspective it is conceivable that changes in property rules or practices could necessitate changes in property doctrine without endangering the property regime. It is, for example, no longer fashionable or theoretically credible to argue that property is a pre-social or pre-constitutional right and that every state restriction of property has to be specifically authorised and legitimised.[10] Consequently, a range of regulatory state restrictions of individual property rights can be justified quite easily without having any impact on the stability of the property regime, although they might pose difficulties for a very traditional version of property doctrine. Similarly, it is no longer generally believed that the stability of the property regime or the success of the market depends on the priority and sanctity of private property, and consequently imposition of restrictions upon or even complete removal of certain categories of property resources from the private market can be justified without threatening the stability of the property regime, although doctrine might struggle to explain such a change.[11] My point is that these changes challenge property

[9] See eg GS Alexander, *Commodity and Propriety: Competing Visions of Property in American Legal Thought 1776–1970* (1997), who distinguishes 'propriety' as the status-oriented aspect of property as a mechanism for creating and maintaining social order and justice. LS Underkuffler, *The Idea of Property: Its Meaning and Power* (2003) refers to the 'operative' conception of property that incorporates change as part of the idea of property. JW Singer and JM Beerman, 'The Social Origins of Property' (1993) 6 *Canadian Journal of Law & Jur* 217–48 argued convincingly against the idea that property could be a pre-social right. CM Rose, 'The Comedy of the Commons: Custom, Commerce, and Inherently Public Property' (1986) 53 *Univ Chicago LR* 711–81 argued authoritatively that private property is not always efficient and that commons are not necessarily inefficient.

[10] In ch 2 examples are discussed to demonstrate that some theorists or courts do expect every regulatory restriction to be justified; see particularly O Depenheuer, 'Entwicklungslinien des verfassungsrechtlichen Eigentumsschutzes in Deutschland 1949–2001' in T von Danwitz *et al*, *Bericht zur Lage des Eigentums* (2002) 109–213.

[11] A good example is the German constitutional cases in which large systemic shifts in the property regime were accommodated by explaining how they stabilised rather than threatened the system. The most significant cases involved legislation that removed certain categories of property from the sphere of private ownership altogether for reasons of its extreme public importance: *BVerfGE* 24, 367 (*Deichordnung*) [1968]; *BVerfGE* 42, 263 (*Contergan*) [1976]. In *Deichordnung*, the public interest in the safety of low-lying land from severe flooding justified removal of dyke land from the private property market. In *Contergan*, justice and equality demanded that a private compensation fund be nationalised so that the government could ensure that payments were made to all claimants and not just those who had obtained court rulings in their favour. See further AJ van der Walt, *Constitutional Property Clauses: A Comparative Analysis* (1999) at 132–6.

doctrine when and because the theoretical paradigm of property is outdated or unsophisticated, and often the doctrine could be developed or amended without any serious implications for the stability of the property regime as such.

Three general points emerge from the preceding discussion. The first is that small changes in the property regime brought about by regulatory state intervention might infringe or threaten the personal security of individual property holders but should not, unless their cumulative effect is extremely large, normally threaten the stability of the entire property regime because they are counterbalanced by systemic controls. These changes should not threaten the integrity of property doctrine either, because they can usually be explained and assimilated within existing doctrine as incremental or interstitial developments of existing rules and practices. Unless their cumulative effect is remarkable,[12] changes in the property regime brought about by state interventions of this kind are relatively uninteresting for my analysis.

The second general point is that large-scale, transformative changes in the property regime are sometimes morally, politically or constitutionally sanctioned or required because of social or political transitions that render central tenets or characteristics of the property regime illegitimate or untenable. Changes of this kind would necessarily pose a larger or smaller threat to the stability of the entire property regime (in the sense of changing it fundamentally) and the authority of property doctrine (as a supposedly coherent exposition of the regime). In such cases the efficacy of state interventions aimed at bringing about the intended reforms should not be resisted or minimised because of the threat to systemic stability or doctrinal integrity, since the change was politically or constitutionally intended and therefore has to be implemented; in these instances, the integrity of doctrine must be of secondary value. Some examples from South African land reform law discussed in chapters four and five resemble this kind of change.

In systems where large-scale, transformative changes in the property regime are not morally or politically required or authorised, even quite radical changes might still be systemically unproblematic if they are sanctioned by other policy or statutory powers; these changes should then not be resisted or minimised purely because they pose a threat for property doctrine, although resistance might be indicated if they are perceived to threaten the stability of the regime. To some extent, this and the previous category can overlap in the sense that smaller radical changes can be implemented against the backdrop of a large-scale transformation process, as is the case in post-apartheid South Africa. The majority of interesting examples from South African, English and German law discussed in chapters four and five fall into this category: Some change was intended, but not necessarily large-scale systemic change; the changes often impose fairly dramatic burdens on existing property holdings and therefore involve doctrinal contradictions or inconsistencies but do not necessarily threaten the stability of the entire property

[12] The due process amendments made to eviction of tenants in the form of forfeiture of the tenancy in English law illustrate the cumulative effect of apparently small incremental changes; see ch 4, section II.C.

regime. However, if the relevant reformist laws are interpreted and applied from the perspective of the integrity of mainstream property doctrine, the intended changes could be either resisted or minimised and the reforms might fail to reach their intended goals.

C. The Rights Paradigm and Eviction

Following up on the points above and in chapter one, chapter two describes the theoretical framework within which property is usually theorised as the 'rights paradigm', a rhetorical and doctrinal framework that explains the relative value and power of property interests in a way that justifies the rights-centred (and often ownership-centered) outcome of particular property disputes. Within this paradigm, property interests are valued according to their status as strong rights, weak rights, or no-rights, on the understanding that property rights are stronger than personal rights; that rights always trump no-rights; and that stronger rights always trump weaker rights or no-rights. This abstract description of the rights paradigm reflects often unarticulated assumptions about the nature of property and its role in society; the reality of the legal system is often more complex than these assumptions suggest. Although it abstractly oversimplifies the status of property rights, the paradigm has real rhetorical, logical and affective power in thinking about property. The rhetoric and logic of the rights paradigm tend to privilege and entrench the status quo and the hierarchy of vested rights, while resisting change in the form of state interventions that might threaten or undermine this hierarchy. This dynamic reduces the chances of significant change or transformation for the sake of justice.

The implications of this theoretical approach are applied to the example of eviction law in chapter three. The most significant characteristic of the rights paradigm is that the hierarchical power of stronger property rights, and particularly property ownership, traditionally inspired and justified property rules and practices that allow property owners or holders of strong property rights (such as an unqualified right to possession) to assert their rights to exclusive possession by evicting anyone who cannot prove a stronger right in defence. Most importantly, the right to evict is usually exercised without any reference to contextual factors such as the general socio-political context or the particular personal circumstances of the occupier. A central hypothesis of this book is that significant reforms of property law involve or include state interventions that were intentionally designed to ensure that property owners' rights to exclusive possession cannot be exercised abstractly. Social or historical justice often dictates that owners or holders of strong property rights be prevented from evicting certain persons or groups even when the claimants can satisfy the abstract requirements for a possessory claim, purely because of contextual considerations such as the general socio-economic situation or the particular personal circumstances of the occupiers. If restrictions of this nature are imposed on the right to claim possession, one can speak of a justice-oriented reform of property law, especially in so far as the restrictions cannot be explained as a logical aspect of the rights paradigm (that is, 'normal' regulatory restrictions). If these justice-dictated restrictions become more widespread and impose stronger limitations on the right to claim possession from someone with a weaker right or no right, it is possible that they could indicate a significant challenge to the rights paradigm; in extreme cases they could threaten the integrity of the paradigm and point towards a paradigm shift.

In the course of the first three chapters I therefore developed the argument that eviction is an institution where one can usefully investigate the hypotheses set out earlier. In view of the three general points identified in the previous section I am particularly interested in two kinds of state intervention (in the shape of legislation or policy): firstly, interventions that authorise large-scale reforms that would change the whole property regime fundamentally (and that would therefore also challenge existing property doctrine about eviction); and secondly, interventions that do not authorise large-scale systemic reforms but that still bring about radical changes that challenge the integrity of existing property doctrine. As was noted earlier, smaller radical changes of this kind can be implemented against the backdrop of a larger transformative agenda. Both categories of reform can change the law regarding eviction and thus have interesting implications for my analysis, particularly in so far as they undermine or challenge the rights paradigm. Apart from legislation, case-law is a source of information that should highlight the existence of such challenges and the courts' response to them.

II. Overview of Results

In view of the first section of this chapter, my project can therefore be explained as an analysis of instances where property rules and practices have changed or are changing in ways that either qualify the rights paradigm significantly or challenge its integrity altogether in the sense that they contradict fundamental tenets of the paradigm. Chapters four, five and six therefore review legislation and case-law regarding the right to exclusive possession and eviction in three different sets of circumstances, namely landlord–tenant law (chapter four), unlawful occupiers of residential property (chapter five) and other related or similar areas of property law where owners are prevented from enforcing their right to exclusive possession (acquisitive prescription and adverse possession, public access to private property, significant building encroachments and dispossession of weak landowners; chapter six).

Summarised very briefly, the results of the three substantive chapters were as follows. Firstly, as far as landlord–tenant evictions are concerned (chapter four), tenants are protected against eviction by extensive statutory frameworks in German and English law. The protective measures include due process requirements (on termination of the lease as well as on eviction as such) as well as substantive provisions that can either delay or prevent eviction if its effects are judged to be unfair. There are some examples where eviction is delayed or prevented purely because of the personal circumstances of the occupier or the general social and economic context, even though the landlord is able to satisfy all the normal formal requirements for a possession order. Similar provisions exist in South African law, but despite a strong anti-eviction provision in the Constitution and the history of apartheid evictions, they are much less extensive in number and scope than the English or German examples, and for the most part they are restricted to due process. As far as eviction of unlawful occupiers is concerned (chapter five), all three jurisdictions (English law, German law and South African law) have promulgated some statutory protection to ensure due process, but in this case South African legislation is the most extensive. On the other hand it is clear from the overview that unlawful occupation is much less of a problem in the other jurisdictions because of more extensive housing programmes that were developed over the last three decades. An important point appearing in this chapter is the importance of political action, including demonstrative unlawful occupation of unused property and resistance against eviction, in campaigning for better housing and land use policies and laws. The chapter brought to light that unlawful occupiers are indeed sometimes protected against eviction purely because of their personal circumstances, and that the rights paradigm is therefore qualified to the extent that these extraneous considerations are allowed to resist the enforcement of the stronger right to possession. The chapter also indicated that political action, in the form of political protest and demonstrative unlawful occupation of land or buildings, plays a significant part in bringing about changes in the law in this particular area, albeit outside of and therefore in conflict with the law. In so far as these actions have been successful their impact on change in the property regime has been mostly political and social rather than legal; they tend to convince policymakers and legislatures rather than courts.

In chapter six it appeared that the exclusivity of ownership is not always protected equally strongly. In the cases of adverse possession or acquisitive prescription and encroachment by building, a landowner can lose her property rights by operation of law, even when the occupier was a bad faith possessor, for policy reasons. Similarly, there are examples that show that some landowners are less well protected simply because of their weak social or political status. In other cases, landowners may be prevented from exercising their right to exclusive possession and may be obliged to allow public or individual access to their land for policy reasons. In accordance with the theoretical framework set out in chapter three, most of the anti-eviction measures described in these chapters are purely regulatory in their nature and effect, in the sense that they merely adjust the scope and extent of private property (and specifically exclusivity) for the sake of balancing these rights with other, competing rights or to accommodate policy goals. However, in a smaller number of cases, the right to enforce exclusivity is restricted much more extensively, by either delaying or preventing a landowner from exercising her stronger right to possession, purely because of the general social and economic context or because of the personal circumstances of the occupier and the effect that eviction would have on her and her family or community. In these latter instances, the restrictions pose a challenge to the rights paradigm to the extent that they cannot be explained as normal, regulatory restrictions on property rights within that paradigm.

These substantive chapters suggest two broad conclusions. The first is that ownership and similar strong property positions, considered from the perspective of weak and marginal property holders, are in fact not nearly as strong as the rhetoric of the rights paradigm might suggest; the supposedly powerful right to exclusive possession is in fact subjected to surprisingly many weak, marginal and non-property interests for policy reasons that are unrelated to the abstract, hierarchical legal merits of either the claimant's or the defendant's rights. The second broad conclusion is that this corrective perspective from the margins needs to complement the traditional strong-rights focus of property doctrine if real and meaningful transformation of the property regime is to be considered, discussed and promoted imaginatively, effectively and systemically. If the power of strong property interests is in fact subject to qualifications on policy grounds it is easier to argue in favour of further or stronger justice-inspired reforms of the property regime—the existing qualifications of and challenges to the rights paradigm create space within which further reform is possible or becomes easier. The three substantive chapters therefore develop the position adopted in the first three chapters by identifying existing qualifications of the rights paradigm and pointing out how these qualifications undermine the force of the paradigm and thereby create space for further justice-oriented reforms.

In one important respect the results of the substantive analysis should not be surprising: It was always clear that ownership and other property rights are in fact subject to (often substantial) regulatory restrictions and limitations. It also stands to reason that some of those regulatory restrictions would have been imposed in view of justice considerations embodied in, for example, housing policy dictated by the exigencies of social and economic circumstances—the analysis in chapter four indicates that landlord–tenant reforms have been introduced by legislation in South Africa, Germany and England since at least World War I. Small changes in the rules and practices of eviction could solve or alleviate some of the problems surrounding homelessness, social and economic vulnerability and inequality that have inspired reform in this area. However—and this is the crucial point—the rhetoric and logic of the rights paradigm can only accommodate legislative interventions imposed in terms of justice considerations in so far as they are relatively minor in scope and as long as they fit or can be accommodated into the doctrinal structure of the property hierarchy. Accordingly, the gradual (and by now practically universal) imposition of due process requirements that subject the cancellation of residential leases and the execution of eviction orders to judicial control and to general fairness standards could be accommodated within the paradigm with relative ease.[13] Like many other regulatory controls over the use, develop-

---

[13] One interesting and significant qualification on this point is highlighted in ch 4, section II.C, text accompanying n 52.

ment and exploitation of property in land, these limitations of property rights in land could be explained as lawful exercises of the police power, serving the legitimate state purpose of ensuring public health and safety and guaranteeing equality before the law and administrative justice. Incremental developments that subject the property holder's right of exclusive possession to due process controls can be reconciled with the paradigmatic notion that strong rights trump weaker rights or no-rights, and the corresponding doctrinal rule that the owner (or the holder of the stronger right to possession) can claim possession (and thus eviction) purely on the basis of the (absolute or relative) strength of her right and regardless of extraneous factors such as the historical context, the general socio-economic climate or the socio-economic or personal circumstances of the occupier. Some of these changes might strain the paradigm more than others, but by and large they can be accommodated.[14]

However, as soon as legislative regulation of the landlord–tenant relationship restricts the landlord's right to exclusive possession purely on the basis of policy considerations informed by general socio-economic conditions or the personal circumstances of the occupier (that is, circumstances unrelated to the landlord's right and out of her control), it becomes more difficult (and eventually impossible) to explain the restrictions as a 'normal' part of the rights paradigm because these restrictions fundamentally undermine the absolutist assumptions and the general rights-focused personal autonomy logic of the rights paradigm. Again, the more restrictions there are of this nature and the stronger their impact on the rights of landowners, the more significant the threat that is posed to the paradigm; at some point the weight of restrictions could become unbearable and a paradigm shift might be indicated. Even in the absence of such a shift, mainstream doctrine would be stretched to explain restrictions of this nature without compromising central tenets of the rights paradigm. In the process of undermining mainstream doctrine or tradition, these challenges to the rights paradigm open up theoretical space within which change can be imagined and explained more freely and creatively, thereby enhancing the prospects of further and more meaningful changes.

The main thrust of the analysis in the substantive chapters (chapters four, five and six) is therefore not the (fairly trite) conclusion that there are in fact instances where the rights of landowners are subjected to the competing interests of other, weaker land users for policy reasons. The point is, rather, the less obvious conclusion that there are instances where the rights of landowners are subjected to sometimes significant qualifications for the sake of justice-inspired policy considerations, unrelated to the merits of the competing claims and out of the landowner's control, and that these restrictions cannot be accommodated or explained in the rights paradigm without rendering the paradigm's central tenets relative to an extent not compatible with its own foundations. The point of these restrictions—in the form of instances where the owner cannot enforce her stronger right to exclusive possession—is not that they restrict ownership but that they do so in a way and for reasons that deny

---

[14] See n 12 above.

and contradict the basic tenets of the rights paradigm. To explain and justify these impositions on the right of landowners and other holders of strong property rights at all adequately it is necessary to refer to and rely upon factors and considerations that are not traditionally regarded as relevant or important within the rights paradigm, such as the age or health of the occupier, the existence of an economic slump or the availability of alternative housing. In short, as soon as these marginal features of property interests gain enough currency and weight in fact to require explaining their impact on property doctrine, they force us to reconsider the very foundations of the rights paradigm and, with it, the current property regime. At that point we are in a position where it becomes both easier and more fruitful to contemplate large-scale reforms or transformation of the property regime and of property law from the perspective of justice. Imagining radical transformation of the law is easier from a marginal theoretical perspective, in other words from the perspective of marginal property interests and with attention to property conflicts in marginal settings, because this perspective reveals theoretical manoeuvring space that is either denied or invisible within the rhetorical and logical confines of the paradigm.

In the landlord–tenant context (chapter four) the majority of tenant-friendly statutory interventions can be explained as 'normal' regulatory controls and there are just a small number of restrictions that contradict current doctrine to the point where they undermine the rights paradigm but, surprisingly, there are a few reasonably clear instances where extraordinary restrictions on eviction are enforced for the protection of unlawful occupiers (chapter five). On the other end of the scale there are surprisingly many examples of instances where ownership is either trumped by other, weak competing interests or simply overridden for efficiency or utility reasons; neither of these exceptions can be explained adequately in terms of current doctrine and they therefore also stretch the rights paradigm (chapter six). Despite the fact that the really significant examples of paradigm-challenging restrictions are few and far between, their mere existence is sufficient to allow us room and opportunity for fruitful theoretical discussion.

The analysis of legislation and policy changes in the three substantive chapters shows that legislation in a variety of areas actually transforms eviction into a discretionary right that could be denied, even when the owner or landlord can satisfy all the common law and statutory requirements, simply and purely because of extraneous or subjective factors such as the historical, social and economic context within which eviction takes place and the personal or social circumstances of the occupier and the effect that eviction will have on her and her family or community. These changes, I argued in chapters four and five, challenge fundamental tenets of the rights paradigm in that they remove the power of rights from the equation when deciding an eviction conflict. Explaining them within the context of rights requires a fundamental shift or paradigmatic revolution. Both the paradigmatic notion of rights and the doctrinal logic of eviction are undermined when (and to the extent that) the right to claim possession is qualified by these extraneous factors, and when the extraneous factors are completely unrelated to the relative merits of the parties' claims to possession, totally out of the property holder's control and purely based on justice or fairness considerations such as the historical or political context or the effect of eviction on weak or vulnerable persons or groups, the threat to the integrity of the paradigm becomes stronger. When the beneficiaries of the shift are not only holders of weaker rights but unlawful (and even bad faith) occupiers, it becomes even more likely that a paradigm shift is indicated, depending upon the scope of the restriction. Although these restrictions provide interesting space for theoretical analysis and discussion in any event, the question whether they actually pose any threat to the stability of the property regime or the integrity of property doctrine or the rights paradigm depends on the context within which they occur, the number and scope of these changes and the reasons and justifications for introducing them.

In view of these considerations two preliminary and general conclusions could be postulated. Firstly, it seems bearably clear that the South African land reform programme and the changes in property holdings, land use policy and land law it involves do not necessarily pose any threat to the stability of the property regime as such, although the reform programme obviously foresees some dramatic changes in the regime of property holdings and therefore potentially threatens the security of individual land holdings. However, given the strict constitutional and legislative framework within which these reforms are to be implemented, there are enough checks and balances to justify (and, where necessary, compensate) the individual losses. Secondly, it could be said that at least some of the more radical restrictions on the right to evict that were introduced as part of the South African land reform programme, contextualised by the abolition of apartheid and legitimised and authorised by the 1996 Constitution, cannot be encapsulated within the doctrinal framework of the rights paradigm. Although many of the reforms introduced as part of the land reform programme can indeed be accommodated within and reconciled with the traditional rights-dominated property doctrine, at least some reforms are in fact or potentially so radical and significant that they do not fit within that framework because they question or undermine its fundamental tenets. To force interpretation and application of these radical or significant reforms into the restrictive framework of mainstream doctrine is inevitably to rob them, and the constitutional and statutory instruments behind them, of their transformative potential and intention. Equally, to read and interpret these measures restrictively from the doctrinal perspective of the strong property holder is to assume that restrictions and interferences with the status quo must be minimal, which in turn results in exactly the restrictive approach that would prevent these measures from realising their transformative potential and purpose. The fairly widespread notion that the transformative legislation has to be interpreted and applied purposively should therefore enjoy special attention in the field of land reform to ensure that the land reform laws are not robbed of their efficacy by unsuitable traditional or paradigmatic interpretation.[15]

---

[15] I do not expand on the notion of purposive interpretation of new property laws here; see further AJ van der Walt, *Constitutional Property Law* (2005) at 22–42.

In other jurisdictions, similar restrictions have been imposed upon the right to evict, but then without the historical justification and the political intention that chacterise the South African situation. When the European Convention on Human Rights 1950 was made applicable to English law through the promulgation of the Human Rights Act 1998, the property and housing provisions of the Convention were superimposed upon a property regime that was already qualified by protective legislation that subjected the right to evict to extensive due process and substantive fairness restrictions. Moreover, the adoption of the Human Rights Act 1998 was not accompanied by a major political and constitutional revolution from an authoritarian to a democratic regime (as might arguably be the case for some new members of the European Union who have to reform their law in view of the Convention). As a consequence, the effect of the anti-eviction provisions in the European Convention (and the case-law on those provisions) on the existing English law of eviction is qualitatively different from the effect of the constitutional and statutory anti-eviction provisions in South African post-apartheid law. Judged purely from a contextual perspective, (at least some of) the South African provisions must be regarded as large, systemic, paradigmatic shifts intended to revolutionise the existing regime, while the English developments could be seen as small, incremental developments intended to qualify and develop existing law without revolutionising it. There are indications that at least some commentators think that a relatively major shift in the English property regime is necessary, but the moral and political case for such a shift has to be made independently with reference to the context. Of course, it is possible to argue that both English and German law have already gone through paradigmatic or doctrinal revolutions much earlier, when post-war housing shortages and the rise of labour and social democratic politics inspired the respective governments to adopt anti-eviction reforms of property law roughly similar to some of the protective measures now being developed for post-apartheid South African law. At least in German law it is indeed apparent that constitutional property theory did experience something like the paradigmatic revolution described above during the 1970s and 1980s, partly in the wake of social democratic politics and legislation, but it is a different question whether that revolution has affected German private law theory and doctrine as well. The mere scope and depth of English tenant protection since the 1970s indicates that legislation introduced there also resembles some kind of major policy shift, which is arguably now being reversed as a result of a return to new liberal economic policies. It is also possible to argue that the counter-reforms now taking place in English and German law under the influence of new liberal economic policy are perhaps larger and more significant, at least in some respects, than is apparent from the surface, and that this trend might reverse the developments made in the 1970s and 1980s, but that is a different story that requires more intensive analysis than could be undertaken here.

Anti-eviction restrictions imposed upon ownership or strong property rights could therefore indicate either a smaller, doctrinally unproblematic incremental development of property law or a larger, doctrinally contentious and hence potentially revolutionary paradigm shift, depending (at least in part) on the social and political context. The historical, social and political context and the extent to which the existing distribution of property is contentious and contested could be an indication whether the shift is incremental or revolutionary; similarly, the fact that anti-eviction restrictions are aimed at ensuring due process rather than substantive, justice- or fairness-inspired suspension of the right to evict could indicate that the shift is incremental rather than systemic. The fact that a property holder is allowed to evict tenants holding over or unlawful occupiers from her property but forced to do so by way of prescribed (and possibly judicially overseen) eviction procedure does not contradict or undermine the basic tenets of the rights paradigm. Similarly, the fact that an existing, already extensive statutory scheme of tenant protection is expanded to include a further category of vulnerable tenants or to fine-tune the existing protective scheme does not pose any new problems for the rights paradigm (which has already been amended, perhaps significantly, by the introduction of the scheme), even if the protection implies that the rights holder is prevented from evicting the tenants in question purely because of justice or fairness considerations. However, when substantive anti-eviction measures are introduced as part of a new protective scheme that is clearly intended to facilitate and promote large-scale policy interventions in the existing property regime, the indications are that these measures could possibly (depending upon their scope and nature and the context) be intended to bring about major change in the property regime that would require an equally major paradigm shift in property theory. Similarly, when the scope and effect of these arguably paradigmatic changes are reduced by the introduction of new policies,[16] this shift in policy direction could again signify a (larger or smaller) reversal of the challenge posed to the paradigmatic integrity of liberal property doctrine and theory.

The implication of these considerations is that the incidence, nature, scope and effect of changes in the property regime must be determined and assessed with sensitivity to the context. Generally speaking, due process restrictions on the exercise of property rights should not be significant enough to indicate a paradigm shift, but even more substantive restrictions could bring about merely incremental changes if they occur in the context of an already significantly qualified property regime. In a transformative regime, where there may be strong political and constitutional motives for paradigmatic changes to the property regime, either due process or substantive restrictions could amount to a paradigm shift if they are significant enough and if they challenge the mainstream doctrine or practice strongly enough.[17]

---

[16] It was suggested in ch 4, section II.C that recent developments in English law, whereby the number of public housing units has been reduced and the protection of short-term private tenancies cut back, could indicate exactly such a reversal of protective policies.

[17] It was argued in ch 4, section II.C that the introduction of due process requirements in landlord–tenant eviction law had such a radical effect on the established institution of forfeiture of a lease that it brought about a substantive change in the property relationship.

The most significant implication of the analysis in the substantive chapters of this book for property doctrine and theory is not that ownership and strong property rights are restricted, but rather that some of these restrictions occur in a setting and to an extent that render the basic tenets of mainstream property doctrine and theory contradictory or so relative as to become meaningless or contingent. The challenges for mainstream property doctrine and theory are twofold. On the one hand, the analysis in the substantive chapters suggests that the incidence, nature, scope and implications of the changes in property law set out there can best be perceived and interpreted from an unconventional perspective that takes marginal property interests and conflicts as its point of reference, instead of focusing on centrality or presence, as the rights paradigm tends to do. From a conventional perspective the changes and shifts discussed in the chapters above are either overlooked or downplayed, while a perspective from the margins underlines their challenging and undermining effect on the law and their implications for property doctrine and theory. Secondly, this perspective from the margins not only indicates that property doctrine and theory have shifted in certain significant ways, but also suggests a way forward for efforts to justify and explain further shifts and changes that might be required by justice and fairness considerations. The marginal perspective therefore creates space for further critical reconsideration of important property issues.

III. Property in the Margins

A. The Role of Centrality Thinking

Thus far the discussion has been mostly about change in the property regime, which was described earlier as the combination of property holdings and the property rules and practices that uphold them. It is necessary to repeat that paradigmatic change of the kind discussed here involves at least three different kinds of change. Firstly, it could involve change in the actual distribution of property holdings and in the status and force of the rights involved. As far as the South African land reform programme is concerned, restitution, redistribution and tenure reform initiatives all involve changes that are supposed to actually alter the current distribution of property holdings; both legislation and policy play an important part in bringing about change of this nature. A second kind of change involves the law—in a constitutional system characterised by the rule of law, dramatic changes in property holdings will inevitably also imply paradigmatic changes in property law; in some cases it is impossible to make the changes without changing the law. Legislation obviously features prominently in effecting this kind of change as well; new or amended legislation could have a bigger or smaller and a more or less obvious and clear-cut impact on existing law. New anti-eviction legislation that explicitly overrides the common law (such as the Prevention of

Illegal Eviction from and Unlawful Occupation of Land Act 19 of 1998) is a good
example of an explicit, high-impact amendment of existing law in a specified area.
A third kind of change involves legal doctrine and theory; the underlying and for-
mative framework within and through which the (old or changed) law is understood and implemented. This is the area that is perhaps most resistant against
change, in the sense that it takes big and convincing contradictions and anomalies,
brought about by dramatic changes in property holdings or the law, to successfully
challenge and eventually shift or amend the paradigm within which doctrine and
theory function.

One of the central hypotheses in this book is that property doctrine (embodied
in what I described as the rights paradigm in chapter two) resists meaningful
change to the extent that it is still dominated by what I have elsewhere described
as the logic of centrality.[18] The core of my hypothesis about centrality is that we,
as owners and users of property, unreflectively accept that private property naturally holds a central place in society through its importance in the free market
economy, which we simply assume to be an indispensable element of a liberal
society. As lawyers, we also accept, often equally unreflectively, that property is a
central organising concept in law and legal theory. Because of these assumptions
we are unwilling or slow to adopt or accept legal developments that do not reflect
and correspond with the central position of property in society and in legal thinking and, to the extent that such developments might be necessary or beneficial for
social change, we tend to resist or inhibit change.

As a quality of the property regime, centrality indicates that property occupies
a central position in and exercises important functions in the social system. On
the one hand, centrality means that property is assumed to be central to the
human condition and hence to societal organisation. Centrality links the power
that follows from having property to essential human and social values such as
desert, human flourishing or utility. The central role that is assigned to property
in upholding and safeguarding these values explains and justifies the otherwise
startling inequalities that follow from the unequal distribution of property in
society.[19] Although marginal social and economic positions such as poverty and
dependence are no longer treated with the same disdain and condescension as
in the nineteenth century, these conditions still carry some stigma of
physical, mental or moral weakness or shortcoming; just like the central position
of having property is still associated with personal, social and moral worth or

---

[18] This section of the chapter is based partly on passages from the as yet unpublished AJ van der
Walt, 'Property and Marginality' in GS Alexander and E Peñalver (eds), *Law and Community* (forthcoming, 2009).

[19] The seminal argument in support of the personhood-centrality of property is MJ Radin,
'Property and Personhood' (1982) 34 *Stanford LR* 957–1015, although CA Reich, 'The New Property'
(1964) 73 *Yale LJ* 733–87 had something similar in mind. See further LS Underkuffler, *The Idea of
Property: Its Meaning and Power* (2003) 38–46 with regard to what she describes as the 'common
conception of property', reflecting something to the same effect. Gregory Alexander probably had
something similar to my observations in this paragraph in mind when he wrote 'The Concept of
Property in Private and Constitutional Law: The Ideology of the Scientific Turn in Legal Analysis'
(1982) 82 *Columbia LR* 1545–99.

superiority.[20] Even when the status of not having property and requiring state or social support is regarded sympathetically as the unavoidable and personally un-blameworthy outcome of some natural disaster or irresistible social, economic or political force, its description in terms of emergency, dire straits or desperate circumstances tends to confirm the normality of having property and the abnormality of need, poverty and marginality. Having property is just assumed to be the natural state of affairs; not having it is ascribed to some defect or shortcoming, which may be caused either by inability or sloth or by a natural or social disaster or emergency. In either event, it is not natural. Assigning the status of having property to the centre and not having property to the margins of social normality justifies the unequal distribution of property and power in society, not only when not having property is related to the personal shortcomings of the have-nots but also when it is accepted more sympathetically as the result of some natural or social disaster that upset the normal course of events.[21]

Ownership or property famously acts as a fence that protects the individual against outside threats; this protective function of property and the central role that it plays in recognising and upholding social, economic and legal patterns of privilege depends for its rhetorical power and its legal efficacy upon the presence of property on one side of the conflict as much as on its absence on the other. In what follows I argue that even critical theories that deny the liberal link between moral desert and property and that advocate social redefinition and significant redistribution of property tend to group property, power and normality versus poverty, weakness and abnormality in a hierarchical configuration that tends to position the first group in the centre and the second on the margins of society and the law, thereby failing to unsettle the assumed 'normality condition' of liberal tradition.

Apart from its social function, centrality also means that having property is the key to the hierarchical regime of property rights (and, by extension, to a large part of the system of rights as a whole)—having ownership (or other rights) in property triggers a whole series of legal entitlements and privileges, just as its absence implies exclusion from those entitlements and privileges. Thus, property is central to the regime in that the presence of property equals and justifies recognition and protection of social, economic and legal autonomy and power, whereas absence of property self-evidently translates into and justifies the continued existence of social, economic and legal weakness, vulnerability and dependence. The centrality of property in the system of rights means that the presence or absence of property decides cases—in this sense, property is central in that the outcome of legal disputes depends upon the presence (or absence) of property. In this (particularly doctrinal) perspective, having property (and enjoying the privileges and powers

[20] See further T Ross, 'The Rhetoric of Poverty: Their Immorality, Our Helplessness' (1991) 79 *Georgetown LJ* 1499–547; LA Williams, 'Welfare and Legal Entitlements: The Social Roots of Poverty' in D Kairys (ed), *The Politics of Law: A Progressive Critique* (3rd edn, 1998) 569–90. I return to this point below.
[21] I use the notion of 'normality' in the sense developed by RJ Coombe, '"Same as it Ever Was": Rethinking the Politics of Legal Interpretation' (1989) 34 *McGill LJ* 603–52.

resulting from it) is sometimes regarded as a self-evident result that follows logically and inevitably upon satisfying certain technical legal acquisition requirements, whereas not-having property (and absence of these privileges and powers) follows naturally and inevitably from not having complied with those requirements. Once the requirements have been met, property simply 'is there'; otherwise it simply is not. Even more importantly, legal implications and results inexorably follow from that 'simple' ontological 'fact'.[22] In the process, we tend to forget that individuals and communities find themselves in the margins of the property regime and of society for a variety of reasons—some because they are indeed socially weak (the elderly, children, the sick); some because they have been deliberately marginalised by society through unjust social, economic or political processes (apartheid history looms large in this respect; so does the position of the gypsies); others because of natural or economic disaster; still others by choice, because they resist and challenge the legitimacy and fairness of the social, economic or political system and its effects on people. Far from being a simple fact, the privilege and power that come with having property and belonging to the centre of the property regime and society can be an accident of nature, the result of social, economic or political discrimination or a matter of political choice. In a free and open democratic society that values plurality and difference, the impact and meaning of the property regime on each of these groups should be considered when we ask whether the property regime is just and whether it needs to be changed or transformed.

In addition to the social and legal aspects mentioned above, centrality also signifies that property fulfils an organising role in legal thinking. Property embodies the organising framework or paradigm for all rights in the sense that the presence of a (particularly exclusionary) right is generally regarded as the central fact that triggers a whole series of doctrinally linked and legally conclusive results. Property becomes a model right that influences the way in which we think and argue about rights and law in general. The boundary- or fence-like role widely ascribed to property is the best example of centrality-inspired thinking on legal rhetoric.[23]

B. Realist and Critical Decenterings

Historically sensitive readers would have identified centrality logic as a kind of formalist thinking and might counter that this kind of thinking has become irrelevant.

[22] The analysis in ch 6, particularly with regard to acquisitive prescription, encroachment by building and weak owners, suggests quite strongly that this logic is not as natural or as inexorable as it may seem, since both the acquisition or assignment and the denigration of strong property rights often result from pure policy decisions not informed by the relative rights of the parties or the logic of rights.

[23] See particularly H Botha, 'Metaphoric Reasoning and Transformative Constitutionalism' (2002) *TSAR* 612–27; (2003) *TSAR* 20–36 (specifically on the power of 'container' rhetoric); P Schlag, 'Rights in the Postmodern Condition' in A Sarat and TR Kearns (eds), *Legal Rights: Historical and Philosophical Perspectives* (1997) at 263–304 (particularly on the 'analytical aesthetic' of legal thinking); CM Rose, *Property and Persuasion: Essays on the History, Theory, and Rhetoric of Ownership* (1994) (specifically the power of fence or boundary rhetoric).

Similarly, the rather one-dimensional Lockean or utilitarian justification for private property inherent in the centrality thesis is now outdated, if not discredited. However, my argument is that centrality remains a powerful force in legal thinking through the rhetoric and logic of the rights paradigm. Although we started moving away from it, centrality logic has become embedded in the law so deeply that realist and other modernist or post-modernist critiques of formalism[24] could not displace it completely, especially in civilian systems where realism was less influential.[25] Even in post-realist circles, utilitarian analysis adheres to the aesthetics of centrality thinking, merely replacing the crude liberal justification of private property on the basis of desert with the subtler distributive logic of utilitarian or efficiency calculus that still regards having property as normal and central to the social and legal system. Property theory based on the notion of human flourishing—still a significant and influential school of thinking, even in post-liberal circles—is firmly embedded in centrality logic, despite its trenchant realism-inspired critique of formalism. Similarly, while the centrality logic of classic formalism was displaced to a certain degree by Marxian and post-structuralist critiques, it retains a hold on legal thinking through the stabilising, tradition-enhancing and reform-inhibiting influence of legal doctrine and legal culture.[26] The de-centring of law as a science, accurately predicted by OW Holmes in 1897,[27] has indeed taken place, at least in the North American context, but the economic and social principles and methodologies upon which legal thinking was subsequently based often resulted in a new formalism that is vulnerable to the same criticism that the realists raised against classical legal thinking. The first move of modernism away from metaphysics and

[24] The realist impatience with metaphysics and formal doctrinal reasoning based on abstract legal axioms precipitated the emphasis on empiricism that would eventually inform the realists' critique of classical legal reasoning. A striking illustration of the anti-metaphysical de-centring of law in realism is FS Cohen, 'Transcendental Nonsense and the Functional Approach' (1935) 35 *Columbia LR* 809–49. In critical legal studies an important legacy of this critical de-centring tendency is the indeterminacy thesis and the notion of reification; see eg D Kairys, 'Introduction' in D Kairys (ed), *The Politics of Law: A Progressive Critique* (3rd edn, 1998) 1–20 at 4; AC Hutchinson, 'Introduction' in AC Hutchinson (ed), *Critical Legal Studies* (1989) 1–11 at 4.

[25] JWG van der Walt, *Law and Sacrifice: Towards a Post-Apartheid Theory of Law* (2005) at 2 points out that American realism's critique of formalism was influenced by R von Jhering's critique of German Pandectism, as indicated by extensive references in FS Cohen, 'Transcendental Nonsense and the Functional Approach' (1935) 35 *Columbia LR* 809–49 to R von Jhering, 'Im juristischen Begriffshimmel' in *Scherz und Ernst in der Jurisprudenz* (1909). See G Minda, *Postmodern Legal Movements: Law and Jurisprudence at Century's End* (1995) 13–23 on American formalism and its critics; F Wieacker, *Privatrechtsgeschichte der Neuzeit* (2nd edn, 1967) 430–58 on German Pandectism. Compare H Botha, 'Democracy and Rights: Constitutional Interpretation in a Postrealist World' (2000) 63 *THRHR* 561–81 at 563–7 on formalism in public law; AJ van der Walt, 'Ownership and Personal Freedom: Subjectivism in Bernhard Windscheid's Theory of Ownership' (1993) 56 *THRHR* 569–89 on Pandectism in private law.

[26] I already referred to the transformation-inhibiting role of legal culture in the South African context in ch 1, n 41, citing K Klare, 'Legal Culture and Transformative Constitutionalism' (1998) 14 *SAJHR* 146–88 at 166–7, 166–72; RJ Coombe, '"Same as it Ever Was": Rethinking the Politics of Legal Interpretation' (1989) 34 *McGill LJ* 603–52.

[27] OW Holmes, 'The Path of the Law' (1897) 10 *Harvard LR* 457–78; republished (1997) 110 *Harvard LR* 991–1009. In (1997) 110 *Harvard LR* 991–1009 at 1001 Holmes stated: 'For the rational study of the law the black-letter man may be the man of the present, but the man of the future is the man of statistics and the master of economics.'

'transcendental nonsense' therefore did not really succeed in de-centring scientific thinking; it merely replaced deductive with inductive formalism and shifted the law's reliance on truth and certainty from metaphysical to empirical foundations. The development sometimes described as the interpretive or linguistic turn, resulting from critiques of the empirical methodology embraced by the realists and their contemporaries,[28] could have precipitated a potentially larger de-centring of law as a science but, although legal thinking has felt the effect of these developments, the linguistic turn has had remarkably little direct effect on legal doctrine and hence its effect in displacing centrality thinking was negligible. For the most part, legal doctrine remains firmly locked into centrality logic informed either by formalism or by some sort of economic or utilitarian calculus. Especially in the civil law jurisdictions, neither realism nor the linguistic turn has had a paradigm-shifting effect on legal doctrine, even though both movements have penetrated legal theory. In North American law, realism has had a profound effect but its legacy is pragmatic and utilitarian rather than critical. In English law, the situation is comparable to the civil law jurisdictions; neither realism nor post-structuralist thinking has made a paradigm-shifting impact on legal doctrine, although it has influenced legal theory. Sadly, and for whatever reasons, legal theory does not have much impact on either legal doctrine or policy.

In this book I am interested in de-centring that implies shifting the focus of the law, both as a science and as a social institution, away from the centre and towards the margins, at least in part. Partly to avoid the obvious misfit between legal theory and legal doctrine, I attempted in the three substantive chapters to initiate my

---

[28] The linguistic or interpretive turn in the social and human sciences, based on observation of the mutual dependency of language and thinking and the impossibility of describing the outside world objectively from a neutral Archimedes point, was influenced by developments in the natural sciences, particularly the realisation that even the most stringent scientific experiment and observation were subject to limitations deriving from the observer's double or biased position. The notion of uncertainty caused by observer position had its origin in the so-called Heisenberg uncertainty principle, formulated by Werner Heisenberg in 1927: The more precisely the position of a sub-atomic particle is determined, the less precisely its momentum is known at the same instant, and vice versa. Heisenberg's uncertainty principle does not imply that every scientific observation is uncertain, but rather indicated the limits of certainty in observing sub-atomic events from a particular position. By electing to observe either the wave or the particle picture, the observer 'disturbs untouched nature' and renders it impossible to observe nature 'as it really is', inducing Heisenberg to conclude that the 'path' of a sub-atomic particle comes into existence only when we observe it. I am indebted to my colleague JHS Hofmeyr for this information. In socio-linguistics, the same principle is known as the '(language) observer's paradox', referring to the researcher's double role of participant in the conversation(s) that she uses as data and as a *posteriori* observer or interpreter of the same data. The term 'observer's paradox' is from W Labov, *Language in the Inner City: Studies in the Black English Vernacular* (1972). I am indebted to Christa van der Walt for this information. See further in this regard RJ Coombe, '"Same As It Ever Was": Rethinking the Politics of Legal Interpretation' (1989) 34 *McGill LJ* 603–52 at 606, with reference to TS Kuhn, *The Structure of Scientific Revolutions* (1962) and P Feyerabend, *Against Method: Outline of an Anarchistic Theory of Knowledge* (1978). The link between post-structuralist developments in the social sciences and earlier developments in the natural sciences has been related to legal methodology in the South African context before by DP Visser, 'The Legal Historian as Subversive or: Killing the Capitoline Geese' in DP Visser (ed), *Essays on the History of Law* (1989) 1–31, especially at 11, 14. The information in this footnote is based upon AJ van der Walt, 'Legal History, Legal Culture and Transformation in a Constitutional Democracy' (2006) 12 *Fundamina* 1–47 at 21, fn 56.

analysis from a place that holds analytical value and interest for both theory and doctrine, namely the response of legal rules and practice to the interests of persons and groups that are regarded as marginal and irrelevant in mainstream law. In one sense, OW Holmes predicted a de-centring of this kind when he stated: 'If you want to know the law and nothing else, you must look at it as a bad man, who cares only for the material consequences which such knowledge enables him to predict.'[29] Holmes' 'bad man' image was destined to attract criticism from the mainstream, not least because he described the law as nothing more complicated than prediction of outcomes.[30] One could also ascribe a certain cynicism to the bad man's approach to law and argue that this cynical, perhaps even manipulative, approach fits much more comfortably with the fundamental assumptions of liberal (pragmatist or utilitarian) thinking than with the de-centring critique of the realists. For that reason alone, I would not like to hitch my argument to the Holmes image of the bad man, although his argument illustrates the point of de-centring the focus of the law.

Holmes' argument could, if sheared of its pragmatist foundations, point us towards a theoretical development that can destabilise our unreflective tendency to focus on the holders of rights, the essential, the principle, the rule, the normal case. Focusing on the position and legal interests of the bad man shifts the focus of the law away from the 'normal' case and onto the marginal, the outlier. This could be extended to a more general de-centring of the subject in law, a shift that is presaged in some of the more critical work of the realists,[31] although its philosophical implications would only become clear much later and in a different theoretical context, under the auspices of post-modernism.[32] Legal doctrine, with its focus on

[29] OW Holmes, 'The Path of the Law' (1997) 110 *Harvard LR* 991–1009 at 993. See ch 1, n 49 and accompanying text, where I have already raised the Holmes argument.

[30] In 'The Path of the Law' (1997) 110 *Harvard LR* 991–1009 at 994 Holmes explained that law was about prediction of outcomes, something that the 'bad man' is more aware of than anybody else: 'prophecies of what the courts will do in fact, and nothing more pretentious, are what I mean by the law'. JP Diggins, *The Promise of Pragmatism* (1994) at 342–59 points out that Holmes was a pragmatist, although he personally thought that most pragmatists 'lacked tough-mindedness and allowed sentiment to do the work of thought'.

[31] Arguably the most visible feature of this de-centring in critical realism is the focus on poverty and welfare issues, with particular attention to the social origins of poverty, as embodied in the political programme of the realism-inspired New Deal. For post-realist continuation of this interest in welfare and poverty issues see eg LA Williams, 'Welfare and Legal Entitlements: The Social Roots of Poverty' in D Kairys (ed), *The Politics of Law: A Progressive Critique* (3rd edn, 1998) 569–90; W Simon, 'The Invention and Reinvention of Welfare Rights' (1985) 44 *Maryland LR* 1–37; W Simon, 'Rights and Redistribution in the Welfare System' (1986) 38 *Stanford LR* 1431–516. However, critical theorists did not simply accept the realist critique unquestioningly; see eg GS Alexander, 'The Concept of Property in Private and Constitutional Law: The Ideology of the Scientific Turn in Legal Analysis' (1982) 82 *Columbia LR* 1545–99 for a critical assessment of the 'scientific turn' that accompanied the shift of focus to poverty and welfare issues in realist thinking.

[32] The theoretical potential of de-centring the subject was unveiled by E Lévinas, *Totality and Infinity: An Essay on Exteriority* (1969), pointing out that traditional Western notions of knowledge proceed from the presence and identity of the self and thus reduce 'the Other' to that identity. Lévinas steered post-modern legal theory away from centrality thinking when he insisted upon the priority of confrontation with the Other. I am indebted to W le Roux and K van Marle, 'Postmodernism(s) and the Law' in C Roederer and D Moellendorf (eds), *Jurisprudence* (2004) 354–81 at 368 for this explanation of Lévinas.

principles and norms, obviously does not work well in the margins and hence this kind of de-centring has had little effect on doctrinal thinking. As could be expected, doctrinalists avoid the margins; they focus on the principle, the rule, the central and the essential. In the margins, the law does not feature as guarantor of the rights of the upright citizen, the property-owning and contract-concluding entrepreneur, the Wasp family man or the owner of 40 acres and a mule. Here, the legal cast is made up of an unfamiliar and often rather unsavoury bunch that do not normally feature prominently (or at all) in legal discourse, at least not as far as principles are concerned: criminals, outlaws, political protestors, squatters, gypsies, the homeless, the sick, the poor, the elderly, the immigrant, the ex-slave, the handicapped, women and whoever else is vulnerable and weak or unusual and ill-fitting in the face of the law. The law has always found it difficult to deal with representatives of this group, mostly because they 'normally' encounter the law only in conflict with ownership and other vested rights (fugitive slaves, trespassers, squatters, intruders and encroachers) or when they demand exceptional treatment and accommodation founded not in law but in moral obligation and compassion (children, the poor, the homeless, the hungry, the unemployed, the sick and the disabled). In the margins where these groups feature, the law mostly shines in its absence, its shortcomings, its inability to include, to safeguard and to protect those who do not themselves occupy central positions in law because of their status or possessions. For them, the law is normally either present in its status as protector of others' rights and punisher of those who infringe those rights or, in a few exceptional cases, as the mediator or regulator of emergency relief or disability programmes initiated by the state or civil society. For the law, these individuals and groups are normally either criminals or beggars; they do not receive justice so much as either punishment or benefaction.

The realist and post-modern shift of focus away from the strong and powerful who are most likely to influence the making and enforcement of law, towards those who have least influence on the law and who mostly experience it from a position of exclusion, resistance, poverty, weakness, vulnerability and suffering has indicated a third way of thinking about power, privilege and status in law.[33] Traditionally, the law knew only two ways in which to deal with marginal groups: prescribing and enforcing rules that govern their (mostly unlawful) interaction with the property rights of the privileged, or ignoring them completely for being marginal and hence irrelevant to the business of property rules and principles. In exceptional cases, the law might administer emergency or disability relief programmes initiated for the benefit of these groups, but it never dispenses justice on the basis of the value of their property interests. However, from a de-centred

---

[33] The most striking illustration of the resulting de-centring of the legal subject in realism is RL Hale, 'Coercion and Distribution in a Supposedly Non-Coercive State' (1923) 38 *Political Science Qly* 470–94, pointing out the effect and role of power and coercion in a legal regime supposedly based on equality and liberty. In critical legal studies a significant legacy of this de-centring is critical race theory and critical feminist theory, which further developed the critique of mainstream legal theory from the perspective of the marginal legal subject; see eg PJ Williams, *The Alchemy of Race and Rights* (1991).

perspective, it becomes possible to think about marginal individuals and groups in a different way by allowing their interests and their lack of property (and hence power) to influence the formulation, interpretation and application of law, on the basis of proper consideration of their particular situation, their needs, their status, their beliefs or their customs. In the margins, these individuals and groups appear as persons rather than just positions; they acquire depth and character. Considering the legal value and power of property interests that do not translate into recognised property rights is not possible within the rights paradigm, but it is possible (and inevitable) in the margins.

In the margins, the law inevitably acquires a liminal quality, as Ruti Teitel described it.[34] This liminal quality of law, in so far as we recognise it, means that we are compelled to work on and deal with the limits, the margins, the fringes of the law and whoever or whatever we find there. We cannot simply accept (as classical legal thinking does) that law is about the essential, the central, or the normal, and we cannot simply ignore the margins of the law and those who feature on them.[35] This requires recognition of the somewhat unusual and disturbing notion that property law is not exclusively or even primarily about owners and holders of rights, but about those who do not own property and whose lives are shaped and affected by the property holdings of others; those who are required to respect property and who are owned as or through property. In the margins, property law is as deeply concerned with absence of property; no-property; not-property; as it is with property.[36] In the margins, absence of property can be just as important

---

[34] RG Teitel, *Transitional Justice* (2000) describes law in transition as both settled and unsettled, restrained and restraining, historically and politically contingent (at 6), partial, provisional, limited and symbolic in nature, and best understood in its liminal quality as law 'in between regimes' (at 215, 220). Teitel uses the term 'liminal' to refer to the forward- and backward-looking quality of transitional law that renders it separate from its predecessor but also informed by prior injustice in forming a notion of what is just (at 6–7, 196). I regard her analysis valuable for transformational (as opposed to transitional) situations or analysis of law as well; alternatively, my argument assumes that all law is always transitional, at least in part. When JWG van der Walt, *Law and Sacrifice: Towards a Post-Apartheid Theory of Law* (2005) refers to the understanding of law as sacrifice he has something similar in mind, particularly in so far as his analysis focuses on the blurring of the boundaries of law (at 5); on the destructive effect of presence and representation in law (at 8, 24); and on plurality and its de-centring effects (at 8–11).

[35] During the 1970s and 1980s neo-Marxism and post-structuralism resulted in the same de-centring thinking that Holmes and the realists inspired in American critical legal studies circles; a forceful example is to be found in the pages of the leftist legal journal *Recht & Kritiek* published by Dutch legal academics and activists between 1975 and 1997. An article on squatting illustrates the marginality thesis I am presenting perfectly: GE van Maanen, 'Balanceren op de Grens van de Rechtsorde' ('Balancing on the margins of the legal order') (1982) 8 *Recht & Kritiek* 467–71 argued at 469: 'Met andere woorden ik veronderstel een mogelijkheid tot grensverlegging binnen de rechtsorde, bijvoorbeeld veranderingen in het denken over het eigendomsbegrip [. . .] Of je het nu leuk vindt of niet, je bevindt je *in* deze rechtsorde. Je kunt hooguit proberen de grenzen te verleggen door te balanceren op de grens van de rechtsorde. Maar je kunt er niet uit.' ('In other words, I presuppose the possibility of a certain shifting of boundaries within the legal order, for example changing thinking about ownership. Whether you like it or not, you find yourself within this legal order. You can at best try and shift the boundaries by balancing on the margins of the legal order, but you cannot escape from it.')

[36] According to Hohfeldian analysis, the correlative of a claim-right is a duty and the opposite a no-right; the correlative of property would therefore be the duty to respect others' property and the opposite would be no-property. I cannot enter into a discussion of Hohfeld here, but his analysis of the

and significant in deciding disputes as the presence of property, depending on the context. In the terminology of contemporary legal theory, the best context within which to discuss ownership is not condominium development or owner-ship of valuable urban air space, but ownership as it appears in its absence, in its confrontation with poverty, slavery or unlawful occupation of land and buildings.[37]

Shifting the theoretical focus of property law to the margins is not a magic recipe that will necessarily bring about more responsive property thinking. Two examples illustrate the problems with marginality thinking. On the one hand, pro-gressive theorists who questioned the notion of rights gravitated towards what became known as needs-based theory,[38] focusing legal analysis on the needs of weak and marginalised people instead of on the rights of the rich and powerful. These de-centring theories emphasised the obligations that accompany and are implicated by property, instead of simply relying on the entitlements and power enjoyed in terms of it.[39] In a wider context, this line of thinking coincided nicely with broader post-realist de-centring arguments to the effect that ownership entails obligations as well as rights and, more particularly, that it brings with it a certain social and environmental responsibility—ownership as absolute dominion was replaced by ownership as stewardship; absolute ownership was replaced by ownership that is subject to legal restrictions and to social and ethical obligations. By engaging in theoretical analysis and practical lawyering in support of workers, the homeless, receivers of state welfare and other marginalised groups, needs-based theorists from this group succeeded in shifting the attention of lawyers, lay people and policymakers alike towards the fringes of society and the margins of the law. That in itself was a laudable and worthwhile exercise, but it did not succeed in dislodging the rights-based centring of law in the mainstream paradigm of legal thinking. Despite its de-centring intentions and its social focus, needs-based dis-course always retained an air of exceptionalism; social justice appeared as some-thing that ethical and responsible property owners had to do in addition to enjoying their powerful and privileged position. Responsibility qualified the

fundamental conceptions of law illustrates the issues; see WN Hohfeld, 'Some Fundamental Legal Conceptions as Applied in Judicial Reasoning' (1913) 23 *Yale LJ* 16–59; 'Fundamental Legal Conceptions as Applied in Legal Reasoning' (1917) 26 *Yale LJ* 710–70.

[37] This insight was brought home to me by Robert Cover's book on slavery, which is about property as much as slavery: RM Cover, *Justice Accused: Antislavery and the Judicial Process* (1975). For my reac-tion to this insight see AJ van der Walt, 'Rendition/Eviction: a Post-Apartheid Reflection' (2005) 15 *Law & Critique* 321–44.

[38] The original anti-rights essay was M Tushnet, 'An Essay on Rights' (1984) 62 *Texas LR* 1363–403. A more nuanced early needs-based analysis based on constitutional notions of self-government is FI Michelman, 'The Supreme Court 1968 Term—Foreword: On Protecting the Poor through the Fourteenth Amendment' (1969) 83 *Harvard LR* 7–59. On Michelman's theory of social justice see AJ van der Walt, 'A South African Reading of Frank Michelman's Theory of Social Justice' (2004) 19 *SAPL* 253–307.

[39] For a later exploration of needs discourse in the South African constitutional context see D Brand, 'The "Politics of Need Interpretation" and the Adjudication of Socio-Economic Rights Claims in South Africa' in AJ van der Walt (ed), *Theories of Social and Economic Justice* (2005) 17–36; S Liebenberg, 'Needs, Rights and Transformation: Adjudicating Social Rights' (2006) 17 *Stell LR* 5–36.

notion of ownership but did not affect its centrality in the hierarchy of rights. Needs-based theory also met with strong criticism: Liberals claimed that it misrepresented rights-talk,[40] while activists on the left said that it ignored the strategic benefits of rights-talk for minorities[41] and that it reflected and helped to entrench a paternalistic and insulting attitude towards poverty and the poor.[42]

A second, related, shift that contributed to the de-centring of property but ultimately failed to dislodge the rights paradigm completely was the critical tendency to emphasise the social origins (and hence contingency) of property as a social artefact.[43] Social origins theory argues that state limitation of property holdings is legitimate not only when exercising the state's police power in protecting public health and safety, but also when the limitations are specifically designed to accommodate the particular social and economic needs and circumstances of non-owner groups and individuals; considerations that are traditionally relegated to the margins of the law for being irrelevant.[44] By focusing on the paradox that property simultaneously protects individual security and privilege and serves (or at least has to take account of) the public good, social origins theory established that property is not only inherently limited by social obligations, but that those obligations could extend beyond the requirements of public health and safety to embrace the (even conflicting) interests (and needs) of others.[45] Theorists thinking along similar lines, but inspired by a more radical Hohfeldian departure from liberal rights theory, produced a version of rights theory that still functions within the discourse of rights but de-centres it by placing stronger emphasis on social relationships and

---

[40] J Waldron, 'Rights and Needs: The Myth of Disjunction' in A Sarat and TR Kearns, *Legal Rights: Historical and Philosophical Perspectives* (2nd edn, 1997) 87–109.

[41] Eg PJ Williams, 'Alchemical Notes: Reconstructing Ideals from Deconstructed Rights' (1987) 22 *Harvard Civil Rights–Civil Liberties LR* 401–33; K Crenshaw, 'A Black Feminist Critique of Antidiscrimination Law and Politics' in D Kairys (ed), *The Politics of Law: A Progressive Critique* (3rd edn, 1998) 356–80.

[42] T Ross, 'The Rhetoric of Poverty: Their Immorality, Our Helplessness' (1991) 79 *Georgetown LJ* 1499–1547; see also GS Alexander, 'Socio-Economic Rights in American Perspective: The Tradition of Anti-Paternalism in American Constitutional Thought' in AJ van der Walt (ed), *Theories of Social and Economic Justice* (2005) 6–16.

[43] The pivotal social origins article is JW Singer and JM Beerman, 'The Social Origins of Property' (1993) 6 *Canadian Journal of Law & Jur* 217–48.

[44] In *Brisley v Drotsky* 2002 (4) SA 1 (SCA) at paras 42–6 the South African Supreme Court of Appeal decided that s 26(3) of the Constitution (nobody shall be evicted from their home without a court order, and a court shall only grant an eviction order having considered all the circumstances) did not grant the courts the discretion to deprive a landowner of an eviction order based on the personal circumstances of the occupier and her family; in the absence of explicit statutory provisions, the personal circumstances of the occupier are not 'relevant circumstances' and an eviction order is granted purely with reference to proof of ownership and possession (the classic requirements). See chs 2 and 4 for a discussion of this decision.

[45] The theoretical basis in critical legal studies is Duncan Kennedy's notion of the fundamental contradiction; see D Kennedy, 'Form and Substance in Private Law Adjudication' (1976) 89 *Harvard LR* 1685–778 at 1713–24 ('sense of contradiction'); D Kennedy, 'The Structure of Blackstone's *Commentaries*' (1979) 28 *Buffalo LR* 209–382 at 211–13 (notion of the fundamental contradiction); P Gabel and D Kennedy, 'Roll over Beethoven' (1984) 36 *Stanford LR* 1–55 at 15–16 (abandoning the fundamental contradiction).

care.[46] The examples of social protection legislation discussed in chapters four and five are, for the most part, illustrative of the influence that the social origins and responsibility thinking has had in property law. However, this does not mean that centrality thinking has been replaced by social responsibility thinking. The problem with de-centring the focus of property law on the basis of its social origins or its foundation in relationship is that the de-centring ultimately remains focused on the social need to care for others, especially others in dire straits, as an exceptional (but ethical) reaction to exceptional needs. The propertied Self remains the norm; the have-not Other the exception. The process of caring for those in need does no more than remind the rich and powerful that they have a duty of conscience not to forget the needs of the less privileged. This is particularly true with reference to needs-based theories that focus on poverty and the survival needs of the poor or those who find themselves in dire emergencies. Of course it is important to recognise the social responsibilities of ownership and the obligation to assist people in emergency and other socially and economically extreme circumstances of need, but the question is whether we have made a really significant shift by simply adding concern for the poor to mainstream ownership thinking as an afterthought. In this sense, property lawyers have arguably noticed the margins, but we have not mastered the art of balancing on the very edge of the legal order yet. In so far as theoretical shifts in property theory rely on needs-based, social origins or relationship thinking they have succeeded in amending property discourse and thinking, but they have not displaced the rights paradigm. For that, an even more radical departure from traditional property thinking is required.

C. Balancing on the Edge

The remaining question is, how do we conceptualise marginality or no-property as an organising principle that is relevant to property law and theory in a wider context and more forcefully than ethical or social concern for the weak and the poor? How do we conceptualise marginality in property or, stated differently, how do we practise property in the margins by balancing on the very edge of property law? Marginality involves legal positions not characterised or dominated by the presence of rights, possessions, privilege and power. Thinking and arguing about property in a way that takes the persons in those positions and their interests and circumstances seriously means, at the very least, that we have to try and think away the power and the centrality of rights, entitlements and privileges and to imagine

---

[46] The primary rights as relationships article is J Nedelsky, 'Reconceiving Rights as Relationship' (1993) 1 *Rev Const Studies* 1–26, where she proposed the theory of rights as relationship; an idea that relies on realist thinking and that goes beyond Tushnet's rights critique in that it redefines rights instead of abandoning rights discourse for needs discourse. For strong property-related analysis in the same theoretical vein see JW Singer, *The Edges of the Field: Lessons on the Obligations of Ownership* (2000); most recently JW Singer, 'After the Flood: Equality and Humanity in Property Relations' (2006) 52 *Loyola LR* 243–343.

a legal order not dominated by the hierarchies built on the distinction between their presence or absence.

In one of its recent decisions the South African Constitutional Court signalled the importance for social and legal transformation of breaking loose from the hierarchies embedded in legal tradition:[47]

> In sum, the Constitution imposes new obligations on the courts concerning rights relating to property not previously recognised by the common law. It counterposes to the normal ownership rights of possession, use and occupation, a new and equally relevant right not arbitrarily to be deprived of a home. The expectations that ordinarily go with title could clash head-on with the genuine despair of people in dire need of accommodation. The judicial function in these circumstances is not to establish a hierarchical arrangement between the different interests involved, privileging in an abstract and mechanical way the rights of ownership over the right not to be dispossessed of a home, or vice versa. Rather it is to balance out and reconcile the opposed claims in as just a manner as possible taking account of all the interests involved and the specific factors relevant in each particular case.

The Court referred to need in its reference to 'people in dire need of accommodation', but the explanation of the 'new obligations' imposed on courts by the Constitution genuinely attempts to break away from a centrality logic that is dominated and determined by abstract and hierarchical rights-thinking, privileging either ownership over 'home interests' or vice versa. In other words, the Court makes it clear that the new obligation imposed by the Constitution does not allow courts to simply follow the presence or centrality logic of ownership or rights, but neither does it allow them to simply follow the absence or mercy logic of need and emergency. In this way it might be possible to account for marginality in property law without simply reducing marginality to poverty, need and weakness—in other words, it becomes possible to conceive of property in the margins without the discussion being dominated by the mere absence of property or the conceptual counterpoint of property.

The decision of the Constitutional Court also makes it clear that to account for marginality does not imply ignoring or simply overriding or undermining ownership or property rights. Property law is not possible without attention, at some level, to property rights and the power that they entail. Similarly, my quest in this book is not to ignore property rights or ownership or even necessarily to weaken their legal power, but to imagine a perspective on property that includes, in a meaningful way, the interests of those who are not 'normally' considered part of the property elite, without automatically reducing them to the status of weakness and dependency.

In this perspective, marginality is not limited to poverty, need, or even necessarily the absence of property—at least in some cases, marginality and absence of property indicate surprisingly strong positions that deserve more focused and

---

[47] *Port Elizabeth Municipality v Various Occupiers* 2005 (1) SA 217 (CC) at para 23 (references omitted). See the discussion of this decision in ch 5.

serious attention from legal theory. To think about property in the margins also implies taking note of the strong positions that sometimes feature in the margins,[48] particularly when they are founded on direct rejection of or confrontation with the dominant property regime. I quite like the term 'property outlaws' that was coined by Peñalver and Katyal,[49] referring as it does to the fact that no-property positions are sometimes founded in the powerful action of political activists, squatters and land invaders who later become folk heroes and national idols because they opposed and rejected social, legal and political structures or traditions. Apart from the examples discussed by Peñalver and Katyal, the Western European politically inspired urban squatting movement of the 1980s is another instructive case in point,[50] as are the South African land reform cases involving resistance to eviction under the apartheid regime.[51] Refusal to abide in the conventional property structures and roles of mainstream society could therefore be an indicator of marginal property positions that deserve special attention from property theorists.

One important aspect of theorising property in the margins is that one sometimes has to look outside of the narrow confines of the law. In some instances, the political context is more relevant, and political rather than legal action is called for to promote and protect weak, marginal land rights—both the urban squatting cases of the 1980s and the South African land struggle under apartheid demonstrate that the law sometimes simply does not reach far enough and that change is possible only through political action.[52] The squatting cases also demonstrate that political action of this nature could well involve conscious deliberate illegal action and that there is a risk that enforcement of the infringed rights might involve criminal and civil action against the demonstrators or squatters. In the Dutch *kraken* movement of the 1980s the demonstrators deliberately accepted the risk and used the resulting court cases to drum up political and social support for their cause. As the squatter cases in chapter five and the historical references[53] demonstrate, there are significant indicators that both legal and illegal political action to demonstrate against an unjust property regime can be successful in changing the regime, albeit sometimes in the long run. Political protest against unjust property regimes is primarily addressed to political actors such as governments, policymakers and legislature and will therefore not necessarily sway or influence courts or theorists, but it is equally important for a marginal perspective on property and, as has been proven, it can be effective in changing the law.

---

[48] In his inaugural lecture, Paul Cilliers argued convincingly, from the perspective of complexity theory, that modest or relative positions do not necessarily have to be weak: P Cilliers, 'Do Modest Positions Have to be Weak? A View from Complexity'. A version of the lecture was published as P Cilliers, 'Complexity, Deconstruction and Relativism' (2005) 22 *Theory Culture Society* 255–67 (available online at http://tcs.sagepub.com/cgi/content/abstract/22/5/255) (accessed 4 September 2007).

[49] EM Peñalver and SK Katyal, 'Property Outlaws' (2007) 155 *Univ Pennsylvania LR* 1095–186. See ch5, section II. for a discussion of their arguments.

[50] See the discussion in ch 5, section II.

[51] I discuss the case-law in ch 5, section III.

[52] I discuss the cases and materials in ch 5, sections II. and III.

[53] See n 54 below.

Focus on strong marginal property positions should also remind us that marginal property interests have, historically speaking, in certain instances become dominant property rights in the mainstream because of social, economic and political changes and developments, both legal and political. By reminding property lawyers of these often denied or forgotten events it becomes possible or easier to imagine or accept similar changes again, even though they might appear impossible or even unthinkable in the everyday slog of property practice. These shifts in property status still occur, and they often originate in what are considered marginal positions at the time; sometimes they involve political action that might include unlawful or illegal acts of defiance.[54] A stronger focus on the margins of property and on the faultlines and breakdowns in historical continuity enables us to notice and remember these marginal but very important changes in legal status and, by remembering them, we are enabled to imagine their recurrence in future, in cases when they might support the bringing about of a more just and equitable property regime.[55]

A marginal perspective on strong marginal positions in property requires attention for marginal aspects of property law; instead of focusing on property (security) and contract (exchange) we should look at marginal positions such as those of the weaker parties in landlord and tenant law and squatting law, where the primary focus is not the position and the rights of the owner-landlord but the status and legal position of tenants and squatters. In addition to big property developments we should also focus attention on the squatter huts and slave cottages that represent powerful and significant property loci. During apartheid the South African property syllabus never included apartheid legislation; that was seen as politics, best left to the politicians. As a consequence, property law was always typically the white law of the business district and the suburbs; never the struggle law of the forcibly evacuated black spots or the rural areas destroyed by migrant labour and political neglect. This failure of South African property lawyers prevented the timely development of more inclusive and critical property doctrine and theory that could have avoided—or at least opposed—the abuses and injustices of apartheid land law. This situation is changing, not only in South Africa but elsewhere as well, as more and more journal articles and books focus on marginal property interests and positions.

Critical analysis of strong marginal positions in property should also be aware that property rules and practices are often contingent and contested rather than clear and consensual. Schnably argued, with regard to the supposed virtues of the private family home as a locus where property enables the fostering of person-

[54] W van Iterson, 'Beschouwingen over Rolverwisseling of Eigendomsverschuiving' in *Verslagen en Mededelingen van de Vereniging tot Uitgave van het Oud-Vaderlands Recht* XII, no 3 (1971) 407–66 describes processes in post-feudal Dutch law where ownership 'shifted' from feudal landlords to vassals by force of social and economic changes. Compare *James v United Kingdom* [1986] 8 EHRR 123; *Hawaii Housing Authority v Midkiff* 467 US 229 (1984).

[55] Some authors even argue that strategic illegal action should be supported for efficiency reasons; see ch 6, section II.C and compare LA Fennell, 'Efficient Trespass: The Case for "Bad Faith"' Adverse Possession' (2006) 100 *Northwestern Univ LR* 1037–96.

hood, that the suburban family home is not just a heart-warming symbol of all that is good and necessary about private property; it is also a contested space that entrenches and hides inequality, such as gender oppression and family violence, racial and class inequality and exclusion, and bad town planning favouring the economic domination of the white middle class.[56] Because critical awareness of marginality requires awareness of the existence and effects of social or political disputes, hierarchies that privilege rights over marginal interests may often look normal or unproblematic.[57] Marginal property interests often resemble or are even recognised as rights, but when assessed against their socio-political background they are weak and marginal because they do not fit into the mainstream hierarchy of rights, allowing them to be dominated by ownership in what looks like a perfectly logical and neutral logic. In this context it will no doubt be useful to approach analysis of property status from the perspective of what Johan van der Walt describes as alterity and plurality, which means that we cannot afford to see the hegemony of the normal, the everyday or the mass consensus as a norm; we have to leave room for otherness, for difference.[58] Marginality thinking has its own logic in that it forces one to look for the paradox and the contradiction rather than for broad theory and grand narrative, for diversity rather than uniformity, for dissent rather than consensus, for conflict and chaos rather than consent and order. In other words, it directs our attention to faultlines and disputes or historical breakdowns rather than concentrating on or searching for the golden thread of continuity. In a very real sense, a marginality perspective requires us to make a fundamental switch in what we regard as important or central in law.

A further implication of marginality thinking in property theory is that it should focus our attention much more on the social position, economic status and personal circumstances of the parties involved in property relations or disputes and less on their legal status or established property rights. Marginal people such as criminals, outlaws, the homeless, the weak, the poor, the elderly and the handicapped, but also the politically defiant, often have no rights and therefore they cannot enter the dogmatic syllogism to compete in a classic legal battle about property. The interests that they do have might either not be recognised by law or, if they are recognised, might be protected weakly because these interests enjoy a lower status than mainstream rights. The result is that we do not recognise or see the rights that they do have or the challenges they address to the property regime we accept as something normal and equitable. A focus on the margins therefore should involve more than just having sympathy or greater understanding for those in the margins because of their social context; it should include developing an eye for the power and status of their position in the margin and the reasons for their

---

[56] S Schnably, 'Property and Pragmatism: A Critique of Radin's Theory of Property and Personhood' (1993) 45 *Stanford LR* 347–407; in response to MJ Radin, 'Property and Personhood' (1982) 34 *Stanford LR* 957–1015.

[57] See to the same effect RJ Coombe, '"Same As It Ever Was": Rethinking the Politics of Legal Interpretation' (1989) 34 *McGill LJ* 603–52.

[58] JWG van der Walt, *Law and Sacrifice: Towards a Post-Apartheid Theory of Law* (2005) at 11–17.

challenge to the regime. Recent property literature suggests that, like in social science literature in general,[59] there is an increasing interest in the property status and the possible protection of people who occupy land unlawfully, whether for economic, political or social reasons;[60] indicating a shift towards marginal interests in property law. My aim is to strengthen the impulse of that shift.

How much change is necessary to bring about greater justice and equity in the property regime? As I stated in chapter one, this is not a question that can or should be answered in the abstract; the context within which property disputes arise is crucial. As far as the examples discussed in the substantive chapters are concerned, one could at most say that a long history of unequal and discriminatory or oppressive property relations, for example in South African land law under apartheid, obviously requires more reform and stronger transformative measures than in the absence of such a history. However, at the same time it is just as true that a long history of protective legislation and proactive housing policies does not guarantee faultless equality and justice in the property regime; the discussion of English landlord–tenant law suggests that recent shifts in housing policy might endanger gains that have been made earlier. The section on weak owners in chapter six is particularly worrying and requires further analysis because it suggests that there are owners of land who do not enjoy the same protection as other owners, despite the presence of statutory or even constitutional equality and property guarantees. If these owners are vulnerable to unjust eviction even within the framework of the rights paradigm there is a serious problem that requires critical reconsideration of the social and political situation and the underlying reasons why the law not only countenances but apparently entrenches what appear to be remnants of discrimination and inequality. At the same time, the policy reasons for which apparently strong ownership positions are subjugated to the interests of weak or no-property interests in cases like encroachment by building, adverse possession and public access cases deserve further attention, particularly if they could point towards possibilities for further justice-inspired changes in the rights paradigm and the property regime.

In the end, the one general conclusion that does appear possible is that property rhetoric and the logic of rights are perhaps the greatest causes for concern. The

---

[59] I pointed out in ch 1 that Mari Matsuda's proposal to study 'the actual experience, history, culture, and intellectual tradition of [especially black] people' holds promise for critical theorising about other forms of marginalisation such as poverty or gender, especially since these forms of marginality are connected. I also referred to the historical work of Eric Hobsbawm and Charles van Onselen as examples of socio-historical research that selects as its central focus the shady underworld of social bandits and politically marginalised groups rather the central figures of rich and powerful property owners. See MJ Matsuda, 'Looking to the Bottom: Critical Legal Studies and Reparations' (1987) 22 *Harvard Civil Rights–Civil Liberties LR* 323–99 at 325; EJ Hobsbawm, *Bandits* (2nd edn, 2000); C van Onselen, *The Seed is Mine: The Life of Kas Maine, A South African Sharecropper 1894–1985* (1996); C Van Onselen, *The Fox and the Flies: The World of Joseph Silver, Racketeer and Psychopath* (2007).

[60] Lorna Fox pointed out that the 'home' interest of residential tenants or defaulting debtors is important to them even if it is not recognised or protected as strongly by the law as the investment interests of the landlord or the creditor; see L Fox, *Conceptualising Home: Theories, Laws and Policies* (2007).

substantive chapters indicate that there are surprisingly many statutory and policy interventions in the property regime that are intended to bring about greater justice and equity, but that these interventions sometimes fail (or are restricted) because their effect on (especially uncodified) legal tradition and doctrine is uncertain. Despite clear statutory and policy declarations to the effect that ownership and other land rights are not absolute, and although most theoretical and doctrinal property texts now at least pay lip service to the notion that absolutism is dead, doctrinal texts often still hold on to supposedly clear and natural rules and practices that simply confirm and entrench the presumptive power of the rights paradigm. It is obviously difficult to change established legal tradition and culture.

I will end the final chapter where I started the first one, namely by discussing the transformation of law and society in post-apartheid South Africa. In his seminal essay on transformation and legal culture in post-apartheid South Africa, Karl Klare stated that the new Constitution 'invites a new imagination and self-reflection about legal method, analysis and reasoning consistent with its transformative goals'.[61] The place to start transforming the property regime in post-apartheid South Africa was obviously the abolition of apartheid land laws and the development of well-considered restitution, redistribution and housing policies, supported by suitable social and economic reforms and land reform legislation. Most of that has been done. However, that is not enough. In order for the new policies and laws to succeed and meet their targets, the law needs to change, and that cannot be accomplished purely through legislation. In addition to legislation it is also necessary to change the legal culture, the rhetoric, logic and unarticulated assumptions within which the law functions. To change these deep paradigmatic structures of the legal culture we have to imagine the alternatives, and that is only possible if we turn our attention away from the centre and towards the margins. By balancing upon the very edge of the property order we are able to see not only the power of privileged established property positions, but also the effect of this power on others who do not share in it. By imagining property law that takes the interests of those in the margins seriously even though it does not fit the syllogism of rights, we may be able to adapt or redirect our thinking and talking about property in ways that could enable us to insist on the simultaneous promotion of rights and justice in the property regime.

---

[61] K Klare, 'Legal Culture and Transformative Constitutionalism' (1998) 14 *SAJHR* 146–88 at 156.

BIBLIOGRAPHY

Books and Journals

A

Abas, P, *Asser's Handleiding tot de Beoefening van het Nederlands Burgerlijk Recht: Bijzondere Overeenkomsten* (2007) Deventer: Kluwer, 'Huur', §§ 199–236.

Ackerman, BA, *Private Property and the Constitution* (1977) New Haven: Yale University Press.

—— *Social Justice in the Liberal State* (1980) New Haven: Yale University Press.

Agambin, PA, 'Right of Landlord Legally Entitled to Possession to Dispossess Tenant without Legal Process' 6 *ALR* 3d 177 (2006) 1–7.

Albertyn, C and Goldblatt, B, 'Facing the Challenges of Transformation: Difficulties in the Development of an Indigenous Jurisprudence of Equality' (1998) 14 *SAJHR* 248–76.

Alcoff, L and Mendieta, E, *Identities: Race, Class, Gender, and Nationality* (2003) Oxford: Blackwell Publishing.

Alexander, GS, 'The Concept of Property in Private and Constitutional Law: The Ideology of the Scientific Turn in Legal Analysis' (1982) 82 *Columbia LR* 1545–99.

—— *Commodity and Propriety: Competing Visions of Property in American Legal Thought 1776–1970* (1997) Chicago, IL: University of Chicago Press.

—— 'Critical Land Law' in S Bright and J Dewar (eds), *Land Law: Themes and Perspectives* (1998) Oxford: Oxford University Press 52–78.

—— 'Socio-economic Rights in American Perspective: The Tradition of Anti-paternalism in American Constitutional Thought' in AJ Van der Walt (ed), *Theories of Social and Economic Justice* (2005) Stellenbosch: African Sun Media 6–16.

—— *The Global Debate over Constitutional Property: Lessons for American Takings Jurisprudence* (2006) Chicago, IL: University of Chicago Press.

Alexander, GS and Skàpska, G (eds), *A Fourth Way. Privatization, Property, and the Emergence of New Market Economies* (1994) New York: Routledge.

Allen, T, *Property and the Human Rights Act 1998* (2005) Oxford: Hart Publishing.

Ankum, JA, Spruit, JE and Wubbe, FBJ (eds), *Satura Roberto Feenstra Sexagesum Quintum Annum Aetatis Complenti an Alumnus Collegis Amicis Oblata* (1985) Fribourg: University Press Fribourg.

Aquinas, T, *Summa Theologica* (German/Latin edn, PHM Christmann (ed), 1953) Heidelberg: Gemeinshaftsverlage FH Kerle, Graz: A Pustet.

B

Badenhorst, PJ, Pienaar, JM and Mostert, H, *Silberberg & Schoeman's The Law of Property* (4th edn, 2003; 5th edn, 2006) Durban: Butterworths.

Bakker Schut, PH, Prakken, T and de Roos, T 'Politiek Protest in de Rechtszaal' (1984) 10 *Recht & Kritiek* 33–62.

Baron, JB, 'Property and "no Property"' (2006) 42 *Houston LR* 1425–49.

Bartlett, RH, *The Mabo Decision; With Commentary and the Full Text of the Decision in* Mabo and Others v State of Queensland (1993) Sydney: Butterworths.

Bartolus de Saxoferrato *Commentaries on the Corpus Iuris Civilis* (1596) Venice: Andreas Torresanus

Baur, F, Baur, JF and Stürner, R, *Sachenrecht* (17th edn, 1999) Munich: CH Beck.

Bennett TW, Dean WHB, Hutchison DB, Leeman I, and Van Zyl Smit D (eds), *Land Ownership—Changing Concepts* (1986) Cape Town: Juta (also published as 1985 *Acta Juridica*).

Benton, S, 'Section 25 of Constitution will Help Land Reform' *BuaNews* 28 October 2005, http://www.eprop.co.za/news/ article.aspx?idArticle=6472 (accessed 18 June 2008).

Birks, P, 'The Roman Law Concept of Dominium and the Idea of Absolute Ownership' (1985) *Acta Juridica* 1–37.

Blackstone, W, *Commentaries on the Laws of England, Book 2* (11th edn, 1791) London: A Strahan & W Woodfall.

Bosman, L, 'Grondteikens Moet Ander Doelwitte in Ag Neem' *Landbouweekblad* (11 November 2005) 106.

Botha, H, 'Democracy and Rights: Constitutional Interpretation in a Postrealist World' (2000) 63 *THRHR* 561–81.

—— 'Metaphoric Reasoning and Transformative Constitutionalism' (2002) *TSAR* 612–27; (2003) *TSAR* 20–36.

—— 'Freedom and Constraint in Constitutional Adjudication' (2004) 20 *SAJHR* 249–83.

Botha, H, van der Walt, AJ and van der Walt, JWG (eds), *Rights and Democracy in a Transformative Constitution* (2003) Stellenbosch: African Sun Media.

Bouckaert, B and Depoorter, BWF, 'Adverse Possession: Title Systems' in B Bouckaert and G De Geest (eds), *Encyclopedia of Law and Economics*, http://encyclo.findlaw.com/ (accessed 15 June 2008), 1200: 18–31

Brand, D, 'The "Politics of Need Interpretation" and the Adjudication of Socio-economic Rights Claims in South Africa' in AJ van der Walt (ed), *Theories of Social and Economic Justice* (2005) Stellenbosch: African Sun Media 17–36.

Bright, S, 'Ending Tenancies by Notice to Quit: The Human Rights Challenge' (2004) 120 *LQR* 398–403.

—— (ed), *Landlord and Tenant Law: Past, Present and Future* (2006) Oxford: Hart Publishing.

—— *Landlord and Tenant Law in Context* (2007) Oxford: Hart Publishing.

Brudner, A, *The Unity of the Common Law: Studies in Hegelian Jurisprudence* (1995) Berkeley, CA: University of California Press.

Bruinsma, JF, 'Ongehoorzaam in en buiten de Rechtsorde' (1983) *NJB* 125–8.

Budlender, G, 'Justiciability of the Right to Housing: The South African Experience' in S Leckie (ed), *National Perspectives on Housing Rights* (2003) The Hague: Martinus Nijhoff 207–19.

Budlender, G, Latsky, J and Roux, T, *Juta's New Land Law* (1998) Cape Town: Juta.

Burmeister, J et al (eds) *Verfassungsstaatlichkeit: Festschrift für Klaus Stern zum 65. Geburtstag* (1997) Munich: CH Beck.

Butler, A, *Cyril Ramaphosa* (2007) Johannesburg: Jacana Media.

Butt, P, *Land Law* (3rd edn, 1996) Sydney: LBC Information Services.

C

Caldwell, LK, 'Rights of Ownership or Rights of Use? The Need for a New Conceptual Basis for Land Use Policy' (1975) 6 *Environmental LR* 409–25.

Carey Miller, DL (with Pope, A), *Land Title in South Africa* (2000) Cape Town: Juta.

Caterina, R, 'Some Comparative Remarks on *JA Pye (Oxford) Ltd v The United Kingdom*' (2007) 15 *European Rev of Private Law* 273–9.

Cilliers, JB and Van der Merwe, CG, 'The "Year and a Day Rule" in South African Law: Do our Courts Have a Discretion to Order Damages instead of Removal in the Case of Structural Encroachments on Neighbouring Land?' (1994) 57 *THRHR* 587–93.

Cilliers, P, 'Complexity, Deconstruction and Relativism' (2005) 22 *Theory Culture Society* 255–67 (http://tcs.sagepub.com/cgi/content/abstract/22/5/255) (accessed 4 September 2007).

Clarke, D, 'Long Residential Leases: Future Directions' in S Bright (ed), *Landlord and Tenant Law: Past, Present and Future* (2006) Oxford: Hart Publishing 171–90.

Cohen, FS, 'Transcendental Nonsense and the Functional Approach' (1935) 35 *Columbia LR* 809–49.

Cohen, MR, 'Property and Sovereignty' (1927) 13 *Cornell LQ* 8–30.

Coombe, RJ, '"Same as it Ever Was": Rethinking the Politics of Legal Interpretation' (1989) 34 *McGill LJ* 603–52.

Cooper, WE, *Landlord and Tenant* (2nd edn, 1994) Cape Town: Juta.

Corbett, MM, 'Trust Law in the 90s: Challenges and Change' (1993) 56 *THRHR* 262–70.

Cover, RM, *Justice Accused: Antislavery and the Judicial Process* (1975) New Haven: Yale University Press.

Cowen, DV, *New Patterns of Landownership. The Transformation of the Concept of Landownership as Plena in Re Potestas* (1984) Johannesburg: University of the Witwatersrand, Faculty of Law.

Crenshaw, K, 'A Black Feminist Critique of Antidiscrimination Law and Politics' in D Kairys (ed), *The Politics of Law: A Progressive Critique* (3rd edn, 1998) New York: Basic Books 356–80.

Cross, CR and Haines, RJ (eds), *Towards Freehold: Options for Land and Development in South Africa's Black Rural Areas* (1988) Cape Town: Juta.

Cunningham, R, Stoebuck, W and Whitman, D, *The Law of Property* (1984) St Paul, MN: West Publishing.

D

Depenheuer, O, 'Der Mieter als Eigentümer' (1993) 46 *NJW* 2561–4.

—— 'Entwicklungslinien des verfassungsrechtlichen Eigentumsschutzes in Deutschland 1949–2001' in T von Danwitz, O Depenheuer and C Engel, *Bericht zur Lage des Eigentums* (2002) Berlin: Springer 109–213.

De Vos, P, 'A Bridge too Far? History as Context in the Interpretation of the South African Constitution' (2001) 17 *SAJHR* 1–33.

Didiza, T, Address, National Land Summit, Johannesburg (27–30 July 2005), http://land.pwv.gov.za/publications/news/speeches/Land%20Summit.2005.01.doc (accessed 18 June 2008).

Dietlein, J, *Die Lehre von den grundrechtlichen Schutzpflichten* (1992) Berlin: Duncker & Humblot.

Diggins, JP, *The Promise of Pragmatism* (1994) Chicago, IL: University of Chicago Press.

Du Plessis, L, '"Subsidiarity": What's in the Name for Constitutional Interpretation and Adjudication?' (2006) 17 *Stell LR* 207–31.

Du Preez, M, *Oranje Blanje Blues: 'n Nostalgiese Trip—Vrye Weekblad 88–94* (2005) Cape Town: Zebra Press.

Du Toit, P, 'Vrae oor Hanekom se Grondhervorming', *Finansies & Tegniek* (15 June 1995) 106.

Dukeminier, J and Krier, JE, *Property* (5th edn, 2002) New York: Aspen Publishers.

E

Edwards, M, 'Application for Order for Possession of Land: Whether Defendant could Raise as Defence a Claim of Infringement of Art. 8 of the European Convention on Human Rights' (2005) *J Planning & Env Law* 1241–52.

Elvin, D, 'Human Rights and Property Law' (Nov 2005) Landmark Chambers, http://www.landmarkchambers.co.uk/upload/docs/Blundell_Elvin_June-2006.pdf (accessed 18 June 2008).

Engel, C, 'Die Soziale Funktion des Eigentums' in T von Danwitz, O Depenheuer and C Engel, *Bericht zur Lage des Eigentums* (2002) Berlin: Springer 9–107.

Epstein, RA, 'Past and Future: The Temporal Dimension in the Law of Property' (1986) 64 *Washington Univ LQ* 667–722.

F

Feenstra, R, 'Historische Aspecten van de Private Eigendom als Rechtsinstituut' 1976 *RM Themis* 248–75.

—— 'Hugo de Groot's Eerste Beschouwingen over *Dominium* en over de Oorsprong van de Private Eigendom: *Mare Liberum* en zijn Bronnen' 1976 *Acta Juridica* 269–82.

—— 'Der Eigentumsbegriff bei Hugo Grotius im Licht einiger mittelalterlicher und spätscholastischer Quellen' in O Behrends, M Diesselhorst, H Lange, D Liebs, JG Wolf and C Wollschlaeger (eds), *Festschrift für Franz Wieacker zum 70. Geburtstag* (1978) Gottingen: Vandenhoeck & Ruprecht 209–34.

—— *Ius in Re: Het Begrip Zakelijk Recht in Historisch Perspectief* (Thorbecke-Colleges no 4) (1979) Leiden: Universitaire Pers/Zwolle: WEJ Tjeenk Willink.

Fennell, LA, 'Efficient Trespass: The Case for "Bad Faith" Adverse Possession' (2006) 100 *Northwestern Univ LR* 1037–96.

Feyerabend, P, *Against Method: Outline of an Anarchistic Theory of Knowledge* (1978) Los Angeles: Verso.

Flockton, C, 'Employment, Welfare Support and Income Distribution in East Germany' in C Flockton and E Kolinsky (eds), *Recasting East Germany: Social Transformation after the GDR* (1999) London: Routledge 33–51.

—— 'Policy Agendas and the Economy in Germany and Europe' in C Flockton, E Kolinsky and R Pritchard (eds), *The New Germany in the East: Policy, Agendas and Social Developments since Unification* (2000) London: Routledge 61–86.

Fox, L, *Conceptualising Home: Theories, Laws and Policies* (2007) Oxford: Hart Publishing.

G

Gabel, P and Kennedy, D, 'Roll over Beethoven' (1984) 36 *Stanford LR* 1–55

Gevisser, M, *Thabo Mbeki: The Dream Deferred* (2007) Johannesburg: Jonathan Ball.

Gildenhuys, A, 'Evictions: A Quagmire for the Unwary' 1999 (Sep) *Butterworths Property Law Digest* 5–11.

—— *Onteieningsreg* (2nd edn, 2001) Durban: Butterworths.

Giliomee, H, *The Afrikaners: Biography of a People* (2003) Charlottesville, VA: University of Virginia Press.

Giliomee, H and Elphick, R, *The Shaping of South African Society, 1652–1840* (2nd edn, 1989) Middletown: Wesleyan University Press.

Gordon, RW, 'Paradoxical Property' in J Brewer and S Staves (eds), *Early Modern Conceptions of Property* (1996) London: Routledge 95–110.

Gramsci, A, 'The Intellectuals' in *Selections from the Prison Notebooks 5* (1971) New York: International Publishers.

Gray, K, 'Property in Thin Air' (1991) 50 *Cambridge LJ* 252–307.

—— 'Human Property Rights: The Politics of Expropriation' (2005) 16 *Stell LR* 398–412.

—— 'There's no Place like Home!' (2007) 11 *Journal of South Pacific Law* 73–88.

Gray, K and Gray, SF, 'The Idea of Property in Land' in S Bright and J Dewar (eds), *Land Law: Themes and Perspectives* (1998) Oxford: Oxford University Press 15–51.

—— *Elements of Land Law* (4th edn, 2005) Oxford: Oxford University Press.

Gretton, GL, '*Pye*: A Scottish View' (2007) 15 *European Rev of Private Law* 281–8.

Grotius, H, *Inleidinge tot de Hollandsche Rechts–Geleerdheid* (1619–1621), F Dovring, HFWD Fischer and EM Meijers (eds) (1952) Leyden: Universitaire Pers.

H

Hale, RL, 'Coercion and Distribution in a Supposedly Non-Coercive State' (1923) 38 *Political Science Qly* 470–94.

Harpum, C, *Megarry & Wade The Law of Real Property* (6th edn, 2000) London: Sweet & Maxwell.

Harris, CI, 'Whiteness as Property' (1993) 106 *Harvard LR* 1707–91.

Harris, JW, *Property and Justice* (1996) Oxford: Oxford University Press.

Hart, HLA, *The Concept of Law* (1961) Oxford: Oxford University Press

Helmholz, RH, 'Adverse Possession and Subjective Intent' (1983) 61 *Washington Univ LQ* 331–58.

Helmholz, RH, 'More on Subjective Intent: A Response to Professor Cunningham' (1986) 64 *Washington Univ LQ* 65–106.

Hobsbawm, EJ, *Bandits* (2nd edn, 2000) London: Weidenfeld & Nicholson.

Hogan, G and Whyte, G, *JM Kelly: The Irish Constitution* (4th edn, 2003) Dublin: Butterworths.

Hohfeld, WN, 'Some Fundamental Legal Conceptions as Applied in Judicial Reasoning' (1913) 23 *Yale LJ* 16–59.

—— 'Fundamental Legal Conceptions as Applied in Legal Reasoning' (1917) 26 *Yale LJ* 710–70.

Holmes, OW, 'The Path of the Law' (1897) 10 *Harvard LR* 457–78; republished (1997) 110 *Harvard LR* 991–1009.

Home, R, 'Land Titling and Urban Development in Developing Countries: The Challenge of Hernando de Soto's *The Mystery of Capital*' (2003) 2 *Journal of Commonwealth Law & Legal Education* 73–88.

Honoré, AM, 'Ownership' in AG Guest (ed), *Oxford Essays in Jurisprudence* (1961) Oxford: Oxford University Press 107–47.

Hughes, D, and Davis, M, 'Human Rights and the Triumph of Property: The Marginalisation of the European Convention on Human Rights in Housing Law' (2006) Nov/Dec *Conveyancer & Property Lawyer* 526–52.

Hutchinson, AC, 'Introduction' in AC Hutchinson (ed), *Critical Legal Studies* (1989) Totowa, NJ: Rowan & Littlefield 1–11.

I

Immink, PWA, '"Eigendom" en "Heerlijkheid": Exponenten van Tweёrlei Maatschappelijke Structuur' (1959) 27 *Tijdschrift Rechtsgeschiedenis* 36–74.

J

Jacobs, HM (ed), *Private Property in the 21st Century: The Future of an American Ideal* (2004) Northampton, MA: Edward Elgar.

Josson, M, *Schets van het Recht van de Zuid-Afrikaanse Republiek* (1897) Gent: Vanderpoorten.

K

Kahn, E, Havenga, M, Havenga, P and Lotz, J, *Principles of the Law of Sale and Lease* (1998) Cape Town: Juta.

Kairys, D, 'Introduction' in D Kairys (ed), *The Politics of Law: A Progressive Critique* (3rd edn, 1998) New York: Basic Books 1–20.

Kaser, M, *Das römische Privatrecht* (2nd edn, 1971) Munich: CH Beck.

Keightley, R, 'The Impact of the Extension of Security of Tenure Act on an Owner's Right to Vindicate Immovable Property' (1999) 15 *SAJHR* 277–307.

Kennedy, D, 'Form and Substance in Private Law Adjudication' (1976) 89 *Harvard LR* 1685–778.

—— 'The Structure of Blackstone's *Commentaries*' (1979) 28 *Buffalo LR* 209–382.

Klare, K, 'Legal Culture and Transformative Constitutionalism' (1998) 14 *SAJHR* 146–88.

Kommers, DP, *The Constitutional Jurisprudence of the Federal Republic of Germany* (2nd edn, 1997) Durham, NC: Duke University Press.

Küchenhoff, E, 'Demonstrative Hausbesetzungen' (1981) *Berliner Mieter-Zeitung* 9–10

—— 'Zur Strafbarkeit von Hausbesetzungen' (1981) *Demokratie und Recht* 300–1.

Kuhn, TS, *The Structure of Scientific Revolutions* (1962; 2nd edn, 1970) Chicago, IL: University of Chicago Press.

L

Labov, W, *Language in the Inner City: Studies in the Black English Vernacular* (1972) University of Pennsylvania Press.

Langa, P, 'Transformative Constitutionalism' (2006) 17 *Stell LR* 351–60.

Le Roux, W, 'Bridges, Clearings and Labyrinths: The Architectural Framing of Post-Apartheid Constitutionalism' (2004) 19 *SAPL* 629–75.

Le Roux, W and Van Marle, K, 'Postmodernism(s) and the Law' in C Roederer and D Moellendorf (eds), *Jurisprudence* (2004) Cape Town: Juta 354–81.

Lévinas, E, *Totality and Infinity: An Essay on Exteriority* (1969) Pittsburgh, PA: Duquesne University Press.

Lewis, C, 'The Prevention of Illegal Squatting Act: The Promotion of Homelessness?' (1989) 5 *SAJHR* 233–9.

—— 'The Modern Concept of Ownership of Land' 1985 *Acta Juridica* (also published as TW Bennett, WHB Dean, DB Hutchison, L Leeman and D Van Zyl Smit (eds), *Land Ownership: Changing Concepts* (1986) Cape Town: Juta) 241–66.

Liebenberg, S, 'The Right to Social Assistance: The Implications of *Grootboom* for Policy Reform in South Africa' (2001) 17 *SAJHR* 232–57.

—— 'Needs, Rights and Transformation: Adjudicating Social Rights' (2006) 17 *Stell LR* 5–36.

Luba, J, 'Residential Possession Proceedings and Article 8 (Part 2): The Impact on the Private Sector' (2002) 6(2) *L&T Rev* 9–12.

M

Maasdorp, AFS, *The Institutes of Cape Law*, Part 3 The Law of Things (1903) Cape Town: Juta.

Mahomed, I, 'The Future of Roman-Dutch Law in Southern Africa, Particularly in Lesotho' 1985 *Lesotho LJ* 357–65.

Mahoney, MR, 'Segregation, Whiteness, and Transformation' (1995) 143 *Univ Pennsylvania LR* 1659–84.

Marais, H, *South Africa: Limits of Change. The Political Economy of Transformation* (1998) Cape Town: University of Cape Town Press.

Matsuda, MJ, 'Looking to the Bottom: Critical Legal Studies and Reparations' (1987) 22 *Harvard Civil Rights–Civil Liberties LR* 323–99.

Merrill, TW, 'Property Rules, Liability Rules and Adverse Possession' (1985) 79 *Northwestern Univ LR* 1122–54

Michelman, FI, 'Property, Utility and Fairness: Comments on the Ethical Foundations of "Just Compensation' Law" (1967) 80 *Harvard LR* 1165–258.

—— 'The Supreme Court 1968 Term—Foreword: On Protecting the Poor through the Fourteenth Amendment' (1969) 83 *Harvard LR* 7–59.

—— 'Formal and Associational Aims in Procedural Due Process' in JR Pennock and JW Chapman (eds), *Due Process (NOMOS XVIII)* (1977) New York: New York University Press 126–71.

—— 'Property as a Constitutional Right' (1981) 38 *Wash & Lee LR* 1097–114.

—— 'Possession vs Distribution in the Constitutional Idea of Property' (1987) 72 *Iowa LR* 1319–50.

—— 'Takings, 1987' (1988) 88 *Columbia LR* 1600–29.

—— 'The Bill of Rights, the Common Law, and the Freedom-friendly State' (2003) 58 *Univ Miami LR* 401–48.

Milo, JM, 'On the Constitutional Proportionality of Property Law in The Netherlands' (2007) 15 *European Rev of Private Law* 255–63.

Minda, G, *Postmodern Legal Movements: Law and Jurisprudence at Century's End* (1995) New York: New York University Press.

Moseneke, D, 'The Fourth Bram Fischer Memorial Lecture: Transformative Adjudication' (2002) 18 *SAJHR* 309–19.

Mostert, H and Fitzpatrick, P, '"Living in the Margins of History on the Edge of the Country" Legal Foundation and the Richtersveld Community's Title to Land' 2004 *TSAR* 309–23, 498–510.

Mukheiber, A, 'The Effect of the Rental Housing Act 50 of 1999 on the Common Law of Landlord and Tenant' (2000) 21 *Obiter* 325–50.

Munzer, SR, *A Theory of Property* (1990) Cambridge: Cambridge University Press.

—— 'Property as Social Relations' in SR Munzer (ed), *New Essays in the Legal and Political Theory of Property* (2001) Cambridge: Cambridge University Press 36–75.

Murray, C and O'Regan, C (eds), *No Place to Rest: Forced Removals and the Law in South Africa* (1990) Oxford: Oxford University Press/Cape Town: Labour Law Unit, University of Cape Town.

N

Nedelsky, J, *Private Property and the Limits of American Constitutionalism: The Madisonian Framework* (1990) Chicago, IL: University of Chicago Press.
—— 'Reconceiving Rights as Relationship' (1993) 1 *Rev Const Studies* 1–26.
Norman, C, 'Compulsory Purchase Compensation: Limitation after *Pye v United Kingdom*' 2006 (Apr) *J Planning & Env Law* 454–62.

O

O'Connor, P, 'The Private Taking of Land: Adverse Possession, Encroachment by Buildings and Improvement under a Mistake' (2006) 33 *Univ of Western Australia LR* 31–62.
—— 'An Adjudication Rule for Encroachment Disputes: Adverse Possession or a Building Encroachment Statute?' in E Cooke (ed), *Modern Studies in Property Law, Vol IV* (2007) Oxford: Hart Publishing 197–217.

P

Peñalver, EM, 'Property as Entrance' (2005) 91 *Virginia LR* 1889–972.
—— 'Reconstructing Richard Epstein' (2006) 15 *William & Mary Bill of Rights J* 429–37.
Peñalver, EM and Katyal, SK, 'Property Outlaws' (2007) 155 *Univ Pennsylvania LR* 1095–186
Pienaar, JM, 'Recent Developments Relating to Automatic Review Proceedings in the Land Claims Court' (2001) 34 *De Jure* 162–71.
Pienaar, JM and Mostert, H, 'Uitsettings onder die Suid-Afrikaanse Grondwet: Die Verhouding tussen Artikel 25(1), Artikel 26(3) en die Uitsettingswet (Deel 1)' 2006 *TSAR* 277–99.
Pienaar, JM and Muller, A, 'The Impact of the Prevention of Illegal Eviction from and Unlawful Occupation of Land Act 19 of 1998 on Homelessness and Unlawful Occupation within the Present Statutory Framework' (1999) 10 *Stell LR* 370–96.
Pieterse, M, 'What do we mean when we Talk about Transformative Constitutionalism?' (2005) 20 *SAPL* 155–66.
Platzky, L and Walker, C, *The Surplus People: Forced Removals in South Africa* (1985) Johannesburg: Ravan Press.
Pogany, IS, *Righting Wrongs in Eastern Europe* (1997) Manchester: Manchester University Press.
Pope, A, 'Encroachment or Accession? The Importance of the Extent of Encroachment in Light of South African Constitutional Principles' (2007) 124 *SALJ* 537–56.
Posner, RA, *Economic Analysis of the Law* (6th edn, 2003) New York: Aspen Law & Business.
Potgieter, JM, 'The Role of the Law in a Period of Political Transition: The Need for Objectivity' (1991) 54 *THRHR* 800–97.
Powelson, JP, *The Story of Land. A World History of Land Tenure and Agrarian Reform* (1988) Cambridge, MA: Lincoln Institute of Land Policy.
Proudhon, PJ, 'Avertissement aux Propriétaires' in C Bouglé and H Moysset (eds) *Oeuvres Complètes de PJ Proudhon*, vol XIV (new edn, 1938) Paris: Librairie Marcel Riviére.

Q

Quack, F (ed), *Münchener Kommentar zum BGB* Band IV *Sachenrecht* (1986) Munich: CH Beck.

R

Radin, MJ, 'Property and Personhood' (1982) 34 *Stanford LR* 957–1015.

—— 'Time, Possession, and Alienation' (1986) 64 *Washington Univ LQ* 739–58.

—— 'Market-Inalienability' (1987) 100 *Harvard LR* 1849–937.

—— *Contested Commodities* (1996) Cambridge: Cambridge University Press.

Radley-Gardner, O, '*Pye (Oxford) Ltd v United Kingdom*: The View from England' (2007) 15 *European Rev of Private Law* 289–308.

Rawls, J, *A Theory of Justice* (1971) Cambridge, MA: Belknap Press of Harvard University Press.

Reehuis, WHM and Heisterkamp, AHT, with Van Maanen, GE and De Jong GT, *Pitlo Het Nederlands Burgerlijk Recht, Vol 3, Goederenrecht* (11th edn, 2001; 12th revised and expanded edn, 2006) Deventer: Kluwer.

Reich, CA, 'The New Property' (1964) 73 *Yale LJ* 733–87.

Republic of South Africa, Department of Land Affairs, *White Paper on South African Land Policy* (1997) http://land.pwv.gov.za/legislation_policies/white_papers/_docs/White%20Paper%20land%20policy.doc (accessed 11 March 2008).

Robertson, M, 'Land and Human Rights in South Africa (A Reply to Marcus and Skweyiya)' (1990) 6 *SAJHR* 215–27.

Rose, CM, 'The Comedy of the Commons: Custom, Commerce, and Inherently Public Property' (1986) 53 *Univ Chicago LR* 711–81.

—— *Property and Persuasion: Essays on the History, Theory, and Rhetoric of Ownership* (1994) Boulder, CO: Westview Press.

—— 'Canons of Property Talk, or, Blackstone's Anxiety' (1998) 108 *Yale LJ* 601–32.

Ross, T, 'The Rhetoric of Poverty: Their Immorality, Our Helplessness' (1991) 79 *Georgetown LJ* 1499–1547.

Roux, T, 'Chapter 7: The Extension of Security of Tenure Act' in G Budlender, J Latsky and T Roux, *Juta's New Land Law* (1998) Cape Town: Juta.

—— 'Continuity and Change in a Transforming Legal Order: The Impact of Section 26(3) of the Constitution on South African Law' (2004) 121 *SALJ* 466–92.

—— 'Pro-Poor Court, Anti-Poor Outcomes: Explaining the Performance of the South African Land Claims Court' (2004) 20 *SAJHR* 511–43.

Rowan-Robinson, J, 'Working Together for Access' in P Jackson and DC Wilde (eds), *Property Law: Current Issues and Debates* (1999) Aldershot: Dartmouth Ashgate 1–13.

Ruffert, M, *Vorrang der Verfassung und Eigenständigkeit des Privatrechts* (2001) Tubingen: Mohr Siebeck.

S

Sachs, A, *Protecting Human Rights in a New South Africa* (1990) Oxford: Oxford University Press.

Sagaert, V, 'Prescription in French and Belgian Property Law after the *Pye* Judgment' (2007) 15 *European Rev of Private Law* 265–72.

Schall, H, 'Hausbesetzungen im Lichte der Auslegung des § 123 StGB' (1983) 3(6) *Neue Zeitschrift für Strafrecht* 241–7.

Schlag, P, 'Rights in the Postmodern Condition' in A Sarat and TR Kearns (eds), *Legal Rights: Historical and Philosophical Perspectives* (1997) Ann Arbor: University of Michigan Press 263–304.

Schnably, S, 'Property and Pragmatism: A Critique of Radin's Theory of Property and Personhood' (1993) 45 *Stanford LR* 347–407.

Scholtens, JE, 'Infringement and Protection of Ownership' 1956 *ASSAL* 129–36.

Schoombee, JT, 'Group Areas Legislation: The Political Control of Ownership and Occupation of Land' 1985 *Acta Juridica* 77–118.

Schotmans, A, 'De Middelburgse Fopspeen Herwogen' (1982) 8 *Recht & Kritiek* 463–6.

Schrage, EJH, *Koop Breekt Geen Huur: Enige Grepen uit de Geschiedenis van het Geleerde Recht inzake de Gevolgen van de Vervreemding van een Verhuurde Zaak* (1984) Deventer: Kluwer.

Schutte, RM and Vranken, JBM, 'Gebruik van Woonruimte en Woonrecht' in JJM De Vries, RM Schutte and JBM Vranken, *Eigendom en Woonrecht* (1981) Deventer: Kluwer 65–127.

Scott, S, 'Recent Developments in Case Law Regarding Neighbour Law and its Influence on the Concept of Ownership' (2005) 16 *Stell LR* 351–77.

Scott, TJ and Visser, D (eds) *Developing Delict: Essays in Honour of Robert Feenstra* (2000) Cape Town: Juta (also published as *Acta Juridica* 2000).

Sen, A, *Resources, Values, and Development* (1984) Cambridge, MA: Harvard University Press.

Simon, W, 'The Invention and Reinvention of Welfare Rights' (1985) 44 *Maryland LR* 1–37.

—— 'Rights and Redistribution in the Welfare System' (1986) 38 *Stanford LR* 1431–516.

Singer, JW, 'Legal Realism Now' (1988) 76 *California LR* 467–544.

—— *Property Law: Rules, Policies, and Practices* (1993; 3rd edn, 2002) Boston: Aspen Law & Business.

—— 'No Right to Exclude: Public Accommodations and Private Property' (1996) 90 *Northwestern Univ LR* 1283–497.

—— 'Property and Equality: Public Accommodations and the Constitution in South Africa and the United States' (1997) 12 *SAPL* 53–86.

—— *The Edges of the Field: Lessons on the Obligations of Ownership* (2000) Boston, MA: Beacon Press.

—— *Entitlement: The Paradoxes of Property* (2000) New Haven, NJ: Yale University Press.

—— 'After the Flood: Equality and Humanity in Property Relations' (2006) 52 *Loyola LR* 243–343

Singer, JW and Beerman, JM, 'The Social Origins of Property' (1993) 6 *Canadian Journal of Law & Jur* 217–48.

Sprankling, JG, 'An Environmental Critique of Adverse Possession' (1994) 79 *Cornell LR* 816–84.

Stern, K, *Das Staatsrecht der Bundesrepublik Deutschland*, vols I–V (1994–2005) Munich: CH Beck.

Stern, K, 'Die Grundrechte und ihre Schranken' in P Badura and H Dreier (eds), *Festschrift 50 Jahre Bundesverfassungsgericht, Vol 2 Klärung und Fortbildung des Verfassungsrechts* (2001) Munich: CH Beck 1–34.

Swadling, W, 'Property: General Principles' in P Birks (ed), *English Private Law, Vol I* (2000) Oxford: Oxford University Press 203–384.

Swain, S and Clarke, A, 'Negotiating Postmodernity: Narratives of Law and Imperialism' (1995) 6 *Law & Critique* 229–56.

T

Teitel, RG, *Transitional Justice* (2000) Oxford: Oxford University Press.

Ten Berg-Koolen, J, 'Invoering van de Naamloze Dagvaarding; de Kraker Gekraakt?' (1987) 10 *NJB* 306–14

Terreblanche, SJ, *A History of Inequality in South Africa, 1652–2002* (2002) Scottsville: University of Natal Press.

Thibaut, AFJ, 'Über Dominium Directum und Utile' in *Versuche über Einzelne Theile der Theorie des Rechts* (1817, reprint 1970), Aalen, vol I, part II, 67–9.

Thomas, JAC, *Textbook of Roman Law* (1976) Cape Town: Juta.

Thomas, Ph J, 'The Rental Housing Act' (2000) 33 *De Jure* 235–47.

Tomann, H, 'Germany' in P Balchin (ed), *Housing Policy in Europe* (1996) London: Routledge 51–68

Tushnet, M, 'An Essay on Rights' (1984) 62 *Texas LR* 1363–403.

U

Underkuffler, LS, 'On Property: An Essay' (1990) 100 *Yale LJ* 127–48.

—— *The Idea of Property: Its Meaning and Power* (2003) Oxford: Oxford University Press.

United Kingdom Law Commission, *Report on Forfeiture of Tenancies* (1985) Law Com No 142.

—— *Termination of Tenancies Bill* (1994) Law Com No 221.

—— *Termination of Tenancies for Tenant Default* (2006) Law Com No 303.

United Nations, South Africa Human Development Report (2003).

V

Van den Bergh, GCJJ, *Eigendom: Grepen uit de Geschiedenis van een Omstreden Begrip* (2nd edn, 1988) Deventer: Kluwer.

Van der Merwe, CG, *Sakereg* (1979; 2nd edn, 1989) Durban: Butterworths.

Van der Walt, AJ, 'The Effect of Environmental Conservation Measures on the Concept of Landownership' (1987) 104 *SALJ* 469–79.

—— 'Towards the Development of Post-Apartheid Land Law: An Exploratory Survey' (1990) 23 *De Jure* 1–45.

—— 'De Onrechtmatige Bezetting van Leegstaande Woningen en het Eigendomsbegrip: Een Vergelijkende Analyse van het Conflict tussen de Privaat Eigendom van Onroerend Goed en Dakloosheid' (1991) 17 *Recht & Kritiek* 329–59.

—— (ed), *Land Reform and the Future of Landownership in South Africa* (1991) Cape Town: Juta.

—— 'Der Eigentumsbegriff' in R Feenstra and R Zimmermann (eds) *Das römisch-holländische Recht* (1992) Berlin: Dunker & Humblot 485–520.

—— 'Squatting and the Right to Shelter' (1992) *TSAR* 40–55.

—— 'Ownership and Personal Freedom: Subjectivism in Bernhard Windscheid's Theory of Ownership' (1993) 56 *THRHR* 569–89.

—— 'Tradition on Trial: A Critical Analysis of the Civil-Law Tradition in South African Property Law' (1995) 11 *SAJHR* 169–206.

—— 'Unity and Pluralism in Property Theory: A Review of Property Theories and Debates in Recent Literature' 1995 *TSAR* 15–42.

—— 'Subject and Society in Property Theory: A Review of Property Theories and Debates in Recent Literature' 1995 *TSAR* 322–45.

—— 'Rights and Reforms in Property Theory: A Review of Property Theories and Debates in Recent Literature' 1995 *TSAR* 493–526.

—— 'Marginal Notes on Powerful(l) Legends: Critical Perspectives on Property Theory' (1995) 58 *THRHR* 396–420.

Bibliography

Van der Walt, AJ, 'Un-doing Things with Words: The Colonization of the Public Sphere by Private Property Discourse' 1998 *Acta Juridica* (also published as G Bradfield and D Van der Merwe (eds), *'Meaning' in Legal Interpretation* (1998) Cape Town: Juta) 235–81.

—— *Constitutional Property Clauses: A Comparative Analysis* (1999) Cape Town: Juta/Kluwer International.

—— 'Compensation for Excessive or Unfair Regulation: A Comparative Overview of Constitutional Practice Relating to Regulatory Takings' (1999) 14 *SAPL* 273–331.

—— 'Property Rights and Hierarchies of Power: A Critical Evaluation of Land-Reform Policy in South Africa' (1999) 64 *Koers* 259–94.

—— 'Modernity, Normality, and Meaning: The Struggle between Progress and Stability and the Politics of Interpretation' (2000) 11 *Stell LR* 21–49, 226–43.

—— 'Dancing with Codes—Protecting, Developing, Limiting and Deconstructing Property Rights in the Constitutional State' (2001) 118 *SALJ* 258–311.

—— 'Exclusivity of Ownership, Security of Tenure, and Eviction Orders: A Critical Evaluation of Recent Case Law' (2002) 18 *SAJHR* 372–420.

—— 'Exclusivity of Ownership, Security of Tenure, and Eviction Orders: A Model to Evaluate South African Land-Reform Legislation' (2002) *TSAR* 254–89.

—— 'Protecting Social Participation Rights within the Property Paradigm: A Critical Reappraisal' in E Cooke (ed), Modern *Studies in Property Law, Vol II* (2003) Oxford: Hart Publishing 27–41.

—— 'A South African Reading of Frank Michelman's Theory of Social Justice' (2004) 19 *SAPL* 253–307 (also published in H Botha, A Van der Walt, and J Van der Walt (eds), *Rights and Democracy in a Transformative Constitution* (2003) Stellenbosch: African Sun Media 163–211).

—— 'Striving for the Better Interpretation: A Critical Reflection on the Constitutional Court's *Harksen* and *FNB* Decisions on the Property Clause' (2004) 121 *SALJ* 854–78.

—— 'The Property Clause in the New Federal Constitution of the Swiss Confederation 1999' (2004) 15 *Stell LR* 326–32.

—— *Constitutional Property Law* (2005) Cape Town: Juta.

—— 'Ownership and Eviction: Constitutional Rights in Private Law' (2005) 9 *Edinburgh LR* 32–64.

—— 'Property Theory and the Transformation of Property Law' in E Cooke (ed), *Modern Studies in Property Law, Vol III* (2005) Oxford: Hart Publishing 361–80.

—— 'Rendition/Eviction: A Post-Apartheid Reflection' (2005) 15 *Law & Critique* 321–44.

—— 'Transformative Constitutionalism and the Development of South African Property Law' (2005) *TSAR* 655–89; (2006) *TSAR* 1–31.

—— 'Legal History, Legal Culture and Transformation in a Constitutional Democracy' (2006) 12 *Fundamina* 1–47.

—— 'Developing the Law on Unlawful Squatting and Spoliation' (2008) 125 *SALJ* 24–36.

—— 'Property, Social Justice and Citizenship: The Transformation of Property Law in Post-Apartheid South Africa' (2008) 19 *Stell LR* 325–46.

—— 'Replacing Property Rules with Liability Rules: Encroachment by Building' (2008) 125 *SALJ* 604–40.

—— 'Property and Marginality' in GS Alexander and E Peñalver (eds), *Law and Community* (forthcoming, 2009).

Van der Walt, AJ and Kleyn, DG, 'Duplex Dominium: The History and Significance of the Concept of Divided Ownership' in DP Visser (ed), *Essays on the History of Law* (1989) Cape Town: Juta 213–60.

Van der Walt, JWG, 'The Critique of Subjectivism and its Implications for Property Law: Towards a Deconstructive Republican Theory of Property' in GE van Maanen and AJ van der Walt (eds), *Property Law on the Threshold of the 21st Century* (1996) Antwerpen: Maklu 115–59.

Van der Walt, JWG, *Law and Sacrifice: Towards a Post-Apartheid Theory of Law* (2005) London: Routledge Cavendish.

Van Iterson, W, 'Beschouwingen over Rolverwisseling of Eigendomsverschuiving' in *Verslagen en Mededelingen van de Vereniging tot Uitgave der Bronnen van het Oud-Vaderlandsch Recht* XIII, no 3 (1971) 407–66.

Van Maanen, GE, 'Kraken als Onrechtmatig Daad, of: De Grensoverschrijdende Speculant' (1981) 7 *Recht & Kritiek* 5–17.

—— 'Balanceren op de Grens van de Rechtsorde' (1982) 8 *Recht & Kritiek* 467–71.

—— *Eigendomsschijnbewegingen: Juridische, Historische en Politiek-Filosofische Opmerkingen over Eigendom* (1987) Nijmegen: Ars Aequi Libri.

Van Onselen, C, *The Seed is Mine: The Life of Kas Maine, A South African Sharecropper 1894–1985* (1996) Johannesburg: Jonathan Ball.

—— *The Fox and the Flies: The World of Joseph Silver, Racketeer and Psychopath* (2007) London: Jonathan Cape

Vilhjálmsdóttir, HD, 'Housing Support and Public Housing Funds in Iceland and Abroad' (2004) 4 *Monetary Bulletin* at http://www.sedlabanki.is/lisalib/getfile.aspx?itemid=2866 (accessed 9 June 2008).

Visser, DP, 'The "Absoluteness" of Ownership: The South African Common Law in Perspective' 1985 *Acta Juridica* (also published as TW Bennett, WHB Dean, DB Hutchison, L Leeman and D Van Zyl Smit (eds), *Land Ownership: Changing Concepts* (1986) Cape Town: Juta) 39–52.

—— 'The Legal Historian as Subversive or: Killing the Capitoline Geese' in DP Visser (ed), *Essays on the History of Law* (1989) Cape Town: Juta 1–31.

Von Jhering, R, 'Im juristischen Begriffshimmel' in *Scherz und Ernst in der Jurisprudenz* (1909) Boston: Adamant Media Corp.

W

Waldron, J, *Liberal Rights: Collected Papers, 1981–1991* (1993) Cambridge: Cambridge University Press.

—— 'Rights and Needs: The Myth of Disjunction' in A Sarat and TR Kearns (eds), *Legal Rights: Historical and Philosophical Perspectives* (2nd edn, 1997) Ann Arbor: University of Michigan Press 87–109.

Wessels, JW, *History of the Roman-Dutch Law* (1908) Grahamstown: African Book Company.

West, C, *Prophesy of Deliverance! An Afro-American Revolutionary Christianity* (1982) Philadelphia: Westminster Press.

Wieacker, F, *Privatrechtsgeschichte der Neuzeit* (2nd edn, 1967) Göttingen: Vandenhoeck & Ruprecht.

Wieling, HJ, *Sachenrecht* (1992) Berlin: Springer

Williams, LA, 'Welfare and Legal Entitlements: The Social Roots of Poverty' in D Kairys (ed), *The Politics of Law: A Progressive Critique* (3rd edn, 1998) New York: Basic Books 569–90.

Williams, PJ, 'Alchemical Notes: Reconstructing Ideals from Deconstructed Rights' (1987) 22 *Harvard Civil Rights–Civil Liberties LR* 401–33.

—— 'Spirit-Murdering the Messenger: The Discourse of Fingerpointing as the Law's Response to Racism' (1987) 42 *Univ Miami LR* 127–57.

Williams, PJ, *The Alchemy of Race and Rights* (1991) Cambridge, MA: Harvard University Press.

Willmore, C, 'The "Right to Roam": An Empty Dream?' in P Jackson and DC Wilde (eds), *Property Law: Current Issues and Debates* (1999) Aldershot: Dartmouth Ashgate 14–47.

Willoweit, D, 'Dominium und Proprietas—zur Entwicklung des Eigentumsbegriffs in der mittelalterlichen und neuzeitlichen Rechtswissenschaft' (1974) *Historisches Jahrbuch des Görres-Gesellschaft* 131–56.

Wordie, JR, 'The Chronology of English Enclosure 1500–1914' (1983) 36 *The Economic History Rev* 483–505.

Wunsh, B, 'May Lessee Quit Premises on Sale of Them?' (1990) 107 *SALJ* 384–7.

Z

Ziff, B, *Principles of Property Law* (4th edn, 2006) Toronto: Carswell.

Ziff, B and Rao, PV (eds), *Borrowed Power. Essays on Cultural Appropriation* (1997) New Brunswick, NJ: Rutgers University Press.

Zimmermann, R and Visser, DP, 'Introduction: South African Law as a Mixed Legal System' in R Zimmermann and DP Visser (eds), *Southern Cross: Civil Law and Common Law in South Africa* (1996) Oxford: Oxford University Press 1–30.

Websites

http://www.unicef.org/infobycountry/southafrica_statistics.html (accessed 18 June 2008)

http://www.busrep.co.za/ (accessed 29 January 2007).

http://www.info.gov.za/otherdocs/1996/gear.pdf (accessed 18 June 2008)

http://en.wikipedia.org/wiki/Squatter (accessed 18 June 2008)

http://www.surreycc.gov.uk/sccwebsite/sccwspages.nsf/LookupWebPagesByTITLE_RTF/Parliamentary+enclosure?opendocument (accessed 18 June 2008)

http://www.achr.net/Evictions%20Asia/Eviction%20Law.html (accessed 16 July 2008)

http://www.austlii.edu.au (accessed 16 October 2008)

INDEX

Introductory Note

References such as '178–9' indicate (not necessarily continuous) discussion of a topic across a range of pages. Wherever possible in the case of topics with many references, these have either been divided into sub-topics or only the most significant discussions of the topic are listed. Because the entire volume is about 'property', the use of this term (and certain others occurring throughout the work) as an entry point has been minimised. Information will be found under the corresponding detailed topics.

aboriginal land claims/rights, 11, 197, 205, 207
absence of property, 232, 238, 242
absolute ownership, 15, 29, 34–7, 179, 239
absoluteness, 25, 33–4, 36, 39, 49, 71–2
absolutism, 16, 34–7, 247
access, public, 52, 76, 170–1, 194–5, 199, 222
accommodation, alternative, 81, 101–2, 106, 121, 123, 150, 157
accommodations, public, 172, 190–2, 195
acquisition of ownership, 38, 170, 173–5, 181, 183, 204
acquisitive prescription, 52, 170, 172–88, 201, 222–3
  American Midwest, 182–7
  English law, 176–82
  South African law, 172–6
activists, 146, 192, 238, 240
adverse possession, 143, 169–70, 172–88, 199, 201, 204
  American Midwest, 182–7
  English law, 176–82
  South African law, 172–6
  transfers, 187, 209
adverse user, 170, 172–3, 176, 178, 181, 183
agricultural land, 2, 115, 123, 126, 129, 194, 197
Alexander, GS, 4, 10, 12, 16–17, 36–7, 39, 92–3
alternative accommodation, availability of, 81, 101–2, 106, 121, 123, 150, 157
alternative housing, 68–9, 226
American law:
  adverse possession, 182–7
  'property outlaws', 144–5
  public access, 190–2
anti-eviction legislation/measures, 75, 78–80, 82–4, 118–19, 122–3, 153–4, 228–9
  see also eviction
anti-eviction principle, 119, 122–3, 126
apartheid, 1–4, 12–13, 60–3, 65, 67–9, 114–15, 159
  evictions, 62, 64–5, 223

ideology, 60–1, 63, 67
land law, 25, 62–3, 65, 67, 129, 146, 205–6
politics, 2, 4, 6, 25, 64, 68, 211
system, 1–2, 7, 18
arbitrary eviction, 43, 57, 73, 84, 96, 117, 119
assumptions, 4–5, 12, 22, 31, 39–40, 200, 215–18
assured shorthold tenancies, 100–1, 103, 130
Australia, 11, 53, 55, 179, 184, 201, 207
availability of alternative accommodation, 81, 83, 101–2, 106, 121, 123, 134

bad faith, 65–6, 170, 173–4, 178, 180, 182–3, 185–8
  possessors, 170, 173, 175, 181–3, 186–7, 223
Badenhorst, PJ, 32–3, 57, 72, 115–17, 129, 172–3, 188
balance:
  of convenience, 171, 204
  fair, 50–1, 91, 112, 129, 181, 194–5, 198
Baur, F, 33, 53, 55, 57, 71, 87–8, 202–3
beliefs, cultural, 197–8
Bennett, TW, 6, 11, 53, 71–2
black South Africans, 2–3, 62–3, 65–7, 117, 167, 196–7, 205–6
  see also apartheid
Blackstone, W, 15–16, 36, 38–9, 52
bona fide see good faith
Botha, H, 8, 24, 105, 233–4
Bouckaert, B, 186
breach of the peace, 88, 138, 141–2
Bright, S, 11–12, 24, 28, 35–6, 38–9, 96–105, 108–11
Brisley case, 43–6
Budlender, G, 6, 117, 120, 123, 126–8
building encroachments, 169, 171, 199–205, 222
  Dutch law, 202–3
  English law, 201–2
  German law, 202–3
  South African law, 199–201
bundles of rights, 35, 37, 53, 72, 189–91

burden of proof, 58, 120, 124, 167
burials, 197–8

cancellation of leases/tenancies, 43, 47, 56,
      86–91, 95, 129, 131–2
Caterina, R, 174, 180–2
centrality, 37, 50, 230–6, 240–2
change in property law, 214–21
children, 149, 151, 165, 167, 233, 237
circumstances:
   personal, 27–8, 44, 58–9, 73–4, 81, 112–13,
      223
   relevant, 43, 45, 68, 83, 118–21, 123, 147–50
   social, 56, 75, 81, 83, 89, 151, 226
   surrounding, 73, 105
Civil Codes, 33, 48–9, 55, 80, 85–9, 91, 202–3
civil law systems, 28–30, 34–5, 37–40, 53–5,
      92–9, 98–9, 179–81
civil partners, 98
civil possession, 172–4
   open, 175
Cohen, FS, 35, 234
colonial dispossessions, 38, 206
common-good restrictions, 70–1
common law, 18–19, 35–8, 43–6, 63–7, 115–17,
      119–26, 151–4
   English/Anglo-American, 35–6, 38–9, 50,
      53–4, 56–7, 79, 99–100
   evictions, 63, 65, 67, 126, 131
   and Prevention of Illegal Eviction from and
      Unlawful Occupation of Land Act 19 of
      1998 (PIE), 151–2
   property rights, 35–7, 56, 119, 125
   requirements, 44–6, 120, 172
   Roman-Dutch, 63
   traditions, 28, 37, 44–5, 63, 65–6, 69,
      169–70
   uncodified, 18, 34, 96
commons, 189–90, 193, 219
compensation, 38, 55, 70–1, 87, 160, 195,
      198–205
competitive interferences, 39
compulsory sale, 200–1
consent, 33–4, 39, 42–3, 123, 129, 150, 172–3
conservatism, doctrinal, 116, 130–1
constitutional democracy, 1, 8–14, 41, 235
constitutional law, 84, 93, 231, 236
constitutional obligations, 17, 20, 69, 118, 129,
      156, 160
constitutional property, 20, 49, 90–3, 96, 196,
      228
constitutional provisions, 19–20, 40, 42, 44–5,
      51, 83, 118
constitutionalism, transformative, 8–10, 18, 20,
      63, 212, 233–4, 247
continuation of leases, 88–90, 202
control, 43–4, 61–2, 70–1, 80–1, 83, 89–90,
      189–90

due process, 81, 100, 104, 115, 122, 127,
      129–30
   exclusive, 123, 188–9
   landowner's, 56, 89, 119, 130, 160, 190, 225
   legislative, 82, 90, 135
   regulatory, 46, 73–4, 81, 126, 129, 134–5, 224
convenience, balance of, 171, 204
Cooke, E, 48, 94, 199, 201
Coombe, RJ, 18, 232, 234–5, 245
cooperation, 170, 172–3, 177
court orders, 99–102, 104–6, 118–19, 127–8,
      147–8, 158, 164
covenants, 54, 58, 99
Cowen, DV, 32–3, 71–2
cultural appropriation, 11
cultural beliefs, 197–8
culture, 23, 205, 246–7
current distribution of property rights, 10, 16,
      76, 209, 212, 215, 230
customary land rights, 205
customary law, 19, 157–8
customary marriages, 157–8

damage, 3–4, 88, 128, 194–5, 208
damages, 199–201
de Vries, JJM, 138, 140–1
death, 86–7, 97–8, 100, 134, 148, 157
decentrings, 233–41
defences, 24, 44–6, 55, 58, 110, 142, 161–3
democracy, 1–3, 6, 20, 24, 68
   constitutional, 1, 8–14, 41, 235
demolition, 49, 102, 146, 150, 200–3
   orders, 199–200
demonstrative unlawful occupation, 223
deprivation, 3, 58, 73, 120, 122, 125, 198
development:
   economic, 109, 206–7
   incremental, 35, 216, 218, 225, 228
   interstitial, 26, 34, 218, 220
Dewar, J, 35–6, 39
direct ownership, 30, 32, 54
disabled persons, 149, 151
discretion, 44–7, 54, 68–9, 81–3, 111, 120–1, 153
discrimination, 1, 62, 67, 113, 190–2, 246
dispossession, 54, 64, 106, 180, 205, 207, 222
   colonial, 38, 206
   post-colonial, 38
   unlawful, 67
distribution of property rights, 10, 16, 76, 78–9,
      209, 212, 215
doctrinal conservatism, 116, 130–1
doctrinal developments, 17, 19, 22, 25
doctrinal differences, 28, 36–7
doctrinal framework, 27, 52, 213, 218, 221, 227
doctrinal logic, 18, 21, 26, 28, 94, 132, 214
doctrinal traditions, 19, 21, 75, 213
doctrine:
   existing, 21–2, 25, 213–14, 220

mainstream, 27, 189, 218–19, 221, 225, 227, 229–30
domain, eminent, 171, 206–7, 217
dominant property regime, 30, 77, 243–4
dominium, 29–30, 33, 35, 38, 54, 179
due process:
  controls, 81, 100, 104, 115, 122, 127, 129–30
  regulation, 99–100, 131
  requirements, 80, 100, 104–5, 128–9, 148, 222, 224
Dutch law, 33, 53, 84, 88–9, 137–8, 141–2, 203
  see also Netherlands
  building encroachments, 202–3
  eviction of unlawful occupiers, 137–41

economic context, 44, 54, 58, 73–4, 83, 132–3, 223
economic development, 109, 206–7
economic efficiency, 175–6, 187, 204
economic growth, 4–5, 7, 10–11, 14
economic justice, 19, 24, 160, 199, 239–40
economic liberalism, 37, 39, 50
economic liberty, 29, 37, 85
economic policies, 4–5, 109, 214
economic power, 3, 60, 73, 78, 207
economic privilege, 1–2, 13
economic reforms, 3–5, 7, 10, 12–14, 16–18, 20, 133
economic stability, 3–4, 10
economic transformation *see* social and economic transformation
economic use, 88–9
efficiency, 7, 186, 208–9, 226
  economic, 175–6, 187, 204
effluxion of time, 97, 99–100, 175, 177
Eigenbedarfskündigung, 47, 89–90
elasticity of ownership, 72
eminent domain, 171, 206–7, 217
enclosure, 193–4
encroachments *see* building encroachments
English courts, 50, 106–7, 114, 143, 162–3, 165, 167
English law, 50–1, 53–6, 84–5, 96–8, 105–6, 112–14, 200–1
  acquisitive prescription, 176–82
  adverse possession, 176–82
  building encroachments, 201–2
  common law, 38–9, 50, 54, 56–7, 77, 79, 99–100
  eviction of unlawful occupiers, 143–4
  gypsies/travellers, 161–4
  land law, 28, 35, 38, 94, 98, 103, 178–9
  landlord-tenant law, 96, 246
  public access, 193–5
  tenant protection, 96–113
entitlements, 29, 32–3, 35, 48–9, 73, 188, 194–5
Epstein, RA, 15, 37
equality, 2, 6, 8, 12, 14, 148, 190–2

equity, 202, 209, 246–7
estates, doctrine of, 98, 157–8, 179, 189
  doctrine of, 98
European case-law, gypsies/travellers, 164–6
European Convention on Human Rights, 11, 50, 55, 84–5, 104, 114, 161–2
European Court of Human Rights, 11, 50–1, 106–8, 110–12, 162–5, 167, 180–1
European Social Charter, 165–6
European Union, 14, 16, 20, 181, 228
eviction, 51–70, 72–8, 80–6, 110–19, 121–31, 144–67, 221–3
  acquisitive prescription *see* acquisitive prescription
  adverse possession *see* adverse possession
  American 'property outlaws', 144–5
  apartheid, 62, 64–5, 223
  arbitrary, 43, 57, 73, 84, 96, 117, 119
  and building encroachments, 199–205
  challenge of, 70–6
  common law, 63, 65, 67, 126, 131
  Dutch law, 137–41
  English law, 96–113, 143–4
  German law, 84–96, 141–3
  gypsies/travellers, 108, 133, 161–6
  in landlord-tenant law, 77–132
  orders, 43–5, 56–8, 72–3, 118–25, 127–8, 146–57, 160
  and political power, 60–70
  politically inspired urban squatters, 135–46
  power of, 54, 61, 69
  private, 61, 64, 159
  and public access, 188–99
  right to evict as incident of ownership, 53–60
  and rights paradigm, 53–76, 221–2
  and socio-economic power, 60–70
  South African law, 114–30
    land reform law, 146–61
  state(-enforced/supported/sponsored), 64, 66–8
  sundry limitations, 169–210
  unlawful occupiers, 80, 84, 133–67
  and weak owners, 205–7
excludability, 189–90
  South African law, 195–9
exclusive control, 123, 188–9
exclusive possession, 32, 42, 53, 58–9, 75–6, 188–9, 221–5
exclusivity, 59, 70–1, 76, 173, 192–3, 196–7, 223
  and public access, 188–90
execution, 105, 120, 122
existing doctrine, 21–2, 25, 213–14, 220
existing property holdings, 4, 7, 14, 16, 18–19, 75, 213
existing property interests, 9–10, 13–14, 16, 183
existing property regime, 6, 11, 13–15, 209, 214, 216, 229
expiration of leases/tenancies, 86, 100, 129, 176

Index

exploitation of property, 215, 217, 225
expropriation, 12, 181, 197–8, 201, 205–7, 217
    unconstitutional, 198
extraneous factors, 102, 225–6

factual possession, 180, 189
fair balance, 50–1, 91, 112, 129, 181, 194–5, 198
fairness, 77, 82, 127, 149, 175–6, 209, 229–30
families, 86, 89, 95, 107, 143, 148–50, 197–8
family members, 87–8, 98, 106, 127–8, 197–8
Feenstra, R, 30
Fennell, LA, 174–5, 177, 182–7, 209, 244
feudal land law, 30, 50, 94, 175, 244
feudalism, 30, 35, 48, 94
fixed-term tenancies, 86–9, 100, 105, 128
    see also periodic tenancies
Flockton, C, 90, 141–2
forced removals, 2, 59–61, 65–8, 74, 115, 154,
    205–6
forfeiture, 54, 57, 97, 99–100, 104–6, 220, 229
formalism, 234–5
former tenants, 42, 56, 80–2, 95, 102, 125–6,
    134
Fox, L, 11–12, 24, 42, 71, 98, 246
free markets, 40–1, 48, 60, 219
free speech, 191–2, 195, 199
free will, 30–1, 34, 142
freedom, 8, 16, 19, 93, 113, 191, 193
functional splitting of ownership, 94

gateways, 110, 112, 163
German Landlord–Tenant case, 46–50
German law:
    building encroachments, 202–3
    Civil Code, 33, 48, 86, 92, 141, 202–3
    constitutional law, 48–9, 71, 95, 113
    constitutional property law, 92–3, 96
    eviction of unlawful occupiers, 141–3
    Federal Constitutional Court, 42, 48, 54,
        85–6, 90–1, 94, 207
    private law, 48, 53, 85, 92, 94–5, 188
    tenant protection, 84–96
globalisation, 10, 12, 14, 20, 212
good faith, 69, 172, 174–5, 180, 182–3, 186
governments, 4–5, 19, 57, 61, 78–80, 158–60,
    183
gravesites, 197–8
Gray, K and SF, 35–6, 50–1, 53–5, 97–100,
    176–81, 189–90, 193–5
gross negligence, 203
Grotius, H, 29–30, 32, 36, 48, 59, 94
grounds for possession, mandatory, 101–2
group areas, 62, 66, 206
groups, marginalised, 11–12, 23, 109–11, 161,
    166–7, 183, 236–9
growth, economic, 4–5, 7, 10–11, 14
gypsies/travellers, 107–9, 111, 133–5, 161–6,
    207, 233, 237

English case law, 161–4
European case-law, 164–6

hardship, 44, 46, 86, 89, 91, 95, 111
Harpum, C, 99, 113
health and safety, 61–2, 68, 71, 151, 154–5, 225,
    240
hierarchical power, 56, 204, 221
hierarchical privileging, 78–9, 169
hierarchical supremacy of ownership, 32, 34, 36,
    140
hierarchies, 29, 35, 40, 55–6, 77–8, 221, 242
    property, 28, 30, 32–4, 36, 54, 77, 81
historical context, 13, 81, 147, 167, 199, 225
Hohfeld, WN, 35, 40, 238–40
Holmes, OW, 22–3, 177, 234, 236, 238
homelessness, 118, 136, 139–40, 143–5, 147,
    156–7, 166–7
Honoré, AM, 53, 72, 189
House of Lords, 11, 42, 50–1, 105, 107–12,
    162–4, 179–81
housing, 2–3, 68–9, 85, 118, 140–2, 154–9,
    165–6
    alternative see alternative accommodation;
        alternative housing
    policies, 41, 55, 80, 103, 131, 135–7, 246–7
    public, 79, 103, 143
    shortages, 11, 75, 83–4, 90, 131, 136–7, 140
    social, 90, 105, 111, 142–3
human rights, 5, 14, 51, 60, 212–13

ideology, apartheid, 60–1, 63, 67
imperium, 35, 38
incremental development, 35, 216, 218, 225, 228
indefeasible title, 177–8
individual property holdings, 79, 187, 215,
    217–18
individual security see personal security
inequality, 1–2, 7, 9, 14, 62–3, 211–12, 245–6
    see also equality
informal land rights, 129, 147
information, 124, 148–9, 153, 186
injunctive relief, 200–2
injustices, 1, 4, 7, 14, 21, 60, 211–12
insolvency, 86–7
integrity of property doctrine, 38, 217, 220, 227
intention, 47, 91, 109, 124, 129, 179–81
    owner's, 128, 170, 172
interdicts, permanent, 195–6
interests:
    of landlords/owners, 91, 95, 111, 114
    marginal, 82, 245–6
    of tenants, 43, 79, 81, 91–3, 95, 113
interference:
    competitive, 39
    with rights, 19, 109–10, 112, 162–3, 165, 181,
        192
interstitial developments, 26, 34, 218, 220

266

invasions, 64, 66, 121, 124, 136–8, 146, 151
  physical, 189, 192
  unlawful, 64, 124, 126, 134, 136, 146, 150–2

Jackson, P, 193–5
judicial discretion *see* discretion
judicial review, 47, 51, 86, 89–90, 108–9, 114,
  162–3
justice, 9, 11–12, 14–16, 208–9, 211–13, 229–30,
  246–7
  economic, 19, 24, 160, 199, 239–40
  social, 20, 23–4, 74, 105, 239

Kairys, D, 232, 234, 236, 240
Katyal, SK, 136, 144–5, 173, 183–5, 192–3, 209,
  243
Kennedy, D, 7, 39, 240
Klare, K, 8, 18, 212, 234, 247
knowing trespass, 170, 173, 182, 184–8
knowledge, doctrine of, 59, 116
Kolinsky, E, 90, 142
kraken, 134, 136–40

labour tenants, 4, 118, 122, 124, 127, 129
land invasions *see* invasions
land redistribution *see* redistribution
land reform, 4–5, 11, 19, 25, 67, 121–2, 194
  laws, 57, 115, 119–20, 122–6, 148–9, 154,
   160–1
  programme, 19, 75, 117, 227
land rights, 5, 25, 52, 74–5, 117, 121, 160
  aboriginal, 197, 207
  customary, 205
  informal, 129, 147
land title *see* title
land use, 61, 135, 223, 227
  management/planning, 71, 135, 158
  segregated, 62–3, 66, 206
landlessness, 22, 146–7, 175, 187–8, 194
landlord-tenant law, 77–80, 82, 84–6, 88, 102,
  116, 130–4
  English, 96, 246
  eviction in, 77–132
  landlord-tenant relationships, 46, 54–6, 76,
   78, 82, 85–6, 105
  legislation, 51, 55, 73, 78–9, 83, 95–6, 123–4
  tenant protection
   comparative overview, 82–114
   in South African law, 114–30
landlords, 42–4, 46–7, 53–5, 86–99, 101–7,
  112–17, 127–9
  feudal, 175, 244
  interests of, 91, 95, 111, 114
  private, 61, 101
  proprietary power, 50, 55, 99
  public, 112, 144, 163
landowners, 29–34, 47–60, 70–8, 119–29,
  137–43, 169–78, 186–206

control, 56, 130, 160, 190, 225
interests of, 91, 95, 111, 114
neglectful, 174–8, 184, 186
private, 64, 67, 150, 159, 206
public, 107, 159
rights, 46, 50, 91, 107, 162, 198, 202
weak, 52, 169, 171–2, 205–9, 217, 222, 233
landownership *see* ownership
lawful occupiers, 43, 45, 56, 115, 122–3, 125–6,
  148
le Roux, W, 8, 236
legal culture, 18, 234, 247
legal order, 176, 184, 238, 241–2
legal systems, 4, 18, 20, 22, 27–8, 40–2, 212
legislative control, 82, 90, 135
legislative interventions, 73, 78–9, 81–2, 94, 97,
  137, 166
legislature, 48–50, 107, 111, 114, 126, 152–3,
  196–7
liberalism, economic, 37, 39, 50
liberty, economic, 29, 37, 85
licences, 11, 30, 73–4, 105, 161–2, 179–80,
  194
limitation principle, 176–8, 182
limited real rights, 28–30, 32, 93
local authorities, 64–5, 69, 108–10, 143, 149–51,
  154–9, 163–4
logic, 27–8, 31–2, 34–6, 81, 213–14, 233–4,
  245–7
  doctrinal, 18, 21, 26, 28, 94, 132, 214
  syllogistic, 27–8
long-term protected occupiers, 127–8
long-term stability, 96, 209–10
loss of ownership, 170, 181
lunch counter sit-ins, 136, 144–6

mainstream doctrine, 27, 189, 218–19, 221, 225,
  227, 229–30
mala fide see bad faith
mandatory grounds for possession, 101–2
marginal interests, 82, 245–6
marginal perspective, 21, 25, 159, 214, 230,
  243–4
marginal property interests, 81, 224, 226, 230,
  244–5
marginalisation, 7, 23, 75, 78, 108, 112, 133
marginalised groups, 11–12, 23, 109–11, 161,
  166–7, 183, 236–9
marginality, 23–5, 121, 197, 232, 239, 241–2,
  245–6
markets, 185–7, 216, 219
  free, 40–1, 48, 60, 219
marriages, customary, 157–8
Michelman, F, 28, 63, 105
morality, 15–16, 74
Mostert, H, 11, 125, 147, 152
municipalities *see* local authorities
Munzer, SR, 35

native title, 205
necessity, 4, 19, 92, 136, 142–6
needs-based theories, 239–41
negative obligation, 118–19
neglectful landowners, 174–8, 184, 186
negligence, gross, 203
neighbour law, 25, 70, 200
neighbouring land, 25, 199, 201
Netherlands, 57, 136–7, 143, 146, 165, 180–1
    see also Dutch law
New Zealand, 11, 179, 184, 201
no-property, 238, 241, 243, 246
    see also absence of property
non-owners, 33–4, 39, 50, 60, 174, 187, 196
non-ownership interests/rights, 34, 56, 78, 81,
    85, 93
non-use, 145–6
    see also land use
normal science, 22, 25, 218
nuisance, 25, 128, 164, 170, 189, 195–6, 199

obligations:
    constitutional, 17, 20, 69, 118, 129, 156, 160
    negative, 118–19
observer's paradox, 235
occupation interests, 41, 77, 129
occupation rights, 54, 58, 99, 109, 116–18,
    121–2, 126–8
occupation, unlawful *see* unlawful occupation
occupiers, 52–8, 73–5, 118–28, 136–9, 147–9,
    151–61, 197–8
    personal circumstances of, 46, 123, 155
    unlawful *see* unlawful occupiers
    vulnerable, 74–5, 118
onus of proof *see* burden of proof
open civil possession, 175
operative conceptions of property, 16–17, 219
owners *see* landowners
    neglectful *see* neglectful landowners
owners of record, 176, 185–7
ownership, 25–36, 38–42, 46–55, 70–8, 92–4,
    175–6, 237–42
    absolute, 15, 29, 34, 36–7, 179, 239
    acquisition of, 38, 170, 173–5, 181, 183,
        204
    direct, 30, 32, 54
    elasticity of, 72
    exclusivity of *see* exclusivity
    functional splitting of, 94
    hierarchical supremacy of, 32, 34, 36, 140
    loss of, 170, 181
    model, 37, 39–40, 42, 47, 96
    paradigm, 36, 47, 50, 55, 72, 79, 113
    power of, 31, 78, 206–7
    presumptive power of, 50, 59, 94
    private, 4, 16, 40–1, 48, 60, 63–4, 94
    and right to evict, 53–60
    rights, 30, 39, 46, 50, 52, 71, 91

paper owners, 173, 176, 180
    see also owners of record
paradigm of ownership, 36, 47, 50, 55, 72, 79,
    113
paradigm shifts, 74, 79, 82, 119, 121, 225–7,
    229–30
peace, breach of the, 88, 138, 141–2
peaceful transition, 5–7, 20
Peñalver, E, 9, 15, 136, 144–5, 183–5, 192–3, 243
periodic tenancies, 98, 100–2, 105, 128
permanent interdicts, 195–6
permission, 54, 74, 77, 123, 127, 162–3, 197–8
    precarious or revocable, 22, 73, 102, 129, 172,
        174
person in charge, 124, 128, 148, 197
personal circumstances, 27–8, 44, 58–9, 73–4,
    81, 112–13, 223
personal rights, 27–9, 32, 93, 221
personal security, 3, 6–7, 10, 15, 59, 96, 215
physical invasions, 189, 192
    see also invasions
Pienaar, JMF, 58, 117, 125, 147, 152, 174–5,
    197–8
police power, 62, 70–1, 155, 171, 225, 240
political action, 137, 142–4, 147, 167, 223,
    243–4
political change, 1–3, 5–7, 9, 14, 17, 21,
    212–14
political context, 9, 24, 27, 75, 122, 197, 229
political power, 1, 9, 20, 53
    and eviction, 60–70
political reform, 3, 8–9, 13, 19–20, 161
political transformation, 1, 3–5, 7, 9–11, 13, 16,
    217
politically inspired urban squatters, 135–46
possessio civilis see civil possession
possession, 32–5, 53–60, 98–102, 105–14, 160–4,
    172, 175–82
    adverse *see* adverse possession
    civil *see* civil possession
    exclusive, 32, 42, 53, 58–9, 75–6, 188–9, 221–5
    factual, 180, 189
    orders, 101–2, 105, 107–8, 112, 223
    reclaiming/recovery of, 11, 82, 99, 101, 112,
        131–2, 173
    requirement, 172, 174, 180
    undisturbed, 67, 73, 160, 202
    unlawful, 35, 141, 173, 177, 183
possessors, bad faith, 170, 173, 175, 180–3,
    186–8, 223
possessory claims, 40–2, 221
post-apartheid South Africa, 12, 18, 25, 67, 115,
    117, 247
poverty, 2, 7, 23, 145–6, 231–2, 236–7, 239–42
power:
    economic, 3, 60, 73, 78, 207
    hierarchical, 56, 204, 221
    police, 62, 70–1, 155, 171, 225, 240

political, 1, 9, 20, 53, 60–70
rhetorical, 30–1, 42, 232
socio-economic, 60–70
precarious or revocable permission, 73, 102, 129, 172, 174
prescription, 76, 170–1, 173–6, 181–2, 187–8, 204
acquisitive *see* acquisitive prescription
presumptive power, 39, 41, 50–1, 54, 59, 81, 120
Prevention of Illegal Eviction from and Unlawful Occupation of Land Act 19 of 1998 (PIE), 147–51
case law, 151–9
effect on common law, 151–2
private evictions, 61, 64, 159
private land, 64, 68, 117, 150, 170, 183, 192–3
private landlords, 61, 101
private landowners, 64, 67, 150, 159, 206
private law, 37–8, 48–51, 78–9, 84–6, 92–7, 113–14, 180–2
private ownership, 4, 16, 40–1, 48, 60, 63–4, 94
private property, 14–18, 36–8, 49–50, 169–70, 188–93, 217–19, 222–3
private sector, 98, 100–3, 106–7, 113, 130
private sector tenancies, 106, 130
privatisation, 79–80
procedural restrictions, 80, 138
procedural safeguards, 123, 164–5
proof, burden of, 58, 120, 124, 167
propertisation, 189–90
property:
absence of, 232, 238, 242
constitutional, 20, 49, 90–3, 96, 196, 228
current distribution of, 16, 209, 215
exploitation of, 215, 217, 225
unequal distribution of, 231–2
unlawful occupation of *see* unlawful occupation
property doctrine, 20, 26, 35, 214, 217–20, 222, 230–1
mainstream, 27, 219, 221, 230
property hierarchies, 28, 30, 32–4, 36, 54, 77, 81
property holders, 93, 96, 183, 214, 220, 225–6, 229
property holdings, 10, 15, 17, 23, 211–12, 217, 230–1
current distribution of, 212, 230
existing, 4, 7, 14, 16, 18–19, 75, 213
protection of existing, 14, 19, 75, 213
property interests, 9, 13, 27–9, 77, 89–90, 113, 207–8
existing, 9–10, 13–14, 16, 183
hierarchy of, 30, 33, 36, 207
marginal, 81, 224, 226, 230, 244–5
power of, 37, 221, 238
private, 10, 16, 38
'property outlaws', 144–5, 243
property owners *see* landowners

property ownership *see* ownership
property regime, 13–21, 209–13, 215–20, 222–4, 226–31, 233, 245–7
existing, 6, 11, 13–15, 209, 214, 216, 229
property relations, 31, 147, 159, 241, 245–6
property rhetoric *see* rhetoric
property rights, 4, 11–14, 24, 26–30, 70–1, 214–15, 223–5
current distribution of, 10, 16, 76, 209, 212, 215, 230
strong, 27, 31, 77–8, 169, 205–9, 221, 225–6
weak, 24, 27, 205, 208–9, 221
property status, 23, 92, 244–6
property theory, 1, 9, 12–17, 21, 23–5, 214–15, 219
and transformation, 12–26
proportionality, 11, 50–1, 104, 108, 112, 165
proprietary power, landlords, 50, 55, 99
proprietary sovereignty, resolute defence of, 50–1, 55, 109
protected occupiers, long-term, 127–8
protected periodic tenancies, 98, 100
protection:
of property interests/rights, 10, 14, 19, 75, 85, 154, 213
of tenants *see* tenant protection
protective legislation, 56, 75, 78, 102, 130, 132–3, 228
protest, 47, 136, 144–6, 167, 192, 216
Proudhon, PJ, 22, 211
public access, 52, 76, 170–1
American law, 190–2
English law, 193–5
and eviction, 188–99
and exclusivity, 188–90
South African law, excludability post-apartheid, 195–9
public accommodations, 172, 190–2, 195
public health *see* health and safety
public housing, 79, 103, 143
see also social housing
tenants, 83, 103
public interest, 14–16, 31, 34, 46, 49–50, 90–2, 151
public landlords, 112, 144, 163
public landowners, 107, 112, 159
public purposes, 40, 170–1, 201, 206, 217
public sector tenancies, 98, 100–3, 106
purchasers, 58, 87, 114, 116–17

Qazi case, 50–1
qualifications, 31–2, 75–6, 81–3, 131–3, 171–3, 208–10, 224–5

racial segregation, 1, 3, 60, 62, 64, 136, 144
see also segregated land use
re-entry right, 50, 54, 58, 99–100, 105
real rights, limited, 28–30, 32, 93

real servitudes *see* servitudes
realism, 72, 94, 234–8
reasonableness, 25, 101–2, 106, 113, 200
reclaiming/recovery of possession, 11, 82, 99,
  101, 112, 131–2, 173
record, owners of, 176, 185–7
recovery of possession *see* reclaiming/recovery of
  possession
recreational access, 170, 193–5
redistribution, 5–6, 10, 117, 176, 185, 187,
  230
reform legislation, 17, 39, 52, 69, 74, 97, 115
reforms, 3–4, 9–10, 13–14, 16–22, 31–2,
  211–16, 227–8
  economic, 3–5, 7, 10, 12–14, 16–18, 20,
    133
  political, 3, 8–9, 13, 19–20, 161
  significant, 8–10, 14, 52, 76, 79, 82, 166
registered land, 176, 178–9
registered proprietors, 178–9
  see also owners of record
registration, 116, 178–9, 181–2
regulatory controls, 46, 73–4, 81, 126, 129,
  134–5, 224
regulatory restrictions, 16, 39–40, 48, 71, 84,
  219, 224
rei vindicatio, 56–7
relative title, 30, 35–6, 38, 40, 53, 176
relevant circumstances, 43, 45, 68, 83, 118–21,
  123, 147–50
religion, 102, 113, 197
removals, forced, 2, 59–61, 65–8, 74, 115, 154,
  205–6
residence, 87, 122, 127–8, 164, 198
residential tenancies, 46, 101, 104–5, 115,
  124–6, 129, 246
residuarity, 32, 72
resources, 155–6, 166, 189–90, 215
responsibilities, 16, 52, 86, 91, 93, 143, 157–9
restrictions:
  anti-eviction, 228–9
  common-good, 70–1
  procedural, 80, 138
  regulatory, 16, 39–40, 48, 71, 84, 219, 224
  substantive, 80, 118, 130, 229
review *see* judicial review
rhetoric, 21, 26–8, 31, 33–4, 81, 132–3,
  217–18
rhetorical power, 30–1, 42, 232
right of occupation *see* occupation rights
right to evict and ownership, 53–60
  see also eviction
right to roam, 193–5
rights:
  land, 5, 25, 52, 74–5, 117, 121, 160
  occupation, 54, 58, 99, 109, 116–18, 121–2,
    126–8
  personal, 27–9, 32, 93, 221

strong, 27, 31, 77–8, 169, 205–9, 221,
  225–6
weak, 24, 27, 205, 208–9, 221
rights paradigm, 27–41, 77–86, 129–33, 169–73,
  203–10, 222–7
  and eviction, 53–76, 221–2
  illustrations, 41–52
roam, right to, 193–5
Robertson, M, 5–6
Roman-Dutch common law, 63
Roman-Germanic law, 28, 35, 84, 87, 94, 169,
  175
Roman law, 29, 49, 172, 174
Ruffert, M, 49, 92–4
rural land, 45, 115, 118, 134–5, 147
  lawful occupiers of, 125–7

sacrifices, 204, 206–7, 217, 234, 238, 245
safety *see* health and safety
Sagaert, V, 181–2
sale, 58–9, 98, 104, 116, 128, 150, 196
  compulsory, 200–1
  in execution, 86–7, 98, 116, 149–50
science, law as, 234–5
security:
  individual *see* security, personal
  of ownership, 49, 76, 175, 179, 187, 217
  personal, 3, 6–7, 10, 15, 59, 96, 215
  of tenure, 58, 67, 99–100, 114, 117–18, 122,
    198
segregated land use, 62–3, 66, 206
segregation, racial, 1, 3, 60, 62, 64, 136, 144
servitudes, 29–30, 173, 198, 203, 216
shifting of landownership, 175
shorthold tenancies, assured, 100–1, 103,
  130
significant building encroachments
  see building encroachments
Singer, JW, 35–6, 39–40, 54–5, 58–9, 182,
  190–2, 240–1
sit-ins, lunch counter, 136, 144–6
Skweyiya, Z, 5–6
social and economic transformation, 5–6, 8, 10,
  25, 43, 74
social and political transformation, 1–12
social circumstances, 56, 75, 81, 83, 89, 151,
  226
social context, 123, 160, 198, 245
social housing, 90, 105, 111, 142–3
social justice, 20, 23–4, 74, 105, 239
social origins, 21, 236, 240–1
socio-economic context, 42, 56, 77, 81, 169
socio-economic power and eviction, 60–70
sole and despotic dominion, 36, 38
South African law:
  acquisitive prescription, 172–6
  adverse possession, 172–6
  building encroachments, 199–201

excludability, 195–9
  public access, 195–9
  tenant protection in, 114–30
sovereignty, 35, 38
sovereignty, proprietary, 50–1, 55, 109
squatters, 64–6, 147, 170–1, 176–8, 183–4
  urban, 135–46
squatting movements, 136–7, 243
stability, 4–7, 9–11, 17, 19–20, 59–60, 75–6
  economic, 3–4, 10
  long-term, 96, 209–10
  in property law, 214–21
  systemic, 6–7, 10, 15, 21, 59, 76, 215
state(-enforced/supported) evictions, 64,
      66–8
state interventions, 213, 216–17, 220–2
state organs, 19, 61, 63–4, 119, 149–50, 158
statutory protection, 81, 94, 106, 108, 110,
      223
  of tenants, 130–1
strong property rights, 27, 31, 77–8, 169, 205–9,
      221, 225–6
stronger claim, 28, 35, 38, 76–7, 176–8
subsidiarity, 151–2
substantive restrictions, 80, 118, 130, 229
succession, 98
suitable alternative accommodation *see*
      alternative accommodation, availability
      of
superiority, 57, 59, 65, 197, 232
surrounding circumstances, 73, 105
syllogistic logic, 27–8
systemic stability, 6–7, 10, 15, 21, 59, 76, 215

Teitel, RG, 10, 24, 238
tenancies, 54–7, 80–1, 97–102, 104–10, 112–13,
      134, 162
  assured shorthold, 100–1, 103, 130
  fixed-term, 100, 128
    see also tenancies, periodic
  periodic, 98, 100–2, 105, 128
  private sector, 106, 130
  public sector, 98, 100–3, 106
  residential, 46, 101, 104–5, 115, 124–6, 129,
      246
tenant law *see* landlord-tenant law
tenant protection, 79
  comparative overview, 82–114
  English law, 96–113
  German law, 84–96
  in South African law, 77, 114–30
tenants:
  former, 42, 56, 80–2, 95, 102, 125–6, 134
  interests of, 43, 79, 81, 91–3, 95, 113
  labour, 4, 118, 122, 124, 127, 129
tenure, 44, 53, 57, 75, 114, 122–5, 127–8
  security of, 58, 67, 99–100, 114, 117–18, 122,
      198

termination of leases/tenancies, 56–8, 82–3, 89,
      99–101, 103–5, 116–18, 127–31
time, effluxion of, 97, 99–100, 175, 177
title, 22, 32, 105, 175–80, 182, 184–6, 189
  absolute, 35
    see also absolute ownership
  indefeasible, 177–8
  native, 205
  relative, 30, 35–6, 38, 40, 53, 176
tolerated trespassers, 102
tradition, 16–17, 41, 49, 51–2, 65, 92, 133
transformation:
  political, 1, 3–5, 7, 9–11, 13, 16, 217
  and property theory, 12–26
  social and economic, 5–6, 8, 10, 25, 43,
      74
  social and political, 1–12
transformative constitutionalism, 8–10, 18,
      20, 63, 212, 233–4, 247
transformative setting, 1–2, 4, 6, 8, 10, 12,
      26
transition, peaceful, 5–7, 20
travellers *see* gypsies/travellers
trespass(ers), 76, 163–5, 170–1, 182, 185–7,
      201–2, 208
  knowing, 170, 184–5
  tolerated, 102

uncodified common law, 18, 34, 96
unconstitutional expropriation, 198
Underkuffler, LS, 16–17, 39, 50, 59, 189–90,
      219, 231
undisturbed possession, 67, 73, 160, 202
unequal distribution of property, 231–2
United Kingdom *see* English law
United States *see* American law
unlawful invasions, 64, 124, 126, 134, 136, 146,
      150–2
unlawful occupation, 41, 124, 134–5, 137,
      141–2, 146–7, 152
  demonstrative, 223
  politically inspired, 11, 135–6
unlawful occupiers, 43–4, 72–7, 106–7
  American 'property outlaws', 144–5
  anti-eviction protection in South African
      land reform law, 135–46
  Dutch law, 137–41
  English law, 143–4
  eviction, 80, 84, 133–67
  German law, 141–3
unlawful possession, 35, 141, 173, 177, 183
unlawful squatters *see* squatters
urban areas, 2, 62, 114, 126, 136–7
urban land/property, 45, 115, 127, 135,
      145–6
urban squatters, politically inspired, 135–46
US law *see* American law
users, adverse, 170, 172–3, 176, 178, 181, 183

Index

utilitarian perspective, 55, 175, 184, 234–6
utility, 184, 208–9, 231

van Maanen, G, 22, 33, 37, 139–41, 145, 238
vested holdings/rights/interests, 6, 11, 14, 24,
   133, 167, 211
vulnerability, 73, 151, 161, 167, 206, 232,
   237

vulnerable occupiers/tenants, 74–5, 91, 118, 130,
   160, 229

weak owners, 52, 169, 171–2, 217, 222, 233
   and eviction, 205–7
weak rights, 24, 27, 205, 208–9, 221
Willmore, C, 193–5
women, 149, 151, 157–8, 167, 237

VEGETARIAN
INDIAN COOKING
WITH YOUR INSTANT POT®

75 TRADITIONAL RECIPES THAT ARE
EASIER, QUICKER AND HEALTHIER

MANALI SINGH

FOUNDER OF COOK WITH MANALI

PAGE STREET
PUBLISHING CO.

PAGE STREET
PUBLISHING CO.

First published in 2018 by
Page Street Publishing Co.
27 Congress Street, Suite 105
Salem, MA 01970
www.pagestreetpublishing.com

Distributed by Macmillan, sales in Canada by The Canadian Manda Group.

22   21   20   19   18   1   2   3   4   5

ISBN-13: 978-1624146459
ISBN-10: 1624146457

Library of Congress Control Number: 2018940350

Cover and book design by Meg Baskis for Page Street Publishing Co.
Photography by Manali Singh

Printed and bound in China

TO MY MUMMA—
I MISS YOU

Introduction　　6

FAVORITE TAKEOUTS　9

Butter Paneer
(Indian Cottage Cheese in a Buttery Sauce)　10

Chana Masala (Chickpea Curry)　13

Navratan Korma (Vegetables &
Nuts in a Creamy Cashew Sauce)　15

Dal Makhani (Creamy Black Lentils)　19

Palak Paneer
(Indian Cottage Cheese & Spinach Curry)　20

Matar Mushroom (Mushrooms
& Green Peas in a Creamy Tomato Sauce)　23

Dal Tadka (Mixed Lentils with Spices)　24

Paneer Tikka Masala
(Indian Cottage Cheese in a Creamy Tomato Sauce)　27

Vegetable Biryani
(Basmati Rice with Veggies & Fragrant Spices)　29

Achari Mixed Vegetables
(Mixed Vegetables with Pickle Masala)　33

LENTILS & BEANS　35

Spinach Dal (Lentils with Spinach)　36

Sambar (South Indian Lentil Stew)　39

Black-Eyed Pea Curry with Kale　40

Jackfruit with Chana Dal　43

Kashmiri Rajma (Kidney-Bean Curry)　44

Moong Dal with Cabbage & Dill
(Lentils with Cabbage & Dill)　47

Panchmel Dal (Five-Lentil Mix with Spices)　48

Tomato Butternut Squash Dal　51

Spiced Chickpea Salad　52

Khatti Meethi Gujarati Dal (Sweet & Sour Lentils)　55

Sookha Kala Chana (Spiced Black Chickpeas)　56

HEARTY MEALS　59

Aloo Gobi (Spiced Potatoes & Cauliflower)　60

Vegetable Khichdi
(Mixed Lentils & Rice Porridge)　63

Gatte Ki Sabzi (Chickpea Flour Dumplings Curry)　64

Banarsi Dum Aloo (Creamy Baby Potatoes Curry)　67

Paneer Lasagna
(Spiced Indian Cottage Cheese Lasagna)　69

Kadai Tofu (Spiced Tofu with Bell Peppers)　70

Soya Jalapeño Keema Tacos
(Vegan Minced Soya Granules Tacos)　73

Gobi Matar Korma
(Cauliflower & Green Peas Coconut Curry)　74

Panchporan Spinach Kadhi
(Yogurt Soup with Five Spices)　77

Masala Baingan
(Spiced Baby Eggplants with Coconut)　78

Curried Black Bean Burrito Bowl　81

Dal Dhokli (Whole-Wheat Noodles in Lentil Stew)　82

Tofu Broccoli Asparagus in Fenugreek Sauce　85

Quinoa Curd Rice (Spiced Quinoa with Yogurt)　86

Cilantro Mint Paneer　89

Dal-Chawal-Aloo Sabzi
(Layered Meal with Rice, Lentils & Potatoes)　90

Ven Pongal
(Rice & Lentil Porridge with Peppercorns)　93

30 MINUTES OR LESS   95

Matar Paneer
(Indian Cottage Cheese & Green Peas Curry)   96

Dal Dhania Shorba (Lentil Cilantro Soup)   99

Jeera Aloo (Cumin Potatoes)   100

Tehri (Spicy Potato & Peas Pulao)   103

Tofu Mango Coconut Curry   104

Masala Mac & Cheese (Spiced Mac & Cheese)   107

Turmeric Masala Doodh (Spiced Turmeric Milk)   108

Beans & Beets Poriyal
(Spiced Green Beans & Beets with Coconut)   111

INDIAN STREET FOOD   113

Pav Bhaji
(Mashed Spiced Vegetables with Dinner Rolls)   114

Aloo Chana Rolls (Spiced Potato & Chickpea Wraps)   117

Vegetarian Momos (Vegetarian Dumplings)   121

Mushroom Garlic Fried Rice   122

Spicy Masala Corn   125

Vegan Hot & Sour Soup   126

Sweet Potato Chaat with Cilantro Mint Yogurt Chutney   129

SNACKS & SIDES   131

Saag (Spiced Creamy Greens)   132

Tofu Bhurji (Indian-Style Scrambled Tofu)   135

Masala Chai   136

Tomato & Date Chutney   139

Masala Hummus (Spiced Hummus)   140

Mint Cashew Pulao
(Spiced Basmati Rice with Mint & Cashews)   143

Khatti Meethi Pumpkin Sabzi (Sweet & Sour Pumpkin)   144

Idlis (Steamed Rice Lentil Cakes)   147

Khaman Dhokla
(Steamed Savory Chickpea-Flour Cakes)   149

DELECTABLE DESSERTS   153

Rice Kheer (Indian Rice Pudding)   154

Kesar Elaichi Shrikhand (Saffron Cardamom Yogurt)   157

Kalakand (Spiced Milk Fudge)   158

Zarda (Sweet Rice)   161

Eggless Tutti Frutti Cake   162

Pumpkin Coconut Halwa (Pumpkin Coconut Pudding)   165

Masala Chai Crème Brûlée   166

Rose Pistachio Cheesecake   169

Mango Coconut Tapioca Pudding   172

INDIAN COOKING BASICS   175

Paneer (Indian Cottage Cheese)   176

Ghee (Clarified Butter)   179

Dahi (Yogurt)   180

Ginger-Garlic Paste   183

Buttons on the Instant Pot   184

Instant Pot Accessories   185

Indian Cooking Ingredient Notes   185

Acknowledgments   187

About the Author   188

Index   189

INTRODUCTION

I wouldn't be exaggerating if I said that every Indian household is likely to have a pressure cooker. It is one kitchen gadget no Indian can survive without. In fact, when I was moving to another country to get my MBA, my mom's main concern was that I should not forget to pack my pressure cooker! She was so concerned that she ended up packing the cooker in my handbag and it eventually was removed from my luggage at the airport! You see, Indians eat lentils, beans and chickpeas on a daily basis, so for us it's like you can cook—not to mention survive—only if you have a pressure cooker.

When I first was introduced to the Instant Pot, I was intimidated. But very soon I realized that this electric cooker was so much more user-friendly than the traditional pressure cooker that I had been using all my life. There was less guesswork, more consistent results, no loud whistles—I was hooked!

As I began experimenting more and more with the Instant Pot, I realized that there's so much that you can do with one pot. Initially, I only made soups and dals, but soon I started using the pot for pretty much everything. Over the next few months, I became so hooked on the Instant Pot that I would joke with my husband that I couldn't remember the last time I had turned on my gas stove.

This book covers some of my favorite Indian recipes. There are basic Indian recipes that I grew up eating and ones that are made in Indian homes on a daily basis. Then there are recipes you would find on the menu of your favorite Indian restaurant. There are hearty, comforting meals, some fun fusion recipes and desserts. All the recipes in this book are vegetarian and a lot of them are vegan. Basic Indian food is predominantly vegetarian/vegan, so if you are making

a shift toward a plant-based diet or are just trying to eat more veggies, Indian food is your gold mine!

These recipes are for anyone who loves Indian food or wants to try cooking Indian food at home. Cooking Indian is not as challenging as people assume it to be, and the Instant Pot makes it that much easier.

Contrary to the popular notion, the recipes in this book are not very spicy. Sure, they have a lot of spices (how else would you cook Indian!?) but they aren't very hot. I am not a fan of super spicy food and that is reflected in my cooking. If you enjoy really spicy food, increase the number of chilies and up the spices in the recipes per your taste.

Some of the ingredients used in these recipes may not be available at your local grocery store. If you can't find a particular ingredient, head over to the nearest Indian grocery store and you should find everything there. These ingredients are also readily available online. If there's an ingredient that you've never cooked with before, check the Indian Cooking Ingredient Notes (page 185) for more information on what they are.

If you are new to using the Instant Pot, I recommend that you check out the resources at the end of the book before you begin cooking. The Buttons on the Instant Pot section (page 184) gives you information on the settings and modes for the Instant Pot, and the Instant Pot Accessories section (page 185) tells you about helpful add-ons you may want to purchase. If you're a pro with the Instant Pot, feel free to dive right in and start cooking!

I hope the recipes in this book inspire you to get into the kitchen, use your Instant Pot and cook the best Indian meal of your life!

Manali Singh

FAVORITE TAKEOUTS

The recipes in this chapter are those that you find on the menu of your favorite Indian restaurants. Whether it's the creamy Butter Paneer (page 10)—paneer pieces simmered in a tomato cashew sauce, or the aromatic Vegetable Biryani (page 29)—basmati rice cooked to perfection and flavored with fragrant spices like saffron, each dish is infused with a lot of flavors. This chapter also has some of my favorite dals, like Dal Makhani (page 19)—black lentils cooked to a creamy consistency with spices and lots of garlic, ginger, onions and tomatoes. It's my absolute favorite and if you have never tried it, you are missing out!

These favorite takeouts go well with naan, roti or any flatbread of your choice. They also go equally well with rice. Dal Tadka (page 24), a mix of three lentils tempered with spices, especially goes well with boiled rice.

Indian dishes have robust flavors and I hope you will enjoy all of them in these restaurant-style recipes. They are all really easy to make in the Instant Pot. I like the fact that all these dishes retain the same flavor as they would if cooked on the stovetop.

BUTTER PANEER

(INDIAN COTTAGE CHEESE IN A BUTTERY SAUCE)

SERVES: 3–4

Have you ever wondered how to make restaurant-style butter paneer at home? Yeah, with that finger-licking good creamy tomato sauce? This recipe is one of my favorites just because it's so easy! The sauce is made with tomatoes, garlic and ginger and flavored with garam masala, cardamom and a touch of honey.

4 large tomatoes, roughly chopped

4–5 cloves garlic, roughly chopped

1-inch (25-mm) piece ginger, roughly chopped

1 green chili, or to taste

8 raw cashews

4 green cardamoms, crushed

¼ tsp red chili powder, adjust to taste

½ tsp garam masala, divided

1 tsp salt, divided

½ cup (120 ml) water

2 tbsp (30 g) unsalted butter

1 tbsp (15 g) tomato paste

2½ tbsp (38 ml) heavy cream

1½ tsp (11 g) honey

½ tsp kashmiri red chili powder, for color

1 cup (225 g) paneer, cut into cubes

1 tbsp (1 g) cilantro, chopped

1 tsp kasuri methi (fenugreek leaves), crushed

To the inner pot of your Instant Pot, add the tomatoes, garlic, ginger, green chili, cashews and green cardamoms. Add the red chili powder, ¼ teaspoon garam masala, ½ teaspoon salt and water. Close the lid and press the manual or pressure-cook button, and cook on high pressure for 5 minutes. Do a quick-pressure release. Open the pot and purée the contents using an immersion blender, or wait for 10 to 15 minutes or until the mixture has cooled down a bit and then purée using a regular blender and return to the pot.

Press the sauté button, then add the butter, tomato paste, heavy cream, honey, the remaining ¼ teaspoon garam masala, kashmiri red chili powder and the remaining ½ teaspoon salt. Mix to combine, then stir in the paneer cubes. Add the cilantro and kasuri methi and let the curry simmer for 2 more minutes.

Serve the butter paneer with butter naan!

MAKE IT VEGAN: Replace the paneer with tofu, the butter with vegan butter and the heavy cream with coconut cream.

CHANA MASALA

(CHICKPEA CURRY)

SERVES: 4

Chana masala is one of the most popular Indian curries. Raw chickpeas are soaked overnight and then cooked along with onion, tomatoes and a special blend of spices. Cooking with raw chickpeas is essential for getting that authentic taste. It makes the chana masala so much more flavorful compared to what you would get if you used canned chickpeas. This chana masala is everyone's favorite, including my husband!

Making the chana masala spice mixture to use in this recipe is optional. You can use store-bought instead if you'd like.

FOR THE CHANA MASALA SPICE MIXTURE

2 tbsp (10 g) coriander seeds

1 tbsp (9 g) cumin seeds

1 tbsp (12 g) dried pomegranate seeds

1 tsp black peppercorn

2 black cardamoms

8 cloves

3–4 dried red chilies

2-inch (5-cm) cinnamon stick

1 tsp ginger powder

FOR THE CHANA MASALA CURRY

1¼ cups (263 g) dried chickpeas

2 tbsp (30 ml) vegetable oil

1 bay leaf

3 green cardamoms

½-inch (13-mm) cinnamon stick

1 sprig mace

1 large red onion, finely chopped using a food processor

1 small green chili, finely chopped

3–4 cloves garlic, minced

1½-inch (38-mm) piece ginger, two-thirds minced, one-third julienned

2 large tomatoes, puréed

½ tsp turmeric powder

½ tsp cumin powder

1 tsp coriander powder

2 tsp (4 g) chana masala

¼ tsp red chili powder, optional

1¼ tsp (8 g) salt, or to taste

2 cups (473 ml) water

2 tbsp (30 ml) lemon juice

2 tbsp (2 g) cilantro, chopped

½ tsp kasuri methi (fenugreek leaves), crushed

¼ tsp garam masala

1 tsp ghee, optional

(continued)

CHANA MASALA (CONT.)

Soak the dried chickpeas in 3 cups (720 ml) of water overnight. In the morning, drain, then rinse the chickpeas.

For the chana masala spice mixture, dry roast the coriander seeds, cumin seeds, pomegranate seeds, black peppercorns, black cardamoms, cloves, red chilies and the 2-inch (5-cm) piece of cinnamon stick in a pan over medium heat until the spices are fragrant and become golden in color, 5 to 6 minutes. Let the mixture cool and then transfer it to a spice grinder. Stir in the ground ginger and grind until powdered and well combined. If you are making this ahead, or for another recipe, store the chana masala spice mixture in an airtight container at room temperature.

Press the sauté button on the Instant Pot. When it displays hot, add the vegetable oil, bay leaf, green cardamoms, ½-inch (13-mm) piece cinnamon stick and mace. Sauté for a few seconds until the spices are fragrant.

Add the onion and green chili and cook for 2 to 3 minutes until the onion is soft. Then add the minced garlic and ginger and cook for another minute or so. Stir in the puréed tomatoes, cover with a glass lid and cook for 2 to 3 minutes. Add the turmeric powder, cumin powder, coriander powder, 2 teaspoons (4 g) chana masala and red chili powder. (Using red chili powder is optional; it makes the dish spicier.)

Let the spices cook with the tomato–onion masala for 2 more minutes, and then add the soaked chickpeas along with the salt and water. Stir to mix everything together. Close the lid of the pot, making sure the pressure valve is in the sealing position. Press the manual or pressure-cook button and cook at high pressure for 25 minutes. Let the pressure release naturally.

Open the lid, and add the lemon juice and cilantro. Also stir in the kasuri methi and garam masala. You can serve the chana masala at this point or do the extra step of tempering the dish, which makes it extra flavorful. To temper, heat 1 teaspoon of ghee in a pan over medium heat. When the ghee is hot, add the ginger juliennes, and cook until the ginger turns golden brown in color. Pour the tempering over the chana masala.

Serve the chana masala over rice and enjoy.

MAKE IT VEGAN: Replace the ghee with oil in the tempering.

NAVRATAN KORMA

(VEGETABLES & NUTS IN A CREAMY CASHEW SAUCE)

SERVES: 4

This is a very rich dish named as a tribute to the nine jewels of emperor Akbar's court. Navratan korma usually has an assortment of nine veggies/nuts/garnishing ingredients, hence the name (nav = nine and rattan = jewels). This dish has a white gravy made of onions, cashews and cream. This rich and creamy curry is often served at special occasions.

½ cup (70 g) raw cashews

2 medium white onions, halved

1-inch (25-mm) piece ginger

1 heaping cup (140 g) cauliflower florets

1 large carrot, cut into rounds

10–12 green beans, cut into ½-inch (13-mm) pieces

¼ cup (35 g) frozen green peas

¾ cup (150 g) paneer, cut into cubes

2 tbsp + 1 tsp (35 ml) ghee, divided

1 bay leaf

½-inch (13-mm) cinnamon stick

3 green cardamoms

3 cloves

2 green chilies, sliced

1½ cups (360 ml) water

½ tsp garam masala

½ tsp coriander powder

1¼ tsp (8 g) salt, or to taste

Pinch of cardamom powder

¼ cup (60 ml) heavy cream

12–15 whole almonds

1–2 tbsp (9–18 g) golden raisins

A few saffron strands

Pomegranate arils, for garnish

Soak the cashews in 1 cup (240 ml) of water for 15 to 20 minutes, then drain. Bring a pan of water to boil. Add the onions to the boiling water. Boil for 3 to 4 minutes until the onions are very soft, then drain. Using a blender, grind the onions, cashews and ginger to a fine paste. You may add 1 to 2 teaspoons of water while grinding if the mixture is too thick. Set the paste aside.

Put the cauliflower, carrots, beans and peas in the steamer basket of the Instant Pot. (I do not steam the paneer, but feel free to add the paneer to the vegetables.) Pour 1 cup (240 ml) of water in the inner pot of your Instant Pot and then place the steamer basket inside. Close the lid, making sure the pressure valve is in the sealing position, and then press the steam button. Set the time to 2 minutes on high pressure. Do a quick-pressure release.

Carefully remove the steamer basket from the pot. All the veggies should be nice and soft. Set them aside. Drain all the water from the pot, dry it with a paper towel and then place it back into the Instant Pot. Press the sauté button, and when the pot displays hot, add 2 tablespoons (30 ml) of ghee. Add the bay leaf, cinnamon stick, green cardamoms and cloves. Sauté for a few seconds until the spices are fragrant, and then add the prepared onion–cashew paste. Add the sliced green chilies and cook for 2 to 3 minutes. Then add the water and all the steamed veggies and paneer and stir to combine. Add the garam masala, coriander powder, salt and cardamom powder. Mix to combine all the spices. Cover the pot with a glass lid and let simmer for 2 minutes. Stir in the heavy cream.

(continued)

NAVRATAN KORMA (CONT.)

In a small pan, heat the remaining teaspoon of ghee over medium heat. When the ghee is hot, add the almonds, raisins and saffron strands. Cook until the raisins swell up and the almonds are toasted, about 1 minute. Transfer the tempering to the Instant Pot and stir to combine. Transfer the navratan korma into a serving dish and garnish with pomegranate arils. Serve with naan.

NOTE: Pineapple is often used in navratan korma. If you would like, add ¼ cup (45 g) chopped pineapple just before serving.

MAKE IT VEGAN: Replace the paneer with tofu and the heavy cream with coconut cream or milk.

DAL MAKHANI
(CREAMY BLACK LENTILS)

SERVES: 4

Dal makhani is one of India's most popular lentil dishes. Black lentils are cooked until creamy and fragrant. Dal makhani is my husband's favorite dal and we love this Instant Pot version. A lot of dal makhani recipes include kidney beans; if you want to include them, simply replace ¼ cup (55 g) of black lentils with kidney beans and soak them overnight along with the dal. We love that version just as much!

1 cup (220 g) whole black gram lentils/urad dal sabut

2 tbsp (30 ml) ghee

1 bay leaf

2–3 green cardamoms

1 tsp cumin seeds

1 medium red onion, finely chopped

2 tsp (12 g) ginger–garlic paste (see page 183)

¼ cup + 1 tbsp (75 ml) store-bought tomato purée

3½ cups (840 ml) water, divided

¾ tsp garam masala

½ tsp cumin powder

½ tsp red chili powder

1¼ tsp (8 g) salt, or to taste

1½ tsp (5 g) kasuri methi (fenugreek leaves), crushed

1 tbsp (15 g) unsalted butter

1 tbsp (15 ml) heavy cream

MAKE IT VEGAN: Replace the ghee with oil, the butter with vegan butter and the heavy cream with nondairy milk.

Wash and soak the lentils in 3 cups (720 ml) of water overnight. In the morning, drain and rinse the lentils and set it aside.

Press the sauté button. When the pot displays hot, add the ghee, bay leaf and green cardamoms and sauté for a few seconds until the spices are fragrant. Add the cumin seeds, let them sizzle for a few seconds and then add the chopped onion. Cook the onion for 2 minutes until soft and translucent, and then add the ginger–garlic paste. Cook for another minute and then add the tomato purée. Add ½ cup (120 ml) of water and let the mixture cook for 3 to 4 minutes. Add the garam masala, cumin powder, chili powder and salt. Cook for 1 minute, then add the soaked lentils to the pot. Toss the lentils with the masala and then add the remaining 3 cups (720 ml) of water to the pot. Stir and close the lid. Press the bean/chili button, and cook on high pressure for 35 minutes, making sure the pressure valve is in the sealing position. Let the pressure release naturally for 15 minutes and then do a quick release.

Open the lid and press the sauté button. Mash some of the lentils using a potato masher, then add the kasuri methi, butter and heavy cream to the dal. Let it all simmer for a minute or two. Garnish with cilantro (if desired) and serve with naan.

NOTES: I recommend using store-bought tomato purée here for that perfect creamy dal makhani texture. If you can't get it, purée 2 medium tomatoes and use them in the recipe.

PALAK PANEER

(INDIAN COTTAGE CHEESE & SPINACH CURRY)

SERVES: 3–4

Palak paneer is a popular Indian curry in which cubes of paneer are simmered in a spiced spinach-based sauce. This popular curry is not only delicious but also a great way to eat your greens. I know of people who don't like spinach otherwise but would happily gulp down bowls of palak paneer!

I love how easy it is to make palak paneer in the Instant Pot—you don't even need to chop the spinach! This dish is lightly spiced, and the fresh flavors of paneer and spinach taste great with just about any flatbread.

2 tbsp (30 g) ghee or unsalted butter

½ tbsp (8 ml) vegetable oil

1 tsp cumin seeds

2 green chilies, chopped

¼ tsp asafetida

2 small onions, chopped

5–6 cloves garlic, chopped

1-inch (25-mm) piece ginger, chopped

2 medium tomatoes, chopped

1 lb (455 g) spinach leaves

½ cup (120 ml) water, divided

1¼ tsp (8 g) salt, or to taste

1 tsp garam masala

1½ tbsp (22 ml) heavy cream

10.5 oz (300 g) paneer, cut into cubes

Press the sauté button. When the pot displays hot, add the ghee (or butter) and oil. Add the cumin seeds and let them sizzle for a few seconds. Add the chopped green chilies and asafetida and cook for a few more seconds. Next, add the onion, garlic and ginger, and cook until the raw smell of ginger and garlic goes away, around 2 minutes. Stir in the chopped tomatoes and cook for another 2 to 3 minutes.

Add the spinach to the pot. There's no need to chop it, you can just add it straight to the pot. Stir until the spinach leaves have wilted; this will take around 1 to 2 minutes. Add ¼ cup (60 ml) of water and the salt. Stir and close the pot with its lid. Press the manual or pressure-cook button and cook on high pressure for 3 minutes, making sure the pressure valve is in the sealing position.

Let the pressure release naturally for 3 minutes and then do a quick release. Using an immersion blender, purée the contents of the pot until creamy. Press the sauté button. Add the remaining ¼ cup (60 ml) of water along with the garam masala and the heavy cream. Add the paneer cubes and let it simmer for 2 minutes. Serve with any bread of your choice. We love to eat it with paratha.

MAKE IT VEGAN: Replace the paneer with tofu, the ghee with oil and the heavy cream with coconut milk.

NOTES: A lot of people like pan-frying their paneer before adding it to the curry. If you wish to, simply pan-fry the paneer cubes in 1 to 2 teaspoons (5 to 10 ml) of oil or ghee before tossing them into the Instant Pot.

MATAR MUSHROOM

(MUSHROOMS & GREEN PEAS IN A CREAMY TOMATO SAUCE)

SERVES: 2

This is one recipe that even the mushroom haters will eat! My husband, who doesn't touch mushrooms, cannot have enough of this dish. Sliced white mushrooms are cooked with green peas in a tomato-cashew-based sauce. The sweetness of the green peas pairs perfectly with the mushrooms. My favorite way to eat matar mushroom is with a plain paratha.

¾ cup (100 g) frozen green peas

¼ cup (60 ml) milk, almond or regular

¼ cup (25 g) cashews

2 medium tomatoes

1 small red onion

3 cloves garlic

½-inch (13-mm) piece ginger

1 tbsp (15 ml) oil of choice

1 bay leaf

½ tsp coriander powder

½ tsp garam masala

¼ tsp red chili powder, or to taste

¼ tsp turmeric powder

½ tsp kashmiri red chili powder, optional

¾ tsp salt, or to taste

2-3 cups (150–200 g) white mushrooms, sliced

¾ cup (180 ml) water

½ tsp kasuri methi (fenugreek leaves), crushed

½ tsp sugar

Soak the frozen green peas in warm water for 10 minutes, then drain. Soak the cashews in warm milk for 15 minutes. In a blender, pulse the tomatoes and the cashew-milk mixture into a purée. Scoop out the purée and set aside. Using the same blender, grind the onion, garlic and ginger to a smooth paste (you may need to add a couple of tablespoons of water).

Press the sauté button. When the pot displays hot, add the oil and then add the bay leaf. Sauté for a few seconds, and then add the prepared onion-ginger-garlic paste to the pot. Cook the paste for 3 to 4 minutes until the smell of onion disappears. Add the tomato-cashew paste, stir and cover the pot with a glass lid and cook for 3 minutes. Add the coriander powder, garam masala, red chili powder, turmeric powder, kashmiri red chili powder (if using) and salt. Mix to combine and cook the spices with the masala for another minute or so.

Stir in the sliced mushrooms and green peas and cook for 1 minute. Add the water, stir and close the pot with its lid. Press the manual or pressure-cook button, making sure the valve is in the sealing position. Cook on high pressure for 2 minutes, then release the pressure quickly. Unlock the lid, then add the crushed kasuri methi and sugar and mix to combine. Enjoy with roti or naan.

NOTE: You can adjust the amount of water to your preference. I like more sauce in the matar mushrooms and hence added ¾ cup (180 ml) of water. For a thicker sauce, add ½ cup (120 ml) of water.

DAL TADKA

(MIXED LENTILS WITH SPICES)

SERVES: 4

I make dals every day in my kitchen. While I usually cook the simple yellow dal, sometimes I like to change things up and make dal by mixing up some lentils. This dal tadka has three kinds of lentils that are cooked along with spices and tomatoes, and then finely tempered with a tadka of cumin seeds, ghee, garlic, onion and green chilies. Tadka is the process of adding whole spices to hot oil or ghee to bring out their flavors. Tadka can be done either at the beginning or (more commonly) toward the end of the preparation of the dish. Tadka can consist of spices like cumin seeds, mustard seeds or even curry leaves and red chilies. The tadka in this recipe definitely enhances the flavor of this dal!

½ cup (105 g) split pigeon peas/ toor dal

½ cup (105 g) split red lentil/ masoor dal

¼ cup (50 g) split moong beans/ moong dal dhuli

1-inch (25-mm) piece ginger, finely chopped

2 green chilies, finely chopped

2 medium tomatoes, chopped

3½ cups (840 ml) water, divided

½ tsp turmeric powder

1¼ tsp (8 g) salt, or to taste

1 tbsp (15 ml) ghee

1 tbsp (15 ml) oil of choice

1 tsp cumin seeds

4 cloves garlic, finely chopped

¼ tsp asafetida

¼ tsp kashmiri red chili powder, optional

3 dried red chilies, broken

2 small red onions, finely chopped

½ tsp garam masala

1 tsp kasuri methi (fenugreek leaves), crushed

2 tbsp (2 g) cilantro, chopped

Wash and rinse the dals and then add them to the inner pot of your Instant Pot. Add the chopped ginger, green chilies, tomatoes and 3 cups (720 ml) of water. Add the turmeric powder and salt and mix to combine. Close the lid, making sure the valve is in the sealing position, and then press the manual or pressure-cook button. Cook on high pressure for 7 minutes and let the pressure release naturally.

Open the lid and press the sauté button. Add the remaining ½ cup (120 ml) of water to the dal at this point if you think it's too thick. Let the dal simmer while you prepare the tadka. Heat the ghee and the oil in a small pan on medium heat. When hot, add the cumin seeds and let them sizzle for a few seconds. Then add the garlic, asafetida, kashmiri red chili powder and dried red chilies. You may break the red chilies before adding them to the tadka for an extra kick of flavor. When the garlic starts to brown, about 1 minute (be careful not to burn it), add the chopped onions. Cook the onions for around 2 minutes until they are soft and translucent. Pour the tadka over the top of the simmering dal.

Add the garam masala, kasuri methi and cilantro and mix well. Let the dal simmer for a minute or two. Enjoy dal tadka with rice!

MAKE IT VEGAN: Replace the ghee with oil.

PANEER TIKKA MASALA
(INDIAN COTTAGE CHEESE IN A CREAMY TOMATO SAUCE)

SERVES: 4

Tikka masala is the most well-known Indian sauce in the Western world. Surprisingly, its origin is British and not Indian. Paneer cubes are marinated with yogurt and spices and then tossed in a creamy tomato curry. Make sure to use thick plain yogurt for marinating the paneer cubes. The plain yogurt that you buy at any grocery store is good to use here, just make sure it isn't watery.

FOR THE PANEER MARINADE
10.5 oz (300 g) paneer, cut into small cubes
1¼ tsp (4 g) garlic, finely chopped
1¼ tsp (4 g) ginger, finely chopped
1 tsp coriander powder
½ tsp garam masala
½ tsp smoked paprika
½ tsp red chili powder
¼ tsp salt
3 tbsp (68 g) thick plain yogurt

FOR THE CURRY
1 tbsp (15 ml) vegetable oil
1 tbsp (15 g) unsalted butter
¾ tsp cumin seeds
1-inch (25-mm) cinnamon stick
1 large red onion, roughly chopped
4–5 large cloves garlic, roughly chopped
1-inch (25-mm) piece ginger, roughly chopped
4 large tomatoes, roughly chopped
1½ tsp (3 g) curry powder
¼ tsp garam masala
1 tsp salt, or to taste
1 tbsp (13 g) sugar
1 cup (240 ml) water
¼ cup (60 ml) heavy cream
½ tsp red chili powder
½ tsp kashmiri red chili powder, for color
2 tbsp (2 g) cilantro, chopped

(continued)

PANEER TIKKA MASALA (CONT.)

Place the paneer cubes in a large bowl and then add the garlic, ginger, coriander powder, garam masala, smoked paprika, red chili powder and ¼ teaspoon of salt. Add the yogurt and toss to combine. Remember to use thick yogurt here; if you don't have thick yogurt, strain your regular yogurt for an hour or so before using in the recipe. The yogurt shouldn't be watery or else it won't coat the paneer cubes. Stir to coat the paneer cubes well with the marinade. Cover the bowl with plastic wrap and refrigerate for a minimum of 30 minutes or up to 4 hours. You may also marinate the paneer overnight.

While the paneer is marinating, make the curry. Press the sauté button and then use the adjust button to set sauté to "more." When the pot displays hot, add the oil and the butter and then the cumin seeds and cinnamon stick. Let the cumin seeds sizzle for a few seconds and then add the chopped onion, garlic and ginger. Sauté for around 3 minutes, until the onions turn light golden brown in color. Add the tomatoes, curry powder, garam masala, 1 teaspoon of salt and sugar. Give it a good stir, cover the pot with a glass lid and let it cook for 3 to 4 minutes. Then add the water and stir. Close the pot with its lid, making sure the valve is in the sealing position. Press the manual or pressure-cook button and cook on high pressure for 2 minutes. Do a quick-pressure release.

Open the lid, and using an immersion blender, purée the contents of the pot to a smooth sauce. If you don't have an immersion blender, let the sauce cool for 10 to 15 minutes, purée using a regular blender, and return to the Instant Pot. Press the sauté button again. Add the heavy cream, red chili powder and kashmiri red chili powder.

Stir in the marinated paneer cubes. For extra flavor, you may toss the paneer cubes in a skillet over medium heat with a little oil until dark brown on both sides, and then add them to the curry. Let the paneer cubes simmer in the curry for 2 to 3 minutes. Stir in the cilantro.

Serve paneer tikka masala with your favorite naan!

MAKE IT VEGAN: Replace the paneer with tofu, the yogurt with vegan yogurt, the butter with vegan butter and the heavy cream with coconut milk.

VEGETABLE BIRYANI

(BASMATI RICE WITH VEGGIES & FRAGRANT SPICES)

SERVES: 4

Fragrant basmati rice cooked with vegetables and spices is one of the most famous Indian dishes worldwide. Traditionally, biryani is cooked on low heat with layers of veggies and rice. However, you can achieve the same flavors using your Instant Pot. The only time taken for this biryani is the minimal prep work!

1 cup (240 ml) plain whole-milk yogurt

1 cup (225 g) paneer, cut into 1-inch (25-mm) cubes

1 large carrot, cut into 1-inch (25-mm) pieces

10 green beans, cut into 1-inch (25-mm) pieces

1 cup (155 g) cauliflower florets, cut into 1-inch (25-mm) florets

1 medium potato, cut into 1-inch (25-mm) pieces

2 tbsp (2 g) cilantro, chopped

2 tbsp (2 g) mint, chopped

2 green chilies, chopped

2 tsp (12 g) ginger–garlic paste (see page 183)

1 tsp garam masala

½ tsp red chili powder

½ tsp turmeric powder

1 tsp biryani masala or garam masala

¾ tsp salt

1½ cups (300 g) basmati rice

1½ cups (360 ml) water

2 medium red onions, thinly sliced (or ½ cup [25 g] ready-to-use fried onions)

3 tbsp + 1 tsp (50 ml) ghee, divided

5 green cardamoms

2 black cardamoms

1-inch (25-mm) piece cinnamon stick

1 bay leaf

4 cloves

8 peppercorns

½ tsp cumin seeds

Generous pinch of saffron strands, dissolved in 3 tbsp (45 ml) warm milk

2 tbsp (2 g) cilantro, chopped

2 tbsp (2 g) mint, chopped

1½ tsp (8 ml) rose water or kewra water

Biryani masala or garam masala, to sprinkle on top

Salt, to sprinkle on top

(continued)

VEGETABLE BIRYANI (CONT.)

Whisk the yogurt in a large bowl until smooth. Add the paneer, carrot, green beans, cauliflower, potato, cilantro, mint, green chilies, ginger–garlic paste, garam masala, chili powder, turmeric, biryani masala and salt and mix until all the veggies and spices are well combined. Cover with plastic wrap and place the bowl in the refrigerator for 35 minutes. Rinse the basmati rice three to four times, and then soak it in 3 cups (720 ml) of water for 35 minutes.

While the veggies are marinating and the rice is soaking, make the fried onions. Skip this step if using ready-to-use fried onions. Heat 2 tablespoons (30 ml) of ghee in a pan over medium heat. When the ghee is hot, add the sliced onions and fry until the onions turn dark golden brown. This will take around 10 to 12 minutes. You may add a pinch of salt to speed up the cooking process. When the onions are caramelized, remove the pan from heat.

Drain the rice and set it aside.

Press the sauté button. When the pot displays hot, add 1 tablespoon (15 ml) of ghee. Add the green cardamoms, black cardamoms, cinnamon stick, bay leaf, cloves, peppercorns and cumin seeds. Sauté for a few seconds until the cumin seeds sizzle and the spices are fragrant. Add the marinated veggies and mix to combine. Place half of the fried onions on top of the veggies. Then place the drained rice on top to cover the veggies. Pour the water all around the edges of the rice, but don't add water directly in the center and do not stir the rice. Top the rice with the saffron milk, the remaining fried onions, cilantro, mint, remaining 1 teaspoon of ghee and rose water. Sprinkle salt and the biryani masala on top. Close the lid and then press the manual or pressure-cook button and cook on high pressure for 6 minutes, making sure the pressure valve is in the sealing position. Let the pressure release naturally for 2 minutes and then do a quick release.

Open the lid and scoop out the biryani from the bottom, making sure you get both the veggies and rice in each serving. Enjoy with a side of raita.

MAKE IT VEGAN: Replace the yogurt with coconut cream or thick coconut milk to marinate the veggies. Also, replace the ghee with oil and use nondairy milk to make the saffron milk.

ACHARI MIXED VEGETABLES

(MIXED VEGETABLES WITH PICKLE MASALA)

SERVES: 2

Pickles are the perfect accompaniment to Indian meals. We always had five to six types of pickles in my house when I was growing up, and most of them were homemade. This recipe uses spices that are commonly used in making pickles, like fenugreek, fennel, cumin, onion seeds and mustard seeds. The addition of yogurt gives this dish a tangy flavor.

1 tsp fennel seeds

1 tsp cumin seeds

½ tsp kalonji (onion seeds)

½ tsp mustard seeds

¼ tsp fenugreek seeds

2 medium tomatoes

1 green chili

8 cashews

1 tbsp (15 ml) oil of choice

⅛ tsp asafetida

1 tsp ginger–garlic paste (see page 183)

½ tsp coriander powder

¼ tsp red chili powder

¼ tsp turmeric powder

¾ tsp salt, or to taste

1 cup (245 g) whole-milk plain yogurt

½ tsp cornstarch

1 tsp pickle masala, optional

1 medium potato, diced small (½-inch [13-mm] pieces)

1 large carrot, cut into rounds

1 cup (130 g) cauliflower florets

¼ cup (35 g) frozen green peas

¼ cup (60 ml) water

½ tsp kasuri methi (fenugreek leaves), crushed

1–2 tbsp (15–30 ml) heavy cream, optional

Mint leaves, for garnish

In a small pan over medium-low heat, dry roast the fennel seeds, cumin seeds, kalonji, mustard seeds and fenugreek seeds for 2 to 3 minutes, stirring often until fragrant. Be careful not to burn the spices. When roasted, transfer to a spice grinder and grind to a fine powder. Set aside.

In a blender, purée the tomatoes with the green chili and the cashews, then set aside. Press the sauté button and when the pot displays hot, add the oil, asafetida and the ginger–garlic paste. Sauté for 30 seconds and then add the puréed tomato and cashew mixture and stir to combine. Cook for 3 to 4 minutes and then add the coriander, red chili powder, turmeric, salt and the pickle spice powder you prepared earlier. Cook for 1 minute.

Whisk the yogurt with the cornstarch; this ensures the yogurt doesn't separate when you add it to the hot pot. Add the yogurt with the tomato mixture, stirring continuously until all of it is nicely combined. Add store-bought pickle masala (if using) and mix. Add the potato, carrot, cauliflower and peas and mix until nicely coated with the masala.

Let the veggies cook for 1 minute. Add the water and then close the lid, setting the pressure valve to the sealing position. Press the manual or pressure-cook button and then use the adjust button to select "low pressure." Cook on low pressure for 3 minutes, then do a quick-pressure release. Open the lid and add kasuri methi. You may add heavy cream to make it creamier and richer in taste. Garnish with mint and serve with naan or paratha.

LENTILS & BEANS

For me, there's nothing more comforting than a bowl of dal (lentils) and rice. Growing up, there was some kind of dal on the table every day for our lunch and dinner. Because Indian families eat so much dal, we make this dish in several different ways.

The everyday dal is almost always vegan. In my house, we always had simple dal with a tadka of cumin seeds and garlic. But there's so much more that you can add to your dal to make it more flavorful and more nutritious. Have you ever tried a sweet dal? If not, then you have to try the Khatti Meethi Gujarati Dal on page 55. It's lightly sweetened with jaggery and is definitely comfort food for the soul.

One of my other favorites from this chapter is the Kashmiri Rajma (page 44). Rajma, a spicy bean curry, was a staple in my house growing up. In fact, rajma with rice is such a classic combination that in Delhi and surrounding areas, you can find street vendors selling plates of rajma-rice everywhere. The rajma recipe in this chapter is a little different from the traditional one because I have used a few different spices, which makes it so much more flavorful!

If you are not too keen on eating greens like spinach and kale, adding them to dals is always a good idea. Spinach Dal (page 36) and Black-Eyed Pea Curry with Kale (page 40) are both a great way to eat those healthy greens!

SPINACH DAL

(LENTILS WITH SPINACH)

SERVES: 2

This is a healthy everyday dal with spinach. My mom always added those veggies which we wouldn't eat otherwise to dal. We would happily eat those veggies in our dals. In this recipe, the dal is lightly seasoned and most of its flavor comes from the use of fresh garlic and spinach. The tempering of cumin, mustard, tomato and garlic goes so well with the greens!

1 tbsp (15 ml) oil of choice

½ tsp cumin seeds

¼ tsp mustard seeds

3 cloves garlic, finely chopped

1 green chili, finely chopped

1 large tomato, chopped

1½ cups (145 g) spinach, finely chopped

¼ tsp turmeric powder

½ tsp salt, or to taste

¼ cup (50 g) split pigeon peas/toor dal, rinsed

¼ cup (50 g) split red lentil/masoor dal, rinsed

1½ cups (360 ml) water

¼ tsp garam masala

1–2 tsp (5–10 ml) lemon juice

Cilantro, for garnish

Rice, for serving

Press the sauté button. When the pot displays hot, add the oil and then the cumin seeds and mustard seeds. Let the seeds sizzle for a few seconds and then add the garlic and green chili. Sauté until the garlic starts to turn golden brown. Add the tomato and let it cook for 1 minute. Add the chopped spinach and mix well. Add the turmeric powder and salt and cook for 1 to 2 minutes. Add the rinsed dals and give it a stir. Add the water and close the pot with its lid.

Press the manual or pressure-cook button and cook for 10 minutes on high pressure, making sure the pressure valve is in the sealing position. Let the pressure release naturally for 5 minutes and then do a quick-pressure release. Open the pot and add the garam masala, lemon juice and cilantro. If you prefer a thinner consistency to your dal, you may add more water at this point. Serve hot with boiled rice!

SAMBAR
(SOUTH INDIAN LENTIL STEW)

SERVES: 3

This classic dish is loaded with veggies; here I have used tomato, onion, okra, carrots and drumsticks. The drumstick tree is widely cultivated in India and the fruits or seed pods of the tree, known as drumsticks, are commonly used in South Indian cooking in stews and curries. You can find fresh or frozen drumsticks at Indian grocery stores.

You may also add veggies like pumpkin, eggplant and potato to this stew. Instead of cooking the lentils and veggies together, I have cooked them at intervals using the Instant Pot, so that the veggies don't become too mushy. And of course, a simple tadka is a must at the end to finish off the sambar! The ingredients list might look long but this dish is super simple to put together.

If you can't find sambar masala at stores near you, you'll find a quick recipe to make it at home in the note.

½ cup (105 g) split pigeon peas/toor dal

3½ cups (840 ml) water, divided

¼ tsp turmeric powder

1¼ tsp (8 g) salt, divided, adjust to taste

1 medium tomato, diced

1 carrot, cut into rounds

1 small red onion, diced

5 okras, cut into 1-inch (25-mm) pieces

6 drumsticks

¼ tsp turmeric powder

Small piece of jaggery, optional

3–4 tsp (6–8 g) sambar masala, adjust to taste

1 tsp tamarind paste

2–3 tsp (10–15 ml) oil of choice

½ tsp mustard seeds

¼ tsp asafetida

15 curry leaves

1 green chili, sliced

1 tbsp (1 g) cilantro, chopped

To the inner steel pot of the Instant Pot, add the toor dal, 1 cup (240 ml) of water, turmeric powder and ½ teaspoon of salt. Close the pot, then press the manual or pressure-cook button and cook on high pressure for 8 minutes, making sure the pressure valve is in the sealing position. Let the pressure release naturally.

Open the pot and add the tomato, carrot, onion, okras, drumsticks, 2½ cups (600 ml) of water, turmeric powder, jaggery, sambar masala, tamarind paste and ¾ teaspoon of salt. Stir to combine. Close the lid again, press the manual or pressure-cook button and cook on high pressure for 5 minutes. Do a quick-pressure release.

Prepare the tadka while the veggies are still cooking. In a small pan over medium heat, add the oil. When hot, add the mustard seeds. Let them pop and then add the asafetida, curry leaves and green chili. Sauté for a few seconds and then transfer the tadka to the cooked sambar and stir to combine. Garnish with cilantro. Enjoy with idlis, dosa or rice!

NOTE: For a quick sambar masala, in a pan over medium heat, dry roast 1 tablespoon (13 g) chana dal, 1 tablespoon (13 g) coriander seeds, 2 dried red chilies, ½ teaspoon cumin seeds, ½ teaspoon mustard seeds and 1 clove. Let cool, then grind to a powder.

BLACK-EYED PEA CURRY WITH KALE

SERVES: 4

This is the kind of curry that you would find in every household in India on a daily basis— simple flavors, no extra fat or spices, not to mention vegan. In short, simple comfort food for the soul. I have added kale to this curry to make it even more nutritious.

1 cup (197 g) dried black-eyed peas

1 tbsp (15 ml) oil of choice

½ tsp cumin seeds

1 medium red onion, chopped

4–5 cloves garlic, finely chopped

1-inch (25-mm) piece ginger, finely chopped

1 green chili, finely chopped

2 large tomatoes, chopped

1 tsp coriander powder

½ tsp turmeric powder

¼ tsp garam masala

1 tsp salt, or to taste

1½ to 2 cups (360 to 480 ml) water

2–3 cups (60–90 g) kale, chopped

2 tsp (10 ml) lime juice

Rice or quinoa, for serving

Wash and soak the black-eyed peas in 3 cups (720 ml) of water for 3 to 4 hours. Drain and rinse the peas and set them aside.

Press the sauté button. When the pot displays hot, add the oil and the cumin seeds and let them sizzle for a few seconds. Then add the onion and sauté until soft, around 2 minutes. Add the garlic, ginger and green chili and cook until the ginger and garlic start turning light golden brown in color, about 1 minute. Add the tomatoes and cook for 3 to 4 minutes, until the tomatoes are soft. Add the coriander powder, turmeric powder, garam masala and salt. Cook for 1 minute. Add the black-eyed peas along with ½ cup (120 ml) of water, give the curry a good stir and close the pot with its lid. Press the manual or pressure-cook button and cook on high pressure for 20 minutes. The pressure valve should be in the sealing position. Let the pressure release naturally for 10 minutes and then do a quick-pressure release.

Open the pot and press the sauté button. Add the kale and let simmer for 2 to 3 minutes. Stir in the lime juice and serve the curry over rice or quinoa!

NOTE: If you're in a rush, you can soak the black-eyed peas for an hour only. In that case, I would cook the black-eyed peas for 30 minutes on manual high pressure or bean/chili mode and then do a natural pressure release.

JACKFRUIT WITH CHANA DAL

SERVES: 2—3

I have very fond memories of eating my mom's jackfruit and chana dal kebabs. Mom made these spicy patties using jackfruit and lots of whole spices. We used to eat it with cilantro chutney or ketchup. I have tried to incorporate the same flavors in this dish—it has lots of whole spices but in case you can't find some of them, you can omit. Jackfruit has a meat-like texture, so if you are a meat lover who is trying to eat more veggies, give jackfruit a try.

½ cup (104 g) split chickpeas/chana dal

4 green cardamoms

4 cloves

2 black cardamoms

7–8 black peppercorns

2 tsp (10 ml) oil of choice

½ tsp cumin seeds

2 bay leaves

½-inch (13-mm) piece cinnamon stick

2 dried red chilies

4 cloves garlic, chopped

2 medium tomatoes, chopped

20-oz (567-g) can jackfruit, drained, rinsed and diced

1 tsp coriander powder

¼ tsp turmeric powder, optional

¾ tsp salt, or to taste

¾ cup (180 ml) water

1–2 tsp (5–10 ml) lemon juice

Cilantro, for garnish

Rinse and soak the chana dal in 1 cup (240 ml) of water for 40 minutes. Lightly crush the green cardamoms, cloves, black cardamoms and black peppercorns using a mortar and pestle and set aside. Drain the dal and transfer it to another bowl.

Press the sauté button. When the pot displays hot, add the oil and then add the cumin seeds, bay leaves, cinnamon stick, crushed spices (cardamoms/cloves/peppercorns) along with the dried red chilies. Sauté for a few seconds until the spices are fragrant and then add the chopped garlic. Cook for 1 minute or until the garlic starts turning light golden brown in color and then add in the tomato.

Cook the tomato for 2 minutes and then add the chana dal, jackfruit, coriander powder, turmeric powder (if using) and salt and mix to combine. Cook for 1 minute and then add the water. Close the pot with its lid and set the pressure valve to the sealing position. Press the manual or pressure-cook button and cook on high pressure for 10 minutes. Let the pressure release naturally.

Open the pot and press the sauté button. If you want to get rid of a little of the water that's in the pot, let it simmer for 2 minutes on sauté. This is optional; if you want a little liquid in your dish, you may skip this step. Stir in the lemon juice, garnish with cilantro and serve.

NOTE: If you don't have the whole spices, add ½ teaspoon of garam masala instead.

KASHMIRI RAJMA

(KIDNEY-BEAN CURRY)

SERVES: 4

This curry features kidney beans cooked with spices like fennel and ginger. The spices used here are a little different from the punjabi rajma masala, and that's what makes this recipe so special. There are several kinds of kidney beans available in the market and, for this recipe, I have used Kashmiri kidney beans. They are a little smaller in size compared to regular kidney beans. You may of course use the regular kidney beans, but I think the smaller ones cook so much better in the Instant Pot.

1 cup (210 g) kashmiri kidney beans

2 tbsp (30 ml) oil of choice

½-inch (13-mm) piece cinnamon stick

4 green cardamoms

3 cloves

½ tsp cumin seeds

⅛ tsp asafetida

1 medium red onion, finely chopped

1 tbsp (15 g) ginger-garlic paste (see page 183)

3 medium tomatoes, puréed

1 tsp coriander powder

¼ tsp red chili powder, or to taste

1 tsp kashmiri red chili powder

¾ tsp ginger powder

¾ tsp fennel powder

¼ tsp garam masala

1 tsp salt, or to taste

3 cups (720 ml) water

2-3 tbsp (2-3 g) cilantro, chopped

1 tsp ghee, for serving (optional)

Rice, for serving

Soak the kashmiri kidney beans in 3 cups (720 ml) of water for 4 hours, or overnight. If you are in a rush, soak in boiling hot water for 1 hour. Drain the water and set aside.

Press the sauté button. When the pot displays hot, add the oil, cinnamon stick, green cardamoms, cloves and cumin seeds. Sauté for a few seconds until the cumin seeds sizzle and the spices are fragrant. Add the asafetida and onion and cook for 2 minutes until soft. Add the ginger-garlic paste and cook for 1 minute. Stir in the tomato purée, mix well and then cover the pot with a glass lid and cook for 3 to 4 minutes. Remove the lid and add the coriander powder, red chili powder, kashmiri red chili powder, ginger powder, fennel powder, garam masala and salt. Mix well and cook for 1 minute. Add the kidney beans and 3 cups (720 ml) of water. Add the cilantro, stir well and close the pot with its lid. Press the manual or pressure-cook button and cook for 35 minutes on high pressure. Let the pressure release naturally.

Open the lid and press the sauté button. Use the adjust button to set sauté to "more." Using a potato masher, mash some of the beans as the curry simmers. This will thicken the curry and infuse more flavors. Let it simmer for a couple of minutes. Add a teaspoon of ghee, optional, before serving and enjoy the rajma with rice (the best combination!).

NOTE: For this recipe, I use the small jammu or kashmiri kidney beans. If you have to use regular kidney beans, choose the lighter-colored ones. The darker-colored ones take a long time to cook.

MOONG DAL WITH CABBAGE & DILL

(LENTILS WITH CABBAGE & DILL)

SERVES: 2

This is a simple dish made with moong dal, green cabbage and fresh dill. Lightly spiced, and easy on the stomach, you will love this with a simple side of roti.

2 tsp (10 ml) oil of choice

½ tsp mustard seeds

1 small red onion, chopped

2 green chilies, sliced

5 cups (500 g) cabbage, shredded

½ cup (110 g) split moong bean/ moong dal dhuli, rinsed

½ tsp turmeric powder

½ tsp salt, or to taste

⅓ cup (80 ml) water

¼ cup (3 g) fresh dill, chopped

Garam masala, to sprinkle

Roti or flatbread, for serving

Press the sauté button. When the pot displays hot, add the oil and the mustard seeds. After a few seconds, when the mustard seeds start to pop, add the onion and sliced green chilies. Cook for 2 minutes until softened. Add the shredded cabbage, mix well and cook for 1 minute. Add in the moong dal, turmeric powder and salt and mix well. Add the water and close the pot with the lid. Press the manual or pressure-cook button and cook on high pressure for 5 minutes, making sure the valve is in the sealing position. Let the pressure release naturally for 5 minutes and then do a quick-pressure release. Open the pot, add the chopped dill, sprinkle with garam masala and mix well. Serve hot with roti or flatbread of your choice.

PANCHMEL DAL

(FIVE-LENTIL MIX WITH SPICES)

SERVES: 4

Panch means "five" and mel means "mix," so for this recipe we mix together five types of dals. You may use a different combination of dals, but these are the ones that I like the best—split black gram, split red lentil, split chickpeas, split pigeon peas and split green gram. I have flavored this dal with lots of fresh ginger. It's lightly spiced and tastes great with rice or roti.

1¼ cups (250 g) mixed dal (¼ cup [50 g] each of split black gram [urad chilka], split red lentil [masoor], split chickpeas [chana], split pigeon peas [toor] and split green gram [moong chilka])

1 tbsp + 1 tsp (20 ml) ghee, divided

1 bay leaf

4 green cardamoms

3 cloves

1 tsp cumin seeds

2 dried red chilies

¼ tsp asafetida

2-inch (5-cm) piece ginger, finely chopped

1 green chili, chopped

1 large tomato, chopped

½ tsp turmeric powder

1 tsp salt, or to taste

3 cups (720 ml) water

2 tbsp (2 g) cilantro, chopped

2 tsp (10 ml) lemon juice

Rinse the dals and soak them in 3 to 4 cups (720 to 960 ml) of water in a large bowl for 30 minutes. Drain, then set aside the dal mix.

Press the sauté button. When the pot displays hot, add 1 tablespoon (15 ml) of ghee to the pot and then add the bay leaf, green cardamoms, cloves and cumin seeds. Sauté for a few seconds, until the spices are fragrant and the cumin seeds sizzle. Add the dried red chilies (break them for extra heat; I add them whole) and asafetida and sauté for a few seconds. Add the chopped ginger and green chili and cook for a minute or two, until the ginger starts changing color. Stir in the tomato, mix well and cook for 2 minutes, until the tomatoes are a little soft. Add the soaked dal, turmeric powder and salt. Mix well, then add the water and close the lid. Press the manual or pressure-cook button and cook on high pressure for 7 minutes, with the pressure valve in the sealing position. Let the pressure release naturally for 10 minutes and then do a quick-pressure release.

Open the pot, stir the dal and add the remaining 1 teaspoon of ghee, cilantro and lemon juice. Serve panchmel dal hot with boiled rice or pulao.

MAKE IT VEGAN: Replace the ghee with oil.

TOMATO BUTTERNUT SQUASH DAL

SERVES: 4

This is a simple dal made with red lentils, tomatoes and butternut squash. I like making this dal during the fall and winter when squash is in season. This dal is very lightly spiced so that you can fully appreciate the natural flavors of the tomato and squash.

2 tsp (10 ml) oil of choice

½ tsp mustard seeds

½ tsp cumin seeds

⅛ tsp asafetida

1 green chili, sliced

2 dried red chilies, broken

1½ tsp (3 g) ginger, finely chopped

10–12 curry leaves

2 medium tomatoes, chopped

2 cups (300 g) butternut squash, diced into 1- to 1½-inch (25- to 38-mm) pieces

¾ cup (145 g) split red lentils/masoor dal

2½ cups (600 ml) water, divided

½ tsp turmeric powder

1 tsp salt, or to taste

1 tbsp (1 g) cilantro, chopped

1½ tsp (7.5 ml) lemon juice, or to taste

Press the sauté button. When the pot displays hot, add the oil and then the mustard seeds and cumin seeds. Let the mustard seeds pop for a few seconds and then add the asafetida, green chili and broken dried red chilies. Sauté for a few seconds, then add the ginger and curry leaves and cook for a minute or two until the ginger starts turning light golden brown. Stir in the tomatoes and squash. Cook for 2 minutes. Add the lentils and mix well. Add 1 cup (240 ml) of water, the turmeric powder and salt and mix well. Secure the lid, close the pressure valve and press the manual or pressure-cook button. Cook for 6 minutes on high pressure. Naturally release pressure for 5 minutes and then do a quick-pressure release.

Open the pot, press the sauté button and add the remaining 1½ cups (360 ml) of water along with the cilantro and lemon juice. Let it simmer for 2 minutes. Serve the tomato butternut squash dal warm over boiled rice for a comforting meal.

NOTE: The size of the pieces of butternut squash is important. Make sure each piece is at least 1 inch (25 mm) so the squash won't get mushy and dissolve in the dal. This is also why you add only 1 cup (240 ml) of water at first to cook the dal, and then add the remaining amount later.

SPICED CHICKPEA SALAD

SERVES: 2–3

This spiced chickpea salad features peanuts, fresh coconut and a touch of lime and honey! I make this salad often for lunch. It's rather simple to put together, has fresh flavors and is also packed with protein!

1 cup (205 g) dried white chickpeas, soaked overnight

2½ cups (600 ml) water

1 tbsp (15 ml) oil of choice

½ tsp mustard seeds

1-inch (25-mm) piece ginger, chopped

2 dried red chilies, broken

2 tbsp (32 g) raw peanuts

10–12 curry leaves

¼ tsp garam masala

½ tsp salt, or to taste

¼ cup (22 g) grated coconut

2–3 tsp (10–15 ml) lime juice

1½ tsp (7 ml) honey

Cilantro, for garnish

Pomegranate arils, for garnish

Wash and soak the chickpeas in 3 cups (720 ml) of water overnight. Drain the water, transfer the soaked chickpeas to the inner steel pot of your Instant Pot and add the 2½ cups (600 ml) of water. Close the pot with its lid and press the bean/chili button, making sure the pressure valve is in the sealing position. Cook for 25 minutes on high pressure, then let the pressure release naturally. Open the pot, drain the water and set aside the cooked chickpeas.

Press the sauté button. When the pot displays hot, add the oil and mustard seeds. Let the mustard seeds pop for a few seconds and then add the chopped ginger and the broken dried red chilies. Cook for a minute or two until the ginger turns light golden brown, and then add the peanuts. Cook for 1 to 2 minutes, until the peanuts change color. Add the curry leaves, stir and then add the boiled chickpeas back into the pot. Add the garam masala, salt and grated coconut and mix well. Stir in the lime juice, then unplug the Instant Pot. Add the honey and stir again. Garnish with the cilantro and pomegranate arils and serve.

KHATTI MEETHI GUJARATI DAL

(SWEET & SOUR LENTILS)

SERVES: 4

You will find a touch of sweetness in a lot of Gujarati recipes and this khatti (sour) and meethi (sweet) Gujarati dal is no exception. It is seasoned with cumin, mustard and ginger and is lightly sweetened with jaggery. The ingredient list may look long but it is really easy to put it all together. This dal has a very thin consistency; it should always be pourable. This is a staple dal in the state of Gujarat in India and is eaten with phulka or rice.

¾ cup (155 g) split pigeon peas/ toor dal

4 cups (960 ml) water, divided

½ tsp turmeric powder

1 tbsp (16 g) peanuts

1 small tomato, chopped

½-inch (13-mm) piece ginger, grated

2 green chilies, sliced

¼ tsp red chili powder, or to taste

1¼ tsp (8 g) salt, or to taste

2 tbsp (24 g) jaggery, grated

2 tbsp (30 ml) lemon juice

1½ tbsp (1.5 g) cilantro, chopped

1½ tbsp (22 ml) oil of choice

½ tsp mustard seeds

¼ tsp cumin seeds

¼ tsp fenugreek seeds

¼ tsp asafetida

2 cloves

½-inch (13-mm) cinnamon stick

8–10 curry leaves

Rice or roti, for serving

Rinse the dal until the water turns clear, and then add it to the inner steel pot of the Instant Pot, along with 2 cups (480 ml) of water and the turmeric powder. Tie the peanuts in a muslin cloth or place them in a small steel bowl, and place that in the pot along with the dal. Close the lid, press the manual or pressure-cook button and cook on high pressure for 7 minutes. Let the pressure release naturally.

Open the pot, remove the peanuts from the pot and then mash the dal using a potato masher or immersion blender. Gujarati dal should be very smooth, with no visible dal particles.

Press the sauté button and then add the tomato, ginger, green chilies, red chili powder, salt, jaggery and lemon juice into the pot. Also add the remaining 2 cups (480 ml) of water and the cilantro. Let the dal simmer for 5 minutes.

For the tadka, heat the oil in a small pan over medium heat. When the oil is hot, add the mustard seeds, cumin seeds and fenugreek seeds. Let them sizzle for a few seconds, until the mustard seeds start to pop. Then add the asafetida, cloves, cinnamon stick and curry leaves. Cook for a few seconds and then transfer the tadka to the boiling dal. Stir and serve with rice or roti.

SOOKHA KALA CHANA

(SPICED BLACK CHICKPEAS)

SERVES: 3

For this recipe, kala chana, also known as black chickpeas, is cooked with lots of dried spices. This recipe is traditionally made in India during the fasting festival of Navratri. Ever since I can remember, I have enjoyed kala chana with sooji halwa (semolina pudding) and poori (whole-wheat deep-fried bread); it's like these dishes can't be enjoyed any other way! Enjoy this dish with Pumpkin Coconut Halwa (page 165) and poori.

1 cup (200 g) black chickpeas/
kala chana

3 cups (720 ml) water

1½ tsp (5 g) salt, divided

1 tbsp (15 ml) ghee or oil

1 bay leaf

3 green cardamoms

½ tsp cumin seeds

1-inch (25-mm) piece ginger, cut
into thin juliennes

2 green chilies, sliced

1 tsp coriander powder

¼ tsp garam masala

¼ tsp cumin powder

¼ tsp dried mango powder/
amchur

Cilantro, for garnish

Pumpkin Coconut Halwa
(page 165), for serving

Poori, for serving

Wash the black chickpeas and place them in the pot along with the water and 1 teaspoon of salt. Close the pot with its lid and press the bean/chili button. Set the time to 40 minutes, making sure the pressure valve is in the sealing position. Let the pressure release naturally.

Open the lid, drain the water and put the cooked chickpeas in another bowl. Wipe the steel pot and place it back into the Instant Pot. Press the sauté button. When the pot displays hot, add the ghee to the pot and then add the bay leaf and green cardamoms. Sauté for a few seconds until the spices are fragrant, and then add the cumin seeds and let them sizzle for a few seconds. Add the ginger and green chilies and cook for 1 to 2 minutes, until the ginger starts changing color. Next, add the coriander powder, garam masala, cumin powder and dried mango powder along with 1 tablespoon (15 ml) of water. Cook for a few seconds and then add the cooked black chickpeas back into the pot. Stir until the chickpeas are well coated. Add ½ teaspoon of salt and mix well. Garnish with cilantro. Serve with halwa and poori!

NOTE: If you don't have amchur, add 1 teaspoon of lemon juice instead.

HEARTY MEALS

Hearty meals with different flavors and seasonings are sure to entice your taste buds. Most of these dishes taste great with flatbreads, like paratha or naan, or they are great with rice or quinoa if you want to keep it gluten free. Indian food is not all about curries, and these dishes are a testimony to that!

While there's the classic Aloo Gobi (page 60) that I love and is almost always a part of my Indian thali, there's also a fun Paneer Lasagna (page 69). Have you ever tried a lasagna with Indian flavors? Make sure to check it out! Kadai Tofu (page 70) and Banarsi Dum Aloo (page 67) are two more hearty dishes, both of which make excellent weeknight meals. If you want something really comforting, then try the Vegetable Khichdi (page 63), a mix of lentils and rice with a dollop of ghee, which was often on the table for our lunches and dinners when I was growing up. It's so comforting and so good for you!

ALOO GOBI

(SPICED POTATOES & CAULIFLOWER)

SERVES: 4

This is a simple yet classic Indian dish in which potatoes and cauliflower are cooked together with spices. Everyone has their own way of making aloo gobi, but this one is my personal favorite—with lots of ginger, garlic and tomatoes. It's mildly spiced with garam masala and is made a little tangy with the addition of dried mango powder.

1 tbsp (15 ml) vegetable oil

½ tsp cumin seeds

1 large red onion, finely chopped

1½ tsp (9 g) ginger–garlic paste (see page 183)

2 medium tomatoes, chopped

1 tsp coriander powder

½ tsp turmeric powder

½ tsp dried mango powder/amchur

¼ tsp red chili powder, or to taste

¼ tsp garam masala

¾ tsp salt, or to taste

2 medium potatoes, diced into 1-inch (25-mm) pieces

3–4 tbsp (45–60 ml) water

1 medium head (500 g) cauliflower, cut into medium to large florets

2 tbsp (2 g) cilantro, chopped, plus more for garnish

Press the sauté button. When the pot displays hot, add the oil and the cumin seeds and let them sizzle for a few seconds. Add the chopped onion and cook for 2 to 3 minutes until soft and translucent. Add the ginger–garlic paste and cook for another minute, then add the tomatoes and cook for 2 minutes until the tomatoes are soft. Add the coriander powder, turmeric powder, dried mango powder, red chili powder, garam masala and salt and mix to combine. Cook the spices for 30 seconds, and then add 2 tablespoons (30 ml) of water along with the diced potatoes.

Toss the potatoes so they are coated with the masala. Cover the pot with a glass lid and let the potatoes cook for 3 to 4 minutes, stirring them once or twice in between. Remove the glass lid, add 3 to 4 tablespoons (45 to 60 ml) of more water and mix well to deglaze the pot. Place the cauliflower florets on top. Do not stir. Sprinkle 2 tablespoons (2 g) of cilantro on top of the cauliflower, but do not stir. Close the pot with the lid, making sure the pressure valve is in the sealing position. Press the manual or pressure-cook button and then use the adjust or pressure level button to set the pressure to "low." Cook on low pressure for 3 minutes, then do a quick-pressure release.

Open the pot and gently mix the cauliflower with the potatoes and the masala. You may press the sauté button to dry off excess water. Transfer the aloo gobi to a serving bowl, garnish with more cilantro and serve. This dish tastes best with plain roti or paratha.

NOTE: In case the pot doesn't come to pressure (it may happen sometimes!), just add a couple of tablespoons of more water, close the lid and cook on low pressure for 3 minutes. Do not add too much water or the aloo gobi will turn very watery. The tomatoes also release a lot of water when pressure cooked, so you don't need a lot of water here.

VEGETABLE KHICHDI
(MIXED LENTILS & RICE PORRIDGE)

SERVES: 4

Healthy and comforting traditional Indian khichdi is made with white rice and lentils. It is lightly spiced and soft in consistency. In India, we eat khichdi whenever we want something comforting, as well as easy to digest. I have added lots of vegetables like tomato, carrot, beans, potato, spinach and peas to this khichdi to make it more wholesome. It's often served with pickles and yogurt.

2 tsp (10 ml) ghee

1 bay leaf

½ tsp cumin seeds

⅛ tsp asafetida

1-inch (25-mm) piece ginger, chopped

2–3 cloves garlic, chopped

1 medium tomato, chopped

1 large carrot, diced

7–8 green beans, chopped

1 small potato, cubed

¼ cup (35 g) frozen green peas

½ tsp turmeric powder

⅛ tsp red chili powder, or to taste

½ cup (100 g) white rice, drained and rinsed

¼ cup (50 g) split red lentils/masoor dal, drained and rinsed

¼ cup (55 g) split moong beans/moong dal, drained and rinsed

1¼ tsp (8 g) salt, or to taste

3 cups (720 ml) water

½ cup (25 g) spinach, chopped

½ tbsp (7.5 ml) lemon juice, optional

Cilantro, for garnish

Yogurt and pickles, for serving

Press the sauté button. When the pot displays hot, add the ghee to the pot, then add the bay leaf and cumin seeds. Let the cumin seeds sizzle for a few seconds and then add the asafetida and sauté for 5 seconds. Add the ginger and garlic, sauté for 30 seconds, then add the tomato, carrot, green beans, potato and green peas. Stir to combine. Add the turmeric powder and red chili powder and mix, then add the rice, lentils and beans. Stir to combine. Then add the salt and water. Close the lid and then press the rice button, making sure the pressure valve is in the sealing position. This will automatically cook on low pressure for 12 minutes. Let the pressure release naturally.

Open the lid, press the sauté button, then stir in the chopped spinach. Mix until the spinach is wilted and combined, around 1 minute. Add the lemon juice, optional, and garnish with cilantro. Enjoy this vegetable khichdi with yogurt and pickles on the side.

GATTE KI SABZI

(CHICKPEA FLOUR DUMPLINGS CURRY)

SERVES: 3

Chickpea dumplings in a tangy yogurt-based curry is a popular curry from the state of Rajasthan. It's great for days when you have no veggies in your refrigerator! Spiced dumplings made with chickpea flour are first boiled in water and then simmered in a spicy curry. If you like tangy dishes, then you must try this one!

FOR THE GATTE (CHICKPEA DUMPLINGS)

1 cup (102 g) garbanzo bean flour/besan

¼ tsp carom seeds

¼ tsp red chili powder

¼ tsp garam masala

½ tsp turmeric powder

½ tsp coriander powder

½ tsp salt

Pinch of asafetida

2–3 tbsp (30–45 g) yogurt

1 tsp vegetable oil, plus more to grease your hands

FOR THE YOGURT CURRY

1 medium onion

3 garlic cloves

1-inch (25-mm) piece ginger

1 tbsp (15 ml) vegetable oil

½ tbsp (7 ml) ghee

½ tsp cumin seeds

4 cloves

1 green chili, sliced

½ tsp coriander powder

½ tsp turmeric powder

¼ tsp red chili powder

¼ tsp garam masala

¾ tsp salt, or to taste

¾ cup (185 g) plain yogurt, whisked and at room temperature

¾ cup (180 ml) water

1 tbsp (1 g) cilantro, chopped

Bread, for serving

To the inner pot of the Instant Pot, add 5 to 6 cups (1.25 to 1.5 L) of water and then press the yogurt button. Then press the adjust button until the screen displays "boil." Close the pot with the lid; the pressure valve can be venting or sealing. While the water is boiling, make the chickpea dumplings (gatte). In a large bowl, put the garbanzo bean flour, carom seeds, red chili powder, garam masala, turmeric powder, coriander powder, salt and a pinch of asafetida. Mix until well combined. Add the yogurt, 1 tablespoon (15 g) at a time, and mix to form a dough. Add more yogurt only if the dough isn't coming together. Also add 1 teaspoon of oil to the dough and mix to combine. Grease your hands with a little oil before you start kneading—this makes it easier to handle the sticky dough. Knead the dough in the bowl until it comes together to form a smooth yet stiff dough. Divide the dough into four equal parts and shape each part into a log, 4 to 5 inches (10 to 13 cm) long.

(continued)

GATTE KI SABZI (CONT.)

When you hear the beep signalling that the water has come to a boil, open the lid and add the dough logs to the hot water. Close the lid again, making sure the pressure valve is in the sealing position. Press the manual or pressure-cook button. Cook on high pressure for 15 minutes. Do a quick-pressure release. Remove the gatte carefully from the water using tongs. You will know the dough is done when you insert a knife inside it and it comes out clean. Cut all four logs into small pieces, around ½ inch (13 mm) each. At this point, you may leave them as such or shallow fry them. To fry them, lightly spray a pan with oil and then toss the gatte on it, stirring often until they are golden on both sides. You may also deep fry them.

To make the curry, discard the water in which you boiled the gatte, wipe the inner steel pot and place it back into the Instant Pot. In a blender, purée the onion, garlic and ginger until a paste forms. Press the sauté button and wait until the pot displays hot. Add the oil and ghee, followed by cumin seeds. Let the cumin seeds sizzle for a few seconds, then add the prepared onion–ginger–garlic paste. Also add the cloves and sliced green chili. Sauté the paste until the raw smell of ginger and garlic goes away, around 3 minutes. Add the coriander powder, turmeric powder, red chili powder, garam masala and salt along with 2 tablespoons (30 ml) of water. The water will help keep the spices from burning. Sauté for a minute and then stir in the whisked yogurt. Stir the yogurt continuously until it is well combined. Cook for a minute and then add the prepared gatte to the pot. Add the water and close the pot with the lid. Press the manual or pressure-cook button, making sure the pressure valve is in the sealing position, and cook on high pressure for 3 minutes. Do a quick-pressure release.

Open the pot, add cilantro and serve this tangy gatte ki sabzi with your bread of choice.

NOTE: You may add more water if you prefer a thinner curry.

BANARSI DUM ALOO
(CREAMY BABY POTATOES CURRY)

SERVES: 2—3

Dum aloo refers to a royal Indian dish made with potatoes. It's cooked in different ways in different parts of India. For example, Kashmiri dum aloo is flavored with fennel and ginger, while in the Banarsi dum aloo here, the potatoes are cooked in a creamy onion–tomato-based curry. This dish tastes great with naan.

¼ cup (30 g) cashews

1 medium red onion

2 large tomatoes

1 lb (455 g) baby potatoes

¼ tsp smoked paprika

½ tsp turmeric powder, divided

1¼ tsp (7 g) salt, divided, to taste

2 tbsp (30 ml) oil of choice, divided

1 bay leaf

3 green cardamoms

3 cloves

1½ tsp (9 g) ginger–garlic paste (see page 183)

½ tsp coriander powder

½ tsp garam masala

½ tsp red chili powder, or to taste

1 tbsp (17 g) tomato ketchup

2 tbsp (30 g) plain yogurt, whisked and at room temperature

½ cup (120 ml) water

Cilantro, for garnish

MAKE IT VEGAN: Replace the yogurt with vegan coconut yogurt or skip the yogurt.

Soak the cashews in warm water in a small bowl for 15 minutes, then drain. While they are soaking, in a blender purée the onion, adding 3 to 4 tablespoons (45 to 60 ml) of water to make a fine paste. Remove the paste from the blender and set aside. In the same blender, no need to clean it first, purée the tomatoes and cashews and set aside.

Wash and peel the baby potatoes and then pierce them all over using a fork. We do this so that the spices and flavors will seep inside the potatoes while they cook. Toss the baby potatoes with ¼ teaspoon each of smoked paprika, turmeric powder and salt, making sure the potatoes are evenly coated with the spices.

Press the sauté button. When the pot displays hot, add 1 tablespoon (15 ml) of oil to the pot and then add the potatoes. Sauté for 4 minutes or until lightly browned. Remove the potatoes from the pot and set them aside.

To the same pot, no need to clean it, add the remaining 1 tablespoon (15 ml) of oil. Add the bay leaf, cardamoms and cloves and sauté until the spices are fragrant. Add the puréed onion and let it cook for 5 minutes, stirring often or until the raw smell of onion goes away. Add the ginger–garlic paste, and cook for another 2 minutes. Add the puréed tomato–cashew paste, then cover with a glass lid and cook for 2 to 3 minutes. Add the coriander powder, garam masala, red chili powder, ¼ teaspoon turmeric powder and remaining 1 teaspoon salt. Stir the spices and cook for 1 minute. Stir in the tomato ketchup, then add the yogurt, stirring continuously until well combined. Add the water and the sautéed potatoes. Mix well, then close the lid. Press the manual or pressure-cook button and cook on high pressure for 5 minutes, with the pressure valve in the sealing position. Let the pressure release naturally for 5 minutes and then do a quick-pressure release. Garnish with cilantro and serve dum aloo with naan or rice.

PANEER LASAGNA
(SPICED INDIAN COTTAGE CHEESE LASAGNA)

SERVES: 4

Love lasagna? Then try this Indian-inspired version! This vegetarian lasagna has layers of paneer, spiced pasta sauce and, of course, cheese. Comfort food doesn't get better than this!

2 tsp (10 ml) vegetable oil

1 small onion, chopped

2 large cloves garlic, chopped

1 green chili, chopped

1 small red pepper, chopped

1 medium tomato, chopped

¾ tsp garam masala, divided

⅛ tsp turmeric powder

⅛ tsp black pepper

½ tsp salt, or to taste

2 cups (200 g) grated paneer

2 tsp (1 g) kasuri methi (fenugreek leaves), crushed, divided

24-oz (680-g) jar of traditional pasta sauce

½ tsp cayenne pepper

¼ tsp cardamom powder

2 tbsp (30 ml) heavy cream or half & half

1 tbsp (15 g) unsalted butter

3–4-oz (85–114-g) no-boil lasagna sheets

2 cups (200 g) shredded mozzarella cheese

Cilantro, for garnish

Lightly spray a 7-inch (18-cm) springform pan and set it aside.

Heat the oil in a medium pan over medium heat. When hot, add the onion, garlic and green chili and sauté for a minute or two, then add the red pepper and tomato. Cook for 1 to 2 minutes, then stir in ¼ teaspoon garam masala, turmeric powder, black pepper and salt. Mix well and then add the grated paneer. Stir until everything is well combined, then add 1 teaspoon of kasuri methi. Remove the pan from the heat and set it aside. You may also do this step in your Instant Pot on the sauté mode.

Put the pasta sauce in a small pan over medium heat. Add the cayenne pepper, ½ teaspoon garam masala, cardamom powder, heavy cream, butter and 1 teaspoon kasuri methi. Stir and let it all heat for a minute or two. Remove pan from heat and set it aside.

Spread a thin layer of sauce in the bottom of the springform pan, then top with a layer of lasagna noodles (you will have to break them to fit into the pan), one-third of the paneer mixture and one-quarter of the mozzarella cheese. Repeat the same layers two more times—sauce, noodles, paneer mixture and cheese, pressing down each time to make sure it is compact. End with a thick layer of sauce and the last one-quarter of the mozzarella cheese. Cover the springform pan with a sheet of aluminum foil, making sure to spray the foil with a little nonstick spray so that the cheese doesn't stick to it. Pour 1½ cups (360 ml) of water into the inner steel pot of the Instant Pot and then place the Instant Pot's trivet inside. Make an aluminum foil sling—a long piece of foil folded twice or thrice lengthwise. Wrap the sling around the springform pan, then, using the sling, carefully lower the springform pan into the Instant Pot and place it on top of the trivet. Close the lid and then press the manual or pressure-cook button. Set the time to 20 minutes on high pressure, making sure the pressure valve is in the sealing position. Let the pressure release naturally.

Open the pot and then remove the springform pan carefully from the pot using the sling. At this point, you may pop the pan into the oven to broil for 2 minutes. This is just to brown the cheese and is an optional step. Let the lasagna sit at room temperature for 10 minutes before serving. Top with fresh cilantro and serve!

KADAI TOFU
(SPICED TOFU WITH BELL PEPPERS)

SERVES: 4

Kadai masala is made by grinding roasted coriander seeds, dried red chilies, cardamom and cloves. This kadai tofu has all these fragrant spices cooked along with tofu and bell peppers. It tastes better when the tofu has soaked in all the flavors, so it's a good idea to make this in the morning and serve it for dinner.

3 tbsp (18 g) coriander seeds

8 small dried red chilies

5 cloves

5 green cardamoms

2 tbsp (30 g) unsalted butter

½ tbsp (7 ml) oil of choice

½ tbsp (5 g) grated garlic

½ tbsp (5 g) grated ginger

2 small red onions, cubed

4 large tomatoes

1 tsp salt, or to taste

½ tsp kashmiri red chili powder

¾ cup (180 ml) water, divided

1 small red bell pepper, diced, divided

1 small green bell pepper, diced, divided

16 oz (455 g) extra-firm tofu, cubed

1½ tsp (1 g) kasuri methi (fenugreek leaves), crushed

1 tsp sugar

3 tbsp (45 ml) heavy cream

2 tbsp (1 g) cilantro, chopped

In a small pan over medium heat, dry roast the coriander seeds, red chilies, cloves and green cardamoms until fragrant, around 5 to 6 minutes. Remove the pan from the heat and then transfer the roasted spices to a spice grinder and grind to a fine powder. Set aside.

Press the sauté button. When the pot displays hot, add the butter and oil to the pot and then add the garlic and ginger and sauté for a few seconds. Add the onion and sauté for 2 minutes until softened. Add the tomatoes, mix well and let cook for 2 to 3 minutes. Next, add the salt, kashmiri red chili powder and the prepared kadai masala spice mix. Mix until well combined and then add ½ cup (120 ml) of water and half of the diced bell peppers, reserving half of the peppers to add later. Close the pot, making sure the valve is in the sealing position, and then press the manual or pressure-cook button. Cook on high pressure for 4 minutes. Do a quick-pressure release.

Open the pot and press the sauté button. Use the adjust button to set sauté to "less." Add the remaining ¼ cup (60 ml) of water and then stir in the cubed tofu and the remaining half of the bell peppers. Add kasuri methi, sugar, heavy cream and cilantro and simmer for 3 to 4 minutes on low sauté. Serve kadai tofu with naan.

MAKE IT VEGAN: Replace the butter with oil and the heavy cream with coconut milk.

SOYA JALAPEÑO KEEMA TACOS
(VEGAN MINCED SOYA GRANULES TACOS)

SERVES: 8–10 TACOS

Keema refers to minced meat; however, our vegan version has keema made of soya granules. Keema with soya granules is spiced with jalapeños, taco seasoning and garam masala. Serve these tacos with lots of sliced onion, more jalapeños and cilantro for an easy weeknight meal.

2 cups (150 g) soya granules

½ cup (70 g) frozen green peas

1 tbsp (15 ml) oil of choice

1 medium red onion, chopped

2 tsp (12 g) ginger–garlic paste (see page 183)

3 jalapeños, sliced, plus more for garnish

1 tbsp (17 g) tomato paste

¾ tsp taco seasoning

½ tsp garam masala

½ tsp coriander powder

1 tsp salt, or to taste

1 cup (240 ml) water

2–3 tbsp (2–3 g) cilantro, chopped, plus more for garnish

2–3 tsp (10–15 ml) lime juice

8–10 small corn tortillas

Sliced onions, for garnish

Salsa, for garnish

Diced avocados, for garnish

Lime wedges, for garnish

Soak the soya granules in 3 cups (720 ml) of warm water for 20 minutes. They will absorb almost all the water, but this step is important to make sure that the granules stay moist when you make the keema. Soak the peas in warm water for 5 minutes.

Press the sauté button. When the pot displays hot, add the oil and then add the chopped onion. Cook the onion for 2 minutes until softened and then add the ginger–garlic paste and cook for another minute. Add the sliced jalapeños and cook for 30 seconds. If you'd like it to be less spicy, you can de-seed the jalapeños. Lightly squeeze water from the soaked soya granules and add them to the pot (don't add the water in which they were soaked) along with the green peas. In a small bowl, mix the tomato paste with 2 tablespoons (30 ml) of water, then add it to the pot, along with the taco seasoning, garam masala, coriander powder and salt, and mix until well combined. Add the water and close the lid. Press the manual or pressure-cook button and cook on high pressure for 4 minutes. Let the pressure release naturally for 5 minutes and then do a quick-pressure release. Remove the lid, add the cilantro and lime juice and mix. If there's excess water in the pot, press the sauté button and let the keema simmer for 2 to 3 minutes to get rid of it.

To serve, warm the tortillas and fill them with the prepared keema filling. Top with sliced onions, jalapeños, cilantro, salsa and diced avocados and serve with extra lime wedges on the side.

NOTE: If you don't have tomato paste on hand, purée one large tomato to use in this recipe.

GOBI MATAR KORMA

(CAULIFLOWER & GREEN PEAS COCONUT CURRY)

SERVES: 4

Korma refers to a yogurt- and coconut-based curry. Traditionally, making korma involves a number of steps, but this Instant Pot version gets it done rather quickly. My favorite way to eat this cauliflower–peas korma? With paratha—it's just the best combination!

3 large tomatoes

4 large cloves garlic

1-inch (25-mm) piece ginger

1 green chili

12 raw cashews

1½ tbsp (22 ml) oil of choice

1 bay leaf

3 green cardamoms

6–7 peppercorns

3 cloves

1 large red onion, chopped

1½ tsp (6 g) coriander powder

1 tsp garam masala

½ tsp red chili powder, or to taste

½ tsp turmeric powder

1 tsp salt, or to taste

¼ cup (60 g) plain yogurt, at room temperature

½ cup + 2 tbsp (150 ml) coconut milk

¼ cup (60 ml) water

1 large head cauliflower, cut into medium- to large-sized florets

½ cup (70 g) frozen green peas

Cilantro, for garnish

Using a blender, purée the tomatoes, garlic, ginger, green chili and cashews to a smooth paste. Set aside.

Press the sauté button. When the pot displays hot, add the oil and then add the bay leaf, green cardamoms, peppercorns and cloves. Sauté for a few seconds until the spices are fragrant and then add the onion. Cook the onion until soft, around 2 minutes, and then add in the puréed tomato–ginger–garlic–cashew paste that you prepared earlier. Cook for 2 minutes and then add the coriander powder, garam masala, red chili powder, turmeric powder and salt. Stir to combine the spices and cook them for 30 seconds. Add the yogurt, whisking continuously until it's well combined with the curry. Make sure the yogurt is at room temperature before you add it to the masala.

Add the coconut milk and the water and mix to combine. Add the cauliflower florets and peas and toss to combine them with the masala. Close the lid and press the manual or pressure-cook button, making sure the pressure valve is in the sealing position. Use the adjust or pressure-level button to set to low pressure and cook on low pressure for 3 minutes. Do a quick-pressure release.

Open the pot, give the korma a stir and adjust spices and salt to taste. Garnish with cilantro and serve.

MAKE IT VEGAN: Skip the yogurt and add ½ cup (120 ml) of water.

PANCHPORAN SPINACH KADHI

(YOGURT SOUP WITH FIVE SPICES)

SERVES: 4

Kadhi is a garbanzo-bean flour– and yogurt–based dish widely popular in North India. The traditional kadhi is always served with pakodas (fritters), which are deep fried and then dunked in the kadhi. But I prefer the plain kadhi without the fritters. This one has some added spinach for a healthy twist and is spiced with panchporan, which literally means five spices. To make sure the yogurt doesn't separate while cooking in the Instant Pot, use room-temperature yogurt, add salt at the very end, cook on soup mode and mix in a little cornstarch to bind the yogurt.

1 cup (245 g) plain yogurt, at room temperature

5 tbsp (45 g) garbanzo bean flour/besan

4¾ cups (175 g) spinach; 3¼ cups (100 g) whole, 1½ cups (75 g) chopped

¼ tsp turmeric powder

½ tsp red chili powder

1 tsp cornstarch

5 cups (1.2 L) water, divided

2½ tsp (12 ml) oil or ghee

1¼ tsp (3 g) panchporan mix (¼ tsp each of cumin seeds, fenugreek seeds, fennel seeds, mustard seeds and onion seeds; if you don't have all of these, use 1 tsp cumin seeds and ¼ tsp fenugreek seeds)

2 dried red chilies

1 tsp finely chopped ginger

1 green chili, optional

¼ medium red onion, chopped

1¼ tsp (8 g) salt, or to taste

In a blender, purée the yogurt, garbanzo bean flour, 3¼ cups (100 g) spinach, turmeric powder, red chili powder, cornstarch and 4 cups (960 ml) of water. Set the batter aside.

Press the sauté button. When the pot displays hot, add the oil and the panchporan spice mix. Let the seeds sizzle for a few seconds and then add the dried red chilies, ginger and green chili, if using. Sauté until the ginger starts turning golden brown. Add the chopped onion and sauté for a minute or two until the onion turns soft.

Stir in the prepared kadhi batter, whisking it for 2 minutes until it is well combined with the spices. Close the lid and press the soup button, making sure the pressure valve is in the sealing position. Cook for 10 minutes on high pressure. Let the pressure release naturally for 10 minutes and then do a quick-pressure release. Open the pot and press the sauté button. Add 1 cup (240 ml) of water. You can add more or less water, depending on what consistency you want for your kadhi. Add the salt and 1½ cups (75 g) chopped spinach, mix well and let it simmer for 2 to 3 minutes. Serve the spinach kadhi with rice.

MASALA BAINGAN

(SPICED BABY EGGPLANTS WITH COCONUT)

SERVES: 4

This dish features stuffed baby eggplants cooked in a spicy coconut masala. Eggplant is cooked in several ways in India and this is one of the easiest ways you can make masala baingan in no time. The stuffing includes coconut powder, coriander, cumin and garam masala, giving it a great flavor.

¼ cup (20 g) dried coconut powder

1 tbsp (7 g) coriander powder

1 tsp cumin powder

½ tsp red chili powder

½ tsp garam masala

¼ tsp turmeric powder

1 tsp salt, divided

10–12 (500 g) baby eggplants, each eggplant 2 to 2½ inches (5 to 6.5 cm) in length

1 tbsp (15 ml) oil of choice

½ tsp mustard seeds

1 medium red onion, chopped

1 tsp ginger–garlic paste (see page 183)

2 medium tomatoes, chopped

¾ cup (180 ml) water, divided

Cilantro, to garnish

NOTE: If your eggplants are larger (more than 3 inches [7.5 cm] in length), it might take more time for the eggplants to cook; it may take 5 to 6 minutes on high pressure after adding the eggplants.

In a bowl, mix the coconut powder, coriander powder, cumin powder, red chili powder, garam masala, turmeric powder and ½ teaspoon salt. Wash the baby eggplants and pat them dry. Make crosswise and lengthwise slits through the flesh of each eggplant, but without cutting all the way through. Carefully open the eggplants up and put some of the coconut mixture in each. Reserve some of the coconut stuffing to use in the curry. Set the stuffed eggplants and reserved stuffing mixture aside.

Press the sauté button. When the pot displays hot, add the oil and the mustard seeds and let them heat until they start to pop. Add the onion and cook for 2 minutes until soft and translucent. Add the ginger–garlic paste and cook for 1 minute, then add the tomatoes and ¼ cup (60 ml) of water. Cook the tomatoes for 2 minutes until they turn soft, and then add the reserved coconut stuffing. Cook for 1 minute and then add ½ cup (120 ml) of water and ½ teaspoon of salt and mix well. Place the stuffed eggplants on top of the masala (do not stir) and close the lid. Set the pressure valve to sealing and then press the manual or pressure-cook button. Cook on high pressure for 4 minutes. Do a quick-pressure release.

Open the pot, garnish masala baingan with cilantro and serve. I like to place the masala at the bottom and then the eggplants on top when I serve this dish. Enjoy with roti or rice.

CURRIED BLACK BEAN BURRITO BOWL

SERVES: 2

This is an easy one-pot meal—the beans, veggies and rice are cooked together at the same time using the pot-in-pot method. I love this meal on busy days, when I really want something on the table quick. My favorite way to eat this burrito bowl is with guacamole and salsa and I highly recommend not skipping them!

1 cup (200 g) white rice

2 tsp (10 ml) oil of choice

1 bay leaf

2 cloves garlic, chopped

1 medium white onion, sliced

1 jalapeño, deseeded and chopped

15-oz (445-ml) can black beans, drained and rinsed, or 1½ cups (258 g) cooked black beans

1 green pepper, sliced

¼ tsp smoked paprika

¼ tsp cumin powder

½ tsp curry powder

⅛ tsp cayenne pepper, or to taste

½ tsp salt, or to taste

½ cup (68 g) frozen sweet corn

1½ cups (360 ml) water, divided

Juice of half a lime

Guacamole, for garnish

Salsa, for garnish

Cilantro, for garnish

Tortilla chips, for garnish

Wash and rinse the rice until the water turns clear. Transfer it to a glass or steel container that will fit inside your Instant Pot. Set it aside.

Press the sauté button. When the pot displays hot, add the oil to the pot and then add the bay leaf, garlic, onion and jalapeño. Sauté for 2 minutes until the onion is soft. Add the black beans and sliced green pepper and mix. Add the smoked paprika, cumin powder, curry powder, cayenne pepper and salt and mix. Then stir in the frozen corn along with ½ cup (120 ml) of water. Place the Instant Pot's trivet inside the inner pot and then place the container with the rice on top. Add 1 cup (240 ml) of water to the rice container. Close the pot with its lid. Press the manual or pressure-cook button and cook on high pressure for 6 minutes, making sure the pressure valve is in the sealing position. Let the pressure release naturally for 5 minutes and then do a quick-pressure release.

Open the lid, carefully remove the rice container from the pot and fluff the rice using a fork. Add lime juice to the beans and veggies and mix. Press saute to dry off excess water, if needed. To serve, put the rice, beans and veggies in a large bowl. Top with guacamole, salsa, cilantro and tortilla chips and enjoy.

DAL DHOKLI

(WHOLE-WHEAT NOODLES IN LENTIL STEW)

SERVES: 2–3

Spiced wheat-flour noodles (dhokli) are simmered in thin Gujarati dal and are lightly spiced with turmeric, red chili powder and carom seeds, and best of all, are easy to make at home! You can make the noodles while the dal is cooking and then later, simply boil the noodles along with the dal for a comforting meal. For extra flavor, add a teaspoon of ghee before serving.

FOR THE DAL

2 tsp (10 ml) oil of choice

½ tsp cumin seeds

½ tsp mustard seeds

¼ tsp fenugreek seeds

3 cloves

½-inch (13-mm) cinnamon stick

1 tsp finely chopped ginger

1 green chili, finely chopped

10–12 curry leaves

½ cup (104 g) split pigeon peas/toor dal

2 cups (480 ml) water

1 tbsp (16 g) raw peanuts

1½ tbsp (18 g) jaggery, grated

½ tsp turmeric powder, divided

⅛ tsp red chili powder, or to taste

1 tsp salt, divided, to taste

FOR THE DHOKLI

½ cup (65 g) whole-wheat flour/atta

1½ tbsp (14 g) garbanzo bean flour/besan

¼ tsp red chili powder

Pinch of carom seeds

½ tbsp (7.5 ml) vegetable oil

2¼ cups (300 ml) water, divided

1½ tbsp (22 ml) lemon juice

Cilantro, for garnish

Press the sauté button. When the pot displays hot, add the oil to the pot and then add the cumin seeds, mustard seeds, fenugreek seeds, cloves and cinnamon stick. Let the seeds sizzle for a few seconds and then add the ginger and green chili. Sauté for a minute until the ginger starts changing color. Add the curry leaves and then add the dal. Stir and then add 2 cups (240 ml) of water, peanuts, jaggery, ¼ teaspoon turmeric powder, red chili powder and ¾ teaspoon salt. Mix until everything is well combined. Close the pot with the lid and then press the manual or pressure-cook button and cook on high pressure for 8 minutes. The pressure valve should be in the sealing position. Let the pressure release naturally.

While the dal is cooking, make the noodles (dhokli). In a large bowl, mix the whole-wheat flour, garbanzo bean flour, ¼ teaspoon turmeric powder, red chili powder, carom seeds and ¼ teaspoon salt. Add the vegetable oil and mix well, then add ¼ cup (60 ml) of water, a little at a time, kneading to form a smooth dough. Let the dough rest for 5 minutes and then divide the dough into two equal parts. Roll each half into a thin circle, 8 to 9 inches (20 to 23 cm) across. Using a pizza cutter, cut long strips, each around 1½ inches (38 mm) wide. Then cut diagonally across the strips, making diamond-shaped dhoklis. You will get 25 to 30 dhoklis and each one will be of a different size. Set them aside.

When the pressure has released, open the pot and use an immersion blender to purée the dal until you don't see any lentil particles; it should look like a soup. Blend in short bursts and don't overblend; the soup should still have a little texture. Add 2 cups (240 ml) of water and the lemon juice to the dal and press the sauté button. In 2 minutes, when the dal starts to bubble slightly, add the dhoklis to the pot, a few at a time. After you have added all the dhoklis, close the pot again. Press the manual or pressure-cook button and cook on high pressure for 3 minutes, then do a quick-pressure release. Garnish dal dhokli with cilantro and serve.

TOFU BROCCOLI ASPARAGUS IN FENUGREEK SAUCE

SERVES: 3

Fenugreek (methi) parathas/flatbreads were a staple in my house during the winter. When in abundance during the winter, methi is also used in a number of curries. It pairs especially well with sweeter veggies like green peas, but in this recipe I have paired it with tofu, broccoli and asapargus. I have used fresh methi as well as dry methi (kasuri methi) in this curry. Fenugreek is a bit on the bitter side, so adding the cream helps to balance the flavors.

1 yellow onion, quartered

15 cashews

3 cloves garlic

1-inch (25-mm) piece ginger

1 green chili

4 green cardamoms

1½ cups (360 ml) water, divided

1½ tbsp (22 ml) oil of choice

1 bay leaf

1 tsp coriander powder

¼ tsp garam masala

¼ tsp turmeric powder

¼ tsp red chili powder

1 tsp salt, or to taste

1½ cups (55 g) fenugreek leaves, stems removed (use leaves only), chopped

6 oz (170 g) extra-firm tofu, cubed

1 tsp kasuri methi (fenugreek leaves), crushed

¼ cup (60 ml) heavy cream

½ tsp sugar

1 cup (65 g) broccoli florets

10 thin asparagus stalks, hard end removed and then cut into 1-inch (25-mm) pieces

Place the onion and cashews into the steamer basket. Pour 1 cup (240 ml) of water in the inner pot of your Instant Pot and then place the steamer basket inside it. Close the lid, set the pressure valve to the sealing position and then press the steam button. Steam on high pressure for 2 minutes. Do a quick-pressure release.

Transfer the steamed onion and cashews to a blender and add the garlic, ginger, green chili, green cardamoms and ½ cup (120 ml) of water and purée to a smooth paste.

Press the sauté button. When the pot displays hot, add the oil and then add the bay leaf along with the prepared onion paste. Cook the onion paste for 4 to 5 minutes, until there's no smell of raw onion, and then stir in the coriander powder, garam masala, turmeric powder, red chili powder and salt. Cook for 1 minute, then add the chopped fenugreek leaves and cook for another 1 to 2 minutes. Add 1 cup (240 ml) of water and the tofu, mix well and then close the lid. Press the manual or pressure-cook button and cook on high pressure for 3 minutes. Do a quick-pressure release.

Open the lid and press the sauté button. Use the adjust button to set sauté to "more." Add the kasuri methi, heavy cream, sugar, broccoli florets and asparagus. Cover the pot with a glass lid and let it simmer for 4 to 5 minutes. Serve warm with naan.

MAKE IT VEGAN: Replace the heavy cream with coconut cream.

QUINOA CURD RICE

(SPICED QUINOA WITH YOGURT)

SERVES: 2–3

Curd rice is total comfort food! Rice is mixed with yogurt and tempered with curry leaves, mustard seeds and pomegranate arils. This recipe is a spin on the traditional curd rice—I have replaced rice with quinoa to make it more wholesome.

1 cup (180 g) quinoa

1½ cups (360 ml) water

¾–1 cup (180–240 ml) milk

2 cups (490 g) plain yogurt, whisked

3 tbsp (24 g) carrot, finely chopped

3 tbsp (28 g) green pepper, finely chopped

1 green chili, chopped, optional

1½ tsp (3 g) ginger, finely chopped

¾ tsp salt, or to taste

2 tbsp (22 g) pomegranate arils

3 tsp (15 ml) oil of choice

1 tsp mustard seeds

1 tbsp (16 g) raw peanuts

2 tsp (8 g) split black gram lentils/urad dal dhuli

⅛ tsp asafetida

2 dried red chilies

10 curry leaves

Cilantro, to garnish

Rinse the quinoa well for 2 to 3 minutes. This is important to get rid of that slightly bitter taste. Place the quinoa in the inner steel pot of your Instant Pot along with the water. Close the lid and press the manual or pressure-cook button. Cook on high pressure for 1 minute and let the pressure release naturally.

Open the lid, fluff the quinoa with a fork and transfer it to a large bowl. When the quinoa has cooled slightly, add the milk, yogurt, carrot, green pepper, green chili (if using), ginger and salt. Mix until everything is well combined. Add the pomegranate arils and mix again.

Using a small pan over medium heat, or on the sauté mode in the Instant Pot, heat the oil and when the oil is hot, add the mustard seeds and let them heat for a few seconds until they pop. Then add the peanuts and cook until they start turning golden brown, about 1 minute. Add the lentils and asafetida and cook until the dal starts changing color, about 1 minute. Add the dried red chilies and curry leaves and stir. Remove the pan from the heat and pour the tempering over the curd quinoa. Stir to combine. Garnish with cilantro if desired.

NOTE: Let the quinoa and seasonings sit together for a couple of hours before you serve this dish. This allows the flavors to mix. I personally love this dish chilled; I refrigerate for 3 to 4 hours before serving.

CILANTRO MINT PANEER

SERVES: 4

This recipe combines the flavors of cilantro and mint chutney with paneer in a yogurt-based sauce. If you are tired of eating paneer in a tomato-onion-based curry or simply want to try a new paneer recipe, then you must give this one a go!

1½ cups (30 g) cilantro, roughly chopped

¾ cup (15 g) mint leaves

1 small red onion

2 green chilies

15 cashews

1-inch (25-mm) piece ginger

2 cloves garlic

¼ tsp ground black pepper

1¼ cups (300 ml) water, divided

1 tbsp (15 ml) oil or unsalted butter

1 bay leaf

¾ tsp cumin seeds

½ cup (125 g) yogurt, whisked with ¼ tsp cornstarch

½ tsp cumin powder

½ tsp coriander powder

¼ tsp crushed red pepper, for extra heat, optional

½ tsp salt, or to taste

2 tsp (10 ml) heavy cream

Garam masala, to sprinkle

½–¾ tsp sugar, adjust to taste

1 cup (225 g) paneer, cut into cubes

Tandoori roti, for serving

Sliced onions, for serving

In a blender, grind together the cilantro, mint leaves, onion, green chilies, cashews, ginger, garlic, black pepper and ¼ cup (60 ml) of water to form a smooth paste. Set it aside.

Press the sauté button. When the pot displays hot, add the oil, bay leaf and cumin seeds and let the cumin seeds sizzle for a few seconds. Then add the prepared cilantro–mint paste to the pot and cook for 2 to 3 minutes, until the raw smell of the onion in the paste goes away. Whisk the yogurt with the cornstarch and then add it to the pot. Stir continuously as you add the yogurt until all of it is well combined. Cook for 2 minutes. Add cumin powder, coriander powder, crushed red pepper and ¾ cup (180 ml) of water and cook for a few seconds. Close the lid, making sure the valve is in the sealing position, and then press the soup button and cook for 3 minutes on high pressure. Do a quick-pressure release.

Open the pot, stir the curry and press the sauté button. Add ¼ cup (60 ml) of water along with the salt, heavy cream, garam masala and sugar. Mix well and then add the paneer cubes. Let the curry simmer for 2 minutes. We love this cilantro mint paneer with tandoori roti and sliced onions on the side.

DAL-CHAWAL-ALOO SABZI

(LAYERED MEAL WITH RICE. LENTILS & POTATOES)

SERVES: 2

Whenever we come back from a vacation, this is the first meal that I make in my Instant Pot. It's like we are dying to eat basic Indian food after a break and it can't get more basic than this! There are three parts to this meal—dal (lentils), chawal (rice) and aloo sabzi (spiced potatoes). The fact that I can make all three things in the pot at the same time makes this recipe one of my favorites. This is a simple meal, very lightly spiced and comforting for the soul.

1 cup (200 g) basmati or any other white rice

3 to 3½ cups (720 to 840 ml) water, divided

3 medium potatoes, diced into small pieces, ½ inch (13 mm) or less

¼ tsp cumin powder

⅛ tsp turmeric powder

⅛ tsp red chili powder

¾ tsp salt, divided

Pinch of black salt

Pinch of garam masala

1 tsp oil of choice

½ tsp cumin seeds

1 green chili, chopped

1 small red onion, chopped

½ cup (105 g) split pigeon peas/ toor dal

¼ tsp turmeric

1 tbsp (1 g) cilantro, chopped

2 tsp (10 ml) lemon juice

Wash the rice until the water turns clear, then add the rice and 1½ cups (360 ml) of water to a steel container and set aside. I use my stackable steel containers for this recipe, but you may use Pyrex containers as well.

In another steel container, toss the potatoes, cumin powder, ⅛ tsp tumeric powder, red chili powder, ¼ teaspoon salt, black salt and garam masala with 1 tablespoon (15 ml) of water to combine. Set aside.

Press the sauté button. When the pot displays hot, add the oil and then add the cumin seeds. Let the seeds sizzle for a few seconds, then add the green chili and onion and cook for 1 to 2 minutes. Stir in the dal, ¼ teaspoon turmeric and ½ teaspoon salt. Mix well and then add 1½ to 2 cups (360 to 480 ml) of water, depending on the consistency you prefer for the dal. Place the Instant Pot's trivet inside the pot and then place the stackable steel containers, with the rice in one and potatoes in another, on top of the trivet. Close the lid. Press the manual or pressure-cook button and cook for 7 minutes on high pressure, with the pressure valve in the sealing position. Let the pressure release naturally.

Open the lid and remove the stackable containers carefully from the pot. Add cilantro and lemon juice to the potatoes and mix well. Serve the dal, rice and potatoes together for a comforting meal.

VEN PONGAL

(RICE & LENTIL PORRIDGE
WITH PEPPERCORNS)

SERVES: 3

Pongal is a dish made by cooking rice and lentils together, much like khichdi but with different seasoning. This dish is seasoned with curry leaves and whole black peppercorns. Ven pongal is commonly eaten for breakfast in south India along with coconut chutney and a cup of hot filter coffee.

1 cup (200 g) long-grain rice

⅓ cup (72 g) split moong beans/ moong dal dhuli

1½ tbsp (22 ml) ghee

1 tsp cumin seeds

Generous pinch of asafetida

1 tsp whole black peppercorns (or crushed if you don't like biting into the peppercorns)

10 raw cashews

1½ tsp (3 g) ginger, finely chopped

10–12 curry leaves

4 cups (960 ml) water

1 tsp salt, or to taste

Coconut Chutney (page 147), for serving

Rinse the rice and dal together in a bowl. Drain, rinse and set aside.

Press the sauté button. When the pot displays hot, add the ghee then the cumin seeds and let them sizzle for a few seconds. Add a pinch of asafetida along with the peppercorns, cashews and ginger. Sauté until the ginger and cashews begin to change color, about 1 minute. Add the curry leaves and mix, and then add the rinsed rice and dal. Toss to combine the rice and dal with the seasoning and then add the water and salt and close the pot with the lid. Press the rice button, making sure the pressure valve is in the sealing position. This will automatically cook on low pressure for 12 minutes. Let the pressure release naturally.

Serve with a side of Coconut Chutney (page 147) and filter coffee.

MAKE IT VEGAN: Replace ghee with oil.

30 MINUTES OR LESS

Sometimes all you have is 30 minutes to get food on the table. And that's when these quick meals come in handy. After a long day at work, the last thing you want to do is slog for hours in the kitchen. With these easy and quick recipes, you can get your dinner done in 30 minutes or less. And what's even better is that the leftovers make great lunches!

There are so many Indian recipes that you can make rather quickly in your Instant Pot, like the classic Matar Paneer (page 96), fresh paneer cubes cooked with green peas and simmered in a tomato-based curry, or the very fragrant Jeera Aloo (page 100), diced potatoes tossed with lots of cumin seeds.

There is also the Turmeric Masala Doodh (page 108), which will surely make you feel better after a long day at work. You can make this golden milk within minutes in your Instant Pot, and it is just so comforting and very good for you with all the anti-inflammatory properties of turmeric.

MATAR PANEER

(INDIAN COTTAGE CHEESE &
GREEN PEAS CURRY)

SERVES: 2

Paneer is cooked in so many different ways in India. One of the most popular recipes is matar paneer—a combination of soft paneer and sweet green peas. We always made matar paneer during the winter when fresh green peas were in season. The peas imparted so much flavor to this dish and paired beautifully with the paneer. However, since you cannot always get fresh peas, I have used frozen green peas in this recipe.

1 tbsp (15 ml) ghee

1 tbsp (15 ml) vegetable oil

½-inch (13-mm) cinnamon stick

2 bay leaves

½ tsp cumin seeds

1 large red onion, roughly chopped

3–4 cloves garlic, roughly chopped

1-inch (25-mm) piece ginger, roughly chopped

1–2 green chilies, chopped

3 medium tomatoes, chopped

¼ tsp turmeric powder

½ tsp garam masala, divided

¼ tsp red chili powder

¾ tsp salt, or to taste

1 tbsp (15 g) plain yogurt

½ tsp sugar

1 cup (240 ml) water

½ cup (70 g) frozen green peas, soaked in warm water for 5 minutes

1 cup (225 g) paneer, cut into cubes

¼ tsp kashmiri red chili powder, for color (optional)

1 tbsp (1 g) cilantro, chopped

Naan, for serving

Press the sauté button. When the pot displays hot, add the ghee and oil and then the cinnamon stick, bay leaves and cumin seeds. Sauté for a few seconds until the cumin seeds sizzle, then add the chopped onion and sauté for 2 to 3 minutes until the onion is soft. Add the garlic, ginger and green chilies and cook for another 1 to 2 minutes.

Add the tomatoes, cover the pot with a glass lid and cook for 4 to 5 minutes. Then add the turmeric powder, ¼ teaspoon garam masala, red chili powder and salt and mix. Stir in the yogurt and sugar and mix. Add the water and close the pot with the lid. Press the manual or pressure-cook button, and cook on high pressure for 2 minutes, with the pressure valve in the sealing position. Do a quick-pressure release.

Open the pot, remove the bay leaf and cinnamon stick and use an immersion blender to purée the contents. You can also purée using a regular blender when the mixture has cooled down for 10 to 15 minutes—just transfer it back to the Instant Pot after blending.

Press the sauté button and then add the green peas and cubed paneer. Stir in the remaining ¼ teaspoon garam masala and the kashmiri red chili powder. Adjust the salt and consistency of the curry (add ¼ cup [60 ml] of water for thin curry) at this point and let the matar paneer simmer for 2 to 3 minutes. Add the chopped cilantro and mix. Serve with naan or any bread of choice.

MAKE IT VEGAN: Replace the paneer with tofu and the ghee with oil. Skip the yogurt.

DAL DHANIA SHORBA
(LENTIL CILANTRO SOUP)

SERVES: 2

This lentil cilantro soup is so perfect for cold days—its simple comforting flavors are just what you need to warm up! It is made with moong dal, is lightly spiced and garnished with fresh cilantro and lemon juice. I have used moong dal here because it's light and easily digestible.

1 tsp oil of choice

½ white onion, finely chopped

¼-inch (6-mm) piece ginger, finely chopped

1 small green chili, finely chopped

¼ tsp turmeric powder

¼ tsp cumin powder

⅛ tsp red chili powder, optional

½ cup (100 g) split moong bean/moong dal dhuli, rinsed

2–2½ cups (480 to 600 ml) water, divided

¾ tsp salt, or to taste

2 tsp (10 ml) lemon juice, or adjust to taste

1 tbsp (1 g) cilantro, chopped

Lemon wedges, for serving

Press the sauté button. When the pot displays hot, add the oil and the onion. Sauté for 1 minute and then add the ginger and green chili. Sauté for 1 more minute and then add the turmeric, cumin and red chili powder (if you'd like more heat). Sauté for 30 seconds and then add the moong dal. Cook the dal with the spices for 1 minute, and then add 2 cups (480 ml) of water and the salt, and stir to combine. Close the lid and press the manual or pressure-cook button. Cook on high pressure for 5 minutes with the pressure valve in the sealing position. Let the pressure release naturally for 10 minutes and then do a quick-pressure release.

Open the pot and use an immersion blender to blend the dal to a smooth consistency. This is a shorba, so you don't want to see any particles of dal in there. Add ½ cup (120 ml) of water at this point if you want a thinner consistency (shorba is supposed to be quite thin). Squeeze in the fresh lemon juice. Pour into serving bowls, garnish with cilantro and lemon wedges and serve.

JEERA ALOO

(CUMIN POTATOES)

SERVES: 3–4

Boiled potatoes tossed with cumin seeds and turmeric makes a simple yet flavorful dish. This quick and easy dish is the perfect accompaniment to any Indian meal. I love these potatoes with my dal and roti.

2 large russet potatoes, cut in half and skin left on

1 tbsp (15 ml) oil of choice

1¼ tsp (3 g) cumin seeds

2 tsp (3 g) coriander seeds, roughly crushed

2 green chilies, sliced

1-inch (25-mm) piece ginger, chopped

½ tsp turmeric powder

⅛ tsp red chili powder, or to taste

½ tsp salt, or to taste

2 tsp (10 ml) lemon juice

Cilantro, to garnish

Rice, dal or bread, for serving

Add 1 cup (240 ml) of water to the inner steel pot of your Instant Pot. Place the Instant Pot's trivet inside the pot, then place the potatoes, cut side up, on top of the trivet. Secure the lid and set the pressure valve to the sealing position. Press the manual or pressure-cook button and cook on high pressure for 10 minutes. Let the pressure release naturally for 5 minutes and then do a quick-pressure release. Carefully remove the potatoes from the trivet. When they have cooled down a bit, peel the potatoes and dice them into small pieces.

Drain the water from the inner pot, wipe it dry and then place it back into the Instant Pot. Press the sauté button, and when the pot displays hot, add the oil and then the cumin seeds. Let the seeds sizzle for a few seconds, then add the coriander seeds and green chilies. Sauté for a few seconds and then add the ginger. Sauté for a minute or two until the ginger starts turning a light golden color. Add the potatoes, turmeric powder, red chili powder and salt and mix, until all the potato pieces are well coated with the spices. Mix gently so you don't mash too many potatoes. Unplug the pot, add the lemon juice and toss to combine. Garnish with cilantro and serve jeera aloo with rice, dal or any bread of choice like paratha or poori.

TEHRI
(SPICY POTATO & PEAS PULAO)

SERVES: 2

Tehri takes me back to my childhood. My grandmother used to make this whenever we visited her during our summer break. The aroma of basmati rice cooked with spices like cardamom, cinnamon and cloves was intoxicating. The addition of potatoes and peas makes this a complete meal in itself.

1 cup (200 g) basmati rice

1½ tbsp (22 ml) oil of choice

¾ tsp cumin seeds

1 bay leaf

2 green cardamoms

2 black cardamoms

2 cloves

4-5 black peppercorns

½-inch (13-mm) cinnamon stick

Small piece of mace, optional

1 red onion, sliced

2 green chilies, chopped

1½ tsp (9 g) ginger-garlic paste (see page 183)

1 large potato, cubed

¼ cup (35 g) frozen green peas

¼ tsp turmeric powder

¼ tsp coriander powder

1½ cups (360 ml) water

1 tsp salt, or to taste

Cilantro, to garnish

Garam masala, to sprinkle

Yogurt, for serving

Chutney, for serving

Rinse the basmati rice until the water turns clear. Set it aside.

Press the sauté button. When the pot displays hot, add the oil and then the cumin seeds, bay leaf, green cardamoms, black cardamoms, cloves, black peppercorns, cinnamon stick and mace, if using. Sauté for a few seconds until the spices are fragrant and the cumin seeds sizzle. Add the onion and green chilies and cook for 2 minutes, then add the ginger-garlic paste and cook for 1 minute, or until the raw smell of the ginger and garlic subsides.

Add the potato and green peas and give it a good mix. Stir in the turmeric powder and coriander powder, then add the water and the salt and mix again. Add the rice on top of the water, but do not stir. Close the pot with its lid and then press the rice button, making sure the pressure valve is in the sealing position. On the rice mode, the Instant Pot will automatically cook on low pressure for 12 minutes. Let the pressure release naturally. Open the lid, add the cilantro and then sprinkle the garam masala on top. Serve with yogurt and chutney on the side.

TOFU MANGO COCONUT CURRY

SERVES: 2

Do you love mangoes and coconut? Then you will love this spiced vegan curry with tofu! This curry has a sweet taste that is well balanced with all the spices and seasoning—a comforting curry for cold nights!

8 oz (227 g) extra-firm tofu, cubed

¼ tsp smoked paprika

¼ tsp crushed red pepper

1¼ tsp (8 g) salt, divided

⅛ tsp ground black pepper

2 tbsp (30 ml) oil of choice, divided

½ tsp mustard seeds

2 dried red chilies

½ medium white onion, diced

1½-inch (38-mm) piece ginger, grated

¾ cup (177 ml) mango purée, fresh or canned

½ cup (120 ml) coconut milk, lite preferred, may also use full fat

1 tsp curry powder

¼ tsp red chili powder, optional

½ cup (120 ml) water

Juice of ½ lemon

Cilantro, to garnish

Desiccated coconut flakes, to garnish

Press the tofu with a heavy object for 10 to 15 minutes to get rid of excess moisture, and then cut it into cubes. Toss the tofu cubes with smoked paprika, crushed red pepper, ¼ teaspoon salt and ground black pepper. Press the sauté button. When the pot displays hot, add 1 tablespoon (15 ml) of oil to the pot, then add the spiced tofu cubes and cook for 4 minutes, or until lightly browned on all sides. Remove the tofu cubes to a bowl and set aside. Add another tablespoon (15 ml) of oil to the pot, there's no need to clean it first, then add the mustard seeds. Let the mustard seeds pop and then add the dried red chilies. Sauté for a few seconds, then add the onion and ginger. Cook the onion and ginger for a minute or two until the onion turns a little soft. Add the mango purée, coconut milk, curry powder and red chili powder, optional, then add 1 teaspoon of salt and let it all cook for a minute or two. Add the water along with the sautéed tofu cubes and close the lid. Press the manual or pressure-cook button and cook on high pressure for 3 minutes, with the pressure valve in the sealing position. Then do a quick-pressure release.

Stir in the lemon juice, then transfer the curry to a serving bowl. Garnish with cilantro and desiccated coconut flakes and serve. This tastes great with jasmine rice or brown rice.

MASALA MAC & CHEESE

(SPICED MAC & CHEESE)

SERVES: 6

Classic American comfort food gets an Indian makeover in this masala macaroni and cheese. Flavored with Indian spices, this is comfort food at its best and is also one of the easiest dishes that you can make in your Instant Pot!

2 tbsp (30 g) unsalted butter

1 medium yellow onion, chopped

2 green chilies or jalapeños, chopped

1 tsp ginger–garlic paste (see page 183)

16 oz (454 g) elbow macaroni

4 cups (460 ml) water

½ tsp turmeric powder

½ tsp cumin powder

¼ tsp red chili powder

½ tsp garam masala

1½ tsp (10 g) salt, or to taste

½ cup (120 ml) heavy cream

½ cup (120 ml) whole milk

2 cups (170 g) shredded cheese (I use a mix of Monterey Jack and mild cheddar)

2 tbsp (2 g) cilantro, chopped

Smoked paprika, for serving

Lemon wedges, for serving

Press the sauté button. When the pot displays hot, add the butter and let it melt. Add the onion and green chilies and sauté for 2 minutes until the onion is soft. Add the ginger–garlic paste and cook for another 30 seconds or so, then add the elbow macaroni and water to the pot. Add the turmeric powder, cumin powder, red chili powder, garam masala and salt, stir, then close the pot with the lid. Press the manual or pressure-cook button and cook on high pressure for 4 minutes, with the pressure valve in the sealing position. Then do a quick-pressure release.

Open the lid, press the sauté button and then add the heavy cream and milk to the pot. Stir to combine and then add the shredded cheese, a little at a time, making sure it melts before you add more. Finally, add the cilantro. Transfer to serving bowls, sprinkle smoked paprika on top and serve with lemon wedges.

NOTE: You may use any cheese of choice. Also, evaporated milk would work in place of the cream and milk.

TURMERIC MASALA DOODH

(SPICED TURMERIC MILK)

SERVES: 2

Whenever I was sick or got the flu, my mom would make me drink haldi wala doodh (turmeric milk). It's just amazing to see how this humble drink I grew up drinking has gained so much popularity over the years in the Western world. This turmeric milk is flavored with cinnamon, cardamom, nutmeg and a little bit of ginger—the spices make it really comforting.

2¼ cups (540 ml) milk of choice

¾ tsp turmeric powder

1-inch (25-mm) cinnamon stick

⅛ tsp nutmeg powder

⅛ tsp ground ginger

3 green cardamoms, slightly crushed

1 tbsp (5 g) ground cashew (optional), for a creamier texture

⅛ tsp ground cardamom

1 tbsp (13 g) sugar, or sweetener of choice

Add 1 cup (240 ml) of water to the inner steel pot of your Instant Pot. Place the Instant Pot's trivet inside the pot and then place a steel or glass container on the trivet. To the steel or glass container, add the milk, turmeric powder, cinnamon stick, nutmeg powder, ground ginger, green cardamoms and ground cashew, if using. Give the milk a quick stir and then close the pot with the lid. Press the manual or pressure-cook button and cook on high pressure for 3 minutes, with the pressure valve in the sealing position, then do a quick-pressure release.

Open the lid, add the ground cardamom, sugar (or sweetener of choice) and stir well. Carefully remove the container from the Instant Pot and then strain the milk using a sieve. Transfer the turmeric milk to serving glasses. Serve warm.

BEANS & BEETS PORIYAL

(SPICED GREEN BEANS & BEETS WITH COCONUT)

SERVES: 2—3

Poriyal in south Indian cuisine refers to sautéed vegetables flavored with a generous amount of fresh grated coconut. This easy poriyal has green beans, beetroot and, obviously, lots of coconut. This simple dish tastes great with roti or can be a perfect accompaniment to any Indian meal.

1 cup (200 g) green beans, cut into ½-inch (13-mm) pieces

1 large beetroot, diced small, around ½-inch (13-mm) pieces

1½ tbsp (22 ml) oil of choice

½ tsp mustard seeds

2 tsp (12 g) split and dehusked black gram lentil/urad dal dhuli

2 tsp (12 g) chana dal

2 dried red chilies, broken

⅛ tsp asafetida

10–12 curry leaves

⅛ tsp turmeric powder

½ tsp salt, or to taste

⅓ cup (34 g) fresh grated coconut

Roti or bread of choice, for serving

Add 1 cup (240 ml) of water to the inner steel pot of your Instant Pot. Place the chopped green beans and beetroot in a steamer basket and then place the steamer basket inside the pot. Close the lid, making sure the pressure valve is in the sealing position. Press the steam button and set the time to 2 minutes on high pressure. Do a quick-pressure release. Carefully remove the steamer basket from the pot and then transfer the steamed veggies to another bowl.

Drain the water from the steel pot and transfer it back into the Instant Pot. Press the sauté button, and when the pot displays hot, add the oil and then the mustard seeds, letting them heat for a few seconds until they pop. Add the urad dal and chana dal and cook for 1 to 2 minutes, until they turn golden in color. Then add the dried red chilies and asafetida and sauté for a few seconds. Add the curry leaves, stir, then add the steamed veggies, turmeric powder and salt. Toss the veggies until they are well combined with the seasonings, then add the fresh grated coconut and mix well. Transfer to a serving dish and serve with roti or any other bread of choice.

INDIAN STREET FOOD

Indian street food is my favorite kind of food. It is so flavorful and spicy and I can never have enough. Other than Indian chaat (the common term for spicy Indian street food), wraps, dumplings and Indo-Chinese are also very popular on Indian streets, and most of the street food in India is vegetarian! I have shared some of my favorites here, the Vegetarian Momos (dumplings) (page 121) being my favorite. The best way to enjoy them? With hot sauce!

The Sweet Potato Chaat with Cilantro Mint Yogurt Chutney (page 129) is another favorite. The steamed sweet potatoes tossed with my favorite chutney and pomegranate arils create an explosion of flavors and can be enjoyed as a snack or even as a quick lunch.

If you are a fan of Indo-Chinese food, then you are going to love the famous Vegan Hot & Sour Soup (page 126) and Mushroom Garlic Fried Rice (page 122) in this chapter. They are my go-to recipes in the Instant Pot when I am craving Indo-Chinese!

PAV BHAJI
(MASHED SPICED VEGETABLES WITH DINNER ROLLS)

SERVES: 4–5

With spicy mashed veggies served with dinner rolls and a dollop of butter, pav bhaji is one of the most popular Indian street foods—and it's my favorite too! I always prefer making eggless dinner rolls (known as ladi pav) at home when I make pav bhaji, but of course if you don't have the time, you can always serve it with regular burger buns instead.

FOR THE PAV BHAJI MASALA

4 tbsp (20 g) coriander seeds

2 tbsp (18 g) cumin seeds

5 dried red chilies, adjust to taste

8 cloves

1 tbsp (9 g) fennel seeds

3 black cardamoms

2-inch (5-cm) cinnamon stick

1½ tsp (6 g) turmeric powder

2 tsp (6 g) ground black pepper

1½ tbsp (18 g) dried mango powder/amchur

½ tsp ground ginger

2 tsp (12 g) black salt

FOR THE PAV BHAJI

2-inch (5-cm) piece ginger

8–10 cloves garlic

3 green chilies

4 tbsp (60 g) butter, divided, plus more for serving

1 tsp cumin seeds

2 large red onions, chopped

5 medium tomatoes, chopped

1 tsp kashmiri red chili powder, or to taste

3 medium potatoes

½ head (255 g) cauliflower

1 cup (140 g) frozen green peas

1 medium green bell pepper

¾ cup (180 ml) water

2 tsp (12 g) salt, or to taste

1 tsp kasuri methi (fenugreek leaves), crushed

2 tbsp (30 ml) lemon juice

Fistful (14 g) cilantro, chopped

Dinner rolls/pav, for serving

Chopped onion, for serving

Lemon wedges, for serving

(continued)

PAV BHAJI (CONT.)

Dry roast the coriander seeds, cumin seeds, dried red chilies, cloves, fennel seeds, black cardamoms and cinnamon stick in a pan on medium heat until fragrant, around 3 to 4 minutes. Let the mixture cool, then transfer to a spice grinder. Stir in the turmeric powder, ground black pepper, dried mango powder, ground ginger and black salt. Grind until powdered and well combined. Store the pav bhaji masala in an airtight container at room temperature.

Using a blender, grind the ginger, garlic and green chilies to a paste using about a tablespoon (15 ml) of water, then set aside.

Press the sauté button. When the pot displays hot, add 2 tablespoons (30 g) of butter and then add the cumin seeds. Let the cumin seeds sizzle for a few seconds and then add the onions. Sauté for 3 to 4 minutes, or until the onions are soft and turn light golden brown in color. Add the prepared ginger–garlic–chili paste and cook for another 2 minutes. Add the tomatoes and cook for another 3 to 4 minutes. Add 2½ tablespoons (20 g) pav bhaji masala and kashmiri red chili powder and mix until well combined. Cook for 1 minute and then add the potatoes, cauliflower, green peas and green bell pepper. Stir, then add the water and the salt; mix well. Close the pot with the lid and then press the manual or pressure-cook button. Cook on high pressure for 8 minutes, with the pressure valve in the sealing position. Let the pressure release naturally.

Open the lid and, using an immersion blender, grind the veggies coarsely—don't turn it into a smooth paste. If you don't have an immersion blender, you can use a potato masher. After mashing the veggies, press the sauté button again and then add 2 tablespoons (30 g) of butter, kasuri methi, lemon juice and cilantro. Let it simmer for 2 to 3 minutes.

To serve the pav bhaji, toast the dinner rolls with butter. You may also sprinkle some leftover pav bhaji masala on the rolls while heating them. Serve with dinner rolls, chopped onion, butter and lemon wedges.

MAKE IT VEGAN: Replace the butter with vegan butter.

ALOO CHANA ROLLS

(SPICED POTATO & CHICKPEA WRAPS)

SERVES: 6 LARGE WRAPS

On roadsides in India, you will find all kinds of rolls—from egg rolls to paneer rolls to chicken rolls and so much more. All of them are spicy and most of them are accompanied with cilantro mint chutney. These aloo chana rolls are filled with a spicy potato and chickpea mixture, cilantro mint yogurt chutney and sliced onions.

FOR THE CILANTRO MINT YOGURT CHUTNEY

2 bunches (75–100 g) cilantro, larger stems removed

½ cup (18 g) mint leaves

2 green chilies, or to taste

1-inch (25-mm) piece ginger

¼ tsp cumin powder

¼ tsp chaat masala, optional

½ tsp salt, or to taste

Pinch of black pepper

1 tbsp (15 ml) lemon juice

1 tsp sugar, or to taste

⅓ cup (81 g) yogurt

FOR THE ALOO CHANA

1 tbsp (15 ml) oil of choice

1 tsp cumin seeds

1½ tsp (3 g) coriander seeds, crushed

1-inch (25-mm) piece ginger, chopped

1 small red onion, chopped

1 green chili, chopped

2 medium tomatoes, chopped

2 medium potatoes, diced

15.5-oz (439-g) can chickpeas, drained (or 1½ cups [228 g] boiled chickpeas)

¼ tsp red chili powder

½ tsp cumin powder

½ tsp garam masala

¾ tsp salt, or to taste

1 tbsp (1 g) cilantro, chopped

¼ cup (60 ml) water

6 whole-wheat wraps (I use large wraps, around 9 inches [23 cm])

FOR THE ONION TOPPING

1 medium white onion, sliced

1½ tsp (7 ml) lemon juice

Pinch of chaat masala

Pinch of black salt/kala namak

(continued)

ALOO CHANA ROLLS (CONT.)

To make the cilantro mint yogurt chutney, add the cilantro, mint leaves, green chilies, ginger, cumin powder, chaat masala, salt, black pepper, lemon juice, sugar and yogurt to a blender and blend until the chutney is smooth. You can add a tablespoon (15 ml) of water if necessary to help blend, but the chutney should be thick, not thin or watery. Taste and adjust the seasonings if necessary. Store in the refrigerator in an airtight container for up to a week.

Press the sauté button. When the pot displays hot, add the oil and then the cumin seeds and crushed coriander seeds. Let them sizzle for a few seconds, then add the ginger and cook for 1 minute, or until the ginger starts turning a light golden brown in color. Add the onion and green chili and cook for 2 minutes, or until the onion is soft. Then add the tomatoes and cook for 2 more minutes. Add the diced potatoes, chickpeas, red chili powder, cumin powder, garam masala and salt. Cook for 1 minute, then add cilantro and the water and close the lid. Make sure the pressure valve is in the sealing position and then press the manual or pressure-cook button. Cook on high pressure for 6 minutes. Let the pressure release naturally for 5 minutes and then do a quick-pressure release.

Open the lid and check the potatoes. They should be quite soft (almost mushy)—that's exactly how we want them for this recipe. Press the sauté button and let the mixture simmer for 2 minutes so that any excess water dries off.

Meanwhile, in a small bowl, toss the sliced onion with lemon juice, chaat masala and black salt. Heat up the wraps according to the directions on the package.

To assemble, take one wrap and spread 1 to 2 teaspoons (15 to 30 ml) of the cilantro mint yogurt chutney all over. Then place 3 to 4 tablespoons (45 to 60 g) of the prepared potato chickpea filling on top, and then top it with the prepared sliced onions and an extra drizzle of chutney, around ½ teaspoon. Fold the wrap to form a roll. Serve the rolls with more chutney or ketchup.

NOTE: For extra crunch, you may also add sliced cabbage and carrots to the onion topping.

VEGETARIAN MOMOS
(VEGETARIAN DUMPLINGS)

SERVES: 18–20 MOMOS

Momos are dumplings popular in south-Asian countries. While the traditional ones are filled with meat, I have, of course, made a vegetarian version. These are stuffed with shredded cabbage, peppers and carrots. I love them with chili oil, or you can also eat them with Szechuan sauce. I made the dough for these dumplings from scratch, but to cut short the cooking time, you may use ready-to-use dumpling wrappers.

FOR THE DUMPLING DOUGH

2 cups (264 g) all-purpose flour

½ tsp salt

2–3 tsp (10–15 ml) vegetable oil

6–7 tbsp (90–105 ml) water

FOR THE STUFFING

1 tbsp (15 ml) vegetable oil

2 large cloves garlic, finely chopped

2 stalks spring onion, finely chopped, white and green parts separated

1 green chili, finely chopped

2 cups (200 g) shredded cabbage

½ cup (60 g) grated carrot

½ cup (72 g) green pepper, finely chopped

1½ tsp (7 ml) soy sauce

½ tsp rice or white vinegar

¼ tsp salt, or to taste

¼ tsp black pepper

Pinch of white pepper powder, optional

In a large bowl, mix the flour with salt and 2 teaspoons (10 ml) of oil. Rub the oil into the flour using your fingers. Start adding water, little by little, and knead to form a smooth dough. You may use a little more oil if the dough is sticking too much while kneading. Pour a few drops of oil over the top of the dough and cover it with a cloth. Let it rest for 30 to 45 minutes.

While the dough is resting, make the stuffing. Press the sauté button, then use the adjust button to set it to "more." When the pot displays hot, add the oil, then add the garlic, spring onion whites and green chili and cook for 1 minute, or until the garlic starts turning golden brown in color. Add the cabbage, carrot and green pepper, mix well, then cook for 2 more minutes. Stir in the soy sauce, vinegar, salt, black pepper and white pepper powder, mix and cook for 1 minute. Unplug the Instant Pot, then add the spring onion greens, mix well and set aside.

After the dough has rested, divide it into twenty equal parts. Each part should weigh 20 to 22 grams. Roll each dough ball into a thin circle. Remember to roll it thin or else the momos will be too thick, which doesn't taste that great! Place 1 to 1½ tablespoons (15 to 21 mg) of the stuffing in each circle, do not overfill, and then make the pleats and seal the momo. Repeat until all the momos are stuffed.

Place 1 cup (240 ml) of water in the Instant Pot. Working in batches, arrange about half of the stuffed momos on a steamer basket and then place the steamer basket inside the pot. Close the lid and then press the steam button and steam for 10 minutes on high pressure, making sure the pressure valve is in the sealing position. Let the pressure release naturally for 2 to 3 minutes and then release the remaining pressure manually. Remove the momos carefully using tongs. You know they are done when they aren't sticky. Steam the remaining batch of stuffed momos in the same way. Enjoy them with chili oil or Szechuan sauce.

MUSHROOM GARLIC FRIED RICE

SERVES: 2

While I love all kinds of fried rice, this Indo-Chinese rice loaded with garlic and mushrooms is my absolute favorite. This is an easy and quick meal, and it's also great to pack in your lunchbox.

1¼ cups (260 g) jasmine rice

1¼ cups (300 ml) water

1½ tbsp (22 ml) toasted sesame oil

1 tbsp (10 g) minced garlic

4 spring onion stalks, chopped, white and green parts separated

1 medium red bell pepper, diced

8 oz (227 g) white mushrooms, thinly sliced

2 tbsp (30 ml) soy sauce

⅛ tsp white pepper powder, or to taste

1 tsp rice or white vinegar

1 tsp Sriracha, or to taste

½ tsp salt, or to taste

Rinse the rice for 2 minutes, or until the water turns clear. This is important to get rid of the excess starch. Place the rinsed rice into the inner steel pot of the Instant Pot and then add the water, stir and close the lid. Make sure the pressure valve is in the sealing position and then press the manual or pressure-cook button. Cook on high pressure for 3 minutes. Let the pressure release naturally for 10 minutes and then do a quick-pressure release. Fluff the rice with a fork and transfer it to another bowl. Set aside.

Now press the sauté button (there's no need to clean the pot). When the pot displays hot, add the toasted sesame oil. Then add the garlic and sauté until it starts turning a light golden color. Add the spring onion whites and the bell pepper and cook for a few seconds, then add the sliced mushrooms. Cook for 2 to 3 minutes until the mushrooms become soft and turn a nice golden brown. Add the soy sauce, white pepper powder, vinegar and Sriracha. Mix to combine the seasonings, then add the cooked rice back into the pot. Add the salt and mix until everything is well combined. Finally, add the spring onion greens and mix.

Serve as a side or main dish with any of your favorite Indo-Chinese recipes!

SPICY MASALA CORN

SERVES: 4

If you ever visit a movie theater or mall in India, especially in the metropolitan cities, you will definitely come across food carts selling masala corn, which is sweet corn with Indian spices. It's the perfect movie-time snack and can easily be made in the Instant Pot.

4 ears corn

1 tbsp (15 g) unsalted butter, cut into small pieces

1 jalapeño, deseeded and finely chopped

1 tsp chaat masala

½ tsp red chili powder, or adjust to taste

½ tsp black salt

¼ tsp salt, or to taste

2 tbsp (2 g) cilantro, chopped

½ tbsp (7 ml) lemon juice, or to taste

Place 1 cup (240 ml) of water into the inner steel pot of the Instant Pot and then place the Instant Pot's trivet inside. Lay the four ears of corn on the trivet. Close the pot with its lid and press the steam button, making sure the pressure valve is in the sealing position. Steam for 5 minutes on high pressure. Do a quick-pressure release. Remove the corn carefully from the pot using tongs.

Cut the corn kernels off the cob while it's still warm. Transfer the corn kernels to a large mixing bowl. Add the butter and stir. Because the corn is still warm, the butter will melt and mix easily. Next, add in the jalapeño, chaat masala, red chili powder, black salt and regular salt. Stir to combine. Finish off by mixing in the cilantro and lemon juice. Place in individual cups and enjoy.

MAKE IT VEGAN: Replace the butter with vegan butter.

VEGAN HOT & SOUR SOUP

SERVES: 3

This is the most common soup that you will find on Indo-Chinese food trucks in India. I have always been a fan, maybe because of all the veggies in this soup. It is flavored mostly with soy sauce, a little black pepper and hot chili sauce for that heat. I have kept this soup really thick because that's how it usually is in India, but you may make it thinner by reducing the amount of cornstarch.

1 tbsp (15 ml) vegetable oil

1-inch (25-mm) piece ginger, finely chopped

5–6 cloves garlic, finely chopped

2 tbsp (13 g) chopped celery

5 white mushrooms, sliced

1 large carrot, cut into thin slices

¼ head (150 g) cabbage, sliced

3 tbsp (45 ml) soy sauce

1 tsp rice or white vinegar

1 tsp hot chili sauce, like Sriracha

¼ tsp black pepper

½ tsp brown sugar

¾ tsp salt, or to taste

3½ cups (840 ml) water, divided

2½ tbsp (20 g) cornstarch

Chopped green onions, for garnish (optional)

Press the sauté button. When the pot displays hot, add the oil, then add ginger, garlic and celery and sauté for 1 to 2 minutes. Add the sliced mushrooms and carrot and cook for 1 minute, then add the cabbage. Toss the cabbage with the remaining veggies until it shrinks, around 1 minute. Add the soy sauce, vinegar, hot chili sauce, black pepper, brown sugar, salt and 3 cups (720 ml) of water. Stir everything together and close the pot with the lid. Press the manual or pressure-cook button and cook on high pressure for 2 minutes, then do a quick-pressure release.

While the soup is cooking, mix the cornstarch with 3 tablespoons (45 ml) of water. Stir well to dissolve the cornstarch. Open the lid and press the sauté button. Then add the cornstarch slurry to the pot, stir the slurry again before adding, as cornstarch settles at the bottom after a while, and mix well. Add ½ cup (120 ml) of water and mix. Let the soup simmer for a minute or two and then transfer it to serving bowls and garnish with green onions, if desired. Enjoy!

NOTE: This soup will become quite thick later on; add water as needed when reheating.

SWEET POTATO CHAAT WITH CILANTRO MINT YOGURT CHUTNEY

SERVES: 2

This is my favorite way to eat sweet potatoes—so flavorful! Boiled sweet potatoes are tossed with a spicy cilantro yogurt chutney, sev (a kind of savory snack made with chickpea flour) and fresh pomegranate arils. You may also toss the sweet potatoes in a little ghee or oil for extra flavor once they are boiled.

2 large sweet potatoes

1½ tbsp (23 g) cilantro mint yogurt chutney (see page 117)

2 tsp (10 ml) lemon juice

Sprinkle of chaat masala

Sprinkle of salt

2 tbsp (6 g) sev, optional

2 tbsp (22 g) pomegranate arils

Cilantro, for garnish

Add 1 cup (240 ml) of water to the inner pot of your Instant Pot. Place the Instant Pot's trivet inside and then place the sweet potatoes on top of the trivet. Close the lid and then press the manual or pressure-cook button. Cook on high pressure for 15 minutes with the pressure valve in the sealing position. Let the pressure release naturally.

Open the lid and carefully remove the sweet potatoes from the pot using tongs or gloves. If you use tongs, the skin of the sweet potatoes might come off in few places while you are lifting them out, so be very careful when lifting them up. Let them cool down a bit and then dice. Place the sweet potatoes in a serving bowl and drizzle the cilantro mint yogurt chutney on top. Sprinkle with the lemon juice, chaat masala, salt and sev. Finally, garnish with pomegranate arils and fresh cilantro and serve.

NOTE: For extra flavor, you may toss the diced, cooked sweet potatoes in 2 teaspoons (10 ml) of oil or ghee until they are caramelized!

SNACKS & SIDES

I am sure I am not the only who is always looking for some quick and easy sides to go with my meals. These sides are the perfect accompaniment to your Indian meals. I especially love the Saag (page 132)—creamy mixed greens spiced with masala and topped with ghee!

The Instant Pot is also great for making Indian snacks like Kaman Dhokla (steamed savory chickpea-flour cake) (page 149), Idlis (page 147), Tomato & Date Chutney (page 139) and Masala Hummus (page 140). These snacks are perfect for those afternoon hunger pangs and they are also great to serve guests at parties.

This chapter also includes the very popular Masala Chai (page 136), made with cardamom, fennel, cloves and peppercorns. In India, anything and everything can be solved over a cup of chai!

SAAG
(SPICED CREAMY GREENS)

SERVES: 4

Saag means puréed greens and in India, the word saag often refers to the saag made in northern parts of India in the winter. It's made with greens like spinach, mustard greens and fenugreek and is enjoyed with makki ki roti (a flatbread made with maize flour). I have used a mix of spinach, mustard greens, turnip greens and collards in this recipe, but you may use other combinations. This saag is lightly spiced and makes a wonderful side.

2 tbsp (30 ml) ghee, divided

1-inch (25-mm) piece ginger, chopped

4 large cloves garlic, chopped

1 green chili, chopped

1 medium red onion, chopped

2-inch (5-cm) radish, cut into rounds

1 medium tomato, chopped

1 lb (454 g) mixed greens (mix of spinach, mustard greens, turnip greens and collards)

¼ tsp turmeric powder

¼ tsp cumin powder

¼ tsp coriander powder

⅛ tsp red chili powder, or to taste

¾ tsp salt, or to taste

¼ cup (60 ml) water

Press the sauté button. When the pot displays hot, add 1 tablespoon (15 ml) of ghee to the pot and then add the ginger, garlic, green chili and onion. Sauté for 2 to 3 minutes, then add the radish and tomato and mix well. Add half of the greens and mix until the leaves wilt and there's room to add more, and then add the remaining half. Stir in the turmeric powder, cumin powder, coriander powder, red chili powder and salt, then mix well. Add the water and close the pot with the lid. Press the manual or pressure-cook button and cook on high pressure for 10 minutes, making sure the pressure valve is in the sealing position. Let the pressure release naturally.

Open the pot and use an immersion blender to purée the contents to a smooth paste. You may also use a regular blender, just make sure the greens cool down for 15 minutes before you purée them in a blender or they will splatter all over. Serve with the remaining 1 tablespoon (15 ml) of ghee drizzled on top.

MAKE IT VEGAN: Replace the ghee with oil.

TOFU BHURJI

(INDIAN-STYLE SCRAMBLED TOFU)

SERVES: 2

This is tofu scramble made the Indian way! It is a quick vegan scramble spiced with mustard, cumin, turmeric and garam masala. Ginger and cilantro give this scramble a fresh taste that makes it ideal for breakfast. You can use this scramble on top of bread or as a filling inside a wrap.

2 tsp (10 ml) oil of choice

½ tsp cumin seeds

¼ tsp mustard seeds

1 tsp grated ginger

1 green chili, finely chopped

1 small onion, finely chopped

5–6 curry leaves

1 tomato, chopped

¼ tsp turmeric powder

½ tsp garam masala

¾ tsp salt, or to taste

10 oz (284 g) extra-firm tofu, crumbled

¼ cup (35 g) frozen green peas

¼ cup (60 ml) water

2 tbsp (2 g) cilantro, chopped

1 tsp lemon juice, optional

Press the sauté button. When the pot displays hot, add the oil and then add the cumin seeds and mustard seeds. Wait a few seconds until the mustard seeds pop and the cumin seeds sizzle and then add the ginger and green chili. Sauté for 30 seconds and then add the onion and curry leaves. Cook for 2 minutes or until the onion is softened.

Add the tomato, turmeric powder, garam masala and salt. Mix and cook for 1 minute. Crumble the tofu with your hands and add it to the pot along with the green peas. You may soak the green peas in warm water for 10 minutes before adding to the recipe. Mix to combine and then add the water, stir, and close the pot with its lid.

Press the manual or pressure-cook button and cook on high pressure for 2 minutes, making sure the pressure valve is in the sealing position. Do a quick-pressure release. If there's some excess water or if the scramble looks too wet, press the sauté button and cook for 1 to 2 minutes until the water dries off. Add the cilantro and mix. Enjoy the tofu scramble on its own or on top of toast. You may also squeeze in some fresh lemon juice.

MASALA CHAI

SERVES: 2

Chai is not a drink but rather an emotion in India. Everything in India happens around a cup of chai. Whether you are happy or sad, chai is your constant companion. Everyone has a personal preference when it comes to chai—some people do not like any spices in their chai (just plain milk, water and tea) while others (like me!) cannot have their chai without spices. Similarly, some like milky tea, while others like strong tea with much less milk. This recipe makes masala chai in a way I like it, but feel free to make changes and adjust according to your taste.

5 green cardamoms

3 cloves

7–8 black peppercorns

¾ tsp fennel seeds

1½ cups (360 ml) water

½ cup (120 ml) milk

2 tsp (2 g) loose black tea leaves

2 tsp (8 g) sugar, or to taste

Add the green cardamoms, cloves, black peppercorns and fennel seeds to a mortar. Crush the spices slightly using the pestle and set it aside. Take a glass or steel container that will fit inside your Instant Pot and add the water, milk, black tea leaves, sugar and the crushed spices to it. Cover the container with foil.

Add 1 cup (240 ml) of water to the inner steel pot of the Instant Pot and then place the Instant Pot's trivet inside. Place the chai container on top of the trivet and lock the lid, making sure the pressure valve is in the sealing position. Press the manual or pressure-cook button and set the time to 3 minutes on high pressure. Let the pressure release naturally for 5 minutes and then do a quick-pressure release. Pour the chai through a strainer into cups and serve hot.

NOTES: Like more milk in your chai? Use 1 cup (240 ml) of water and 1 cup (240 ml) of milk. Like stronger chai? Cook on high pressure for 5 minutes. Want to add ginger to your chai? Add ginger powder or thin strips of ginger. Do not crush or grate the ginger, it might curdle the chai when it boils.

TOMATO & DATE CHUTNEY

SERVES: 1⅓ CUPS (320 ML) CHUTNEY

I have fond memories of my mom making this sweet chutney (with a hint of spice) and serving it to us with plain paratha. That truly was the best breakfast ever! This chutney is a great accompaniment to any Indian meal, but my personal favorite is to eat it with paratha and a cup of chai.

2 tbsp (30 ml) vegetable oil

¾ tsp mustard seeds

4 tomatoes, diced

8 medjool dates, chopped

¼ cup (50 g) brown sugar, or to taste

¼ tsp red chili powder

¼ tsp garam masala

¾ tsp cumin powder

⅛ tsp ground ginger, optional

1 tsp salt, or to taste

1–2 tbsp (10–20 g) golden raisins, optional

Press the sauté button. When the pot displays hot, add the oil and then the mustard seeds, letting them heat for a few seconds until they pop. Add the tomatoes, stir, then close the pot with the lid. Set the pressure valve to the sealing position and press the manual or pressure-cook button. Cook on high pressure for 10 minutes, then do a quick-pressure release.

Open the lid. The tomatoes should have released a lot of liquid. Press the sauté button and use the adjust button to set it to "more." Add the dates, brown sugar, red chili powder, garam masala, cumin powder, ground ginger (optional) and salt. Cook the chutney for 5 minutes, stirring often. Add the golden raisins and cook for another 5 to 7 minutes, until the chutney thickens quite a bit. Transfer to an airtight container and let it cool. It should keep well in the refrigerator for 2 weeks. Enjoy it with paratha or any other type of bread.

MASALA HUMMUS

(SPICED HUMMUS)

SERVES: 6

Classic hummus is made spicy with garam masala, cumin powder, coriander powder and chili powder! Enjoy it with chips or on your sandwiches.

1 cup (210 g) dried chickpeas

4 cups (960 ml) water

1 tsp salt, divided

4–5 cloves garlic

1 green chili

¼ cup (62 g) tahini

1 tsp garam masala

¼ tsp red chili powder, optional

½ tsp cumin powder

¼ tsp coriander powder

2 tbsp (30 ml) olive oil

2 tbsp (30 ml) lemon juice

Chopped cilantro, for serving

Extra-virgin olive oil, for serving

Smoked paprika, for serving

Soak the dried chickpeas overnight. In the morning, drain the water and rinse the chickpeas. Place them in the inner steel pot of your Instant Pot and add the water and ½ teaspoon salt and close the lid. Press the manual or pressure-cook button and cook on high pressure for 20 minutes. Make sure the pressure valve is in the sealing position. Let the pressure release naturally.

Drain the cooked chickpeas, reserving the water in which they were cooked. Transfer the chickpeas to a food processor along with the garlic, green chili, tahini, garam masala, red chili powder (if using), cumin powder, coriander powder and 5 tablespoons (75 ml) of reserved chickpea cooking water. Pulse to combine.

Add the olive oil, lemon juice and ½ teaspoon salt (or adjust to taste). Mix until combined. Place hummus in a serving bowl and top with cilantro, extra-virgin olive oil and smoked paprika.

MINT CASHEW PULAO

(SPICED BASMATI RICE WITH MINT & CASHEWS)

SERVES: 2

This refreshing pulao made with fresh mint and cashews goes so well with any Indian curry or even plain yogurt. The recipe calls for ½ cup (18 g) of packed mint leaves but if you aren't a huge mint fan, you can also use half mint and half cilantro.

1 cup (200 g) basmati rice

½ cup (18 g) packed mint leaves

1 green chili

1-inch (25-mm) piece ginger

1 tbsp (15 ml) oil of choice

1 bay leaf

2 cloves

2 green cardamoms

½ tsp cumin seeds

20 raw cashews

1 medium onion, sliced

1 cup (240 ml) water

½ tsp salt, or to taste

Wash the rice with cold water until the water turns clear. Soak in 2 cups (480 ml) of water for 15 minutes, then drain the water and set the rice aside.

In a blender, purée the mint leaves, green chili, ginger and 3 to 4 tablespoons (45 to 60 ml) of water. It should be a fine purée and come to around ½ cup (120 ml). If the mint purée does not equal ½ cup (120 ml), add enough water to make ½ cup (120 ml) of liquid total.

Press the sauté button. When the pot displays hot, add the oil and then the bay leaf, cloves, green cardamoms and cumin seeds. Sauté for a few seconds until the cumin seeds sizzle and the spices are fragrant. Add the cashews and cook until they turn light golden brown in color, about 1 minute. Add the onion and cook for 3 minutes or until the onion turns light golden in color. Then add the prepared mint purée and the rice to the pot. Stir and cook for 1 minute. Add the water and salt and close the lid. Press the manual or pressure-cook button with the pressure valve in the sealing position. Cook on high pressure for 6 minutes. Let the pressure release naturally. Open the lid, fluff the pulao with a fork and serve with a side of raita.

KHATTI MEETHI PUMPKIN SABZI
(SWEET & SOUR PUMPKIN)

SERVES: 3

The only way we would eat pumpkin as kids was when it was made in this way: sweet and sour and spiced with masalas. This pumpkin tastes amazing with paratha (whole-wheat flatbread) or poori (deep-fried whole-wheat bread).

2 tsp (10 ml) oil of choice

¼ tsp fenugreek seeds

¼ tsp mustard seeds

2 dried red chilies

1 sugar pumpkin (about 2 lb [990 g]), diced into 1½–2-inch (4–5-cm) pieces

¼ tsp turmeric powder

⅛ tsp red chili powder, optional

½ tsp coriander powder

½ tsp garam masala

½ tsp salt, or to taste

1½ tsp (6 g) dried mango powder/ amchur

1 tbsp (13 g) sugar

½ cup (120 ml) water

Poori, for serving

Paratha, for serving

Press the sauté button. When the pot displays hot, add the oil and then the fenugreek seeds and mustard seeds. Let the mustard seeds pop for a few seconds and then add the dried red chilies. You may break them before adding for extra spice in your dish. Add the diced pumpkin, turmeric powder, red chili powder (if using), coriander powder, garam masala, salt, dried mango powder and sugar. Toss the pumpkin until it is well coated with the spices. Add the water, close the lid and press the manual or pressure-cook button. Cook on high pressure for 6 minutes and then do a quick-pressure release. Serve the khatti meethi pumpkin sabzi with poori or paratha.

IDLIS
(STEAMED RICE LENTIL CAKES)

SERVES: 16—18 IDLIS

This is a traditional south Indian breakfast! I didn't grow up eating idlis because I was born and brought up in north India, but I have always had a huge inclination toward south Indian food. One of the most common south Indian dishes are idlis, which is like a steamed rice–lentil cake. They are traditionally made by fermenting rice and lentils. I love my idlis with coconut chutney. Once you have the idli batter ready to go, you can get these idlis on the table in less than 15 minutes!

You will need an idli stand for this recipe. You can find them online or at Indian grocery stores. This recipe will make enough idli batter for two batches of idlis. Make another batch right away, or store the rest in the refrigerator for three to four days.

FOR THE IDLIS
½ cup (100 g) split and dehusked black gram lentil/urad dal dhuli

1 tsp fenugreek seeds/methi seeds

2 cups (400 g) idli rice (short-grain rice)

1½–2 cups (300–420 ml) water, divided

1 tsp salt

FOR THE COCONUT CHUTNEY
1 cup (240 g) freshly grated or desiccated coconut

1-inch (25-mm) piece ginger

1–2 green chilies

½ tsp salt, or to taste

½–¾ cup (120–180 ml) water

2 tsp (10 ml) vegetable oil

¾ tsp mustard seeds

Pinch of asafetida

½ tsp split and dehusked black gram lentil/urad dal dhuli

2 dried red chilies

10–15 curry leaves

Put the urad dal and fenugreek seeds in a large bowl. Rinse three to four times and then soak in 1 cup (240 ml) of water for 5 to 6 hours, or overnight. In another bowl, add the rice and rinse until the water turns clear, then soak in 4 cups (960 ml) of water for the same amount of time as the dal.

Drain the water from the dal first, then transfer the soaked dal and fenugreek seeds to a high-speed blender. A Blendtec or Vitamix works really well. Add ½ to ¾ cup (120 to 180 ml) of water and blend on medium-high speed for 1 minute, until you have a fine paste. Transfer to the steel pot of your Instant Pot. Drain the rice. Rinse the blender and add the rice and ¾ to 1 cup (180 to 240 ml) of water. Grind to a coarse paste. Add the rice to the steel pot and mix well with the lentil batter. Add a few tablespoons of water at a time, up to about ¼ cup (60 ml), to make a thick, pourable batter. Do not add too much water, as you don't want it to be watery. Using your hands, add the salt to the batter and mix for 2 to 3 minutes. Mixing the salt by hand aids in the fermentation process. The batter will be somewhere between the 3 to 4-cup mark in your Instant Pot.

Place the steel pot back into the Instant Pot and press the yogurt button. Set the time to 12 hours and place the lid on top. The pressure valve can either be in the sealing or venting position. After 12 hours, the batter should have fermented and doubled in volume. It will be around the 8-cup mark or even higher. If it hasn't fermented, press the yogurt button again and set the time to 2 hours or until it's fermented. Use fermented batter to make idlis and dosas.

(continued)

IDLIS (CONT.)

Spray an idli stand with nonstick spray or brush it with a little oil. Fill each cavity of the idli stand with the prepared idli-dosa batter. You should be able to get 16 to 18 idlis out of 4 cups (960 ml) of the batter. You can save the rest of the batter for another use. Pour 1 cup (240 ml) of water into the inner steel pot of your instant pot and then place the idli stand inside the Instant Pot and close the lid. Press the steam button and let it steam for 12 to 13 minutes, with the pressure valve in the venting position. When the valve is in the venting position, the Instant Pot does not display the timer, so you have to time it manually. After 12 to 13 minutes, unplug the Instant Pot. The pressure valve will come down within a minute or two. Open the lid and carefully remove the idli stand from the pot. Remove idlis from each cavity and serve with coconut chutney and chai or coffee.

For the chutney, pulse together the coconut, ginger, green chili, salt and the water to a fine paste in a blender. Transfer the chutney to a bowl. To make the tempering for the chutney, add the oil to a small pan over medium heat. When the oil is hot, add the mustard seeds and let them pop for a few seconds, then add the asafetida, urad dal and dried red chilies. Sauté for a few seconds until the dal starts turning golden brown in color. Add the curry leaves (it will sizzle a lot, so add the curry leaves, then quickly move away from the pan), sauté for a few seconds and then remove the pan from the heat. Transfer the tempering to the bowl of coconut chutney and mix. Serve coconut chutney with idlis and dosa.

NOTE: The same batter used for the idlis could also be used to make dosas, which are rice and lentil crepes filled with spiced potatoes and other veggies.

KHAMAN DHOKLA

(STEAMED SAVORY CHICKPEA-FLOUR CAKES)

SERVES: 4 (12–16 PIECES)

Dhokla is a steamed savory cake that tastes so good with chai and is also great to serve at parties! This popular snack is traditionally made by fermenting garbanzo bean–flour batter for hours, but, in this instant version, we get soft and spongy khaman within minutes. I have used a combination of fruit salt (eno) and citric acid, which gives the perfect result every time.

1¼ cups (130 g) chickpea flour/besan

2 tbsp (28 g) semolina/sooji

1 tbsp + 1½ tsp (19 g) sugar, divided

¾ tsp salt, divided

¼ tsp turmeric powder

1 tsp grated ginger

3 green chilies, 1 minced, 2 sliced

2½ tbsp (37 ml) vegetable oil, divided

½ tsp + ⅛ tsp citric acid

Pinch of baking soda

1½ cups (360 ml) water, divided

1¼ tsp (8 g) fruit salt, commonly known as eno

1½ tsp (3 g) mustard seeds

1 tsp sesame seeds

10–12 curry leaves

1 tsp lemon juice

Desiccated coconut, for garnish

Lightly spray a 7- to 8-inch (18- to 20-cm) steel bowl with nonstick spray. Pour 1½ cups (360 ml) of water in the inner pot of your Instant Pot and then press the sauté button. Use the adjust button to set sauté to "more." While the water boils, make the batter for the dhokla.

In a large bowl, stir together the chickpea flour, semolina, 1 tablespoon (13 g) of sugar, ½ teaspoon salt, turmeric powder, grated ginger and 1 minced green chili. Mix well and then add 1½ tablespoons (22 ml) of oil and rub with your fingers so that the oil mixes well with everything. Mix in the citric acid and baking soda, then add 1 cup (240 ml) of water. Mix for a couple of minutes until it is well combined. Finally, add the fruit salt (eno) and mix again until the batter is well combined; it will increase in volume after you add the fruit salt. Pour the batter into the prepared steel bowl and cover the container with foil.

When the water in the Instant Pot is boiling, press the cancel button and then place the Instant Pot's trivet inside the pot. Place the prepared bowl on top of the trivet. It's very important to steam the dhokla as soon as you mix the fruit salt into the batter; do not wait or else the dhokla will not get spongy. Close the lid and then press the steam button. Set the time to 20 minutes, making sure the pressure valve is in the sealing position. Do a quick-pressure release.

Carefully remove the pan from the Instant Pot. Remove the foil and let the dhokla sit for 10 minutes and then flip it over a serving plate. Let it cool on the plate and in the meantime, make the tempering.

(continued)

KHAMAN DHOKLA (CONT.)

Heat 1 tablespoon (15 ml) of oil in a small pan on medium heat. When the oil is hot, add the mustard seeds and let them pop for a few seconds. Then add the sesame seeds and cook for 30 seconds until they start changing color. Add curry leaves and 2 sliced green chilies; the curry leaves will splutter a lot, so be careful and move away from the pan once you have added them. Remove the pan from the heat. Add ½ cup (120 ml) of water, 1½ teaspoons (6 g) of sugar, ¼ teaspoon salt and lemon juice, then put the pan back on medium heat. Let it all come to a boil, then remove from the heat.

Cut the dhokla into pieces. Pour half of the prepared tadka over all of the dhokla pieces. It might look like a lot of water, but the flour will absorb it all and you need this much water for soft dhokla. Now pour the remaining half of the tadka onto the cut edges of the dhokla so that they get soft from all sides. Transfer the dhokla to a serving plate lined with a paper towel and let sit for 10 to 15 minutes. Then, sprinkle with the coconut and serve. Dhokla tastes great when chilled! I love to serve it with cilantro chutney.

NOTES: You may substitute citric acid with 1 teaspoon of lime juice, but keep in mind that citric acid does give the best results. I do not like using baking soda in place of fruit salt here as it leads to a soapy taste. You can steam the khaman dhokla in advance and store in an airtight container. Prepare the tadka only 10 to 15 minutes before serving.

DELECTABLE DESSERTS

One of my favorite parts about the Instant Pot is all the cool desserts that you can make in it! It is really a convenient way to make desserts, especially during the holidays when your oven is busy with so many other things. Also, it allows you to make desserts with hands-free cooking time. The classic Indian kheer, which would take quite a bit of monitoring on the stovetop, is a breeze to make in the Instant Pot, where you just have to dump everything together and then forget about it.

This chapter has my favorite desserts like the classic Rice Kheer (page 154) and Pumpkin Coconut Halwa (page 165) and also some fun fusion recipes like Masala Chai Crème Brûlée (page 166)! My favorite, though, is the Rose Pistachio Cheesecake (page 169). It's just so good with a cup of coffee!

RICE KHEER
(INDIAN RICE PUDDING)

SERVES: 4

If there's one dessert that's made in every Indian household, it has to be kheer. This is the easiest way to make kheer—you just have to dump everything together and then let the Instant Pot do its thing! This classic Indian rice pudding is flavored with cardamom and nuts.

5 cups (1.2 L) whole milk

⅓ cup + 1 tbsp (84 g) basmati rice, rinsed

½ cup (100 g) granulated white sugar

1 tbsp (10 g) golden raisins

2 tbsp (17 g) broken cashews

½ tsp cardamom powder, divided

Sliced pistachios, for garnish

To the inner steel pot of your Instant Pot, add the milk, rice, sugar, raisins, cashews and ¼ teaspoon cardamom powder. Stir and close the lid, making sure the pressure valve is in the sealing position. Press the porridge button; it will automatically cook for 20 minutes at high pressure. Let the pressure release naturally. Open the pot and give everything a good stir.

Press the sauté button, and then add the remaining ¼ teaspoon cardamom powder and mix. Let the kheer simmer for 2 to 3 minutes until it thickens and becomes creamy. You can add more sugar to taste at this point. Garnish with sliced pistachios and serve hot or cold. The kheer will get thicker as it cools down.

NOTE: I recommend using whole milk for creamier kheer. Also, kheer tastes best when chilled and is even better the next day.

MAKE IT VEGAN: Replace the whole milk with almond milk. You may also use coconut sugar in place of white sugar.

KESAR ELAICHI SHRIKHAND
(SAFFRON CARDAMOM YOGURT)

SERVES: 3–4

Shrikhand is Indian-style Greek yogurt that is flavored with cardamom and saffron. The traditional process of making shrikhand is quite long and takes days. For this quicker Instant Pot version, we make sweetened yogurt and then strain it to get thick yogurt to make shrikhand.

4 cups (960 ml) whole milk

2 tsp (14 g) plain yogurt

1 cup (240 ml) sweetened condensed milk

½ tsp cardamom powder

Pinch of saffron strands, crushed and dissolved in 1 tsp warm milk

Sliced pistachios and almonds, for garnish

NOTE: Saffron gives a better color and flavor the next day, so it's a good idea to make this a day in advance.

Line a strainer with a muslin cloth or cheesecloth.

Add the milk to the inner steel pot of your Instant Pot. Close the lid; the pressure valve can either be sealing or venting. Press the yogurt button and then press the adjust button until the display says "boil." You will hear a beep when the milk has come to a boil and the display screen will say "yogt." This should take 15 to 16 minutes. Open the lid and check the temperature of the milk; it should be 180°F (82°C) or more. If not, press the sauté button and wait until the milk reaches this temperature or above.

Remove the inner steel pot and transfer it to a sink or a bigger pot filled with cold water. Whisk the milk continuously until it reaches a temperature of 100 to 110°F (38 to 43°C). This will take 5 to 10 minutes.

Put the starter yogurt in another bowl and add ¼ cup (60 ml) of the slightly cooled milk; whisk to combine. Add the condensed milk and mix until well combined. Transfer this mixture to the remaining milk in the inner steel pot and mix well.

Place the inner pot back into the Instant Pot and close the lid. Press the yogurt button and set the time to 7 hours. The pressure valve can be in the sealing or venting position. The Instant Pot will start the counter and after 7 hours it will display "yogt," which means your yogurt is done. Transfer the yogurt to the refrigerator for a couple of hours. When the yogurt is chilled, transfer it to the lined strainer. Place a large bowl beneath the strainer and let the yogurt strain for 3 to 4 hours.

After 4 hours, the yogurt should be quite thick. Transfer to a large bowl and add the cardamom powder to it. Add the saffron milk to the yogurt and mix. Garnish with pistachios and almonds and serve.

KALAKAND

(SPICED MILK FUDGE)

SERVES: 12 PIECES

This Indian milk fudge is made with fresh chena (paneer). Traditionally, first the milk is curdled to make chena and then that chena is cooked with milk until it reaches a very thick consistency. In this recipe, we cut short the process by using condensed milk. This milk-based dessert tastes best when fresh and should be consumed within 3 to 4 days.

8 cups (2 L) whole milk

2 tbsp + 1–2 tsp (35–40 ml) distilled white vinegar

14-oz (400-g) can sweetened condensed milk

¼ tsp cardamom powder

½ tsp rose water, optional

Pistachios, for garnish

NOTE: Don't try to cook this on normal sauté; it will stick to the pot even if you stir continuously. Low sauté is the way to go here, even though it takes a little more time. Even on low sauté, make sure to stir continuously or the mixture may stick to the pot.

Line a 6-inch (15-cm) square pan with aluminum foil and spray with a nonstick spray. Set it aside. Place a cheesecloth over a strainer.

Place ¼ cup (60 ml) of water into the inner steel pot of the Instant Pot. This is optional, but a little water at the bottom makes sure that the milk does not stick to the bottom of the pot. Add the milk and close the lid. Press the yogurt button and use the adjust button until the screen displays "boil." The pressure valve can either be sealing or venting. It will take about 30 minutes for the milk to come to a boil.

When the milk has boiled, you will hear a beep. Open the pot and start adding vinegar to the milk. Keep stirring as you add the vinegar until the milk curdles. The milk will separate completely and you will see clear whey. At this point, remove the inner pot and drain the milk into the prepared strainer. All the chena will be collected in the cheesecloth. Squeeze as much water as you can from the chena and then tie the cloth and let it hang for 10 minutes. Then, remove the chena from the cloth and break it apart into crumbles.

Rinse and wipe the inner steel pot and put it back into the Instant Pot. Press the sauté button and then use the adjust button to set sauté to "less." Add the crumbled chena, condensed milk, cardamom powder and rose water (if using) and mix everything until well combined. Stir continuously; the mixture will start to thicken up and after 15 to 17 minutes, it will thicken considerably and leave the sides of the pot.

Transfer the mixture to the prepared square pan. Use a knife to spread it evenly. Sprinkle chopped pistachios on top. Let it chill in the refrigerator for at least 3 hours before cutting into pieces.

ZARDA

(SWEET RICE)

SERVES: 4

Have you ever had sweet rice? This is a royal Indian dessert made only for special occasions and festivals. The sweet rice with flavors of saffron and rose and garnished with nuts, dried fruits and coconut is indulgence at its best!

1 cup (200 g) sella basmati rice, choose the XL variety

½ cup (120 ml) whole milk

Generous pinch of saffron strands

2 tsp (10 ml) ghee

15 cashews, chopped in half

15 almonds, chopped in half

1–2 tbsp (10–20 g) golden raisins

5–6 green cardamoms

5–6 cloves

¾ cup (150 g) granulated white sugar

¾–1 cup (180–240 ml) water

2 tsp (10 ml) rose water

2–3 tsp (3–5 g) desiccated coconut

Cherries or tutti frutti (candied papaya), for garnish

Edible silver leaves, for garnish

Rinse the basmati rice until the water turns clear. Soak the rice in 2 cups (480 ml) of water for 30 minutes and then drain the water and set the rice aside.

Heat the milk in a small saucepan over medium heat, but do not allow it to come to a boil. Add the saffron strands and set aside.

Press the sauté button and when it displays hot, add the ghee and then the cashews, almonds and raisins. Sauté for a few minutes until the nuts turn light golden brown in color and then remove the nuts and raisins from the pot and set them aside. To the same pot, add the cardamoms and cloves and sauté for a few seconds until fragrant. Add the soaked and drained basmati rice and sauté with the spices for 30 seconds. Add the sugar, ¾ cup (180 ml) of water (or 1 cup [240 ml] if you prefer softer rice) and the saffron milk. Stir for 1 minute until the sugar dissolves. Add the rose water and close the lid. Press the manual or pressure-cook button, with the pressure valve in the sealing position. Cook on high pressure for 6 minutes. Let the pressure release naturally.

Open the lid, let the rice cool down a bit and then fluff with a fork. Add the fried nuts and raisins to the rice. Sprinkle with desiccated coconut and garnish with cherries or tutti frutti. Decorate with edible silver leaves and serve.

MAKE IT VEGAN: Replace the ghee with coconut oil and the milk with almond or coconut milk.

EGGLESS TUTTI FRUTTI CAKE

SERVES: 8

This classic Indian tea-time cake is studded with tutti frutti. This was my favorite cake growing up and my sister and I would gobble down the entire packet in one go. This is so easy to make in the Instant Pot; it is super moist with a hint of vanilla, pineapple and cinnamon. The tutti frutti is candied papaya, but any other nuts or dried fruits would work, too!

1 cup + 2 tbsp (144 g) all-purpose flour

2 tbsp (18 g) cornstarch

¼ tsp ground cinnamon

Pinch of nutmeg

1¼ tsp (6 g) baking powder

½ tsp baking soda

¼ tsp salt

1 cup (245 g) plain yogurt

¾ cup (150 g) granulated white sugar

½ cup (120 ml) vegetable oil

1 tsp vanilla extract

½ tsp pineapple essence

1 cup (120 g) tutti frutti

Powdered sugar, for serving (optional)

NOTE: If you don't have pineapple extract, use 1½ teaspoons (7 ml) of vanilla extract.

Spray a 6-cup bundt pan or a regular 6-inch (15-cm) round pan with nonstick spray. Make a sling out of aluminum foil by taking a long piece, approximately 2 feet (60 cm), and fold it twice or thrice lengthwise.

Add 1½ cups (360 ml) of water to the inner pot of the Instant Pot and then place the Instant Pot's trivet inside.

In a bowl, sift together the flour, cornstarch, cinnamon, nutmeg, baking powder, baking soda and salt.

In a separate bowl, using a whisk or a stand mixer, whisk together the yogurt and sugar until the sugar dissolves completely. Add the oil, vanilla extract and pineapple essence and mix to combine. Add the sifted dry ingredients and mix until just combined; do not overmix the batter. Fold in the tutti frutti. If your batter looks too thick to pour, you may add 1 tablespoon (15 ml) of water at this point.

Transfer the batter to the prepared pan. Cover the pan with aluminum foil. Put the foil sling underneath the pan so that it will be easier to lift the pan out of the Instant Pot when the cake is done. Using the sling, lower the cake pan into the Instant Pot and set it on the trivet. Close the lid, making sure the pressure valve is in the sealing position. Press the manual or pressure-cook button and let it cook for 25 minutes at high pressure. Let the pressure release naturally for 10 minutes and then do a quick-pressure release.

Open the lid and carefully remove the pan using the foil sling. Wait for 5 minutes and then flip the pan over a serving plate to remove the cake. Transfer the cake to a wire rack to cool completely before slicing. Sprinkle some powdered sugar on top (optional) and enjoy!

PUMPKIN COCONUT HALWA

(PUMPKIN COCONUT PUDDING)

SERVES: 4

Halwa is probably the most popular Indian dessert (along with kheer). The most common types of halwa are made using semolina and whole-wheat flour. This one is made using pumpkin, sugar, ghee and coconut. You may use coconut oil in place of ghee to make this vegan, but if you ask me, halwa without ghee is just not the same!

2 tbsp + 2 tsp (40 ml) ghee, divided

4 cups (500 g) pumpkin, cubed, each piece around 1½ inches (38 mm)

½ cup (120 ml) almond milk

½ cup + 2 tbsp (125 g) brown sugar

½ cup (40 g) desiccated coconut powder, plus more for serving

½ tsp cardamom powder

1 tbsp (9 g) broken cashews, plus more for serving

1 tbsp (6 g) sliced almonds, plus more for serving

1 tbsp (10 g) golden raisins

Press the sauté button. When it displays hot, add 2 tablespoons (30 ml) of ghee to the pot, then add the cubed pumpkin. Sauté for 2 to 3 minutes until the raw smell of the pumpkin goes away. Add the almond milk and close the pot with the lid. Press the manual or pressure-cook button with the pressure valve in the sealing position. Cook on high pressure for 5 minutes. Do a quick-pressure release.

Open the pot and press the sauté button. Mash the pumpkin with a fork or potato masher. Then add the sugar and cook for 2 to 3 minutes, stirring continuously. Add the desiccated coconut powder along with the cardamom powder and cook the halwa for 2 to 3 minutes more, stirring continuously until the mixture starts to thicken. Add the cashews, almonds and raisins and cook for another 2 minutes. Stir in the remaining 2 teaspoons (10 ml) of ghee and mix. Garnish with more nuts and coconut powder, if desired, and serve warm.

MAKE IT VEGAN: Replace the ghee with coconut oil.

MASALA CHAI CRÈME BRÛLÉE

SERVES: 4–5

You won't believe how easy it is to make crème brûlée in your Instant Pot! This chai crème brûlée has flavors of Indian chai infused in a smooth and silky custard topped with a layer of crispy caramelized sugar.

1 cup (240 ml) heavy cream

1 cup (240 ml) milk (whole milk preferred)

3 black tea bags

6 green cardamoms

6 whole black peppercorns

4 whole cloves

1-inch (25-mm) piece cinnamon stick

¼ tsp ground ginger

5 large egg yolks

6 tbsp (75 g) granulated white sugar

1 tsp vanilla extract

Pinch of salt

4 tbsp (60 g) caster or superfine sugar

Add 1½ cups (360 ml) of water to the inner steel pot of the Instant Pot and then place the Instant Pot's trivet inside the pot. To a small steel or glass container, add the heavy cream, milk, tea bags, green cardamoms, black peppercorns, cloves, cinnamon stick and ground ginger. Give a quick stir and place the container in the Instant Pot on top of the trivet. Close the lid, making sure the pressure valve is in the sealing position and then press the manual or pressure-cook button. Set the time to 1 minute on high pressure. Release the pressure quickly, open the lid and remove the container carefully from the pot. Let it sit for 10 to 15 minutes for the flavors to infuse. Meanwhile, drain the water from the inner steel pot, wipe it and place it back into the Instant Pot.

In a large bowl, whisk together the egg yolks with granulated white sugar, vanilla extract and a pinch of salt. Whisk until the mixture turns a pale yellow. Strain the cream–milk mixture into another bowl and discard the solids. Add the strained cream–milk mixture a little at a time into the egg–sugar mixture, stirring continuously. When everything is well combined, pour the liquid into 4 to 5 ramekins (3 to 4 ounces [90 to 120 ml] each). Cover each ramekin with a piece of aluminium foil.

(continued)

MASALA CHAI CRÈME BRÛLÉE (CONT.)

Add 1 cup (240 ml) of water to the inner steel pot and then place the Instant Pot's trivet inside. Place the prepared ramekins on top of the trivet; you may stack them if necessary. Close the lid and press the manual or pressure-cook button, with the pressure valve in the sealing position. Cook on high pressure for 7 minutes. Let the pressure release naturally for 10 minutes and then do a quick-pressure release. The crème brûlée should be set but still trembling in the center. Carefully remove the ramekins from the pot and let them cool. If there's condensation on top of the foil, discard the foil. Referigerate for 4 hours or overnight.

When chilled, take the ramekins out of the refrigerator and let them sit at room temperature for around 15 minutes. Divide the caster sugar equally among the ramekins, and spread evenly on top. Use a culinary torch to caramelize the sugar and form a hard and crispy top. If you do not have a kitchen torch, you may do this step in the oven set to broil. Serve immediately.

ROSE PISTACHIO CHEESECAKE

SERVES: 6

This creamy, decadent cheesecake flavored with rose water and pistachios is made right in the Instant Pot! This is one of the best cheesecakes I have ever made, Instant Pot or not! There are little chunks of pistachios in the filling and the crust is made of Biscoff cookies. You may use graham crackers or any other cookie of choice if you can't find Biscoff.

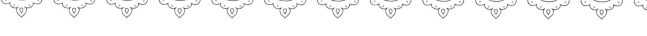

20 Biscoff cookies

3 tbsp (45 g) unsalted butter, melted and cooled slightly

16 oz (454 g) cream cheese, at room temperature

⅔ cup (135 g) granulated white sugar

1 tsp vanilla extract

2 tbsp (30 ml) rose water

½ cup (70 g) raw, unsalted shelled pistachios, roughly ground with some bits and pieces of pistachios remaining

2 tbsp (30 ml) heavy cream, at room temperature

1 tsp all-purpose flour

2 large eggs, at room temperature

2 tbsp (12 g) ground pistachio powder, for garnishing

Candied dried rose petals, for garnishing

Lightly spray a 7 x 3-inch (17 x 8-cm) springform pan with nonstick spray. Make a sling out of aluminum foil by taking a long piece, approximately 2 feet (60 cm), and fold it twice or thrice lengthwise. Take the cream cheese, eggs and heavy cream out of the refrigerator and place on your kitchen counter for at least 2 hours, but preferably 4 hours. It's very important to have these ingredients at room temperature in order to make the perfect cheesecake.

Pulse the Biscoff cookies in a food processor until they turn into fine crumbs. Transfer the cookie crumbs to a large bowl and then add the melted butter and mix until well combined and the crumbs feel like wet sand. Transfer the crumb mixture to the prepared springform pan. Press the crumbs into the bottom of the pan, using the back of a measuring cup to press it really tight. Place the pan into the freezer while you make the filling.

Beat the cream cheese on medium speed for 1 to 2 minutes using a stand or hand mixer until completely smooth. Add the sugar, vanilla extract and rose water and mix for 30 seconds, until well combined. Add the roughly ground pistachios along with the heavy cream and flour and mix to combine. Add the eggs and mix at medium speed until just combined. Do not overmix the batter; it's a good idea to mix the eggs using a wire whisk, just to make sure you don't overmix (thus incorporating too much air into the batter).

(continued)

ROSE PISTACHIO CHEESECAKE (CONT.)

Take the pan out of the freezer and pour the filling on top of the crust. Add 1½ cups (360 ml) of water to the inner pot of the Instant Pot and then place the Instant Pot's trivet inside. Cover the pan with a piece of foil. Put the foil sling underneath the pan so that it will be easier to lift the pan out of the Instant Pot when the cheesecake is done. Using the sling, lower the cake pan into the Instant Pot, and set it on the trivet. Close the pot with the lid and press the manual or pressure-cook button, with the pressure valve in the sealing position. Cook on high pressure for 45 minutes. Let the pressure release naturally.

Carefully remove the cheesecake. The center should still jiggle slightly. Let the cake cool to room temperature, then transfer to the refrigerator to chill overnight or for a minimum of 4 hours. Take the cheesecake out of the refrigerator at least 30 minutes before serving. Garnish with ground pistachio powder and candied dried rose petals (optional) and serve.

MANGO COCONUT TAPIOCA PUDDING

SERVES: 4

I used to love tapioca pearls/sabudana kheer as a child; it was often made in my house during the festive season. This creamy pudding combines the flavor of the sabudana kheer with mangoes! It tastes best when chilled.

½ cup (90 g) tapioca pearls/sabudana

1½ cups (360 ml) water, divided

14-oz (400-g) can of coconut milk

¼ tsp cardamom powder

1 tsp rose water

½ cup + 1 tbsp (135 ml) mango purée, use fresh or canned

3 tbsp (41 g) brown sugar, or to taste

2 tbsp (18 g) broken cashews

1 tbsp (10 g) golden raisins

Sliced pistachios, for serving

Wash the tapioca pearls until the water runs clear and then add them to the inner steel pot of the Instant Pot. Add 1 cup (240 ml) of water and let the tapioca pearls soak in the water for 15 to 20 minutes, with the Instant Pot off. After soaking, plug in the Instant Pot and press the sauté button. Let the tapioca simmer for 5 to 6 minutes or until the tapioca pearls look translucent; they will also begin to float on top. Add the coconut milk and ½ cup (120 ml) of water. Stir and close the pot with the lid. Press the manual or pressure-cook button and then press the adjust button to set pressure to "low." Cook on low pressure for 10 minutes, making sure the pressure valve is in the sealing position. Let the pressure release naturally for 5 minutes and then do a quick-pressure release.

Open the pot and press the sauté button. Use the adjust button to set sauté to "less." Add the cardamom powder, rose water and mango purée and mix well. Then add the brown sugar, cashews and raisins and mix well. Let the pudding simmer for 2 minutes and then switch off the Instant Pot. Chill the pudding before serving. Garnish with sliced pistachios and serve.

INDIAN COOKING BASICS

Ghee, garam masala, paneer—these are just some of the core recipes of Indian cooking. If you have never made Indian before or are new to Indian cooking, these recipes will introduce you to the very basics. These are also commonly used in many of the recipes in this book.

PANEER
(INDIAN COTTAGE CHEESE)

SERVES: 1¹⁄₃ CUPS (300 G)

Paneer is the most popular Indian vegetable without a doubt! It's funny though, because technically it's not a vegetable at all, yet half of the dishes on the vegetarian menu in an Indian restaurant will have paneer. In India, no celebration, no festival is complete without a paneer dish on the menu. It's surprisingly easy to make at home with only two ingredients!

½ gallon (5.7 L) whole milk

2 tbsp + 1 tsp (35 ml) distilled white vinegar

Line a strainer with a cheesecloth.

Add ¼ cup (60 ml) of water into the inner steel pot of your Instant Pot. This is optional, but I recommend doing it because adding a little water at the bottom prevents the milk from burning. Add the milk and then close the pot with the lid. Press the yogurt button and then use the adjust button to set to "boil." The pressure valve can either be in the venting or sealing position.

The Instant Pot will beep when the milk has come to a boiling point; this will take around 25 minutes. Open the pot and then press the sauté button. This is to make sure that the milk remains hot as you add the vinegar. Add the vinegar, 1 tablespoon (15 ml) at a time, mixing well after each addition. At one point, the milk will separate and you will see the solids and whey clearly separated. Stop adding vinegar at this point.

Pour the curdled milk over the cheesecloth in the strainer. Wash the paneer lightly with cold water so that it won't have any taste of vinegar when it's set. Bring the ends of the cheesecloth together and squeeze as much water as you can from the paneer.

Place the paneer, wrapped inside the cheesecloth, on a flat surface and put heavy objects on top of it. I recommend things like a can of black beans along with a mortar and pestle, or books or a cast-iron skillet. Make sure all the areas of paneer are getting equal pressure. Leave it to set for around 2 hours. Remove the paneer block once its set and cut into cubes. Use in any of the paneer recipes in this book.

NOTE: You may also use lemon juice in place of vinegar to curdle the milk. However, in my personal experience making paneer at home for many years, vinegar results in a more solid block of paneer than lemon.

GHEE
(CLARIFIED BUTTER)

SERVES 1¹/₂ CUPS (360 ML)

You can say that ghee is the soul of Indian cooking. In India, curries, parathas, desserts—everything is almost incomplete without the addition of ghee. Ghee is nothing but clarified butter from which the milk solids have been removed. It imparts a wonderful flavor and aroma to any dish.

The traditional way to make ghee is by collecting malai (cream top) from raw milk for days, then churning it to make butter and eventually ghee. This is how it's still made at my home in India. But this Instant Pot version uses store-bought butter to make homemade ghee without much effort.

16 oz (454 g) unsalted butter

Place the butter into your Instant Pot. Press the slow-cook button, then cover the pot with a splash screen or leave it uncovered. Set the time to 1 hour 30 minutes. Don't cover the pot with the lid because you don't want condensation droplets to fall into the pot as the butter melts.

After 1 hour 30 minutes, you should see some foam on top and the milk solids should have settled at the bottom. Cancel the slow-cooker mode and press the sauté button. Cover the pot with a splash screen as the ghee will begin to bubble on sauté mode. Stir occasionally for 9 to 10 minutes—you should see the ghee change its color to a nice golden yellow. Unplug the Instant Pot immediately. Let the ghee cool down a bit in the pot. You will notice the milk solids at the bottom caramelize as the ghee cools down. When the ghee has cooled down a bit, use a strainer to strain it into another container. You don't want any milk solids in your ghee, so straining is a must. Discard the solids (see the note below).

Store ghee in an airtight container at room temperature for several weeks.

NOTE: You may use the milk solids in mashed potatoes or as a topping for pasta and steamed vegetables. My mom used to mix sugar and cardamom powder with the milk solids and eat them as such!

DAHI
(YOGURT)

SERVES: 4 CUPS (960 ML)

Simple homemade yogurt is easy to make in the Instant Pot and so much better, tastier and cheaper! This recipe makes a small batch of yogurt and can easily be doubled or tripled to make more.

4 cups (960 ml) whole milk
2 tsp (14 g) yogurt starter

Add the milk to the Instant Pot. Secure the lid and press the yogurt button, and then press the adjust button to "boil." The pressure valve can either be in the sealing or venting position. You will hear a beep when the milk has come to a boil and the display screen will say "yogt." This will take 15 to 16 minutes. Open the lid and check the temperature of the milk; it should be 180°F (82°C) or more. If it's not yet at that temperature, press the sauté button and wait until the milk reaches this temperature or above.

Remove the pot and transfer it to a sink or a larger pot filled with ice water. Whisk the milk until it reaches a temperature of 100 to 110°F (38 to 43°C). This will take 5 to 10 minutes. In a bowl, whisk the starter and ¼ cup (60 ml) of the cooled milk to combine. Transfer this mixture to the remaining milk and mix well. Place the inner steel pot back into the Instant Pot, close the lid and press the yogurt button. Set the time to 8 hours. After 8 hours, you will hear a beep and the Instant Pot will display "yogt," which means the yogurt is done.

Chill the yogurt in the refrigerator for a few hours and enjoy. We usually make raita (yogurt dip spiced with cumin, black salt and chilies) to enjoy as a side with biryani/pulao or eat it plain with parathas.

NOTE: The yogurt sets at around 6 hours. You can adjust the incubation time up to 12 hours. The longer the incubation time, the tangier the yogurt will be.

GINGER–GARLIC PASTE

SERVES: 1½ CUPS (400 G)

Ginger-garlic paste is a staple in Indian cooking. You can buy it from any Indian store, but the homemade version is so much better and imparts great flavors to curries.

2 cups (200 g) ginger (measured after removing the skin)

1½ cups (200 g) garlic (measured after peeling the skin)

2 tbsp (30 ml) canola, olive or vegetable oil

Peel the ginger and garlic and place them in a blender. You will need a powerful blender for this. Add the oil to the blender and then pulse until the mixture turns into a smooth paste. Transfer the ginger–garlic paste to an airtight container and keep it refrigerated for up to 4 weeks.

BUTTONS ON THE INSTANT POT

The Instant Pot does have a lot of buttons and it can get confusing! Different models may have slightly different buttons, but I will talk about the ones we most commonly use. These are the buttons that I have used in the recipes in this book.

KEEP WARM/CANCEL: This button is used to cancel the current program and choose the next one. You will use this button to end the sauté function before choosing the next cooking program like manual or rice. When the food is cooked, the Instant Pot goes into this mode automatically and keeps the food warm.

SAUTÉ: The sauté button, as the name suggests, is to sauté in the pot. The majority of the recipes in this book use this function. You can use the adjust button to control the heat you want for a particular recipe— from "less" to "more." You can also use this function to get rid of excess water from the pot.

MANUAL: The manual button, which is also the pressure-cook button on some models, is the one you will use all the time. It lets you pressure cook at high or low pressure. Most recipes in this book will call for cooking on high pressure, but a few might need low pressure. You can use the adjust or pressure level button, depending on your model, to adjust the pressure to high or low.

STEAM: This function has a default setting of 10 minutes on high pressure. Time can be adjusted using the adjust button. This setting is great for steaming veggies or dumplings. Remember to use a steamer basket or trivet with this function.

RICE: This is a preset cycle of 12 minutes on low pressure for cooking rice.

BEAN/CHILI: This preset cycle of 30 minutes on high pressure is for cooking beans/legumes. Time can be adjusted using the adjust button.

YOGURT: The preset cycle for this function is 8 hours. Depending on how tart you want your yogurt to be, you can increase or decrease this time. You can adjust yogurt to low or high (which is "boil").

SLOW COOKER: Use this function to slow-cook food. Time can be adjusted using the adjust button.

SOUP: This is a preset cycle of 15 minutes on high pressure. Time can be adjusted using the adjust button.

PORRIDGE: This preset cycle is 20 minutes on high pressure. Time can be adjusted using the adjust button.

MEAT/STEW: The preset cycle for this function is 35 minutes on high pressure. Time can be adjusted using the adjust button.

MULTIGRAIN: This is a preset cycle of 40 minutes on high pressure. Time can be adjusted using the adjust button.

INSTANT POT ACCESSORIES

While there are tons of accessories that you can find online, here are some of my favorites. They have been used in several recipes in this book.

GLASS LID: This is great when you are cooking on sauté mode. Covering the pot will cook the food quicker and will also prevent the food from splattering. You also need the glass lid when using the slow-cooker button, such as when making ghee.

STEAMER BASKET: I use the steamer basket to steam veggies or dumplings. The basket has a hook, which helps lift the basket out of the pot.

EXTRA SEALING RINGS: The Instant Pot sealing ring absorbs the smell of the food that is cooked in the pot. I like to have two rings—one for savory recipes and one for desserts. I really don't want my cheesecake to smell like curry!

STAINLESS STEEL STACKING PANS: These steel pans are great when you are trying to make several things at the same time. You can make layered dishes using the pot-in-pot method and these steel pans are perfect for that.

CAKE PANS: Desserts in the Instant Pot is always a good idea! I love the 7-inch (18-cm) springform pan for cheesecake and the 6-cup Bundt pan for cakes. A round 6-inch (15-cm) cake pan also works well for cakes.

GRIPPER CLIPS: These are super useful for removing pans/pots from the Instant Pot once the cooking is done.

INDIAN COOKING INGREDIENT NOTES

You may not be familiar with every ingredient used in the recipes in this book. I've included notes below on some that may be less well known outside of India. You will be able to find these spices and ingredients at all Indian grocery stores. Many supermarkets have some or all of them, too. If there's something that you can't find in a store, check online.

ARHAR DAL/TOOR DAL (SPLIT PIGEON PEA LENTIL): One of the most popular dals cooked in India; commonly used in dal tadka and sambar.

ASAFETIDA (HING): Adds pungent flavors. Common addition to any tadka in Indian cooking; good for overall digestion.

BLACK CARDAMOM (BADI ELAICHI): Spice with very strong and smoky flavor used in stews and curries. Not to be confused with green cardamom, which has a subtle aroma.

BLACK CHICKPEAS (KALA CHANA): Smaller and darker in color than the more popular white chickpeas. Used in curries and salads.

BLACK SALT (KALA NAMAK): A type of rock salt. Has a pungent smell; commonly used in Indian chaats (street food), chutneys and raita (yogurt dips).

CAROM SEEDS (AJWAIN): Seeds that have a bitter taste and smell somewhat like thyme. Often added to parathas (whole-wheat flatbread) and while cooking with chickpeas and beans because of its digestive benefits.

CHANA DAL (SPLIT BENGAL GRAM): Popular dal, also used in desserts and fritters.

CHICKPEA FLOUR (BESAN): Gluten-free flour commonly used in Indian cooking to make fritters, crepes and dishes like kadhi.

CITRIC ACID: Used in making paneer and steamed cakes like dhokla.

CURRY LEAVES: Actually an herb, not related in any way to curry powder! Used extensively in south Indian cooking to season dals, chutneys, fritters and more.

DRIED MANGO POWDER (AMCHUR): Used to add tangy flavor to dishes.

DRIED FENUGREEK LEAVES (KASURI METHI): Used to flavor curries, naan and pulaos. Leaves are typically crumbled before adding to the dish.

FENUGREEK (METHI): Has a strong and slightly bitter taste. Fresh fenugreek are leaves used in dals, parathas and curries. Fenugreek seeds are used in pickles and for tempering curries, kadhi, etc.

GARAM MASALA: Special blend of spices like cinnamon, coriander, cloves, cumin; used in many Indian dishes.

GHEE: Clarified butter from which the milk solids have been removed. Used to toast parathas, added to curries and dal, used in all sorts of desserts—it's the soul of Indian cooking!

GREEN CARDAMOM (ELAICHI): Most-used spice in Indian desserts and in chai; has a sweet and subtle flavor. Seeds are often crushed and used in powdered form.

GREEN CHILIES: Slender green chilies added to curries, pickles and chutneys for flavor and spice; also eaten raw! In the United States, Thai chilies are a good substitute.

IDLI RICE: Short-grain rice used for making idlis.

JAGGERY: Unrefined sugar obtained from raw, concentrated sugarcane juice. Used in desserts and in dals to even out the flavors (especially in the state of Gujarat).

KALONJI: Seeds with a nutty onion flavor; used in pickles, on top of naan and other flatbreads.

MASOOR DAL (RED LENTILS): Everyday lentil made in Indian homes, used whole and split.

MOONG DAL (MOONG BEANS): Often used to make khichadi and other sorts of porridge; also used in desserts. Can be used whole (moong sabut), with skin on (moong chilka) and washed without skin (moong dhuli).

PANEER: Indian cottage cheese made by curdling milk. Hugely popular in India and always on the menu!

ROSE WATER: Used in flavoring desserts and milk-based desserts and beverages.

TAMARIND: Used for its tangy flavor in chutneys. It's also used in curries and stews like sambar.

TUTTI FRUTTI: Candied dried papaya used in baked goods like cakes, cookies and buns.

URAD DAL (BLACK GRAM): Used whole (urad sabut), with skin (urad chilka) and split without skin (urad dhuli). Whole urad dal used to make dal makhana; urad dhuli used to make idlis and dosas.

ACKNOWLEDGMENTS

If you had told me 5 years ago that I would be writing a cookbook, I would have probably laughed out loud and called you crazy! Never in my weirdest dreams had I imagined writing a cookbook. I wrote this cookbook during the toughest time of my life, right after losing my mom. There were a lot of tears and hard work on my part, but this book wouldn't have been possible without the support and encouragement of the incredible people in my life.

My mumma, the most amazing, wonderful, kind-hearted woman I know. You left me last year physically, but your blessings and words motivated me every day while writing this cookbook. During your prayer meet, so many of your friends came up to me and told me how proud you were of me and my blog. That was the day I decided to write this cookbook, because I knew it would make you proud. Thank you for always believing in me and teaching me that there's no shortcut to success. You have taught me that no matter what, you can achieve anything if you put your heart and soul into it. Your place in my life can never be replaced and I miss you every second, but I hope wherever you are, this book makes you proud. I love you the most in this world.

My husband, Sarvesh. Thank you for being my biggest cheerleader. If not for you, this book wouldn't have been possible. Thank you for making all those timetables and grocery lists well in advance so that I could work through the week. Thank you for those 6 a.m. grocery trips even when you had a packed day at work. You are the most amazing husband in the world and you are my biggest blessing. This book is as much yours as it is mine.

My dad, thank you for always believing in my dreams. You have always encouraged me to follow my dreams and also taught me to never give up no matter what. It was only due to your encouragement that I had the courage to write this book, right after losing mom.

To my wonderful in-laws, thank you for always being so supportive and showering me with so much love and affection. Your guidance has helped me at every step while writing this book.

To my brothers and sister, Ayush, Kush and Arushi. Thank you for motivating me every day while writing this cookbook. You all believed in me and this cookbook, more than I believed in it.

To my best friends, Himani, Money and Misha. Thank you for always being there for me. You guys have always pushed me to do my best. I can't thank you guys enough for just being you.

My readers, you guys are another big reason why this book came into existence. I appreciate each and every one of you who visit my blog, try my recipes and always encourage me to keep going. Thank you so much.

To my blogging friends, thank you for every comment you have ever left on my blog. Most importantly, thank you for making me a part of this community. You are all amazing.

To my recipes testers, thank you so much for taking the time to test some of these recipes. I thank you all from the bottom of my heart for your time and feedback.

And last but not the least, to Lauren, Meg, Will and the entire team at Page Street Publishing. Thank you so much for believing in me and giving me this opportunity. Thank you for being so supportive throughout this journey.

ABOUT THE AUTHOR

Manali Singh is the face behind the blog: Cook With Manali (https://www.cookwithmanali.com). She started the blog in 2013 as a place to document all her recipes. She shares vegetarian and vegan recipes from all around the world and believes in cooking from scratch.

When not doing recipe creation or food photography, she loves watching Bollywood movies. She is married to her best friend of 16 years and lives with him in Seattle. Her work has been frequently featured on Buzzfeed, Huffington Post, Yahoo, MSN and more.

Don't hesitate to reach out to her through email at manali@cookwithmanali.com or on social media with any questions or feedback.

FACEBOOK: https://www.facebook.com/cookwithmanali

INSTAGRAM: https://www.instagram.com/cookwithmanali/

PINTEREST: https://www.pinterest.com/cookwithmanali/

INDEX

almonds
Kesar Elaichi Shrikhand (Saffron Cardamom Yogurt), 157
Navratan Korma (Vegetables & Nuts in a Creamy Cashew Sauce), 15–16
Pumpkin Coconut Halwa (Pumpkin Coconut Pudding), 165
Zarda (Sweet Rice), 161
asparagus, for Tofu Broccoli Asparagus in Fenugree Sauce, 85
avocados, for Soya Jalapeño Keema Tacos (Vegan Minced Soya Granules Tacos), 73

beetroot, for Beans & Beets Poriyal (Spiced Green Beans & Beets with Coconut), 111
bell peppers, for Pav Bhaji (Mashed Spiced Vegetables with Dinner Rolls), 114–116
beverages
Masala Chai, 136
Turmeric Masala Doodh (Spiced Turmeric Milk), 108
Biscoff cookies, for Rose Pistachio Cheesecake, 169–171
black beans, for Curried Black Bean Burrito Bowl, 81
black-eyed peas, for Black-Eyed Pea Curry with Kale, 40
broccoli, for Tofu Broccoli Asparagus in Fenugree Sauce, 85
butternut squash, for Tomato Butternut Squash Dal, 51

cabbage
Moong Dal with Cabbage & Dill, 47
Vegan Hot & Sour Soup, 126
Vegetarian Momos (Vegetarian Dumplings), 121
cakes
cake pans, 145

Eggless Tutti Frutti Cake, 162
Idlis (Steamed Rice Lentil Cakes), 147–148
Khaman Dhokla (Steamed Savory Chickpea-Flour Cakes), 149–150
Rose Pistachio Cheesecake, 169–171
carrots
Achari Mixed Vegetables (Mixed Vegetables with Pickle Masala), 33
Navratan Korma (Vegetables & Nuts in a Creamy Cashew Sauce), 15–16
Quinoa Curd Rice (Spiced Quinoa with Yogurt), 86
Sambar (South Indian Lentil Stew), 39
Vegan Hot & Sour Soup, 126
Vegetable Biryani (Basmati Rice with Veggies & Fragrant Spices), 29–30
Vegetable Khichdi (Mixed Lentils & Rice Porridge), 63
Vegetarian Momos (Vegetarian Dumplings), 121
cashews
Achari Mixed Vegetables (Mixed Vegetables with Pickle Masala), 33
Banarsi Dum Aloo (Creamy Baby Potatoes Curry), 67
Butter Paneer, 10
Cilantro Mint Paneer, 89
Gobi Matar Korma (Cauliflower & Green Peas Coconut Curry), 74
Mango Coconut Tapioca Pudding, 172
Matar Mushroom (Mushrooms & Green Peas in Creamy Tomato Sauce), 23
Mint Cashew Pulao (Spiced Basmati Rice with Mint & Cashews), 143
Navratan Korma (Vegetables & Nuts in a Creamy Cashew Sauce), 15–16
Pumpkin Coconut Halwa (Pumpkin Coconut Pudding), 165

Rice Kheer (Indian Rice Pudding), 154
Tofu Broccoli Asparagus in Fenugree Sauce, 85
Turmeric Masala Doodh (Spiced Turmeric Milk), 108
Ven Pongal (Rice & Lentil Porridge with Peppercorns), 93
Zarda (Sweet Rice), 161
cauliflower
Achari Mixed Vegetables (Mixed Vegetables with Pickle Masala), 33
Aloo Gobi (Spiced Potatoes & Cauliflower), 60
Gobi Matar Korma (Cauliflower & Green Peas Coconut Curry), 74
Navratan Korma (Vegetables & Nuts in a Creamy Cashew Sauce), 15–16
Pav Bhaji (Mashed Spiced Vegetables with Dinner Rolls), 114–116
Vegetable Biryani (Basmati Rice with Veggies & Fragrant Spices), 29–30
celery, for Vegan Hot & Sour Soup, 126
cheddar cheese, for Masala Mac & Cheese (Spiced Mac & Cheese), 107
cheesecake, as Rose Pistachio Cheesecake, 169–171
cheese, cheddar, for Masala Mac & Cheese (Spiced Mac & Cheese), 107
cheese, cream cheese, for Rose Pistachio Cheesecake, 169–171
cheese, Monterey Jack, for Masala Mac & Cheese (Spiced Mac & Cheese), 107
cheese, mozzarella, for Paneer Lasagna (Spiced Indian Cottage Cheese Lasagna), 69
cherries, for Zarda (Sweet Rice), 161
chickpeas
Aloo Chana Rolls (Spiced Potato & Chickpea Wraps), 117–118

Chana Masala (Chickpea Curry), 13–14
introduction to, 185
Jackfruit with Chana Dal, 43
Masala Hummus (Spiced Hummus), 140
Panchmel Dal (Five-Lentil Mix with Spices), 48
Sookha Kala Chana (Spiced Black Chickpeas), 56
Spiced Chickpea Salad, 52
chutney
Cilantro Mint Yogurt Chutney, 117–118
Sweet Potato Chaat with Cilantro Mint Yogurt Chutney, 129
Tomato & Date Chutney, 139
coconut
Beans & Beets Poriyal (Spiced Green Beans & Beets with Coconut), 111
Idlis (Steamed Rice Lentil Cakes), 147–148
Spiced Chickpea Salad, 52
Zarda (Sweet Rice), 161
cookies, for Rose Pistachio Cheesecake, 169–171
corn
Curried Black Bean Burrito Bowl, 81
Spicy Masala Corn, 125
cream cheese, for Rose Pistachio Cheesecake, 169–171
crème brûlée, as Masala Chai Crème Brûlée, 166–168
curry
Banarsi Dum Aloo (Creamy Baby Potatoes Curry), 67
Black-Eyed Pea Curry with Kale, 40
Chana Masala (Chickpea Curry), 13–14
Gatte Ki Sabzi (Chickpea Flour Dumplings Curry), 64–66
Gobi Matar Korma (Cauliflower & Green Peas Coconut Curry), 74
Kashmiri Rajma (Kidney-Bean Curry), 44
Matar Paneer (Indian Cottage Cheese & Green Peas Curry), 96

Palak Paneer (Indian Cottage Cheese & Spinach Curry), 20
Paneer Tikka Masala (Indian Cottage Cheese in a Creamy Tomato Sauce), 27–28
Tofu Mango Coconut Curry, 104

dates, for Tomato & Date Chutney, 139
dill, for Moong Dal with Cabbage & Dill, 47
drumsticks, for Sambar (South Indian Lentil Stew), 39
dumplings, as Vegetarian Momos (Vegetarian Dumplings), 121

eggplants, for Masala Baingan (Spiced Baby Eggplants with Coconut), 78

fudge, as Kalakand (Spiced Milk Fudge), 158

garlic
Black-Eyed Pea Curry with Kale, 40
Butter Paneer, 10
Cilantro Mint Paneer, 89
Curried Black Bean Burrito Bowl, 81
Dal Tadka (Mixed Lentils with Spices), 24
Gatte Ki Sabzi (Chickpea Flour Dumplings Curry), 64–66
Gobi Matar Korma (Cauliflower & Green Peas Coconut Curry), 74
Jackfruit with Chana Dal, 43
Kadai Tofu (Spiced Tofu with Bell Peppers), 70
Masala Hummus (Spiced Hummus), 140
Matar Mushroom (Mushrooms & Green Peas in Creamy Tomato Sauce), 23
Matar Paneer (Indian Cottage Cheese & Green Peas Curry), 96
Mushroom Garlic Fried Rice, 122
Palak Paneer (Indian Cottage Cheese & Spinach Curry), 20
Paneer Lasagna (Spiced Indian Cottage Cheese Lasagna), 69
Paneer Tikka Masala (Indian Cottage Cheese in a Creamy Tomato Sauce), 27–28

Pav Bhaji (Mashed Spiced Vegetables with Dinner Rolls), 114–116
Saag (Spiced Creamy Greens), 132
Spinach Dal (Lentils with Spinach), 36
Tofu Broccoli Asparagus in Fenugree Sauce, 85
Vegan Hot & Sour Soup, 126
Vegetable Khichdi (Mixed Lentils & Rice Porridge), 63
Vegetarian Momos (Vegetarian Dumplings), 121
Ghee (Clarified Butter)
Dal Makhani (Creamy Black Lentils), 19
Dal Tadka (Mixed Lentils with Spices), 24
Gatte Ki Sabzi (Chickpea Flour Dumplings Curry), 64–66
introduction to, 186
Kashmiri Rajma (Kidney-Bean Curry), 44
Matar Paneer (Indian Cottage Cheese & Green Peas Curry), 96
Navratan Korma (Vegetables & Nuts in a Creamy Cashew Sauce), 15–16
Palak Paneer (Indian Cottage Cheese & Spinach Curry), 20
Panchmel Dal (Five-Lentil Mix with Spices), 48
Pumpkin Coconut Halwa (Pumpkin Coconut Pudding), 165
recipe, 179
Saag (Spiced Creamy Greens), 132
Sookha Kala Chana (Spiced Black Chickpeas), 56
Vegetable Biryani (Basmati Rice with Veggies & Fragrant Spices), 29–30
Vegetable Khichdi (Mixed Lentils & Rice Porridge), 63
Ven Pongal (Rice & Lentil Porridge with Peppercorns), 93
Zarda (Sweet Rice), 161
Ginger–Garlic Paste
Achari Mixed Vegetables (Mixed Vegetables with Pickle Masala), 33
Aloo Gobi (Spiced Potatoes & Cauliflower), 60
Banarsi Dum Aloo (Creamy Baby Potatoes Curry), 67

Dal Makhani (Creamy Black Lentils), 19
Kashmiri Rajma (Kidney-Bean Curry), 44
Masala Baingan (Spiced Baby Eggplants with Coconut), 78
Masala Mac & Cheese (Spiced Mac & Cheese), 107
recipe, 183
Soya Jalapeño Keema Tacos (Vegan Minced Soya Granules Tacos), 73
Tehri (Spicy Potato & Peas Pulao), 103
Vegetable Biryani (Basmati Rice with Veggies & Fragrant Spices), 29–30
green beans
Beans & Beets Poriyal (Spiced Green Beans & Beets with Coconut), 111
Navratan Korma (Vegetables & Nuts in a Creamy Cashew Sauce), 15–16
Vegetable Biryani (Basmati Rice with Veggies & Fragrant Spices), 29–30
Vegetable Khichdi (Mixed Lentils & Rice Porridge), 63
green gram, for Panchmel Dal (Five-Lentil Mix with Spices), 48
greens, mixed, for Saag (Spiced Creamy Greens), 132

honey
Butter Paneer, 10
Spiced Chickpea Salad, 52
hummus, as Masala Hummus (Spiced Hummus), 140

Instant Pot
accessories, 185
buttons, 184

jackfruit, for Jackfruit with Chana Dal, 43
jalapeño peppers
Curried Black Bean Burrito Bowl, 81
Masala Mac & Cheese (Spiced Mac & Cheese), 107
Soya Jalapeño Keema Tacos (Vegan Minced Soya Granules Tacos), 73
Spicy Masala Corn, 125

kale, for Black-Eyed Pea Curry with Kale, 40
kidney beans, for Kashmiri Rajma (Kidney-Bean Curry), 44

lasagna, as Paneer Lasagna (Spiced Indian Cottage Cheese Lasagna), 69
lentils, black gram
Beans & Beets Poriyal (Spiced Green Beans & Beets with Coconut), 111
Dal Makhani (Creamy Black Lentils), 19
Idlis (Steamed Rice Lentil Cakes), 147–148
Quinoa Curd Rice (Spiced Quinoa with Yogurt), 86
lentils, red
Dal Tadka (Mixed Lentils with Spices), 24
introduction to, 186
Panchmel Dal (Five-Lentil Mix with Spices), 48
Spinach Dal (Lentils with Spinach), 36
Tomato Butternut Squash Dal, 51
Vegetable Khichdi (Mixed Lentils & Rice Porridge), 63

macaroni, for Masala Mac & Cheese (Spiced Mac & Cheese), 107
mango purée
Mango Coconut Tapioca Pudding, 172
Tofu Mango Coconut Curry, 104
mint
Cilantro Mint Paneer, 89
Mint Cashew Pulao (Spiced Basmati Rice with Mint & Cashews), 143
Monterey Jack cheese, for Masala Mac & Cheese (Spiced Mac & Cheese), 107
moong beans
Dal Dhania Shorba (Lentil Cilantro Soup), 99
Dal Tadka (Mixed Lentils with Spices), 24
introduction to, 186
Moong Dal with Cabbage & Dill, 47
Vegetable Khichdi (Mixed Lentils & Rice Porridge), 63
Ven Pongal (Rice & Lentil Porridge with Peppercorns), 93
mozzarella cheese, for Paneer Lasagna (Spiced Indian Cottage Cheese Lasagna), 69
mushrooms

Matar Mushroom (Mushrooms & Green Peas in a Creamy Tomato Sauce), 23
Mushroom Garlic Fried Rice, 122
Vegan Hot & Sour Soup, 126

okras, for Sambar (South Indian Lentil Stew), 39
onions, chopped
Palak Paneer (Indian Cottage Cheese & Spinach Curry), 20
Paneer Lasagna (Spiced Indian Cottage Cheese Lasagna), 69
Tofu Bhurji (Indian-Style Scrambled Tofu), 135
onions, green, for Vegan Hot & Sour Soup, 126
onions, puréed, for Gatte Ki Sabzi (Chickpea Flour Dumplings Curry), 64–66
onions, red
Aloo Chana Rolls (Spiced Potato & Chickpea Wraps), 117–118
Aloo Gobi (Spiced Potatoes & Cauliflower), 60
Banarsi Dum Aloo (Creamy Baby Potatoes Curry), 67
Black-Eyed Pea Curry with Kale, 40
Chana Masala (Chickpea Curry), 13–14
Cilantro Mint Paneer, 89
Dal-Chawal-Aloo Sabzi (Layered Meal with Rice, Lentils & Potatoes), 90
Dal Makhani (Creamy Black Lentils), 19
Dal Tadka (Mixed Lentils with Spices), 24
Gobi Matar Korma (Cauliflower & Green Peas Coconut Curry), 74
Kadai Tofu (Spiced Tofu with Bell Peppers), 70
Kashmiri Rajma (Kidney-Bean Curry), 44
Masala Baingan (Spiced Baby Eggplants with Coconut), 78
Matar Mushroom (Mushrooms & Green Peas in a Creamy Tomato Sauce), 23
Matar Paneer (Indian Cottage Cheese & Green Peas Curry), 96
Moong Dal with Cabbage & Dill, 47
Panchporan Spinach Kadhi (Yogurt Soup with Five Spices), 77

Paneer Tikka Masala (Indian Cottage Cheese in a Creamy Tomato Sauce), 27–28
Pav Bhaji (Mashed Spiced Vegetables with Dinner Rolls), 114–116
Saag (Spiced Creamy Greens), 132
Sambar (South Indian Lentil Stew), 39
Soya Jalapeño Keema Tacos (Vegan Minced Soya Granules Tacos), 73
Tehri (Spicy Potato & Peas Pulao), 103
Vegetable Biryani (Basmati Rice with Veggies & Fragrant Spices), 29–30
onions, sliced, for Mint Cashew Pulao (Spiced Basmati Rice with Mint & Cashews), 143
onions, spring
Mushroom Garlic Fried Rice, 122
Vegetarian Momos (Vegetarian Dumplings), 121
onions, white
Aloo Chana Rolls (Spiced Potato & Chickpea Wraps), 117–118
Curried Black Bean Burrito Bowl, 81
Dal Dhania Shorba (Lentil Cilantro Soup), 99
Navratan Korma (Vegetables & Nuts in a Creamy Cashew Sauce), 15–16
Tofu Mango Coconut Curry, 104
onions, yellow
Masala Mac & Cheese (Spiced Mac & Cheese), 107
Tofu Broccoli Asparagus in Fenugree Sauce, 85

Paneer (Indian Cottage Cheese)
Butter Paneer, 10
Cilantro Mint Paneer, 89
introduction to, 186
Matar Paneer (Indian Cottage Cheese & Green Peas Curry), 96
Navratan Korma (Vegetables & Nuts in a Creamy Cashew Sauce), 15–16
Palak Paneer (Indian Cottage Cheese & Spinach Curry), 20
Paneer Lasagna (Spiced Indian Cottage Cheese Lasagna), 69

Paneer Tikka Masala (Indian Cottage Cheese in a Creamy Tomato Sauce), 27–28
recipe, 176
Vegetable Biryani (Basmati Rice with Veggies & Fragrant Spices), 29–30
papaya, for Zarda (Sweet Rice), 161
pasta sauce, for Paneer Lasagna (Spiced Indian Cottage Cheese Lasagna), 69
peanuts
Dal Dhokli (Whole-Wheat Noodles in Lentil Stew), 82
Khatti Meethi Gujarati Dal, 55
Quinoa Curd Rice (Spiced Quinoa with Yogurt), 86
Spiced Chickpea Salad, 52
peas
Achari Mixed Vegetables (Mixed Vegetables with Pickle Masala), 33
Dal Tadka (Mixed Lentils with Spices), 24
Gobi Matar Korma (Cauliflower & Green Peas Coconut Curry), 74
Matar Mushroom (Mushrooms & Green Peas in a Creamy Tomato Sauce), 23
Matar Paneer (Indian Cottage Cheese & Green Peas Curry), 96
Navratan Korma (Vegetables & Nuts in a Creamy Cashew Sauce), 15–16
Pav Bhaji (Mashed Spiced Vegetables with Dinner Rolls), 114–116
Soya Jalapeño Keema Tacos (Vegan Minced Soya Granules Tacos), 73
Tehri (Spicy Potato & Peas Pulao), 103
Tofu Bhurji (Indian-Style Scrambled Tofu), 135
Vegetable Khichdi (Mixed Lentils & Rice Porridge), 63
peppers, green
Curried Black Bean Burrito Bowl, 81
Kadai Tofu (Spiced Tofu with Bell Peppers), 70
Quinoa Curd Rice (Spiced Quinoa with Yogurt), 86
Vegetarian Momos (Vegetarian Dumplings), 121
peppers, jalapeño

Curried Black Bean Burrito Bowl, 81
Masala Mac & Cheese (Spiced Mac & Cheese), 107
Soya Jalapeño Keema Tacos (Vegan Minced Soya Granules Tacos), 73
Spicy Masala Corn, 125
peppers, red
Kadai Tofu (Spiced Tofu with Bell Peppers), 70
Mushroom Garlic Fried Rice, 122
Paneer Lasagna (Spiced Indian Cottage Cheese Lasagna), 69
pigeon peas
Dal-Chawal-Aloo Sabzi (Layered Meal with Rice, Lentils & Potatoes), 90
Dal Dhokli (Whole-Wheat Noodles in Lentil Stew), 82
Khatti Meethi Gujarati Dal, 55
Panchmel Dal (Five-Lentil Mix with Spices), 48
Sambar (South Indian Lentil Stew), 39
Spinach Dal (Lentils with Spinach), 36
pistachios
Kalakand (Spiced Milk Fudge), 158
Kesar Elaichi Shrikhand (Saffron Cardamom Yogurt), 157
Mango Coconut Tapioca Pudding, 172
Rice Kheer (Indian Rice Pudding), 154
Rose Pistachio Cheesecake, 169–171
porridge, as Vegetable Khichdi (Mixed Lentils & Rice Porridge), 63
potatoes
Achari Mixed Vegetables (Mixed Vegetables with Pickle Masala), 33
Aloo Chana Rolls (Spiced Potato & Chickpea Wraps), 117–118
Aloo Gobi (Spiced Potatoes & Cauliflower), 60
Banarsi Dum Aloo (Creamy Baby Potatoes Curry), 67
Dal-Chawal-Aloo Sabzi (Layered Meal with Rice, Lentils & Potatoes), 90
Jeera Aloo (Cumin Potatoes), 100
Pav Bhaji (Mashed Spiced Vegetables with Dinner Rolls), 114–116

Tehri (Spicy Potato & Peas Pulao), 103
Vegetable Biryani (Basmati Rice with Veggies & Fragrant Spices), 29–30
Vegetable Khichdi (Mixed Lentils & Rice Porridge), 63
pudding
Mango Coconut Tapioca Pudding, 172
Pumpkin Coconut Halwa (Pumpkin Coconut Pudding), 165
Rice Kheer (Indian Rice Pudding), 154
pumpkin
Khatti Meethi Pumpkin Sabzi (Sweet & Sour Pumpkin), 144
Pumpkin Coconut Halwa (Pumpkin Coconut Pudding), 165

quinoa, for Quinoa Curd Rice (Spiced Quinoa with Yogurt), 86

radishes, for Saag (Spiced Creamy Greens), 132
raisins
Mango Coconut Tapioca Pudding, 172
Navratan Korma (Vegetables & Nuts in a Creamy Cashew Sauce), 15–16
Pumpkin Coconut Halwa (Pumpkin Coconut Pudding), 165
Rice Kheer (Indian Rice Pudding), 154
Tomato & Date Chutney, 139
Zarda (Sweet Rice), 161
rice, basmati
Dal-Chawal-Aloo Sabzi (Layered Meal with Rice, Lentils & Potatoes), 90
Mint Cashew Pulao (Spiced Basmati Rice with Mint & Cashews), 143
Rice Kheer (Indian Rice Pudding), 154
Tehri (Spicy Potato & Peas Pulao), 103
Vegetable Biryani (Basmati Rice with Veggies & Fragrant Spices), 29–30
Zarda (Sweet Rice), 161
rice, idli
Idlis (Steamed Rice Lentil Cakes), 147–148
introduction to, 186
rice, jasmine, for Mushroom Garlic Fried Rice, 122

rice, long grain, for Ven Pongal (Rice & Lentil Porridge with Peppercorns), 93
rice, white
Curried Black Bean Burrito Bowl, 81
Dal-Chawal-Aloo Sabzi (Layered Meal with Rice, Lentils & Potatoes), 90
Vegetable Khichdi (Mixed Lentils & Rice Porridge), 63

soup
Dal Dhania Shorba (Lentil Cilantro Soup), 99
Panchporan Spinach Kadhi (Yogurt Soup with Five Spices), 77
Vegan Hot & Sour Soup, 126
soya granules, for Soya Jalapeño Keema Tacos (Vegan Minced Soya Granules Tacos), 73
spinach
Palak Paneer (Indian Cottage Cheese & Spinach Curry), 20
Panchporan Spinach Kadhi (Yogurt Soup with Five Spices), 77
Saag (Spiced Creamy Greens), 132
Spinach Dal (Lentils with Spinach), 36
Vegetable Khichdi (Mixed Lentils & Rice Porridge), 63
sweet potatoes, for Sweet Potato Chaat with Cilantro Mint Yogurt Chutney, 129

tacos, as Soya Jalapeño Keema Tacos (Vegan Minced Soya Granules Tacos), 73
tapioca pearls, for Mango Coconut Tapioca Pudding, 172
tea
Masala Chai, 136
Masala Chai Crème Brûlée, 166–168
tofu
Kadai Tofu (Spiced Tofu with Bell Peppers), 70
Tofu Bhurji (Indian-Style Scrambled Tofu), 135
Tofu Broccoli Asparagus in Fenugree Sauce, 85
Tofu Mango Coconut Curry, 104
tomatoes, chopped

Aloo Chana Rolls (Spiced Potato & Chickpea Wraps), 117–118
Aloo Gobi (Spiced Potatoes & Cauliflower), 60
Black-Eyed Pea Curry with Kale, 40
Butter Paneer, 10
Dal Tadka (Mixed Lentils with Spices), 24
Jackfruit with Chana Dal, 43
Kadai Tofu (Spiced Tofu with Bell Peppers), 70
Khatti Meethi Gujarati Dal, 55
Masala Baingan (Spiced Baby Eggplants with Coconut), 78
Matar Paneer (Indian Cottage Cheese & Green Peas Curry), 96
Palak Paneer (Indian Cottage Cheese & Spinach Curry), 20
Panchmel Dal (Five-Lentil Mix with Spices), 48
Paneer Lasagna (Spiced Indian Cottage Cheese Lasagna), 69
Paneer Tikka Masala (Indian Cottage Cheese in a Creamy Tomato Sauce), 27–28
Pav Bhaji (Mashed Spiced Vegetables with Dinner Rolls), 114–116
Saag (Spiced Creamy Greens), 132
Spinach Dal (Lentils with Spinach), 36
Tofu Bhurji (Indian-Style Scrambled Tofu), 135
Tomato Butternut Squash Dal, 51
Vegetable Khichdi (Mixed Lentils & Rice Porridge), 63
tomatoes, diced
Sambar (South Indian Lentil Stew), 39
Tomato & Date Chutney, 139
tomato paste
Butter Paneer, 10
Soya Jalapeño Keema Tacos (Vegan Minced Soya Granules Tacos), 73
tomatoes, puréed
Banarsi Dum Aloo (Creamy Baby Potatoes Curry), 67
Dal Makhani (Creamy Black Lentils), 19
Gobi Matar Korma (Cauliflower & Green Peas Coconut Curry), 74

Kashmiri Rajma (Kidney-Bean Curry), 44
Matar Mushroom (Mushrooms & Green Peas in a Creamy Tomato Sauce), 23
tortillas, for Soya Jalapeño Keema Tacos (Vegan Minced Soya Granules Tacos), 73
tutti frutti
Eggless Tutti Frutti Cake, 162
introduction to, 186
Zarda (Sweet Rice), 161

wraps, as Aloo Chana Rolls (Spiced Potato & Chickpea Wraps), 117–118

yogurt
Achari Mixed Vegetables (Mixed Vegetables with Pickle Masala), 33
Aloo Chana Rolls (Spiced Potato & Chickpea Wraps), 117–118
Banarsi Dum Aloo (Creamy Baby Potatoes Curry), 67
Cilantro Mint Paneer, 89
Dahi (Yogurt), 180
Eggless Tutti Frutti Cake, 162
Gatte Ki Sabzi (Chickpea Flour Dumplings Curry), 64–66
Gobi Matar Korma (Cauliflower & Green Peas Coconut Curry), 74
Kesar Elaichi Shrikhand (Saffron Cardamom Yogurt), 157
Matar Paneer (Indian Cottage Cheese & Green Peas Curry), 96
Panchporan Spinach Kadhi (Yogurt Soup with Five Spices), 77
Paneer Tikka Masala (Indian Cottage Cheese in a Creamy Tomato Sauce), 27–28
Quinoa Curd Rice (Spiced Quinoa with Yogurt), 86
Tehri (Spicy Potato & Peas Pulao), 103
Vegetable Biryani (Basmati Rice with Veggies & Fragrant Spices), 29–30